Paralegal Practice and Procedure

Paralegal Practice & Procedure

FOURTH EDITION

A Practical Guide for the Legal Assistant

DEBORAH E. LARBALESTRIER

Edited and Revised by Linda A. Spagnola, J.D.

PRENTICE HALL PRESS

PRENTICE HALL PRESS
Published by the Penguin Group
Penguin Group (USA) Inc.
375 Hudson Street, New York, New York 10014, USA
Penguin Group (Canada), 90 Eglinton Avenue East, Suite 700, Toronto, Ontario M4P 2Y3, Canada
(a division of Pearson Penguin Canada Inc.) • Penguin Books Ltd., 80 Strand, London WC2R 0RL,
England • Penguin Group Ireland, 25 St. Stephen's Green, Dublin 2, Ireland (a division of Penguin
Books Ltd.) • Penguin Group (Australia), 250 Camberwell Road, Camberwell, Victoria 3124,
Australia (a division of Pearson Australia Group Pty. Ltd.) • Penguin Books India Pvt. Ltd., 11
Community Centre, Panchsheel Park, New Delhi—110 017, India • Penguin Group (NZ), 67
Apollo Drive, Rosedale, North Shore 0632, New Zealand (a division of Pearson New Zealand
Ltd.) • Penguin Books (South Africa) (Pty.) Ltd., 24 Sturdee Avenue, Rosebank, Johannesburg
2196, South Africa
Penguin Books Ltd., Registered Offices: 80 Strand, London WC2R 0RL, England

While the author has made every effort to provide accurate telephone numbers and Internet addresses
at the time of publication, neither the publisher nor the author assumes any responsibility for errors,
or for changes that occur after publication. Further, the publisher does not have any control over and
does not assume any responsibility for author or third-party websites or their content.

PRINTING HISTORY
Prentice Hall Press trade paperback third edition / December 1994
Prentice Hall Press trade paperback fourth edition / July 2009

Prentice Hall Press fourth edition ISBN: 978-0-7352-0433-1

The Library of Congress has cataloged the Prentice Hall Press third edition as follows:

Larbalestrier, Deborah E. 1934–
    Paralegal practice and procedure : a practical guide for the legal assistant / Deborah E.
Larbalestrier.— 3rd ed.
    p.   cm.
    Includes index.
    ISBN 0-13-108564-6
    1. Legal assistants—United States—Handbooks, manuals, etc.   2. Legal secretaries—United
States—Handbooks, manuals, etc.   I. Title.
KF320.L4L363 1994   94-28860
340'.023'73—dc20 CIP

PRINTED IN THE UNITED STATES OF AMERICA

10   9   8   7   6   5   4   3   2   1

This publication is designed to provide accurate and authoritative information in regard to the subject
matter covered. It is sold with the understanding that the publisher is not engaged in rendering legal,
accounting or other professional services. If you require legal advice or other expert assistance, you
should seek the services of a competent professional.

Most Prentice Hall Press books are available at special quantity discounts for bulk purchases for
sales promotions, premiums, fund-raising, or educational use. Special books, or book excerpts, can
also be created to fit specific needs. For details, write: Special Markets, Penguin Group (USA) Inc.,
375 Hudson Street, New York, New York 10014.

This book is dedicated to all those paralegals who have been influenced by Deborah Larbalestrier and all those who, through this fourth edition, will come to know her work. As the revisionist for the fourth edition, I have been moved by her dedication to the profession and consider myself privileged to have been able to work on this update.

—LINDA A. SPAGNOLA, ESQ.

CONTENTS

PREFACE TO THE FOURTH EDITION

It has been more than a decade since the publication of the third edition of *Paralegal Practice and Procedure* and so many things have changed—all of them, I am happy to report, again advancing the state of the profession. Paralegals should be proud of their accomplishments in legal practice and the justice system.

Listed below are some of the new topics covered in the fourth edition, which convey its value as a reference textbook for your office library and a reference guide for the vast and diverse sources available on the Internet.

1. The developments in each state regarding the regulation, certification, and potential licensing of paralegals and the possible implications for the profession. An updated state-by-state list with the relevant websites is included.

2. An expanded discussion on legal ethics for paralegals and their utmost importance in the legal profession. It is vitally important for the paralegal to adhere to the standards in order to preserve and protect the professionalism of paralegals.

3. We have also updated the In-House Training Program. The professional paralegal associations, International Paralegal Management Association, and ABA resources are included and/or the electronic sources are identified.

4. The Legal Research section has been completely updated reflecting the current state of electronic research, including both subscription-based and free Internet resources.

5. We have included a discussion on alternative methods of litigation such as mediation and arbitration (collectively known as ADR), with forms and formats to illustrate their use and to assist the paralegal in preparing these documents for the attorney.

6. Almost all areas of legal practice have been significantly digitized, and electronic resources are referenced in each practice section to direct the paralegal not only to these new sources, but also to information and websites relating to updating it. In this regard the importance of continuing legal education cannot be overstressed.

7. The problems and/or challenges of electronic discovery in litigation have been addressed as well as the various litigation support systems used in the law office.

8. The major changes for filing (almost solely electronically) for bankruptcy under the new rules of the Bankruptcy Abuse Prevention and Consumer Protection Act of 2005 are discussed at length, with many of the forms supplied.

9. The chapter on business organizations has been expanded to include not only corporations, but also the various other models, such as the limited liability company.

In summary, this fourth edition focuses on the information age and the consequent changes in the responsibilities and duties of paralegals. Wherever possible, we have included the electronic resources available to permit the paralegal to perform at optimum levels for thoroughness and efficiency. I have tried to stay true to the original author's organization and style so that her voice would remain in these pages.

Our best advice is to keep current and maintain the passion you have for advancing not only yourself in your career, but also the entire paralegal profession. That is what we have tried to do in writing and revising this book.

On a more personal level, I have had the opportunity to teach and work with some amazing people who are now, I am happy to say, thriving in their paralegal careers. While I may have had some part to play in their education, it is they who have inspired me to constantly strive to improve the profession as a whole. I hope that the paralegals reading this book are likewise informed and inspired.

—Linda A. Spagnola, Esq.

Paralegal Practice and Procedure

PART ONE

General Duties, Practices, and Procedures

CHAPTER ONE

Paralegal Ethics

The Future of the Paralegal Profession

In the third edition, written more than fifteen years ago, Deborah Larbalestrier asked: "What lies ahead for the paralegal profession?" So much has changed in the past fifteen years that it hardly seems possible to answer that question within a single chapter. Not only have paralegals become firmly rooted as necessary to the proper functioning of the law office, but also the profession plays a vital role in the delivery of legal services. Further, since 1994, significant progress has been made in the education of paralegals. Currently, AAfPE's (American Association for Paralegal Education) membership includes over 450 universities, colleges, private schools, and institutions of higher learning, primarily in the United States, although a few members hail from Australia and Canada. Paralegals graduating from these institutions number in the hundreds of thousands and the schools currently enroll more than 50,000 students in their programs. Clearly, the paralegal profession is here to stay.

The profession has made significant strides toward recognition within both the legal community and society at large. Paralegals are well on the road to validation of professional achievement, although there is still more to be done in this regard. Formal certification of some type may benefit all concerned. The paralegal profession has demonstrated its concern for accountability to the organized bar, in the same manner and form as the public demands of attorneys. Additionally, this form of ethical procedure enhances the quality and credibility of its professional conduct. Thus far, there are only a few national paralegal associations that sponsor a certification exam.

NALA (National Association of Legal Assistants) sponsors an entry level "Certified Paralegal" credential along with a newly introduced "Advanced Paralegal Certification." NFPA (National Federation of Paralegal Associations) sponsors its Paralegal Advanced Competency Exam for experienced paralegals only. Both NALS (the Association for Legal Professionals) and AAPI (American Alliance of Paralegals Inc.) also sponsor credentialing examinations, although as of yet, they are not as widely known.

The most interesting development over the past fifteen years has been the creation of state-sponsored paralegal accreditation. Leading the pack is North Carolina; it has set up a State Bar Board of Paralegal Certification which administers and oversees the program. Its goal is to "assist in the development of paralegal standards, raise the profile of the paralegal profession, and standardize the expectations of the public and other legal professionals." Details can be found at www.nccertifiedpara legal.org. Ohio has followed this certification model as well, and details for its program can be accessed at http://downloads.ohiobar.org/pub/pcs.pdf. It is important to note that both of these certification plans are completely voluntary and do not affect the rights of practicing paralegals who are not certified by the states' bar associations. Wisconsin is the only state at this juncture that is proposing a true licensure scheme for paralegals that would prohibit those not licensed from practicing; thereby directly paralleling attorneys.

As only these few states have acted upon regulation issues, one must ask why. The major stumbling block to these various forms of licensing and/or certification continues to be the elusive phrase "practice of law" and its definition. The "practice of law," as traditionally defined by the legal profession, makes no reference to the delivery of legal services to the public. That is to say, it does not specifically say that educated, well-trained, and highly experienced laymen cannot deliver legal services to the general public. In 2002, the ABA's Task Force on the Model Definition of the Practice of Law attempted to respond to these issues surrounding the provision of legal services by non-lawyers. The ABA's conclusion was to direct each state to draft its own definition that included as a basic premise that the practice of law is "the application of legal principles and judgment to the circumstances or objectives of another person or entity." A list of the individual states' determinations regarding what may be considered the "practice of law" can be accessed at www.abanet.org/cpr/model-def/model_def_statutes.pdf.

About half the states have statutory and/or case law definitions of the "practice of law." Other states have taken a case-by-case approach, avoiding a formal definition. There are six generally accepted tasks that are considered the "practice of law" and they are (1) acquiring clients, (2) rendering legal advice, (3) preparing the final draft of legal documents, (4) managing the business of the law firm, (5) representing clients in a court of law, and (6) negotiating and settling legal claims.

There have been attempts made to establish a Code of Ethics for non-lawyers. There are several versions circulating in the paralegal community via paralegal organizations throughout the country, but not under one umbrella like the ABA Code of Professional Responsibility for lawyers, which is adhered to throughout the country. The two most prominent emanate from NALA and NFPA. The full texts of these Model Codes can be accessed at www.nala.org/code.htm and www.paralegals .org/displaycommon.cfm?an=1&subarticlenbr=133 (respectively).

Due to the lack of unanimity or preeminence among these various paralegal organizations, members of the paralegal community must also rely on their common sense, experience, and education to protect themselves, their profession, *and* the attorneys and their clients, to insure the integrity and competence of their performance on the job.

Why the Stumbling Block?

As predicted by the U.S. Labor Department as far back as the late 1980s, the paralegal profession has grown, and is still growing, by leaps and bounds. The DOL projects that in the future the profession will grow much faster than average—approximately 22 percent between 2006 and 2016. *The Occupational Outlook Handbook* for the paralegal profession can be accessed directly at www.bls.gov/oco/ocos 114.htm#outlook.

This growth was and is predicated upon the new job opportunities that have opened up for the utilization of these paraprofessionals, such as in the military, the legal departments of health care organizations, and the police departments of some cities. Add to this the realization finally by attorneys of the economic benefits in hiring a well-trained and educated paraprofessional.

And therein rests the problem.

While there are many independent paralegals who are well-trained, educated, and with years of experience, who just decided to go out on their own for personal reasons, there has also emerged the "legal technician" or "independent paralegal" who it seems is apparently not supervised and/or does not work with attorneys. Some of these individuals have only had "hours" of education, as opposed to "years." In direct response to this problem, both the ABA and the AAfPE have enacted academic standards for paralegal education. However, without a nationally unified body in charge of oversight, these educational standards remain as models only. AAfPE's position statement can be accessed at www.aafpe.org/p_about/ statement.htm#standards. The ABA Standing Committee on Paralegals website (www.abanet.org/legalservices/paralegals) has the Guidelines for Paralegal Education as well as a host of other helpful information. It is alleged that people are operating unchecked or without credentials throughout the country. Still to be decided by the organized bar is whether or not these laypersons are impostors, if they are practicing law without a license, or if they are bona fide paralegals—and how to control them. This question is still being debated on the floors of various state legislatures and bar association committee meetings.

State-by-State Review Regarding Paralegals

Alabama

Paralegals in Alabama are working with the Alabama State Bar Task Force on Allied Professionals to create a definition of "paralegal" and a credentialing program. To stay current on these developments, please visit www.alabar.org/bbc where you can access the latest minutes of the State Board of Bar Commissioners' meetings.

Alaska

In November of 1997, the Alaska State Bar created a Task Force for Equal Access to Civil Justice to address the issue of the unmet legal needs of Alaskans and how to increase the effective use of paralegals. See www.state.ak.us/courts/civjust.pdf for more information. Additionally, the Alaska Supreme Court has adopted a court rule 86, effective July 15, 1996, which allows for the award of paralegal fees under the same rule that allows attorney fees.

Arizona

The Arizona Supreme Court has adopted Rule 31 (a)2A, which affirmatively defines the practice of law. The unauthorized practice of law is governed by Rule 31(a)2B. Further, Arizona is one of the few states that have a separate statutory provision for "Legal Document Preparers" (LDPs) which permits individuals and businesses to prepare legal documents without the supervision of an attorney. These LDPs must be certified pursuant to Rule 31 and Arizona Code of Judicial Administration §7-208. With these regulations in place, "the State Bar of Arizona has the authority to bring an action to enforce rules regarding non-lawyers engaging in the unauthorized practice of law." See www.supreme.state.az.us/cld/pdf/rule%2031%20final%20for%20code%20book.pdf.

Arkansas

While the Arkansas Bar Association has looked into regulation and standards of paralegals, no formal decisions have been made to date. These "paraprofessionals" are regulated through the proper oversight of their supervising attorneys. The onus remains on the attorney, who is ultimately responsible for the paralegal's work product and conduct. For updates, please visit the association's website at www.arkbar.com/index.html.

California

The California Business and Professions Code §6450-6456 defines the paralegal profession. A person may call himself a paralegal if he is "qualified by education, training, or work experience" and is someone "who either contracts with or is employed by an attorney, law firm, corporation, governmental agency, or other entity, and who performs substantial legal work under the direction and supervision of an active member of the State Bar of California." The education, training, continuing legal education requirements, and other specifics are all enumerated within the code. See www.leginfo.ca.gov/cgi-bin/displaycode?section=bpc&group=06001-07000&file=6450-6456. Further, California has created an independent profession, the legal document preparers (LDPs) under the Business and Professions Code §6400(c). These professionals can assist with routine legal tasks, such as typing and filing the paperwork for uncontested divorces, bankruptcies, wills, and similar basic documents without supervision of an attorney. See www.leginfo.ca.gov/cgi-bin/displaycode?section=bpc&group=06001-07000&file=6400-6401.6.

Colorado

The state bar association has approved its Paralegal Committee's *Guidelines for the Utilization of Paralegals*. These guidelines include delineation of duties of paralegals in the many and diverse specialty areas of practice. For further information, see www.cobar.org/page.cfm/ID/106.

Connecticut

Similar to Colorado, Connecticut's Bar Association has developed *Guidelines for Legal Assistants*. It is directed at the supervising attorneys rather than, as the name suggests, at paralegals. See www.ctbar.org/article/articleview/198/1/57.

Delaware

Although the state bar and judiciary have taken no formal steps to regulate the profession, in 2005, the Delaware Paralegal Association implemented the Delaware Certified Paralegal (DCP) Program "in an effort to continue to promote a high level of education and professionalism and to encourage continuing legal education for Delaware paralegals." See www.deparalegals.org/dcpp.php.

Florida

In late 2007, the Florida Supreme Court adopted a voluntary registration program. A practicing paralegal with the required education, training, or work experience may choose to apply to the Florida Bar to gain permission to use the designation "Florida Registered Paralegal" (FRP) under Chapter 20 of the Rules Regulating the Florida Bar. For more details, please visit www.floridabar.org/divexe/rrtfb.nsf/FV?Openview&Start=1&Expand=20#20.

Georgia

As in so many other states, the Committee to Examine the Role of Legal Assistants of the State Bar of Georgia seems to be taking a "wait-and-see" approach to the issue of regulation of paralegals. There are no formal positions taken on the profession; however, the court has issued many advisory ethics opinions on the subject of the unauthorized practice of law by non-lawyers. The Georgia State Bar's web address is www.gabar.org.

Hawaii

While the Hawaii Judiciary is actively involved in access to justice issues, there has been no coordination with the paralegal profession to make those kinds of services more available. Indeed, in 2001, the Hawaii State Bar Association rejected a proposal for mandatory regulation and certification of paralegals as proposed by its own Task Force. To follow these developments, go to www.hawaiiparalegal.org and click "Hot topics."

Idaho

These "paraprofessionals" are regulated through the proper oversight of their supervising attorneys and their relevant Rules of Professional Conduct. The onus remains on the attorney who is ultimately responsible for the paralegal's work product and conduct. For updates, please visit the state bar association's website at www2.state.id.us/ISB.

Illinois

The state has a statutory definition of a paralegal that essentially correlates to the ABA definition. See Chapter 5, provision 70 §1.35 (www.ilga.gov/legislation/ilcs/ilcs3.asp?Act ID=79&ChapAct=5%26nbsp%3BILCS %26nbsp%3B70%2F&ChapterID=2& ChapterName=GENERAL+PROVISIONS &ActName=Statute+on+Statutes%2E).

Indiana

Within its Rules of Professional Responsibility, Indiana specifically promulgated guidelines for the use of non-lawyers assistants. See www.in.gov/judiciary/rules/prof_conduct/ index.html#_USE_OF_NON-LAWYER_ ASSISTANTS. The 2006 proposed legislation regarding the creation of "Registered Paralegals" overseen by the Indiana Supreme Court has not yet been resolved. Similar to other states' programs, in order to qualify for "IRP" status, the candidate must have completed certain educational requirements, be employed by a supervising attorney, and commit to a program of continuing legal education. Updates can be found at www.in .gov/judiciary/rules/proposed/2005/dec-a&d-paralegal.pdf.

Iowa

There has not been much development in the Legal Assistant Committee of the Iowa State Bar Association. Iowa paralegals are encouraged to attain a voluntary national certification credential.

Kansas

While there are no recent developments in official regulation, the Kansas Bar Association has adopted Official Standards and Guidelines for the Utilization of Legal Assistants/Paralegals. See www.ksbar.org/pdf/ laguidelines.pdf. These Guidelines not only provide a definition of "paralegal," but also acknowledge paralegals' contributions and skills to the public. Going further than some other states, Kansas also sets forth educational requirements for paralegals.

Kentucky

The Kentucky Code of Professional Responsibility contains Guidelines for the Utilization of Paralegals and can be accessed at www.kybar.org/documents/scr/scr3/scr_3 .700.pdf. The Kentucky Paralegal Association has developed a voluntary certification. For more information, please visit the association's website at www.kypa.org.

Louisiana

While there are no state bar requirements for a person calling themselves a "paralegal," a practicing paralegal may apply for voluntary certification through the Louisiana State Paralegal Association. See www.la-paralegals .org/3.html.

Maine

Title Four Chapter 18 of Maine's Revised Statutes specifically defines a "paralegal" (aka "legal assistant") and the Access to Justice Committee continues to work on the legal needs of the citizens of Maine.

Maryland

The Maryland State Bar has created a Paralegal Committee to "effectively represent Maryland's paralegals, to promote the paralegal profession within the Maryland legal community, to promote professionalism within the legal community in general, and to support the continuing education and effective utilization of paralegals." For more information, please visit www.msba.org/sec _comm/committees/paralegals. A very helpful element of this particular committee is the posting of their meeting minutes online to enable paralegals to keep apace with new developments in the field.

Massachusetts

This state also still relies upon the supervisory role of the attorney to ensure paralegal competence, rather than an independent regulatory body.

Michigan

The State Bar of Michigan has an active paralegal section whose mission is to provide "education, information and analysis about issues of concern through meetings, seminars, [the website], public service programs, and publication of a newsletter." See www.michbar .org/legalassistants/mission.cfm.

Minnesota

Similar to Michigan, the Minnesota State Bar Association has created a paralegal committee in order to "provide a forum for paralegals, educators, attorneys and other legal professionals to engage in discussion and research relevant to the paralegal profession and the legal community." There are no state-sponsored certifications or judicial regulations in place.

Mississippi

Like so many other states, Mississippi relies upon its Rules of Professional Conduct to ensure proper supervision of paralegals as an ethical duty of the attorney.

Missouri

The Missouri Bar Association has officially adopted a definition of "paralegal" and has created threshold educational standards for the profession to assist attorneys in identifying the basic competencies of paralegals. For

details, please visit www.mobar.org/ece8dc5c -0293-4990-8f54-be7193f99abe.aspx.

Montana

The Montana State Bar Association has an entire section devoted to the paralegal profession and it has six standing committees within that section at www.montanabar .org/displaycommon.cfm?an=1&subarti clenbr=73.

Nebraska

Nebraska also relies on its Rules of Professional Conduct to ensure that paralegals are properly supervised by attorneys, rather than create an independent body for oversight.

Nevada

The State Bar of Nevada's Legal Assistant Division's mission is to "enhance legal assistants' participation in the administration of justice, professional responsibility and public service in cooperation with the State Bar of Nevada." A practicing paralegal may become a member of this division and is expected to take an oath of professionalism and to adhere to the Code of Ethics for Paralegals as promulgated by the division. For more information, please visit www.nvbar .org/sections/sections_legal_assistants_divi sion.htm.

New Hampshire

Although there is currently no official regulation of the paralegal profession, the New Hampshire Bar Association appears to take this issue seriously. For a detailed analysis, please read the article "The State of Paralegal Regulation in New Hampshire" at www.nhbar.org/publications/archives/dis play-journal-issue.asp?id=148.

New Jersey

Perhaps the oldest attempt at officially licensing the paralegal profession emanates from New Jersey. In 1992, the Supreme Court of New Jersey's Committee on the Unauthorized Practice of Law examined the role of paralegals in the delivery of legal services. While the committee recommended that paralegals should be licensed, this licensure program was ultimately, in 1999, declined by the New Jersey Supreme Court. The bar continues to work on paralegal registration in the state.

New Mexico

Rules 20-101 to 20-115 of the Court Rules specifically define who may hold themselves out as "paralegals" and delineates minimum educational standards and competencies. The court recognizes paralegals as "highly trained, highly skilled legal support staff who engage in substantive legal work."

New York

The Bar Association of New York has adopted a definition of a "paralegal," and any paralegal using a "certification" credential must identify from which body that designation was granted (NYSBA Ethics Opinion 695). The state does not have its own regulatory body. The Empire State Alliance of Paralegal Associations (a coalition of many regional groups) has taken certain positions regarding education and regulation, and they can be accessed via www.empire stateparalegals.org/paralegal_utilization.

North Carolina

In 2004, the North Carolina Bar Association adopted "voluntary certification" ("North Carolina Certified Paralegal"). This state bar program sets minimum educational standards, mandates continuing legal education, and requires a certain amount of work experience in order to qualify. Details can be found at www.nccertifiedparalegal.org. Further, the North Carolina Bar has a standing division for legal assistants which can be accessed at http://legalassistantsdivision.ncbar .org.

North Dakota

North Dakota relies upon the attorneys' Rules of Professional Conduct to ensure that paralegals are properly supervised, rather than create an independent body for oversight. There does not appear to be any specially dedicated section of the bar for paralegals at this time.

Ohio

Similar to North Carolina, the Ohio State Bar Association has established a voluntary program for certifying its paralegals. After applying and passing the examination for the designation, a paralegal can use the title "OSBA Certified paralegal." For details, please visit www.ohiobar.org/pub/?articleid= 785.

Oklahoma

The Oklahoma Bar Association has recently created a standing Paralegal Division to "provide an established forum for paralegals to improve skills utilized by the legal team in the provision of legal services and to promote interaction among paralegals and between paralegals and lawyers to develop better ways to serve the needs of clients and the public," available at www.okbar.org/ members/committees/las07.htm. Further, the Oklahoma Bar has recognized that it "has a duty to the public to begin the journey toward responsible regulation of the role paralegals play in the provision of legal services."

Oregon

Several plans for regulation of paralegals in Oregon have met strong opposition by the members of the bar and bench and legislature. At this time, the state relies upon the attorneys' Rules of Professional Conduct to ensure that paralegals are properly supervised, rather than create an independent body for oversight.

Pennsylvania

In April 2008, the state's paralegal organizations through the Keystone Alliance ratified a voluntary credentialing program for Pennsylvania's paralegals. Details can be found at http://keystoneparalegals.org/certification .html. The state has also addressed the potential for the unauthorized practice of law by paralegals, specifically, in Title 42, §2524 of its Revised Statutes. See http://members .aol.com/statutespa/42.Cp.25.html.

Rhode Island

Although there is no state bar committee or state court committee dedicated to the issue, the Rhode Island Supreme Court Provisional Order No. 18 relating to Rule 5.5 (UPL) of the Rules of Professional Conduct establishes the tasks that may be properly delegated to a paralegal. See www.law.cornell.edu/ethics/ri/ code/guidelines_po18.htm.

South Carolina

South Carolina relies upon the attorneys' Rules of Professional Conduct to ensure that paralegals are properly supervised, rather than create an independent body for oversight. There does not appear to be any specially dedicated section of the bar for paralegals at this time.

South Dakota

The South Dakota Supreme Court is in the process of considering an official definition of "paralegal" along with setting forth qualifying requirements in order to use the title "paralegal." Full details can be accessed through the South Dakota Paralegal Association's website, www.sdparalegals.com/ sdpa_prof_develop_website_rpt_2-23-07 .pdf. Further, the South Dakota Rules of Professional Conduct Ch. 16-18 §34.3 directs that attorneys should make "proper use of assistants who are not licensed attorneys [because they] significantly increase the ability of attorneys to provide quality professional services to the public at reasonable cost." The rules detail the ways for attorneys to achieve this goal. See http://legis.state.sd .us/statutes/displaystatute.aspx?type=statute &statute=16-18-34.3.

Tennessee

Tennessee is among those states that rely on their Rules of Professional Conduct to ensure that paralegals are properly supervised by attorneys, rather than create an independent body for oversight.

Texas

In 2006, the State Bar of Texas Board of Directors not only authored its own definition of "paralegal" but also included an enumerated list of standards "which are intended to assist the public in obtaining quality legal services, assist attorneys in their utilization of paralegals, and assist judges in determining whether paralegal work is a reimbursable cost when granting attorney fees." See http://txpd .org/page.asp?p=paralegal%20definition

%20and%20standards. These standards include education, training, work experience, proper delegation of substantive work, and ethical obligations. Further, the Texas Board of Legal Specialization of the Supreme Court of Texas sponsors a voluntary paralegal certification. An applicant must first qualify for the process and then pass the examination in order to become a certified paralegal. The Texas Board goes even further by certifying in individual legal specialty areas. For more information please visit www.tbls.org/default.aspx?tabid=70.

Utah

The Utah State Bar also has an active Paralegal Division which has promulgated both utilization standards and ethical guidelines for paralegals. Please visit www.utahbar.org/sections/paralegals/welcome.html. Utah is also considering the licensure issue very seriously. The bar has created a "Licensing of Legal Assistants Committee" that works in tandem with the Access to Justice Committee to examine the possibility of licensure of paralegals. No action has been taken on the licensure program as of yet; they continue to monitor the national and state developments.

Vermont

Vermont is also among those states that rely on their Rules of Professional Conduct to ensure that paralegals are properly supervised by attorneys, rather than create an independent body for oversight.

Virginia

The Virginia Alliance of Paralegal Associations has promulgated Educational Standards and Professional Responsibility Guidelines for Legal Assistants in the Commonwealth of Virginia. These are standards attendant to voluntary membership in the organization, however. See www.richmondparalegals.org/guidelines.html. Neither the Virginia Bar nor their judiciary has taken a position on the certification of paralegals in the state. Oversight remains the responsibility of the paralegal's supervising attorney under the Attorney Code of Professional Responsibility.

Washington

The state paralegal association (WSPA) continues to monitor the developments. Go to www.wspaonline.com/regulation.htm. The Practice of Law Board of the Washington Bar submitted a proposal, in January 2008, regarding the provision of legal and law-related services by non-lawyers to the Washington Supreme Court. This proposal would create a pilot program in the area of family law. Details on this and other board activities can be accessed at www.wsba.org/lawyers/groups/practiceoflaw/default1.htm.

West Virginia

Currently, there are no developments in the regulation of paralegals in West Virginia. The bar association has a Legal Assistants Committee and minutes of their meetings can be accessed through www.wvbar.org/barinfo/comms. West Virginian paralegals are overseen by their supervising attorneys in compliance with the West Virginia Standards of Professional Conduct.

Wisconsin

The Final Report of the State Bar Paralegal Practice Task Force is currently before the Supreme Court of Wisconsin. It sets forth a true licensure scheme for paralegals similar to those enacted for attorneys. The full text of the report can be accessed at www.wisbar

.org/am/template.cfm?section=research_
and_reports&template=/cm/contentdisplay
.cfm&contentid=36337.

Wyoming

Although the state bar association appears to acknowledge the significance of nation- ally certified paralegals (i.e., through NALA or NFPA), there is currently no state-specific regulation or credentialing system of paralegals. Oversight remains the responsibility of the paralegal's supervising attorney under the Attorney Code of Professional Responsibility.

The Practice of Law by Paralegals

It is apparent that each state is somehow attempting to address the paralegal profession's "official" recognition. There are three distinct issues that arise:

1. The official definition of the "paralegal" as a separate profession and the educational requirements necessary to call oneself a paralegal. There are also questions regarding standardized testing for entry into and maintenance of the profession. Each state must make its own determination as to how the profession should be regulated and the potential candidates certified.

2. The definition and enforcement of the unauthorized practice of law. Paralegals walk a fine line between permitted and prohibited actions on a daily basis, both in and out of the law office.

3. The status of the paralegal in the office hierarchy. As the work of a paraprofessional performing substantive legal tasks (i.e., nonclerical), the court can (and does) award legal fees for paralegal hours. This would indicate that paralegals are professionals in every sense of the word; however the U.S. Department of Labor has taken a position that appears contrary to this. When posed the question whether the paralegal is as an exempt professional or nonexempt employee under the regulations—essentially asking whether paralegals are salaried employees or those that are entitled to overtime compensation—the DOL did not recognize them as exempt. Therefore, the status of the profession is not yet resolved as there remain contradictory determinations from the courts and legislatures.

The delicate situation of the profession can also be hindered by ethical considerations. To establish the appropriate reputation, paralegals must be ever cognizant of their professional responsibility. Presented below are some problems that may have occurred during your office day, and that may bear discussing with your immediate supervisor.

For example, have you ever gone on a date with a client of your attorney? Dated a defendant or a defendant's witness? Have you had what you thought was an "innocent" lunch? *Think about it:* Conflict of interest or not? The next few pages are food for thought.

Fact Situations

1. A paralegal working for a partner in a law firm was asked by his attorney to transfer his billable hours from one client's case to another's and to bill on a separate case for hours he had not worked at all. He approached the senior partner of the firm, who was also the chair of the State Bar Ethics Committee, and requested to be transferred to another attorney. The senior partner approved his transfer and said he would speak to the partner. Months later the situation was repeated with the partner's new paralegal.

2. In the first month of his new job, while going through some files, a probate paralegal found a case that was five years old and had not been worked on for a long time. It appeared that the court dates had been repeatedly postponed and the case forgotten. He pointed out the lack of progress on this case to the attorney. The attorney's response was "We'll get to it when we get to it."

3. A paralegal moved from a plaintiff to a defense PI firm and was asked to work on the same case. He notified his attorney of the situation and was told to use what he knew.

4. A paralegal received a frantic call from a client in a dissolution case who said she'd just found out that her husband had cleaned out their joint checking account. The attorney was out of town. The client asked if she should clean out their joint savings account. The paralegal responded, "Well, I can't give you legal advice, but if I were you I would do it."

5. A client wearing a surgical collar came into his attorney's office to sign some papers regarding his personal injury case. Later on that day the paralegal saw the client walking along the street without the collar. He told the attorney and the attorney told him to ignore it.

Which of the following situations does *not* violate any Code of Ethics for Legal Assistants as adopted by the American Paralegal Association?

a. Ralph worked as a clerk in a law office for ten years. He now has his own paralegal consulting firm.

b. Julie works in a law office under a duly qualified attorney. She drafts legal documents.

c. Ralph is a certified legal assistant and consults with business clients, giving them timely advice.

d. All of the above are in violation of professional ethics.

Which of the following situations does *not* violate any Code of Ethics for Legal Assistants as adopted by The American Paralegal Association?

a. As Mrs. Dalton left the office, Sue and Margaret, legal assistants, discussed her previous divorce package and how it wouldn't apply to her current position. They were standing in the receptionist's area at the time.

b. Sue's mother had some legal problems with a real estate closing so Sue, responding to her mother's request, talked to the real estate attorney to learn some of the facts.

c. Margaret's sister needed a divorce so Margaret prepared all the paperwork for her so she could handle her own.

d. All of the above are in violation of professional ethics.

Which of the following situations does *not* violate any Code of Ethics for Legal Assistants as adopted by The American Paralegal Association?

a. Terry asks his friend Mike to stop at the site of an accident so he can give his paralegal business card to the injured driver. The ambulance is on the scene.

b. Terry asks his friend Mike to stop at the site of an accident so he can give his paralegal business card to the injured driver. The ambulance is *not* on the scene.

c. Terry receives a bonus for every client he brings into the law office. Therefore, he places an ad in the local paper for the law firm.

d. All of the above are in violation of professional ethics.

Which of the following situations does *not* violate any Code of Ethics for Legal Assistants as adopted by The American Paralegal Association?

a. Sam Horn works in a law office as a legal assistant, duly qualified and certified. He prints cards saying: "Law Firm of G, L & M, specialists in litigation and general practice; Sam Horn, certified paralegal."

b. Alexandra Day works in a law office as a legal assistant, duly certified. She prints cards saying: "Alex Day, specialist in litigation and general practice."

c. Becky Night works at an insurance company doing legal research as a certified paralegal. Her cards say: "Becky Night, Certified Legal Research Analyst."

d. All of the above are in violation of professional ethics.

The Paralegal as Notary Public: An Ethical Dilemma

A paralegal acting as a notary public is playing a double role, which is fraught with pitfalls and possible conflicts of interest.

To illustrate this dilemma, consider the following:

1. As you know, the most important obligation a notary has to the public being served is:

   - To judge what acts constitute the practice of law and

   - What acts constitute the practice of a notary public.

2. And further, a notary public is only responsible for:

   - Executing and witnessing documents,

   - Confirming that the signatures are legal, and

   - The truth or authenticity of said signatures.

To do anything else subjects a notary to a possible lawsuit or claim.

On the other hand, the duties and role of a paralegal per se, in general, go far beyond that of a notary public, such as:

- To interview clients—after instruction of attorney;

- The drafting of preliminary and final documents after approval by attorney;

- The conduction of preliminary and final legal research after consultation with the attorney;

- The conduction of investigation of clients and witnesses at the insistence and request of the attorney:

- The necessary and required legwork and follow-up procedures mentioned above and much, much more in some offices.

So that when you put these two professionals into one individual, as a practical day-by-day procedure, separating them is no easy task. Hence, the paralegal who acts as a notary public should ask himself/herself the following questions in order to determine whether stepping into that gray area could be construed as the practice of law:

- Should you charge for it? If so, does the fact that you are being paid cause you to be more careful?

- Do you take more time and give more legal information because you are being paid directly?

- If you are doing this merely as a convenience for the office and do not charge, are you less careful since the ultimate responsibility lies with the boss?

- Do you put more time in and have the tendency to give legal advice because you are trained in the art, if it is being done as part of your job as a paralegal?

- Do you take more time and tend to give legal advice because the client is a friend of yours, or do you feel sorry for clients who are unfamiliar with American law and language and hence do not understand?

- Do you notarize a document because you are told to do so by your employer—such as notarizing a buddy's signature or an unknown client's signature, simply because you have been instructed to do so by your employer?

To further underscore the double role of the paralegal acting as a notary public, consider the following question.

> **Question:** Do paralegals have the notarial problem of having to make decisions and judgments in the course of their work for which there are no instructions? If so, how does a paralegal solve or attempt to solve this problem?
>
> **Answer:** "Using your head" or "common sense" are the phrases often used by the attorney.

This is particularly true when a paralegal should have seen that what his attorney instructed him to do was incorrect, and either advised his attorney tactfully, or gone forward and corrected the mistake. Oftentimes, when a paralegal is left alone, as when the attorney is engaged in trial or is out of the city, he is placed in a position to make decisions without instruction. On these occasions, the paralegal uses his best judgment, resulting from the experience of working closely with his employer, which enables him to answer the question: He solves the problem as the employer would have done had he been on hand to give the instruction. Even then, a paralegal awaits the return of the employer with fear and trepidation, hoping that the right decision has been made.

> **NOTE:** We have found it to be the better part of valor to have another attorney in the office review any and all documents prepared in the absence of your attorney before the same are filed with the court.

Compare this to the role of the paralegal working as a notary public in solving a similar and like problem. The difference is that as a notary you are not required to work under the direct supervision of an attorney; hence your understanding of the law and the particular aspect of a given situation is more vital and crucial. Any decision you make would be final.

EXAMPLE

In the case of a paralegal, let us suppose that the employer has instructed his paralegal to prepare a declaration with supporting Memorandum of Points and Authorities to accompany a motion to be filed in court by Monday and he is leaving the city for the weekend. The paralegal, therefore, has to review the file, the facts of the case, do the legal research, prepare the document in his absence, and have another attorney in the office sign it on behalf of his employer, since paralegals cannot sign legal documents that are filed in the courts. The other attorney, not being familiar with the case, will of course rely heavily on what the paralegal has done and therefore will go blindly forward and sign the document.

This is a classic case in which a paralegal must use judgment to make a decision as to what should be incorporated in the Declaration as well as being sure that the Memorandum of Points and Authorities clearly supports the Declaration in order to win the motion.

Compare this to a notary public, who has the discretion to make the decision to notarize or not notarize a document based on what the client has said. Should the decision be to notarize the document, the notary is taking on the responsibility that what has been stated is the truth as to the facts.

Once that has been done, and the same is recorded, it has become final. The notary is taking a risk, because the client may or may not be a stranger, but this is a professional judgment based on years of experience and expertise. The notary may or may not have it reviewed by any attorney, since he does not work under the direction of an attorney.

CHAPTER TWO

In-House Training Program

Purpose

Law firm management, having been convinced of the need and viability of utilizing paralegals, may find that attorneys do not know how to utilize the special skills of a paralegal efficiently; or how much supervision is necessary; or even what tasks a paralegal can or should be able to perform, without infringing upon the practice of law. The purpose of this chapter, therefore, is to set forth tried and proven duties that can be and are being performed by paralegals without infringing upon the attorney's practice of his profession.

This chapter attempts to address the two remaining problems facing the attorneys, i.e., what and how laypersons should be taught and trained to perform to their optimum; and how to remove the doubts and fears of the attorneys as to what legal tasks a paralegal is capable of performing without encroaching upon the attorneys' bailiwick. This is the fine-line distinction between the paralegal's proper exercise of his skills and knowledge of the law and the unauthorized practice of law.

This chapter is also geared to aiding paralegal managers, coordinators, or liaison attorneys in teaching/training laypersons to become paralegals; or to fine-tuning the skills of a currently practicing paralegal. It is further intended to give these lay individuals the bread-and-butter tools they will need to become viable members of the law firm or team. Recognizing the vital importance that proper oversight of paralegals plays in the workforce, IPMA (International Paralegal Management Association, formerly LAMA, the Legal Assistant Management Association) has gained steady recognition and influence in this field. For more information, visit www.paralegalmanagement.org/ipma.

Introduction

Let us assume that your office is engaged in defense litigation and that you are representing the insurance carrier for the defendant. Let us assume further that negotiations between the parties have failed and your offices are in receipt of all the documents pertinent, including, but not limited to, the summons and complaint, the report of the incident, investigative reports, statements of all witnesses, and any medical reports on file to date. All these documents pertain to a five-car collision.

Continuing with this hypothesis, let us assume that there are three plaintiffs, i.e., the driver of the car, the registered owner of the car, and a passenger. Then let us assume that there are five defendants, all of whom were either drivers or passengers in the respective vehicles.

This is obviously a case requiring analytical ability to determine the right of the parties and, of course, the liability of your client. As such, based on the qualifications and experience of your paralegal as to the theory of law in this type of case, you could give this assignment to him for analysis and evaluation.

To determine this, you would of course have to consider client contact. Could this individual, after the initial client-attorney contact, fill out a report with the client that would be sufficient to obtain the necessary information required and the client's cooperation? Does the paralegal have the proper oral and writing skills?

Another factor to be determined is the nature and extent of the legal research. It is the feeling of some offices that paralegals should not be given in-depth legal research projects. Here again, you should look to the experience and know-how of your paralegal. If instructed properly, a paralegal can successfully pursue and complete any legal research project. In the above hypothesis, a paralegal would be looking to the liability exposure of the client and the negligence on the part of plaintiffs, court rulings, and decisions in other similar and like cases, in order to prepare an evaluation memorandum setting forth these findings and case law.

The customary practice in most medium to large offices is to have a senior lead attorney, an associate attorney, a law clerk, a legal secretary, and a paralegal. This being true, in considering the development of a paralegal program or department, you must ask yourself three questions: (1) Can the legal tasks currently being performed by these individuals be delegated to a layman such as a paralegal? (2) Would this delegation be violative of the duties currently being performed by the senior lead and associate attorney? And (3) Would this delegation deprive the law clerk of the experience he will need for future use in a law practice?

For example, if it is a customary practice for the senior lead attorney to be responsible for "rainmaking" clients for the offices, is it fair and equitable that he be required to do demanding, routine legal tasks on the cases he brings into the office? Is it economically feasible for the associate attorney, who in most offices is responsible for the trial work of said cases, to be responsible for the mundane, routine tasks necessary to defend the client's position? And is it good economics and practical to utilize the services of a law clerk to perform these tasks in a slow methodical manner, when an experienced paralegal can do it in a shorter, more efficient, expeditious manner?

Remember, a paralegal has been trained to be analytical, and for this reason could be delegated the responsibility of analyzing said facts and bifurcating the rights of the various parties, plaintiff or defendant. Depending on your office policy relating to client contact, the paralegal should have developed all the oral skills to enable productive contact. And remember, the paralegal was specifically trained to do legal research. If you are not using the skills of your paralegal in either of the aforementioned categories, your office is wasting a valuable resource.

Establishing a Paralegal Program
Generally

The following is submitted as a flexible step-by-step procedure that can be used in establishing an in-house paralegal training program.

One of the prime factors to be considered is the attorney or attorneys who will be working with the paralegal.

1. The attorney(s) should have an understanding as to what a paralegal is all about and what duties the paralegal is capable of performing. This may entail reviewing the state's or the ABA's Guidelines for the Utilization of Paralegals;

2. The attorney must want to use these special skills;

3. The attorney must be an individual willing to delegate to his paralegal full credit as a valuable member of the legal team;

4. The attorney must be willing to change old habits;

5. The attorney must have an open mind; and

6. The attorney must be willing to recognize the need for a change with the advent of the paralegal into the legal workforce.

Cooperation is the key in this area of transition.

There *must* be a commitment by the firm. This is the key element in the success of an in-house training program. Additionally, the firm must have long-range goals in connection with the in-house training program and in the utilization of its paralegal personnel.

Using the Paralegal to Raise the
Level of Efficiency in the Law Office

Many young associates and/or law students find that certain detailed work, capable of being performed by a paralegal, is incompatible with their education and ultimate desire to become partners in a law firm. And, most often, senior partners prefer to use paralegals for detailed, time-consuming work, since it results in a cheaper, more efficient operation and frees up the young associate or law student to do the things for which he was trained.

This preference on the part of the senior partner stems from the fact that the average young associate or law student was not taught court procedures, preparation of court pleadings, or with whom or where to file said documents once completed. It is accepted that he must learn these things before he can carry his weight in a law office and be considered an integral member of the legal team—unless, of course, he had the good fortune to work as a law clerk during his tenure in law school.

Utilizing the skills of the paralegal to raise the level of efficiency in this regard is feasible and proper. Indeed, the paralegal can act as a liaison between the partner and the young associate since he if trained, can relate to a young associate much better than a young associate can relate to the senior partner. Furthermore, the senior partner does not have the time to train the young associate in areas of court procedure and format of pleadings, etc.; hence the paralegal can be used as a trainer in helping young associates pick up the fine points of this phase of the practice of law. The use of paralegals will also enable the lawyers to enhance the quality of the substantial work for which they were trained. Finally, there is the important economic benefit to be derived from the utilization of paralegals.

Let me give you an example. You have an attorney who charges fixed dollars per hour. This attorney is hypothetically limited to an eight-hour day and probably most of his time would be devoted to one or two—or if you stretch it—maybe three matters.

On the other side of the coin, if the same attorney had a specially trained paralegal, he could organize the work to be performed on five, six, possibly even seven matters, thus devoting perhaps one or two hours to instruction. By utilizing the paralegal who could perform routine duties and complete the matter, an attorney could charge eight hours at his rate and charge a lesser rate for the effective working time of a paralegal under his supervision. It is well documented that an attorney who takes advantage of the special skills of a well-trained paralegal can accomplish much more on behalf of his client at a lesser expense to his client, and still generate more income for the firm.

What does this look like using numbers? This equation is greatly simplified for demonstration purposes.

SCENARIO 1

Employee		Time	Rate	Total Billable
Attorney	Matter 1	2.5	$200	$500
	Matter 2	3.5	$250	$875
	Matter 3	1.0	$200	$200
	Matter 4	2.0	$250	$500
Daily Billable for Firm				**$2,275**

Note that the attorney bills out at a higher rate for more complicated tasks performed on matters 2 and 4.

SCENARIO 2

Instead of doing all the work herself, the attorney delegates some of the initial drafting work for pleadings and interrogatories and some legal research to the paralegal. This frees up time for the attorney either to work longer on a complicated matter or to take on another matter.

Employee		Time	Rate	Total Billable
Attorney	Matter 1	1.0	$200	$200
	Matter 2	4.0	$250	$1,000
	Matter 3	.5	$200	$100
	Matter 4	2.0	$250	$500
	Matter 5	.5	$250	$125
Paralegal	Matter 1	2.5	$75	$187.50
	Matter 3	1.5	$75	$112.50
	Matter 5	5.0	$75	$375.00
Daily Billable for Firm				**$2,600**

Analyzing these scenarios shows that Client 1 saves money by having the paralegal do the initial drafting of the pleadings. (Total cost to the client=$387.50 instead of $500.) The attorney remains responsible for the final submission, but has saved an hour and a half out of his day; he is free to bill out at least $300 on another matter. The same thing happens for matter 3. Further, the attorney is able to review the paralegal's intensive work on interrogatories on matter 5. In sum, the clients have saved money, the attorney can bill out on other matters at a higher rate and handle more matters, and the firm overall makes more money during the day simply by effectively using the paralegal.

Clarification of Roles

From an experienced paralegal's point of view, we have determined that the role of the attorney is as follows:

1. Pinpointing the abilities and skills of the legal team, i.e., associate, paralegal, and legal secretary;

2. Delegating to the team members the tasks the attorney feels, because of their individualized skills, they can perform more efficiently;

3. Instructing each member, together or separately, as to the conclusion desired in the client's matter so that each will understand the integral role his tasks play in the overall picture; and

4. Reviewing the draft and/or legal memoranda, and giving final approval of the work accomplished by each.

Most important, it should be remembered by support staff that an attorney is a very busy individual, rainmaking business for the office, consulting with clients, and advocating their claims before the courts.

The Key

As an aid in determining these special skills and the roles to be played by the members of the legal team, we submit the following Request for Admissions:

1. Admit that the law student's course of study is designed to create a class of persons who will be advocates;

2. Admit that the prime assets of an attorney are his education and resulting specialized ability, judgment, and analytical skills;

3. Admit that it is the exclusive domain of the attorney to direct the course of the lawsuit for the benefit of his client;

4. Admit that a primary role of the attorney is deciding on a course of action based upon his knowledge of the law and the facts of the particular case;

5. Admit that the foregoing is designed to reach the conclusions desired by a client, in compliance with the appropriate limit of regulations or statutory laws pertinent thereto;

6. Admit that, together with the advocacy role and the realization of a client's desire, the role of the attorney is to direct an expeditious and efficient performance on behalf of his client;

7. Admit that the above and foregoing is "The Practice of Law" as defined by the organized bar; and finally,

8. Admit that the above and foregoing being true, then any task that does not require the exercise of an attorney's prime assets, i.e., specialized ability, judgment, and analytical skills, can be performed by a paralegal.

Thus, the role of a senior partner or associate, and perhaps of the law student, would include the following:

1. Determining the facts of the case, or triable issues;

2. Determining the law, rule, or regulation applicable to these facts or issues;

3. Applying the law, rule, or regulations applicable; and

4. Proceeding therefrom to plan the strategy to be utilized in advocating the client's claim or lawsuit.

Qualities to Look for in a Paralegal

- An outgoing personality;

- Ability to communicate, both verbally and in writing;

- Self-reliance;

- Ability to think critically rather than to perform tasks robotically;

- Willingness to accept responsibility;

- Willingness to follow directions;

- Understanding thoroughly not only every step in the prosecution of a claim being handled, but also the critical requirement for *the direct supervision of the attorney at all times*; and

- Specific training in these special skills either through school offerings or in-house training.

Educational Background of Paralegals

For the benefit of the attorneys, and for their review and edification, submitted herewith is a brief description of what paralegals learn in school to prepare them to be members of a legal team. For the benefit of paralegals, this list should serve as a baseline for evaluating an educational offering.

From this course, the attorneys and the paralegals will get a better idea of what legal tasks can be delegated to the non-attorneys on their team.

Both the ABA and AAfPE have taken the position that short-course programs ("weekend wonders") do not fully prepare students to become professional paralegals. However, the lack of any standardization either nationally or by state means that there is a diverse array of educational/training options in the marketplace. In most ABA-accredited paralegal schools, the following course offerings are taught. These courses are normally taught by attorneys and may include a paralegal assistant.

1. INTRODUCTION TO LAW AND/OR TO THE PARALEGAL PROFESSION, which discusses the nature of the law and the legal system. The focus may include either or both the structure and function of the judiciary and/or the paralegals' role within that system. Students are also introduced to the methods of case analysis and legal reasoning. Paralegal and attorney ethics and professional responsibility are generally covered as well. Although many programs also include a stand-alone ethics course and teach ethics across the curriculum.

2. LEGAL WRITING, which concerns itself with basic legal vocabulary, writing logically, and reading for comprehension. The course introduces the students to the conventions of the basic formats used most often in the office, letters, memoranda, case briefs, and the like.

3. LAW OFFICE ADMINISTRATION, which deals with the organization and function of a law firm and the technology associated with running the office and managing cases. Increasingly, this course is taught in a computer lab, as software exists for almost every task and specialty in the practice of law. Further, database administration is essential in case management.

4. LEGAL RESEARCH, wherein the paralegal is introduced to the law library, its organization, and how to use the various resources. Usually the students are given certain problems that require extensive research skills to solve. They are expected to integrate book research, including Shepardizing, as well as computerized research using one of the major databases such as LexisNexis or Westlaw. This culminates in the preparation of case briefs and legal memoranda to reflect upon and effectively convey their findings and to demonstrate their proficiency at both research and writing.

5. LITIGATION. This particular area of the course offering can also be a specialization. It includes the introduction to the preparation of complaints, answers, demurrers and various other pretrial motions, points, and authorities. Additionally, the paralegal learns how to set up various files, including but not limited to document files, legal research files, evidence files, indexing and cross-referencing documents and charts, etc.

- Discovery in this course includes instruction in the five vehicles of discovery, which include the analysis and preparation of interrogatories, answers to interrogatories, requests for production of documents, requests for admissions, and preparing notices of depositions.

- *Trial preparation.* This phase of a litigation course concerns itself with summarization of depositions, interrogatories, analyzing and abstracting documents from the file, preparing the list of exhibits, preparation of the trial book, and preparing the necessary post-trial motions for after trial, such as the notice of appeal, etc.

It should be noted that a paralegal, in pursuing a substantive paralegal education program, also has the opportunity to specialize in other areas, such as, but not limited to wills; trust and estate planning; property (real estate); torts; family law; contracts; workers' compensation; bankruptcy law and procedure; and criminal law and procedure.

As you can tell from the above course listings, the average paralegal program takes at least two to two and a half years to complete, and as such, the paralegal is well-qualified to assist the attorney in the practice of his profession. The ABA and AAfPE course load is a minimum of eighteen hours in legal specialty, and many programs go well beyond that minimum.

Tips for Working Paralegals and Their Supervising Attorneys

If your office is organized into teams, the paralegal should be aware of each member of the team, and be given a synopsis of the case or cases being worked on and their status as well as the role he is expected to play therein. Moreover, it is incumbent upon the paralegal to understand the theory of law in the area, either by an overview discussion of it with the attorney or law clerk, or by doing research on his own.

Once this is accomplished, the attorney should review with the paralegal the client interview sheet to acquaint him with the office policy in the area of client-office relationship and procedure; then specifically that which is personal to each attorney, how he likes the pleadings handled, and the format that each normally uses.

Since the court now allows printed forms of complaints, interrogatories, answers, etc., the attorney should make the paralegal aware of the availability of these documents and the attorney's preference for them—or against them—in order to utilize the paralegal's time more efficiently. This is mentioned since those paralegals trained as a result of institutional training have been taught to draft pleadings from scratch and create the document as opposed to filling in blank spaces on a printed form.

Throughout all of the above, you should not leave out your *valued legal secretary*, for without him, it would not work. He plays a very important role as a member of the legal team and should be requested and permitted to work closely with the paralegal.

Legal Tasks That Can Be Delegated to a Paralegal

For a high-volume litigation office, the following tasks are examples, to which the paralegal is not necessarily limited:

1. Drafting various substantive correspondence such as "bad faith" and/or "demand" letters, which requires a thorough review of the file (see Exhibits A and B, below);

2. Preparing draft complaints for the review, correction, modification, and final acceptance and submission of the attorney;

3. Preparing a draft answer, drafting affirmative defenses, and constructing possible counterclaims;

4. Preparing routine answers to interrogatories, which require the expenditure of a great deal of the attorney's time reviewing the file;

5. Marshaling of interrogatories or requests for admissions, which requires the review and study of a file to produce another time-consuming project;

6. Completing legal research projects and drafting legal memoranda regarding the findings (the extent of these tasks depends on the skill of the paralegal);

7. Preparing certain motions which could either be done in final form at the direction of the attorney or submitted in draft;

8. Drafting of an affidavit for the attorney in support of a motion;

9. Preparing a Memorandum of Points and Authorities in support of a motion; and finally,

10. Doing all of the above, together with the page-lining of depositions, the summary of medical reports, the summary of reporter's transcripts, the indexing of documents, preparation of exhibits, and other trial pleadings.

Exhibit A: Component Parts of a Demand Letter

This letter must be sent by certified mail, return receipt requested.

1. The first paragraph of your demand letter sets forth the purpose of the letter, i.e., a demand for a settlement.

2. This paragraph deals with the liability of the party to whom the letter is being addressed.

3. Some attorneys would set forth at this point the contentions of the party who is sending the letter and sometimes the contentions of the party to whom it is being addressed.

4. This paragraph (which could be more than one) sets forth the injuries of the plaintiff (defendant) and damages sustained.

5. This is normally the conclusion, which could also be a summary of the previous paragraphs, again explaining why the case should be settled at this point for the figure amount offered in the first paragraph. It is suggested, should the occasion arise and you are requested to do a demand letter, that you discuss paragraphs one and five to be sure that the figure amount discussed is correct.

The information for the contents of paragraphs two, three, and four can be found in both your correspondence and pleading files.

Exhibit B: "Bad Faith" Extra Contract Liability

DEFINITION

"No showing of evil motives or intentional misconduct is required, but rather a breach of the covenant of good faith and their dealing implied by law in every contract. It gives rise to tort liability."

FIRST-PARTY CLAIMS

1. Claims under life, health, and disability policy;

2. Claims for damages to an insured's property, homeowner's insurance, commercial casualty policies, third-party claims;

3. When a liability insurer refuses to "defend" the insured against the third party's claim despite the obligation to do so;

4. The third-party case is one in which the "bad faith" cause of action is based on an insurance company's unreasonable handling of, or refusal to settle a third party's claim against the insured under a liability insurance policy.

CHAPTER THREE

The Paralegal's Effectiveness in the Modern Law Office

Social change and need are the factors that have encouraged the advent and use of the legal assistant/paralegal over the past few decades. These factors include:

1. Trend toward specialization in law by attorneys, with concomitant development of subspecialists;

2. Desire of legal secretaries and other non-lawyers for advancement in a recognized profession;

3. Recognition of the legal needs of low- and moderate-income families not adequately served under the old system;

4. Rising costs of legal services, and the need to deliver them more efficiently;

5. Desire of the legal profession to respond positively and reduce the loss of additional areas of their practice to accountants, real estate brokers, and banks;

6. Expanded use of small-claims courts, which removes the need for an attorney and crystallizes the use of paralegals to aid these lay litigants; and

7. Upward trend of the use of Alternate Dispute Resolution (ADR) procedures.

But the most compelling reason for hiring a paralegal was, and is, economic. The use of a paralegal has been a great boon to the increase of the gross income of today's law firm, without raising the cost of delivery of legal services to the public. That use has increased the public's ability to afford an attorney when in need of legal advice.

Change in Hiring Practices and Utilization of Paralegals

Large law firms are setting up "paralegal series" or levels within their offices not unlike the Civil Service Paralegal Series within the state and federal government agencies, which now have supervising paralegals who delegate duties to other paralegals, overseeing their work prior to submission to the attorney for review, change, and so forth.

Law firms often train new paralegals or paralegal trainees or legal secretaries who wish to become paralegals as a promotion vehicle. Such recognition of the duties and responsibilities of paralegalism not only enhances the prestige of the paralegal, but increases salaries and gives the paralegal a feeling of self-fulfillment.

There is an intriguing change in the attitude of today's paralegal. Years ago legal assistants were saying that one of the reasons they were far more employable than the young associate was their staying power; they would not leave the law firm to "go out on their own," as is common practice among young associates after a year or two in a law firm.

Today, we find that there are individual paralegals who freelance their skills, and there are paralegals operating their own "paralegal services" businesses for attorneys on a per-diem or hourly basis or even on a retainer agreement. Furthermore, we find legal secretarial-services companies advertising for and using these independent paralegal contractors to attract attorney business for their legal secretarial operation.

And what is more surprising are the recent surveys and researches that indicate that since there are more employable attorneys in the marketplace than there are employing attorneys (according to legal-placement-service agencies), these young attorneys are seeking job opportunities as paralegals, since that is where the jobs are and what the law firms are hiring.

Impact of Technology

Innovative changes and the exponential growth of both hardware and software technology have radically changed the way in which attorneys practice law. Technology is used daily to handle complex litigation, routine letters and clauses, corporate documents, case management, and billing, to name only a few. This has also radically changed the duties of paralegals and at the same time has expanded the role and effectiveness of the paralegal and his value to the attorney-employer.

Specifically, these diverse software and computer systems are being used in almost every phase of the law practice and every stage of case management.

There is a plethora of the litigation support systems that have become a vital tool in trial preparation, in the discovery process, and in the handling of voluminous documents in complex litigation. Indeed, an entirely new profession has branched off from the traditional paralegal to the IT legal support personnel. The focus of these specialists is to design, implement, and maintain the legal/litigation databases. They may also be involved in training others in the firm on database use and document management.

New Paralegals Entering the Profession

During the peak of the paralegal movement (from about 1968 to 1975), a legal assistant was primarily a legal secretary turned legal assistant after years of legal work experience in a law office or with other law-related background. A letter of recommendation from his attorney-employer was sufficient for enrollment in a school offering a paralegal course. Alternatively, prospective paralegals were those reentering the job market and being trained in-house by their attorney-employers to become paralegals.

A lot has changed since then. Today's would-be paralegal may come from a variety of backgrounds. Although not as prevalent as it once was, some still come directly from high school to be trained in-house and work their way up the training ladder. More likely, the future paralegal may choose to either directly enter a paralegal program at a two- or four-year school and earn a paralegal studies degree, or finish the bachelor's degree in any major and subsequently pursue a post-BA certificate from a qualified institution.

Furthermore, today's paralegal can be in an alternative employment plan, or in a new career for retired persons; this may be a job opportunity for individuals seeking to change careers, such as law students, civil-service employees, armed-forces personnel, and the like.

Most amazing is the prison inmate "attorney" seeking formal education to become a paralegal while still incarcerated in a penal institution.

Changes in Educational Requirements and Benefits

Years ago all a graduating student could hope to receive from a paralegal course was a certificate of completion. Today, a student can receive any of the following: a bachelor of science degree in paralegal studies; an associate's degree in paralegal studies (this may be an AA, AS or an AAS depending on the granting institution); or a post-baccalaureate paralegal certificate or a paralegal certificate. To acquire the basic paralegal certificate now requires an AA degree or its equivalent.

There are other variations of these educational offerings. Many traditional institutions as well as the online schools are offering courses or entire programs via distance learning. The diploma, degree, or certificate earned varies greatly. It is important for the prospective paralegal to investigate all the options available and make the best choice based upon his own needs and the legal employment market in the area. Employers are continually raising their expectations for these vital positions in the legal field.

No matter what course of instruction the candidate ultimately pursues, the message is clear: Paralegals are expected not only to be vocationally trained, but also to be well-educated employees.

General Duties of Today's Paralegals

As the case for "access to justice" grows, paralegals will continue to play an active role in delivery of legal services in the various group and prepaid legal plans and legal clinics.

Moreover, their positive effect can be seen in the various law agencies such as state and federal district attorneys' offices, in public defenders' offices, and even in some correctional institutions.

In some parts of the country, paralegals are now being employed by newspapers and consumer advocate organizations and are even holding legislative positions in state governments.

And as mentioned before, the more experienced paralegals are proliferating as "independent contractors," servicing attorneys on an "as-needed basis" with the assistance of litigation support systems in their homes. Others are opening up their own offices with an in-house attorney on staff.

There is a controversy regarding a newer development, "independent paralegals" who are attempting to offer their services to the public without the supervision of a licensed attorney. Whereas freelance paralegals operate as independent contractors under the direction of an ultimately responsible attorney, "independent paralegals" are held directly accountable and responsible for their own work product. Without regulation, as in California and Arizona for "legal document preparers," the public remains susceptible to their potential malpractice.

Specific Duties of Today's Paralegals

Some specific examples of the extended use and scope of paralegal duties in today's modern law office are:

General

Conduct interviews with clients to gather background information

Draft pleadings and documents

Organize and maintain files

Index or summarize documents or transcripts

Prepare client for court hearing

Update and maintain library materials

Review legal periodicals and material relevant to particular areas of law

Maintain calendar or tickler system

Be responsible for office administration or personnel

Conduct legal research, including procedural, administrative, and case law research

Bankruptcy

Interview clients to obtain information for filing petitions and schedules

Confirm amounts owed to creditors and verify dates incurred

Identify secured and unsecured claims of creditors

Draft and file petitions, schedules, and proofs of claim

Obtain case information from U.S. Bankruptcy Court clerk

Check U.C.C. filings, real property records, and taxes owed

Identify exempt property

Maintain contact with client/debtor and verify compliance with instructions to debtors

Draft, serve, and file debtor's monthly financial statements in Chapter 11 cases

Draft, serve, and file complaints in adversary proceedings

Correspond with creditors, creditors' committee chair, creditors' committee attorney, trustee, and client

Prepare applications and orders including enforcement of stay, restraining sales, reinstatement of utility service, venue, avoiding liens, approving reaffirmation or redemption, and abandonment

Prepare prefiling letters to creditors

Draft and file applications and orders to employ professional persons

Prepare motion to allow claim or objection to claim

Draft and file attorneys' fee applications

Attend Section 341(a) meetings and Chapter 13 Plan confirmation hearing

Maintain log to check off discharge and status of bankruptcy

Business

Check availability and reserve corporate name

Draft and file articles of incorporation

Complete and file qualification of foreign corporations

Draft certificates of authority for foreign corporation

Obtain good standing certificates from secretary of state

Draft bylaws, notices, and minutes or consents for organization meeting

Draft subscription agreements, stock certificates, investment letters, and banking resolutions

Draft shareholder agreements, buy-sell agreements, employment agreements, and stock option plans

Complete and file any assumed name certificates

Draft and file certificates of designation for preferred stock issuances

Complete and file election by small business corporation and subsequent shareholders' consents to such election

Complete and file application for employer identification number, workers' compensation, unemployment insurance, and employer withholding tax registration

Complete and file application for appropriate licenses to operate specific businesses, trade name applications, copyright applications, and financing statements

Order minute book, stock book, and seal

Draft and file application for proper licensing when forming professional or special purpose corporation

Draft response to auditors' information request and prepare for audit

Complete reporting and compliance requirements for multi-state corporations, including qualifying corporation under state law

Secure licenses and permits, e.g., liquor, sales tax, health department, and building permits

Complete change of agent/address forms

Prepare and file annual reports

Maintain a tickler system for annual meetings, payments of bonuses to offices, contribution to pension and profit-sharing plans, exercise of stock options, and filing of annual reports

Draft notices, proxies, affidavits of mailing, agenda, ballots, and oaths of judges of election, for annual meeting

Draft shareholders and directors' minutes

Draft written consents in lieu of meetings

Draft plans and/or resolutions of liquidation or dissolution including required state forms to effect dissolution

Draft articles of merger and plan of merger

Draft closing checklists and closing memoranda

Assist in closing, managing assembly and execution of documents

Prepare closing files and bound volumes

Prepare and file financing statements, U.C.C. agreements, or amendments

Obtain consents to assignments, releases, and signatures on consent resolutions

Draft articles of dissolution

Conduct due diligence investigation

Compile and index documents in corporate transactions

Draft partnership agreements including noncompetition assignment of interests and approval of substituted partner

Draft certificates of limited partnership

Draft and file trade name documents

Draft amendments to partnership agreements, certificates of amendment to certificates of limited partnership, and amended trade name documents

Draft certificates or cancellation of certificates of limited partnership and trade name withdrawals

Draft business organization federal and state tax returns

Collections

Conduct initial review of documents provided by client

Investigate public records for assets, including real estate records and prior judgments

Verify employment

Draft demand letter to debtor

Draft summons and complaint

Draft motions for or in opposition to summary judgment, including memoranda and affidavits in support

Draft judgment, cost bill, and other supporting pleadings

Maintain judgment account worksheet to record payments

Draft notice of demand to pay

Draft, file, and serve documents for judgment debtor examination

Draft, have issued, and serve writ of garnishment, order to release garnishment, and writ of execution

Arrange for indemnity bond for sheriff

Arrange for posting of notice of sale or publication of notice of sale

Maintain communication with sheriff re levy on personal property

Prepare bid and attend sheriff's sale on real property

Obtain certified copy of judgment transcript

Transfer judgment transcript to a different court

Obtain exemplified copy of foreign judgment

Prepare affidavit for transfer of a foreign judgment

Register judgment in a different state

Prepare and file satisfaction of judgment

Criminal

Prescreen prospective new client

Assist in initial interview of client with attorney

Prepare charges or plea for arraignment; make bail arrangements

Obtain discovery (police reports, search warrant, affidavit)

Draft motion compelling discovery or to produce additional documents

Analyze case based on discovery; gather information for plea bargaining

Draft motion for change of venue, demurrer, and motion to set aside indictment

Draft motion to suppress, motion to controvert, motion for civil compromise, and motion for diversion

Draft motion in limine, motion for return of property, motion to postpone trial, and motion to disqualify judge

Prepare for trial, including interviewing and subpoenaing witnesses; examining physical evidence, tangible objects, scene of alleged crime; and coordinating outside investigators and experts

Arrange for diversion, civil compromise, and work release

Draft supplemental memoranda of law and trial memorandum

Attend conference with prosecutor and pretrial conferences with judge and attorneys

Draft jury instructions

Attend and assist at trial

Draft motion in arrest of judgment, motion for new trial, and motion for release pending new trial/appeal

Attend conference with client regarding presentence report

Draft petition for leniency/probation

Research law regarding appealable issues and draft notice of appeal, assignments of error, and arguments

Employee Benefits

Draft qualified plan documents, trust agreements, custodial agreements, money purchase, 401(k), stock bonus, defined benefit plans, and IRA plans

Draft amendments and restatements to plans to bring into compliance with new law and regulations

Draft summary plan description

Draft deferred compensation plans, including nonqualified executive compensation, stock option, and medical reimbursement plans

Draft affiliate adoption statement

Draft notification of participation, election to participate, beneficiary designation, election out of qualified joint and survivor annuity, application for benefits, and election to contribute

Consult with business managers and actuaries to determine contribution and benefit formulas

Prepare schedules showing maximized employer contributions

Draft summary annual report

Draft benefit statement

Draft promissory note and salary assignment for participant loans

Draft board of directors resolutions for plan adoption, adoption of amendments, and fixing contributions

Prepare and file application for IRS determination letter

Prepare and file annual report (5500 series and related schedules)

Prepare PBGC premium forms

Submit descriptive documents to the Department of Labor

Monitor progress of implementation of new plans and amendments to verify that required actions occur on schedule

Draft plan amendments, qualify amendments with IRS, notice to Department of Labor

Coordinate general notice mailings to clients about potential impact of new legal developments on plans

Prepare notices to employees regarding significant changes in plan

Develop and maintain checklists, sets of model plans, administrative documents and letters, and update as new material is developed

Prepare summary of amendments required by new registration and assemble list of plans requiring such amendments

Research interpretive questions on prohibited transactions and qualified and nonqualified plans

Calculate employer contributions and forfeitures and allocate to participant accounts

Determine valuation adjustments and allocate to participant accounts

Calculate participant's years of service for eligibility and vesting

Calculate benefit for terminated participant

Test plan for discrimination, top-heaviness, or Section 415 limits

Terminate plans and qualify terminations with IRS and PBGC

Family Law

Draft petition for dissolution, summons, waiver of service, affidavit as to children, and response

Draft temporary motions, affidavits, and orders

Draft notice to produce

Draft property settlement and separation agreements

Attend initial interview with attorney and client

Complete domestic relations questionnaire form

Arrange for service of documents

Obtain settings for court hearings

Assist client in preparation of monthly income and expense sheet

Arrange for appraisers for real property and personal property

Draft subpoenas and arrange for service

Schedule expert witness interviews and availability at trial

Obtain information for discovery; organize, categorize, and determine completeness of discovery

Draft proposed stipulations

Prepare and record transfer of asset documents

Draft decree of dissolution, accompanying motions, and affidavits

Draft motion and affidavit for modification

Draft petition for adoption and consent for adoption

Draft decree of adoption

Draft petition for name change

Foreclosure

Order foreclosure report and review with respect to priority of lien holders and parties to be served

Locate addresses of parties to be served, draft foreclosure complaint, and arrange service

Draft motion, order of default, judgment, and decree of foreclosure

Draft motion and supporting documents for summary judgment

Draft subpoenas, notices of deposition, and requests for production, and prepare for trial if necessary

Draft presale documents to begin execution, including writ of execution and Draft Bid Sheet for sale

Draft postsale documents, including motion confirming sale, directing sheriff to execute deed, and writ of assistance

Draft deed in lieu of foreclosure

Draft appointment of successor trustee, notice of default and election to sell, and trustee's notice of sale

Set sale date and docket statutory deadlines to be met

Record notice of default and appointment of successor trustee

Prepare, serve, and arrange publication of trustee's notice of sale on grantors, occupants, and subsequent lien creditors

Record all proofs of service, affidavits of mailing, and publication prior to sale

Check for federal tax liens thirty days prior to sale and prepare and serve IRS with notice of nonjudicial sale if necessary

Prepare memorandum of amount due on sale

Prepare trustee's deed, certificate of nonmilitary service, and postsale memorandum; record deed and certificate

Appear at time and place set for sale to postpone sale

Draft and record trustee's deed after sale

Take possession, satisfy, and transmit promissory note and original trust deed to trustee

Intellectual Property

Prepare patent and/or trademark status summary reports

Docket and/or maintain docket system for due dates for responses, renewals, oppositions, Sections 8 and 15 filings, use affidavits, and working requirements

Docket and/or maintain docket system for payment of patent annuities in foreign countries

Conduct patent/trademark searches

Conduct online computer information searches of technical literature for patent/trademarks

Draft trademark registration application, renewal application, and registered user agreements

Draft power of attorney

Draft copyright applications

Research procedural matters, case law, and unfair competition matters

Conduct factual investigation using magazines and trade publications

Conduct prior art search

Conduct patent/trademark searches

Assist in opposition, interference, infringement, and related proceedings

Arrange for visual aids/models/mock-ups for trial use

Maintain files of new products and invention development

Review patent filings with engineers

Draft licenses/agreements regarding proprietary information/technology

Litigation

Draft complaint

Draft answer and/or other defensive pleadings

Draft provisional remedy documents, including injunctions, TROs, and attachments

Draft interrogatories, requests for production, and requests for admissions

Prepare summons and service of process

Draft discovery motions

Draft response to interrogatories, requests for production, and requests for admission

Locate, interview, and obtain statements from witnesses

Arrange for expert witnesses

Arrange for outside investigator

Review documents for response to request for production including screening for relevance and privilege

Control numbering and history of documents produced and received

Obtain/examine public records

Research legislative history

Prepare and serve subpoena duces tecum

Schedule deposition and arrange court reporter

Draft deposition questions and prepare deposition outline

Prepare witness files

Prepare witnesses for deposition

Attend document productions

Attend depositions

Index, digest, and summarize depositions

Follow up after depositions for additional information

Obtain, review, and analyze medical records

Analyze/summarize factual information

Prepare statistical/factual summaries or chronologies

Draft affidavits and declarations

Draft motions for extension of time

Draft demand letters and subpoenas

Organize documents and other physical evidence

Draft legal memoranda and/or briefs, including table of cases, statement of facts, and appendices

Check citations and/or Shepardize

Review briefs for accuracy of factual information

Identify and prepare potential and expert witnesses

Draft stipulation for admissibility of exhibits

Review trial exhibits for evidentiary purposes, relevance, and authentication

Organize trial exhibits

Prepare trial notebooks

Prepare trial subpoenas

Prepare deposition designations

Prepare documents and testimony to use for impeachment

Draft pretrial statements and settlement conference memoranda

Obtain jury list and biographical information on jurors

Draft jury instructions and voir dire

Coordinate witness attendance at trial

Monitor preparation of charts/graphs and other demonstrative evidence for use at trial

Attend trial, noting developments of the case as well as reactions of jurors, witnesses, and opposing counsel during trial

Maintain list of exhibits as mentioned, offered, admitted, or objected to

Draft cost bill

Prepare settlement calculations

Prepare comparative analysis of terms of potential settlement agreements

Draft settlement documents, including releases and dismissals

Supervise postjudgment collections

Draft notice of appeal

Draft factual information for appeal brief

Prepare corrections to trial transcript

Prepare recap or outline of trial transcripts

Maintain and update form files

Probate and Estate Planning

Meet with client and attorney at initial meeting

Answer questions from personal representative, surviving spouse, and other interested parties

Prepare and maintain a calendar system

Locate witnesses to will

Locate and notify heirs and devisees of probate proceeding

Publish appropriate notices to interested persons

Order public records, including birth, death, and marriage certificates

Collect information and/or assets for preparation of inventory and tax returns

Value assets (date of death and alternate valuation date)

Draft inventory, arrange for and attend inventory of safe deposit box

Handle matters re ancillary administrations

Maintain financial records of estate

Prepare and file claims for insurance proceeds and death benefits

Prepare disallowance of claims against the estate and monitor claims, including court files

Correspond with debtors and creditors to obtain pertinent information

Interpret will provisions

Apply for employer identification number and file notices of fiduciary relationship

Prepare and transmit necessary papers to transfer/liquidate assets, including stock, real estate, and motor vehicles

Prepare preliminary income projection and estimate taxes

Prepare state inheritance tax return and federal estate tax return

Prepare individual income tax returns for beneficiaries

Prepare decedent's final federal and state individual income tax returns

Draft federal and state gift tax returns

Prepare state and federal fiduciary income tax returns

Arrange for tax releases and payment of taxes

Draft petitions and orders for partial distribution

Draft accountings

Assist in audit of tax returns including correspondence, affidavits, and statements submitted upon audit

Draft distribution schedule and closing documents

Review documents and tax returns in connection with an ancillary proceeding

Draft tax returns for nonprobate estate

Collect data for estate planning, including current estate plans and assets

Prepare tax calculations for various estate plans

Draft wills, codicils, trust agreements, and amendments

Draft documents necessary to fund trusts

Prepare and record powers of attorney

Draft court documents for conservatorship

Draft inventory and accountings for conservatorship

Draft federal and state tax returns for conservatorship

Draft prenuptial agreements

Draft court documents for guardianships

Make postmortem tax planning calculations

Public Benefits

Represent claimants at SSI (Supplementary Security Income) hearings

Represent claimants at SSD (Social Security Disability) hearings

Research appropriate Social Security law

Assist with Medicare waivers and Medicare appeals

Assist with Social Security overpayment waivers

Locate medical information

Review Social Security file and obtain documentation

Negotiate with landlord and tenant to resolve problems

Assist with consumer fraud complaints and forward to Consumer Protection Division

Obtain documentation for unemployment claim

Real Property

Draft subdivision, condominium, and time-share registrations for in-state and out-of-state registrations

Draft registrations of recreational subdivisions for federal registrations

Organize recording procedures for large-scale recording and prepare draft of opinion letters

Prepare transaction books

Perform financial calculations (amortization, present and future value, discounting, APR)

Maintain current records regarding CPI, APR, Federal Reserve rate, and residential/commercial interest rates

Draft Truth-in-Lending Disclosure statements

Draft and review permits

Draft and review easements

Review surveys and run out legal descriptions to calculate acreage/square footage, locate easements, and determine actuary and adequacy of descriptions

Draft trust, warranty, bargain and sale, and other deeds

Draft notes, mortgages, and contracts of sale

Draft leases, assignments, extensions, and amendments

Draft purchase and sale agreements, letters of intent, earnest money agreements, and addenda

Draft U.C.C. filing, continuations, amendments, extensions, and terminations

Draft security agreements

Order and review title reports, including review of underlying encumbrances and exceptions and endorsement requests

Draft escrow instructions and preliminary closing statements

Review closing statements and documents prepared by escrow officer

Review loan payoff documentation and coordinate disbursement of loan proceeds

Prepare closing memoranda and organize/manage complex closings

Analyze conveyance, security, and lease documents

Review BLM and county records to determine validity of hard rock mineral claims

Review and analyze abstracts of title and chain of title to draft title opinions

Obtain lien waivers and certificates of completion for new construction

Check and review zoning and comprehensive plan designations; obtain letters on designation as closing requirement

Obtain and analyze appraisal information based on market, income, and cost approaches

Obtain canceled note, deed of trust, releases, and recorded original documents

Review title policy, insurance policy, closing statement, and other closing documents after closing and request corrections/revisions

Perform/order U.C.C. and litigation searches at county or state level

Obtain real and personal property tax information for proration and in preparation for appeals to Board of Equalization and Department of Revenue

Research state laws relating to conveyancing, recording, and financial statements

Maintain current zoning ordinances, comprehensive plans, real estate–related form file, and computer databases

Research county records to develop abstracts of title

Securities/Municipal Bonds

Draft registration statement, prospectus offering memoranda, and amendments

Organize filing of registration statement, including coordinating with printer, assembling appropriate copies, and preparing transmittal letters

Monitor distribution of offering memoranda

Draft 1934 Act reports

Draft questionnaire for officers, directors, and principal shareholders

Draft promissory notes, underwriting agreements, trust indentures, and bond purchase agreements

Obtain CVSIP number, NASDAQ, Standard and Poor's, and Moody's Securities Manual listings

Draft Blue Sky memoranda and applications for exemption

Draft legal investment survey

Draft Blue Sky registration

Draft and file applications for registration, including uniform consent to service of process, powers of attorney, and uniform form of corporate resolutions

Notify state securities administrators of SEC effectiveness

Draft and file dealer and/or salesmen registration documents

Perfect securities or dealer exemptions

Prepare memoranda on the availability of exemptions

Research and prepare documents for after-market trading exemptions

Draft and file documents for registering broker/dealers and/or salesmen with NASD, SEC, and state securities commissions

Draft and file documents for renewing or withdrawing the registration of broker/dealers with salesmen

Qualify dealer corporations where applicable

Draft portions of Forms 3, 4, 8, 8-K, 10, 10-K, 10-Q, 13D, and 13G

Prepare drafts of proxy and proxy statements

Prepare "inside trading" precautionary memo to employees

Prepare stock exchange listing application

Draft and file Form 144 and related documentation

Draft exhibits to private placement memorandum, including offeree questionnaire and subscription agreement

Prepare and file notice of sale of securities

Prepare and file for tax shelter registration numbers

Draft lease agreement, loan agreement, agreement of sale, facilities financing agreement ordinance, or contracts

Draft indenture

Draft security agreements (deed, guaranty, mortgages)

Review bond purchase agreement or underwriting agreement

Draft summaries of documents for use in preparing preliminary official statement and official statement

Coordinate with underwriter the accuracy of the statements

Finalize basic documents and distribute for execution

Draft petition and complaint, notice to the public, notice to the district attorney, rule nisi, answers, and validation order

Draft necessary resolutions authorizing the issuance of the bonds

Calculate debt borrowing base, debt service for financing bond issue refunding studies, and conventional mortgage payout schedules

Prepare exhibits to pleadings and resolutions

Send bond form to printer

Proof first galley of the bonds and check manufacturing schedule, coupon amounts, and CVSIP numbers

Check bonds at time of closing and read bond numbered 1

Draft closing papers for issuer including authorizing resolutions, authentication order to trustee, incumbency certificate, nonarbitrage certificates, and CVSIP numbers

Draft company authorizing resolutions and officers' certificates

Prepare tax election (if applicable) and arrange for appropriate filing

Draft recording certificate

Draft financing statements

Attend closing, checking all certificates and opinions, insurance policies, and legal descriptions

Compile the closing transcript

Workers' Compensation

Obtain copy of accident report

Prepare LS-203 and LS-18 forms and transmit to Department of Labor

Draft request for hearing or response

Draft application to schedule date or reply, motion to postpone or response, and demand for documents

Draft trial brief

Organize medical reports, schedule doctor appointments and meetings, and interview doctors

Organize correspondence with attorneys and doctors

Request employer medical mileage reimbursement

Prepare narrative case evaluation

Supervise compliance with demand for documents

Evaluate disability utilizing WCB rules and guidelines

Prepare exhibit list

Check average weekly wage calculations

Draft settlement papers and negotiate settlement

Draft petition for review (WCB)

Draft petition for judicial review

Draft statement of case

Draft issue and fact section of appellate brief

Draft motion for reconsideration

Draft affidavit regarding attorney's fees

Brief new case law and analyze WCB and judicial trends

Litigation Support

As discussed previously, technology has changed the landscape for paralegals and their potential career ladder. Senior paralegals are no longer hitting the top of their field and thinking: "Do I go on to law school? Is this all there is?" They are diversifying their skills into litigation support technologies. From client intake through case management all the way to trial presentation software, law is practiced through technology. What are the qualifications and duties of this new paralegal field?

It requires more than a basic understanding of the litigation process. The litigation support specialist must understand the nuances and details in building the information to be used for the matter and how that information can be presented to the court. To be successful, the litigation support paralegal will have experience or ability to work with the major legal applications such as Concordance, CT Summation, CaseMap/TimeMap, LiveNote, Doculex, Sanction, and TrialDirector. This is in addition to being able to handle other generic technologies, such as Oracle database systems, and other text creation and manipulation software.

The Future of Paralegals

In the 1970s the use of laypeople to assist attorneys in the practice of their profession was a concept; a whisper; an experiment in the law firm and a pilot program in the universities and colleges throughout the country.

The 1980s saw the paralegal profession become a reality. It then set its sights on respectability. It fought for recognition as a true, viable, adjunct legal profession and for some form of licensing or certification. Further, paralegals branched out on their own to serve the public as freelance paralegals, in some instances working directly with the public. Others became independent contractors working for attorneys away from the law office setting, in their own office or at home. Those paralegals, still working within the law office framework, complained of "burn out," of a lack of recognition and acceptance by attorneys as professionals, and of the undereducated paralegals invading the workforce.

In the 1990s improved, updated education and training of these laypersons became the essential goal. The U.S. Department of Labor statistics predicted that the paralegal profession would be the fastest growing profession and that the paralegal workforce would double during those years. This was and continues to be true. While paralegals are not the fastest growing profession any longer, the DOL has projected that their numbers will continue to grow "much faster than average" from 2006 to 2016.

This aim has slowly been brought into sight in these early years of the new millennium. Truly, the new century has brought many new developments in the paralegal profession. Certification or licensing, a needed plan, will certainly continue to progress in each state. Professional distinction is necessary not only to separate and identify an undereducated staff person from the highly educated and skilled paralegal but also so that the attorneys and general public will know the duties that can be performed by each segment of the profession. This certification or other types of regulation will insure the continued future success and expansion of the paralegal profession. It behooves each paralegal to keep current with the educational and technical training requirements for not only advancement of a personal career, but also the advancement of this profession.

CHAPTER FOUR

What the Paralegal Should Know About the Court Systems and Court Procedures

The Court System

Together with a general knowledge of the law, you as a paralegal should have a better-than-average working knowledge of the courts and how they operate. You should know the location, jurisdiction, and venue of all the courts of the city, county, and federal district where you are working. In addition, you should have some knowledge of both the state and federal appellate courts to which cases arising out of and tried in your area may be appealed.

You should be familiar with the rules of procedure for all the courts in which your law office files lawsuits. The rules vary for criminal and civil cases. There are usually special rules for probate, guardianship, family matters, and summary procedure, just to name a few. Every law office must have and use a copy of the appropriate court rules of procedure. It is also probable that the local rules are available online through your state's judiciary website.

The names and addresses of the courthouses, the judges, and the court officials are usually available in local bar association publications and websites, the lawyers' diary (either the hard copy or the electronic version), or directories furnished by local banks or title companies.

Knowledge of the courts and their official rules can be a time-saver in preparing, filing, amending, and obtaining copies of court documents. Courts are inundated with applications and documents; any nonconforming submission is likely to be rejected. It is also critical to ascertain whether the local court will accept electronic filings and requests.

This chapter gives you much of the essential information about the court systems in our country, their jurisdiction and venue, and some practical points and procedures for handling and performing the tasks assigned to you in the course of a day in your law office.

Court systems are created by the federal or state constitutions and, in specific instances, by statutes. The courts operate pursuant to rules of court established by general order of an appropriate court. A local court may also have specific local rules to supplement the general rules. Rules regulate the forms of pleading, time and manner of filing and serving, and other procedural matters.

To determine the jurisdiction of the court, check the constitution or statute that created it. To determine procedure, check the appropriate "court rules." Check state appellate cases that have interpreted the rules, the statutes, and the state constitution.

The word "court" has many meanings. Primarily, it refers to the persons assembled under authority of law at a designated place for the administration of justice.

The persons so assembled are the judge or judges, clerks, marshal, bailiff, court reporter, jurors, and attorneys, all of whom constitute a body of the government. However, it is not necessary that all of the above named individuals be present to constitute a "court," for court is frequently held without a jury.

The word "court" also refers to the judge or judges themselves as distinguished from the counsel or jury. Thus we have the expression, "In the opinion of the court," or "May it please the court." In this sense the word is written without a capital because it is personified when it stands for the judge.

Furthermore, the word "court" is used occasionally to refer to the judge's chambers, or the hall or place where the court is being held. Thus, a spectator is present at court in the courtroom, but the defendant is in court because he is a part of the assembly.

Jurisdiction of Courts

The laws of the United States provide that certain causes of action must be brought in court and have provided a set of guidelines to aid the courts and attorneys in determining in which court an action may be brought. These rules and regulations are called first "jurisdiction" and then "venue." A court may have jurisdiction but not venue, but it cannot have venue without jurisdiction.

Jurisdiction is required in every kind of judicial action. It is the power of a court to hear a particular kind of issue and to tender a binding decision as to the cause before it.

To hear and determine a cause the court must have personal jurisdiction (*personam*) and subject matter jurisdiction (*subjectum*) over the issues and parties involved in the dispute. *In personam jurisdiction* (not to be confused with *in propria persona*, which is the term used when a plaintiff or defendant acts as his own attorney) means the court has authority to render a decision that is binding on the defendant(s). Each defendant must be served with notice of the lawsuit in the manner prescribed by the law. Without personal jurisdiction over the defendant, the court's ruling or final orders cannot be carried out against him.

"Subject matter jurisdiction" means that the court has jurisdiction over the legal issue that is the subject of the controversy. Courts cannot hear any and every kind of case that can be brought. The most common and easily understood division of jurisdiction lies between civil and criminal courts. Courts of general jurisdiction hear a great variety of cases, while courts of limited jurisdiction or specialty courts hear one kind of problem only. For instance, tax courts hear only matters involving tax; they have no jurisdiction to hear a divorce case. Similarly, family courts hear all those types of disputes that arise from domestic situations, not landlord-tenant matters.

Further examples of jurisdiction are:

A magistrate's court has jurisdiction over a traffic violation but cannot hear and determine a case for first degree murder.

or

A county court may not have jurisdiction over a claim for damages that exceed $5,000.

or

An action for damages caused by an automobile collision cannot be brought in a probate court. The probate court only hears matters involving the distribution of estates, therefore it has no subject matter jurisdiction.

or

A foreclosure proceeding dealing with real property can be brought in the county where the property is located even though the mortgagor resides elsewhere, so long as he is served with process in accordance with the law. This is an example of a third type of jurisdiction that applies to the rights and title of property only, *in rem* (the thing) jurisdiction. The court has the power to make a binding determination regarding the status of the property in question without implicating any personal liabilities of potential parties. This often happens in actions to quiet title or other property (real or personal) matters.

It is extremely important to properly serve the defendant with process—usually the Summons and Complaint delivered by either the sheriff or professional process server. Service may be made in any number of other ways, including by mail, by constructive notice by publishing the process in a newspaper, or by substituted service upon an agent who has agreed to accept service for the principal defendant. This often occurs in corporate service by serving the secretary of state. A court has no personal jurisdiction over the matter if the required service of process has not been made. Improper service will result in dismissal of the matter.

Jurisdiction of a court may be "original" or "appellate." The state trial courts have original jurisdiction. At its most basic this means that the trial itself will be heard in that court of original jurisdiction. Trial courts can exercise appellate jurisdiction when the matter has arisen from an inferior trial court or an administrative agency. That is because many state statutes require appeals from these inferior courts to be heard *de novo* (trial over again). Courts of original jurisdiction will hear the evidence presented by both parties and make findings of both law and fact.

After a case has been tried and decided in a court of original jurisdiction, it may be brought into a higher court having appellate jurisdiction for review of the lower court decision on a question of law. Appellate jurisdiction does not include the ability to hear new evidence or make determination of fact. Instead, these courts' function is to determine whether the lower court applied the correct rule of law to the proceedings. If the appellate court finds that the lower court based its decision on the proper application of law, the trial court determination will be "affirmed." If the improper legal standard was used or the proper standard applied incorrectly, then the appellate court can "reverse" and/or "remand" the matter.

While jurisdiction refers to the power of the court to hear the subject matter and render a judgment concerning it, venue refers to the proper place (physical location) for the trial of the particular action. Subject matter and personal jurisdiction of the case are determined by the allegations of fact and the prayer of the complaint and in some cases the amount of damages requested. It is vitally important to check the local rules to determine whether a prayer for a sum certain complies with the jurisdiction of the court, or limits the recovery, or is required or permitted at all.

Venue of Courts

Venue refers to the correct (or incorrect) place for the trial of the particular action (city, county, and so forth) where more than one court has jurisdiction of the subject matter and defendant in the case. Choice of venue is regulated by statute and/or rules of court. Generally speaking, venue is situated where the cause of action arose. For example, in a motor vehicle action the venue is most likely where the accident took place or where the defendant lives. This may or may not be the same county or other venue.

A motion (request) for change of venue may be made when:

1. The action was filed in a county other than the residence of an individual defendant or the principal place of business of a corporate defendant;

2. There is prejudice of the judge which can be arbitrarily challenged once in some states (this is the basis for a motion to rescue in some states);

3. A fair trial cannot be had for various other reasons, such as pretrial publicity;

4. There is substantial inconvenience of producing witnesses and records; or

5. The ends of justice would be best served by a change of venue for some other statutory reason.

The statutes in many states provide for a change of venue on some or all of the preceding grounds and others. Even where there are grounds for change of venue, a judge has some reasonable discretion to grant or deny such a motion.

In California, a Notice of Motion for Change of Venue will take care of some errors regarding jurisdiction. If the motion for change of venue is on the ground of the wrong court, then there must be a Declaration of Merits, as well as the motion itself, and it must be made at the time the answer or demurrer is filed.

If the motion for change of venue is based upon the convenience of witnesses, then a Declaration of Merits is not necessary. In most jurisdictions, a Motion for Change of Venue is a "speaking motion," which is a written motion containing specific allegations of fact and law which will be argued by the attorney for the movant at the hearing of the motion. Check your state statute (code) and local court rules for change of venue grounds and procedure in your area.

State Courts

Now that the technicalities of jurisdiction and venue have been discussed, it is appropriate to move on to the structure of the state court system. It mirrors, for the most part, the structure of the federal system. It is a hierarchical structure which has numerous trial (and lesser) courts at its base. These are the municipal and county courts. One tier above those courts are the appellate courts, which make determinations of law affecting the trial appeal. At the top is the single state supreme court, also an appellate court for the most part, although it too has some original jurisdiction. This is the court of last resort, meaning that its determination is final (at least on the state level).

Appellate Courts

Each state has at least two courts of appeal. Appellate courts may also have some original jurisdiction.

1. The highest court in a state is usually called the supreme court. One of the exceptions to this is the New York Court of Appeals, which is the name of the highest court in the State of New York. The highest court of any state is a court of record and usually has both appellate and original jurisdiction given to it by the state constitution. The original jurisdiction does not include the trial of civil

or criminal cases. It may include original jurisdiction of writs of habeas corpus, writs of mandamus, and writs of prohibition, although such writs are also obtainable originally in lower courts of the state.

The highest court in a state may hear direct appeals designated by the state constitution or statute, and it may exercise discretionary appeal by what is sometimes called *certiorari* to a lower appellate court. The highest court will not usually grant a *writ of certiorari* or discretionary appeal unless there is a conflict of decisions in the lower appellate courts of the state or the question is one involving substantial public interest.

2. "Intermediate appellate courts" in a state court system may be called district court(s) of appeal, superior court(s), special court(s) of appeal, and similar names. Depending on the size and population of the state, it may be divided into a number of appellate districts, and the appellate court may hold regular sessions in all districts or may hold special sessions in each district at various times.

For example, in California, there are three districts, with three justices in each district. Regular sessions are held. Appeals from the superior court, which is a trial court in California, go to the district court of appeals.

The names of both the trial courts and the appellate courts vary from state to state, but the principle is the same. The first appeal from the trial court is usually taken to the intermediate appellate court. Its decision is final, unless the highest court in the state decides to grant a discretionary review or certiorari.

Trial Courts

Each state has trial courts of record that have jurisdiction over criminal and civil matters in each county or judicial district (as in Idaho). The courts are located within the county or district. These trial courts are variously named circuit court, county court, common pleas court, or superior court, among other names.

In addition to the trial courts of general jurisdiction in each county, most counties have special courts that handle particular matters such as probate, juvenile cases, and criminal cases. In some states, such special matters are handled by divisions of the trial court (probate division, criminal division, and so forth).

Each county of a state has lower courts that are not considered courts of record, where minor disputes may be heard without a jury (magistrate's court and justice of the peace).

A county usually has two basic trial courts where jurisdiction depends on the amount of money in controversy, the nature of the dispute, or the seriousness of a criminal charge.

In California, for example, there are principally two trial courts, superior and municipal (comparable to common pleas court and county court in Pennsylvania and circuit court and county court in Florida).

1. *Superior courts:* The superior courts (or court with the same jurisdiction) are the trial courts of general jurisdiction in the judicial system. They have original jurisdiction in all cases and proceedings not otherwise provided for and hear appeals from decisions in the municipal, justice, and small claims courts. (Compare Pennsylvania common pleas courts, Florida circuit courts, and Idaho district courts for similar jurisdiction.)

   The state constitution permits the legislature to establish appellate departments of this court in counties having municipal courts. In California, for example, each county has one superior court, and the number of judges is fixed by the state legislature, varying according to the population. Superior court judges serve six-year terms and are elected in the general election on a nonpartisan ballot by the voters of the county. Vacancies are filled by the governor. Superior court judges are required to be attorneys, admitted to the practice of law for at least five years immediately preceding election or appointment.

2. *Municipal courts:* In California the municipal court has jurisdiction in civil cases where the amount is $25,000 or less and have jurisdiction over misdemeanor criminal cases; a magistrate conducts preliminary hearings in felony cases. The municipal courts also exercise small-claims jurisdiction. (Compare Pennsylvania county courts, Florida county courts, and magistrates division of district courts in Idaho, for similar jurisdiction.)

   The judges are elected for six-year terms on a nonpartisan ballot by the voters in the judicial district in which the court is located. Vacancies are filled by the governor, the same as superior courts. Municipal court judges are also required to be attorneys, admitted to the practice of law for at least five years immediately preceding election or appointment.

3. *Small claims courts:* Small claims is the lowest trial court of record and is consumer-oriented. In California, attorneys cannot appear in this court on behalf of a litigant; only the parties involved in the action are permitted. In some states, attorneys are permitted to appear in small claims court but are not required to present a claim.

   Appeals from small claims court are usually taken to the highest court in the county or district. (Compare the circuit court in Florida, and the superior court in California. Check your state's statute creating the small claims court.)

   Small claims are usually heard before the judge, without a jury. In some states a jury trial can be demanded in a small claims court if the party deposits a required sum of money with the court.

The following is a practical checklist for proceeding with a claim in a state small claims court:

CHECKLIST FOR SMALL CLAIMS COURT

1. Determine the full legal name and address of the person or persons being sued (not a post office box number). This will help determine where the small claim must be filed (venue).

2. Go to the clerk of the small claims court, which is normally part of the county or district court or located in the same building, and fill out the form given.

3. Pay the appropriate filing fee.

4. Arrange for the subpoena or order to be served on the defendant (but not the plaintiff). In some jurisdictions, the plaintiff or the clerk may authorize someone to personally serve the order on the defendant. The subpoena or order will contain the trial date.

5. While waiting for the trial, gather all important documents and have them ready. Contact all potential witnesses and arrange for them to come to the courthouse on the day of the trial or obtain a subpoena from the clerk of the small claims court for any witness who will not come voluntarily. If an interpreter is needed, find out if one is available at the small claims court or if one can be secured through the higher trial court. In some states the higher trial courts have translators available. Otherwise, the plaintiff should bring his own interpreter.

6. Go to the court building early on the day of the trial and ask the clerk *where* your case is being heard. When you get to the courtroom, check the calendar and see that your case is listed.

7. When giving his testimony, the plaintiff should present only the facts, no editorializing or emotion. He must be brief. He should submit all papers and documents that may help his case.

8. If the plaintiff wins, he may ask the defendant courteously for the money awarded him in the judgment.

9. If the plaintiff has difficulty in collecting his money, he should ask the clerk to assist him in obtaining same.

10. In California, the plaintiff is not allowed to appeal if he loses, unless he is ordered to pay as a result of a counterclaim the defendant has filed against him. In some states, either party may appeal from a small claims judgment. Check the state statute creating the court and local court rules to determine the right and time for appeal.

Most states have lower trial courts which are not courts of record. For example: In California justice courts have jurisdiction in civil cases involving minimal amounts and minor criminal cases. Justice court judges, sitting as magistrates, also conduct preliminary hearings in felony cases. Judges of justice courts are elected to six-year terms. Vacancies are filled by the Board of Supervisors (or a similar body in other states). They must either have passed a qualifying examination given by the Judicial Council or must have been admitted to practice law. (Comparable are justice of the peace courts and magistrate's courts in other states, where the justice of the peace or magistrate may be elected or appointed.)

Special Courts

In addition to the regular trial courts here described, a state may have special courts located in each county or court district to handle particular matters, such as probate, juvenile cases, or criminal cases. In some states these specific matters are handled in divisions of the regular trial court.

EXAMPLES

A *probate court* (also called orphan's court or surrogate court in some jurisdictions or the probate division of the higher trial court) would have jurisdiction over the probate of wills and administration of a deceased person's estate and the guardianship of minors and incompetents.

A *criminal court* (also called quarter sessions or *oyer* and *terminer* or the criminal division of the trial court which has jurisdiction of the particular crime) would hear criminal cases with or without a jury and sentence the defendant(s) if found guilty. The defendant in a criminal case is entitled to a jury trial unless he waives it. In most states, the higher county trial court hears felony charges and the lower county trial court hears misdemeanors.

A *juvenile court* (sometimes a division of surrogate court) would have original exclusive jurisdiction of minor children who are alleged to be neglected, dependent, or delinquent (which includes truancy in some states). Some states allow the removal of cases involving serious crimes alleged against juveniles to the regular criminal court for trial and sentencing.

Large cities in a state may have special courts, such as the Philadelphia Municipal Court and the Pittsburgh Magistrates Court in Pennsylvania.

Some states have special courts that have both original and appellate jurisdiction in regard to claims against the state. An example is the Commonwealth Court of Pennsylvania, which has exclusive jurisdiction of such claims and has jurisdiction concurrent with the common pleas courts of others.

State Court Practice and Procedure

The following sample practices and procedures are those used in individual states (most of the examples are from the State of California) and are submitted here by way of example only. The forms and names of pleadings or motions described in this section may differ from state to state, but the caveats and suggestions given in this section are appropriate and applicable to practice and procedure in all state courts.

State court proceedings are conducted for and on behalf of the litigants by attorneys duly licensed to practice in the state where the case is being heard, with few exceptions. Under certain circumstances, it is permissible for a litigant to represent himself in court. Such an appearance by the litigant is called a *pro se appearance*, or it is said that the litigant is appearing *in propria persona*. Courts generally frown on this procedure and encourage parties wishing to follow this practice to obtain the advice and counsel of a licensed attorney before they proceed by self-representation. Advice of counsel is often needed before filing in small claims court, even though the appearance of counsel in the small claims court is not required and may not be permitted.

Certain court documents or papers must be filed in the office of the clerk of the court to start the legal proceeding and to bring it to its final conclusion. These "court papers" consist of a series of written statements of the claims and defenses of the parties to the lawsuit. The written statements that are required (as opposed to permitted) to be filed before a lawsuit (action) is "at issue" (ready to be tried before the court) are called "pleadings." Other court papers or documents that may be filed in addition to or in lieu of pleadings are "motions," "notices," "stipulations," "requests for admissions," other "discovery" documents, as well as court "orders" when signed by the court.

An "action" is commenced when the first pleading is filed with the clerk of the court by the person bringing the action.

Generally, the person who brings the suit is called a "plaintiff." He makes a written statement setting forth the facts that are the basis for his suit. This court paper or written statement is called a "complaint." In certain courts and jurisdictions this written statement is called a "declaration" or "petition." It is the first court paper filed in the office of the clerk of the court to begin the action.

A "summons" or its equivalent, which is a notice that a legal action has been started, is then issued by the clerk of the court and served with a copy of the complaint upon the person against whom the legal action is being brought. That person is called a "defendant."

The defendant responds to the complaint, defending himself against the allegations contained in the complaint by filing a written "answer" in which he admits or denies the facts stated by the plaintiff in the complaint, and may allege further facts which constitute "new matter" in the form of "affirmative defenses" or a "counterclaim."

After the defendant files an answer, the plaintiff may or may not be required to file a "reply" (replication), depending on the rules of court for that particular court.

Instead of filing an answer to a complaint, a defendant may file and argue written motions or demurrers objecting to the complaint on legal grounds. For the purpose of such a motion, the facts alleged in the complaint are considered to be true but not admitted by the defendant. If such a preliminary motion of the defendant is denied by the court, the defendant must file an answer, and the case proceeds as herein described.

Most state courts as well as federal courts allow all parties to seek relevant evidence for use in the trial of the case by formal rules of "discovery." These procedures are governed by the rules applicable to the court where the case is filed. They include "depositions," "interrogatories," and "requests to produce," among others. Any or all of these formal methods of discovery may be used before the trial in addition to any informal investigation of the facts.

When all pleadings have been filed, all pretrial motions disposed of by order of court or withdrawal of the motion, and all pretrial discovery completed, the case is ready for trial. It is "at issue."

When the case is tried, it is submitted to a court and jury or to a court without a jury (nonjury trial) for a final decision. In a jury trial, the judge decides questions of law, and the jury decides questions of fact. In a nonjury trial, the judge decides questions of both law and fact.

This is a critical distinction—the questions of law and of fact. The facts must be properly ascertained before the judge can determine which law should be applied to them. For example, in a murder trial, it must first be ascertained by the jury (the fact-finders) whether the defendant had planned or premeditated the crime. This question of intent is a question of fact. The law to be applied will depend upon that answer. If the defendant planned the murder, the law of murder of the first degree and the accompanying punishments can be applied. If the jury finds that he did not, then it cannot be first degree murder and the laws pertaining to first degree murder cannot be implemented.

In this situation, if the trial court improperly applied the laws regarding first degree murder to a defendant who was found by the fact-finder not to have planned the murder, then the appeal would be based upon that mistaken application. The appellate court does not have the jurisdiction to act as the fact-finder and change the determination whether the defendant did or did not plan the murder. That is a question of fact soley for the trial court's determination.

Pleadings and Motions

In preparing pleadings and motions, the name and location of the court (including the name of the division of the court), the names of the parties, and a place for inserting the case number to be assigned by the clerk of the court must be typed as the heading of the document. That information is called the "caption" or "title" of the case. The caption or title must be typed on all "court papers" to be filed in the case, including orders to be signed by the judge.

Be sure that the name of the court and the names of the parties are correct. Use complete individual names and exact registered corporate names. If a party is not suing or being sued in his individual capacity, indicate the proper capacity.

EXAMPLES

John Doe, Trustee for Richard Roe
or
John Doe and Richard Roe d/b/a
Doe Plumbing Supplies

The foregoing examples are for use in so-called adversary proceedings. In probate and in cases where an action is brought on behalf of or against another person or group, the caption of the case may not contain the names of all parties.

EXAMPLES

In Re:
Estate of John Doe, deceased
or
STATE ex rel. DOE v. ROE

A. Summons and Complaints

The summons is not a pleading. It is the notice of the filing of the first pleading, and it is an instruction to the defendant to answer the pleading (complaint) or be subject to judgment by default.

The filing of the complaint with the clerk of the court sets a litigation matter into motion. A copy of the complaint must be served on a defendant in accordance with applicable law to give the court personal jurisdiction over that named defendant. The defendant has the right to know what allegations are being brought against him so that he can properly answer the Summons and Complaint.

A copy of the complaint is served with the summons by the sheriff or other process server (or in any other manner permitted by rules of court). After service, the server files a "return of service" showing where and when the defendant was served. A copy of the return of service is usually mailed to the office of the plaintiff's attorney.

CAVEAT: When a complaint is filed, the paralegal or other person assigned to the office calendar should set an appropriate date for checking on whether the complaint has been served, if a return of service is not received before that date. Check local rules as to availability of further attempts to serve and possibly better address instructions, and so forth. The defendant does not have to answer the complaint until he is properly served according to the court rules. For more details on preparation and service of summons, see Chapter 5.

After the defendant is duly served, the defendant must take affirmative action or the plaintiff will obtain a judgment by default against the defendant in a *civil* case. This default judgment essentially grants a "win" to the plaintiff. In theory, anything not denied by the defendant is admitted; therefore the defendant has conceded. This default judgment is not hard to reopen by procedural rules, however. Clearly, the defendant must respond to the complaint by filing a pleading or an appropriate motion. A pleading sets forth the party's factual position in the situation at hand, while a motion asks the court for some relief based upon the law. The most common responses of a defendant are discussed in B. and C. in this section.

B. General Demurrer (Motion to Dismiss)

The general demurrer or motion to dismiss attacks the whole complaint or some alleged cause of action or count contained in the complaint on the basis that a cause of action has not been stated. It does not address the factual allegations of the complaint, rather it states that even if all of the factual allegations are true, there is no basis for the lawsuit or, if there is a basis for the suit, that there is a technical problem that bars the suit from going forward. It may be filed in lieu of an answer within the time allowed for filing an answer (see C).

In order to file the general demurrer, the defendant must have proper grounds for the affirmative defenses. Those defenses, among others, are:

1. Statute of limitations

2. Laches

3. Standing to sue

4. *Res judicata*

5. Illegality in a contract action

6. Contributory negligence of assumption of risk in a tort action

The filing of a demurrer or motion to dismiss tolls the time for filing an answer.

CAUTION: Some other pretrial motions do not toll the time for filing a responsive pleading.

Demurrers are not used in some states. Under the Federal Rules of Civil Procedure (F.R.C.P.), and under many state court rules of civil procedure, a demurrer is simply called a Motion to Dismiss because it has the same effect—it dismisses the claim of the plaintiff. The motion to dismiss must state the grounds for dismissal with some particularity, such as the following:

The complaint does not state facts sufficient to constitute a cause of action.

or

The first cause of action does not state facts sufficient to state a cause of action.

or

The complaint does not state facts sufficient to constitute a cause of action in that the alleged cause of action is barred by the Statute of Limitations [or you can state any other defenses appearing on the face of the complaint].

It is wise to prepare a law memorandum in support of a general demurrer or motion to dismiss if the grounds are not obvious.

C. Answer and Counterclaim

Unlike the motion to dismiss or general demurrer discussed in A., which are "motions," the answer of a defendant(s) is a "pleading."

The answer is the first pleading required of the defendant in response to the complaint filed by the plaintiff.

The answer admits or denies the facts alleged in the complaint. Facts showing that the defendant has an affirmative defense to the complaint are also asserted in the answer or such defenses are considered to be waived. In other words, if, in a breach of contract action, the plaintiff has asserted that the contract was signed over six years prior to the commencement of the suit, the defendant has the Statute of Limitations as an affirmative defense. The defendant must assert this defense in his answer or else the court will consider it waived. If the affirmative defenses are pleaded in the answer, the facts are stated under the heading Affirmative Defenses following a paragraph-by-paragraph (numbered as the paragraphs of the complaint that are being answered are numbered) admission or denial of the plaintiff's statement of facts in the complaint.

A counterclaim may be pleaded in the defendant's answer or in a separate document with the same caption of the case. A counterclaim is essentially a complaint by the defendant as against the plaintiff. It may be related or not to the original action brought by the plaintiff. In many states, if a counterclaim is related to the original action, it *must* be brought as a counterclaim or the defendant will be barred from bringing it in a separate action. It is important to check your local rules regarding this "entire controversy doctrine." The counterclaim must state a valid cause of action, just as the original complaint must state a valid cause of action. See Chapter 5.

In addition to his answer and whether or not the answer contained a counterclaim or a counterclaim was separately filed, the defendant may feel that he has a cause of action against a codefendant or against a person not party to the plaintiff's action, which other cause of action arises out of the facts alleged by the plaintiff. If so, he may want to file a cross-complaint as discussed in E. or a "third-party complaint" as discussed in F.

D. Reply

The reply is a pleading by which the plaintiff responds to the answer filed by the defendant. It is necessary in case of certain allegations in the answer, but it is usually not required. If the defendant has asserted a counterclaim, it will be necessary to answer those allegations. Check with your attorney as to whether a reply is necessary when you receive the answer from the defendant's attorney. This is important. If a reply is required, there is a time limit for filing it. Check the court rules of civil procedure. The time is usually the same as the time for the defendant to file his answer to the complaint.

E. Cross-Complaint

A cross-complaint is a separate document, in a separate cover and designated or titled as a cross-complaint. A cross-complaint asserts a claim between defendants or as between plaintiffs. The key is that the parties are on the same "side of the 'v.'" in the original complaint. For example, in a motor vehicle accident, where one motorist sues the driver and passengers of the car that hit him, the passengers (who are defendants) can assert a claim against the driver of the car that they were riding in.

In some jurisdictions, it may be part of the answer and therefore may be entitled Answer and Cross-Complaint. You are cautioned to check your local courts for this procedure. In some state courts and in the federal courts there is a provision in the rules of pleading for a cross-complaint and for a third-party complaint.

Talk to your attorney about these procedures. The cross-complaint must state a cause of action against the cross-defendant. For rules of pleading, see Chapter 6. The rules of pleading applicable to drafting a complaint apply to drafting a cross-complaint.

F. Third-Party Complaint

In many state jurisdictions, a cross-complaint is filed by a plaintiff against another plaintiff or it is filed by a defendant against another defendant. That is also the procedure in the federal trial courts. The cross-complaint may be indemnity or liability arising out of the facts alleged by the plaintiff in the complaint.

A third-party complaint differs because it brings a new party into the cause of action. A third-party complaint is filed by a defendant when he believes a person not made party to the action by the plaintiff is responsible directly to the plaintiff for the facts alleged in the complaint; or is liable over to the defendant by way of indemnity; or is jointly liable with the defendant if the defendant is liable to the plaintiff; or is liable to the defendant in any other way on the facts alleged by the plaintiff.

The third-party complaint must state a cause of action against the third-party defendant. For drafting, see Chapter 6. The rules of pleading applicable to drafting a complaint apply to drafting a third-party complaint.

G. Amended and Supplemental Pleadings

Sometime during the course of civil litigation it may be necessary for you to amend your pleadings or, in the alternative, to file a supplemental pleading upon the discovery of new evidence or information material to the case. Court rules allow certain amendments without leave of court. There is usually a time limit on such an amendment. Pleadings may also be amended by stipulation between the parties or upon motion to the court for leave to amend.

EXAMPLES

You might amend your pleading or file a supplemental pleading in the following circumstances:

1. Where, subsequent to filing your summons and complaint, you have discovered the name of a necessary party-defendant previously described and designated as a "Doe";

2. Where you may have incorrectly spelled the name of a defendant, such as "Schmidt" when it should have been "Smith"; or

3. Where you have omitted alleging facts necessary to state the cause of action.

The time limit for amendments (without stipulation of the parties or order of court) is usually before a responsive pleading, which includes a demurrer or motion to dismiss, if filed.

Amended pleadings should be so designated in the title of the pleading, which follows the caption of the case.

EXAMPLES

Amended Complaint

or

Second Amended Complaint

or

Amended Answer

In most states, if an attorney or party *has entered his appearance in the case*, an amended pleading can be filed and a copy served on the attorney. In such instance, it is not necessary to prepare a new summons or to have the amended pleading served personally on the adverse party.

If an "amended complaint" is filed before the answer to the original complaint is *due*, it may be wise to have the amended complaint served with an alias summons (or its equivalent in your state) to lay the groundwork for a default judgment if the defendant does not appear or fails to file an answer or other responsive pleading. You want your default against the right defendant on the right cause of action.

H. Pretrial Motions

The "demurrer" or "motion to dismiss" (see B) is one of the pretrial motions.

A "motion to strike," a "motion for judgment on the pleadings," and a "motion for summary judgment" are also generally used before trial. These motions are explained in further detail in Chapter 5.

These motions should be used only when you are sure that you have valid grounds for the motion. The motions should not be used as a delaying tactic, but they are often so misused. Improper use of motions can expose the delaying party to sanctions imposed by the court through the procedural rules. The penalties can be grave; at their most potent, the rules permit the judge to dismiss the case as against the imprudent party making the inappropriate motion.

Note that the filing of the foregoing motions, except motion to dismiss, does not toll or extend the time within which the movant is required to file a responsive pleading. For this reason, be sure to flag the statute of limitations on your file and your follow-up procedure to avoid a default being taken against your office, or should you want to take a default against the opposing counsel.

The parties making and opposing a motion for summary judgment are permitted to file affidavits in support of their arguments. If an affidavit is filed, a counter-affidavit should be filed to show that there is a genuine issue of material fact in order to defeat the motion.

Grounds for the request for relief sought must be stated in the motions. A law memorandum in support of the motion may be indicated. The motion will be argued by the attorneys at a hearing on the motion.

I. Post-Trial Motions

Post-trial motions include "motion for new trial," "motion for judgment n.o.v." (notwithstanding the verdict), and "motion to set aside judgment," among other post-trial motions most frequently used. Court rules of civil procedure govern the content and time for making these motions. Essentially, the party is asking the court to overturn the decision in the original trial and either rule in his favor or grant a "do-over" of the entire process.

Grounds for this type of dramatic relief must be stated in the motion. It is imperative in these instances to prepare a law memorandum in support of the post-trial motion. The motion will be argued by the attorneys at a hearing on the motion.

CHAPTER FIVE

What the Paralegal Should Know About Federal Court Practice and Procedure

Federal Courts

The United States is a federal government, meaning that it has a centralized body for creating, administering, and adjudicating the national laws of the country. The fifty states, however, retain significant powers over the citizens of their respective states. The national government is also charged with the responsibility of preserving the governments and laws of the fifty states. It is therefore not unreasonable to say that in its attempt to define or bring into proper relationship the laws of the various states, problems of conflict of laws will arise. We will not discuss these problems and mention them only to give you a broad understanding of the meaning and import of the federal court system.

The federal court system was provided for in Article III of the Constitution of the United States. That article established one supreme court and such other inferior federal courts as Congress "may from time to time ordain and establish."

As a result of the federal Constitution and acts of Congress, the regular federal court system today consists of the following courts:

Federal Court System

1. *U.S. Supreme Court* (which can be accessed directly at www.supremecourtus .gov):

   * The U.S. Supreme Court is the "final arbiter" (the court of last resort) of law in matters arising from the Constitution, federal laws, treaties, or disputes among the states. It does *not* have subject matter jurisdiction for every issue in American jurisprudence. States retain the right to interpret their own laws as long as those state laws do not conflict with the U.S. Constitution.

   * Decisions can *only* be reversed by the Supreme Court itself or by Congressional legislation.

   * The Supreme Court has some "original" jurisdiction in some state/federal disputes, as well as diplomatic matters, *but* the thrust of the court's work is in the *appellate* area. The court reviews decisions from the U.S. Circuit Courts, the highest state courts, and other appellate tribunals.

2. *U.S. Circuit Courts of Appeal:* Under authority of Article III of the U.S. Constitution and Judiciary Act of 1789, there are twelve federal judicial circuits. Washington, DC, makes up its own district in this system. (See 28 U.S.C.A., Section 41.) For a map of the circuits and other relevant information, please visit www.uscourts.gov/courtlinks.

3. *Federal District Courts:* This is the "first level trial" network in the federal court system. There are ninety-four district courts in the United States and its territories. Each state has at least one, and the most populated have up to four, like New York, Texas, and California. These various districts are designated by compass coordinates—i.e., Northern, Southern, Eastern, and Western Districts. For more details about your particular district, please visit www.uscourts.gov/dis trictcourts.html.

In addition to the regular federal courts in the system, there are special federal courts created by Congress from time to time. At the present time, the following are special federal courts:

1. U.S. Court of Appeals for the Federal Circuit (formerly appellate court for the U.S. Court of Claims and U.S. Court of Customs and Patent Appeals, it has national jurisdiction on a variety of federal issues)

2. U.S. Court of Federal Claims (handles causes of action brought by private citizens as against the United States)

3. U.S. Court of International Trade (formerly the Customs Court)

4. Tax Court of the United States (formerly known as U.S. Board of Tax Appeals)

5. U.S. Court of Appeals for the Armed Forces

6. U.S. Court of Appeals for Veteran's Claims

7. District of Columbia Superior Court and District of Columbia Court of Appeals, which have jurisdiction of local district matters

8. District Bankruptcy Courts, which are associated with the federal district courts throughout the states, territories, and the District of Columbia, for the purpose of hearing and administering federal bankruptcy laws (Appeals from the district bankruptcy courts are taken to bankruptcy appellate panels of the U.S. Court of Appeals for the federal circuit in which the district bankruptcy court is located.)

The Supreme Court of the United States

The U.S. Supreme Court is the ultimate authority for the interpretation of federal law and constitutional law as it affects both the federal and all state government actions. It has both appellate and original jurisdiction. It may grant discretionary review (*certiorari*) of cases from the U.S. Court of Appeals of the various U.S. judicial circuits. The "Rule of Four" determines whether a case will be heard by the Supreme Court—that is, four out of the nine Justices must agree that the matter should be heard.

U.S. Courts of Appeal

These twelve courts are located in each of the present eleven U.S. judicial circuits plus the District of Columbia circuit. Every state and territory of the United States (including Guam and Puerto Rico) belongs to one of the eleven judicial circuits.

Appellate jurisdiction includes appeals from the U.S. District Courts and various federal administrative and regulatory agencies. The rules of procedure for the U.S. Circuit Courts of Appeals are promulgated by the U.S. Supreme Court and supplemented by rules made by each circuit for its courts. Check both sets of rules before you proceed with a federal appeal. Follow them exactly or the right to appeal may be lost or prejudicially delayed.

The U.S. judicial circuits and the states and territories that belong to each circuit are as follows:

District of Columbia: District of Columbia

First: Maine, New Hampshire, Massachusetts, Rhode Island, and Puerto Rico

Second: Vermont, Connecticut, and New York

Third: New Jersey, Pennsylvania, Delaware, and the Virgin Islands

Fourth: Maryland, West Virginia, Virginia, North Carolina, and South Carolina

Fifth: Mississippi, Louisiana, and Texas

Sixth: Ohio, Michigan, Kentucky, and Tennessee

Seventh: Indiana, Illinois, and Wisconsin

Eighth: Minnesota, Iowa, Missouri, Arkansas, Nebraska, North Dakota, and South Dakota

Ninth: California, Oregon, Nevada, Montana, Washington, Idaho, Arizona, Alaska, Hawaii, territories of Guam, and Northern Mariana Islands

Tenth: Colorado, Wyoming, Utah, Kansas, Oklahoma, and New Mexico

Eleventh: Alabama, Georgia, and Florida

Compare federal judicial circuits to federal judicial districts, discussed in the following section.

U.S. District Courts

The U.S. district courts are courts of original jurisdiction and are federal trial courts located in every state and territory of the United States and in the District of Columbia.

In addition to their jurisdiction to hear cases involving federal law, these courts also have jurisdiction to hear some state matters if the dispute is between citizens of different states and the amount in controversy exceeds a certain statutory amount. Currently, that minimum amount in controversy is $75,000 under 28 U.S.C.A. §1332. (The Code can be accessed through the Legal Information Institute of Cornell University Law School at http://uscode.law.cornell.edu/uscode.) Under such circumstances, a case may either be started in the federal district court or, if it was started in a state court, it may be "removed" from the state court to the federal district court, if approved by the federal court on a statutory "petition for removal." After removal to the federal district court, the court will apply the substantive law of the state where the cause of action arose but will apply the federal rules of civil procedure to the case after it is removed. See 28 U.S.C.A. §1441. The district court may also review some decisions of some federal agencies.

Some less populated states have just one federal judicial district in the state. The following is a list of the federal judicial districts:

Alabama (Northern, Middle, Southern)

Alaska

Arizona

Arkansas (Eastern, Western)

California (Northern, Eastern, Central, Southern)

Colorado

Connecticut

Delaware

District of Columbia

Florida (Northern, Middle, Southern)

Georgia (Northern, Middle, Southern)

Guam

Hawaii

Idaho

Illinois (Northern, Central, Southern)

Indiana (Northern, Southern)

Iowa (Northern, Southern)

Kansas

Kentucky (Eastern, Western)

Louisiana (Eastern, Middle, Western)

Maine

Maryland

Massachusetts

Michigan (Eastern, Western)

Minnesota

Mississippi (Northern, Southern, Eastern, Western)

Montana

Nebraska

Nevada

New Hampshire

New Jersey

New Mexico

New York (Northern, Southern, Eastern, Western)

North Carolina (Eastern, Middle, Western)

North Dakota

Northern Mariana Islands

Ohio (Northern, Southern)

Oklahoma (Northern, Eastern, Western)

Oregon

Pennsylvania (Eastern, Middle, Western)

Puerto Rico

Rhode Island

South Carolina

South Dakota

Tennessee (Eastern, Middle, Western)

Texas (Northern, Southern, Eastern, Western)

Utah

Vermont

Virgin Islands

Virginia (Eastern, Western)

Washington (Eastern, Western)

West Virginia (Northern, Southern)

Wisconsin (Eastern, Western)

Wyoming

In each federal district, with the exception of Guam and the Northern Mariana Islands, there is at least one federal bankruptcy court. Puerto Rico has two federal bankruptcy courts, and the Virgin Islands district has one.

In addition to the foregoing regular federal courts, various special federal courts are created and done away with by Congress from time to time as it exercises its power under the Constitution to do so.

The following section describes some of those special federal courts, tells how and for what purpose they were created, and what court rules of procedure apply to practice before those courts.

Special Federal Courts

The special federal courts were created by Acts of Congress at various times. The jurisdiction of a special court is determined by the statute that created it. An easy reference guide to congressional acts (called federal statutes) is the U.S. Code Annotated (U.S.C.A.). It is a multivolume set of law books that contains the text of all federal statutes with pocket parts in the back of each book updating it yearly. The websites for the special federal courts are listed below so that you may check the most current information on jurisdiction and procedure for that particular court:

1. U.S. Court of Appeals for the Federal Circuit (www.cafc.uscourts.gov/index .html)

2. U.S. Court of Federal Claims (www.uscfc.uscourts.gov)

3. U.S. Court of International Trade (www.cit.uscourts.gov)

4. Tax Court of the United States (www.ustaxcourt.gov)

5. U.S. Court of Appeals for the Armed Forces (www.armfor.uscourts.gov)

6. U.S. Court of Appeals for Veteran's Claims (www.vetapp.uscourts.gov)

7. District of Columbia Superior Court and District of Columbia Court of Appeals (www.dccourts.gov/dccourts/index.jsp)—Both have jurisdiction of local District of Columbia matters. These courts are in addition to the regular federal district and circuit courts for the District of Columbia, which are also located in the district. The local jurisdiction was transferred from the federal district court to these additional courts by an Act of Congress called the Court Reform and Criminal Procedure Act of 1970.

8. District Bankruptcy Courts (www.uscourts.gov/bankruptcycourts.html)—It is important to check your district's bankruptcy court rules.

Federal Court Practice and Procedure
General Jurisdiction

The district courts in the federal court system have original jurisdiction of actions involving a "federal question" (such as breach of a federal statute or regulation or a violation of the provisions of the Constitution of the United States) and of all criminal actions where the defendant is charged with a federal crime (a crime defined by Act of Congress). Some examples of federal questions or issues are admiralty, maritime, or prize cases; poor bankruptcy proceedings; interstate commerce and antitrust suits; patent, copyright, trademarks, and unfair competition lawsuits under federal acts; civil rights cases based on federal statutes or the Constitution of the United States; and those claims arising out of and under the federal labor acts. Chapter 85 of Title 28 U.S.C.A. §§1330–1369 deals with the specific subject matter jurisdiction of the federal courts.

Special federal courts are courts of "limited jurisdiction," and as a general proposition of law you must spell out, with statutory specificity, the authority of the court to hear the matter. These courts were created by federal statute. For instance, the Court of Appeals for Veteran's Claims has exclusive jurisdiction to review the final decisions of the Board of Veteran's Affairs. Therefore, the applicant to the court must specifically state his status, the relief sought, the fact that there are inadequate alternative means to obtain the relief sought, and the like.

> **NOTE:** Failure to state and prove facts establishing jurisdiction may subject your claim to an automatic rejection at any given point of the proceeding, up to and including the appellate hearing. As the paralegal, therefore, you should read the relevant portions of the U.S. Code, Title 28, regarding all the procedural requirements. These U.S. Code sections set forth the conditions under which a case can be filed in federal courts and are the statutory authority giving the federal court jurisdiction to hear and determine the claim. The annotated version of the statutes will supply you with case law that has interpreted the specific meaning and application of the rules.

Practice and Procedure—General Rules

Federal courts apply "procedural rules" under the Federal Rules of Civil Procedure. They can be easily accessed through the Cornell University School of Law website (www.law.cornell.edu/rules/frcp/#chapter_ii). The "substantive law" will be either the applicable federal law or the law of the state where the incident occurred.

> **NOTE:** A *must*—the federal courts must have "subject matter jurisdiction" to hear the matter in either situation. This means that the underlying cause of action in the

lawsuit is either a federal question or it involves citizens of different states where the amount in controversy exceeds the statutory threshold amount ($75,000).

Federal questions are those matters "arising under" the Constitution—such as a federal statute, a federal/administrative regulation, or an international treaty—and all violations of the Federal Criminal Code.

Types of Jurisdictions Under Federal Rules of Civil Procedure

1. *Subject matter jurisdiction:* These are the types of cases that the court may legitimately hear and decide. As discussed earlier, this can be either general or specific. The district courts have general jurisdiction, while the specialty courts can only hear one type of matter.

2. *Concurrent jurisdiction (diversity):* Joint jurisdiction with the state court. This is permitted by legislation of Congress. As noted earlier, the federal court will use the Federal Rules of Procedure, but will apply the law of the state where the underlying cause accrued.

   In order to sue in federal court on a state claim, the diversity of citizenship requires both that:

   a. The parties are citizens of two (or more) different states; and

   b. The complaint must meet the minimum jurisdictional amount of $75,000 (this is *not* required in a federal question case)

      NOTE: If there are some parties that are diverse and others that reside in the same state, the requirement for complete diversity will not be met.

3. *Jurisdiction over the person* (in personam) falls into two categories and can be based on:

   a. Residence (any person who resides within the jurisdictional area served by the court); or

   b. The Long-Arm Statutes: even though the defendant does not reside in the forum state, that defendant will have significant enough contacts with the jurisdiction to allow service upon him as a matter of public policy if the defendant:

      i. Conducts business within the forum area,

      ii. Commits a tort within the forum area,

      iii. Insures persons or property located within the forum area, or

      iv. Enters into a contract that will be performed within the forum area.

4. *In rem jurisdiction:* The court maintains jurisdiction over property of the defendant within the forum area or any assets of the defendant, and these can be attached or garnished within the court's jurisdiction.

5. *Exclusive jurisdiction:* Cases that can only be tried in a particular court or which only a particular type of court can hear and determine, such as bankruptcy and cases having the United States as a party (Court of Federal Claims).

6. *Ancillary and pendant jurisdiction:* There may be matters that are sufficiently related to the primary action before the court, but are, standing alone, insufficient to invoke the federal jurisdiction of the court. These theories permit the court to hear these cases out of convenience for the parties and efficient administration of jurisdiction.

7. *Removal jurisdiction:* The defendant can force the transfer to federal court of an action originally brought by the plaintiff in state court.

Step-by-Step Procedure in Commencing a Federal Court Action

File a complaint: no technical language needed—just "tell a story." In the federal court—emphasis is placed on "the trial," rather than "forms" needed to "get to trial." Pleadings are construed liberally as to allow a litigant his "day in court." It is vital, however, to relate all the facts necessary to show that the court has jurisdiction and to prove the underlying cause of action in the complaint. See, generally, Rule 8 of the FRCP. Incomplete or vague statements may result in dismissal.

A. Service of Process

1. The clerk will issue a Summons on the defendant or his agent.

2. U.S. Marshal serves the Summons along with the Complaint on the defendant.

3. Pretrial motions

   a. *Motion to Dismiss*

      i. Complaint fails to state a cause of action;

      ii. Denial of jurisdiction (either personal or subject matter) of the court; or

      iii. Other grounds:

         • If granted—the case is dismissed.

         • If dismissed "without prejudice," the plaintiff can refile in the proper court or amend the complaint.

         • If dismissed "with prejudice," the plaintiff cannot amend or refile.

b. *Motion for a More Definite Statement*, which is asking for more specific facts that give rise to the purported claim of the plaintiff because the allegations or facts are too ambiguous (FRCP Rule 12 (e))

c. *Motion to Strike*, which is merely asking the court to strike from the complaint matters (facts) which are not "germane" to the case (FRCP Rule 12 (f))

d. *Motion for General Demurrer*, which admits to all allegations but denies that these allegations state a cause of action. If granted, the case is dismissed.

then

e. *Answer*: Counterclaim against the plaintiff and/or cross-claim against a third party. Plaintiff must file a "reply" to the counterclaim.

B. Pleading Stage

1. Motion for Judgment on the pleadings (FRCP Rule 12 (c)) and

2. Motion for Summary Judgment (FRCP Rule 56).

   a. These can be filed by either party *after* all other pleadings have been resolved. The summary judgment is granted as a "matter of law."

C. Discovery Stage

1. Deposition,

2. Interrogatories,

3. Demand for production of documents,

4. Physical/mental examination or entry onto land, and

5. Request for admissions.

Three Major Methods for Resolving Legal Controversies

Alternatives to Trial (aka ADR—Alternate Dispute Resolution)

A. Negotiation
Concerns itself with discussions or conferences between the parties, seeking to establish the final form of future proceedings or a settlement of the controversy.

1. *Advantages*

   a. It is a "mutual agreement,"

b. It is informal, and

c. It is simple.

2. *Drawback:* It is not binding upon the parties.

B. Mediation

Where the matter is referred to a third party, who will attempt to reconcile the differences between the parties and to settle them through compromise ("win some, lose some"). Give each party a "portion of what that party is seeking." In some circumstances, the mediator is a "fact-finder" who will then issue a conclusion based on the facts as he understands them.

C. Arbitration

This vehicle refers the controversy to a third party chosen by the litigants or one provided by law, whichever is applicable. Here, to avoid going to trial, the result is an "award," the "final resolution" of the controversy. Arbitration is often mandated by law or provided for in an agreement. Hence, you have two types of arbitration: (1) compulsory and (2) voluntary.

The main difference between mediation and arbitration is the role played by the third party. Mediation revolves around the wishes and compromises of the parties. Ultimately, the mediator does not grant relief that is not agreed to by the parties. The mediator works with the parties to resolve the conflict. On the other hand, arbitration involves a neutral third party who collects the evidence presented by the parties to the controversy, but then independently makes his decision based upon his interpretation of the gathered information.

Procedure for Removal of a State Court Action to the Federal Court System

1. Prepare the notice for removal (see 28 U.S.C.A. §1441 et seq. for jurisdictional and procedural requirements). Be sure in your statement that you include the jurisdiction of the federal law giving you the eligibility to file the action in the federal court system. An example of this would be the constitutional requirement that the claim arises under federal law, thereby creating a cause of action for the plaintiff; other examples would be the diversity of citizenship and the amount in controversy.

2. Serve a copy of the Notice of Removal with the federal clerk, together with all pleadings and any orders that were filed in the state court. You might check with the federal court clerk to determine if a filing fee is required. This is peculiar to each district court.

3. Please be advised that you no longer need to obtain from any insurance company a bond to cover costs incurred in this removal process.

4. Give prompt notice to the state court that you have removed the case to the federal court system.

> NOTE: You should file your answer to the pleading (complaint) or the Notice of Removal in the state court *before* the thirty-day statute of limitations has passed. Otherwise, a default judgment can be taken against the client.

5. Thereafter, be sure to notify all parties of the Notice of Removal to Federal Court. Be sure that each and every plaintiff, if more than one, is also notified.

6. As the paralegal, it will be your job to check the file to determine if any state court orders were rendered during the course of the proceeding. If so, please advise the attorney so that he can in turn advise as to whether or not to seek federal court changes in the orders.

7. Be reminded, or take note, that the removed case does not have to be repleaded in the federal district court.

Pleadings and Motions

Most state courts have adopted modern court rules of civil procedure, as well as modern court rules of criminal procedure, that are similar in content to the Federal Rules of Civil Procedure. The trend today is to get away from long technical pleadings and instead submit a plain, simple statement of the facts or defenses to a claim. This is primarily true in the federal court system. Facts sufficing to allege a "cause of action" must be stated after facts that show jurisdiction of the court. Pleadings are simple pleadings in the federal system, and all you have to do is notify the defending party generally what is being alleged against him—ref. Federal Rules of Civil Procedure, Title III, Rules 7 through 16, particularly Rule 8(a), which states:

(A) CLAIMS FOR RELIEF.

A pleading that states a claim for relief must contain:

(1) a short and plain statement of the grounds for the court's jurisdiction, unless the court already has jurisdiction and the claim needs no new jurisdictional support;

(2) a short and plain statement of the claim showing that the pleader is entitled to relief; and

(3) a demand for the relief sought, which may include relief in the alternative or different types of relief.

(This can be accessed directly at www.law.cornell.edu/rules/frcp/rule8.htm.)

A. Summons and Complaint

The summons and a copy of the complaint can be served on the defendant to start the action by any person over the age of eighteen (F.R.C.P. 4(c)(2)). This can either be a professional private process server or a U.S. marshal. Should you wish a marshal to serve the summons and complaint, you must ask the clerk of the court to do so under F.R.C.P. 4(c)(3). This is done by applying to the court clerk with a printed form entitled Request for Personal Service. This is merely a formality as the clerk simply signs and stamps the document—ref. F.R.C.P. 4(c).

> **PRACTICAL HINT:** Service on minors or other persons incompetent to receive personal service must be made on the guardian *ad litem*, or agent, appointed by the court—ref. F.R.C.P. 4(g).
>
> Service on corporations, partnerships, or associations may be made pursuant to F.R.C.P. 4(h). This permits service upon an authorized agent designated as such.
>
> Upon completion of the service of process you should immediately cause the proof of service of the summons and complaint to be filed with the court pursuant to F.R.C.P. Rule 4(l).

B. Answer

After service of the summons and complaint, the defendant has twenty days in which to file a responsive pleading, unless otherwise extended by the court or excepted under F.R.C.P. 12(a). Defenses must be appropriately pleaded or they are waived, with few exceptions.

An answer to be filed by the U.S. attorney or other officer or agency of the government has sixty days in which to file a responsive pleading—ref. F.R.C.P 12(a).

Basically, the answer is the same as that prepared and filed in a state court that has adopted modern court rules of civil procedure. As in a state court answer, you have to admit or deny part of a paragraph, or you can specifically deny part or generally deny part of a paragraph, and so forth. But here too it is deemed admitted if you do not do one or the other.

> **A CAUTIONARY MEASURE:** Note that a denial for lack of information sufficient to form a belief as to the jurisdictional facts is an appropriate challenge and puts the burden of proof on the plaintiff.

Just as in a state court that has adopted modern court rules of civil procedure, "affirmative defenses" should be pleaded in the answer to a federal court complaint as listed in F.R.C.P 8(c). They are:

- Accord and satisfaction
- Arbitration and award
- Assumption of risk
- Contributory negligence
- Discharge in bankruptcy
- Duress

- Estoppel
- Failure of consideration
- Fraud
- Illegality
- Injury by fellow servant
- Laches

- License
- Payment
- Release
- *Res judicata*
- Statute of frauds
- Statute of limitations
- Waiver

Under F.R.C.P. 12(b), you can put certain defenses in your answer, or make a motion to dismiss based upon the following defenses:

1. Lack of jurisdiction of the subject matter

2. Lack of jurisdiction over the person

3. Improper venue

4. Insufficiency of process—meaning that the summons and complaint was improperly issued—ref. F.R.C.P 4(a) and (b)

5. Insufficiency of service of process of summons—meaning that the summons was incorrectly served. In some state courts, such as California, a "motion to quash" is used to raise this question—ref. F.R.C.P. 4(c) through (i).

6. Failure to state a claim upon which relief can be granted. This would be the same as a general demurrer in some state court actions or a motion to dismiss for failure to state a cause of action in other state courts (see Chapter 6).

7. Failure to join an indispensable party. This is important, because even though they are not a party to the action, if they were not brought in as a party-defendant (or party-plaintiff), complete relief could not be given to the parties privy to the lawsuit. Remember that when this party is brought in, you must consider the problems of venue, service of process, and diversity jurisdiction.

Some defenses cannot be waived. They are as follows:

1. Lack of subject matter (see statute creating the federal court),

2. Failure to state a claim upon which relief can be granted (see Chapter 6), and

3. Failure to join an indispensable party (see F.R.C.P. 19 and compare F.R.C.P 20 covering permissive joinder of parties and F.R.C.P. 21 covering the right to add or drop parties).

The defenses that cannot be waived are defenses that concern the jurisdiction of the court. If a court has no jurisdiction it has no power and its judgment is void.

Other affirmative defenses as defined in F.R.C.P. 7(c) must be pleaded or they are waived.

NOTE: The Statute of Limitations, contrary to some popular opinion, is an affirmative defense that must be pleaded or it is waived.

C. Counterclaim

The counterclaim is the pleading filed by a defendant against a plaintiff in the action that states facts that show the defendant also has a legal claim against the plaintiff. (See Chapter 6, "How to State a Cause of Action.") Sections (a) through (f) of the Federal Rules of Civil Procedure govern Counterclaims.

Compulsory counterclaim. The compulsory counterclaim is the claim of defendant arising out of the transaction that is the subject matter of plaintiff's action. It must be brought or you have automatically waived the right of the client to bring it. You do not have to show independent jurisdiction in the federal court; the jurisdiction is satisfied by the plaintiff's claim. The plaintiff has to file and serve a reply to this counterclaim within twenty days of receipt thereof—ref. F.R.C.P. 13(a) and 13(c).

Permissive counterclaim. The permissive counterclaim is the claim of defendant for any other claim he may have against the plaintiff that is not related to the cause of action asserted by the plaintiff. Such claim need not be alleged or alluded to in the original complaint transaction. The only thing it has in common is the parties—ref. F.R.C.P. 13(b) and 13(c).

Counterclaims maturing or acquired after pleading are covered in F.R.C.P. 13(e), which allows a party to supplement his original pleading to include these counterclaims. F.R.C.P. 13(f) permits amendment of the pleadings for an omitted counterclaim where that omission was due to some excusable neglect or oversight.

D. Cross-Claims

A "cross-claim" arises between parties on the same side of a lawsuit. Cross-claims are always "permissive." The test for a cross-claim is that the claim must arise out of the transaction or occurrence that is the subject of the pending lawsuit—ref. F.R.C.P. 13(g) and (i).

An example of a cross-claim in a defendant-against-defendant situation may be under the theory of indemnification, that is, the defendant claims that the other defendant has agreed to hold him harmless against any claim by the plaintiff in the matter.

After the cross-claim has been served, the defending party has twenty days in which to file his answer (sixty days for the U.S. attorney). You do not have to plead facts showing jurisdiction in your cross-claim.

E. Third-Party Complaint

Rule 14(a) of the Federal Rules of Civil Procedure (F.R.C.P.) applies to the bringing in of a third party by a defendant in a federal lawsuit. Section (b) of that Rule applies to bringing in of a third party by a plaintiff. All rules regarding pleadings and procedure in this section on federal practice and procedure apply to the third-party plaintiffs and defendants whether they were brought in by the original plaintiff or the original defendant.

A third-party complaint is filed by a defending party to bring in an outside party he feels is really the person liable for the plaintiff's complaint or the defendant's counterclaim. When your attorney brings in a third party in his client's case, you must have a summons issued and personally served on the new party with a copy of the third-party complaint (which will have a copy of the *original* complaint attached). See F.R.C.P. 14(c) as to third-party practice as it applies to admiralty and maritime court.

The new third-party defendant and you as the third-party plaintiff will then follow the federal practice and procedures as given herein for the original plaintiffs and defendants.

> **NOTE:** A third-party complaint may be filed without leave of court if it is filed not later than ten days after the original defendant's answer is filed. Otherwise, defendant (third-party plaintiff) must get an "order of court" permitting him to file the third-party complaint—ref. F.R.C.P. 14(a).

F. Amended and Supplemental Pleadings

You can amend your original pleading without permission of the court, as long as it is done *before* the defendant files his answer. There is a leeway of about twenty days. Thereafter, you have to prepare a motion for leave to amend. The defendant, of course, would have to file an amended answer if you are granted permission to amend the complaint—ref. F.R.C.P. 15(a).

If a defendant files a motion to dismiss or other preliminary motion objecting to the complaint, the court will usually give you leave to amend the complaint if it grants the motion. See G, titled Pretrial Motions.

The procedure for filing an amended pleading at your request after the defendant has filed his answer is basically the same as in a state court proceeding. You make your regular motion to amend the pleading and attach a copy of the proposed pleading as an exhibit. The judge may want to see what you have amended to determine whether or not to grant your motion.

Check your local federal district court rule to determine whether you must retype the entire amended complaint and refile it after leave to amend is granted.

G. Pretrial Motions

A pretrial motion must be in writing and must state the grounds for the motion with particularity. The motion may be written together with a written notice of hearing on the motion, depending on the local federal district court rules and customs—ref. F.R.C.P. 7(b). Filing of the pretrial motions that are prescribed in Federal Rules of Civil Procedure 12 extend the time for filing an answer until ten days after the court's order on the motion.

1. *Motion for a more definite statement.* If this motion is granted and it is not obeyed within ten days after notice of the order, or such other time as the court may direct, the court may at its discretion strike the pleading or make such other order as it deems just. The motion is used where a pleading is so vague or ambiguous that a party could not reasonably respond to it in a required responsive pleading. The key word is reasonably. Pleading does not require perfect clarity.

   If a motion for more definite statement is granted and the plaintiff obeys the order by filing an amended complaint, the defendant (movant) has ten days from the date the amended complaint is filed to file his answer.

2. *Motion to strike—F.R.C.P. 2(f).* This motion is made before responding to a pleading within twenty days after service of the pleading; as a result of this motion the court may order stricken from any pleading any redundant, immaterial, impertinent, or scandalous matter. In some state courts a motion to strike does not expand the time for filing an answer.

3. *Motion for judgment on the pleadings—F.R.C.P. 12(c).* This motion may be made after the pleadings are closed, but within a time that will not delay the trial of the action.

   CAUTION: This is a dangerous motion, in that if matters outside of the pleadings are presented and admitted into evidence by the court, the motion can be treated as a summary judgment and can be disposed of such as provided in Rule 56. Of course, should this occur, all parties are given notice and a reasonable time within which to present materials pertinent to such a motion by Rule 56.

4. *Motion for summary judgment—F.R.C.P. 56.* This motion will be granted if there are no genuine issues as to any material fact and the moving party is entitled to a judgment as a matter of law. As in the state court system, this motion is normally made after the completion of all discovery. And, similarly, you can obtain a partial summary judgment under federal practice procedures, as in the state court system, to narrow the triable issues of fact.

   The purpose of this motion is, primarily, to achieve a quick, final resolution of a dispute when there is no real necessity for a trial because there are no facts that are in dispute. If the facts, taken in the light most favorable to the non-moving party, indicate that the movant has an unarguable right to the relief sought, then the summary judgment will be granted. Essentially, the court has no need for a fact-finder in this situation, the judge can simply move on to applying the applicable law to the facts and render a decision.

Under Rule 56 of the Federal Rules of Civil Procedure, the parties making and opposing a motion for summary judgment are required to submit affidavits and certifications in support of the motion. The court may also consider depositions and sworn answers to interrogatories filed in the case as supporting evidence for the motion.

When the attorney wishes to proceed with any of the preceding motions, a paralegal should (1) carefully review the file, (2) reread the deposition(s) or the summary digest of the depositions, (3) reread answers to interrogatories and requests for admissions, (4) prepare a statement of undisputed facts for review and submission, (5) read the applicable code sections, (6) check the law applicable to the facts, and (7) then draft the appropriate motion to be reviewed by the attorney before filing.

> **NOTE:** One can also file a motion for partial summary judgment under Rule 56(c) for liability alone (allocation of fault) despite the fact that the amount of the liability is still in dispute. This is often easier to obtain than final summary judgment.

Procedure for Filing Motions

In the federal district court file written motions and notices of hearing thereon not later than five days before the date set for the hearing on the motion—ref. F.R.C.P. 6(d).

Opposing counsel must file any opposing affidavits and memoranda of law at least one day before the date set for the hearings.

> **PRACTICAL HINT:** A law memorandum in support of a motion or opposing a motion is not required by the Federal Rules of Civil Procedure. However, a law memorandum makes your position clearer and saves time for the court. It is always a good idea to provide the court with accurate and concise information. Your task, as the paralegal, is to prepare a law memorandum that is clear, overt, and measurable, particularly if the legal issues raised by the motion are complex or not obviously in your favor.
>
> Your local federal court rules may require filing the original and one copy (or duplicate originals). Some courts are even accepting electronic submissions; indeed, the bankruptcy court is completely electronic. Check these matters with the clerk of your local federal court before proceeding.
>
> On the motion for the production of documents, if the volume of documents is too big to handle practically or if there is controversy as to the need for certain

documents requested, the court clerk will send out an order requiring the parties to meet and decide on what documents should be produced. The parties usually have two weeks to perform or reply to this request. It may be your task to review the documents with your attorney and help draft the joint statement with opposing counsel or his assistant.

Discovery Procedures

Discovery in civil cases in the federal courts is governed by the Federal Rules of Civil Procedure Title V, sections 26 through 37.

A paralegal may be required to:

1. Set depositions dates by notice (see F.R.C.P. 27(2)),

2. Send out sets of written interrogatories (see F.R.C.P. 33),

3. Request production of documents and things and for entry upon land for inspection and other purposes (see F.R.C.P. 34),

4. Prepare notices of a physical or mental examination of a defendant (see F.R.C.P. 35), and

5. Send out a set of requests for admissions (see F.R.C.P. 36).

The scope of federal court discovery is quite broad in that any matter not privileged, which is relevant to the subject matter, is discoverable. There is an important distinction between what is "discoverable" and what is "admissible" during the trial proceedings. That which is discoverable is not always admissible. You can utilize any of the preceding vehicles as much as you want, whenever you want. And, most important, there is no thirty-day rule that all discovery should be completed before trial, as in some court rules.

As a paralegal you should be able to draft some of the discovery documents, subject to review by your attorney. Protection from improper and unduly burdensome discovery can be obtained by order of the federal court in which the action is filed or where a deposition is being taken—ref. F.R.C.P. 26(c).

A. Depositions

"Depositions," oral examinations of a party, are usually taken after the complaint is filed. In certain circumstances they are allowed before the action. See F.R.C.P. 27 and 30.

Depositions have to be noticed by a party-litigant in the action, but you can take the deposition of anybody by giving reasonable notice, whether or not the person to be deposed is a party to the action. If you are requested a deposition of a nonparty, a subpoena may be necessary. If you want documents produced at the deposition, you should describe them with particularity in a *subpoena duces tecum* to a nonparty or in the notice to a party. (A deposition that is solely testamentary (i.e., no documents requested) is referred to as a *subpoena ad testificatum.*)

If you are not sure of the name or the identity of the custodian of records of a corporate or government defendant, merely describe in your *subpoena duces tecum* or notice the subject matter of the deposition and clearly state which pertinent documents you wish presented at the deposition. Thereafter, it is incumbent upon the corporation or government entity to designate a person to come to the deposition with the proper documents.

A transcript of the deposition must be filed with the court clerk immediately after it has been reviewed and signed by the party deposed. The deposed must not only be sworn in prior to giving testimony, but also must certify that the transcript of the deposition to be filed is a true and accurate record of the event. This is important because depositions are admissible as evidence in court and therefore must comply with the evidentiary procedural requirements. During a regular deposition duly recorded before a court-approved officer, all the attorneys may ask any question that is within the general scope of discovery. The federal rule, and some state rules, also allow depositions to be taken on specified questions only. See F.R.C.P. 31. As a paralegal you should be able to draft these questions subject to review by your attorney. See F.R.C.P. 26(c) for Protective Order and F.R.C.P. 37 for Motion to Compel Discovery.

B. Interrogatories

As in the state court system, you can only serve interrogatories on party-litigants. Information requested from nonparties must be obtained through a subpoena or consent. Though urged, but not generally followed, in state courts, in preparing written answers to a set of interrogatories for filing in the federal court, you must type the answer to the interrogatory being answered just below the question.

EXAMPLE

Interrogatory 1. What was the date of the accident?
Answer: July 30, 20___.
Interrogatory 2. What was the time and place of accident?
Answer: On or about 12:15 p.m. at the intersection of Doheny and Olympic Boulevards, Los Angeles, CA.

Interrogatories in a civil case in federal court are governed by Rule 33 of the Federal Rules of Civil Procedure. Some of the provisions relating to interrogatories are:

1. Interrogatories may be filed and served any time after commencement of the action.

2. There is a limit of twenty-five questions to be posed in the request.

3. Unless extended by the court, the time within which to answer a set of interrogatories is thirty days—F.R.C.P 6(e). If they are served by mail, you get an extra three days. An extension of time other than this must be obtained by stipulation of the parties approved by the court or by order of court on motion of a party—ref. F.R.C.P. 6(b) and (d). One exception is where interrogatories are filed so quickly that forty-five days have not passed since the filing of the complaint—ref. F.R.C.P. 33(a).

4. If your attorney has any objections to the interrogatories, he has thirty days after service within which to file the objections or answer the interrogatories. Note that these objections are prepared for his signature, *not* that of the client.

5. If a party fails to answer or object to interrogatories that were served on him by you, your attorney may file a Motion to Compel Further Answers. This can be done at any time, as opposed to the procedure for objection to interrogatories. See F.R.C.P. 37.

C. Requests for Admission

"Requests for admission" can be served anytime after commencement of the action. These are a set of numbered statements presented to the opposing party which he must admit or deny. This is a mechanism to establish uncontested facts. Failure to respond will be deemed an admission of the factual statement and will be admissible as against that party.

The party to whom the request for admission is directed has thirty days to respond per F.R.C.P. 36(a), unless forty-five days have not passed since service of the complaint and summons on him. For example, if plaintiff wants to serve a request early, say ten days after the filing and service of the summons and complaint, the party to whom the request is directed has thirty-five days to respond.

Federal Multidistrict Litigation

The concept of federal multidistrict litigation was created and is governed by statute. See 28 U.S.C. 4207 (see www.law.cornell.edu/uscode/html/uscode28/usc_sec_28_00001407----000-.html). Its purpose was to create a more efficient system for handling very large or class action cases like airplane accidents, injuries from defective products, patent infringements, and investment fraud. The statute creates a federal judicial panel and prescribes the rules for its jurisdiction and proceedings.

A multidistrict claim may be held before the statutory Judicial Panel on Multidistrict Litigation, the members of which are appointed by the chief justice of the

United States. The website for the U.S. Judicial Panel on Multidistrict Litigation can be accessed at www.jpml.uscourts.gov/index.html.

Step-by-Step Procedure for Filing a Multidistrict Litigation Claim

1. Prepare an original and required copies of each document: the claim or summons and complaint, motion for transfer, and a proof of service or notice of opposition pursuant to the Procedural Rules under 28 U.S.C. §1407. Also note that electronic copies are required in the submission.

2. These documents should then be submitted for filing with the clerk of the panel, either by mailing or personal delivery to:

> Clerk of the Panel
> Judicial Panel on Multidistrict Litigation
> Thurgood Marshall Federal Judiciary Building
> One Columbus Circle, NE, Room G-255, North Lobby
> Washington, DC 20002-8004

   NOTE: No document should be left with or mailed to a judge of the panel.

3. Thereafter the clerk of the panel, as in state and other federal court actions, places the date of filing on all documents filed.

4. Copies of motions for transfer of claims or actions should be filed in each district court where an action is pending that will be affected by the motion.

5. Copies of motion for remand should be filed in the district court in which any action affected by the motion is pending.

6. Within ten days of filing of a motion to transfer, an order to show cause (or conditional transfer order), will be issued by the panel. Each litigant or his attorney must give the clerk of the panel, in writing, the name and address of the attorney designated by that litigant to receive service of process and other documents relating to the case being heard by the judicial panel of multidistrict litigation.

   NOTE: Only one attorney shall represent a party-litigant, and any party-litigant not represented shall be served any and all pleadings by mailing to his last known address.

7. In connection with number 6 here, the clerk of the panel shall provide all counsel and party-litigants not represented by counsel with a Panel Service List of names and addresses of the designated attorneys and the parties they represent and the names and addresses of the parties not represented by counsel.

8. See Rule 7.2 of 28 U.S.C. §1407, as to the practice and procedure for filing motions in Multidistrict Litigation Panel.

9. See Rules 9 and 10 of 28 U.S.C. §1407, regarding conditions and provisions for the practice and procedure relating to "tag-along actions."

NOTE: Paralegals will find the checklist from the JPML particularly helpful.

CHECKLIST FOR FILING A NEW MDL MOTION

FOR 28 U.S.C. §1407 TRANSFER

Court Rules Judicial Panel on Multidistrict Litigation cited @ 199 F.R.D. 425

☐ Motion must consist of at least two actions with common questions of fact pending in two different federal district courts.

☐ Motion shall be captioned "BEFORE THE JUDICIAL PANEL ON MULTIDISTRICT LITIGATION" followed by a brief descriptive caption of the new litigation (Rule 7.1(e)). *See Sample M-1.*

☐ Final page of each pleading shall contain the name, address, phone number of the attorney and shall include the name of each party represented.

☐ Brief (memorandum) in support of motion may not exceed 20 pages. *See Sample M-2.*

☐ Schedule of Actions must include the complete name of each action, listing the full names of each party (do not shorten with "etc." or "et al.") and shall also include any additional parties such as movants, intervenors, etc.; the district court and division; the civil action number; and the judge assigned for each action. *See Sample M-3.*

☐ Proof of Service shall indicate service of papers on the clerk of each district court that may be affected by the motion and shall include the name and address of each attorney served and the party represented by each. Double-check the proof of service against the schedule of actions to make sure each party has been listed with counsel or, if counsel are unknown, serve the party directly. If unable to obtain the address of a party, you must state so in the proof of service (Rule 5.2(a) and (b)). *See Sample M-4.*

☐ Excessive exhibits are not helpful and generally do little to assist the Panel in ruling on a motion for transfer. Exhibits exceeding 50 pages should be bound separately from the motion papers. DO NOT include as exhibits copies of the Panel's own orders or pleadings that are readily available through PACER or CM/ECF.

☐ Provide the Panel with one courtesy copy of each complaint and docket sheet for the cases on your motion. This will facilitate processing of the motion papers.

☐ An Oral Argument Statement is not required, however, one may be submitted with the motion papers.

CHAPTER SIX

How to State a Cause
of Action in a Civil Case

What Is a Cause of Action?

A cause of action is the legal or equitable right to recover damages or other claimed relief in a court action. The statement or allegation of the facts sufficient to support or deny that relief from the court are stated in pleadings prepared in accordance with the rules of court in which the legal action alleging the cause of action is filed.

The right to bring a legal action in any court is the right to seek judicial relief for the cause of action in the jurisdiction of the court in which a legal action is filed.

The facts alleged in the pleadings must be proved or admitted before the plaintiff in the cause of action can recover.

It might be noted at this point that some state and local rules differ from the federal rules in that they require the complaint to state facts sufficient to state a "cause of action," whereas the federal court uses the word "claim for relief"—F.R.C.P 8(a). There are also some causes of action that must be pleaded with specificity. It is not enough to set forth merely enough facts to give the defendant(s) notice of the claim; the details must be set forth clearly as well. This most often occurs in claims of fraud and claims requesting "special damages."

What Are the Elements of a Cause of Action?

To recover damages or other relief from a court, you must allege (state) facts in a complaint that, if admitted or proved at the trial, would entitle the plaintiff to a final judgment after trial of the case.

The legal elements of a cause of action are found in case law, statutes, and government regulations.

Monetary damages are recovered in an action "at law." Other relief may be obtained in an action "in equity."

The factual elements of the cause of action must be stated in the complaint in numbered paragraphs. Each factual element will receive its own number. This enables the other parties to respond most efficiently. To state a cause of action in a pleading, the facts must show the right of the plaintiff to recover. The first paragraphs state facts that show the court's jurisdiction of the subject matter and of the parties. The following paragraphs state the facts in logical (chronological) order, showing that the client has a right to recover for legal reasons.

The legal elements of the cause of action are argued by the attorneys to the court and explained by the court to the jury (if there is one) in the trial of the case. The factual elements are presented in court to the fact-finders directly. If this is the jury, they will make their own decisions regarding the veracity and reliability of the evidence presented.

During the initial interview with the client (in some offices this is done by the paralegal), the attorney will hear the basic facts relating to the client's problem. From those facts, he will decide, as a matter of law, whether the client has a cause of action over which some court has jurisdiction.

NOTE: Before the attorney can decide the foregoing, he may require the paralegal to interview the client further to get additional facts, documents, and other information that is necessary to decide whether the client does have a cause of action. The attorney or the paralegal may also do some preliminary legal research to determine whether the client has a "case which will stand up in court" (cause of action). See Chapters 7 and 8.

The facts are as important as the law in stating a cause of action. The facts stated in a pleading must show that the defendant had a legal duty to the plaintiff which he breached without legal excuse. A legal excuse for breaching a legal duty to the plaintiff under the facts stated by the plaintiff in his complaint is called an affirmative defense. The defendant's affirmative defense(s) consists of facts alleged by defendant in his answer that, if proved at the trial, show that plaintiff is not entitled to recover even if he suffered injury inflicted by the defendant, because the defendant's actions were legally excused.

AB, while driving to work, ran a red light and hit CD's vehicle from the rear, causing personal injuries to CD. In this instance, CD has a legal right to recover against AB, since AB violated a statute prohibiting drivers of automobiles to run red lights. As a result of violating the state statute, AB intruded upon CD's right to safe driving on the highway, causing CD personal injury and resultant damage to CD's vehicle.

AB had a duty to obey the law and, in not obeying the law, breached his duty to CD, giving rise to a good cause of action for personal injuries and property damage. It would be up to the courts to determine the extent of the damage being sought, thereby giving CD the relief prayed. If the facts of the accident are different, AB may have an affirmative defense.

EXAMPLE

AB was making an illegal left turn from the right lane when CD hit the side of the car being driven by AB because CD was exceeding the speed limit.

In the second example, both parties violated their respective duties to obey the law. If the complaint filed states that CD struck the side of the other car because CD was exceeding the speed limit or committing other violations, it may state a cause of action against CD. But if CD, in his answer, alleges that AB was making an illegal left turn from the right lane, CD has stated an affirmative defense to the cause of action stated by AB. That affirmative defense is "contributory negligence" or "comparative negligence," depending on the law of the state where the accident happened. It is important to determine whether your state is a contributory or comparative negligence state. In contributory negligence, fault on the part of a party will deny him the relief sought. In comparative negligence, the percentage of fault will be allocated between the parties and the recovery will be reduced by that amount (i.e., if the plaintiff is found to be 40 percent negligent in causing the accident and the total recovery would be $100,000 without that negligence, the plaintiff is only entitled to receive $60,000—the amount not attributable to his own wrongdoing).

Basic Causes of Action at Law

Causes of court actions at law are divided into two basic categories that are important to determine in which court the legal action should or must be filed:

Local Actions

Local actions usually include those actions dealing with real property. The court is exercising its *in rem* jurisdiction. Examples are quiet title action, action to gain possession of real property, foreclosure of a trust deed or mortgage, or any other action to determine an interest in real property.

Where two or more owners seek a division of a piece of real property for purposes of a sale, but cannot agree how to divide it, or who is entitled to what size share. This is a typical partition suit.

or

Where a person claims by adverse possession against the present owner of a piece of property. An action in ejectment or an action to quiet title may be appropriate. Both actions are called "real actions."

"Local actions" must be brought in the county where the property is located or where the local action arose. Interestingly, marriages are considered a local action and therefore many states consider their jurisdiction over them to be over that *rem* for divorce proceedings.

Transitory Actions

Transitory actions, on the other hand, deal with personal injury, with personal property, and with breach of contract. These actions may be filed in the county where at least one of the defendants resides or the cause of action accrued. These are actions that can be tried anywhere the defendant can be found and served with process in accordance with the local rules. In a transitory action the substantive law of the place where, for example, the accident took place is applied. The court hearing the case follows its own procedural law.

Typical transitory actions may be filed as follows: A personal injury may be filed in either the county where the accident occurred or in the county where the defendant lives; a breach of contract action may be filed in any county where one of the defendants lives or where the contract was entered into, or in the county where the contract was to be performed or substantially performed.

State statutes may prescribe "venue" (as opposed to jurisdiction) for bringing transitory actions, particularly where corporations are involved. Check state venue statutes and see the Chapter 4 discussion of venue under court procedures.

Basic Causes of Action in Equity

In most civil cases, the party-litigants suffering harm are seeking money awards to alleviate their loss and/or pain and suffering. Though this would appear to be the norm, there are times when a "money damage award" will not and does not make the individual whole or redress the harm. In such event he may file a complaint in equity. These courts hearing a case in equity can make an order to prevent irreparable injury and give relief where a court of law will not or cannot. A court hearing an equity case may order the return or delivery of property or the performing or refraining from doing some other act.

Courts of equity consider the equitable rights of both parties. They weigh what is and what is not fair. For example, issuance of an injunction is not a matter of right but rests in the discretion of the court, which will consider whether greater injury will result to defendant from granting the injunction than would be caused to plaintiff by refusing the injunction.

The most important prerequisites to filing an action in equity are as follows:

1. The plaintiff does not have an adequate remedy at law (i.e., monetary recompense).

2. The plaintiff is suffering, or is about to suffer, an irreparable harm.

Courts award equitable remedies only where monetary damages are inadequate. Therefore, if a money award alone will satisfy the damages caused, do not file your lawsuit in a court of equity. You do not have a cause of action in equity in such case.

Another consideration of the equity courts may be whether the court decree, if ordered, will be feasible to enforce. It may be entirely possible that what the plaintiff is entitled to is not possible to give him. For instance, if the plaintiff is entitled to receive the rare, irreplaceable, and invaluable painting that he contracted to buy, but the defendant sold it to an innocent "good faith" third-party purchaser, it will be impossible for the court to order it over to the plaintiff.

In an equity case, the court hears the case without a jury. The court makes findings of both fact and law as the basis for its final order. The court may, in some cases, allow a jury to hear a certain factual phase of the case if the judge believes it would be necessary, on his own motion or on the motion of a party to the case.

The basic relief that an equity court may give, if the plaintiff states a cause of action entitling him to equitable relief, may be one or more of the following: injunction, specific performance, rescission, or reformation.

Injunction

An "injunction" is an order of court directing a party to a cause of action in equity to refrain from doing some act. It acts as a "stop order." There are several types of injunctions:

1. A temporary restraining order (TRO) which acts immediately to order the defendant to refrain from acting. This can be applied for by the plaintiff even

before the commencement of suit and without notice to the defendant. This is granted for a short period of time and only in limited and exigent circumstances. The plaintiff must set forth the facts of the emergency situation in order to receive this drastic relief.

2. A preliminary injunction may be granted either before or during trial. The plaintiff must demonstrate the urgent need to preserve the status quo until final determination on the merits can be made.

3. A permanent or temporary injunction may be granted after the hearing and may be made a part of the final order of the court in the case. The permanent injunction forever bars the defendant from taking the action(s) complained of, while the temporary injunction sets a time limit after which the defendant is able to act as he wishes.

EXAMPLE

Covenants not to compete are often placed in employment contracts. They prohibit the employee from working for another competing company after the employee leaves the original employer. Assuming that the departing employee has trade secrets or other proprietary information, the original employer may apply for an injunction to prevent the departing employee from accepting employment and working for the competitor. If the original employer can prove that it would suffer harm in the marketplace if this employee is able to work for the competitor, the court may order an injunction as against that employment. These are usually only temporary, as the court does not want to constrain a person's ability to engage in his livelihood.

Specific Performance

This is a typical equitable remedy available to a plaintiff in cases arising from contractual relationships. As opposed to the stop order of an injunction, this is an order to "do something"—to perform some specific act. The overriding consideration is still whether the legal remedy (money damages) is adequate, and furthermore, whether the consideration bargained for is unique and thereby irreplaceable. This is the court's decision.

EXAMPLES

The court may order the defendant to execute a deed for real property to the plaintiff where defendant had agreed to sell to the plaintiff but has since refused to sell without any legal excuse (affirmative defense).

or

Let us assume that the client's complaint for specific performance is based on a personal service contract wherein the defendant, when promising to perform a unique service for plaintiff, had either expressly or impliedly promised not to perform this service for anyone else. This is called a "negative covenant" or promise and thus, by enjoining the breach of this negative covenant, the court has indirectly ordered specific performance of the contract. The defendant may not perform for anyone else at the time and/or place where he had agreed to perform for plaintiff.

Such negative covenants arise most often in the fields of entertainment, television, or motion-picture production.

Rescission

"Rescission" is an equitable remedy whereby plaintiff seeks to avoid the existence of a contract.

The primary consideration of rescission is whether the grounds for rescission occurred *at* or *before* the time the contract was entered into by the parties.

The usual basis for a complaint for rescission are:

1. Mutual mistake—both parties were operating under incorrect assumptions as to the basic premise(s) of the contract. The facts constituting the mistake must be stated with specificity in the complaint.

   In the case of a "unilateral mistake," the courts will not order a rescission of a contract for a unilateral mistake unless the nonmistaken party knows, or should have known, of the mistaken party's mistake. The court will, however, grant an equitable rescission for a unilateral mistake not known by the defendant if the degree of hardship incurred by plaintiff by having to perform the contract outweighs the expectancies of the defendant. To do otherwise, it is felt, would be unjust enrichment.

2. Misrepresentation or fraud—the plaintiff must show that the defendant intentionally or recklessly misled the plaintiff regarding the material element(s) of contract, he knew that the plaintiff would rely upon it, and the plaintiff was harmed by relying on that misinformation. Again, this must be pleaded with specificity.

NOTE: When drafting a complaint in equity for rescission, get all the facts you must allege to comply with that pleading requirement. You cannot just state that defendant committed fraud. That is the legal conclusion that the attorney has to prove by introducing evidence of the facts you allege.

Reformation

Reformation is the equitable remedy for reforming or changing a written contract by decree to conform to the original intent of the parties. This occurs when the writing does not state exactly what the parties meant it to state.

The difference between reformation and rescission is that in rescission there is a finding that no original, valid contract existed, as it was entered into only because of a mistake, misrepresentation, or fraud.

In reformation there is a valid original contract that simply does not conform to the true intent of the parties as it is mutually understood. In essence, it is an error in the drafting, not in the intent of the parties.

To state the cause of action, the complaint must allege the facts of the contract as written and the actions or events that show what the parties *both* intended.

Who Are the Parties to a Cause of Action?

There are basically two parties to any lawsuit in a civil action: the moving party, which is the plaintiff who initiated the action, and the nonmoving party or defendant against whom the action is being brought.

A plaintiff can be any person or legal entity that has a legal, legitimate grievance against another; be this an executor, administrator, trustee, relator, conservator, guardian or guardian *ad litem*, or other person who is acting for another—ref. F.R.C.P. 17(a). A plaintiff is usually represented by a lawyer, but he may act in *propria persona* (in his own behalf as in the "do-it-yourself divorce" or in a small claims court). Every plaintiff must follow the rules of court that apply to his cause of action.

Situations and circumstances may arise in these civil actions where each of the parties here described may play double or identical roles. This occasion may arise when the defendant here referred to files a cross-complaint, thereby becoming both a defendant and a cross-complainant in the same action, wherein he is seeking affirmative relief based on the allegations of fact contained in plaintiff's complaint.

The plaintiff above referred to would then be plaintiff and cross-defendant, and must respond to the allegations in the cross-complaint.

Another person or legal entity may enter into this same lawsuit as an "intervenor," a third or outside party privy to the subject matter and facts seeking relief; or arising out of the same transaction he may be brought into the lawsuit by one of the present parties. These additions of parties would be done by court motion establishing them as a necessary or permissive party to the action, or it could be done by stipulation between the parties—ref. F.R.C.P. 17 through 25.

Other names given to a plaintiff or defendant in an action before the courts are petitioner, declarant, or relator.

EXAMPLE

A party seeking a dissolution of marriage (divorce) or a writ of mandamus, or writ of prohibition, or writ of *habeas corpus* as used in criminal cases, or writ of review, which is the appeal vehicle used in industrial cases, is called a "petitioner" instead of a plaintiff.

The defendant in the preceding actions is called a "respondent," but some states may still refer to such defending party as defendant.

The moving party in appellate procedures is called an "appellant" and the defending party may be called either a respondent or an appellee, since the policy as to this name designation varies from state to state, or may be interchangeable.

By whatever name, the moving party must state a cause of action.

Joinder of Parties

In a lawsuit the question of who or what constitutes an "indispensable party" (or a "conditionally necessary party," or a "compulsory joinder," or a "permissive joinder") is a matter of legal interpretation and argument. As such, it is a continuing dispute among the judiciary and attorneys. If the question is raised by any of the parties, your attorney has to make a court appearance on a motion. If your attorney raises the question, it would be necessary for you to prepare the appropriate notice and motion with accompanying affidavits and case authority. Or in lieu thereof, prepare a demurrer (if applicable in your state). Either method will allow your attorney to go to court and argue his point. Copies of these documents are to be served on opposing counsel, as court rules require.

A. Compulsory Joinder

Compulsory joinder is applicable if a court determines a party to be "materially interested" and the absence of such party will cause substantial prejudice to the court and all other parties concerned. In this case, the party must be made a party to the action or else the action may be barred. Often, the attorney of record must certify that, to his knowledge, he has joined all necessary parties. See your local court rule comparable to F.R.C.P. 19.

B. Permissive Joinder

Permissive joinder allows persons to join in the action if they allege facts entitling them to relief on some ground of privity to the original transaction that is the subject of the lawsuit. If they are not joined, they still retain their right to sue the current parties in a separate lawsuit. See your local court rule comparable to F.R.C.P. 20.

Who Must State the Cause of Action?

In order to succeed in a legal action, the plaintiff or petitioner must have the "capacity to sue." The person who has the legal capacity to sue states the cause of action in the complaint or petition.

EXAMPLES

1. An incompetent does not have the capacity to sue in his own name. An incompetent is a person who has been "adjudged" legally incompetent by a court. It means that the person does not have the capacity to understand the proceedings and their significance. Incompetency or ignorance or inefficiency are not synonymous.

2. A minor does not have the capacity to sue in his own name. It should be noted that the age of majority is eighteen in most states, but the age of majority may be higher in some states. It is important to double-check the rules.

3. A corporation (or other entity) has the capacity to sue in most states only if it is duly registered as a domestic corporation or registered as a foreign corporation doing business in the state.

Practical Duties of the Paralegal in Determining and Creating Capacity to Sue

A. Minor or Incompetent

Before filing a complaint for a minor or incompetent, the lack of capacity to sue must be cured. The duty of the paralegal would be to draft the petition for appointment of a guardian *ad litem* for the minor or appointment of a conservator or guardian for the senile or incompetent. This petition should be prepared and signed by the parties at the time of drafting.

A guardian has the same power as the person he represents with an exception: Any compromise or settlement or satisfaction of judgment must be approved by the court. The guardian is instructed to proceed in the best interests of his ward. Check your local state statutes in this regard.

If a "guardian of the property" (to be distinguished from a "guardian of the person") has been appointed by the court that adjudged the person incompetent, that guardian has the capacity to sue on behalf of the incompetent ward in any other action. That guardian may be an individual or a corporation (such as a bank that is authorized to conduct trust business). It is not necessary to file a petition for a new appointment in the present cause of action.

NOTE: State the facts and date of appointment of that guardian in the complaint or petition that is filed after the facts alleging jurisdiction are stated and before the facts alleging the cause of action. The same pleading procedure applies where another court has formerly appointed a guardian of the property of a minor plaintiff.

B. Corporation

As you know, a corporation is considered to be a legal entity with full power to sue or be sued. Foreign corporations (those not incorporated in your state) have similar or like rights to sue or be sued. But if a corporation has not registered to do business in a state, it may not have the right to bring a lawsuit, though it may have the right to defend against a lawsuit. The important thing to determine, therefore, is whether the plaintiff corporation has complied with the state regulations relating to incorporation and/or registration of a foreign corporation to do business in the state where it is bringing the action.

A "de jure corporation" is a corporation formed in compliance with the rules and regulations of applicable state law.

A "de facto corporation" is an organization that exercises corporate powers and franchises under color of law, absent compliance with the rules and regulations of state law for forming or continuing as a de jure corporation. The elements necessary for a de facto corporation are as follows:

1. A valid law that encompasses the assumed rights,

2. An attempt on the part of the organizers to incorporate under such law, and

3. Overt exercise of these purported powers.

The effect of omission to comply with state registration statutes and whether or not a de facto corporation may be created without filing articles of incorporation depends on the terms of state statutes that govern incorporation. Those statutes vary from state to state.

NOTE: The importance of checking the exact corporate status of a corporation before allowing it to file as a plaintiff is that its existence as a legal entity may be challenged by the defendant and a counterclaim of the defendant against the individual incorporators or stockholders may be asserted. Also check the corporate status of all defendants you are suing. Get and *use* the *exact* registered corporate name and corporate status. A judgment against a defendant with an inaccurate corporate name may cause serious problems in collecting the judgment. This information is usually available through your state's secretary or treasurer.

Also note that even if the corporation cures the registration defect(s) after the lawsuit is filed, its right to sue or defend may not be retroactive in some states. This problem is especially critical if the statute of limitations will soon run out on the corporation's claim.

C. Partnership or Business Using Assumed Name

A partnership may sue in its partnership name and/or in the names of all the general partners.

NOTE: If a partnership's name is a fictitious name, the name must have been registered or filed under the Fictitious Names Act in the state where it does business. Check the state statute for registration requirements. For a "limited" partnership, see the state statute. Failure to register the fictitious name creates problems similar to those discussed here as to failure to properly register a corporation.

An individual may do business under an assumed or fictitious name. For immediate clarity and under most court rules, the caption of a legal action may name John Doe d/b/a Atlas Plumbing Supplies as plaintiff. Instead of that, the plaintiff's real name alone may be used as plaintiff, but it should be alleged in the body of the complaint, following *either caption*, that "the plaintiff was doing business as Atlas Plumbing at all times pertinent to the complaint."

See the foregoing note regarding registration of a fictitious partnership name. The same law and caution applies to an individual person doing business under an assumed or fictitious name.

D. Government Entity

A government entity may have a cause of action in a court against another government entity or against an individual or against any other defendant.

When a government entity is the plaintiff, it may use its own name as plaintiff or it may, under certain statutes, bring an action on behalf of someone else.

EXAMPLES

1. Criminal case charging a federal crime or violation of federal law—*United States v. John Doe.*

2. Criminal case charging a state crime or violation of state law—*State of Florida v. John Doe.*

3. Case by one state against another state—*State of West Virginia v. Commonwealth of Pennsylvania.*

4. Case by a state, on behalf of an individual, for violation of a consumer protection statute, environmental protection statute, or other protective statute, based on information—*State of New York* EX REL. *John Doe v. ABC Corporation.*

Where your attorney's client has a cause of action against a government entity as the defendant, the "doctrine of sovereign immunity" must be considered before filing the legal action.

As a general rule, in the absence of statutory authority or consent, the doctrine of sovereign immunity exempts federal and state agencies and their political subdivisions from liability resulting from injury or damage arising out of their exercise of government duties that would include construction in public streets, highways, and the like. It should be noted that "consent statutes" have not received nationwide acceptance and furthermore that a dispute still exists as to whether this type of immunity exempts municipalities in general.

By way of example as to how these consent statutes work, under California law before you can bring a lawsuit naming one of the preceding entities as a defendant, you must first obtain its permission (or consent) by filing a petition or claim for damages. This petition or claim is either a printed form or typewritten document, depending on the entity involved. Within the document you set forth the facts of the case that justify naming the entity as the defendant, which include, but are not necessarily limited to, the following:

1. How the incident occurred,

2. An estimate of the damages caused, and

3. The extent of the injuries received.

The statutory procedure for filing this type of claim is found in the statutes or code of your state. Consent statutes that waive sovereign immunity usually contain instruction on *whom*, *where*, and *when* to serve the complaint. After the complaint is filed in the appropriate court, the rules of that court govern the proceedings. Some consent statutes set maximum limits for recovery against the government entity. Some of these statutes allow recovery of a judgment higher than the statutory limit but require an action of the state legislature to authorize payment of the additional judgment amount in excess of the statutory monetary limit.

It is also worth noting that government employees in their individual capacity are immune from suit if and when they are carrying out their duties of governmental employment. For example, the municipal building inspector generally cannot be sued by a homeowner where that inspector failed to find the defect(s) in a project that he inspected. This has engendered some controversy in that it insulates the employee for acts of professional negligence.

Pleading a Cause of Action

The cause of action must be stated in the complaint or petition that will be filed in court by the plaintiff or petitioner to commence the action.

The form, filing, and service of the complaint or petition are governed by the rules of the court in which the complaint or petition is to be filed. The content of the complaint depends upon the nature of the plaintiff's claim.

What to Incorporate in the Complaint

What is a complaint? A complaint, in civil practice (as opposed to a criminal complaint) is the first pleading of a plaintiff. It is a concise statement of the facts constituting the cause of action. Each material allegation of fact must be stated distinctly and be separately numbered.

The purpose of a complaint is to give the defendant information of all material facts upon which the plaintiff relies to support his demand for legal relief.

As indicated above, the information submitted in a complaint is a clear, precise, and accurate presentation of the transaction between the parties and a statement of the plaintiff's grievance.

The complaint must contain certain "ultimate facts." It need not contain "evidentiary facts," which may be necessary to prove the ultimate facts. This is particularly true in federal court complaints. The complaint should not state conclusions of law—ref. F.R.C.P. 7 and 8 and your comparable state court rules.

The courts have established certain rules, as follows:

- An ultimate fact is an "action" or "event" that may be proved by presenting "evidentiary facts" leading to that ultimate fact.

- A "conclusion of fact" is an expected consequence inferred from a given set of facts.

- A "law" is a "principle" that determines whether a particular action or event is legal or illegal in the jurisdiction where the action or event occurs.

- A "conclusion of law" is a statement that certain actions or events comply with or violate a law.

EXAMPLES

1. A speed limit is a law.

2. That the defendant was driving his automobile at a rate in excess of seventy miles an hour is an ultimate fact.

3. Testimony that defendant's car was going more than seventy miles an hour and a picture of car tire marks on the pavement on the road at the scene of the accident are evidentiary facts of the ultimate fact that defendant was traveling seventy miles an hour at the time of impact.

4. A statement that the defendant's driving at seventy miles an hour was a violation of his legal duty to plaintiff is a conclusion of law.

5. Whether a photograph of the car tire tracks is admissible in evidence at the trial is a conclusion of law.

Some conclusions of fact may be stated in a complaint as ultimate facts. They are: malice, intent, knowledge, and comparable state court rules.

Allegations of fact in the complaint should normally be based on and stated as "actual knowledge."

Where actual knowledge can not be obtained by reasonable investigation, material facts may be stated on information and belief.

EXAMPLE

Let us examine the case of Mary Pitts, hospital nurse, who wants to file a slander suit against her former employer, XYZ Hospital. In her complaint, she will claim defamation of character resulting from a publication of defamatory remarks.

The publication in this instance could have been a memorandum circulated throughout the hospital, or a letter of recommendation to a prospective new employer containing defamatory remarks, thereby causing Mary Pitts to be denied the new employment.

In the ordinary course of events, Mary Pitts would not have been present when the publication was disseminated. She might not know the exact words used in the letter. She would of necessity have to allege "on information and belief," the ultimate fact of the publication and its content since she would not have had direct or personal knowledge of the same.

This type of hearsay allegation is often necessary within the medical malpractice area of the law or in an equity action for an accounting. In a medical malpractice action, the party bringing the suit must rely on the opinions of others—medical experts—since the average layman knows nothing about medical practice and procedures. So any allegation made as to wrongs committed or injury suffered by way of medical malfeasance, negligence, and so forth, would have to be on information and belief, or the lack of it.

In the preceding examples, it is important to note that the moving party has neither actual nor constructive knowledge of the facts alleged. (Constructive knowledge is information that one is presumed to know generally since it is a matter of public record.)

The wording for the type of allegations described here would be "Plaintiff is informed and believes, and based upon such information and belief, alleges . . . ," or "Plaintiff does not possess sufficient information to allege ultimate facts, as the only source of information is in the sole custody and control of the defendant, but plaintiff believes that . . ."

A. Stating More Than One Cause of Action in the Complaint

Separate claims in a complaint are alleged in separate "counts."

A plaintiff may have one or more legal claims based on the same set of facts. The claims may be alternative *or* cumulative. They do not have to be consistent with each other either. Each claim must be stated in a separate count.

In drafting a complaint, all causes of action arising out of the same set of facts must be pleaded, or the ones not pleaded are "waived." Other unrelated claims may also be pleaded against the opposing party, but they are not waived if not pleaded; recall the discussion regarding compulsory and permissive claims. See the joinder of claims F.R.C.P. 18.

Each count is numbered as one, two, three, or Count 1, Count 2, and so forth. The consecutive numbering of the paragraphs in each count does not begin with one in each count.

EXAMPLE

Paragraph 9 may be the first paragraph in Count 2 but is still numbered 9 in the plaintiff's claim for relief or recovery of damages.

EXAMPLE

Count 1—Negligence; Count 2—Intentional Tort, and so forth might be included in a complaint to recover damages for personal injuries.

B. Incorporating Facts in the Complaint by Reference

Exhibits incorporated in the complaint. In lawsuits based on a written instrument, most courts permit the parties to attach a true copy of the document to the complaint as an exhibit. The exhibit is then incorporated into the complaint by reference to it in one of the numbered paragraphs of the complaint.

EXAMPLE

Plaintiff and defendant entered into a written contract on January 17, 20—, a copy of which is attached hereto as Exhibit "A" and made a part hereof by reference as though fully set forth herein.

NOTE: Be doubly sure that all allegations in the complaint referring to the attached document(s) are a word-by-word, line-by-line exact quotation, since the slightest deviation may subject your complaint, or that portion of it, to a motion to dismiss (demurrer). In such a case, the document controls. The allegations that inaccurately describe the exhibit documents may be subject to motion to strike.

Allegations from other counts incorporated in the complaint. The facts alleged in one count contained in a complaint may be incorporated by reference in other counts in facts, which must be specifically alleged in a new count.

A SAFETY MEASURE: Here again, you must be careful that you are re-alleging *all* the proper factual allegations to state a cause of action in the new count and not limiting yourself to the allegations pertinent only to the first count.

EXAMPLE

Count 1—Negligence. Count 2—Intentional Tort or punitive damages: Plaintiff incorporates herein by reference all of the allegations contained in Paragraphs 1, 2, 3, 4, and 5 of its First Cause of Action (Count 1) as though the same were fully set forth herein.

The conduct of the defendant was intentional, willful, and wanton and in complete disregard for the right of . . . and so forth.

C. Defenses Appearing on the Face of the Complaint

As the purpose of any complaint or petition filed in behalf of the plaintiff is to present his legal claim to the court, it should not contain or set forth any possible defenses to the allegations contained herein. In other words, do not do the work of the defendant or educate him. However, the facts alleged must be true and complete enough to state a cause of action.

Defenses, such as the Statute of Limitations and the Statute of Frauds, even if they appear on the face of the complaint, must be responded to by the defendant. Recall that if the defendant does not assert those defenses, he has waived them.

Drafting the Complaint

We now know what a complaint is, the purpose of a complaint, and the types of facts and allegations to be incorporated therein. Now we can proceed to place them in proper order and to come up with a final product.

The following will be explained in an elementary fashion for the benefit of those persons who have not heretofore been required to actually draft a complaint and follow through with the procedures involved therein. These examples follow F.R.C.P. 10.

Basically, legal documents filed with the court are on legal-size paper with a printed margin. There are several word processing programs that have pleading templates included in even the most basic versions or available through the system's website. Windows Office online has at least thirty different complaints available. Use extreme caution when using templates however, as they may not be accurate, complete, or in compliance with your local rules.

A. Caption

Representative: In upper left-hand corner place the attorney's name, address, telephone number, and representative capacity (attorney for plaintiff or defendant, and so forth) in some states. In other states that information appears at the end of the complaint.

Name of court: At or on about line 8 (depending on your local court procedure and rules) the name of the court is centered in all capital letters. In some states the court's name appears to the right of center at the top of the complaint.

Parties to the action: To the left, at or about line 11, is (are) first the name(s) of the plaintiff(s); below, in the middle, is the word "versus" or "against" or an abbreviation thereof, "v." or "vs." After the abbreviation and directly below the name of the plaintiff(s) is (are) the name of the defendant(s).

Filing information and title: To the right, on or at line 11, type a space for the court case number and directly below this type the title of the document.

EXAMPLE (FROM AN ACTUAL CASE FROM THE OFFICE OF THE NEW YORK ATTORNEY GENERAL)

Complaint for Breach of Contract
SUPREME COURT OF THE STATE OF NEW YORK
COUNTY OF NEW YORK

—————————————————————————————-x
THE PEOPLE OF THE STATE OF NEW YORK
by ELIOT SPITZER, Attorney General of   **COMPLAINT**
the State of New York,
Plaintiff,   Index No.
- against -
STATEN ISLAND UNIVERSITY HOSPITAL and
CHAPS COMMUNITY HEALTH SERVICES INC.,
Defendants.
—————————————————————————————-x

NOTE: In some courts, the title of the document is typed in all capital letters in the center immediately below the other caption information.

B. Body of the Complaint

The introductory paragraph of the complaint identifies the plaintiff and is not numbered. "Plaintiff, the People of the State of New York, by Eliot Spitzer, Attorney General of the State of New York, complaining of the above-named defendants, alleges upon information and belief, that:"

After the introductory paragraph you incorporate the knowledge gained in the prior section of this chapter as it relates to the inclusion or exclusion of ultimate or evidentiary facts or pleading conclusions of law that may be demurrable or factual conclusions that may be accepted. As a result, the body of a complaint is normally divided into the following five categories:

1. Fictitious name or Doe clause if necessary

2. Jurisdiction of the court over the subject matter

3. Agency clause (if your court rules require it)

4. Allegations (statements) of ultimate facts that show that plaintiff has a cause of action

5. Prayer

If applicable, attach any of the following exhibits:

1. The verification (if your court rules require it or the attorney desires it)

2. Proof of certificate of mailing

Proof of certificate of mailing is normally at the bottom of the document and signed by the secretary responsible for mailing the complaint if it can be served by mail. Ordinarily, the complaint must be served personally with a summons. In that case a certificate of mailing is not typed on the document.

First paragraph—fictitious name or Doe clause: The purpose of this clause is to enable the moving party to file his complaint against and serve an unknown or undiscovered defendant prior to the running of the Statute of Limitations. The moving party must allege this ignorance in the complaint as a separate allegation, otherwise he is forever barred to join such defendant in the lawsuit. The allegation is made in a separate numbered paragraph.

SPECIMEN FICTITIOUS NAME CLAUSE

The true names or capacities, whether individual, corporate, associate, or otherwise, and defendantship of defendants DOES I through ____, inclusive, are unknown at the time of the filing of this complaint to plaintiff, who therefore sues said defendants by such fictitious names and will ask leave of court to amend this complaint to show their true names or capacities and defendantship when the same have been ascertained. Plaintiff is informed and believes, and based upon such information and belief, alleges that each defendant designated herein as a DOE was responsible, negligently or in some other actionable manner, for the events and happenings referred to herein that proximately caused injury to plaintiff as hereinafter alleged.

Second paragraph—jurisdiction of the court over the subject matter: This is a separate numbered paragraph that sets forth the authority of the court to hear and determine the controversy.

Note that there is a statement when setting forth the jurisdiction over individuals and an alternative one for corporate entities.

Individual Residence Requirement

2. Plaintiff is now, and at all times herein mentioned has been, a resident of the County of _____ , State of _____ .

Corporation Residence Requirement

2. Defendant is now, and at all times herein mentioned has been, a corporation duly organized and existing under and by virtue of the laws of the State of _____ .

or

Defendant is now, and at all times herein mentioned, a corporation duly organized and existing under and by virtue of the laws of the State of Delaware and licensed and authorized to do business in the State of _____ , having its principal office in the City and County of _____ .

Third paragraph—agency clause: The purpose of this paragraph is to pinpoint the responsibility for the wrong or injury committed by defendant and anyone else whose name and/or capacity you may not know at the time of filing the complaint.

A further purpose is to anticipate that that individual may have been part of a larger entity, and since you do not know this for a fact, you include a "Doe" as an agent to accommodate the unknown individual or entity.

EXAMPLE

John Greu and Does I and II, and each of them.

To allege or state a possible agency relationship between the parties, including course and scope of employment together with, consent and permission "of each of them," the following sample clauses may be used:

EXAMPLES

Sample Agency Clause

At all times herein mentioned, defendant, and each of them, was the agent, servant, and employee of each remaining defendant and was at all times herein mentioned acting within the course, scope, and authority of said agency, service, and employment.

Sample Permission Clause

Plaintiff is informed and believes, and thereon alleges that at all times herein mentioned, defendant, and each of them, was driving the subject vehicle with the consent, permission, and knowledge of each of the other remaining defendants.

Fourth and following paragraphs—allegations of ultimate facts that gave rise to the cause of action and resulting damages: In these paragraphs you spell out in detail, with specificity and in chronological order, the events and happenings that led to the wrong or breach of duty and the resulting damage caused thereby.

> NOTE: You may want to read this entire chapter before drafting the complaint. In these paragraphs state the date, place (and time if applicable) of the actions and events creating defendant's negligence or his breach of contract, and reliance on statements or acts of defendant, and any other factual elements of the cause of action.

Each of the foregoing should be separately stated in a distinctly numbered paragraph. *Never* lump them into one paragraph.

EXAMPLES

Sample Separate Paragraphs

1. At all times herein mentioned _____ Street, at or near its intersection with _____, was a public street and highway in the County of _____, State of _____.

2. On or about _____ plaintiff _____ was operating his automobile in an _____ direction on _____ street in the County and State aforesaid.

3. At said time and place, defendants, and each of them, so negligently managed, operated, and controlled their said motor vehicle in a _____ direction along and their vehicle to collide with [the rear, broadside, etc.] plaintiff's automobile, thereby proximately causing severe and serious physical injuries to plaintiff, all to his damage in the sum of _____ ($_____).

> NOTE: These are the paragraphs wherein you establish the situs, place the defendant at the scene of the incident, and spell out the negligent acts of the defendant that caused injury, irreparable harm, breach of contract, wrongful death, and so forth, and "general damages."

If "special" or "consequential" damages were suffered, the facts causing those damages should also be set out in separate paragraphs.

Last paragraph of each count in complaint—prayer: This is a statement of the relief, damages, restitution, or other action by the court that is requested by the plaintiff.

EXAMPLES

Sample Prayer in a Complaint for Special Damages

WHEREFORE, plaintiff prays for judgment against defendant, and each of them, as follows:

1. General damages in the sum of $ _____;

2. For sums incurred and to be incurred for [medical treatment, etc.; repairs; maintenance; delays in construction, etc.] in conformity to proof;

3. Loss of income incurred and to be incurred [from rents, loss of ability to work, etc.] in conformity to proof;

4. Loss of sums incurred to repair automobile, building, etc.

5. [Optional: punitive damages; exemplary damages; special damages, etc.]

6. Costs of suits;

7. For such other and further relief as to the court seems just and proper in the premises.

or

For General Damages

WHEREFORE, plaintiff demands judgment against the defendant for damages in excess of five thousand dollars ($5,000) [or the lowest jurisdictional amount for the trial court in which the legal action will be filed] plus costs of this proceeding and interest [where applicable].

Signature: Complaints in civil actions require the signatures of both the attorney and the plaintiff(s) in some jurisdictions. In other jurisdictions, the signature of the attorney alone is sufficient. In some jurisdictions a petition to a special court may require the petitioner's signature or verification and a complaint to the regular trial court may not. Check your local court rules to determine what signatures are required. F.R.C.P. 11 requires the following contact information be included: the signer's address, email address, and telephone number.

Verification of complaint: Simply stated, a "verification" is a statement that follows the complaint and is dated and signed by the plaintiff, who declares thereby (in some states under penalty of perjury) that to the best of his knowledge and belief everything contained in the answer or complaint is true and correct. Check local court rules for need for verification of a complaint.

After drafting the complaint, prepare a summons for each defendant. The summons is a separate document that is served on *each* defendant with a copy of the complaint.

Procedure for Filing a Cause of Action

1. Prepare original complaint to file with the court, one copy to be served on each defendant named (with extra copies for the Does) and one office copy.

2. If the same is to be verified, either

   a. Have client come in to review the document and then sign, or

   b. Mail a copy along with the original to client for signature.

   > **PRACTICAL HINT:** It has been our experience that it is best to have the clients come in, since they invariably have questions that are easier to answer face-to-face as opposed to over the telephone. Also, this removes the possibility of losing the original or having it marred by coffee or a child's play in the home of the plaintiff or answering defendant. Furthermore, most laymen have difficulty in signing a document in the right place or fail to date it, both of which are of great importance. Otherwise, you merely have to return it to the client for one or the other reason, or both. For proper execution, having him come into the office saves time, particularly if you have a Statute of Limitations problem.

3. After the foregoing has been accomplished, prepare and attach a copy of the summons to each copy of the complaint with a paper clip, except the copies that are attached permanently with a staple.

4. File the original complaint, with appropriate filing fee, in the office of the clerk of the court and have the original summons issued. You should check the filing fee with the appropriate court clerk since filing fees vary from county to county and state to state.

5. Have a copy of the summons and complaint served on each defendant. If service is to be made on a minor or incompetent, you not only bring the action in the name of the guardian *ad litem* who was appointed by the court, but you serve it upon the named guardian *ad litem*. This does not obviate the necessity for naming the minor or incompetent in the caption of the lawsuit. It merely means he is not served with the service of process. See Chapter 7 for manner of service.

   > **NOTE:** Of prime importance here is the notation of the date and time on which the foregoing was filed for each defendant. *Reason:* All summonses and complaints must be served within a certain period or a plaintiff may be forever barred from serving any unserved defendant or prosecuting the claim of plaintiff. You should check your local court rules in this regard.

   The service of process is your activity of the case. A case can be dismissed for lack of activity thereon. Should this happen, your attorney can and must appear in court to show cause why the matter should not be dismissed. Your duty in this regard is to systematically audit your attorney's active files and keep them updated to guard against this possibility. Failure to do this brings on malpractice lawsuits and increases malpractice insurance rates and premiums. State laws do vary as to the legal consequences of failure to serve a summons properly.

6. When the sheriff or process server (see Chapter 4 on court procedure) files his "return of service" of the complaint and summons, check it to see that the defendant was served. Then make a notation of the date of service on your office calendar so that a "default judgment" can be prepared if the defendant does not file an answer by the answer date stated in the summons.

The next chapter deals with pretrial court proceedings after the complaint and summons have been served.

CHAPTER SEVEN

Pretrial Practice and Procedure

Chronology of Pretrial Practice and Procedure

Pretrial practice and procedure are governed by rules of court, usually promulgated by the highest court in the state.

Most, if not all, state courts have adopted court rules of civil procedure similar to the Rules of Civil Procedure adopted by the federal courts.

Reference to the federal civil rules is made in this book by using the short citation form "F.R.C.P." and the section number of the federal rule. Check your comparable state rule in your state court rules. While the rules may appear the same, there are important particularities that must be adhered to in order to properly bring an action in that court. Also check local state court rules that may supplement the general state court rules but cannot do away with them.

In Chapter 6, "How to State a Cause of Action in a Civil Case," the proper drafting of a complaint was covered. After the complaint has been drafted, it must formally enter into the judicial system.

The first court procedure in a civil action (whether at law or in equity) is to file the complaint in the office of the clerk of the court where the lawsuit is to be heard or tried. That is called "commencement of the action."

Representative court procedures are discussed in more or less chronological order in the sections of Chapters 4 and 5 titled "State Court Practice and Procedure" and "Federal Court Practice and Procedure."

In this chapter you will find more details and practical hints for preparing, filing, and serving court papers.

Service of Process (Civil)

A matter cannot be tried until the complaint is "served" on all the defendants who are to be bound by the final judgment. Indeed, it does not become a lawsuit until the formal commencement of the action by service of process. If any defendant is not served, he does not have to do anything in a court case even though he is named as a defendant in the "caption" of the case—ref. F.R.C.P. 4 and state statute providing for "constructive" or "substituted" service in certain cases instead of "personal service." That is because he is not a party to the action unless he is properly served.

The case can proceed against other defendants who have been served, if the one(s) not served is (are) not a "necessary party" (as opposed to a "permissive party")— ref. F.R.C.P. 19 and 20. The case cannot proceed unless all necessary parties have been served.

The service may be by personal service of process or substituted service (as by advertising a notice of the action in the local newspaper a required number of times), *depending on the nature of the case.*

EXAMPLES

A local action affecting real property located in the county where the action is brought can be served by constructive service if the defendant cannot be found after diligent search. Most courts require that an Affidavit of Diligent Search be filed with the clerk of the court before constructive service is binding.

or

A state statute may provide that the secretary of state or other state official may be served with a complaint filed against an out-of-state motorist for an automobile accident that happened in the state. The sheriff in the county where the office of the state official is located serves (usually two) copies of the complaint on the official, who then notifies the defendant by mail of the action.

Summons

A. Purpose and Use of Summons

What is a summons? A summons is a form that is used to give notice to a defendant of an action pending against him in the court that issues it.

The summons is prepared by you and signed in the name of the clerk of the court or his deputy, and it directs the sheriff or marshal or other lawfully appointed person to personally serve the defendant (or an adult member of his household or other person designated or allowed by statute to accept service) with the notice that an action has been filed against the defendant in the court named in the summons.

The summons contains the number of days before, or a certain day on which, the defendant must appear or answer or otherwise plead in response to the complaint (a copy of the complaint must be served with the summons).

The name of the court in which the defendant must appear (such as small claims court) or respond to by a pleading or motion appears in the captions of both the summons and the complaint. Very often, the summons also must include a list of the legal services offices available in the state should the defendant not have an attorney or is not able to afford one.

The Federal Rules of Civil Procedure have included, as an appendix, many of the basic forms that are available online. The following sample comes from a shortcut on the U.S. Courts website (www.uscourts.gov/rules/cvforms2.htm):

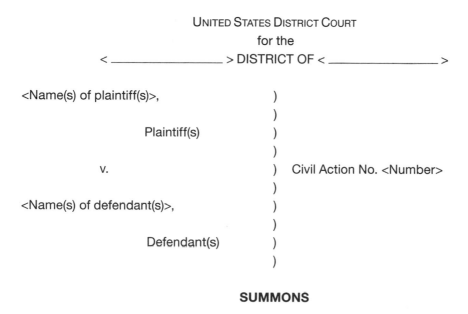

UNITED STATES DISTRICT COURT
for the
< _____ > DISTRICT OF < _____ >

<Name(s) of plaintiff(s)>,   )
)
            Plaintiff(s)   )
)
      v.   )   Civil Action No. <Number>
)
<Name(s) of defendant(s)>,   )
)
            Defendant(s)   )
)

SUMMONS

To: <Name of the defendant>

A lawsuit has been filed against you.

Within 20 days <Use 60 days if the defendant is the United States or a United States agency, or is an officer or employee of the United States allowed 60 days by Rule 12(a)(3)> after service of this summons on you (not counting the day you received it), you must serve on the plaintiff an answer to the attached complaint or a motion under Rule 12 of the Federal Rules of Civil Procedure. The answer or motion must be served on the plaintiff's attorney, <Name of Plaintiff's Attorney>, whose address is <Address of

Plaintiff's Attorney>. If you fail to do so, judgment by default will be entered against you for the relief demanded in the complaint. You also must file your answer or motion with the court.

Date: <Date>   <Signature of Clerk of Court>

_____

Clerk of Court

(Court Seal)

If a defendant fails to answer or otherwise plead or appear within the specified time limit shown on the face of the summons, the plaintiff can file a motion and secure a default judgment.

EXAMPLE

In a California state court, you should file a Request for Entry of Default Judgment with the court, in duplicate, together with the original summons and proof of service. (This is on the reverse side of the summons.) These documents should be accompanied with an Affidavit of Nonmilitary Service and Memorandum of Costs.

Most summonses have a thirty-day returnable period. However, there are some kinds of suits for which the return period in which to answer (or otherwise plead or move) may be shorter or longer. This is why it is vital to always check your local rules for your particular action.

When the time allowed for serving an original summons has expired because it was not able to be served upon the defendant in a traditional manner, you may want to apply for an "alias summons," if your jurisdiction still uses this form (the Federal Rules do not) or you may be able to use constructive service as described earlier.

NOTE: An alias summons is a duplicate of the initial summons issued by the court; that is, you merely cause the original summons to be reissued with the *same* caption, parties, and court case number with the addition of the word "alias" placed just preceding the word "summons." This is the procedure followed should the initial original summons be lost, misplaced, damaged, prematurely filed with the court for safekeeping, or not served within the allotted time as described earlier. An affidavit setting forth the circumstances under which one of these occurred should accompany your request for issuance of an alias summons.

B. Preparation of a Summons

The heading and caption on the summons should be *exactly* the same as on the complaint. This holds true for all of the documents drafted during litigation; the caption, including the docket number, must be identical on all of them. The exception to this rule is when you have a long list of defendants, in which case it is usually permissible to list them either up to and including the name of the defendant you want served, or just the first-named defendant followed by the phrase "et al." In either case the name of the defendant to be served must appear on the body of the summons (spelled and complete, as it is in the caption of the complaint).

In most states unknown defendants can be sued as "John or Jane Doe" in the case of individuals or "ABC corporation" in the case of businesses. The "Doe" names are included in the caption of the summons even though a summons cannot be presently served on them. In the body of the "Doe" summons, type the following notation:

You are hereby served in the within action as the person named herein as "Doe I."

In all states, the name of the defendant plus the name of any person who is allowed by law to accept substituted service for him individually or for a corporation must appear in the body of the summons. Only the defendant's name appears in the caption of the summons. Where a resident agent or registered agent is to be served as a substitute for service on a corporation as its principal office, the name in the body of the summons might be:

Richard Roe, as registered agent for ABC Corporation, a Florida corporation. (Give the registered agent's address if it is not the same as the corporation's address.)

or

John Doe, Insurance Commissioner for the State of Florida Tallahassee, Florida

for

XYZ Casualty Insurance Company
(Give the correct home office address for the insurance company even though it is out of state.)

By preparing a summons accurately and in accordance with the rules for personal service or substituted service, the paralegal can save his attorney valuable time and money and ultimately preserve the legal rights of the client.

When the attorney says "sue this corporation" (or limited liability company or partnership) the following preliminary steps *must* be taken:

1. Get a status report from the department of state in the state where you believe the corporation (or other legal entity) is incorporated or from your department of state if it is a domestic corporation.

2. Read the status report to get the name and address of the registered agent for service of process of a domestic corporation.

3. If it is a foreign corporation, check with your department of state to see if it is "registered" to do business in your state and, if so, who is its resident agent for service of process.

4. In all the preceding cases get *and use* the *exact registered corporate* name in the summons and complaint captions. Many businesses have one name that is the official registered name, but use a different commercial name. For example, Salvatore's Pizzeria Restaurant & Catering Company LLC may be publicly known and advertised only as "Sal's Pizza."

If you are not 100 percent sure of your own client's exact registered corporate name, it is wise to check so you will use its correct name as plaintiff in the caption of the summons and the complaint.

If you are preparing a summons for an individual who does business under a fictitious or assumed name, you may just use his individual name in the summons. If the claim is for a contract or activity conducted by him in the fictitious name, use both in the summons and in the complaint.

EXAMPLE

John Doe d/b/a Atlas Plumbing Supplies

C. Proof of Service of Summons and Complaint

If a sheriff, marshal, constable, or individual process server makes the service, he must file a certificate or affidavit of service that is often on the reverse side of the summons or may be on a separate printed form or one that has been typed up. Or, in lieu of proof of service, one may file a written admission or acknowledgment of service by the defendant. Any typed form must contain the complete caption of the case and court number heretofore assigned, and be signed (and notarized if out-of-state), or declared under penalty of perjury.

A standard form looks like:

Return of Service

Service of the Summons and complaint was made by me

NAME OF SERVER *(PRINT)* and TITLE

On this _____ day of _____, 20____
DATE

Check one box below to indicate appropriate method of service:

☐ Served personally upon the defendant. Place where served:

☐ Left copies thereof at the defendant's dwelling house or usual place of abode with a person of suitable age and discretion then residing therein.
Name of person with whom the summons and complaint were left:

☐ Returned unexecuted:

☐ Other (specify):

Declaration of Server

I declare that the foregoing information contained in the Return of Service is true and correct under penalty of perjury under the laws of the United States of America.
Executed on:

_____
Date

_____
Signature of Server
Address of Server

D. Appearance of Defendant

If a defendant or an attorney for the defendant files an "appearance" in the case or files any responsive pleading in the case, that is proof that the defendant was served or had notice of the case, unless it is a special appearance only to object to service. There is also a form of waiver of service that essentially circumvents the formalities of the summons. If the defendant is amenable to service, he may simply sign and return the waiver as acknowledgment of receipt of the complaint. The form from the federal rulemaking website follows:

AO 399 (03/08) Waiver of the Service of Summons

UNITED STATES DISTRICT COURT

for the

_____ District of _____

_____ Plaintiff v. _____ Defendant	} Civil Action No. _____

Waiver of the Service of Summons

To:
(Name of the plaintiff's attorney or unrepresented plaintiff)

I have received your request to waive service of a summons in this action along with a copy of the complaint, two copies of this waiver form, and a prepaid means of returning one signed copy of the form to you.

I, or the entity I represent, agree to save the expense of serving a summons and complaint in this case.

I understand that I, or the entity I represent, will keep all defenses or objections to the lawsuit, the court's jurisdiction, and the venue of the action, but that I waive any objections to the absence of a summons or of service.

I also understand that I, or the entity I represent, must file and serve an answer or a motion under Rule 12 within 60 days from _____, the date when this request was sent (or 90 days if it was sent outside the United States). If I fail to do so, a default judgment will be entered against me or the entity I represent.

Date _____   _____
                                        (Signature of attorney or unrepresented party)

                                        Printed name

                                        Address
                                        Email address
                                        Telephone number

Duty to Avoid Unnecessary Expenses of Serving a Summons

Rule 4 of the Federal Rules of Civil Procedure requires certain defendants to cooperate in saving unnecessary expenses of serving a summons and complaint. A defendant who is located in the United States and who fails to return a signed waiver of service requested by a plaintiff located in the United States will be required to pay the expenses of service, unless the defendant shows good cause for the failure.

"Good cause" does not include a belief that the lawsuit is groundless, or that it has been brought in an improper venue, or that the court has no jurisdiction over this matter or over the defendant or the defendant's property.

If the waiver is signed and returned, you can still make these and all other defenses and objections, but you cannot object to the absence of a summons or of service.

If you waive service, then you must, within the time specified on the waiver form, serve an answer or a motion under Rule 12 on the plaintiff and file a copy with the court. By signing and returning the waiver form, you are allowed more time to respond than if a summons had been served.

If the appearance is general, the defendant must comply with the rules of court in responding to the pleadings from then on or he may suffer a default judgment. A defendant cannot waive subject matter jurisdiction, but he may waive personal jurisdiction by constructively waiving "service of process" by his actions in defending a case. He essentially has submitted to the authority of the court to render a binding decision that is enforceable against him. In some courts the defendant's attorney may file a "special appearance" for the purpose of attacking jurisdiction or service of process only, but the special appearance should be drafted by the attorney. *Do not use a general appearance form for this purpose; a general appearance submits to the jurisdiction of the court.*

Use of Responsive Pleadings

A defendant may respond to a complaint by filing an answer or a motion objecting to the complaint on one of the various grounds. This is where the defendant must make a decision to either try to avoid the lawsuit or become involved in the merits of the case. In many cases, the defendant will attempt to do both. It is the attorney's job to assess the strength of the defendant's position in either circumstance and counsel appropriately. See Chapter 4 on court procedures.

Answer and Counterclaim

A. Purpose of Answer and Counterclaim

The defendant's answer, with or without affirmative defenses, plays a vital role in raising issues of fact in the pending litigation. The defendant does this by denying the truth of at least some material allegations of the complaint and/or by pleading affirmative defenses to the allegations contained in the complaint. The defendant is not required to answer evidentiary facts or conclusions of law, but he can and perhaps should deny them by stating that he "has no knowledge as to their veracity or accuracy."

As paralegal, the attorney may want you to prepare a "motion to strike" those facts and/or other allegations that are not relevant, unnecessary, prejudicial, or otherwise unacceptable—ref. F.R.C.P. 12(f).

> **CAUTION:** Under the federal rules, the filing of a motion to strike tolls the time for filing a responsive pleading. The non-moving party has ten days after either the motion to strike was denied or the plaintiff has "corrected" his pleadings to conform to the motion for a more definite statement. See F.R.C.P. 12(a)(4). In some state courts, the motion to strike does not toll the time unless a "motion for more definite statement" or "motion to dismiss" is also filed. Check your state court rules comparable to F.R.C.P. 12 (a) through (h) on this point.

A counterclaim may or may not be included in the defendant's answer. See Chapter 4, the sections on State Court Practice and Procedure and Federal Court Practice and Procedure.

A counterclaim may be created as a separate document with the caption of the case or, in the alternative may be included in the answer following the affirmative defenses, if any. The caption will change to reflect this inclusion of the counterclaim. See Chapter 6, "How to State a Cause of Action in a Civil Case."

> **CAUTION:** If your office represents the plaintiff and the defendant files a counterclaim against him, you must respond as the counter-defendant. The same rules apply to counter-defendants (original plaintiffs) as apply to original defendants regarding responses and waivers. Prepare an answer to counterclaim, using the same principles discussed in this section for filing an answer to the original complaint.

The defendant may or may not allege facts in his answer to show that he has an affirmative defense, but he may do so. If he does not plead an available affirmative defense, he waives it—ref. F.R.C.P. 8(c).

THE MOST COMMON AFFIRMATIVE DEFENSES

1. Accord and satisfaction

2. Arbitration and award

3. Assumption of risk

4. Contributory negligence

5. Comparative negligence (in states where that defense in a negligence case is available)

6. Discharge in bankruptcy

7. Duress

8. Estoppel

9. Failure of consideration

10. Fraud

11. Illegality

12. Injury by a fellow servant

13. Laches

14. License

15. Payment

16. Release

17. *Res judicata*

18. Statute of frauds

19. Statute of limitations

20. Waiver

In addition to the common affirmative defenses listed, most of which can be pleaded in an action at law, there are certain affirmative defenses peculiar to equity. One of them is the "doctrine of unclean hands." This doctrine stems from the common law and stands for the proposition that he who seeks equity, must do equity. Essentially, the doctrine will deny relief to a party who has not acted fairly and blamelessly in the transaction at issue. A court of equity will carefully scrutinize the conduct of the plaintiff in determining whether equitable relief should be granted.

This doctrine operates under the general concepts of:

1. Balancing the damages and injuries,

2. Hardship on the defendant or third party as opposed to the rights of the plaintiff, and

3. Fairness to all parties.

In an action at law, the statute of limitations (statutory time for that particular type of claim has run) is an affirmative defense.

In an action in equity the court may consider the statutory time limitations but will not necessarily enforce them or require their application. The court will establish a justification for exempting the matter from the strictures of the statute in order to effectuate a fair result.

Equity does not concern itself with the "passage of time," but with the effect of the passage of time on the rights of the defendant.

If the defendant can convince the court that though the statute of limitations has not run, but the plaintiff has "unreasonably delayed" in filing the action to the prejudice of defendant's rights, plaintiff may be barred from bringing the suit. This is the defense of "laches" and it effectively serves to shorten the statute of limitations.

It may prevent the claimant from asserting his request for some particular equitable relief.

If the defendant, in his answer, does include facts tending to show an affirmative defense, a "reply" by plaintiff may not be required, but it may be permissible. If this reply is allowed without order of court, many attorneys like to play it safe by filing one that denies the factual allegations made in the affirmative defense paragraphs of the defendant's answer. Note that the Federal Rules do not allow a reply to be filed in such case except by order of the court. See F.R.C.P. 7(a)(7). It will be necessary to check your state court rule, which describes the pleadings allowed in its courts either on a party's own initiative or by leave of court.

Special courts, such as probate and juvenile courts, may have different rules for pleading. Again, it cannot be overemphasized to check the rules of the particular local court in which you are filing. See other chapters of this book for special court procedures.

B. Drafting Answer and Counterclaim

An answer must be filed within the prescribed time (usually thirty days) after the summons and copy of complaint are served on the defendant, unless a preliminary motion objecting to the complaint has been filed.

Whether the counterclaim is included in the defendant's answer or it is drafted as a separate document, the counterclaim must state a cause of action against the plaintiff/counterdefendant or it will be subject to the same preliminary motions as a complaint. See Chapter 6, "How to State a Cause of Action in a Civil Case."

The answer itself, including affirmative defenses, if any, should be drafted in accordance with the court rules of the court in which it is to be filed. This means that it should be asserted in numbered paragraphs so that the plaintiff/counter-defendant can efficiently reply to the allegations. For filing an answer in federal courts, see F.R.C.P. 7 (a)(c) and 8(b), (c), and (d). Your state court will have comparable rules.

The first step in drafting an answer is the meticulous reading of the complaint that you are answering. The second is to decide what allegations must be admitted and what allegations must be denied in the answer and which you cannot make any determination upon as you do not have the appropriate information to answer.

> **NOTE:** We have found it a good practice to note your denials and admissions in the margin of the complaint for quick review, recounting, and rechecking with your boss. It also makes it easier to decide on your affirmative defenses to the complaint.

It may be necessary to talk to the client about the facts alleged to determine whether they can be admitted or denied. Certain harmless or incontrovertible facts may be admitted.

If harmful facts must be admitted because they are true, the attorney may want to settle the case or the defendant may have an affirmative defense to those facts.

This is a strategic decision that is solely within the purview of the attorney to make. The paralegal must be very careful in discussing this issue with the client so he does not cross the line into the unauthorized practice of law.

If no answer is filed, all the facts in the complaint are admitted by that silence. Any facts that are not denied in the answer are admitted. Facts admitted in the answer are admitted for all purposes in the lawsuit. Some court rules treat a general denial as no answer and as an admission. Other court rules allow a general denial.

The federal court rules and many state court rules treat a statement of "without knowledge or information to form a belief as to the truth of paragraph" (the corresponding paragraph in the complaint) as a denial.

In most courts any numbered paragraph of the complaint may be admitted in part and denied in part in an identically numbered paragraph in the answer (qualified denial).

Denials are sometimes categorized as "general denials," "qualified general denials," and "specific denials."

NOTE: The key in answering a complaint is you must either deny or admit each allegation. Failure to do either as to any allegation is considered an admission as to the truth of the allegations so omitted.

A general denial is a simple, uncomplicated, one-sentence denial of all the allegations in a complaint, but it is not recommended. Most courts require a numbered list of denials that correspond to the enumerated allegations in the complaint.

EXAMPLE

This answering defendant denies each and every allegation contained in the complaint, and the whole thereof.

In some states the defendant may take advantage of this type of denial only if he can do so in good faith. That is, have a bona fide reason for denial.

If the reason is not bona fide, the general denial is treated as an admission.

The reason is simple: There are probably known and undeniable truths contained in the complaint, even if they are only the basic facts of identification and jurisdiction.

A qualified general denial is a combination of admission of particular allegations and a general denial of a particular paragraph of a complaint.

EXAMPLES

In answer to Paragraph IV, defendant admits that he has his principal place of business in Los Angeles, California, but denies each and every other allegation contained in said paragraph.

or

In answer to the allegations contained in Paragraph IV, this answering defendant admits the allegations beginning on line 12, on page 4, with the word "herein," and denies each and every other allegation contained in said Paragraph IV.

A specific denial is a denial of each paragraph of the complaint. Some paragraphs may be admitted.

EXAMPLE

Paragraph I is denied.
Paragraph II is *admitted.*
Paragraph III is denied.
(and so forth, for each paragraph)

Any of these types of denial may be made on "information and belief" or on "lack of information and belief."

EXAMPLE

In answering Paragraph IV, this answering defendant is informed and believes that the allegations contained herein are untrue and, based upon such information and belief, denies generally and specifically the truth of each and every allegation contained in Paragraph IV.

Note that since this denial is based upon information and belief, it is in the conjunctive, and neither information alone nor belief alone will suffice—you have to have both to successfully resist a special demurrer or comparable motion, as either used alone is not a denial.

While the use of the denial mechanism based on information and belief seems a likely or easy way to go, it is primarily used where the defendant cannot honestly deny or admit with any certainty any of the allegations for one reason or another. (Your attorney can help you here since these facts will no doubt be brought out in the initial client-attorney interview, so check with him.)

If the defendant, in truth or in fact, has knowledge or can obtain the knowledge required by the allegation, a denial on information and belief or lack of information and belief will not stand and will probably be subject to a motion to strike. So, though the defendant may not have personal knowledge, if the subject matter is of public record, it is presumed that the defendant has constructive knowledge, making his denial or lack of information and belief invalid and a sham since he had a means of acquiring the knowledge. For example, if the plaintiff alleges that the accident took place at the corner of Main and Broad Streets, but the defendant is not familiar with the area, he cannot rely upon lack of information or belief. He can either revisit the accident site to verify the address or he can rely upon the accident report prepared by the responding officer.

The third step in drafting an answer is to determine whether your client has an affirmative defense.

> **NOTE:** An interview with the defendant after he has also read the complaint is a *must*. The attorney and/or the paralegal may ask the client the questions and get the documents from the client that are necessary for the attorney to decide whether one or more affirmative defenses should be pleaded in the answer. At this interview, the client should also be questioned about facts that might be the basis for a counterclaim against the plaintiff or the bringing in of a "third-party defendant" or a "cross-defendant."

Some examples of pleading affirmative defenses follow:

AFFIRMATIVE DEFENSE (PAYMENT)

1. Before commencement of this action, defendant discharged plaintiff's claim by payment of the amount claimed.

AFFIRMATIVE DEFENSE (STATUTE OF FRAUDS)

1. The agreement alleged in the complaint was not in writing and signed by the defendant or by any person authorized to act for the defendant.

2. The agreement was alleged to be a lease for more than one (1) year—to wit, five (5) years.

3. The statutes of this state require a lease for more than one (1) year to be in writing.

AFFIRMATIVE DEFENSE (RELEASE)

1. On November 1, 20—, and after plaintiff's claim in this action accrued, plaintiff released defendant from that claim by a written release, a copy of which is attached hereto, made part hereof and marked Exhibit A.

> **NOTE:** Photocopy the written release. Attach a photocopy to each copy of the answer. Put the original in the evidence file for use at trial.

The fourth step is to decide whether a counterclaim should be included or filed separately. The decision to file a counterclaim, cross-complaint, or third-party complaint may be postponed, but the answer or motion objecting to the complaint *must* be filed within the time limits imposed by the applicable rules. When all the facts are gathered and the decisions are made as here described, and it has been decided that an answer is to be filed, the actual drafting of the answer (and, if applicable, the affirmative defenses and counterclaim) begins.

C. Filing and Serving Answer and Counterclaim

The answer must be drafted, typed, filed, and served within the time prescribed by the applicable court rules (ten, fifteen, twenty, or thirty days in various states and types of cases), if no demurrer or motion objecting to the complaint is filed.

The section following this one discusses motions that may be filed in lieu of an answer, among others. Chapter 4 also has some suggestions on this matter in the sections on court procedure.

> NOTE: The time allowed by court rules in any state for filing an answer is not much time for accomplishing all the tasks and decisions described in Drafting Answer and Counterclaim. Sometimes a client fails to bring in a complaint served on him until several days after the service. It is then particularly important to get organized and approach the matter methodically in order not to miss any details. This is when the paralegal can be essential and most effective.

In any case, regardless of the client's delay, he will expect your attorney to make a proper legal response on his behalf. It may be necessary for you to arrange for an extension of the time for filing an answer by calling the office of opposing counsel.

If you are able to get opposing counsel to agree to the extension of time (because your attorney is out of town or trying another case, or the like), it is imperative to confirm the extension of time in writing. The additional time requested must be reasonable in order not to unduly delay the progress of the case.

We have found it a very good idea to make an original and copy of this confirming letter, with the following phrase at the bottom adjacent to the signature line:

I Agree to the Above Extension of time for _____(party) to Respond to the within Request

_____ _____
(date)

There follows a space for the signature of opposing counsel and a line for the date, as indicated here.

See Chapters 4 and 5 under state and federal court procedures for further general tips and warnings as to the preparation and filing of an answer or alternative motions.

At the time of filing the answer and/or counterclaim with the clerk of court, you must also mail or deliver copies of same (including copies of the exhibits attached and incorporated in the original answer and/or complaint) to counsel for each party to the lawsuit that has entered on appearance in the lawsuit, as well as on opposing counsel (unless there are so many parties that the court has made an order limiting this usual requirement).

NOTE: In some multiple-party cases, the court may excuse mailing copies to every party if the expense and time would be too burdensome. Electronic submission to all parties may be an effective alternative. This option must be agreed to by the parties and may require a written consent order of the court. While electronic submissions may be more convenient, they are susceptible to security and privacy concerns.

When the answer is filed, the plaintiff may or may not have to reply under your court rules (see Chapter 4 on court procedures). In any case, use your office calendar or index to note that the client file should be pulled on a certain future date if nothing happens in the meantime.

NOTE: If no actions have been taken in a case that has been commenced, some court rules allow dismissal for want of prosecution after a certain period of inactivity. The plaintiff may lose his right to pursue his legal rights if he does nothing to advance the matter through the justice system. See the court rules for a time at which this drastic action can be taken in your court. *But,* index your case file to be pulled long before that. Index the file to be pulled a short time after the next pleading from opposing counsel is required.

D. Pretrial Motions Concerning Pleadings

Court rules govern the form and time for filing certain common pretrial motions. A pretrial motion is a written request to the court asking the judge to take some action in the matter. It is usually signed by the attorney, not by the client, because motions usually involve questions of law and/or legal procedure about which the attorney has the requisite knowledge. Clients, on the other hand, sign off on papers that contain factual allegations, as they are the ones with the most personal knowledge of those events.

Most court rules require the "grounds" (reasons for the motion to be stated with "particularity" as to law and/or fact, as applicable) in the motion. The attorneys for the parties argue the motion at a hearing.

1. *Motion to dismiss.* This motion is filed for reasons similar to those stated in a demurrer to the complaint, which is still used in some states.

   Under the federal court rule, F.R.C.P. 12(b), and many state court rules, a motion to dismiss (demurrer) may raise the following defenses:

   a. Lack of jurisdiction of subject matter

   b. Lack of jurisdiction over the person

   c. Improper venue

   d. Insufficiency of process

   e. Insufficiency of service of process

f. Failure to state a claim upon which relief can be granted (or failure to state facts sufficient to constitute a cause of action)

In some states one may also move to dismiss or demur to a complaint on the basis of an affirmative defense *if* the facts constituting that affirmative defense appear on the face of the complaint.

Another commonly used defense is that of *res judicata*, which means that "the thing has been decided." This is a rule of law that bars the re-litigation of the same cause of action between the same parties. You can raise this defense, if not discernible on the face of the complaint, in your answer by attaching the judgment rendered in the prior action.

Contrary to the rule for stating the general demurrer, in utilizing a "special demurrer," you must point out with specificity the defect in the pleading where other than a failure to state a cause of action is the issue. For example, defect as to form, which means a cause of action exists but there are curable defects in setting forth the cause of action, may be subject to a special demurrer, comparable to a motion to strike in other jurisdictions.

A special demurrer or a motion to strike is important, since unless it is raised by way of a demurrer or motion, the defendant waives his right to object to a "defect in form." Only the right to raise "defects in substance" can be raised at a later time during the course of the proceeding. For example, in a complaint alleging fraud, it is necessary to set forth all the details in order to show every element of the offense is met—it must be pleaded with particularity. If, however, the plaintiff omits to show facts that would show that the defendant had the intent to defraud, the defendant can move for a more definite statement (special demurrer) or simply answer that which he understands the plaintiff to be alleging, thereby waiving this defect in the form of the pleading. If, however, the defendant later discovers evidence that would repudiate the plaintiff's claim (the plaintiff did not, in fact, rely on the statements made by the defendant), then the defendant may bring that evidence forward at any time. That is a substantive problem with the plaintiff's claim.

A special demurrer may be filed to force a plaintiff to state facts in the complaint, which if set forth would afford the defendant the opportunity to file a general demurrer. That is comparable to a motion for more definite statement in other states and the federal courts.

A motion for more definite statement or a special demurrer for the purpose of getting more essential facts might state:

It cannot be ascertained from the complaint herein whether the contract on which the alleged cause of action is founded and referred to is written or oral.

This fact is particularly relevant to the defendant's available affirmative defenses—in this case, the statute of frauds.

2. *Motion to strike.* This motion is made to get the court to strike all parts or all of a pleading that is defective in form.

The federal court rules and many court rules provide that a motion to strike can be brought either by the court itself or by the opposing party. It can challenge any "insufficient defense" or those statements that are redundant, immaterial, impertinent, or scandalous. See F.R.C.P. 12(f). The meaning of these words, except the word "impertinent," is for the most part the common meaning of the word. Impertinent, as used in the court rule, means the matter should not be in the pleading as a matter of form as, for example, it is superfluous or unintelligible as stated or not appropriate because it is irrelevant to the cause of action or defense.

A motion to strike an answer because it "does not state a sufficient defense" serves the same purpose that a motion to dismiss a complaint for failure to state a claim or cause of action serves. It was noted earlier that a general demurrer can be used for either of those purposes in the State of California or states where demurrers rather than motions are used to object to pleadings.

An example of the use of the motion to strike is when the plaintiff's complaint asks for punitive damages in a matter in which he is not entitled. As the attorney is aware, punitive damages are not awarded where they are not specifically permitted by statute for a particular cause of action. Therefore, to ask for them is irrelevant and impertinent.

The motion to strike can be effectively utilized against a pleading. If a complaint is verified and defendant files a general denial, plaintiff can file a motion to strike the answer on the ground that it is not a verified answer. Conversely, if someone other than the party to the action verifies the complaint, defendant can make a motion to strike the improper verification. This illustrates why it is critical for the paralegal to pay close attention to the details of the pleadings, both procedural and substantive, in order to best protect the interests of the client.

3. *Motion to compel.* This motion is normally used when either party fails or refuses to answer interrogatories or requests for admissions. The moving party simply files a motion requesting the court to "compel" the opposing party to answer and to apply sanctions, which are normally penalties in the form of a monetary award if the party fails to answer as ordered. Another sanction the court may impose is to dismiss a complaint or strike an answer of the party who fails to comply with the order.

These motions are more common in large litigation matters where there is a great deal of information to be produced and, increasingly, a vast amount of electronic discovery to be made. The complexity was demonstrated in *Eastman Kodak Co. v. Sony Corp.*, 2006 WL 2039968 (W.D.N.Y. 2006) wherein Sony's motion to compel was denied. Sony had requested that Kodak "more specifically correlate information produced electronically via a computer server, CD-ROMs and DVDs, to Sony's document requests." Sony contended that without Kodak marking which files were in response to which production request, Sony would "be deprived of due process because it will be virtually impossible to find relevant documents that have been 'hidden' in the electronic equivalent of approximately 300 million pages of produced documents." The court merely responded that: "[W]hile the court is aware of the substantial amount of time and effort it will take to sort through the information produced," as Sony has acknowledged, "[b]illions of dollars of sales are at issue" in this case, and therefore, it is to be expected that discovery will involve substantial time, effort, and expense."

4. *Motion to quash service of summons.* This is another common type of motion and it is used where there is no jurisdiction of the court over the person, and therefore you may file a "motion to quash" service of the summons. This is known as a "special appearance" and is only used to attack jurisdiction of the court over the person. It does not confer jurisdiction by waiver of the defect—it is a direct challenge to it. This motion to quash must be accompanied by points and authorities to support your contentions; then it is up to the court. Any other type of appearance, that is, another motion, demurrer, answer, or so forth, by a defendant may create personal jurisdiction. In other words, if you plan to file a motion to quash, you cannot also file any other type of pleading in the case, for to do so is to subject the client to the complete jurisdiction of the court in most states. In some states, the question of jurisdiction and other defenses may be raised in a motion to dismiss without that problem if the question of ineffective service is resolved in favor of the movant.

5. *Motion for judgment on the pleadings.* This motion cannot be made until the required pleadings in the case have all been filed and the case is "at issue." "At issue" means ready to be tried but not that the case has been set for trial.

A motion for judgment on the pleadings can be brought at any time after the time for pleadings has closed. See F.R.C.P. 12(c). Most court rules do provide that the motion must be made within such time as not to delay the trial.

This is a noticed motion that should be accompanied by a memorandum of points and authorities and, in most states, a declaration by your attorney in support thereof. You should include in his declaration what order is being requested and the basis of your request. In other words, give the court a good, valid reason and sufficient facts for granting the motion and resultant order.

In all jurisdictions, it is advisable to prepare a law memorandum in support of the motion if your attorney represents the movant or opposing the motion if he does not.

6. *Motion for summary judgment.* In the legal community the motion for summary judgment is considered the most devastating. To the attorney who makes the motion and wins, it is also the sweetest victory. The key: the word "judgment" by

way of a motion. In other words, you are making a request for the court to grant you a judgment against the opposition "without benefit of trial" of the issues. See F.R.C.P. 56.

In the federal courts and in many states this motion may he filed anytime after the expiration of twenty days after the complaint was filed.

Either party can make a motion for summary judgment alleging that there are "no triable issues of facts" or "no genuine issues of material fact." In essence there is only a question of law left for determination and questions of law can be decided by a judge without need for a trial. Courts should and do take this motion very seriously. It is a final judgment that cannot be reopened.

You should know that a motion for partial summary judgment can be filed as to a cause of action or count in some courts. It settles some of the matters in the complaint, but leaves others to be tried in court. See F.R.C.P. 56(d).

EXAMPLE

If in your request for admissions you have received an admission that a contract did in fact exist, that the plaintiff did in fact comply with all the terms of the contract, and that the defendant did in fact breach the contract, you could file for a summary judgment as to liability and remove that issue of liability from the trial of the action. The issue that remains to be tried is the amount of the damages.

As with all motions heretofore discussed, a law memorandum of supporting case authority and statutes, if any, in support of your motion should be prepared. Additionally, the attorney and/or the client may also need to submit a supporting affidavit. This declaration "must be made on personal knowledge, set out facts that would be admissible in evidence, and show that the affiant is competent to testify on the matters stated." See F.R.C.P. 56(e)(1). The content of this declaration is the ammunition for your summary judgment. Your attorney can win or lose his motion on the declaration alone. Hence, it should state, succinctly and in chronological sequence, the facts of the case, to aid the court in reaching its decision in your favor; that is, that there are no triable issues as to any material fact to be determined and that the moving party is entitled to a judgment as a matter of law. Further, these affidavits can (and should) be supplemented with deposition testimony, answers to interrogatories, and other evidentiary tools.

EXAMPLE

In many states, a contractor must be licensed to practice his trade. Let us say for argument that the plaintiff is a contractor who does not have a license, yet has been practicing his trade. As a result of a dispute with the owner of the property for whom he is building a garage, he has filed a complaint for breach of contract and for damages.

Thereafter, the defendant files his answer to the complaint and as a result of discovery determines that plaintiff was not a licensed contractor. He can then file a motion for summary judgment on the ground that plaintiff was not a licensed contractor at the time of entering into the contract and, furthermore, that plaintiff had not, since and during the pendency of the action, secured a license to practice his trade as required by the laws of the state.

In this connection, you should be sure to obtain a certified document from the proper state authority that indicates that the plaintiff was not a licensed contractor, nor had he applied for such license, and so forth. This could cause a summary judgment victory for your attorney.

A step-by-step procedure for preparing for summary judgment on behalf of the defendant is as follows:

After discussing the file and reviewing the complaint and other documents received through discovery or other means with your attorney who represents the defendant, it must be determined that the case has no merit, or that there is no defense to it. Again, you must show that all of the facts, taken in the light most favorable to the plaintiff (the non-moving party in this case), do not evidence any issues of triable fact. You will need to prepare the necessary documentation to support your motion for summary judgment. The documents to be prepared are:

1. Notice of motion and the motion for summary judgment,

2. Affidavits of your attorney or client, or both (affidavit[s] of facts with necessary exhibits attached and incorporated by reference into the affidavit),

3. Memorandum of law in support of summary judgment, and

4. Cover letter and proof of mailing.

Make sure that declaration(s) or affidavit(s) are signed before a notary. The foregoing package should be filed, and copies of everything in the package must be served on opposing counsel at least ten days prior to the date upon which the motion is set for hearing.

CAUTION: Note that the filing of this motion does not toll or extend the time within which the defendant is required to file a responsive pleading. Be sure, therefore, to flag the regular responsive pleading date on your file and your "come-up" calendar to avoid a default being taken against your office while waiting for the motion day.

Be aware that it is extremely difficult for attorneys to obtain a summary judgment since it, in essence, prevents the losing party from cross-examining witnesses.

If there is a question about even *one* fact material to the cause of action, a court cannot lawfully grant a summary judgment. Immaterial or irrelevant facts will not be undisputed to get a summary judgment.

Common Elements to All Pretrial Motions

In addition to the pretrial motions described earlier there are innumerable pretrial requests that can be made by written motion. Some may be heard *ex parte* (only movant's attorney present) when there are emergent circumstances to warrant such drastic relief. Your attorney will tell you when he needs such motions.

The caption of *all* motions is the regular caption of the case in which the motion is filed.

The nature of the motion is usually stated under the caption as the title in all caps, as:

Motion for continuance, motion for transfer, motion to dismiss, motion to strike, or motion to dismiss third-party complaint [and so forth].

The written motion is filed with the clerk of the court, and a copy of the motion is mailed or delivered to opposing counsel (or all parties, as the case may be). *Be sure to make a copy of the motions for your office file!*

If the motion requires a hearing, a "notice of hearing" may be sent with the copy of the motion or may be made part of it, or the motion may be filed and a hearing date obtained later. Check your attorney's desires and the court rules in this matter. It is very important to adhere to the time periods prescribed by the court rules in determining the "return date" (date of the hearing) of the submitted motion. If you have not allowed sufficient time under the rules, the motion will be pushed back until the next available date on the court calendar. This may be weeks away from the originally intended date. Needless to say, with the busy agenda of your attorney, the rescheduling of a motion hearing will not be met with favor.

PART TWO

General Trial Preparation

CHAPTER EIGHT

Legal Research Tools

This chapter will reintroduce you to the basic traditional tools of legal research, as well as to the most recent, the computerized tools of legal research. This chapter will attempt to discuss what they are, how to use them, and will furnish examples of their finished product. It is intended as a general overview, only because the scope of this material can fill an entire textbook itself.

As you know, your employer will give you a question and you need to find not only an answer but *the* definitive, controlling, most recent answer on the subject as well as the opposing authority. This must be done in the most thorough yet efficient manner possible.

There are many companies involved in supplying computerized tools of legal research, such as Westlaw, LexisNexis, and Loislaw to name a few of the subscription-based online searchable databases. Many states and the federal judiciary have their own searchable databases and these are often free to members of the bar and sometimes even to the general public. There are also many free searchable databases on the Internet, although they do not contain nearly the same quality or quantity of information as the subscription services. Lexis and Westlaw continue to dominate the subscription database market. There are literally hundreds of other companies supplying specialized electronic databases on CDs and through other media and proprietary websites.

Computerized Tools of Legal Research

The traditional manual legal research approach appears to be fading into the sunset as the number one way in which to accomplish research projects, though there are still some attorneys and paralegals who feel more comfortable using the traditional methods and like to be able to see all of the material in front of them in hard copy. They get self-satisfaction from holding in their hands books that contain their cases. They still like to work with paper as a more concrete source of information. However, used properly, computer research methods can make for faster retrieval, more accuracy, and greater scope of scan and depth of material available in completing a research project. The peril lies in the fact that so much information is available that the researcher gets lost in the sheer volume of it.

And, as we all know, there is always a problem in a law office and there are always emergencies when briefs have to be filed right away. This requires quick citation checking, to determine if the cases are on point and up to date. This is where Lexis's Auto-Cite, or Westlaw's KeyCite, for example, can give you quick information that you cannot get any other way. These citation checkers verify the name and year of the case, parallel citations, and subsequent history, which flags negative treatment and other necessary details.

But this element of the technology merely scratches the surface of the services' capabilities. The two major research providers will be explored in this chapter. For the most part, after learning these methods, you can switch relatively easily between the two and adapt to other systems readily. All of the legal research providers or sites have made attempts at making their systems user-friendly.

General Considerations in CALR
(Computer-Aided Legal Research)

It is critical to have an understanding of the facts and issues at hand before sitting down to the computer to start research. Remember, the computer contains raw material; that is, the full text of cases as written by judges. To this end, your problem analysis must be performed *prior* to seeking retrieval of applicable information for your project. Additionally, it will be necessary to have the traditional tools of a pen and paper handy to record all the various searches and results obtained from the CALR session.

In either a Boolean-type search, which uses a term and connector format, or a natural language format search, the key to success is the formation of the query. It is important to keep track of what keywords you have already used and in what combination, in order to refine your work without repetition. It is also a good idea to note which cases, statutes, or other authority continue to appear in the results or which secondary authorities warrant further review after the primary research is complete. As we all know, clicking link after connecting link leads you so far astray from the original result that it becomes hard to find your way back. The written notes can serve as your bread crumb trail back out of the forest of information.

Boolean searches require the researcher to understand how the database engine interprets the input. Once you have decided on the words that are necessary for your request, it becomes equally necessary for you to figure out how they should appear and how close together or in what relationship they should appear in the case in order to have meaning to you.

Spaces between words in the query string have meaning for the search engine, as do certain "connectors," such as "or," "and," and "w/n," and symbols, such as "*" and "!" The individual system will have a "help with searching" element so that you can learn how to use it most effectively.

As an example of this kind of search, you might enter "free! w/15 speech or press and censor!" The system interprets this as a search for any variation of the word "free," which would include "freedom." It would also look for the word variation of "freedom" within fifteen words around the word "speech," thus attempting to ensure a link between those two concepts in the result. The search also includes "press" that does not have to be correlated to the search for "press" because there is an "or" qualifier, but it would have to be correlated to the search for any variation of the word "censor," including, of course, "censorship," but also "censored" and "censoring."

> **TIP:** These systems search for individual words, not phrases. You should therefore avoid unnecessary words. For example, Xerox Corporation; instead of putting in the entire phrase "Xerox Corporation," you should simply put in the word "Xerox." This is done so that Lexis does not have to search for every occurrence of the word "corporation" which would, of course, bring back hundreds of cases. In fact, it would bring back much more, but the database limits the number of results that will appear.

The natural language search is the one that most people are familiar with, as the majority of the general search engines used every day, like Google, Yahoo!, and Ask, use it. The researcher simply types in a question or string of words without any need for special formats or characters. The same search as above would look like this: "freedom of the press," or "free speech and censorship." You could even enter it as a full question: "When can the constitutional guarantee of freedom of the press be abrogated by a valid act of censorship?" The search engine automatically removes those common words that will appear in so many cases. It can pare down the query to get to the substantive words. It does not interpret the meaning of the query any more than a Boolean search does. Technology has simply made the engine able to sift through the terms more effectively.

It is important to remember that no matter what search engine you are using, it does not actually read the query string. It is looking for the keywords and matching them to the millions of documents in the database and then sorting them by its own sense of relevancy. CALR relevancy means that more of the keywords appear more frequently in the most relevant documents. It is purely a quantitative result, not a quality match. Therefore, the paralegal must carefully read and analyze the results and not jump to a conclusion based upon the CALR findings and prioritization. The most important thing to remember in conducting searches: *You have to understand what the system understands from your input.*

In addition to searching by query strings, for the most part in Lexis, Westlaw, and Loislaw you can define your search parameters as to which particular court the case eminated from, the parties' names, the attorneys involved, the dates within which to conduct the search, whether the query should appear in the majority or dissenting opinion, and many other variables.

Of course, the easiest and most direct access is granted by most every legal database if you search by citation. You simply type in "384 U.S. 436" and the search engine pulls up the *State v. Miranda* decision.

On to the particularities of using each of the major electronic research providers.

LexisNexis

www.lexis.com
The main characteristics of Lexis are:

- Complete and comprehensive research for almost all primary and secondary sources of law

- Shepard's legal citation tools

- Web and email alerts to keep track of developments in your practice area or particular to a case

- Litigation news and reports

The vastness of the information would be daunting to any researcher if Lexis had not made the interface so easy to use. Once you access the Lexis database, you can sort through the various "libraries" (folder and tab subdivisions) of information. Lexis has cases, statutes, and administrative materials in seperate areas, and they are further broken down into subcategories. Further, headnotes and case law summaries are available for more than 4 million cases, federal and state, even unreported cases. So if you know what kind of law (federal, state, or administrative) you are looking for, you may enter the appropriate library.

If you are researching in a particular area of law, the Lexis Search Advisor covers

16,000 legal topics and can assist in the search within primary law. Of course, Lexis also offers the online version of its cite-checker—Shepard's Citations Service, which validates the primary source for currentness and validity.

Also arranged topically are the secondary sources available through Lexis Analytical Materials and Secondary Sources, including the Restatements of Law, *American Jurisprudence 2d* treatises (including CCH and BNA), and hundreds of law reviews.

There are also practical libraries filled with briefs, motions, pleadings, and verdicts for use in practical trial preparation. You are also able to conduct factual discovery in your case, as LexisNexis provides access to approximately 3.8 billion public records.

As the practice of law also concerns itself with current events and the general world of business, the Nexis part of the site "contains newspapers, wire services, business magazines, and newsletters. It supplies information about legal issues not necessarily limited to case-law reporters, for example, the amounts of money awarded in settlements of newsworthy cases."

Mechanical Checklist for Using Lexis

1. *Signing-on:* Visit www.lexis.com for the legal research site. Type in your ID and password. (Do not use the Remember checkbox if you are at a public computer.)

2. *Option of choosing a "Quick Search":* This element on the sign-in page lets you quickly Shepardize, Get, and Print a case (or simply Get), and/or set up a Shepard's Alert which notifies you of any decisions affecting your case.

3. *Library selection:* Decide where and what you need to search. Do you need access to federal statutes, state case law, or administrative decisions? You can choose from many options that will simultaneously search across many kinds of law. You might find the Case Law Summaries and LexisNexis Headnotes section to be the most helpful if you aren't quite sure how to narrow your jurisdictional search just yet. This kind of search also gives you an insight into the key words and phrases used in a particular area of law. This element of Lexis is most like using the traditional digest method of searching for legal authorities.

4. *Search:* You may choose to conduct a search by forming your own query either using terms and connectors or by using natural language. You have the ability to search a single jurisdiction or multiple jurisdictions and have the choice of including topical or secondary materials. The site provides a list from which you may choose the databases you feel appropriate for your needs.

5. *Display:* The results are then compiled for you. The search engine produces results that are categorized for ease of use. For example, the results page indicates how many cases, statutes, administrative materials, law review hits were

found. It then creates a set of tabs so that you can access each kind of legal authority.

6. *Read and analyze*: Determine which cases are most on point with your issue. Tag those that are and then, if necessary, move on to the next step.

7. *Modify:* At the second level you can then modify or refine your request by adding new terms, accessing the thesaurus feature, or changing the databases searched. The "more like this" feature lets you jump off into a new search for cases similar to the on-point ones you have already found. This is the point where your written notes will come in handy to keep track of the different queries and databases searched.

8. *Verify:* Any legal authority that you intend to rely upon needs to be Shepardized, and you should also use the citation format assistant to make sure you are properly citing the case. A summary of the *Miranda* case as Shepardized is included in Figure. 8.1. As you can see, there is a lot of information available through electronic cite-checking that traditionally had to be deciphered or simply could not be included in print format.

9. *Delivery options*: After all the above has been accomplished to your satisfaction, you can then request any number of ways to retain the information. Lexis provides options for hard printing, downloading to your computer file, faxing, or emailing the results.

Figure 8.1
The Restricted Shepard's Summary for the Miranda Decision

Restricted Shepard's Summary:
Miranda v. Arizona, 384 U.S. 436, 86 S. Ct. 1602, 16 L. Ed. 2d 694, 1966 U.S. LEXIS 2817, 10 Ohio Misc. 9, 36 Ohio Op. 2d 237, 10 A.L.R.3d 974 (1966).

Citing References:	
Warning Analyses:	Superseded (3)
Cautionary Analyses:	Criticized (5), Distinguished (687), Limited (1)
Positive Analyses:	Followed (1558), Concurring Opinion (1361)
Neutral Analyses:	Conflict.Authority (1), Dissenting Op. (792), Explained (500), Harmonized (7), Interim Decision (1), Quest. Precedent (102)
Other Sources:	Law Reviews (1), Secondary Sources (2)
LexisNexis Headnotes:	HN1 (700), HN2 (147), HN3 (77), HN4 (572), HN5 (622), HN6 (71), HN7 (213), HN8 (212), HN9 (1073), HN10 (1651), HN11 (28), HN12 (40), HN13 (1624), HN14 (81), HN15 (547), HN16 (1847), HN17 (1072), HN18 (43), HN19 (152), HN20 (3)

lexisONE

www.lexisone.com

LexisONE is a research service offered by Lexis for small firms that do not have the substantive need or financial resources to subscribe to the full-blown Lexis service. The amount of databases available is limited to certain jurisdictions or practice areas and the pricing is based upon individual requests for documents.

Westlaw

www.westlaw.com

Westlaw is an enormous database service owned and operated by the Thomson-West Publishing Company, a powerhouse in print media as well. Its scope is comparable to that of Lexis. Westlaw's main benefit stems from the fact that it is tied into its own proprietary system of organizing the print information that attorneys are so familiar with—the West Key system. Its libraries cover all the jurisdictions in the United States and just about every practice area imaginable, in both primary and secondary source materials.

It also retains its classic West Headnotes that represent the opinions of the courts and use the language of the court as fully as possible. Westlaw also has a citation verification system—KeyCite, which not only supplies the history and treatment of the case but also includes "depth of treatment stars," which indicate how extensively a case discussed the case you KeyCited. For example, four stars indicates that the citing case discussed your KeyCited case extensively, while one star means that the citing case only mentioned it. See Figure 8.2 for an *abridged* Key-Cite session on Miranda.

Figure 8.2
KeyCite Result List for the Miranda Decision (abridged and excluding court documents)

History

    Direct History

☐ ➡ 1   KeyCited Citation:
        Miranda v. Arizona, 384 U.S. 436, 10 Ohio Misc. 9, 86 S.Ct. 1602, 16 L.
        Ed.2d 694, 10 A.L.R.3d 974 (U.S.Ariz. Jun 13, 1966) (NO. 759, 760, 761, 584)

        Rehearing Denied by

☐ H 2   California v. Stewart, 385 U.S. 890, 87 S.Ct. 11, 17 L.Ed.2d 121 (U.S.Ariz.
        Oct 10, 1966) (NO. 584, OCT. TERM 1965)

Figure 8.2 (*continued*)

Negative Citing References (U.S.A.)

Superseded by Statute as Stated in

☐ ▶ 3   U.S. v. Dickerson, 166 F.3d 667 (4th Cir.(Va.) Feb 08, 1999) (NO. 97-4750)
★ ★ ★ ★ HN: 76,77,78 (S.Ct.)

☐ H 4   People v. Banks, 2000 WL 33519258 (Mich.App. Apr 21, 2000) (NO. 211439,
216965) ★ ★ HN: 1 (S.Ct.)

Disagreement Recognized by

☐ H 5   Ashford v. State, 147 Md.App. 1, 807 A.2d 732 (Md.App. Sep 12, 2002) (NO.
1856 SEPT.TERM 2001) ★ ★ ★ ★ ★ HN: 58,62,82 (S.Ct.)

Called into Doubt by

☐ ▶ 6   U.S. v. Mora, 98 F.Supp.2d 466 (S.D.N.Y. May 30, 2000) (NO. 98 CR. 1407
(MBM))

Declined to Extend by

☐ H 7   State v. McCormick, 778 S.W.2d 48 (Tenn. Sep 25, 1989) (NO. 87) ★ ★ HN:
76,79 (S.Ct.)

☐ ▶ 8   State v. Post, 118 Wash.2d 596, 826 P.2d 172, 60 USLW 2635 (Wash. Mar
12, 1992) (NO. 57846-0), reconsideration denied (Sep 10, 1992)
★ ★ ★ ★ HN: 30,76,79 (S.Ct.)

· · · · ·

Distinguished by

☐ H 22   State v. Gray, 268 N.C. 69, 150 S.E.2d 1 (N.C. Sep 21, 1966) (NO. 7)
★ ★ ★ ★ HN: 74,76,82 (S.Ct.)

☐ C 23   U.S. v. Hill, 260 F.Supp. 139, 19 A.F.T.R.2d 440, 67-1 USTC P 9173 (S.D.Cal.
Sep 29, 1966) (NO. CRIM. 36501) ★ ★ ★

☐ C 24   People v. McCasle, 35 Ill.2d 552, 221 N.E.2d 227 (Ill. Nov 14, 1966) (NO.
38695) ★ HN: 78 (S.Ct.)

☐ C 25   Com. ex rel. Zaffina v. Maroney, 423 Pa. 237, 223 A.2d 678 (Pa. Nov 15,
1966) ★ ★

Figure 8.2 (*continued*)

. . .

Limitation of Holding Recognized by

☐ H 153 U.S. v. Whitehead, 26 M.J. 613 (ACMR May 02, 1988) (NO. ACMR 8700178)
★ ★ ★ ★**HN: 7,67 (S.Ct.)**

☐ ▶ 154 State v. Rosse, 478 N.W.2d 482 (Minn. Dec 20, 1991) (NO. C5-90-1775)
★ ★ ★ ★**HN: 62,67,79 (S.Ct.)**

☐ ▶ 155 Harper v. Virginia Dept. of Taxation, 509 U.S. 86, 113 S.Ct. 2510, 125
L.Ed.2d 74, 61 USLW 4664, 16 Employee Benefits Cas. 2313 (U.S.Va. Jun
18, 1993) (NO. 91-794) ★ ★**HN: 4 (S.Ct.)**

☐ C 156 State v. Mason, 1996 WL 111200 (Tenn.Crim.App. Mar 14, 1996) (NO.
02C-01-9310-CC-00233) ★ ★ ★ ★**HN: 4,67,79 (S.Ct.)**

. . . . . .

Modification Recognized by

☐ C 162 State v. Trujillo, 869 S.W.2d 844 (Mo.App. W.D. Feb 01, 1994) (NO. WD
46122, WD 47710) ★ ★**HN: 82 (S.Ct.)**

☐ ▶ 163 State v. Lewis, 258 Kan. 24, 899 P.2d 1027 (Kan. Jul 14, 1995) (NO. 70,195)
★ ★ ★ ★**HN: 58,62,82 (S.Ct.)**

Negative Citing References (Canada)

Distinguished in

☐ ▶ 164 R. v. Strachan, 1986 WL 596273, 25 D.L.R. (4th) 567, 24 C.C.C. (3d) 205,
1986 CarswellBC 446, 49 C.R. (3d) 289, 21 C.R.R. 193, [1986] B.C.W.L.D.
782, [1986] B.C.J. No. 55 (B.C. C.A. Jan 23, 1986)

☐ C 165 R. v. Edwards, 1986 WL 595298, 1986 CarswellOnt 1015, 31 C.R.R. 343, 2
W.C.B. (2d) 220 (Ont. H.C. Sep 02, 1986)

. . . .

As in most other legal database systems, in doing research with Westlaw, you can
search by words and/or phrases in either a terms-and-connectors or natural language
query, search by party name or by citation. The advantage to searching for a concept
in Westlaw is that you can search by the West Key Number, either in the original
query (if you already know what the Key Number is for your issue) or once you have
located a case. Once a relevant case has been retrieved, you can review the Headnotes, finding the most relevant to your issue. Westlaw provides a link to "most

cited" cases on this point. For example, one of the Key Numbers in the Miranda decision is ☞110k412.2(3)k. *Informing Accused as to His Rights.* By clicking the Most Cited Cases link you can directly access a list of those cases either ordered according to relevancy or most recently cited, and can limit the jurisdiction in which Westlaw performs the search (e.g., individual states, federal, secondary sources, etc.).

Mechanical Checklist for Using Westlaw

1. *Signing-on:* Visit www.westlaw.com for the legal research site. Type in your password and the client ID, which can be either alpha or numeric. It is a way to keep track of your research history on a particular matter and the time spent on it. (Recall: Do not use the Remember checkbox if you are at a public computer.)

2. *Sidebar options:* This element on the homepage lets you quickly Find and Print a case, KeyCite, and/or perform a database search to quickly access the database you need. It also allows you to save certain databases as your "favorites" so you can jump straight to them after signing on.

3. *Tab selection:* Westlaw lets you customize your search options by letting you add tabs to access search sessions in certain jurisdictions or topical areas. This is again where you decide where and what you need to search. You may also access the Site Map to choose what and where you need to search. This is also the area where you can directly perform a KeyCite search.

4. *Search:* You may choose to conduct a search by forming your own query either using terms and connectors or by using natural language. You have the ability to search a single jurisdiction or multiple jurisdictions and have the choice of including topical or secondary materials.

5. *Display:* The results are then compiled for you as a list with direct links to the found materials.

6. *Read and analyze:* Determine which cases are most on point with your issue. Tag those that are and then, if necessary, move on to the next step. Remember to keep track of how many links you click on! They will take you farther away from your original search results. While this may ultimately benefit your research, you should know where you have been to avoid repetition and to find your way back should you go too far afield.

7. *Modify:* At the top of the results list you can modify or refine your request by adding new terms, accessing the thesaurus feature, or changing the databases searched.

8. *Verify:* Any legal authority that you intend to rely upon needs to be KeyCited. The flags at the top of the case display indicate the treatment it has received. It

may be green (good law), yellow (some negative treatment), or red (overturned or otherwise no longer valid for at least one point of law). For example, the *Miranda* case has a yellow flag due to all the modifications, distinctions, and other treatment it has received since its decision.

9. *Delivery options:* After all the above has been accomplished to your satisfaction you can then request any number of ways to retain the information. Westlaw also provides options for hard printing, viewing the actual reporter image as a PDF, downloading to your computer file, saving on Westlaw, faxing, or emailing the results.

It is very important to know that both Lexis and Westlaw offer excellent online training modules specifically for paralegals. Lexis sponsors an entire community for paralegals that offers not just research, but practice management tools and discussion boards. It can be accessed directly at http://law.lexisnexis.com/communityportal/default.aspx?g=QfsTyLJ1USs=.

Westlaw has a variety of e-learning courses for paralegals to learn to navigate and use the Westlaw site most effectively. Paralegals may also earn certificates of completion from Westlaw to document their proficiency in CALR.

FindLaw

www.findlaw.com

This is West Thomson's free legal research website that has both federal, state, and topical search capabilities. It is geared toward users who are not legal professionals. The extent of the results will be more limited than with a subscription-based service, but can serve as a good jumping-off point. FindLaw provides summaries and citations in response to the queries. There is also a Forms section that permits downloading of common documents. The site also has an extensive searchable database that allows visitors to find a lawyer in their jurisdiction and who practices in specialty areas.

Loislaw

www.loislaw.com

Wolters Kluwer has also created a subscription-based legal research resource to compete with the major players, Westlaw and Lexis. It claims to simplify the potentially overwhelming research process by its jurisdictional organization located on the home navigation page. It takes the researcher on a step-by-step process to complete the query, whereas Westlaw and Lexis have all the options for the search-scope on one page. Its scope is broad, but not as comprehensive as either of the two market leaders. Its purpose is to be more streamlined than the other database services to "control research costs, enhance productivity, and increase the return on investment."

Loislaw also provides citation and updating services through its GlobalCite and LawWatch services. GlobalCite notifies the user whenever there are citing references to the case that has been viewed, provides a link to that list of documents, and has "treatment codes" to indicate how the viewed case has been subsequently handled by the citing sources. LawWatch permits the user to set up a notification whenever Loislaw's daily updates include new documents satisfying certain predetermined search criteria.

LII/Legal Information Institute

www.law.cornell.edu
The Legal Information Institute is a free (although they encourage donations) legal research initiative sponsored by the Cornell University Law School. Its coverage is impressive. Researchers can choose to search by subject in the Law About . . . menu, by types of law in either the Constitution and Codes or Court Opinions sections, or by Source of Jurisdiction. Very helpfully, the site contains an Introduction to Basic Legal Citation by Peter W. Martin, which explains and gives examples of both *BlueBook* and ALWD (Association of Legal Writing Directors) styles and formats.

ABA Legal Technology Resource Center

www.abanet.org/tech/ltrc/lawlink/home.html
This site provides a "jumpstation," essentially a list of hyperlinks, that will directly access a vast array of electronically available legal resources. It contains links to federal and state official resources, which include statutes, codes, evidentiary, and procedural rules; international legal information; the bar and paralegal associations of every state; educational and employment opportunities; ethics resources, including the model rules and all of the state codes; surveys and statistics; legal news; and various other reference resource sources.

Traditional Tools of Legal Research

While online legal research is the most current and accessible, it may not always be the easiest or best method for you. As previously illustrated, the amount of information is enormous and, if you are not careful, can become overwhelming. An online researcher must be careful to use his time effectively. It is very easy to get lost or carried away by following link after link. Book research allows you to keep multiple resources at a time open for comparison, whereas electronic research can only display one piece of information on the screen. Further, book research is best when you have a lot of reading to do. A treatise is much easier to read in print when you need to familiarize yourself with a new or complex area of law.

Some law firms have extensive private law libraries. Even a solo practitioner usually has a modest law library, even if it must be tucked away in the wall shelves in his office. Most counties or courts have a law library open to attorneys, and sometimes to the general public.

The traditional tools of legal research are the books and multivolume sets of case reports, statutes, and legal forms contained in those libraries.

The tools of legal research are divided into two basic categories:

1. Primary sources—come from the actual creators of the law. Primary law comes from the three branches of the government (either federal or state)—the legislature (statutory law), the executive (administrative regulations), and the judiciary (case law).

2. Secondary sources—this material is an interpretation or commentary on the law. It is not the law itself. The law is coming to you secondhand, hence the name "secondary source."

What you must understand is the hierarchy and organization of legal authorities in order first to find them and then to determine what is binding law and what is persuasive logic.

Primary Sources Used in Legal Research

A. Constitutions
The primary authority that limits both federal and state statutory law and the decisions of all the courts is the Constitution of the United States. The various constitutions of the several states may limit the authority of the state's legislature in addition to, but not in derogation of, the U.S. Constitution. These state constitutions are very often much longer and more detailed than the Federal Constitution.

The U.S. Code Annotated contains the text of the U.S. Constitution and citations to federal cases that interpret it or construe it.

B. Statutory Law
Statutes are enactments of a state legislature (state statutes) or of the U.S. Congress (federal statutes). These statutory sources are given the most weight (aside from constitutional issues) in a given legal conflict. The reason is that these laws were written by the people's representatives in Congress and should reflect the majority's

opinion on the subject matter. If the statute is applicable, it will control the outcome of the matter.

Your sources for determining applicable statutory law are described below:

1. "Annotated statutes" are privately printed statutes in codified form that contain the actual text of the statutes, plus comments and citations to court cases that have interpreted the particular section of the statute under which the case citation (and brief summary of the point of law) is printed.

   For example, the U.S. Code Annotated (U.S.C.A.) has fifty titles, from Agriculture to War. The U.S.C.S. (U.S. Code Supplement, formerly Federal Case Annotated) is similarly arranged.

2. "Sessions laws," or "public acts or codes," are officially printed by each state and by Congress after each legislative session. They are usually printed chronologically, but some states also print an official code that contains the laws in topical order. The federal official code of laws passed by Congress is called the U.S. Code. It is arranged alphabetically by topic.

C. Administrative Regulations

The executive branch has rule-making authority as delegated by Congress to the administrative agencies. These specialized agencies clarify the broader statutory authority and explain how a piece of legislation is to be enforced and applied. They are subordinate to statutory law.

Each agency publishes its proposed rules in the Federal Register, for review and comment from the parties that will be affected by their enactment.

D. Case Law

"Case law" (also known as "common law" or "judge-made law" consists of written court opinions (usually appellate courts). It makes up the majority of legal research as it often interprets statutes and regulations, to which it is subordinate. A judge cannot change what the law states, he can only interpret it to fit the facts at hand and ensure a just result.

Just as any changes to statutes or regulations must come from the body that created them or a superior one, courts are bound to a hierarchy of authority as well. The Supreme Court is the ultimate decision-making body for interpreting the law. The U.S. Supreme Court binds all other courts below it and the supreme courts of the states. The state supreme courts are the final decision-maker for issues of state law, and all lower courts in their jurisdiction are bound by their interpretations. This is the concept of "legal precedent."

Legal precedent must be understood in order to interpret your findings and apply them appropriately to your case at hand. The lower courts have a definite hierarchy and relationship among themselves. Let's speak in terms of the federal system, as the hierarchy in the state judicial system is easy to understand because it is a simple linear hierarchy. In the federal system, there are appellate-level courts in the thirteen circuits. These circuit courts of appeal are all on equal footing with one another, so that a decision in one circuit is not mandatory authority in another. For example, the 3rd Circuit Court does not have to follow the legal precedents set in the 9th Circuit, although that authority is *persuasive.* Similarly, the district courts are only persuasive authority to one another if they are of the same rank. The twist comes when discussing the weight of authority between a district court and a circuit court that controls a different jurisdiction. That authority, even though it comes from a court of higher rank, is merely persuasive precedent to a lower court that is not within its "family" circuit. Mandatory authority therefore emanates from a higher court that has appellate jurisdiction over that lower court. See Figure 8.3 for a graphic representation of this relationship. These concepts become very important once you sit down to write the memorandum of law.

Figure 8.3

	Supreme Court	
Mandatory		Mandatory
↙		↘
3rd Circuit	←Persuasive →	**9th Circuit**
Mandatory ↓	Persuasive ✕	Mandatory ↓
District of New Jersey	←Persuasive →	**Northern District of California**
Mandatory ↓		Mandatory ↓
Any party before the courts of New Jersey		**Any party before the courts of California**

Your sources for case law are:

1. The State Reports, if your state has official state reports. The cases for one state are printed in chronological order in consecutively numbered volumes by that state.

2. The National Reporter System (West Publishing Company). All state cases are printed in more or less chronological order in consecutively numbered volumes, grouping decisions of several states in reporting units of the system, such as:

GEOGRAPHICAL

Pacific Reporter	New York Reporter	Southern Reporter
Atlantic Reporter	North East Reporter	South Western Reporter
California Reporter	North West Reporter	

All federal cases are reported in consecutively numbered volumes, grouping decisions of various levels and types of federal courts, in:

Supreme Court Reporter

Federal Court Reporter

Federal Supplement

The real question is how does one find case law in the books, if they are compiled chronologically? That is where the digest system comes in. The digests are arranged topically, very much like an encyclopedia, and organized by West's Key system. There are three ways to access these volumes: (1) by descriptive words about your topic, (2) by "words and phrases," and (3) by case name. The first method is used most frequently, as it allows for the most flexibility. The "words and phrases" volume only indexes cases that legally define a word or phrase as a "term of art." It does not contain all words and phrases used in legal decisions. It is only useful when the issue in the case turns upon a particular judicial interpretation of that "term of art." The last option only works if you have the full case name, which is rare, and if you did, you could more easily pull it up online.

So, back to the descriptive word index. If you wanted to find in the books cases that dealt with the *Roe v. Wade* fourteenth amendment rights to abortion, you would simply use those words relating to the issue as your query. However, in more complex matters, you may find that the word you look up is not there or that it sends you to another term. Persistence will get you the result you need.

Once you have found the appropriate words in the descriptive word index, you will be sent to the actual body of the series—the topical digests, which are arranged alphabetically and follow the Key number system. Therefore, you are not looking up a page number; the Key is the guide. The digest summarizes each issue in the cases reported. Cases often deal with several related issues; therefore, each case may contain numerous references to a single key number. For example, a complex case such as *Roe v. Wade* will appear more than once under a headnote listing. Each summary applies an element of the case to that headnote topic. These case summaries will help you determine which cases you will then need to go retrieve from the reporters so that you can read the entire case. A digest summary is never a substitute for reading the entire case where you intend to rely on that case.

NOTE: All of these sources, the digests, reporters, codes, etc., can and should be periodically updated by "pocket parts" or other cumulative supplements. The books simply cannot be reprinted as quickly as law is being made. It is critical to check these as well for the most recent developments or changes to the law.

Secondary Sources Used in Legal Research

If you find yourself unfamiliar with the area of law in which you must perform research, the secondary research resources (either online or in print) may be the right jumping-off point. It is important to bear in mind that these sources are at most only persuasive in nature and, unless there are *no* cases on point, should not be used in memoranda of law submitted to the court. There is only one exception to this rule—the Restatements. They are so highly regarded as definitive authority in their areas of law, that they are even cited by judges in their decisions.

The major secondary sources are:

1. *Restatements:* These are not law; they summarize all the significant rules of law that the majority of jurisdictions follow. They are used to track trends in the progress of law and can be used to "predict" a case of first impression in your state where there is no precedent.

2. *Treatises* (for example, the "Hornbook" series): These are used to understand a subject of law more clearly. They are very detailed scholarly books that trace the evolution of an area of law and how the principles apply in theory. They help the researcher understand how to apply the rules to his given situation.

3. *Annotated law reports* (for example, the American Law Reports): The ALR helps to pinpoint areas of the law which are controversial. They can be thought of as the opposite of the Restatements, which discuss well-established points of law. Because the ALR is organized chronologically (not by subject as is the Restatements), the researcher must go to the index to find the topic and then to the actual volume containing the case. The annotations to the case will then lead your search to more primary authority.

4. *Legal encyclopedias* (e.g., *American Jurisprudence* and the *Corpus Juris Secondum*): This resource is used to gain a basic understanding of the legal topic, much like a regular encyclopedia is used for general knowledge. It is also helpful to gain familiarity with the catchphrases used in a topic of law (e.g., "attractive nuisance" in torts) so that the researcher can form a better query.

5. *Legal dictionaries* (like *Black's*): They define the "terms of art," Latin phrases, and how words are used in the legal context. Even common words have different legal meanings apart from their everyday usage.

6. *Legal periodicals* (professional journals, magazines, and legal newspapers): They contain not only general information articles about the practice of law, but also very recent court decisions.

7. *Form books* (often referred to as "practice series"): They provide the basic format for the many kinds of legal documents that may need to be prepared.

Uniform System of Citation

You have completed your legal research by using computer tools or traditional tools. Now you are preparing a law memorandum or legal brief that will contain "citations" to primary or secondary sources of law. It is important to understand the purpose and benefits of using proper citation format. Legal writing is a form of technical writing that must adhere to certain rules of style and format. It is heavily dependent upon the source of the information to uphold the argument. That is why citations are used. The readers of your writing must be able—at a glance—to determine the weight of your authorities as they relate to the subject at hand. They do this by seeing your citations. Additionally, it is important that they be able to locate that same information in order to read it as a whole for themselves—so they must be able to locate that information quickly and without confusion as to the reference.

First, you must check the rules of the court to which the document is to be submitted, to determine its citation preference, if any. There are two generally accepted formats, the traditional *BlueBook* from the Harvard Law Review Association, which can be purchased as a hard copy or accessed online at www.legalbluebook.com, and the *ALWD Citation Manual*, information about which can be accessed at www.alwd.org. For the most part, the citations look similar, but there are differences that make either one or the other the acceptable format in your jurisdiction.

The general formula is to give the *full name of the case*, volume of the reporter, name of the reporter, page where the case starts (date). For example, *Miranda v. Arizona*, 384 U.S. 436, 86 S.Ct. 1602, 16 L.Ed.2d 694 (1966). In this citation all three U.S. Supreme Court reporters are used.

In a federal reporter, it will not be possible to determine what court the case came out of, so you need to include that in the parenthetical information. For example, *Bridgeport Music Inc. v. Universal Music Group Inc.*, 440 F.Supp.2d 342 (S.D.N.Y. 2006). The Federal Supplement reports all district court cases, so it is necessary to indicate that the case was decided in the Southern District of New York (S.D.N.Y.).

In either citation format, there are some general rules. Citations are generally set apart from sentences. They are treated as their own independent sentence (even though the spell/grammar checker is going to flag them as fragments). Therefore they start with a capital letter and end with a period. If the citation appears within a long sentence, it is treated as an independent clause and set apart with commas or other appropriate punctuation. Similarly, if two or more citations are joined together, they are separated by semicolons. Finally, all proper names within the citation are capitalized (with the exception of words like "and" and "the"). There are also rules for abbreviating longer, common words in case titles. You will need to look these up in the rules for your citation format.

Getting into the habit of using the prescribed forms for citation will take a paralegal one step closer to perfection. The attorney will love it.

Writing Effectively

Writing is a difficult skill to develop. Most people are intimidated by the written word since, unlike the spoken word, it has permanency. Moreover, to develop your skill requires constant practice, practice, and more practice. Most of us lack the ability to express ideas in writing, and this expression is essential to professional success.

Hence, emphasis will be given to your thought processes; the fundamentals of legal vocabulary, grammar, punctuation; proper citation form; writing logically; and effective reading for comprehension.

Any journalistic student will tell you that there are five "W" questions that should be answered in any writing project. They are who, what, why, when, and where. Never assume that answers will come later.

When you are given a writing assignment, the first thing you must determine, or clearly understand, is the purpose for the document. You must ask yourself exactly what it is you want from the court. Do you want the court to grant or deny a motion? Do you want the attorney to settle the case? Do you want to persuade the attorney that he is in a no-win situation? Do you want the appellate court to rule in your favor? Do you want to appease the anxieties of the client? All of these are affected by your writing skills, or lack thereof.

The most important lesson in *any* writing assignment:

Do not twist facts. Do not omit unfavorable facts or inflate some and hide others.

Once you have determined the purpose of the project, then think it through and decide upon the message to be transmitted. Also remember that appearance matters. Clear formatting in appropriate fonts is essential; the reader should not be distracted by clutter or rambling.

Your writing must be clear and concise. Avoid ambiguities. Avoid superfluous words. Avoid being verbose. Use lead-in words and phrases that make the ideas flow smoothly and carry over to the next paragraph. In the art, these are called transition phrases or connector words.

General Correspondence

While much of the daily office correspondence is the legal secretary's area of expertise, all members of the firm are expected to be able to compose professional letters. Most attorneys these days even compose their own letters—you as a paralegal will be expected to do so as well.

There are some basic formatting guidelines, and, of course, most word processing systems have templates that have these embedded in them.

As with all business correspondence, the addressee should appear at the top left with the date. A little quirk of the legal profession is to also include the method of delivery. This is not a minor detail but can be part of evidence or proof of compliance with a court rule (e.g., some summonses can be sent via Certified mail, RRR).

Next is the "Re:" line. This tells the reader (or opener of the letter) what the general subject of the letter is. In this way, a secretary can open all incoming mail and then properly deliver the mail to the attorney handling that matter. If it is a litigation matter, generally the name of the lawsuit is the "Re:" line along with the reason for the letter. (Depending on the office, the file number may appear here as well.)

EXAMPLE

Re: *Smith v. Jones*, Docket number PP1234
Second Request for Answers to Interrogatories.

If a letter has more than one page (and you'll find attorneys write lots of these letters), then you must create a header, with the attorney's name and page number, for the subsequent pages. The same holds true for exhibits. But be careful that the pagination does not interfere with the integrity of the exhibit (and never attach an original, unless you must file one with the court). The reason for all of this is clear: You always want to make sure that if a bunch of letters gets dropped on the floor or misfiled, you can easily recreate the documents.

Attorneys do not have time or patience to read long-winded, rambling letters, so it is important to organize your thoughts. First, tell the reader why you are writing: Is it a follow-up to a telephone call, are you merely enclosing requested documents, is it in response to a conference or a settlement offer? Give the reader an indication as to the content of the rest of the letter. Be sure that you deal with only one topic per paragraph.

If you are answering a specific question posed by the recipient—quote that question and when it was posed to you. ("In your letter of May 1, 2009, you asked . . .")

If this is the first time you are writing to this person, introduce your firm and the party it represents.

If the letter contains legal advice, do *not* sign it even if the attorney specifically asked you to draft it. Recall the Unauthorized Practice of Law rules. You must have your attorney sign it.

Every office has certain letters that go out on a regular basis. It will be helpful to look at your own firm's letters for the format and tone of this correspondence. The broad categories of letters include:

1. *Informational letters:* Usually these are sent to the client in order to either let him know of a particular happening in the case or to "hold his hand" and let him know that while things are moving slowly, they are indeed moving.

2. *Advice or opinion letters:* Remember, paralegals may not sign this kind of letter.

   This type of letter relates the lawyer's opinion of the case and what action should be taken in furtherance of the issue. These letters serve as mini legal memoranda because the lawyer needs to discuss relevant legal principles and apply them to the client's matter.

   All the formalities of a legal memorandum may apply here as well, meaning that the referenced law must have proper citations.

3. *Demand letters:* These are the most formal as they are letters sent to the opposition demanding that a certain action, like payment or performance, be taken. The letter states *why* the reader must take that action demanded by the letter. In addition, the letter includes how the action must be accomplished and the time limit on the action.

   A very specific kind of demand letter is the *demand for settlement* (in personal injury cases). It includes:

   a. Description of the plaintiff,

   b. Facts of the case,

   c. Theories of liability and recovery,

   d. Description of the plaintiff's damages,

   e. Statement of the amount of damages, and

   f. Analysis of damages and demand of settlement amount. However, note that this must not include an ultimatum—settlement negotiations are often in the works after the letter is written.

   Settlement letters set the stage for any possible trial. These letters should never be boastful about the winning record of the attorney, nor should they have a threatening tone. As always, keep it professional.

   They take much longer to draft, and the firm must have a lot of information regarding the case before one can be drafted. This is where your note-taking skills are going to come in handy.

The Case Brief

Case briefs are summarizations of the opinions you have read and decided are needed to further your case preparation. They are tools that allow you, your attorney, and other staff to easily reference the case without having to read the entire opinion. This can be a great time-saver, particularly when your office handles similar matters and the case briefs can be referenced again and again.

There is a particular format generally followed throughout the legal community. It separates the opinion into four distinct parts: the facts, the issue(s), the holding(s), and the reasoning. Each section gets its own subheading so that the relevant information is easily accessed. As a general rule, the case brief should be just that—brief! Go for the 10 percent rule. The brief should only contain 10 percent of the number of pages as the original opinion (e.g., a ten-page case should be briefed in only one page—a fifty-page case should be briefed in less than five pages).

The subdivisions and functions of the case brief:

1. *The facts:* You must identify what the material/important facts are. These have a direct effect upon the case. For example, the weather conditions in a contract dispute are irrelevant, but they can be vital to a car accident.

   There two types of facts:

   a. *Occurrence facts*: These are the facts that describe what happened between the parties to the lawsuit.

   b. *Procedural facts*: This is a story of what happened to the case once it started its journey through the legal system. Most reported cases are on appeal, so these facts tell you how and why the case was heard at this level.

2. *The issue(s):* The court must determine what the correct legal standard is to apply to the problem before it, and was it applied properly at the trial level? This has nothing to do with the guilt or liability of the particular parties before the court. You are trying to determine how that same precedent can or should be applied in your case.

3. *The holding:* How did the court resolve the legal issue before it? This is the court's determination of the proper standard of law to be applied in this factual situation. Judges base their determination by looking for statutory authority first, then, if there is none, the judge will apply fundamental ideals of right and wrong (equity).

4. *Reasoning* (the most important part of the brief!): The bulk of the court's opinion is its explanation of *why* it arrived at that outcome (holding). The judge sets forth how the legal standard applies in that case. This is the application of the law to the facts—something you will be expected to do when you draft a legal

memorandum. Also note how the court ultimately treated the case—its judgment. Did it affirm, reverse, or remand the case?

The Legal Memorandum

The purpose of a legal memorandum is to inform your attorney or other members of the law firm of the status of the law, giving both sides of the question. You may make a recommendation, if possible, and if not, then be sure to so state. If the law is clear on the issue raised, a conclusion is proper.

The amount of time that it will take to draft a legal memorandum will vary greatly depending on your experience in both research and writing and the complexity of the matter at hand. It could take as little as three or four hours or as much as several days of concentrated, uninterrupted work. When given a legal research problem, give yourself time to get acclimated to the task and for complete understanding. Do not be afraid to ask questions as you are being instructed. Most attorneys prefer that you ask the questions prior to commencement of the job, rather than during the performance, and certainly not after completion. To do otherwise causes irritation. To follow the former shows alertness and humility.

As an aid to taking notes we suggest you develop abbreviations of the words often used by your attorney. This will be of extreme value in discussing the assignment and later in reading and making notes about the cases. For example:

π = plaintiff (pi symbol)

Δ = defendant (delta symbol)

K = contract

bfp = bona fide purchaser

c/p = community property

x = comp-cross-complaint or cross-complaint

PI = personal injury

S/L = Statute of Limitations

S/F = Statute of Frauds

In drafting the legal memorandum we suggest the following:

1. Develop an approach by using an outline or chart. This will not only enable you to clearly understand what it is your attorney wants, but it will help you determine what method you should use to get the desired result.

2. Pick out the phrase or theory that clearly sets forth the proposition or issue you want to support. When attacking the legal research project, determine whether the matter is most likely governed by statute or case law.

3. Do your research. Find out if there is a time constraint. Remember you must be thorough but time-efficient as well.

4. Take notes to keep track of your progress.

5. Should the case be on target, cite-check (Shepardize or KeyCite) it again. Failure to do so may cause your attorney to walk into court and get mud on his face if the case has been overruled or superseded by another more recent decision.

6. Compile the cases in relevancy order, bearing in mind whether the authority is mandatory or persuasive, its recentness, and subsequent treatment.

7. Draft case briefs for those cases that you intend to rely on.

The Format of the Legal Memorandum

1. *Heading*

   a. Caption (centered at the top of the page—stating the kind of memo—"internal memo of law")

   b. To:

   c. From:

   d. Date:

   e. Case or Client:

   f. File number:

   g. Docket number:

   h. Re: a brief description of the assignment

2. *Statement of assignment.* A complete statement of your assignment. This will include any restrictions imposed by your boss—meaning, did he only ask you to research recent cases or cases in your state? This lets the reader know what the boundaries of the assignment are. This also clarifies your understanding of the assignment.

3. *Issue/question(s) presented.* This is the question that your memo will answer. You must include the law in question. For example, "under N.J.S.A. 3:19-2(a) can a person . . ." Often a certain phrase or word will need to be defined—this is called the "element in contention." What constitutes a "holographic will"? Has

the testator "signed" the will by marking with his initials? (This is where you could have used the "words and phrases" digest!) It is important to tie the most important facts into the question presented. Additionally, if you have a multi-part question, start with the most important and most broad, then assume you will lose on that point and form your next question that must be answered. "If our client is found not to have signed his will, what are the intestate succession rules in New Jersey and to whom will the estate devolve?"

4. *Short answer.* Keep it brief—usually without reference to law (that is saved for your discussion). In this way, the reader can find out whether it is worth it to read the rest of the memo!

5. *Statement of facts.* This is perhaps one of the most important parts of the memo. Recall often that cases revolve around tiny details. Cases apply or do not apply depending on every part of the surrounding circumstances. You must be:

   a. *Concise:* Do not give every last detail—you are to weed through the facts, leaving only the material ones for inclusion. Again, this is a skill unto itself. You should review your facts again after you have completed your memo—that way you will see what you need and what you don't, or vice versa, you will find that which you should have covered and didn't.

   b. *Accurate:* You must tell the truth—not the version you or your client would like to be the case. Of course, in a persuasive memo you can portray the truth in the light most favorable to your client—but you must not be misleading as to the reality of the situation. If there are disputed facts, you must recognize that.

   c. *Organized:* Usually this is done in a chronological fashion to help the reader understand the situation. You are telling the story of how the dispute came to be.

6. *Analysis.* This section is where you synthesize your cases to form a coherent view of the current state of the law. First, present the law that applies and, if applicable, quote the relevant section. Then, make sure that you break the law down into its elemental parts and discuss those elements that are in contention as they relate to your matter. The real work comes in where you discuss the relevant case law interpreting the elements in contention. Lastly, remember to discuss opposing viewpoints and anticipate how the other side will interpret the law. You must include valid strong counterarguments in this type of memo. It is vital that your attorney be prepared. It does not make you look bad if the law is not on your side—it isn't always going to be.

7. *Conclusion.* Give your opinion as to which side has better arguments and how you think the court in your case will likely rule given the facts and the state of

the law. This section can also be used to address whether further facts of your case need to be investigated, further research needs to be undertaken, or whether clients should be contacted regarding certain matters.

8. *Appendix.* This section is not always an element present in a memorandum of law. It is necessary only if you have referred to specific information contained in other sources—like graphs, depositions, photos, or full texts of statutes that were too long to put in the body of the paper. You may also include some further resources should the reader wish to dive into independent research or follow your path to another issue.

Nine Practical Guidelines for Preparing the Legal Memorandum

Pay particular attention to the following:

1. In citing a case, always place the official reports first, but also give the unofficial report citations.

   For example, in California we would cite a case as follows:

   > *People v. Gould* (1971), 54 CA2d 621; 7 Cal Rptr 273; 354 P2d 30 Cal— being the official reports, and the unofficial reports being California Reporter (Cal Rptr) and the Pacific Reporter (P) which includes nine other states outside of California.

2. When you are copying a statute and you find that certain portions of the statute are underlined in the code book, *do not* underline when you quote the statute. The line under the words is not part of the statute. It merely tells the reader that those words are new to the statute. The same applies to the asterisk found in the text of a statute quoted in a code. The asterisk shows the reader that the statute has recently been amended by way of deletions of words. The asterisks are not part of the statute.

3. In setting off quotations, citations, etc., indent on both paragraphs for the single space. Do not use quotation marks when indenting.

4. If you are citing old cases, say so and explain the connection and purpose for the reference to them.

5. One of the greatest pitfalls in citing cases is the use of the words *"supra," "infra,"* and *"ibid."* Know them, their meanings, and use them properly.

   a. *Supra* (always underlined) means that which came before;

   b. *Infra* (always underlined) means that which comes later; and

   c. *Ibid* (always underlined) means on the same page or in the same book.

6. In your discussion use strong phrases such as "it appears that the bulk of authority" or "the bulk of case authority states that" or "the law is clear," etc. Don't be frightened. Let your attorney know you have done your homework.

7. Be relevant; never forget the case you are discussing. Always tie in your case law and authority with the subject matter of your legal memorandum. In other words, do not lose sight of your objective and ramble.

8. In your conclusion, list or refer to or even incorporate your leading citations.

9. Make it readable, interesting, and *brief.*

Thereafter, sit down with your attorney and discuss what you have done, explaining your thinking in reaching your conclusion. Make your discussion practical, not argumentative. Have both sides of the issue, with supporting authority, well in mind. These things will aid your attorney in making a legal determination as to strategy. You are not the final authority—just his sounding board.

CHAPTER NINE

Pretrial Discovery

Purpose and Limits of Discovery

In addition to informal investigation of facts by the attorney and his support staff before trial, as dramatically illustrated by Perry Mason types and comically through *My Cousin Vinny*, there are formal methods for discovery of facts set forth in the rules of civil procedure of the federal courts and many state courts. Those formal rules are explored in this chapter.

As a general proposition, parties to a lawsuit may utilize the vehicles of discovery to obtain facts regarding any issue pertinent to the claim(s) or defenses of the parties to the lawsuit that are not privileged materials.

This discovery by any party can relate to documents, books, objects, physical conditions of things, land or persons, and the identity and whereabouts of individuals who may have information relevant and material to the lawsuit. It is extremely broad so that the matter can be most justly adjudicated without the fear of hidden or secreted facts that may influence the outcome of the matter. The underlying principle is that of fairness to every party. The outcome should not be dependent upon the deceptive skills of an attorney, but rather upon the attorney's persuasive power over the exposure of the truth.

The law is clear that even though the matter revealed through discovery may not be admissible at the time of trial, the discovery process can go forward along that line if the materials sought appear reasonably calculated to lead to the discovery of admissible evidence.

The nature and extent of allowable discovery in state court systems is controlled by statutes court rules and case law interpreting them. The source for these rules of evidence is your state rules of civil procedure, contained within your statutory materials, and your local rules of court, all of which can be found in your office, local law library, or, most conveniently, online through your state's judiciary website. It is imperative that you have the most current version of your local rules and that you double-check them before you make any submission. Discovery in the federal court system is governed by the Federal Rules of Civil Procedure and federal cases interpreting the rules. These rules can be found in your office library, the local law library, and, of course, online. The federal rules of discovery are available at www.law.cornell.edu/rules/frcp/#chapter_v.

These are the five whys of discovery:

1. To obtain additional factual information at the least expense to the client,

2. To negate and avoid surprise documentary evidence or witnesses at the time of trial and to share the results of any investigation to aid settlement of a case,

3. To reduce triable issues, thereby shortening the duration of the trial,

4. To preserve evidence or testimony of witnesses, and

5. To get a preview of opposing counsel's case.

Formal discovery is a search for truth based on those facts that are discoverable.

Due to its importance, it is incumbent upon you as the paralegal to be aware and have a full working knowledge of your local rules and any new changes in the law affecting discovery as it relates to your employer's practice. Any change in the rules will have a result upon the duties performed by you. And in addition, you must be cognizant of and knowledgeable in the use of litigation support systems in the discovery process (see Chapter 12, "Electronic Trial Preparation Procedures") and whether the discovery is admissible into evidence at the time of trial. (See Chapter 10, "Admissibility and Use of Evidence.")

There are certain time limits on discovery. Under the most normal of situations, time is always of the essence in a law office. But trial preparation has greater time restrictions. In most states, absent a stipulation between the parties, all discovery has to be completed within a thirty-day period prior to the date of trial. (You should check your local statutes and codes to determine the applicability of this limitation.) The purpose of this time period is to close all discovery proceedings to give the parties time to prepare for the actual trial of the case.

This exchange of information is so important that F.R.C.P. 26 imposes a duty to disclose certain information to the opposing party even *before* any formal requests are made from another party. Rule 26 also requires that parties confer to discuss the nature and basis of their claims and defenses and make those required disclosures within fourteen days of this conference. The Federal Rules make every effort to not only expedite the process, but also encourage settlement so the matter does not need to go to trial in an overburdened justice system.

It is for this and other reasons that you as the paralegal should start your discovery process immediately upon receipt of an answer, or upon service of the answer. In most states you can serve Interrogatories and Requests for Admissions twenty days after receipt of the answer, as well as schedule a deposition.

Court rules also provide time limits for answering interrogatories and responding to Requests for Admissions or Requests to Produce.

Types of Discovery

There are basically six vehicles or devices of discovery:

1. Interrogatories—a set of written questions served upon a party;

2. Depositions—oral examination and cross-examination of a witness (these are sworn statements that can be used as evidence at trial);

3. Requests for Production of Documents—a list of documents that the serving party believes the opposing party has access to and the serving party needs in order to have a complete set of facts;

4. Requests for Physical and Psychological Exam;

5. Requests for Admissions—a set of written statements of fact in which the serving party directs the opposing party to either admit or deny; and

6. Requests to Enter upon Land.

The exceptions to the right of discovery by any of the foregoing methods are:

1. *"Privileged information."* That is the information received by way of one-on-one conversation or that communicated by written statement (letters, telegrams, and so forth) between client and attorney, husband and wife, doctor and patient, clergyman and parishioner, and the like, as provided in state statutes or case law rules of evidence. These statements must have been made with the intention that they were confidential and part of the special fiduciary relationship between the client and his confidante. Not all information that is communicated between these parties is confidential. It is critical to understand this concept. It will be further detailed in the following chapter, on evidence.

2. *The "work product" of your attorney (and yourself as the paralegal).* Any information that is compiled or otherwise prepared by you or the attorney for litigation is

protected as the attorney's "work product," and this type of material is privileged. There are two types of trial preparations. The first is mental impressions, that is, how the attorney intends to conduct the litigation (strategies, theories of the case, etc.). The second is the informational material that has been collected and organized in a certain way. This may be witness interviews or even the way a nonprotected document was summarized or indexed. The names of the witnesses or the facts underlying the reworked document are not protected, however.

NOTE: Ask your attorney if you are in doubt as to whether you should supply information contained in your office case file.

Interrogatories

Interrogatories are written questions that are submitted to another party to the case. That party must answer the questions in writing and sign under oath. Interrogatories cannot be submitted to a person who is not a party to the case.

Depositions, unlike interrogatories, may be taken of anyone who may have knowledge of facts relevant to the case, even though he (or a corporation) is not a party to the case.

A. Use of Interrogatories

Developing interrogatories is a matter of reasoning. That is to say, you must first determine what it is you are attempting to accomplish and what information you are seeking to obtain from the answers to the questions. You are attempting to secure admissions from the opposing party to remove triable issues of fact. Ask yourself, "Will these questions and/or requested statements result in the disclosure of a fact that I need to prove my case?" If your answer is yes, then you are on the right track.

Technology has greatly improved the method for creating customized, on-target interrogatories. Long gone are the canned, voluminous sets of interrogatories and requests for admissions. Drafting well-written interrogatories can now be done easily and quickly simply by rearranging paragraphs, words, phrases, and/or by the addition of words, phrases, paragraphs, and so forth. Additionally, reliable legal research resources are replete with forms and samples.

B. Drafting Interrogatories

The principles applied in plaintiff interrogatories are the same for both defendant and plaintiff's case. Interrogatories may be served on plaintiffs anytime after the complaint is filed. They may be served on any other party after the plaintiff is served.

Sample procedure for drafting interrogatories after *plaintiff's complaint has been filed:* The defendant has filed an answer. Your office may or may not have taken the deposition of the defendant. Your attorney wants to pin down certain facts with specificity. You are given the task of developing a set of interrogatories to be propounded to the defendant. What do you do?

1. You look to the complaint to determine the contentions of the plaintiff, and the alleged wrongs committed by the defendant. Then you look to the answer of the defendant, together with the affirmative defenses claimed by the defendant.

2. Once you have reviewed the pleadings and feel that you have an understanding of the legal issues involved, you are ready to develop your interrogatories.

3. Retrieve, either from your office files or legal research, a set of standard interrogatories used in that kind of cause of action. Read, review, delete, and modify them as appropriate to your particular set of facts. You will most likely have to add original questions about particular matters you need to discover in your case.

4. You should attempt to draft your interrogatory as a single direct question, phrased to clearly inform the receiver what it is you want to know. The interrogatory can be divided into as many subdivisions as you like to make it more intelligible and easier to answer. However, you must note if your local rules limit the number of interrogatories permitted to be served upon another party. Under the Federal Rules, the number of questions may not exceed twenty-five (including subparts) (F.R.C.P. 33(a)(1)).

5. The first paragraph of the set of interrogatories would be the boilerplate notice paragraph stating the statutory or court rules basis under which the interrogatories are being propounded.

EXAMPLE (FEDERAL RULES)

Plaintiff, pursuant to F.R.C.P. 23, requests that the following interrogatories be answered, under oath, separately and fully, within thirty (30) days by defendant (or plaintiff whichever is applicable).

In addition to this reference to the rule of answering, it is common practice to include a set of definitions, spelling out the definitions of words, phrases, and so forth, and the scope of the questions so as to avoid any misunderstanding of what is being asked and thereby insuring responsive answers. Hence, you should include a paragraph or paragraphs as follows:

EXAMPLE

In answering these interrogatories, you are required to not only furnish such information as you know of your own personal knowledge, but information which is in the possession of your attorneys, investigators, insurance carriers, or anyone else acting on your behalf or their behalf.

or

It is intended by these interrogatories to elicit information not only within your own knowledge but obtainable by you . . .

and

If you cannot answer the following interrogatories in full, after exercising due diligence to secure the information to do so, so state, and answer to the extent possible, specifying your inability to answer the remainder, and stating whatever information or knowledge you have concerning the unanswered portions.

6. The first several interrogatories, of course, will be directed to personal data, that is, name, address, telephone number, occupation or business, and address and telephone number of same (all depending on the nature of the lawsuit), and this could include medical information and educational background. Then come the substantive questions that satisfy the purpose of the interrogatories.

EXAMPLE

Let us say it is an action for breach of contract for the purchase and sale of a piece of real property and the plaintiff is attempting to secure the return of his deposit, claiming that he was unable to secure the loan, or that the application for credit was refused; and furthermore, that his demand for the return of his deposit has been rejected by defendant.

In the above example, you want to establish the demand of the plaintiff *and* the refusal by the defendant, among other things.

Your interrogatories on that point may be drafted as follows:

Interrogatory no. 5: Did plaintiff pay deposit described in the contract, a copy of which is attached to the complaint filed in this action? If so,

a. Amount?

b. When paid?

c. To whom was it paid?

Interrogatory no. 6: Did plaintiff ever demand return of his deposit? If so, when did he demand the return of the deposit?

Interrogatory no. 7: Was (were) the demand (or demands) made in writing or orally?

a. If in writing, to whom was (were) the demand(s) addressed?

b. If orally, to whom was (were) it (they) made?

Interrogatory no. 8: Under what circumstances was (were) the demand(s) made? Describe in detail.

Interrogatory no. 9:

a. If the demand(s) was (were) rejected, by whom was (were) it (they) rejected?

b. Upon what authority did this individual reject the demand(s)?

c. What is the name, address, telephone number, and capacity of the person rejecting the demand(s)?

d. State the basis of the rejection, setting forth with particularity each and every fact relating to the rejection.

Interrogatory no. 10:

a. At the time of the rejection, were there other persons present?

b. If your answer to (a) above is in the affirmative, list the name and address of each and every such person present and their interest in the subject matter of this complaint.

While under your local rules there may not be a limit to the number of interrogatories you may include in a set, they may not be redundant or used for harassment. If the party served with the discovery demands believes that they are being used for such improper purposes, that party may bring a motion for sanctions if the serving party does not agree to rescind them. See F.R.C.P. 11.

C. Answering Interrogatories

The principles are the same for answering the interrogatories propounded to either the plaintiff or the defendant. Both parties are under the same discovery obligations; it does not matter who initiated the lawsuit.

In all jurisdictions that permit interrogatories, the answers must be verified or sworn to.

In some jurisdictions the original of the answers to interrogatories is filed in court and a copy of the answers is sent to all the parties. In other jurisdictions the original and a copy is returned to the attorney who submitted the interrogatories to your client. *Check your court rule.* See F.R.C.P. 33(a) as an example of procedure.

Sample procedure for answering interrogatories: Interrogatories to be answered by your attorney's client are received in the mail or by delivery. They must be fully answered or objected to within the time limit prescribed by your rule of civil procedure (usually thirty days but not more than forty-five days from the date the summons and complaint was served on a defendant if the interrogatories are directed to the defendant). See F.R.C.P. 33(a).

As the paralegal, you need to perform the following actions:

1. Put the *due date* for the answers on the official calendar. Be sure that you have noted an *earlier* (by at least a week) date for meeting with the client to review and verify the final answers.

2. Read the interrogatories and determine whether any of the questions can be answered from documents your client has already provided.

3. Copy the interrogatories and mail them to the client with an explanatory letter or have the client come into the office to answer the questions.

4. After having obtained the answers to the set of interrogatories from the client, either by way of an interview or through the mail, the paralegal's role is one of review and rewording (rewording should not change the *content* of the answer). You do this by comparing the answers given with the factual, supporting documentation in the file and by making follow-up telephone calls to the client or other source of the client's information (such as his bookkeeper or tax accountant). It is also wise to compare the answers to any answers formerly given by the client in a deposition, to avoid inconsistency.

> **PRECAUTIONARY MEASURE:** Any deviation between the answers submitted by the client and the documents in your file, as well as any unanswered questions, should be called to the attention of the attorney.
>
> If any questions are improper (irrelevant, confidential, harassment, and the like), consult the attorney. He may want to object to a particular interrogatory rather than answer it. If the question is objected to, the reason for the objection must be stated with specificity. A motion for a protective order may be required as provided in F.R.C.P. 26(c). Be sure to check your state's comparable rule. See Figure 9.1 for the Motion for a Protective Order.

5. If there is no objection to an interrogatory, it must be answered completely to avoid a motion to compel by counsel when he receives the answers.

6. If counsel has provided an electronic copy of the interrogatories, you may be able to insert the answers directly in that document. Otherwise, full and complete answers should be provided with the corresponding interrogatory number as originally served.

7. Have the client read and sign the typed answers or the verification. Where the rules require the answer to be sworn to, make sure the notary has signed.

8. Prepare the notice of filing or the notice of answer to interrogatories (as your court rule requires). The caption appears at the top of the notice and the typed and signed answers to interrogatories are attached.

9. File the original answers and send copy of notice of filing with a copy of the answers to all parties *or* file the notice of answers to interrogatories and send a copy of the notice and a copy of the answers to all parties (depending on your court rule as discussed earlier).

Protective Orders

If you in protecting your client are unwilling to answer the interrogatories due to the sensitive and/or confidential nature of the response requested, you must show "good cause" why the court should intervene and prevent or stop the discovery being requested or demanded.

Some of the grounds you can use in the motion for protective order or your attorney's declaration in support of the motion for a protective order, are:

1. The discovery category is too broad, or is irrelevant;

2. The discovery requested has been received and is presently in the possession or under the control of defendant (plaintiff);

3. Further discovery would be harassment, time-consuming, expensive, and/or would work undue hardship on defendant (plaintiff); and

4. Further discovery would unnecessarily delay trial because of party's delay in seeking that discovery.

If it is a motion for a protective order relating to a medical examination, the ground could be that it would be dangerous to both the health and welfare of the client; but if it is allowed, that it be restricted to one examination for the benefit of all parties in the action, and so forth.

After a protective order is obtained, the other party may prepare and serve new interrogatories or requests and/or take further deposition asking different questions that do not violate the court's protective order.

Some protective orders protect against part of a discovery document and allow and require answer or response to other parts.

EXAMPLE

A request to produce in a negligence action where punitive damages are not alleged includes copies of defendant's income tax. Plaintiff's income tax returns may be relevant where loss of wages is an element of damages.

Figure 9.1
Motion for Protective Order Limiting Interrogatories.
(Choose only those objections which apply.)

Attorneys for Plaintiffs

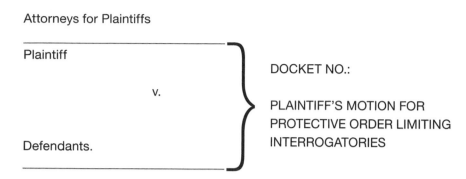

Plaintiff

v.

Defendants.

DOCKET NO.:

PLAINTIFF'S MOTION FOR
PROTECTIVE ORDER LIMITING
INTERROGATORIES

Plaintiff, by counsel, pursuant to the Rules of this Court, respectfully requests the court to enter a protective order limiting discovery based upon the following grounds:

1. Defendant's Interrogatories are overly broad, unduly burdensome and irrelevant insofar as such Interrogatories request the production of documents and the recitation of facts that do not relate, concern nor are aware likely to relate to or concern any relevant information or matter in dispute.
2. Defendant's Interrogatories are being used for harassment, are oppressive and would result in undue expense, it being estimated that answering such interrogatories would require _____ hours of Plaintiff's time to identify responsive information and prepare answers,
3. Defendant's Interrogatories request information which is or was in the possession of the Defendant, his agents, servants or employees and as such are repetitive of the information already acquired by the Defendant.
4. Defendant's Interrogatories request information that constitutes trade secrets or other confidential information for which the Plaintiff is entitled to retain privately, and if made public would embarrass or compromise the Plaintiff, or would impair the Plaintiff's commercial competitive position in the market.
5. Plaintiff, in good faith, has attempted to resolve these issues with the Defendant without the need for court intervention, but these efforts have been to no avail. The documentation of these efforts has been attached hereto as Exhibit A and the attorney of record has supplied the certification of same.

WHEREFORE, Plaintiff requests that the court enter its protective order limiting discovery as against those Interrogatories propounded by the Defendant and objected to by the Plaintiff and further, awarding to Plaintiff all costs and fees associated with this motion.

Requests for Admissions

As you progress through the discovery procedures, it will become increasingly apparent that certain items in the litigation are not disputed and other items may be admitted prior to the trial of the action, pursuant to court rules allowing requests for admissions to be made by either party.

These undisputed facts could conceivably be grounds for either a partial summary or final summary judgment.

A. Use of Requests for Admissions

In any event, despite the fact that some of the allegations stated in the complaint may be undisputed, if they are an integral part of the defense planned by your attorney, you should attempt to pinpoint and document them to avoid having to argue them at the time of trial.

Or you may be sure of some evidentiary facts that you know are true but may be easier to prove by admission, rather than by formal proof at trial.

Sometimes opposing counsel will "stipulate" (agree without argument or motion) as to the truth of such facts. Most often, he will not.

In a formal effort to obtain an admission that opposing counsel refuses to stipulate, you may prepare and file a document titled Requests for Admissions, ref. F.R.C.P. 36.

This vehicle of discovery, like the Summary Judgment, is considered to be one of the most devastating in the litigation procedure, since opposing counsel has only four choices: to admit the matter; to deny the matter; to refuse to admit or deny the matter; or to object. The most devastating consequence may result from the failure to answer at all. If the party upon which the Request is served fails to answer, all the statements are deemed *admitted* as against him.

If he admits the matter, it is a judicial admission and admissible into evidence; if he denies the matter, the moving party can make a motion requiring opposing counsel to pay the costs of proving the matter if it is proved at the time of trial. If opposing counsel wants neither to admit or deny the matter, he is required by law to respond. He must convince the court, by formal objection in the form of a motion, that he has made a reasonable investigation before he is allowed such a response. If he objects, he has to prove the objection is based on lack of personal knowledge, and this is hard to do if he has raised it in the complaint.

B. Time for Filing and Responding to Requests for Admissions

If a request for admissions is served on your attorney, you must act immediately. He *must* read it. He *must* do something or the facts and application of the law to the facts (if included in the request) are admitted. Your local court rules of civil procedure provides a return date for the answer or objection. Remember, it is vital to the survival of your case to answer these requests or else face a deemed admission.

Generally, this document can be filed and served on opposing counsel anytime after service of the summons or after an appearance of opposing counsel in the action.

C. Drafting Requests for Admissions

The following examples for requests for admissions are based on the action for a breach of contract as referenced in the interrogatory section:

SAMPLE OPENING PARAGRAPH

With reference to the set of requests for admissions served upon you herewith for each request that you deny, explain fully all facts upon which such denial is based, including, but not limited to, specific acts or concrete possibilities or examples of situations. Mere conclusions or speculations or erroneous rumors without basis of fact are not sufficient answers.

Request for Admission 1: Admit that you entered into the agreement with plaintiff on January 27, 20—, for the purchase of the subject real property, which agreement appears on Exhibit A to the complaint filed in this action.

Request for Admission 2: Admit that plaintiff applied to the First National Bank for the loan described in the agreement and that he signed the necessary preliminary documents, as required by law to approve his application for a loan covering the balance of the purchase price of said real property.

Request for Admission 3: Admit that the First National Bank refused to make the loan described in Admission 2 to the plaintiff.

Request for Admission 4: Admit that plaintiff's ability to secure the loan was a condition precedent to the agreement described in Admission 1.

Request for Admission 5: Admit that you had an attorney review the aforementioned agreement prior to your execution thereof.

Request for Admission 6: Admit that plaintiff's first demand for the return of his deposit was made on or about February 27, 20—.

Request for Admission 7: Admit that plaintiff showed you a copy of his application for loan and the written denial of the loan by the First National Bank at the time he made his first demand described in Admission 6.

Request for Admission 8: Admit that the date on the written denial of loan by the First National Bank was February 25, 20—.

The rules of civil procedure provides that the failure to respond to these requests within the time allowed will result in that the same must be deemed admitted. But this warning must be included in the request for admissions. Thereafter, if opposing counsel fails to respond, send out a registered letter or a certified letter that your office is deeming the answers to be admitted based upon that code section. This method is a *must* because you must certify that you acted in good faith rather than designed to take unfair procedural advantage.

> **NOTE:** What should you do with a request for admission when in doubt? When in doubt: deny. These are life-and-death matters, and we have found that it is the better part of valor to deny them rather than admit them. Otherwise, check with your boss to see if he, in his strategy, wants to admit some of them.

Depositions

A deposition is an oral examination and cross-examination of any person (not necessarily a party) who may have information *or* evidence relative to the issues of fact in a legal action. For the most part, it resembles the traditional taking of testimony at trial.

What distinguishes a deposition from the other types of discovery is the fact that it is the only vehicle of discovery that permits you to take the testimony of an individual who is not a party to the action.

The testimony is taken out of court at a convenient location (usually the office of the attorney who demands the deposition). The testimony is taken under oath administered by the qualified person designated to record (and usually transcribe) the deposition.

A. Setting the Deposition

1. *The deposition of an individual can be taken:*

   a. Upon oral examination (F.R.C.P. 30) or

   b. Upon written questions (F.R.C.P. 31). The most common is the oral examination. This deposition is the only vehicle of discovery that parallels open court testimony. It includes cross-examination. It is for this reason that some people call it a "mini-trial."

2. *A deposition may be demanded and held:*

   a. By any party in the action;

   b. At any time after the service of the summons and complaint until the case is set for trial; and

   c. Against any party (by written request or, if necessary, by motion) or non-party (by subpoena).

   There are two methods for obtaining serving an opposing party—by demand or stipulation. There are times when you should demand via a formal notice rather than making a request. To demand the taking of a deposition you will prepare a notice of taking deposition or a subpoena for deposition. This latter procedure is done either to protect your office (or client) to ensure that the defendant will be present if he or his attorney have been uncooperative (which happens), or to make it more convenient for your attorney's scheduled office appointments or court appearances. In using this latter procedure, a date is picked at your convenience, usually ten days' notice away from the date upon which you have set the deposition.

3. *The deposition of a nonparty witness may be taken:*

   a. By issuance and service of a subpoena showing the time and place of the deposition for taking his testimony. This is the *subpoena ad testificatum*. He need not bring supporting documents.

   b. By issuance and service of a *subpoena duces tecum* for production of documents at the time of the taking of the deposition. That is the form of subpoena that requires the witness to bring documents described generally or specifically in the *subpoena duces tecum*.

4. *Practical tips in setting the deposition are:*

   a. To take the deposition of a corporate entity, you need only serve the notice of taking the deposition on the attorney representing the corporation if it is party to the action, just as you do in the case of an individual party.

   b. Check the geographical limitations set by the applicable court rules or state code of civil procedure to determine the restrictions for taking the deposition of a nonparty who resides in the state. In California, for example, a deposition can be taken only in the county of residence of a nonparty or no more than seventy-five miles from his place of residence. When setting the deposition of such a nonparty, you would serve the subpoena on him requiring him to appear at a designated time and place in his required geographical area. If necessary, you may be able to obtain special permission from your local trial court requesting the sister state court to issue a subpoena directing the attendance of the individual at the deposition.

   c. Always plan to depose nonparty witnesses. Since you cannot send interrogatories to nonparty witnesses, you *must* take the deposition to preserve their testimony. This procedure is a little more complicated than for disposing witnesses who are parties, but necessary.

   To save time and money the deposition on written questions referred to may be used when a nonparty witness is out of state and submitted to the court reporter where witness resides, who thereafter reads the questions to the witness and transcribes the answers—ref. F.R.C.P. 31.

In any and all events, the moving party has the full responsibility for sending to the court all transcripts of depositions and making all the arrangements as to place of deposition and obtaining the transcript of the proceedings.

STEP-BY-STEP PROCEDURE

For example, if you want the deposition to be held on June 21, you should prepare and mail out your notice prior to, but no later than, June 10, with proof of mailing.

Concurrently with filing your notice, you should arrange for a court reporter to be present at the time and place set in the notice. It is best to confirm this by a letter or other appropriate writing addressed to the reporting agency or reporter.

Key measures for deposing nonparty litigants:

1. First, you must prepare and have issued a subpoena for deposition (*subpoena duces tecum* if you are seeking the testimony plus records, documents, and so forth), which is served on the proposed witness with the date of the deposition thereon.

2. Then, you also prepare, file, and serve the notice of taking deposition of the witness. This notice is served on all parties, keeping in mind the time restriction heretofore mentioned.

3. The sticky part here is the date. Before you send the notice to all parties, *you must first know that the witness has been served.* If for any reason he is not served within the time allowed to complete your ten-day notice to the opposing party, you must reset the date to allow for the service of the notice to all parties. This can be difficult, especially if the witness knows you are trying to serve him and is avoiding service.

4. After the preceding procedure has been followed, the procedure for taking the deposition of a nonparty witness is the same as that for taking the deposition of a party witness.

5. Those who can attend a deposition during these proceedings are only the attorneys for both or all parties, the person who is to be deposed, any other interested party-litigant, and a court reporter. This proceeding is normally held in the offices of the attorney for either party. It is not a public proceeding even though it resembles a mini-trial. The attorneys are able to object to the questions at the time that they are made. If there is a substantial dispute as to the propriety of the question, a "judge-on-call" may be available to render a decision over the telephone so that the deposition can proceed.

B. Summarizing a Deposition

The purpose of summarizing: Summarizing a deposition or making a digest of the facts elicited from the testimony given in a deposition is used as a tool by your attorney before and at the trial of a lawsuit to:

1. Make voluminous testimony more manageable (condensing it);

2. Verify crucial or disputed facts in a case, that is, how fast was the defendant driving, or how many drinks did defendant have, and so forth;

3. Provide the attorney a quick index of testimony;

4. Facilitate the attorney's direct and cross-examination of the witness who gave the deposition while that witness is on the stand during trial;

5. Aid the attorney to quickly detect inconsistent testimony (this is important if he wants to impeach or discredit a witness during the course of examination or cross-examination);

6. Lay the foundation for a motion to produce or for requests for admissions during the discovery process; and

7. Pinpoint questions of fact that should be further developed by interrogatories or further deposition.

Suggested guidelines in preparing a deposition summary:

1. Listen carefully to instructions from your attorney and take notes of the points he wants verified.

2. Determine the foregoing in specifics and establish why it is important.

3. Read through the entire deposition in a cursory way attempting to spot testimony regarding these points. (If time permits, note the page and line where you spotted the testimony and any apparent inconsistencies.)

4. If possible (or applicable) read the deposition of another material witness for comparison, noting the page and line of any statement made relative to the points in issue which either confirm or contradict particular statements of the witness.

5. Reread the deposition which you are summarizing slowly and carefully to get the overall context of the subject matter clearly in mind, paying particular attention to the conversations before and after each point or issue raised.

6. Once again, make brief notations of your findings relating to the inconsistencies, including line(s) and page(s) involved.

7. Read two to five pages ahead of yourself to allow the testimony to fall into place and/or make sense to you. Do not dive head-on into reading, attempting to digest it all at once—this is fatal.

8. Since the first few pages (normally) are preliminary statements of identification laying the foundation for the actual testimony, you can pass over them, and should.

9. If applicable, or as an aid to the attorney, draw a schematic map or diagram or chart to help explain.

10. Ignore the "objections" made by the attorneys while taking of the deposition.

11. Write a brief, more or less chronological narrative of what the witness testified to (if possible).

12. Make a list of lines and page numbers where particular answers were important to a point in issue (state the point).

EXAMPLE

Demand for return of deposit made:

     Page 25   Line 20

     Page 46   Line 13

Credit application a condition of the contract:

     Page 49   Line 12

     Page 66   Line 14

Preparing Your Summaries

Since a major part of your job is summarization of medical reports, depositions, interrogatory responses, request for admissions, and perhaps responses to a request for production of documents, it is appropriate that we discuss in some detail the manner in which and the approach to prepare these summaries.

While it can be argued that there is no black-and-white way, or set rule, for developing a summary, there are some basics which you can adhere to . . . a skeleton, if you will.

A "summary" (like a brief) is what the word says. If you are given a transcript that contains one thousand pages, turning in to the attorney a five-hundred-page summary is out of the question. The same is true of a deposition. So how do we reduce it? *That is the question.* We submit the following tried and proven methodology:

Transcripts and Depositions

1. When given an assignment by your attorney, be sure you understand just what it is the attorney is seeking, e.g., inconsistency in testimony, rulings of the court on objections, etc.

2. Cursorily review the first ten pages or so of the transcript, to get a feel of it. If the transcript is short, quickly review the entire document before commencing your summary.

3. Home in to only those things which are germane to the subject about which your attorney is concerned. I caution you not to think for your attorney; and do not interpret what the witness stated under oath. If necessary, to make the point, quote verbatim what the witness or client or defendant stated.

4. *Do not* paraphrase a statement made by a defendant. Paralegals do not make judgments as to what should be included in a summary; this is for the attorney alone. If you feel that something has been stated or emphasized which would be a benefit to the attorney, it is suggested that you make a side note on a separate sheet of paper of this fact.

5. Determine what format your office uses or should use given the particular transcript. For critical witnesses, the more detailed topical organization may be warranted rather than the simpler page-and-line method. In Figure 9.2 you will notice that the testimony is arranged by topic and does not solely follow consequential pages.

Figure 9.2

Deposition Summary
of
Monica Lewinsky
Senate of the United States sitting for the trial of the Impeachment of William Jefferson Clinton, President of the United States

February 4, 1999

Topic Page: Line	Summary

EXAMINATION BY MR. BRYANT

General Background

1: 17–21	Current Residence
2: 1–15	Review of college education & degree earned

Washington Internship

2: 18–21	Reason for pursuing an internship at the White House
2: 23–29	Application process for internship
2: 30	Internship begins July 10, 1995

White House Access

3: 12–16	Distinction between the pink & blue passes of the White House.
3: 20–21	Access held by Ms. Lewinsky (pink- limited to Old Executive Bldg.)
7: 13–17	President's comment as regards to Ms. Lewinsky's pink pass
29: 11–18	Discussion of Waves pass and how Ms. Lewinsky would gain this access to meet with President Clinton

Figure 9.2 (*continued*)

Nature of Seeking Job Opportunities in New York

16: 10–14	President suggest it may be more difficult for the public to "find" Monica if working in New York opposed to Washington
16: 22–26	President Clinton requests that Monica prepare a "Wish List" of people she would like to work with.
17: 1–5	Monica prepares a list and hands over to Ms. Currie.
55: 15–20	November 7, after signing her Affidavit Monica proceeds to New York to resume interviewing

Encounters with President Clinton

4: 22–28	Initial encounter with President Clinton in November 1995
6: 14–21	First point in time Ms. Lewinsky spoke with President Clinton
12: 13–17	Means Monica used to transport from Pentagon to White House for meetings with the President.
12: 24–31	Meetings were arranged with the President through Ms. Betty Currie, the President's secretary
12: 32–33	Visitations were off the record. To ensure nature of the visits would remain unknown.
19: 13–20	December 6, 1997 Monica receives another meeting with President. She requested this meeting one day prior after contacting Mr. Jordan post interview.
19: 20–30	Social encounter with President at White House Christmas Party
29: 31–34	Arrangement of meetings with President Clinton through Betty Currie
30: 1–5	Weekend meetings with President Clinton while Monica worked at the Pentagon
32: 11–17	Depiction of incident where the President first made physical contact with Ms. Lewinsky

Telephone Conversations with President

20: 11–14	Prior to her meeting with on December 6, 19897 Monica engaged in a telephone call with the President.
20: 21–30	Description of verbal altercation during the phone call between Monica and the President.
21: 2–5	President appeared angered by Monica's reaction to an earlier incident.
23: 3–5	December 17, 1997 President Clinton contacted Ms. Lewinsky
23: 14–17	President informs Monica during the phone call she is named as a witness in the Paula Jones case.
27: 13–16	President relays concerns to Monica that phone conversations may be tapped.

Figure 9.2 (*continued*)

31: 15–20   After morning phone conversation with the President, it was understood Monica would deny her relationship with the President to the Jones Lawyers.

Nature of Relationship with President Clinton

10: 12–15   Ms. Lewinsky confides with others on details of her relationship with President Clinton

11: 24–30   Brief description of physical nature of relationship with President

28: 12–18   Explanation of emotional perspective regarding issues relating to Paula Jones, Kathleen Willey.

35: 12–20   Lewinsky characterizes her relationship as physical absent of sexual intercourse.

Interrogatory/Request for Admissions

Summarizing these discovery documents can be the most difficult of the legal tasks assigned, in that you *must* set forth the answer of the respondent as stated. *Do not paraphrase it or state what you assumed they meant to say.* If you feel that there is an inconsistency in the answers, note or flag it for your attorney's attention.

When doing these types of summaries, you should have the questions and statements, as well as the answers, before you. You should attempt to include the question or statement in the summary of your responses so that your attorney will know what was being asked and answered.

Medical Reports

These are the easiest summaries to do since, unless otherwise requested, the only thing you are looking for is past history of a preexisting injury, or an injury similar to the one at hand and the corresponding treatments including drugs. Remember, the attorneys have medical experts to read and analyze these medical records and explain what they mean. This is not your job.

Production of Documents and Things

If other discovery is to be effective and your attorney is to be successful in the trial of the action, he must be aware of the existence of any pertinent documentation relevant to the subject matter of the lawsuit. In some cases, copies are sufficient, such as copies of medical reports supplied by a hospital.

Your client may know of the existence of such documents and who might have custody of them. (Question the client about this.) Or you may discover the existence of such documents during other discovery, such as during a deposition or in an answer to an interrogatory.

These documents could have been discovered by you when receiving the answers to the interrogatories heretofore received and/or through reviewing, summarizing, or digesting the various depositions. If so discovered, you can move for their production, copying, and inspection through the use of a notice or request to produce, compelling a party to produce relevant documents for inspection. You may also force a party-litigant or nonparty to permit inspection of tangible evidence such as machinery, real property, and the like.

A notice or request to produce does not usually have to state reasons for the production. If the notice or request is attacked by a motion for a protective order made by opposing counsel, then reasons must be given.

The federal court rules and many state rules do not require that reasons be stated in the notice or request to produce. See F.R.C.P. 34. The request must list the items to be inspected either by individual item or by category and must describe the item or category with reasonable particularity so that the person served or the custodian of the records requested (or other appropriate personnel) is able to identify and obtain them.

The request or notice to produce can be used to inspect stationary objects or objects too big or heavy to move, such as machinery or a large number of stored items, as well as documents. The most recent change has been the addition of access to electronically stored information. See F.R.C.P. 34(a)(1)(A).

Real estate may also be inspected in response to a request to produce.

Sample language for drafting a request for production of documents and things and real property under F.R.C.P. 34 follows in Figure 9.3.

Figure 9.3
Request for the Production of Documents and Entry upon Land

Attorneys for Plaintiffs

_____	
Plaintiff	DOCKET NO.:
v.	PLAINTIFF'S REQUEST TO PRODUCE BOTH DOCUMENTS AND THINGS AND TO INSPECT REAL ESTATE
_____	
Defendants.	

Figure 9.3 (*continued*)

Pursuant to Federal Rule of Civil Procedure 34, plaintiff, _____ , requests defendant, _____, to respond within thirty (30) days to the following requests:

1. That defendant produce and permit plaintiff to inspect and to copy each of the following documents:

    (Here should be listed the documents, either individually or by category, a succinct, clear description of each.)

    (Also here should be stated the time, place, and manner of making the inspection and other related acts.)

2. That defendant produce and permit plaintiff to inspect and to copy, test, or sample each of the following objects:

    (Here should be listed the objects, either individually or by category with a clear, succinct description of each object.)

    (Here again, you should state the time, place, and manner of making the inspection and other related acts.)

3. That defendant permit plaintiff to enter (describe property to be entered) and to inspect and photograph, test or sample (briefly describe that portion of the real property and objects to be inspected).

    (Here, again, you should set forth the time, the place and the manner of making the inspection and any other related acts.

(Signature)

_____

Attorney for Plaintiff

Address

CERTIFICATE OF SERVICE (on the parties)

_____

Attorney for Plaintiff

Have the attorney sign the request and the certificate of service. File the original of the request to produce and mail copies of it to the party to whom it is directed. Most court rules require that copies must be mailed to all parties (unless excused by court order and when the parties are numerous).

Physical and Mental Examination

A notice and motion for physical and mental examination of a party is used primarily in personal injury, medical practice, and workmen's compensation litigation, since it is in these types of lawsuits and claims that the mental and physical condition of a litigant becomes an issue.

Those matters are also an issue in a proceeding for appointment of a guardianship for an alleged incompetent, but special court rules apply in such a proceeding.

As a paralegal you will know of an expert in the medical field pertinent to the injury who can and may be used prior to and at the time of trial. Opposing counsel may want to, and normally does, use his own medical expert. Opposing counsel will prepare and file the motion in such case. Or the attorneys for both sides may agree to use the same doctor. The person to be examined must also agree or it will be necessary to get a court order for the examination.

Once the examining physician has been agreed upon by the parties, or the court has made an order, the moving party usually makes the appointment with the doctor for the party. The moving party is usually the defendant's attorney, and the party to be examined is usually the plaintiff or claimant.

The procedure for forcing the physical or mental examination of a party in a federal court action is provided in F.R.C.P. 35.

In both state and federal courts good cause must be shown for requiring the examination, which is obviously an invasion of privacy if it has not been consented to by the party to be examined, even if his consent could be implied by filing a lawsuit claiming physical or mental injury.

Therefore, if it is determined by your attorney that a physical examination is desired, it can be obtained by making a motion, on notice as prescribed by law, to be served on all the parties. In California, this motion too should be accompanied by a declaration stating the reason for the request (the showing of good cause) and a memo of points and authorities in support thereof.

The physician performing the examination is required to submit a detailed, narrative report, which in a workers' compensation case is to be served on all parties, and in a personal injury or medical malpractice case mailed, upon request, to the party examined. The party being examined may submit any previous medical reports and X-rays for the use and benefit of said physician.

> **NOTE:** Even if the physician files a report, you can still take his deposition. As a general rule the purpose of this type of motion for a physical or mental examination is to secure a copy of the doctor's findings and conclusions after examination where the defendant believes that the injuries complained of or sustained by plaintiff are not as severe as indicated.

As a plaintiff paralegal you should be aware that your client must comply with any order of court for a physical or mental examination. He has also waived the doctor-patient privilege in this circumstance, and opposing counsel has a right to see the medical report.

Organizing the Medical Record[1]

A large stack of medical records looks like a forbidding mass of scrawled handwriting and endless paper. You will find that in the copying process pages sometimes become mixed up. A copy service will usually number stamp the bottom of the page, so you have another frame of reference even if the pages are out of order. Many times the copying is very poor, making reading the record almost impossible. If erasures in the record are suspect, the original may have to be examined.

The secret to any task of this nature is organization. Not only will being organized make the report on the hospital records clearer, it will let you know, before starting the attack on the records, whether you possess every record you need, or whether you will have to complete the records by requesting the missing portions.

In tackling any record, you may want to get a clear picture of what it is about by reading the legible portions first and the scribbles next. Paper Post-it notes serve well to mark pages and passages as you begin the task.

The separate sections—for example, the doctor's orders—can then be chronologically summarized. The summary of each section should correlate when completed to give the total picture of each day spent at the hospital. If there are any discrepancies, they should be detectable when the summaries are compared in their chronological sequences.

Medications ordered should be listed, and it should be noted whether they were ordered and given or ordered and not given. Time of medicating could be very important, but realize that with the problem of contemporaneous charting, the time the medication is listed as given (usually when on medical rounds) is an approximation in most cases.

Allergies should be singled out on any charting so mistakes are avoided. If there was more than one hospitalization on the patient, check to see if the allergy to be avoided is the same.

An entire case can turn on the meaning of an abbreviation. When requesting documents from a hospital, be sure to request their manual for documenting medical records and their list of approved abbreviations.

When your summary of each day and stage of treatment is completed, the history of the patient and what was done to the patient should become clear.

A. Ownership of Records

In general, hospitals own their records. Physician's records belong to the physician. But this does not mean the patient does not have the right to review these records.

B. How Errors Are Made

Because of stressful working conditions, each and every department in a hospital has the possibility of making one or more errors daily. For example, just follow the route of the drug distribution system in a hospital.

Procedure	Possible Errors
1. Doctor orders meds for patient.	Medication may be inappropriate to treat illness. Prescription may be ambiguous or written incorrectly. Patient may be given meds or wrong dose of right meds.
2. Nurse incorrectly transcribes the doctor's orders.	
3. Drug ordered but not given.	
4. Extra dose error.	
5. Wrong time error.	
6. Wrong delivery mode.	Delivery mode includes: oral, sublingual (beneath the tongue), intranasal, inhalation therapy, intracutaneous, IM, IV, intra-arterial, intracardiac, intrathecal, rectal, vaginal, topical

C. Ask, What Happened?

Ask yourself why do we have this case? What type of case is this? It will save you much time in reading medical records if you know the degree of scrutiny expected by the litigation involved. For example, if the hospital, doctor, and/or dental records are in the file because of treatment given after a hit-and-run, the information that is most relevant would be diagnosis, the type of treatment given, and was there a trip to the emergency room or was the client/patient hospitalized for any length of time?

Document the time and expense involved, type of treatment, and if there is any outpatient charting to be done and kept elsewhere in the hospital. Did the injured take any medication? Did he use recreational drugs? Was he working with machinery? Or did the patient have severe allergies?

Freedom of Information Act

Products liability: In a products liability case involving a pharmaceutical, you may also have to subpoena the pharmacy records, including the record of buying the medication and information as to lot and batch. More technical information will be needed to assist the expert witness. Begin thinking of what material you may want to request to assist you in the case.

The Freedom of Information Act (FOIA) requires almost all federal agencies to release information requested by citizens. A list of Principal FOIA Contacts at Federal Agencies is available from the Department of Justice FOIA website (www.usdoj.gov/oip/foiacontacts.htm). Of particular relevance to product liability issues are the Departments of Health and Human Services FOIA contact (www.hhs.gov/foia) and its subdivision of the Food and Drug Administration (www.fda.gov/foi/default.htm).

Medical malpractice: It is understood that the strictest scrutiny of hospital records will be necessary for a medical malpractice case. This process will demand several readings of the record to re-create the picture as it was at the time of injury. Careful examination of the record could also tell you if there is a malpractice or not. But do not rely on the strictest scrutiny alone. Keep in mind all the factors that have to be discovered to show malpractice, and above all use common sense.

If your office has a computer that you can program to extract information, you can assemble it page by page and then retrieve it by department and have each department summary at hand.

What Else Are You Looking For?

The extent of injury/disability is corroborated by objective medical findings.

Objective	Subjective
Examiner can observe, by sight, touch, sound (scar, atrophied limb)	Determination of the existence of a condition depends solely upon patient's response (headache)

- When a claim is based on totally subjective complaints, see if the client is consistent. Lack of consistency suggests fabrication.

- Is there a pattern? Is there evidence of normal progressive healing?

- If diagnosis is based solely on patient history and subjective complaints, there is no actual medical corroboration of injury or disability.

- Objective language should always be used in the chart. A note that says a patient uses excessive pain medication, without an indication of an actual amount of pain medication and which medication is taken may be subject to dispute.

Organization Is the Secret

- Find out what type of case you are working on. Keep in mind the problems of proof you will have to face sometime in this case. Ascertain what degree of scrutiny is expected of you.

- Chronological order for all departments in the medical file reconstructs what was being done and any improvement or lack of improvement. Make certain there are no pages or major portions missing. If there are records missing, ask why and find them.

- If the handwriting is driving you mad, read the legible parts first, mark the rest with Post-its or colored paper clips, then fill in the blanks.

- Remember, each section of the chart should correlate with the other sections of the chart.

- Dental records are the easiest of medical records to read. Before beginning, familiarize yourself with a chart of the teeth and the numerical significance given to each tooth to identify it.

- If a case requires the records of the administrative portion of the hospital, be sure and get the hospital procedures as guidelines. If the hospital is one of the defendants, do not forget to get the corporate guidelines and find out which services are contracted for (e.g., janitorial), insurance coverage, etc.

- Records from a doctor's office may not be as extensive as the hospital records, but may be just as revealing in preparing your case. Sometimes a doctor will write the amount he is going to charge the patient somewhere on the page with his diagnosis. This could be extremely damaging in certain cases.

- At times, a doctor writes his uncertainty into the record noting some symptoms and then adding "other problems," opening the door for an accusation of incompetence.

- If the words "ordered a thorough workup" are in the record without any indication of what was ordered and what the doctor considers a thorough workup, the rest of the chart will be a big guessing game, as it will be hard to surmise what was done and what was or was not found. This can make the doctor culpable for "padding" the bill if unnecessary tests are included in this workup.

- If a prescription record must be obtained from a local pharmacy, do not be satisfied with just the computer printout you may receive. When filled, the front of the prescription becomes a legal document. This front side should reveal name of patient, address, phone, age (sometimes), name of drug, amount, directions, refill instructions, and signature of doctor; and for controlled substances, federal narcotics number of physician.

- The pharmacist may write the price on the front. But the back of the prescription may reveal information about what transpired: number of refills given; whether generic was dispensed; if the store was short in stock and how many were dispensed; if compounding was necessary, the amount of ingredients compounded; etc. Be certain to check both sides.

- If medical records are from another state or part of the country, there may be some difference in abbreviations and meanings. If this is the case, then you need to have the hospital manual listing the meanings and abbreviations that are part of staff protocol.

- Sometimes the writing will be absolutely impossible to decipher. Don't frustrate yourself by fixating on those words. They may or may not eventually be read. Just try to do your best on all the other parts of the record.

Records Separate from Patient Medical Record

There are other types of medical records you may or may not require for your case that will not be in the hospital record. They will not be in the doctor's office records either. Some of them may be in the consulting physician's office records on your patient, the visiting nurse records, or the school nurse or employment infirmary records.

If you have a problem with medical equipment or a medical device, you will need maintenance records; request forms; engineering preventive maintenance records; manufacturer's guidelines for maintenance; and lot, batch, and serial numbers of equipment.

Since a hospital has policy manuals for everything it does, it is best initially to subpoena a list of the tables of contents of the hospital's manuals and then request the manuals that apply to your case. Hospital policies are evidence of the standard of care.

Some courts recognize that strict liability can be applied to a hospital when mechanical and administrative services are considered separate from medical service, eliminating the sales/service dichotomy.[2]

You may need every clue to have all the pieces of the puzzle fall into place. Above all, if you are convinced the answer is somewhere in these hieroglyphics, keep looking, you will find it. If what you are seeking is not in the medical records, other sources to inspect are:

- Hospital bylaws
- Department protocols

- Risk management records

- Procedure manuals for each department

- JCAHO (Joint Commission on Accreditation of Healthcare Organizations) manual[3]

- State licensing requirements

- Federal requirements

Lawyers have their own language just as doctors have their own language. While medical terms are Latin and Greek in their origin, it is hoped the resources listed above will make them understandable.

Discovery Enforcement Orders (Sanctions)

A. The Deposition

Court rules provide for enforcement of deposition discovery where a party-litigant has noticed a deposition or sent out a set of interrogatories requiring the adverse party to attend the deposition or answer the interrogatories. Should the defending party fail to respond to either, the moving party may make an application to the court requesting the court to do so. See F.R.C.P. 37.

If a party fails to show up for his deposition, the court on written motion of a party may:

1. Strike all or portions of any pleading heretofore filed by the defendant

2. Dismiss the complaint or portions thereof

3. Enter a judgment by default against the defendant and in favor of plaintiff

4. Grant such other and further relief as to the court deems just and proper, including but not limited to attorney's fees

The only recourse open to a moving party when a nonparty witness fails to appear for the taking of his deposition is a "motion for contempt of court." This is proper since, if you recall, a nonparty witness has to be subpoenaed to attend a deposition, and therefore his failure or refusal to comply with the subpoena is in contempt of court.

During a deposition, a witness who has appeared for the deposition and is being deposed may refuse to answer one or more questions, or an attorney may object to certain questions but allow his client to answer.

If the client refuses to answer or his attorney does not allow him to answer, opposing counsel has a right to apply to the court for an "order to compel" the answer—see F.R.C.P. 37(a)—as well as file a motion for sanctions for failure to comply with the court's order to compel.

B. Interrogatories or Requests to Produce

Answers to interrogatories and responses to requests to produce (as well as answers given to depositions) are useful to your attorney not only at the time of the trial of the action, but in nailing down the contentions of the parties and the testimony of prospective witnesses before the trial. For that reason the court rules providing for compelling a party to answer interrogatories and respond to requests to produce are important to him.

Hence, if the defending party either fails to respond at all or only answers incompletely to any question (such as if, in answering, he has admitted that he has expert witnesses or that he plans to call such witnesses, but he has failed to give you the requested names and addresses of those expert witnesses), you are in a position to make a motion to compel the party to give the names and addresses, or otherwise completely answer particular questions. See Figure 9.4 for a sample of this type of motion.

Figure 9.4

Attorneys for Plaintiffs

_____	
Plaintiff	DOCKET NO.:
v.	
	PLAINTIFF'S MOTION TO COMPEL
_____	MORE DEFINITE ANSWERS TO
Defendants.	INTERROGATORIES

Pursuant to the rules of civil procedure, plaintiff by and through his undersigned attorney, respectfully requests this court for an order requiring the Defendant to provide full and complete answers to the plaintiff's interrogatories served on ___ (date) ____.

1. As to interrogatory #5, defendant's answer is incomplete and unresponsive as the defendant did not provide any factual basis for his assertions.
2. As to interrogatory #8, defendant has merely attached documents in response to this question, but has not provided any information as to the source or chain of custody of these documents. Further, there remain unanswered questions in these interrogatories that the documents themselves do not answer.
3. As to interrogatories #12–15, the moving party further requests the court for an order compelling the defendant to answer those interrogatories to which he objected. The plaintiff refers the court to its supporting brief filed herewith which demonstrates that

Figure 9.4 (*continued*)

the defendant's objections are without merit and the plaintiff is entitled to the information sought.

Plaintiff, in good faith, has attempted to resolve these issues with the Defendant without the need for court intervention, but these efforts have been to no avail. The documentation of these efforts has been attached hereto as Exhibit A and the attorney of record has supplied the certification of same.

Further, plaintiff requests that this court award to plaintiff all costs and fees associated with this motion.

(Signature)

_____

Attorney for Plaintiff

Address

CERTIFICATE OF SERVICE (on the parties)

_____

Attorney for Plaintiff

Electronic Discovery (e-Discovery)

The most dramatic changes in litigation have been the result of the use of technology in every aspect of our lives. Increasingly, records are not kept on paper, but rather electronically in word processing documents, emails, databases, and a multitude of software systems. On December 1, 2006, the Federal Rules of Civil Procedure were changed to reflect the reality that almost all records that will be created for and needed in litigation are created electronically and so a means to access these documents was required. This is the system of e-discovery.

There are serious implications to this that you must understand and be able to convey to your clients. Parties have an obligation to preserve their electronically stored information as soon as litigation is anticipated over a matter. The Federal Rules impose a "litigation hold" on the retention of this electronic information.

Data is also not necessarily stored in an accessible manner. Backups or data that has been stored in now-outdated platforms or operating systems may be random and unindexed. This kind of information is considered inaccessible because it would cause undue burden and expense to create a way to retrieve and organize it.

Further, the Delete key never really deletes information from an information system. There are ways to detect and re-create that information and any tampering that may have been done to it. The very fact of the attempted modification or deletion may be discoverable and has implications for spoliation of evidence. F.R.C.P. 37(f) address the concerns of "routine document retention, deletion or overwriting."

Adding to the complications of producing the masses of electronic data is the issue of "metadata," where the information about the information is stored. This is where the evidence regarding deletions or modifications is found. It is the underlying structure that supports the information that you see in the display.

There has been such extensive coverage of all the nuances of e-discovery and of course, most of it can be found on the Internet in electronic form. It would be impossible to cover the subject in just part of this chapter. Further, at the time of printing, it may be already outdated! Keeping updated in this developing area of law (it changes as the technology changes) is essential. This is where Continuing Legal Education conferences and sessions are invaluable. A good place to start is the Federal Judiciary Committee's webpage, which lists an extensive array of articles on this subject (www.fjc.gov/public/home.nsf/autoframe?openform&url_l=/public/home.nsf/inavgeneral?openpage&url_r=/public/home.nsf/pages/196).

For a state-by-state list of the new e-discovery rules, go to www.ediscoverylaw .com/2008/01/articles/resources/current-listing-of-states-that-have-enacted-ediscovery-rules.

CHAPTER TEN

Admissibility and Use of Evidence

Theory and Concept of Evidence

The paralegal should have a thorough working knowledge and understanding of the *basic* rules of evidence that govern the admissibility or inadmissibility of facts, documents, testimony, and so forth. That basic knowledge will help develop evidence through discovery procedures when the paralegal is aiding the attorney in preparing for trial. This chapter will address only those elements of evidence relevant to the duties performable by a paralegal in an on-the-job situation.

The Federal Rules of Evidence can be accessed at www.law.cornell.edu/rules/fre. Further, most states (thirty-eight of fifty) have adopted the Uniform Rules of Evidence. The full text of the Uniform Rules and the links to the individual state rules can be found at (www.law.cornell.edu/uniform/evidence.html).

In addition, because of the overwhelming increase in the use of computers in both legal research and fact gathering, the effect and use of computer evidence will also be discussed and samples will be shown relating to the admissibility of computer data as well as testimony or more traditional documentary evidence.

In this connection, the paralegal must know what rules affect the admissibility or inadmissibility of traditional evidence, as well as what those rules provide in regard to the admissibility, inadmissibility, or acceptability of that evidence. Expert testimony explaining the programming of software, data compilation, and operation of computer systems is often necessary and relevant in complex modern litigation.

Facts are the backbone of any case. Evidence is the means used to prove an ultimate fact. Evidentiary facts are the bits and pieces of fact presented to a court during the trial for the purpose of proving the ultimate facts necessary to allow the plaintiff to recover or the defendant to prevail in the case.

The rules of evidence are designed to do the following:

1. Set up a series of rules by which the court can referee court procedure or, if you like, by which a lawsuit can be tried and

2. More important, to insure that whatever testimony is received and presented to the court, oral or documentary, is trustworthy, reliable, and relevant information.

Evidence is anything offered to prove the existence or nonexistence of a fact. It may be oral testimony, writings, photographs, charts, or the like.

What are some of the elements of admissible evidence? It

1. Must be relevant to the issues,

2. Must be something that can be perceived,

3. Must tend to prove or disprove a relevant fact, and

4. Must be useful to the trier of fact in rendering a decision as to the truth of the ultimate fact that is sought to be proved by the offered evidentiary fact.

Types of Evidence
Documentary Evidence

Documents are written pieces of evidence, and they must be authenticated in one of three ways in order to be admissible at trial. They must be certified, judicially noticed, or testified to.

A. Exemplified or Certified Documents

This type of document may be a public document of one type or another, such as a deed, a birth certificate, or a death certificate, with an official seal stamp thereon. These documents have a high degree of reliability for the truth because the custodian of the document can demonstrate a clear chain of possession and they are easily verifiable.

Since it is well known that documentary evidence often has much more impact on a jury than oral testimony of a witness, the paralegal has the double duty and responsibility to see that all documents to be used as evidence by the attorney are: (1) gathered together in one place and (2) are exemplified or certified by the proper authority if necessary to make them admissible without testimony of the custodian of the public record.

A. By attestation of the clerk of the court, with the seal of the court affixed; or the officer in whose custody the record is legally kept, under seal of his office. *A* is "certification."
B. By a certificate of the chief judge or presiding magistrate of the court, to the effect that the person so attesting the record is the clerk of the court, or that he is the officer in whose custody the record is required by law to be kept, and that his signature to the attestation is genuine. *B* is "exemplification."
C. By notarization before a duly licensed notary public, etc. *C* is "notarization."

If opposing counsel does not or may not agree to stipulate to the admissibility of a certified copy of a document, it is best for the paralegal to obtain an exemplified copy, unless the document is part of the record in a case or other situation where the court can take judicial notice of it.

B. Judicial Notice of Documents

The court, at the trial, may take "judicial notice" of certain public documents, such as the documents in the files of its own or other courts in the state where it is located. Its purpose is to avoid unnecessary formalities where it is clear that the document is what it purports to be and there is very little possibility that the parties can or would object to its admission. This can also include common documents from reliable public sources, such as maps and newspapers. Check the rules of evidence in your jurisdiction for judicial notice.

Some court rules require that a written request for judicial notice be filed before trial. If so, prepare for that document.

As a practical matter, it is wise also to get a certified copy, which may or may not be admissible but is a convenient way of learning the exact contents to the document that the court is judicially noticing.

C. Authenticated by Testimony

During the trial of the action, if the attorney wishes to introduce a document that has not been exemplified or judicially noticed as authentic, he must lay the foundation for the introduction of that document. He must prove by the sworn testimony of someone who has personal knowledge of the origin and retention of the document that the document is what he alleges it to be and means what he claims it to mean.

Take, for example, a promissory note. The attorney has to satisfy the court that it is the duly executed promissory note entered into between the parties. He can do this by several different means:

1. One of the parties can testify to the fact that the promissory note was executed in his presence;

2. One of the parties can give testimony as to his signature on the document; or

3. A third party, as a notary or other subscribing witness, can identify the document by testifying that it was signed in his presence.

EXAMPLE

Q: Mr. Brown, I show you this paper and ask you if you recognize it.

A: Yes.

Q: Did you see anyone sign it?

A: Yes.

Q: Who signed it?

A: The defendant, John Jones.

Q: When did he sign it?

A: On October 15, 20—.

Q: After that paper was signed by the defendant, what did he do with it?

A: He gave it to me.

Q: Has it been in your possession since then?

A: Yes.

The document would then be offered into evidence because the two elements for admission have been satisfied—verification of authenticity and proof of chain of custody. It is not enough to know that the witness recognizes it, but also that its integrity has been maintained because the witness knows where it has been, who could have had access to it, and that it was not altered.

D. Electronic Evidence (e-Evidence)

The admission of electronic documentary evidence, in particular email, is somewhat more complicated. While emails have overtaken much of the correspondence in both the personal and business spheres, they are not as reliable as traditionally written documents. Anyone with access to a computer and your personal information can assume your identity and send emails in your name. Indeed, some emails do not contain the sender's name at all. Email just does not have the same formality and integrity, as it can be manipulated and edited very easily without those alterations being facially perceptible.

For this reason, it becomes essential to authenticate through testimony the electronic documents that you intend to rely upon at trial. Affidavits, depositions, stipulations can all be used to verify the accuracy of the information contained in the e-evidence. It is also wise to check the most recent case law in your jurisdiction for those electronic sources that can be "self-authenticated" under your jurisdiction's version of FRE 902. This may include the URL or other identifying information as to the source of the information.

Demonstrative Evidence

"Demonstrative evidence" is non-documentary evidence that can be exhibited or shown to the court. It can be any sort of tangible object or demonstration that would tend to prove the existence of an underlying, ultimate fact. It must also be authenticated before it can be considered for admission. Again, the party offering the object must prove that it is what it purports to be. In some cases, a model or replica of the object can serve as evidence. It must be made clear to the court and stipulated between the parties that this is the case.

When would a model be acceptable? When the substitution has no effect on the purpose of its admission. If the question is whether a certain model of fire extinguisher could douse a kitchen grease fire, then another fire extinguisher of the same model could be discharged to determine if it also had the same capacity. As the original had already been discharged, it would not be possible to use it for a subsequent demonstration.

Computer re-creations through animations are also a kind of demonstrable evidence. This evidence makes the concepts easier to visualize and understand than oral testimony. Again, the use of technology has and continues to change the character of litigation. Recall that the creators of demonstrable evidence will have to testify to its veracity and accuracy.

Before and during the trial, the paralegal may have to keep track of for the attorney the whereabouts of the demonstrative evidence. Its integrity and accessibility at the moments when it is needed can be the responsibility of the paralegal.

Testimony

Testimony is the oral response to oral questions asked by the attorneys during the trial. The answers must be statements of fact, not opinion, unless the witness has been qualified as an expert on the given subject.

To qualify a witness as an expert, the attorney may introduce at the trial any or all of several criteria as the qualifying groundwork: education, experience, recognition by associations and organizations in the field, and/or authorship of publications on the subject.

The proposed expert usually testifies to these. His statements are taken as true unless they are objected to by opposing counsel. Prior to trial, opposing counsel may want to stipulate that the witness is an expert or he may not.

NOTE: When arranging for calling an expert witness who has not testified as a witness in court before, it is best to explain to him before the trial that he should have this information immediately available, preferably in writing, to refresh his recollection at the time of trial.

A review of the two following cases will demonstrate the importance of the testimony of an expert witness in the trial of a case and its intersection with technology. The first case, *West v. Martin*, 11 Kan. App.2d 55, 713 P.2d 957 (1986), is a case in which an attempt was made to use computer evidence to form an expert opinion and as demonstrative evidence. However, the computer information could not be properly admitted because it was not admitted through the appropriate expert.

In this matter, the expert attempting to rely on computerized test material was an orthopedic surgeon. The test in question was the Minnesota Multiphasic Personality Inventory, which is scored and interpreted by a computer and which the expert claimed he routinely used to aid him in the diagnosis and evaluation of his patients. The court held that the test was inadmissible as hearsay. "The analysis or interpretive summary make the computer the declarant of the hearsay evidence." Therefore, the expert, although he was familiar with the test, did not perform the analysis; he had to rely upon the computerized results. Experts cannot testify as to their own opinion when it is based upon hearsay, even when that hearsay emanates from a computerized analysis. The doctor as an expert witness was not the appropriate witness to lay the foundation for the admission of that test.

By contrast, the admission of computer-generated animation as demonstrable evidence can have a significant impact if properly admitted through an expert. See *Commonwealth of Pennsylvania v. Serge*, 586 Pa. 671, 896 A.2d 1170 (2006).

The defendant was convicted of first degree murder of his wife. Part of the evidence against him was a computer-generated animation (CGA) that was based upon the expert opinion of the state's forensic pathologist, which was in turn based upon the forensic and physical evidence available. The evidence was deemed admissible because the person responsible for its content was available at trial to authenticate the demonstrable evidence.

A CGA should be admissible if it satisfies the [evidentiary] requirements. When the CGA is used to illustrate an opinion that an expert has arrived at without using the computer, the fact that the visual aid was generated by a computer does not matter because the witness can be questioned and cross-examined concerning the perceptions or opinions to which the witness testifies. In that situation, the computer is no more or less than a drafting device.[4]

Circumstantial Evidence

"Circumstantial evidence" is indirect evidence. It proves the circumstances surrounding the fact rather than the fact itself. The fact-finder must make a logical connection between the offered evidence and the ultimate fact that needs to be established. In other words, it is one step removed from proof of the fact. This is why it is critical to establish a clear link between the circumstances and the inferences that can be drawn therefrom. Circumstantial evidence may consist of any type of evidence, as documentary or demonstrative or testimony.

But, as in admitting direct evidence of a fact, the circumstantial evidence must be of some probative value. It must tend to prove that the main fact is true because it creates a reasonable factual inference that the main fact is true, and it must come from a reliable source.

EXAMPLE

"Testimony" that a defendant in a criminal case was seen running away from the house where someone was killed a few minutes after the killing occurred
and
Demonstrative evidence that he laundered his clothes in bleach immediately afterward, and so forth.

If you must prove a case by circumstantial evidence, you must be sure the evidence you offer would lead a reasonable person to infer that the ultimate fact you are trying to prove is true. You may have to prove more than one circumstantial fact, and you will need to prove it to the standard applicable in the kind of case you are trying. In other words, the circumstantial evidence in a criminal case would have to demonstrate that the underlying fact was true "beyond a reasonable doubt." The potential perils of how this evidence should be presented was aptly demonstrated in the O. J. Simpson case. The bloody glove was circumstantial evidence; the fact that those designer gloves were labeled as O. J. Simpson's size and that he owned a pair just like them should have been enough to lead a reasonable person to believe that they could have been his. However, once the prosecution permitted him to try them on, they lost control over the evidence, and the defendant was able to dispel the inference that the jury could have made by showing that they did not fit his hands.

In *In re James D.*, 116 Cal. App. 3d 810, 172 Cal. Rptr. 321 (1981), the defendant was found to have stolen property in his home. Without any direct evidence that the defendant took the jewelry, the prosecutor was able to prove the case by circumstantial evidence. The court inferred that the defendant knew the property was stolen, because it was found in his possession soon after the it was stolen and its presence there was not explained satisfactorily by the defendant. These were the suspicious circumstances that surrounded his possession of the stolen jewelry.

Rules of Evidence

It is generally stated that all evidence that is *relevant* is admissible unless it is excepted by the rules of evidence applicable in the court where the case is being tried. Relevant evidence is that offer of proof that has "any tendency to make the existence of any fact that is of consequence to the determination of the action more probable or less probable than it would be without the evidence." See F.R.E. 401. This sounds very broad, but in practice, relevant evidence must also be *admissible* in order to be used in the prosecution or defense of a case. Relevant evidence will not be deemed admissible for one of two reasons: (1) there is a defect in its acquisition or authentication or (2) under Rule 403, "if its probative value is substantially outweighed by the danger of unfair prejudice, confusion of the issues, or misleading the jury, or by considerations of undue delay, waste of time, or needless presentation of cumulative evidence."

Relevant Evidence

The first hurdle to be overcome in determining whether some evidence will be useful and admissible is to establish its relevancy. While the fact that it was dark and rainy on the night a contract was entered into may be completely accurate and reliable, it is irrelevant to the cause of action for a breach of contract. On the other hand, that same fact is relevant in a case involving a car accident, as the conditions of sight distances and road surface may have influenced the occurrence.

Since a paralegal will be dealing with the facts of a case and doing the legal research to support the theory and strategy for the attorney, we will deal at some length with illustrative ways in which allegations should and can be supported by the weight of evidence. To do this we shall use a hypothetical case and address ourselves to it for clarity.

Assuming we have alleged negligence on the part of the defendant, the matters to be considered when trying to find evidence of that negligent conduct on the part of a defendant may be as follows:

1. That the conduct of defendant fell below the standard of care of an ordinary prudent man;

2. That there was a violation of a statute;

3. That defendant failed to perform a duty other than one prescribed by statute;

4. That by defendant's failure to perform reasonably and with ordinary care, a duty that he volunteered to perform proximately caused plaintiff's injury;

5. That defendant violated a duty that was prescribed by a contract;

6. Judicial notice; and

7. Application of the doctrine of *res ipsa loquitur*.

STATEMENT OF FACTS (HYPOTHETICAL)

Jane Jones and her baby, passengers on the Silver Meteor from Washington, DC, to Miami, Florida, were killed in a collision between the Silver Meteor and the Blue Special, both trains owned and operated by Southern Trains. Jane Jones and her baby purchased first class tickets from Washington, DC, on December 28, 2003. The trip was uneventful until the Silver Meteor reached the outskirts of the little town of Blainey, South Carolina, where the collision occurred. Several coaches were derailed, and as a result of the derailment, Jane Jones and her baby were crushed to death between the seats of the coach in which they were riding.

These are the facts you have obtained from the husband of the decedent. Your attorney now asks you to prepare a memorandum of law to establish negligence on the part of the defendant. You immediately know that it is a wrongful death action. Where do you start?

You might start with establishing step 5 in the list, "defendant violated a duty that was prescribed by a contract." Since we know the burden will be on your attorney to prove that the decedent had a legal right to be on the train, we must establish privity of contract. To do this you must have evidence of the purchase of first class tickets by Jane Jones and baby.

You therefore will do any of the following (or you may rely on the presumption discussed here):

1. Secure duplicate copies of the ticket, if they are available;

2. Secure a copy of passenger list and have it authenticated by the appropriate officer or agency;

3. Subpoena copies of this list for copying by way of deposition or by a notice and motion for production of documents (see Chapter 9, "Pretrial Discovery");

4. If the tickets were purchased with a credit card or other means, secure copies of the invoice utilizing the procedures in step 3; or

5. The husband could testify that he bought the tickets, gave them to his wife, and put her and the baby on board the train.

Once you have established decedent's legal right to be on the train, your attorney can show that the defendant violated a duty of care in its negligent operation of an inherently dangerous instrument—that is, a railroad train. See Steps 2, 3, and 7 on page 209.

To aid you with this phase (if you cannot get the evidence that Jane Jones was lawfully on the train), you should have a "presumption of law" in her favor. "A presumption of law is a rule of law that courts and judges shall draw a particular inference from a particular fact, or from particular evidence, unless and until the truth of such inference is disproved . . . a rule which, in certain cases, either forbids or dispenses with any ulterior inquiry." (*Black's Law Dictionary*, Revised Fourth Edition,

West Publishing Co.). A presumption of law may be "absolute" or "rebuttable."

The presumption of law involved in our facts is the rebuttable presumption that Jane Jones was lawfully aboard the Silver Meteor. The presumption is that all passengers aboard a passenger train are there lawfully. Presumption is the same as evidence that is presented to show that Jane Jones and her baby purchased a ticket and boarded the train at Union Station in Washington, DC. Either the presumption or the evidence will shift the burden or proceeding to the party seeking to establish the contrary, that is to say, that Jane Jones and her baby did not purchase a ticket and board the train at Union Station in Washington, DC, thereby not being lawfully upon the train at the time of the collision.

A legal passenger contract has now or will be established by your investigation here described, or your attorney has decided or will decide to rely on the presumption of lawful passage as discussed.

The most important question for your consideration in establishing negligent conduct on the part of the defendant in this case is the application of the doctrine of *res ipsa loquitur*, "the thing speaks for itself." Even though you are not an attorney, you should basically understand this doctrine and how and when it is applicable.

If your attorney intends to rely on this doctrine, he does not have as great a burden of producing evidence to establish negligence on the part of the railroad.

However, the following facts should be investigated to determine:

1. *That the accident that occurred was the type of accident that would not have occurred had it not been for the negligence of the defendant.* An investigator might also have an on-site investigation to determine if the rails were defective; whether the brakes on the train were defective; whether they needed repairs; whether the trainman was drunk or had been drinking; whether he had poor eyesight; whether he wore glasses and, if so, whether he had them on at the time of the collision, and so forth. If the doctrine of *res ipsa loquitur* applies, you do not have to prove the exact nature of a defect in the train or exactly what the employee did wrong.

2. *That the defendant (or agent, servant, employee) had exclusive control of the train.* To establish this, secure names, addresses, and capacity or title of the person driving or manning the train at the time of the collision and the immediate supervisor; get copies of payroll sheets and personnel files, and so forth. This information may be obtained by interrogatories directed to the railroad defendant.

3. *That the plaintiff in no way contributed to the accident, either voluntarily or otherwise.* You might establish this by seeking out survivors of the accident who may have witnessed the plaintiff and her baby, talked to her, aided her in some way, sat next to her on the train, and so forth. Contributory negligence is an affirmative defense that must be raised by the railroad company, but it doesn't hurt to be ready.

The facts of our case indicate a case for *res ipsa loquitur. Reason:* The trains were both wholly within the exclusive control of the defendant, and they are dangerous instruments. The attorney will decide what evidence he wants to present.

Now you must find some evidence of the fact that Jane Jones and her baby are dead as a result of the collision of the train in which they were lawful passengers *and* that the collision was the legal fault of the defendant railroad company.

You will not have to get evidence that a train is an inherently dangerous instrument. The attorney will ask the court to take judicial notice of that fact.

What is judicial notice? There are two types: facts that the court is bound to notice and facts that the court may notice (discretionary with the court). See your state code of evidence to determine which applies to the fact you want the court to judicially notice.

You will check the law as to the duty of a railroad to its lawful passengers (as opposed to hobos hitching a ride, fellow employees, and so forth). Is it an insurer or must you prove negligence? If you must prove negligence, does the doctrine of *res ipsa loquitur* apply?

Generally, if a dangerous instrument is in the sole custody and control of the defendant, the doctrine of *res ipsa loquitur* does apply.

Best Evidence Rule

This term may be a little misleading; it can also be called the "original document" rule. It applies only to tangible evidence, such as writings, recordings, and photographs, in order to prove their contents. For example, the best evidence of a written document is the original of the signed contract, deed, note, or so forth, if you are trying to prove the contents of the document.

Secondary evidence is admissible if the "best evidence" (the original document) is unavailable because it has been lost, destroyed, or is simply unobtainable. It is important to note that duplicates are often admissible. It is only when there is a genuine issue as to the authenticity of the offered duplicate that it is unacceptable. See F.R.E. 1003.

In *Seiler v. Lucasfilm Ltd.*, 808 F.2d 1316 (Cal. App. 1986), the plaintiff's drawings were considered "writings" under the best evidence rule. The plaintiff's claim was based upon copyright infringement by Lucasfilm of his drawings in the movie *The Empire Strikes Back*. However, the plaintiff could not produce his original drawings and so he had the burden of proving their loss or destruction through no fault of his own in order to submit his "reconstructions" of his original works. He failed to make this showing, and therefore, the court held that the matter was too susceptible to fraud or other bad faith to permit the secondary evidence of his "reconstructions" to be admissible.

A summary or chart of a voluminous document may be admissible, only if the original document would also be admissible. See F.R.E. 1006. This is often the case with electronic information stored in huge databases. The original must be available for inspection by all the parties and the court should they require it. The underlying principle of the best evidence rule is that of reliability and accuracy.

Parol Evidence Rule

"Parol (oral) evidence" is not admissible to alter or vary the terms of a written instrument. Courts let the writings speak for themselves. The language of the document should contain all the necessary information. This is a rule of substantive law and concerns itself with proving contested issues involving the content of a written instrument introduced in evidence at the time of trial.

The writing is considered to contain all the terms of the parties; therefore, no other evidence of the contents can be produced. This is usually contained in a "merger clause" in the document itself that specifically states that there are no other understandings between the parties other than those expressed therein.

Exceptions to the Parol Evidence Rule

1. If there is a mistake or imperfection in the writing and this imperfection is alleged by a statement to that effect in the pleadings;

2. Where the validity of the writing is the fact in dispute;

3. Where subsequent oral agreements concerning the writing are admissible; or

4. Where the writing is patently ambiguous but definite enough to be enforceable, for example, where a contract is entered into due to the fraud of one of the parties, the complaining party will be able to introduce evidence of the intentional misrepresentations of the other party by parol evidence. The fraudulent inducement creates a defect in the formation of the agreement. The complaining party is not challenging the contents of the writing by parol evidence; he is claiming that the writing is itself invalid.

Check your state code and case law to determine which, if any or all, of the foregoing are exceptions to the parol evidence rule in your state and how they have been construed by case law.

Hearsay Rule

"Hearsay evidence" is not generally admissible even though it may be relevant to the case. Hearsay evidence consists of out-of-court statements made by someone other than the "declarant" (the one testifying at the trial or hearing). It is a secondhand repetition of something that was heard from another. The prohibition against hearsay hinges upon reliability issues. After all, secondhand information is the basis for gossip.

If the declarant is asked to testify to such out-of-court statements, opposing counsel will object. If the witness gives testimony as to such statements, a verbal motion to strike may be granted.

Exceptions to the Hearsay Rule

Exceptions to the hearsay rule are based on the fact that certain hearsay may be reliable because of the circumstances under which the statement was made or written by someone other than the witness. Some examples are:

1. Excited utterance by another at the time of the accident or event (no time to think or scheme during the *res gestae*);

2. Statement for purposes of medical diagnosis or treatment made by patient to doctor where the patient has waived the doctor-patient privilege and the doctor is testifying or the medical report containing patient's statements is put in evidence;

3. Business records kept in the ordinary course of business, even though the witness did not make the entries at the time;

4. Records of vital statistics to prove the fact of birth, marriage, death, causes, and so forth;

5. Absence of public record or entry to prove that none was made;

6. Records of religious organizations to prove a birth or death;

7. Marriage, baptismal, or similar certificates;

8. Family records such as notations of significant family incidents in the family Bible;

9. Statements in ancient documents;

10. Market reports and commercial publications to prove a business trend or other business fact;

11. Reputation in the community concerning boundaries or general history of the community, where that is a relevant issue; and

12. Reputation in the community, where that is a relevant issue.

For a better understanding and explanation of the exceptions to the hearsay rule as well as other exceptions, we refer you to the Federal Evidence Code 28 U.S.C.A. 802, including the federal case law following that section of the U.S. Code in that annotated volume. Also, there are some excellent articles on the subject of hearsay and electronic documents, like email, available on the Internet. There is Law.com's *Legal Technology Journal* (www.law.com/jsp/legaltechnology/edd.jsp) and an article by Joan Feldman, president of Computer Forensics Inc., "Everything you wanted to know about email discovery, but were afraid to ask" (www.forensics.com/pdf/everything .pdf), and, of course, the *ABA Journal of Legal Technology* keeps you apace with the latest developments in the law (www.abajournal.com/topics/legal+technology) and general evidentiary issues (www.abajournal.com/topics/evidence).

Proving a Prima Facie Case

A prima facie case is one in which all the elements of the claim can be shown by the facts presented "at first view." This means that unless the facts are rebutted by the defendant, the plaintiff will win.

Your job as the paralegal will be to:

1. Research the elements necessary to prove the cause of action;

2. Establish factual evidence that corresponds to proving each element of the cause of action; and

3. Account for and rebut any defenses that the opposition may posit.

In an employment discrimination case the plaintiff would need to prove the following in a prima facie case:

1. She was a member of a protected class under the relevant statutory authority, e.g., race, gender, religion, etc.,

2. The job opportunity was open,

3. She met the minimum qualifications for the job or promotion,

4. She was not hired or she was terminated from a position for which she was qualified, and

5. The job remained open, or a person of another race, gender, or religion was hired for it.

Given these facts, the plaintiff has made a prima facie showing. However, the defendant has the opportunity to offer a nondiscriminatory reason for the rejection or termination of employment. If the defendant employer can offer some proof of this contention, then the plaintiff has the opportunity to prove that these were not the true reasons for exclusion, but rather a pretext for discrimination. See *Texas Dep't of Community Affairs v. Burdine*, 450 U.S. 248, 101 S.Ct. 1089 (1981).

Elements of Evidence as to Witnesses

The major portion of any courtroom testimony is from the mouths of lay witnesses with a few experts thrown in. It is for this reason that the laws of evidence are extremely strict when accepting or not accepting what a witness states as to the facts of a case. We will merely hit the highlights of the various facets of lay and expert witness testimony but will delve into detail about how you produce these witnesses at a trial.

There are two major rules governing witness testimony—*competency* and *privilege*. These are further broken down into ten or twelve subdivisions, which we do not believe have significance to a paralegal on a job situation.

Competency

As a general rule any and every person is qualified to be a witness and no one is disqualified to testify in any matter.

1. *Disqualification* of a witness must be based on a statutory ground. For example, one who is incapable of understanding the duty of a witness to tell the truth; or one who is incapable of expressing himself concerning the subject matter as to be understood either through interpretation or otherwise. However, with a statutory provision, competency of witness to testify is a matter to be determined by the court and depends solely upon his (the witness's) capacity to understand the oath and to perceive, remember, and communicate that which he remembers.

2. *Personal knowledge of witness:* Even if a witness is competent, he can only testify to facts of his personal knowledge. And personal knowledge has been defined as "a present recollection of an impression derived from the exercise of the witnesses' own senses." (2 *Wigmore, Evidence*, Section 657 (1940)) This being true, then any testimony by a witness that is outside of his personal knowledge would be inadmissible.

   Therefore, the testimony of any witness must meet the following test:

   a. He must be able to testify so as to be understood;

   b. He must understand the nature and responsibility of the oath administered, and

   c. He must have personal knowledge of the facts to which he is giving testimony (this statement is not true of an expert witness).

Let us skip to the next big category of restrictions:

Privileges

The reasons for invoking privileges as to witness testimony are due to matters of public policy, stable social order, and for religious reasons. That is why today anything said between an attorney and his client is considered "privileged information," as is anything said between the minister and his parishioner, priest and a penitent person, and why a wife (or husband) cannot be forced to testify against her husband (his wife). As you can see then, the mere fact that a witness is competent to testify does not mean that everything the witness has to say or knows can be inquired into.

When you get into the area of a witness "taking the Fifth" or refusing to testify because of some privilege, no presumption of guilt or innocence arises from the exercise of this privilege; and the fact that a witness has claimed the same cannot be used against him in any way.

The major and general provisions relating to privileges are as follows (your state may have other statutory privileges; you might check them if necessary):

1. No privileges exist except those established by statute.

2. A privilege is waived unless raised at the earliest practical moment.

3. No one is permitted to comment on a person's invoking of a privilege.

4. Certain types of communications are presumed to be confidential, and the party attacking the privilege has the burden of producing evidence of nonconfidentiality.

5. The trial court may require disclosure of the allegedly privileged matter in chambers.

To demonstrate some of the above, let us take an actual case situation and see how all this fits.

STATEMENT OF FACTS

John Jones was a visitor at the home of one Frank Williams, along with Harvey Evans and Earl Smith. While at the home of Frank Williams, they were served several drinks. During the course of the evening, several girls came in and there were more drinks served. Later in the evening, when everyone was in high spirits, John Jones, it is alleged, made some improper advances to Mrs. Williams. An argument ensued between Jones and Williams and there were some fisticuffs—however, Evans and Smith succeeded in separating the combatants, and Jones left the house.

Later Jones returned and was readmitted to the house. The prior tension between Williams and Jones still existed and made the other remaining guests uneasy. Shortly after his arrival Jones approached Williams and stated that he, Jones, did not like the way he was being treated and thereupon pulled a pistol from his pocket and shot Williams. Williams was rushed to the hospital and was pronounced "dead on arrival." Jones was arrested and charged with murder.

Let us say for discussion that you are now a paralegal in a criminal law office and have received the above facts from the client. A cursory review of the facts indicates that the testimony of the witnesses to the alleged murder is going to be crucial. What do you look for? What documents do you prepare?

The character witnes: In the case at hand, the defense may call character witnesses for the purpose of showing the general reputation of the accused, but the testimony of the character witness is confined to the reputation the party bears in his own community—where he lives and is personally known to the people at the time of the act.

So you look for evidence to support the fact that "John Jones was a visitor," and then "several girls came in" indicating that he was not personally known by them and he did not live in the community.

The reason—a person's reputation in some place distant from one's home is not admissible. The witnesses must have had an opportunity for observation of the habits and manner of life of the accused, which makes the character witness competent to form an opinion.

Character of the accused: As a general proposition of law, the character of a person cannot be shown for the purpose of proving his conduct. The exception to this rule allows the accused in a criminal case to prove such traits of character as tend to make it improbable that he would or could have committed the crime charged.

Therefore, search and find character witnesses who can testify to his good character in the community where he resides and works.

The expert witness: In the instant case, the testimony of the doctor who attended the deceased and pronounced his death would be necessary in the determination of the cause of death of the deceased. However, before expert evidence can be given, the one proposed to give the evidence must be qualified to testify as to his knowledge and his opinion in the case for the benefit and guidance of the jury. There is a distinction between "expert testimony" as to fact and "expert testimony."

One embraces persons by reason of special opportunity for observation (like the doctor who pronounced John Jones DOA), who are therefore able to judge the nature and effect of certain matters better than persons who have not had opportunity for similar and like observation.

For example, a person of ordinary intelligence, who is accustomed to seeing automobiles travel at various rates of speed, may testify as to the speed of an ordinary automobile. These witnesses are not really experts in the strict sense of the word, but are only *specially qualified witnesses.* This point is made to direct your attention to the possibility of the "doctor who pronounced John Doe DOA." Was he an intern? What is his professional background? What type of expert? This would be your evidence research to possibly negate his testimony.

The other class embraces those persons who by reason of a special course of training or education are qualified to give an opinion in certain matters of a peculiar nature and value—a value much greater than persons not specially trained on the subject, for example, speed of an Indianapolis 500 racing car as opposed to the speed of an ordinary automobile, i.e., a Volkswagen.

How many cases of "dead on arrival" had the doctor handled? Was this his first case? What are his qualifications to make the judgment?

Deposition of a witness: In the statement of facts given, Earl Smith, a witness to the shooting, is a student at the University of Buffalo at New York and by virtue of that fact will be physically unable to give oral testimony in the case. In situations of this kind where a witness is physically, mentally, or for some other adverse reason incapable of attendance at a trial, the party for whom he is to testify is permitted to take his testimony by deposition; provided, however, that the person against whom the evidence is to be given has the opportunity to cross-examine the witness when the examination is taken.

In this connection, the deposition would be arranged either by way of a stipulation between the parties, or by way of Notice of the Taking of Deposition so that opposing counsel has an opportunity to arrange for said deposition or oppose the taking of same. For this reason, the Notice of Taking Deposition should be prepared and mailed to opposing counsel no less than ten days prior to the date of the taking of the deposition—e.g., if you plan to take the witness's deposition on May 18, 20—, then the Notice, with proof of service, should be mailed out by May 8, 20—. If the statute requires that it be a thirty-day notice, then if the date is May 18, 20—, the Notice should be mailed out April 18, 20—.

CHAPTER ELEVEN

Trial Preparation and Procedure

This chapter discusses the practical duties of the paralegal before a trial begins. It covers the steps to be taken before the trial is opened. It includes gathering and assembling actual evidence and the preparation of the numerous procedural witness interviews.

It must be remembered that some trials are held without a jury. In such case, the judge hears the case and decides both the facts and the law.

In some states a party must demand a jury trial in a civil case if he wants one. If that is so, the jury trial may be demanded in writing at the end of a pleading, or a separate demand for jury trial may be filed. F.R.C.P. 38 holds this right to a trial by jury under the Seventh Amendment to the Constitution as inviolate. Check your court rules. In other states a jury trial, even in a civil case, is held unless it is waived (just as in a criminal case).

When a case is "at issue" (all necessary pleadings have been filed) and all pretrial motions have been disposed of and discovery has been completed, either party may have the case set for trial. Many courts have rules for handling scheduling conferences and setting trial dates. These procedures are vital for you as the paralegal to understand.

When the pretrial court requires a pretrial conference memorandum, a knowledgeable paralegal is invaluable to the attorney. Such a memo usually requires a statement of the party's contended facts, lists of witnesses' names and addresses, lists of exhibits that will be offered as evidence, and any requests for preliminary rulings of law.

The paralegal is familiar with both the facts and the law of the case by the time the case reaches the pretrial stage if up to that time he has been performing the practical duties described in this chapter.

General Duties of a Paralegal in Trial Preparation

1. Acquisition and organization of trial materials (documentary and demonstrative evidence)

2. Interviewing client(s) and witnesses (make notes and relay attorney's instructions)

3. Setting up or arranging the files:

   a. Court document file (pleadings, motions, orders)

   b. Law memoranda file

   c. Evidence file (documentary evidence)

4. Indexing of file contents

5. Cross-referencing of file contents

6. Making sure the files are up-to-date (this applies to the correspondence file as well as the aforementioned portions of the client file for this case)

Step-by-Step Procedure to Commence a Trial

1. Depending on your local rules, you may need to request the court for a trial date by filing the appropriate document with the court, with a copy to opposing counsel.

2. Upon receipt of the trial date from the clerk of the court, mark it on your desk calendar, on the pertinent case file folder, the office master calendar, and the trial attorney's calendar. (2a) If your court sets a pretrial date, do the same for that.)

3. Advise the client of the trial date and set up an appointment for the client to come in for an office pretrial conference with the attorney.

   a) If your court sets a pretrial date, it usually does not require or allow the client to be present in the pretrial conference, but it usually requests that the client be immediately available to approve or refuse any settlement offer.

4. Advise any witnesses, including experts, of the date, and at the same time, mail to them the appropriate witness fees, if applicable.

5. If applicable, post your jury bond.

6. It is always nice, though not necessary, to also send out a notice of trial to the opposing counsel, if you are the plaintiff.

7. Depending on the nature of your case and your rules of court, the following are some of the documents you, as a paralegal, might prepare in advance for possible use by your attorney for trial:

    a. Written requests for jury instructions to be requested in the case (ask the attorney what special ones he wants). Use full captions of the case and title— Request for Jury Instructions.

    b. Defendant's first-time motion for non-suit, motion to dismiss, or for directed verdict if your court requires those motions to be in writing. (If required and prepared, use the full caption of the case and the appropriate motion title.)

8. Coordinate activities relevant to the trial, such as (1) appointment with witnesses prior to trial and (2) preparation of a profile of witnesses and their testimony.

9. Organize and index the evidence folder.

10. Prepare and locate exhibits.

11. Prepare the trial book.

12. Prepare and organize your investigation file.

13. Assist your attorney in preparing his opening and final arguments, if he desires such help, such as outlining both the plaintiff's and defendant's case from a daily transcript of the court record if it is available; if not, order it.

14. Lastly, confirm that your office has completely complied with any final trial orders that have emanated from the status conferences at the court. A sample can be found as Figure 11.1.

Figure 11.1
Order Re: Status Conference

SUPERIOR COURT OF THE STATE OF CALIFORNIA
FOR THE COUNTY OF LOS ANGELES

_____,	]	CASE NO. _____
	]	
Plaintiff,	]	ORDER RE FINAL
	]	STATUS CONFERENCE
v.	]	
	]	RULE 1106.5
_____,	]	
Defendant.	]	
_____	]	

All counsel must be present and comply with the following prior to trial and *at the Final Status Conference.*

1. MOTIONS IN LIMINE

   All motions in limine must be in writing and served on opposing party and the Court fifteen (15) days prior to the Final Status Conference. Any opposition to the motions in limine must be in writing and submitted to opposing counsel and Court five (5) days prior to the Final Status Conference.

2. JURY INSTRUCTIONS

   All requested jury instructions must be submitted to the Court at the Final Status Conference. Standard printed BAJI instructions should not be retyped. All blanks should be filled in appropriately and all inapplicable material deleted.

3. STATEMENT OF THE CASE AND CAUSES OF ACTION

   a. All counsel must file a short statement of the case (no more than three paragraphs) to be read to the jury indicating the nature of the litigation and a statement of the facts. This is to be presented at the final status conference.

   b. A separate statement shall be filed with the Court at the final status conference indicating by name and number the precise causes of action on which the plaintiff and cross-complainants actually intend to proceed to trial. This statement shall include the names and numbers of abandoned causes of action.

   c. Defendants and cross-defendants shall specify by name and number the affirmative defenses on which they will actually proceed to trial and the affirmative defenses which are being abandoned.

4. TRIAL BRIEFS

   All trial briefs shall be limited to fifteen (15) pages and shall be filed at the final status conference.

5. VOIR DIRE

   Counsel shall submit to the Court, in writing, a list of voir dire questions counsel requests the Court to ask and questions counsel plans to use.

Figure 11.1 (*continued*)

6. STIPULATED FACTS

   Counsel shall meet prior to the Final Status Conference and prepare a list of facts which are not in dispute for the trial.

7. WITNESS LISTS

   Each side shall prepare a list of the names of all witnesses, the order in which they will be called, the nature of their testimony and the anticipated length of their testimony.

8. EVIDENTIARY ISSUES

   Specify in writing any major evidentiary issues anticipated, along with any points and authorities intended to be submitted on any of these issues.

9. EXHIBITS

   a. Provide a complete list of exhibits on the Court's form listing each document and item of physical evidence pre-numbered.

   b. During trial, each exhibit shall be pre-marked in the morning before the jury arrives.

   c. During trial, all exhibits shall be offered at the close of one's case unless a foundational argument is anticipated.

10. DEPOSITIONS

   All original depositions shall be lodged at the Final Status Conference.

DATED:

_____

_____

Gathering and Assembling Evidence and Files
for Use During Trial
Exhibit (Evidence) Folder

It has been our experience that an "exhibit folder" (or evidence folder) should be immediately made up for each client's file, and original documents should be labeled and indexed and placed therein as they come in. This is true even if the case is a simple one, and it is mandatory in a very complex lawsuit. Your attorney must be able to find a document quickly and easily at any given point in the prosecution or defense of the action.

We have found the following procedure to be most helpful in preserving documentary evidence:

1. Maintain the original of any potential exhibit in the exhibit folder with a copy to the (1) evidence file and (2) chronological file folders.

2. Each document should either be scanned into the computer or should be indexed in the appropriate database for cross-referencing.

3. Note the source of exhibit either by stapling or clipping to the copy thereof. *Never* mark or clip the original.

4. Divide into categories, that is, purchase orders, contracts, tax returns, medical reports, and so forth. If it is a matter involving personal injury or malpractice, then you should of course set up a separate medical file with a further division into plaintiff and defendant medical reports, depositions, witnesses testimony, and the like.

5. Before the actual trial the exhibit folder (evidence folder) should be reorganized and placed in chronological order by subject matter and should be clearly marked. Whatever the method, *explain it to the attorney.* You may use an index or tab system. Any clear system should save the attorney from an embarrassing search for documents during the trial.

Pleading Folder

A separate folder for each case should contain the following:

1. Plaintiff's pleadings and motions and a separation division for defendant's pleadings and motions;

2. Summary of the allegations of the complaint;

3. Summary of the answer and affirmative defenses;

4. Summary of your plaintiff's reply, if any;

5. Summary of issues left to be tried; and

6. Summary of facts to be proven at the time of trial.

Trial Brief or Trial Book

A trial brief, if applicable, may be prepared. The brief may either be complete or cover only those issues in dispute. It could be placed in a separate folder with a list of any information about the jury panel and the list of voir dire questions.

In complex litigation, the trial attorney may be given a "trial book" prepared according to specified firm instructions. It may be quite elaborate—color-coded, indexed, and so forth. A good reference is *McElhaney's Trial Notebook* (ABA 3rd ed., 1994). E-forms and binders can be purchased to ease this creative process. Those attorneys and paralegals who are comfortable with technology may even use a completely electronic version of the trial notebook. Very often the legal technology used in the office has the capability of creating a trial notebook from the information it already has. (See Chapter 12, "Electronic Trial Preparation Procedures.") The electronic trial notebook can make finding and cross-referencing information incredibly fast and easy. Further, its capacity cannot be met by conventional paper; there simply is no bulk to deal with.

The following is a general outline for the organization of the trial notebook:

1. Reference
   a. Parties and attorneys (include the names, phone numbers, addresses, etc.)
   b. Court, judge, clerk info
   c. Staff info
      i. All paralegals and attorneys involved
   d. Client information
   e. Witness info
      i. Eyewitnesses
      ii. Experts
   f. Other involved persons (3rd party info)
   g. Opponent attorney info

2. Case summary
   a. Narrative
   b. Factual and legal issues not in dispute
   c. Factual and legal issues in dispute

3. Proof chart (evidence)
   a. Plaintiff's elements of claim and source of proof for every element of the cause of action
   b. Defendant's elements of defense and source of proof for every element of the defense, counterclaim, or affirmative defense

4. Pleadings
   a. Summarization
   b. Major pleadings (as amended), tabbed and color-coded, to designate party propounding, and key sections highlighted
   c. Pretrial orders

5. Last-minute/Important motions

   a. Remaining motions not yet resolved with supporting authority

   b. Authority to oppose any expected last-minute motions by the opposition

6. Jury selection

   a. Juror data sheet

   b. Outline of voir dire questions

   c. Notes

7. Opening statement

   a. Complete text

   b. Outline (use large font)

8. Outline for trial

9. Witnesses

   a. Own witnesses (each with his own tab)

      i. Synopsis of witness information

      ii. Direct examination

         1. Outline of questions (wide margins to add notes)

         2. List of exhibits to be introduced by that witness

         3. Summaries of any prior statements (with reference to its exhibit)

         4. Notes on any conflicting testimony (prior statements, depositions, interrogatories, etc.)

         5. Questions to rehabilitate witness—particularly by harmful cross-examination

   b. Opponent's witnesses

      i. Synopsis of witness information

      ii. Cross-examination

         1. Outline of questions (wide margins to add notes)

         2. List of exhibits to be introduced by that witness

         3. Summaries of conflicting testimony (prior statements, depositions, interrogatories, etc.)

         4. Impeachment information (bias, etc.)

10. Exhibits (can be a separate binder if too big)

    a. Exhibit log

    b. Exhibits (five copies each) in expected order of presentation

        i. Tabbed separately

        ii. Cover sheet for exhibit should include summary of exhibit and relevance, witness needed for introduction, foundation (chain of custody), authority (evidentiary rule on admissibility)

11. Trial motions and supporting authority

    a. Motions for dismissal, directed verdict, etc.

    b. Make sure you have reminders in the *outline* where these motions may be appropriate

12. Jury instructions

    a. One instruction per page including the supporting legal authority

    b. Opposition's proposed instructions
       If there is no jury—request for a copy of "findings of fact and conclusions of law" by judge

13. Closing statement

    a. Complete text

    b. Outline (use large font)

    c. Blank pages to add notes during trial

14. Law

    a. Trial brief covering all significant questions of law concerning issues, evidence, motions, and other trial objections or conflicts

    b. Responses to the opposition's likely arguments—set forth separately for easy reference

15. Notes and to-do list for trial prep

Alternative Dispute Resolution (ADR)

Increasingly, parties are seeking faster and more economical means to resolve their differences out of court. The most common non-adversarial methods of resolving matters are: (1) private negotiation, (2) mediation, and (3) arbitration. The ABA's section on Dispute Resolution can be accessed at www.abanet.org/dispute/home.html.

Negotiation requires no intervention whatsoever by any third person; the parties simply agree to some sort of compromise to keep the matter out of the court system. If this path is chosen, it is absolutely vital that a Memorandum of Settlement and Release be signed.

Mediation is less formal than arbitration. It requires that a third-party neutral hear the matter as presented by the parties and assist them in finding a resolution. The authority to settle the matter ultimately rests with the parties. There are many private mediation services available—check your local bar association for more information.

By contrast, arbitration involves a third-party neutral who will make the final determination in the matter after hearing evidence from both sides. The arbitrator's job is to come up with the best solution to the issue. The American Arbitration Association (www.adr.org) provides these arbitration services from start to finish in a very effective manner that resembles judicial trial.

It is ultimately the attorney and client that must make the determination that avoidance of litigation and resorting to ADR is best. The attorney will need to consider: whether the dispute must be taken to arbitration under a contractual obligation, the amount of the potential award, time elapsed since the cause of action accrued, the amount of time that litigation will take, and evidentiary issues.

How to File for Arbitration

Once it has been determined that arbitration is the best method for resolving the dispute, the following steps will need to be taken under the American Arbitration Association (AAA) rules:

1. File a Demand for Arbitration in triplicate and send to the AAA and the respondent via certified mail, return receipt requested. The respondent will be notified by the AAA of the request and a deadline for his answer and/or counterclaim will be set.

2. Alternatively, if all the parties consent to the arbitration, the claimant may file a Submission to Dispute Resolution.

3. An arbitrator will be selected. The AAA identifies appropriate neutrals to hear the matter and the parties select from that list.

4. Preliminary hearing is held to discuss both substantive and procedural matters.

5. The parties will then be required to exchange information and prepare for the hearings.

6. The matter is heard. All the parties can present testimony and supporting evidence. It is important to note that the formalities of admissibility under court rules are not present here.

7. If necessary, the arbitrator may permit the parties to supplement their documentation after the hearing.

8. Decision and award is rendered and the case is closed.

It is important to note whether you are filing for arbitration voluntarily or by court order. Many courts mandate a settlement conference/submission to arbitration in an attempt to clear the trial calendar. If you are filing under a court order (nonbinding arbitration), you may have further recourse if the arbitration is unsatisfactory to your client.

Court-Ordered Nonbinding Arbitration

Using California by way of example, the following submissions would be used in arbitration that has been ordered after the filing of a claim. Of course, you must check your local court rules for the format, content, and time limits for making these submissions.

Figure 11.2

ATTORNEYS AT LAW
A PROFESSIONAL CORPORATION
Attorneys for Defendant

SUPERIOR COURT OF THE STATE OF CALIFORNIA
FOR THE COUNTY OF LOS ANGELES

_____,	] CASE NO. C_____
Plaintiffs,	] ARBITRATION BRIEF
	] OF DEFENDANT
v.	]
	] DATE: October 17, 20_____
_____,	] TIME: 4:00 p.m.
	] LOCATION: Room 218
Defendants.	]
_____	]

STATEMENT OF THE FACTS

On October 23, 20____, plaintiff _____ injured the tip of his left middle finger at _____ by placing it in the doorjamb of the manager's office door. His parents, _____, voluntarily dismissed their claims for emotional distress caused by the witnessing of this incident.

On the date of the incident, plaintiffs had entered the store for the purposes of collecting what they believed to be their winnings in a Bingo Contest sponsored by the _____. They affixed their game pieces to a place card on a telephone booth ledge next to the manager's office. During this time, Mr. _____

Figure 11.2 (*continued*)

entered and exited the subject door at least two times, the door thus closing at least four times in the presence of the plaintiff and his parents.

The door in question has an automatic closure mechanism. It cannot be manually slammed. When Mr. _____ entered the office door for a third time, plaintiff stuck his finger in the hinge side of the doorjamb where it was crushed by the closing door.

The plaintiff was treated at Kaiser Permanente Hospital by Dr. _____. His medical bills total $310.00.

CONTENTION OF THE PARTIES

Plaintiffs contend that _____ was _____ negligent through its employee, _____, by allowing the subject door to shut upon the plaintiff's finger.

Defendant contends that it is not liable for the plaintiff's injuries as plaintiff knew the dangers inherent by a closing door and further, the plaintiff's parents failed to exercise the proper, reasonable and necessary parental guidance in supervising their son.

STATEMENT OF THE LAW

As a general rule, owners and possessors of commercial property must exercise reasonable care in maintaining their premises in a safe condition for all purposes invited onto those premises. *Restatement* 2d, Torts, Section 283. The duty of care is not violated, however, where the condition is so obvious that it serves as a warning in and of itself, unless the harm was foreseeable despite the obvious nature of the danger. 4 Witken, *Summary of California Law* 2863, Section 594. Defendants have found no cases which classify a door with a closing mechanism as a dangerous condition. To place such a burden upon commercial landowners would render the effective operation of any business impossible.

In his deposition at page 27, line 18 through page 28, line 3, plaintiff stated that he was aware of a family member who had caught her finger in a car door four years prior to this incident. Thus, It appears that plaintiff assumed the risk or was comparatively negligent for his injuries. California *Civil Code* Section 1719. Additionally, his parents should be negligent for their failure to properly supervise their son. *Smith v. American Motor Lodge* (1974) 39 Cal. App. 3d.

EVIDENCE

Pursuant to California *Rules of Court*, Rule 1613, defendant has given notice of its intention to introduce documentary evidence at the Arbitration hearing. A copy of that notice was served and filed concurrently with this Brief.

DATED: September 21, 20____

_____

A PROFESSIONAL CORPORATION

BY _____.

_____

Attorney for Defendant,

_____

Figure 11.2 (*continued*)

ATTORNEYS AT LAW
A PROFESSIONAL CORPORATION
Attorneys for Defendant

SUPERIOR COURT OF THE STATE OF CALIFORNIA
FOR THE COUNTY OF LOS ANGELES

_____,	]	CASE NO. C_____
Plaintiffs,	]	NOTICE OF INTENTION TO
	]	INTRODUCE DOCUMENTARY
		EVIDENCE
v.	]	AT ARBITRATION HEARING
	]	
_____,		DATE: October 17, 20___
		TIME: 4:00 p.m.
Defendants.	]	LOCATION: Room 218
_____	]	

TO PLAINTIFF, _____ AND TO HIS ATTORNEY OF RECORD:

PLEASE TAKE NOTICE that, pursuant to California Rules of Court, Rule 1613, that defendant, _____, intends to introduce the following documents into evidence at the Arbitration hearing set on October 17, 20___, at 4:00 p.m. in Room 218 of this Court, located at 111 North Hill Street in Los Angeles:

1. The Declaration of No Records from Kaiser Permanente Hospital;
2. Plaintiff's Medical Records from Kaiser Permanente Medical Group;
3. Plaintiff's Medical Records from _____, M.D.;
4. Deposition transcripts and Interrogatory responses of _____, _____ and _____ as necessary for impeachment purposes.

DATED: _____, 20___

_____

A PROFESSIONAL CORPORATION

BY _____

_____

Attorney for Defendant,

_____

FOLLOW-UP PROCEDURES FOR COURT-ORDERED ARBITRATION

1. By law, the Arbitrator is supposed to file the award within a ten-day period after the hearing. So, calendar this date.

2. Upon receipt of the Award, if it is not acceptable, file a Request for Trial within 20 days with the appropriate Court. *This may not be extended.*

Or, in the alternative,

3. File an Application to Correct the Award, if needed, within ten days *after* receipt of the Award.

And/or—then,

4. A Motion to Vacate Judgment Entered is appropriate, and must be made within six months *after* Entry of Judgment under Rule 1615(d); C.C.P. 1286.2(a)(b)(c).

Fast Track Litigation

In many states, the courts have adopted what is commonly called "fast track" litigation.

The purpose of the initiation of the fast track litigation procedure is determined by and is based upon the need to motivate trial courts to implement rules to remove the backlog in the hearing of civil trial litigation. Simpler matters are best suited for this designation. Complex litigation may not be.

The real difference is the amount of time permitted for certain procedures and the scope of discovery controlled by case management orders. The court is attempting to compel the attorneys to develop an effective plan to focus on the issues. The purpose is to ensure a more efficient prosecution of the case. In California, the goal is to have 75 percent of the fast track cases resolved within one year of their filing. That is significant since most litigation, if it goes through to trial, drags on for years. The complaints filed in a fast track litigation procedure are served within sixty days of filing, and a proof of service should be filed within sixty-five days of said filing.

Cross-complaints, without a leave of court first being obtained, may not be filed by any party after the at-issue memorandum has been filed; or after the expiration of the deadline as set forth in the Rules.

The At-Issue Memorandum should be filed not later than 140 days of the filing of the complaint.

As it relates to discovery, all discovery should be completed not later than 180 days after the filing of the at-issue memorandum.

With reference to pleadings and motions, all answers shall be filed and served within thirty days of service of the complaint and cross-complaint, unless a motion or demurrer to such pleading has been filed within the statutory period.

In the event that a motion or demurrer is filed, the court will, upon hearing of the motion or demurrer, make appropriate orders regarding the filing of further pleadings.

Any extensions are granted by the court upon a showing of good cause, but the parties may not obtain any extensions by a stipulation.

As to the Notice of Status Conference, it is substantially the same as with other existing cases and shall be sent to the plaintiff following the filing of the at-issue memorandum. This notice shall be sent out by the clerk not more than fifteen days after the filing of said at-issue memorandum and shall schedule the status conference at a time chosen by the assigned I/C judge, but in no event later than forty-five days after the filing of the at-issue memorandum.

Thereafter, the court may refer appropriate cases to judicial arbitration.

Please note that where the court determines that there is a possibility that the plaintiff will not obtain a judgment in excess of $25,000, it may consider, with a counsel stipulation for an amendment to the complaint, transfer of the case to the municipal court.

The court shall set a Mandatory Settlement Conference and shall determine whether it is appropriate for the I/C judge to hear and determine the MSC.

As to the setting of trial dates, this is done by the court as soon as it determines the appropriate time of completion of reasonable discovery and other pretrial preparation and is set in accordance with the California Rules of Court and in accordance with priorities authorized and mandated by law.

100 Days Before Trial Checklist
(California Example)

Name of Case: _____

Case Number: _____

Court and County: _____

Trial Date: _____

Date of Trial Setting Conference: _____

Date of Settlement Conference: _____

Last date of Discovery: _____
(30 days before trial date; Motions until 15 days)

before trial date—CCP, Section _____
224 (a), CRC, Rule 333)

Any further investigation needed: _____
Notification to client/referring attorney: Date completed:

Conference with client: _____
(Date scheduled)

Prepare a schedule of witnesses/ _____
phone numbers:

Preparation of Subpoenas and _____
Subpoenas Duces Tecum:

Notification of witnesses/experts
re trial date: _____

(Referencing weeks)

Jury trial? _____

Has it been requested? _____

Have fees been paid? _____

(14 days before trial)

Have copies of Depositions been
ordered? _____

Demand for Inspection of
Documents: _____

Compliance in Response to Demand for Inspection of Documents: _____

(20 days after service of Demand)

Last day to serve Cross-Questions
to written Depositions: _____

(15 days after service)

Last day to serve redirect questions
rewritten Depositions: _____

(15 days after service)

Last day to serve and file objections
to form of any question: _____

(15 days after service)

Last day to furnish Interrogatories
or Response to any person not
heretofore served who has made a
written request for same: _____

Demand for physical and/or mental
examination of a party: _____

(Schedule exam at least 30 days after
service of Demand)

Response to Demand for physical
or mental examination: _____

(20 days after service of Demand)

Depositions: _____

Prepare Request for Admissions: _____

Prepare list for exchange of expert
witness information: _____

Make Demand for exchange of
information concerning trial
witnesses: _____

(90 days before trial date)

Election for Arbitration filed: _____

Statement of Damages received: _____

Prepare pretrial statement, if applicable: _____

Prepare Exhibits and evidence: _____

Is legal research completed? _____

Prepare draft of Trial Brief, if applicable: _____

Last date to disqualify judge: _____

Prepare and submit Jury Instructions: _____

Prepare outline for voir dire questions: _____

Prepare Case Summary: _____

Prepare any Motions in Limine: _____

Overview of In-Court Trial Procedures

Under our system of justice the parties, plaintiff and defendant, have a right to have a trial either by a judge with a jury or trial before the judge alone.

The following is the procedure of a court trial sitting with a jury:

1. The first thing occurring in a trial with a jury is that the jury is selected and sworn in. At some point in time, your attorney may ask you to prepare what are called voir dire questions, utilized in selecting those persons who will be sitting on jury.

2. Then the opening statements of plaintiff and defense counsels. These are outlines of what the parties will show by the evidence which will be introduced at the time the trial begins.

3. Witnesses are examined by the question-and-answer method. After direct examination, the opposing counsel is given the opportunity to cross-examine the witness. During these two procedures, objections may be made to the questions or the answers by either party.

4. At the conclusion of the plaintiff's case (evidence and witnesses testimony), defendant may move for a "non-suit" or for a "directed verdict" in his favor. This motion may be made on the grounds of insufficient evidence. If the defendant is successful in his motion, the trial terminates at this point.

If, however, the defendant does not make one of the above motions, or either of them is overruled, the defendant will present his evidence in the same manner as did the plaintiff. And again, at the end of the defendant's presentation of his evidence, the plaintiff may move for a directed verdict. It should be noted that the defendant may again make a motion for a non-suit or directed verdict; or make his first motion at the end of his case.

If, in the discretion of the court, the court does not grant either party's motion, the case will be submitted to the jury. At this point counsels for both parties have the opportunity to give their closing arguments prior to the court giving its instructions to the jury.

5. At this point counsels for both parties have an opportunity to request the court to "charge the jury" in a particular manner as it relates to interpretations of the law as applicable to a given set of facts and/or exhibits which have been entered into evidence.

After hearing the closing arguments of both counsels and receiving instructions from the court, the jury retires to consider its verdict.

6. Upon reaching its decision, the jury can give a verdict for the plaintiff or defendant and state the amount. This is known as a "general verdict." If, on the other hand, the jury reports the facts only and leaves to the trial court the application of the law, this is called a "special verdict."

7. At this point either party can file a Motion for a New Trial. The grounds can be based on either error of the court, or that the verdict is excessive or inadequate or contrary to the weight of the evidence.

Other motions that can be heard at this time are entitled Motions for Judgment Notwithstanding a Verdict, normally made by a plaintiff, and Motion in Arrest of Judgment, normally filed by a defendant. These motions are really in the nature of postponed demurrers.

If none of the above motions is granted, the court will enter judgment in accord with the verdict.

8. Thereafter, a "writ of execution" is prepared, which commands the sheriff to attach the property of the defeated party, sell it, and satisfy the judgment out of the proceeds.

However, the losing party may desire to carry the case to the appellate court and hence would file a Notice of Appeal which would require the preparation of briefs directed to the appellate court. In this connection, be aware that there are basically only three briefs that are filed in the appellate court system:

a. The Appellant's Opening Brief,

b. The Respondent's Reply Brief, and

c. The Rebuttal Brief.

NOTE: The trial before a judge alone would follow the same general sequence.

PROGRESS OF A CASE THROUGH TRIAL AND APPEAL

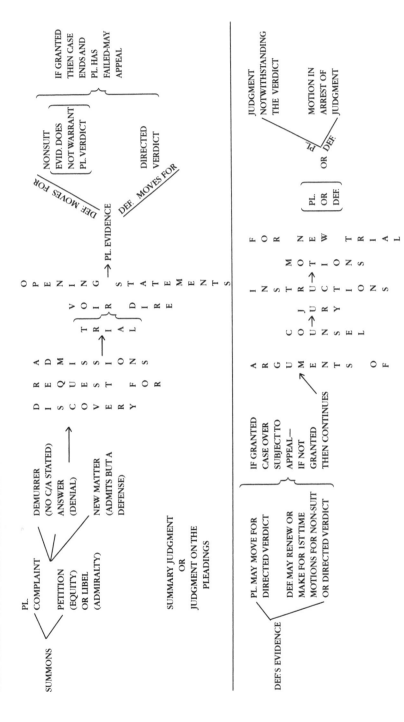

CHAPTER TWELVE

Electronic Trial Preparation Procedures

There once was a time when electronic case management and trial preparation was reserved for complex litigation. Today, almost every matter is input into the office's software systems as a matter of routine. In this chapter we will explore how technology enables an office to better handle complex litigation matters, although the same principles apply to the simpler ones. Basically, complex litigation consists of three important variables:

1. Multiple parties;

2. Multiple causes of action, as in a multiple party incident, wherein you have one or more plaintiffs and one or more defendants and cross-complaints; and

3. A series of cases wherein issues of each are the same.

For example (but not limited thereto), a traffic accident involving multiple cars resulting in multiple injuries and/or multiple deaths; or an antitrust lawsuit wherein a small business is attempting to enjoin a large corporation from performing an act or acts that would prevent the small business from competing fairly in the marketplace; or an attempt to break up the monopoly of a large business in order that small businesses can compete successfully in the open market; or a "class action" suit like those involving recalled pharmaceuticals and diet drugs.

Problems Inherent in Complex Litigation

1. Administration of complex litigation can be a nightmare. The key to successful management and to insurance of an ultimate win of such litigation is organization. For example:

   a. When you have an attorney attempting to handle, process, and otherwise deal with 100,000 sheets (or more) of paper; and/or

   b. Where you have different attorneys trying to handle the same 100,000 sheets (or more) of paper without communication and status report as to who is working on what.

2. A very real problem in complex litigation for the paralegal develops where the plaintiff is a cross-complainant and is served with interrogatories and/or requests for admissions. How do you answer them? The conflict is obvious since if you answer yes as the plaintiff, as the cross-defendant you would be saying no. Caution is the name of the game, and consultation with your attorney is mandatory.

3. Another real problem in complex litigation for the paralegal is documentation processing: how to:

   a. Handle voluminous documents,

   b. Organize voluminous documents,

   c. Index voluminous documents,

   d. Authenticate voluminous documents,

   e. Code voluminous documents, and

   f. Go about retrieving voluminous documents.

4. One of the most important aspects of complex litigation, which could present a real problem if not handled properly, is the awareness, location, and availability of witnesses, expert or otherwise.

   > **VIP HINT:** The paralegal should make sure, far in advance of trial, that key witnesses are available. He should keep the witnesses apprised of the status of the case at all times, either through a status letter or other document, or simply by picking up the phone and talking to them about the case.
   >
   > More important, the paralegal should give all the witnesses, expert and otherwise, sufficient advance notice of the date of trial in order that they may plan their schedules to ensure their presence on the day of trial. Furthermore, as to expert

witnesses, the paralegal should be sure that they have been paid according to their policy and that they have been paid far in advance of the date of trial, to ensure their presence and appearance in court.

NOTE: You should never subpoena a "friendly witness." Have the subpoena, but don't serve it immediately. You inform the witness of the date and time of the trial and hold the subpoena to be served in case of a last-minute foul-up.

Electronic Litigation Support Systems

The main purpose of a "litigation support system" (LSS) or "litigation automation" (LA) is to aid the attorney in the practice of his profession. Technology has permitted the transfer of information from paper to electronic data, which is infinitely easier to work with. There are hundreds of software systems that perform a myriad of functions, all purporting to assist in the creation of client files, and the retention, retrieval, indexing, cross-referencing, and preparation of materials for trial. A staggering alphabetical list of legal software vendors can be accessed at www.digital-lawyer.com/resource/software.html.

With the regular use of the litigation support system the attorney (and his paralegal) is relieved of many time-consuming tasks. Furthermore, it frees the attorney to crystallize or slim-line the substantive issues. Additionally, it gives him time to plan the proper strategy to be used in trial preparation and presentation.

Moreover, attorneys have discovered that a computerized litigation support system is a means of (but not limited to) controlling exhibits during the trial of complex litigation, of locating and identifying exhibits or parts thereof, as well as the time and place of the appearance of the exhibit in the proceeding, and of locating relevant testimony, such as at what page and line in a transcript of an exhibit theretofore entered or in the testimony of a witness the relevant material can be found.

Preliminary Considerations

The first task is to choose a software system (or systems) that is compatible not only with the technical specifications of your hardware, but also the area of specialization (if any) in your office and the way in which information is used. How easy is it to use and is it worth the time that will be needed to spend on the learning curve? It is most beneficial if the primary users are all consulted in this process. Flashy trial presentation software will not be as effective if the system does not also provide for data manipulation and cross-indexing vital to the paralegal's role in prepping the case. Many of the legal vendors will make trial downloads or mini-installations available so that the entire legal team can test drive the software to make sure it works for each particular office.

Next, determine how the users are most likely to use the features:

- What kind of searches can it perform?

- What do the graphical interfaces look like? Do they make sense?

- Do you need mobile capabilities? Must it be accessible outside of the office?

- What are the technical capabilities and/or requirements at the local courthouse?

- How compatible is the software with other systems you may already be using, like the word processing system, email, accounting, calendaring (like Outlook), etc.?

- Do you need it to be customizable? Or is a packaged format satisfactory?

- What are the security parameters? Can you lock down part of the system from other users? Do you need to?

- Does it come with the kind of support you need?

Practical Uses of Case Management Systems

If there is a specific area of paralegal duties that has been extremely affected by computerized practice of law, it is in the area of trial preparation. The gathering together of pertinent documents, the preparation of exhibits, the development of exhibits and exhibit books, trial and appellate briefs—all can now be accomplished much more quickly and efficiently through the use of both standard word processing systems and specialty legal software. Generally speaking, most case management systems perform the following functions:

1. Create client databases that correlate a substantial amount of information to that client (and related others) and automate conflict checks

   - Recall the ethical importance of conflict checks. The office is not permitted to take on a new matter where a current or former client's interest would be compromised by that new representation. Refer to the ABA Model Code of Professional Responsibility 1.7 & 1.8 and your relevant paralegal code of ethics.

2. Generate documents automatically and keep track of all deadlines and parties responsible for responding

3. Integrate a calendar system with a to-do list

4. Provide an area for all case notes—every member of the legal team can update the progress of the case instantly

   - Some systems even have voice recognition software (or it can be obtained separately) so that an attorney can merely dictate his notes and they will appear in the appropriate case without the need for the paralegal or secretary to transcribe dictation.

5. Link and search for relevant law

- You are able to determine prior to trial the attitudes expressed in written opinions of the judge before whom your attorney is to appear as those attitudes relate to cases like the one at bar. Or, if in your attorney's view the judge is questionable, you are now able to place the name of every judge into your computer system and receive every case that he has tried and his decisions or opinions on the subject matter involved. Such information about the judge's attitudes may make your attorney want to make an exception or cause the judge to be relieved or force him to disqualify himself from hearing and determining the present case.

- Another plus in the use of these computer systems is the access to the composition of law firms and the names of attorneys who have tried cases similar to the one at bar. In other words, you can now research the opposition.

6. Keep track of costs and billing. Very often this can be integrated with the billing software as well

7. Customize reports for a variety of uses

8. Synchronize with personal electronic devices or cellular phones

9. Facilitate communications between the legal team players through interoffice email and other options

Characteristics of Case Management Systems

Most systems use either a tab format (as if you were looking at a folder of individual files) or a Windows-type navigation bar. In either instance, the providers are attempting to make creation, retention, and retrieval as easy as possible.

Most often, the information is stored in spreadsheets, which have relationships with other databases in the system. These are referred to as relational databases. They store information in tables that assign different fields to the information. The user is able to then search across the fields in the various databases to pull related information from them. This is where input is critical to the system's functionality. It is imperative that you properly assign the facts to the proper fields; otherwise the computer will simply not be able to find them again.

For example, let's say you have received numerous answers to interrogatories and have properly summarized their contents into the system. Of course, you have already done this with the pleadings. Now, in getting ready for a deposition of a party opponent, you want to run a search for all the disputed facts. You can do this and even create two lists: one of disputed facts from all parties, and one targeting just those disputed allegations from that deponent. The resulting list will cross-reference those facts with their sources as well.

Since all of this is done electronically, no originals have been disturbed. Indeed, the paper file can remain untouched. This saves countless hours in reorganization and copying. Indeed, every piece of paper received can be scanned using OCR (optical character recognition). A further application lets attorneys and paralegals create their own system of organization without impacting any other member of the team's organization. In other words, each person can create his own set of information, containing what he wants and in the format he wants, that best suits his needs. Needless to say, this aids all members of the legal team in better understanding and handling the matter.

Online Information

The paralegal should be aware of both the current in-office litigation support systems being used by law offices, courts, and agencies throughout the country, and also the commercial or outside information systems and databases. While most litigation software is office-based, there is a growing demand in the industry for web-based management systems. The advantage here being accessibility from any Internet connection.

Further, many of the legal research databases offer some sort of case management information. See the discussion regarding computerized legal research in Chapter 8.

The ABA Legal Technology Resource Center has an incredibly comprehensive set of articles available at www.abanet.org/tech/ltrc/lofftech.html. They have divided these Technology Overviews and Comparisons into several categories:

Data Backup: information on data backup needs and solutions

Going Green: ideas for making your office more environmentally friendly

Macintel: using new Intel-based Macs in a legal environment

Records Management: software solutions for managing records and information

Legal Software Purchasing Checklist: suggested steps for researching, purchasing, and implementing software

Case/Practice Management: comparison of solo and small-firm case management solutions

Time and Billing: product comparison including features not normally associated with time and billing applications, focused on the solo and small-firm lawyer

Scanners, OCR, and Document Management: information about scanning, optical character recognition (OCR), and document management software

Calendar and Docketing: applications for lawyers to manage docket and calendar information

Corporate Counsel: management software for corporate counsel

Resources for Legal Technology Research: select bibliography of print and electronic sources to locate reviews, expert advice, vendors, and tips for purchasing software and hardware

To Upgrade or Not to Upgrade: Maximizing Your Technology Dollars: overview of the need for technology planning to control the upgrade cycle of hardware and software in law firms; part of a Chicago Legaltech 2001 panel (For more information, read the upgrade handout from the presentation.)

Computer Rentals: computer rental resource information

Researching Law Office Technology: selected resources to help you stay on top of the latest law office technology

Legal Time Management and Billing Systems

The primary functions of time management systems are in the area of your office docket control for billing and accounting. Many of them are compatible with generic accounting software such as QuickBooks. These programs allow you to not only keep track of the time spent on a matter, but also create customizable reports on individual attorneys. The time can be calculated on many different bases as well—hourly, contingent, transactional, and customized.

Some added bonuses include a "stopwatch" feature that can be engaged to keep track of billable time for each user and remind the user to submit the time into the system.

The production of bills customized for each client is also beneficial. The firm can decide not only what fields are displayed, but also the methods of delivery. For corporate clients, IRS filings and other financial documents can be generated.

On the law office management side, these systems can also create the necessary documents for running the business of law. Employee payrolls, tax documents, government filings, and a variety of other forms can be created.

These systems also ease the ethical burden of trust accounting. Scrupulous records can be generated at a moment's notice, and again, since they are compatible with most accounting software, they can be synchronized and correlated to the banking institution's information.

Trial Presentation Software

When it's time to take the technology out of the office and into the courtroom, trial presentation software can be of great assistance in making your case. Juries are susceptible to the method of presentation of the evidence. The easier it is for them to understand, the more likely a favorable result is.

Many courtrooms are equipped to handle not only generic PowerPoint presentations, but also the legal-specific trial presentation software like TrialDirector, Sanction, TimeMap, TrialMaker, Summation, TrialBook, DirectorSuite, etc. The ABA Legal Technology Resource Center has compiled a comparison chart of some of these programs and describes their capabilities. Please visit www.abanet.org/tech/ltrc/charts/presentationcomparison.html for that information.

There are infinite ways to use these programs. What is clear is that the instant access and graphic presentations to the fact-finders is a key to success, particularly in a "close case." The trial is a chance for the attorneys to show-and-tell their side of the story. Creating these presentations to accurately and effectively reflect the attorney's perception of the case is a talent that needs to be developed. Too much information or information that is not organized properly will ultimately backfire when using this technique.

WHAT SHOULD YOUR TRIAL SOFTWARE BE ABLE TO DO?

- Import and display all necessary files, documents, video clips, and other electronic data;

- Be compatible with standard playback equipment like DVDs and other media systems;

- Transition between documents and graphics to provide a logical sequence to the presentation;

- Display multiple exhibits for ease of comparison;

- Allow annotations;

- Be searchable across several fields at once; and

- Provide enhancement features like highlighting, zooming, pointers, etc., during the presentation.

Imagine the power of offering the video of deposition testimony of the witness, the transcript, and the underlying documentary evidence simultaneously to a jury. The inconsistencies would be instantly obvious. This is the power of trial presentation software. The fact-finder can see all the connections for himself without having a (potentially long-winded) explanation from the attorney.

Bear in mind that all of this information is protected under the attorney work-product rule. The manner in which information is stored, referenced, and presented is protected under the ethics rules, although the underlying facts are not. Take care not to send any preparatory material out of the office. If the opposition needs information, make sure to send it to them in its original form.

The Role of the Paralegal

The paralegal has a dual role in dealing with the electronic information to be used in trial. The initial administration and maintenance of the electronic information may be the responsibility of the paralegal. Accuracy is critical at the input stage, as a document can only be referenced and retrieved if it has been properly marked and stored originally. The substantive work involves the paralegal's ability to search and analyze the available electronic documents in preparing for trial. These duties may also be coupled with implementing and completing legal research projects, such as memorandum of points and authorities, motions to compel further examination, and so forth. It can never be overemphasized: The paralegal's work enables the attorney to concentrate on critical tasks such as strategy and legal applications of law.

Additionally, the role of the paralegal as technical support opens up an avenue for those who are computer literate and technologically adept. A paralegal who is familiar with the software can assist at court with the technology so that the attorney can focus on his personal craft.

Be sure to check for CLE opportunities in this area. NALA sponsors an advanced paralegal certification in Trial Practice and NFPA sponsors a "Tech Institute" to learn about the latest in legal technology.

In line with the foregoing, consider the following specific examples of your role when using any of the litigation support systems.

Step-by-Step Procedure

While your attorney is involved in developing substantive issues, narrowing or focusing on the issues, and planning strategy for presenting his case, you will have the following problems with which to deal:

1. Create a timeline of tasks to be performed. Many trial preparation systems include this as an option. Make note of which team member is responsible for what task and set reminders to follow-up and prepare status reports.

2. Identify logistical issues. Where are all the witnesses? Do they know about the trial date? Have arrangements for their transportation been made? Is the courtroom technology compatible with yours? How are you going to transport the

necessary equipment to the courtroom? Does the judge have any preferences with regard to trial presentations?

3. Summarize, coordinate, and annotate the documents to be used at trial. Make sure that the planned sequence of the exhibits works. If available, include video clips in the presentation and correlate them with the written evidence.

4. Practice the presentation, learn to troubleshoot, eliminate as many technical problems as you can *now*.

5. Update your legal research and check your citations. You could set up an automatic alert through either Lexis or Westlaw for just this purpose.

6. Prepare a persuasive post-trial brief that incorporates a short summary of the pretrial brief and annotated exhibits received in the testimony. This should include pertinent summaries and the pages of the transcript where they were offered. Include the relevant evidence in your trial preparation presentation.

7. Perfect the presentation. Review it with all the attorneys who will (or could be) present at the trial, so they are very familiar and comfortable with it.

8. Prepare the trial notebook—hard copy and/or electronic.

9. Prepare an initial draft of any appeal documents, if applicable, requiring you to select and pull from the computer both parts of a transcript and exhibits you feel will be used or could be used to support your attorney's motion to appeal and which would be incorporated in the appellate record and later used in preparing your appellate brief.

10. Remain calm and practice the trial presentation again!

PART THREE

The Paralegal's Role in Specialty Law Practice

CHAPTER THIRTEEN

How to Handle a Federal Bankruptcy Case

Nature of Bankruptcy

The purpose of the Federal Bankruptcy Act is to provide an honest debtor with a fresh start; as well as to protect creditors from their debtors; to protect creditors from one another; and to convert the debtor's assets in the case to be equally distributed among the creditors. (These assets could include certain state-exempt property belonging to the debtor, leaving the debtor with a complete loss of property and assets. This fact should be considered when determining whether or not to advise a client to file a federal Petition in Bankruptcy.)

On April 20, 2005, President Bush signed into law the Bankruptcy Abuse Prevention and Consumer Protection Act of 2005 ("BAPCPA"). BAPCPA made substantial changes to the Bankruptcy Code. It makes it harder for consumers to use the protections of Chapter 7 (total forgiveness) and instead refers them to discharge of debt under Chapter 13 (repayment under a plan). This plan requires that the petitioner pass the "means test" to determine whether they are eligible for Chapter 7 bankruptcy. The focus of the calculation is to determine whether the petitioner has sufficient means to repay some of their debt and file under Chapter 13. Details on this "means test" follow below.

For the full text of the Federal Rules of Bankruptcy, go to www.law.cornell.edu/rules/frbp/rules.htm#Rule1001, and the official forms can be found at the U.S. Courts website (www.uscourts.gov/bkforms/bankruptcy_forms.html#official).

Jurisdiction

A federal bankruptcy court has jurisdiction over all civil proceedings arising in or related to a bankruptcy proceeding that is held in its court. However, a federal bankruptcy judge can decline jurisdiction. In such case, the debtor would have to rely on state bankruptcy or receivable laws, and a state court would hear the matter and apply the state's bankruptcy laws or its state equivalent. There are ninety-four bankruptcy courts, each state having at least one in its jurisdiction.

Venue (Federal)

Individuals: In the district where the debtor has resided for the longest portion of 180 days prior to the filing of a petition; location of his assets or place of business.

Corporations: In the state where it is incorporated; or where the corporation was licensed to do business and/or where they are actively doing business.

For a directory and contact information for each federal bankruptcy court, please visit www.uscourts.gov/courtlinks or www.findlaw.com/10fedgov/judicial/bankruptcy_courts.html.

The "Means Test"

While the original intent of the provisions of the Bankruptcy Code, as described in *Local Loan Co. v. Hunt,* 292 U.S. 234, 244 (1934), was to give "honest but unfortunate debtors a new opportunity in life and a clear field for future effort," the BAPCPA was intended to curtail unabashed abuse of the process by those who used bankruptcy as an escape even though they may have been able to avoid it.

The older rules assumed that those filing for bankruptcy under Chapter 7 were qualified, and an individual judge would make that final determination. The 2005 rules take this judicial discretion away and replace it with the "means test."

Petitioners who earn more than the median income in their state are subject to this test. They must calculate their disposable monthly income (DMI). See Form 13.1 at the end of the chapter. This calculation is designed to discover whether the petitioner is financially able to repay on his debts in accordance with Chapter 13 bankruptcy. Those whose DMI is less than $100 per month are eligible to file under Chapter 7—just like those persons whose gross income is less than the median. This new means test has been the subject of much criticism (as have some other new provisions).

General Procedures
Petition

To commence a bankruptcy case, the first document to be prepared and filed is the "petition." This petition must be prepared and filed with the federal district of bankruptcy court clerk and then a copy will be sent to the U.S. Trustee in bankruptcy.

Under Rule 1005, the caption must contain the following information:

1. The name of the court (find your appropriate venue given the residence of the petitioner);

2. The title of the case (which includes the debtor's name, last four digits of his social security number, or if a company, the employer ID number, any other tax ID numbers, and all other names used within the last six years before the filing); and

3. The docket number.

Under Rule 1007, the list of creditors contained within the petition should include the names and addresses of all creditors, as well as the account number, if applicable, and the estimated balance due on the accounts. See Figure 13.2 for the petition form.

The schedules of assets and liabilities should be prepared according to 11 U.S.C. §521(1).

The U.S. Bankruptcy Court provides a summary sheet of these forms.

Summary of Schedules

Indicate as to each schedule whether that schedule is attached and state the number of pages in each. Report the totals from Schedules A, B, D, E, F, I, and J in the boxes provided. Add the amounts from Schedules A and B to determine the total amount of the debtor's assets. Add the amounts of all claims from Schedules D, E, and F to determine the total amount of the debtor's liabilities. Individual debtors also must complete the "Statistical Summary of Certain Liabilities and Related Data" form, if they file a case under Chapter 7, 11, or 13.

However, the bankruptcy rules allow the filing of schedules separately, within fifteen days after the petition, if the list of names and addresses of creditors has not been filed with the original petition. Discuss this procedure with your attorney before you file or do not file the schedules concurrently with the filing of the petition. Additionally, there is a provision for amendments to the petition, schedules, and statements up until the close of the case under Rule 1009(a).

Name of Schedule	Attached (Yes/No)	No. of Sheets	Assets	Liabilities	Other
A. Real Property					
B. Personal Property					
C. Property Claimed as Exempt					
D. Creditors Holding Secured Claims					
E. Creditors Holding Unsecured Priority Claims (Total of Claims on Schedule E)					
F. Creditors Holding Unsecured Non-Priority Claims					
G. Executory Contracts and Unexpired Leases					
H. Co-debtors					
I. Current Income of Individual Debtor(s)					
J. Current Expenditures of Individual Debtors(s)					
TOTAL					

Practical Hints

1. When preparing your list of secured creditors, footnote them as follows: If it is a house, then say, "per broker's appraisal of ___of ___," and attach a copy of the appraisal, or if it is an automobile, then say, "per Kelly's Blue-Book, dated ___ of ___, $ ___ retail, $ ___, wholesale."

2. Always include ZIP codes in addresses and complete description of goods claimed, for example, Sony Flat Screen HD 42", Westinghouse refrigerator, Whirlpool, and so forth (with serial number, if possible).

3. As to real property, make the client bring in the deed so that you can personally check it as to plot plan and tract number when recorded, and so forth. Use the legal description in the petition.

4. Before you list the personal property, check out the exemptions allowed under state law; or take the federal exemptions as provided for under 11 U.S.C. §522 either (a) or (b). *You cannot take both.* Make the determination of which is most beneficial to the client before you list the personal property. You must discuss this matter with your attorney and let him make the decision. (It might be the better part of valor if you develop a bible of exemptions and checklists in this regard. See Creditors' Claims and Interest, page 257.)

Practical Step-By-Step Procedures Before Filing Bankruptcy Petition

1. After the initial interview between your attorney and the client, your consultation should be exhaustive. The 2005 bankruptcy rules provide for increased attorney liability in the filings. It is imperative to protect not only your client, but also your office. See Figure 13.3 for a bankruptcy intake questionnaire.

2. In gathering the data needed for the petition, be sure to obtain the following data: name, address, telephone number, and Social Security number of the client; marital status; if a woman, her maiden name, together with the date of marriage (or marriages); if divorced, the date of the legal separation and/or entry of final divorce decree and any child support information. This information could have an effect on what debts are dischargeable or not dischargeable in bankruptcy.

3. Prepare a complete list (and a *complete* list is what is meant) of any and all debts outstanding, current, or in arrears, long past due or delinquent, however old, even out-of-state debts still pending.

4. Discreetly check to see if the balances given to you are on face correct by calling the creditors. The client may be too embarrassed to call and may have inadvertently given you an old invoice or statement.

5. Consult with the client's accountant, since the accountant would have a better understanding of liabilities of the client and have possession of any books and records, financial statements, and/or inventories of the client.

6. Check the judgment section of the court to determine if there are any outstanding judgments or lawsuits pending that the client may feel might not have any bearing on the petition in bankruptcy.

7. Another caution is the "family creditor," who the client says will not cause a problem. Verify the debt owed; obtain documentation if you feel the same is warranted. This might be one of the debts the client wants to protect from a preference suit, as indicated in item 3.

8. If property is involved, be sure that the legal description is correct: in whose name it is owned, and how (joint tenancy or other); when bought, and for how much; and so forth. This data will enable you to complete the filing of a declaration of homestead, if that has not already been done.

9. When all the above has been accomplished, *recheck* the debts with the client, for we often find that after the petition has been prepared and is ready to be filed, the client will call in to add still another outstanding debt. This can be (and is) frustrating to you and your attorney.

10. A suggested office procedure for verifying information with the client is to make a copy of the completed petition and mail it to the client to study and return. A five- to seven-day follow-up is recommended in these situations.

11. After receipt of a notice of the first meeting of creditors, check to see if any of them have been returned for lack of proper address, and if so, determine the correct address and remail the letter by registered return receipt requested in a timely manner in order that the creditor may file his proof of claim.

12. It would also be wise to list any assignees of claims as creditors and all property, regardless of the value. This is because failure to list them on the schedules may constitute a false oath by your client.

13. Finally, check and recheck, and check again to determine if the client has signed each and every page required and that those pages requiring notarization have been notarized. Too many times, petitions are returned by the court merely for lack of a signature. This can be crucial, if time is of the essence.

Credit Counseling

A court can deny the application for discharge for failure to include any of the necessary documents. Further, the petitioner must participate in credit counseling and financial management courses and/or services within the previous six months of filing the bankruptcy petition. The petitioner will also be required to complete some counseling during the pendency of the petition. These requirements serve two purposes, to ensure that the petitioner is first entitled to and needs the bankruptcy discharge and second to provide education on financial management so that it doesn't happen again. Indeed, the bankruptcy rules provide that a petitioner is ineligible to file for another chapter 7 bankruptcy within eight years of discharge.

The rules require that the petitioner obtain a certificate of counseling and review of the petitioner's budget through an approved nonprofit budget and credit counseling agency. Under the provisions of 11 U.S.C. 111, the bankruptcy clerk keeps a list of these approved agencies and instructional courses for personal financial management. Along with the certificate of credit counseling, the petitioner will also need to file a copy of any repayment plan and other pertinent information for use by the trustee in bankruptcy in making determinations in the case.

Creditors' Claims and Interest

Any right to payment, whether or not it is reduced to judgment, is a claim that may enable the creditor to seek payment in the bankruptcy case. Furthermore, the claim is allowed so long as a foreseeable breach, if applicable, gives rise to a right to payment. These creditors can take many forms, and the bankruptcy rules treat them differently depending on the type of security that the creditor holds and the "discharge-ability" of the claim.

Filing Proof of Claim

This filing of a "proof of claim" by a creditor is governed by the Federal Bankruptcy Rules of Procedure 3001 et seq. The form for making this filing is included in Figure 13.4. If it is a claim based upon a writing, that document must also be submitted, and if it is a security interest, the evidence of perfection of that claim must accompany the proof of claim. This perfection would have been done by way of a filing with the secretary of state of the state where the security interest was perfected under that state's commercial code.

A claim is "timely" if it is filed within ninety days after the first date set for the creditors' meeting. See F.R.B.P. 3002(c). There are exceptions and extensions permitted as justice allows or if the creditor is the government.

If your attorney is working for a creditor, you should get a power of attorney to represent the creditor in all matters and to receive all notices and activity and documents flowing in the case. This should be filed along with the proof of claim. See Figure 13.5 for a Power of Attorney in Bankruptcy. The creditor should send all invoices, bills, and bills of lading and a statement of account in dispute as listed on the bankruptcy petition. Furthermore, if the creditor received the claim by way of an assignment, this assignment should be attached to the proof of claim.

The meeting of creditors will be held between twenty and forty days after the petition for bankruptcy has been filed. The trustee will include this notice to the creditors.

The Secured Claim

Bankruptcy filings are affected by a state's version of the Uniform Commercial Code, Article 9, entitled Secured Transactions; Sales of Accounts, Contracts, Rights and Chattel Papers. These secured transactions would include secured personal property but not secured real property. State laws where real property is located determine whether a real property claim is secured.

11 U.S.C. 506 details the requirements for the determination of secured status.

EXAMPLE

Say you have got a house for $100,000 and then you make a down payment of $20,000. The balance due of $80,000 is to be secured by a promissory note and deed of trust. This is recorded where the property is located. Under state law this is a secured obligation. In case of a default, the trustee could ordinarily institute a foreclosure of the debt to satisfy the $80,000. See Scope of Automatic Stay later in this chapter.

EXAMPLE

Let's say that a business needs machinery and fixtures in a factory, and the individual goes to the bank to borrow money to pay for these items. The debtor signs a note for the money, a security agreement, and prepares and files a financial statement under the provisions of the state's version of Article 9 of the Uniform Commercial Code.

The bank *must* perfect this security interest by filing the financial statement with the secretary of state, which is in essence putting the public on notice; or perfect this claim by possession of the security in the business. The perfection of trade fixtures should be recorded in the country in which the property to which it is affixed is located. This is the state law that determines that the bank's claim is a secured claim for personal property in this example.

Then there are lien rights that create security rights such as:

1. A judicial lien plus some type of action by a court: attachment and execution for example.

2. A judgment lien obtained before the ninety-day period preceding the filing and where there was a levy on the property. This achieves the status of a secured claim as well.

3. Statutory liens such as tax liens (outside the ninety-day statutory period) and mechanics liens must be recorded in a timely statutory manner. These are

deemed filed unless they are listed as undisputed or contingent. In Chapter 11 proceedings, these need not be filed in order to share in the distribution of assets. But in Chapters 7 and 13 they must be filed to be considered secured claims.

In no-asset claims, the question becomes moot, since the court and its auditors have determined that the case is a no-asset case, and hence you do not have to file a claim.

The Unsecured Claim

Although a secured creditor does not have to file a proof of claim in order to preserve it, an unsecured creditor does, if it appears to be an "asset" case. This proof of claim must be made within ninety days of the date first set for the creditors' meeting. If the trustee files a "no-asset" report with the court, then there will not be any distribution to the unsecured creditors. A "no-asset" case is one in which all the debtor's assets are exempt and/or subject to valid secured liens. If it is an "asset" case, 11 U.S.C. 507 details the priority order for unsecured claims. Basically, there are two ways to satisfy an unsecured claim under a Chapter 11 filing, which requires a fair and equitable distribution to this class of creditors.

1. Have the plan provide for full and complete payment of the unsecured debt, either through the payment of money or the retention of property of the debtor, equal to the value of the debt; or

2. Under the Chapter 11 plan, do not give property or payment to any class of creditors that may be subordinate to the dissenting creditor.

EXAMPLE

If a dissenting creditor under the plan received payment or property worth only one half of its allowed claim, then the plan may still be considered fair and equitable if all junior or subordinate claims, including partners or stockholders, receive nothing and if no senior class is to receive more than 100 percent of its allowed claims.

The following is a list of allowable unsecured claims:

1. A landlord's claim for loss of future rent resulting from the termination of a lease, which may be for an amount not to exceed the greater of one year or 50 percent of the remaining term of the lease, which does not exceed three years

2. Allowance of employees' salary claim

3. Contingent or unliquidated claims

4. Transfer of voidable transfers of property belonging to the estate, that is, debtor

The following is a list of reasons for disallowed unsecured claims:

1. Unenforceability against the debtor

2. Claim is for the unmatured interest

3. Claim is subject to offset

4. Excess property tax

5. Claim is for services of an insider or an attorney

6. Claim is for a post-petition decree for alimony, maintenance, and support

7. Claim is against employer for employment tax

Equity Interest Holders

"Equity interest holders" under the federal bankruptcy law fall into the following classes:

1. Common and preferred stockholders or

2. Limited and general partners.

To satisfy this class of creditors, the Federal Bankruptcy Code considers a fair and equitable treatment of their claims under the plan of reorganization if it is provided therein that these interest holders receive property equal to the fixed amount of the indebtedness or redemption price or present market value of the interest, whichever is the greater.

Alternatively, the plan, to be fair and equitable to the interest holder, could provide that no compensation be paid to subordinate interest holders, such as common stockholders and general partners. See 11 U.S.C. §1129(b) (2)(c)(ii).

The following are allowable post-petition claims:

1. Gap claims in involuntary cases

2. Claims arising from the rejection of executory contracts or unexpired leases

3. Claims arising from the recovery of property

4. Priority tax claim

5. Allowable post-petition claims under and pursuant to Chapter 13 petitions:

   a. Government proof of claim for taxes that became payable after the case was commenced and still pending

b. Consumer debts that constitute liabilities for property or services necessary for the debtor's performance under the Chapter 13 plan

c. Medical bills that occurred prior to the filing of the petition that relate to an injury of a debtor that has left the debtor incapacitated.

The Role of the Paralegal in Interviewing a Client
In General

1. Attend the initial conference between the client and attorney.

2. Compile and assimilate data.

3. Aid client in completing the initial bankruptcy forms to obtain all pertinent information regarding the client's assets, liabilities, and so forth.

4. If time permits, merely give the forms to the client to complete the information within the privacy of the client's home.

5. If the foregoing is utilized, arrange for a later office appointment to review with the client the information on the sheet prior to discussing it with the attorney for final determination.

Specifics

Because of the recent changes to the bankruptcy rules, the initial interview with the client is vitally important, since these changes offer less protection to petitioners and impose pre-filing requirements.

These new options allow the debtor to take different approaches to obtain this relief from indebtedness, and as such, the requirements and form(s) necessary to be completed are different. It is critical that you are familiar with the vast array of forms required in filing for any type of bankruptcy for your client. If you are in bankruptcy practice, you should bookmark the following websites for constant reference:

1. The U.S. Bankruptcy Code: http://uscode.law.cornell.edu/uscode/html/uscode11

2. Federal Rules of Bankruptcy Procedure: www.law.cornell.edu/rules/frbp

3. Official Bankruptcy Forms: www.uscourts.gov/bkforms/bankruptcy_forms .html#official

4. U.S. Trustee Program: www.usdoj.gov/ust

5. The American Bankruptcy Institute: www.abiworld.org//am/template.cfm?sec tion=home

6. "Bankruptcy Basics," published by the Administrative Office of the Court: www.uscourts.gov/bankruptcycourts/bankruptcybasics.html

Intimate knowledge of the rules and how they apply in your client's particular situation is one of the major reasons why a paralegal should be present at the initial interview. You, as a paralegal, are the one whom the client will be contacting and be working with to complete the forms heretofore referred to, and later you will be verifying the answers with the client's creditors as to the client's outstanding debts, which may be contingent and/or unliquidated claims, and so forth.

> **CAUTION:** In this regard, as it relates to the secured and unsecured claims, you should be careful to verify the nature and extent of the secured interests and what assets were pledged to secure those interests, and, of course, verification of any due and owing state, federal, or other type governmental taxes. In addition, be sure that you verify and tag any property that is exempt under the new bankruptcy laws.

Clients do not always tell the truth. Some do not understand the truth as to whether or not a security interest has been perfected.

The Creditors Meeting

After the petition is filed, the bankruptcy judge appoints an interim trustee, and a regular trustee is elected or designated with full authority to do all those things necessary to protect the assets of the debtor until a determination has been made.

Thereafter, the debtor is required to appear at a public meeting of the creditors in bankruptcy court, often called a "341 meeting," referring to the code section under which it is held. See also F.R.B.P. 2002 and 2003 for specific procedures and time limits. This meeting is normally held between twenty and forty days after the petition is filed. The clerk will mail the notice at least twenty days prior to the meeting. The clerk of the bankruptcy court normally presides over this meeting, unless the creditors vote to designate someone else. They may also elect a regular trustee and/or creditors committee at this point in the proceeding.

The purpose of this meeting is to give the creditors and the trustees a chance to question the debtor (under oath) as to the reason for filing the petition, the assets involved, and any other matters pertinent to the petition and the debtor's right to be discharged in bankruptcy. It is after this meeting that the trustee gains control of the assets to be liquidated. For the most part, the debtor's role in the bankruptcy proceedings is finished after this meeting. The trustee will be responsible for the administration of the bankruptcy estate.

As the paralegal, you should prepare the client for this hearing by causing him to reread the schedules in the petition statement of affairs, go over his account books and bank statements, tax returns, canceled checks, and so forth. *Remember, the attorney will not be with him at this meeting.*

Petitions That Can Be Filed

Bankruptcy petitions are divided into two basic types: voluntary and involuntary. The Federal Bankruptcy Code and the Federal Bankruptcy Court Rules govern who may file and the procedure to be used in filing both types of petition.

Voluntary Petitions

A voluntary petition may be filed by the following persons in the following manner:

A. Individuals

An individual can file a voluntary petition whether or not he is insolvent or eligible to be relieved of the liability for his debts through a discharge in bankruptcy. Further, during the pendency of the action, he is able to convert the case to another chapter if the circumstances so provide.

B. Minors

The foregoing procedure includes minors who have incurred debts for the purchase of the necessities of life and incompetents through their guardians *ad litem*. See F.R.B.P. 1004.1. The only requirement is that the person either reside in the United States and/or have a domicile or place or business or property in the United States. This means that even aliens can file for discharge of their debts as long as they fulfill the foregoing prerequisites.

C. Private Family Trust or Estate

Private family trusts and mismanaged estates cannot file a Chapter 7 bankruptcy petition seeking liquidation.

D. General Partners

Voluntary petitions may also be filed by all the general partners on behalf of the partnership; or a partner may file a voluntary petition either with or without one or more of the other partners. Note, however, that the mere filing of an individual petition by a partner does not discharge the other partners from their personal liabilities to creditors of the partnership.

E. Corporations

Corporations may file a voluntary petition in bankruptcy for the purpose of liquidation and distribution of assets to creditors. This is because the bankruptcy code defines "person" to include a corporation, and as such, a person is eligible to file a liquidation petition. See 11 U.S.C., §101(30), et. seq. However, some businesses may prefer to remain unliquidated and should consider filing under Chapter 11 for reorganization and adjustment of debts. Sole proprietorships are also eligible for this type of relief.

F. Joint Petitions

The only joint petitions (more than one debtor) allowed are in the case of a husband and wife. The effect of a petition on the property rights of the other spouse is determined by the bankruptcy court and *not* by state law.

If only the husband files, remember that the state community property laws are subservient to the bankruptcy court regulations. See Section 302(a) of the Bankruptcy Code.

G. Joint Administration

This procedure occurs when the court orders cases involving two or more related debtors in a partnership or corporation, or the like, to be administered jointly.

Should this occur, joint administration would include the use of a single docket for the administration matters and a joint listing of claims and a combined list and notification of creditors. However, it is possible to file two separate and distinct petitions.

EXAMPLE

Suppose there is a California corporation that owns 100 percent of the stock in a New York corporation, but it has its principal place of business in California and the subsidiary in New York has its principal place of business in California. In this instance, separate petitions must be filed.

H. Consolidation

Consolidation, on the other hand, merges the assets and liabilities of both debtors involved. This procedure is used where there is such a commingling and/or intermingling of assets and liabilities that the court cannot separate them.

Involuntary Petitions (Liquidation)

Under the Code §303, there are only two instances where involuntary petitions may be filed: liquidation under Chapter 7 and reorganization under Chapter 11. This section discusses involuntary petitions for liquidation.

The purpose of filing a petition for liquidation is to assure equal distribution of the debtor's assets among his creditors, without showing preferential treatment. Additionally, this type of petition increases the assets of the debtor to the benefit of a creditor and the voiding of certain liens and encumbrances.

A. Questions to Ask Before You File

1. How is the debtor handling his assets? Are they being squandered or mishandled to such a degree that it compromises the assets?

2. Has the debtor made any recent, questionable transfers of the assets?

   a. Has he sold them for less than they are worth?

   b. Is he transferring them to other creditors in payment for his debts to them?

   c. Are the transfers being made to a related person or subsidiary business?

3. Are other creditors taking actions to secure their interests? Are they seeking further collateral on a loan?

Some of these kinds of transactions can be "undone" if it appears that the transfers were made in an effort to remove assets from the potential bankruptcy estate. Transfers made within two years to "insiders," fraudulent transfers made within one year, and some preferential transfers made within ninety days prior to the filing can be reversed. The assets will be put back into the bankruptcy estate and be eligible for distribution among the creditors.

Another reason to consider an involuntary filing—the creditors may be eligible to recoup attorney fees and legal costs associated with the filing because administrative claims receive priority over all other claims other than those for child support.

B. Who May File

Before taking such a course of action, that is, forcing the debtor to file an involuntary petition, there are certain courses that should be exhausted first.

1. Have you taken any legal action to collect the debt? If so, does the prospect of recovery outweigh the inconvenience and expense of a collection effort?

2. Does the debtor have enough money to pay at least a percentage or partial payment of the total indebtedness? If this is true, you may want to collect by taking the matter to court and seeking redress under the remedies offered under state law.

3. Is your client/creditor aware of the locations of the debtor's assets, and if so, remember that state law provides for post-judgment discovery for this purpose? For example, under state law you have such remedies as garnishment, attachments, receiverships, and other such procedures for protection of your client/creditor.

4. Can the debtor be rehabilitated? In this instance, we are talking about an insolvent debtor who may be able to pay a small fraction of the debts if all his assets

are liquidated and who just may have the ability to improve his economic condition and in the future make periodic payments in larger amounts. If this is the case, the court leans toward giving the debtor the opportunity to do so.

Who may file an involuntary petition? In order to file for an involuntary petition in bankruptcy:

1. There must be three or more entities that hold a claim against that debtor whose claims add up to more than $10,000 more than the value of any lien on property of the debtor securing such claims held by the holders of such claims, or

2. If there are fewer than twelve creditors, with the exclusion of employees or insiders of the debtor, then it only takes one of those creditors who have a claim of at least $10,000.

Reason: These creditors may not be counted by the court because of their special privity with the debtor, such as an employee who might lose his job if the debtor is liquidated in bankruptcy or the insider who might be so closely connected to the debtor (for example, his father or uncle) as to be biased toward the debtor, and so forth. It is for this reason that it is easier for a single outside creditor to commence an involuntary petition against a debtor.

Exact details can be found in §303 of the Code.

NOTE: Secured creditors cannot commence an involuntary bankruptcy case against a debtor, but a partially secured creditor may act as a petitioning creditor to the extent of any deficiencies over and above the value of its secured claim.

After the involuntary petition has been filed, the other unsecured creditors may join in the petition and it will have the same effect as if they originally joined.

How does this affect the debtor? There are two alternatives. The debtor, unless the court orders otherwise, is permitted to continue his affairs and use, acquire, or dispose of property as if this case had not been brought. On the other hand, at the request of a "nervous" creditor, and on proof of necessity, the trustee may take possession of the property to preserve it from loss or to operate the business. The debtor would then be required to post a bond to regain possession and control of the subject property or business.

C. Against Whom Can an Involuntary Petition Be Filed?

Any person, including a corporation, who may file a voluntary petition for liquidation may be the subject of an involuntary bankruptcy case except for farmers and not-for-profit corporations. See 11 U.S.C. §303(a).

It is vital to answer the involuntary petition. If the petition is not opposed, the court will order relief to be granted as against the debtor.

D. Filing an Involuntary Petition Relating to Liquidation

1. At the time of filing the involuntary petition, it should be executed by the petitioners in the office of the clerk of the bankruptcy court, at which time a filing fee is paid. See Figure 13.6 for the involuntary petition.

2. This filing commences a legal action. It should contain allegations made in the form of a pleading. Hence, the petitioners must identify the debtor in the caption, together with any names that he may also have been known by within the previous six years.

3. Furthermore, this involuntary petition should contain the names and addresses of all the petitioners and an allegation asserting the claims each petitioner has against the debtor that would amount to the aggregate sum of $10,000 or more.

4. The service of the summons will issue from the clerk and will take the same form as the service under a voluntary petition. See F.R.B.P. 1010. See Figure 13.7 for the form of the summons.

E. Step-by-Step Procedure After Filing an Involuntary Petition

1. The clerk of the bankruptcy court issues a summons to be served on the debtor, together with a copy of the petition. (It should be noted that it is the petitioner's choice of serving the summons and petition either by personal service or by mail.) Service, however, must be made within ten days from the issuance of the summons. Failure to serve the summons and petition within this time will result in the petitioner's having to obtain a new summons from the court.

2. The service of summons and petition must be made by first-class mail. (As in all other cases, it is suggested that this service by mail be made by certified mail, return receipt requested.)

3. If there is an attempt to make personal service, this personal service may be made by anyone who is an adult and not a party to the bankruptcy proceeding.

F. Step-by-Step Procedure in Preparing an Answer to an Involuntary Petition for Liquidation

1. The debtor in question, whether an individual, corporation, partnership, or general partner, may file and serve an answer.

2. The answer may be in the same form and contain the same type of defenses as in civil actions filed in the federal courts.

4. The answer may include a statement of claim against the petitioning creditor to defeat the purpose of the petition only. This is because an affirmative judgment cannot be sought by way of a counterclaim in a bankruptcy case.

5. The answer must be served and filed within twenty days after the issuance of the summons, unless the time is extended or limited by order of the court for service to be made by publication.

6. *Note that no other pleadings are permitted after an answer is filed and served.* The exception to this rule is when the court orders the petitioners to reply to the answer.

7. As to the debtor, per se, he may make a motion to dismiss the petition for lack of jurisdiction, or for failure to state a claim upon which relief can be granted.

8. The debtor may also file a motion for a more definite statement.

9. The debtor may also make any other motions that are permitted under Rule 12 of the Federal Rules of Civil Procedure.

NOTE: Under Chapter 11, U.S.C. §302(a), permission is given for joint petitions to be filed only against husbands and wives, though in some cases involuntary petitions can be filed against a corporation or other debtors who are closely connected, to be followed by either a joint administration of assets or a complete consolidation of bankruptcy cases.

If the order for involuntary bankruptcy is granted in an involuntary case, the debtor must file a list of creditors per Schedules D, E, F, G, and H in the official forms within fifteen days after the entry of the order.

The Automatic Stay

While the debtor is undergoing the process of bankruptcy, either a total discharge or reorganization, voluntary or involuntary, the court will provide some "shelter." This is the form of the automatic stay which stops *most*, not all, collection actions by the creditors against the property of the debtor. This stay arises out of operation of law—no action needs to be taken by either the debtor or the creditor(s).

A. Scope of the Automatic Stay
The "automatic stay" affects the following:

1. The commencement or continuation of any legal proceeding against the debtor that was or could have been commenced before the filing of a bankruptcy petition is automatically stayed (stopped) when a federal bankruptcy petition is

filed. This includes any judicial, administrative, and arbitration proceeding, whether or not it is before a governmental tribunal. It also applies to every step of a proceeding, including the issuance of a process such as levy, garnishment, and/or other supplemental proceedings.

2. The enforcement of a judgment obtained before the petition was filed, either against the debtor personally or against property of a bankruptcy. In this instance, creditors may not proceed with levy or execution to satisfy any pre-bankruptcy judgment.

3. Efforts to obtain possession of property of the estate, or property from the estate. Property of the estate includes the debtor's property as of the date of the petition. The stay covers these acts so as to give the trustee ample time to discover and evaluate the respective rights in the property before the creditors start grabbing.

4. Any attempt to collect or recover on a claim against a debtor that arose before the bankruptcy petition was filed. The creditors must even stop all telephone calls in an attempt to collect.

5. The settling of any debt that a creditor owes to a debtor against the debtor's liability to the creditor.

6. The commencement or continuation of a proceeding before the U.S. Tax Court concerning the debtor.

> NOTE: The statutory period of time affecting the collection efforts is 180 days. That is to say, collection efforts can be made by the claimant 90 days before the filing of a bankruptcy petition. However, any claim filed or collection efforts made after 90 days or on the 91st day is voided by the filing of the bankruptcy petition.

7. See Federal Bankruptcy Code and Federal Bankruptcy Rules for adversary proceedings in the bankruptcy court.

B. Exemptions from the Automatic Stay
Exemption from the automatic stay are as follows:

1. Criminal actions against the debtor may proceed despite the bankruptcy petition.

2. The collection of alimony, maintenance, and support is not affected by the automatic stay to the extent that it is from property that is not part of the bankruptcy estate.

3. Perfection of a lien or property interest to make it effective against the trustee in bankruptcy under Section 546(b) of the Bankruptcy Code is permitted.

4. Governments may proceed to enforce their police and regulatory powers, such as by prosecuting actions to prevent violations of health, consumer protection, environmental, or other similar laws.

5. Governments also may take steps to enforce injunctions or judgments, other than money judgments, obtained prior to bankruptcy in the exercise of their police or regulatory powers.

6. The automatic stay does not cover certain setoffs or mutual debts and claims relating to commodity claims actions.

7. Despite the automatic stay, the secretary of housing and urban development may commence an action to foreclose on a mortgage insured under the National Housing Act.

8. The automatic stay does not apply to the issuance of a notice of tax deficiency issued by a governmental agency.

Highlights of the Particular Bankruptcy Chapters

The intricacies of the Bankruptcy Code and the Rules of Procedure are too voluminous to be discussed in full. It is imperative that you check your local rules before each and every petition. The necessary resources have been highlighted in this chapter. Now, we will turn to some important aspects of each of the three main bankruptcy chapters: Chapter 7, Chapter 11, and Chapter 13.

Chapter 7: Discharge in Bankruptcy

There are certain categories of indebtedness that free the debtor from forever paying his debts, leaving creditors unable to file any type of civil litigation for repayment of the debts discharged in bankruptcy in the future. Those are dischargeable debts. If no objections are made, 99 percent of the petition is granted a full discharge. There are two ways in which the debtor is denied this relief: (1) Objections from creditors are filed and/or (2) the court finds that the debtor through some fault of his own is not entitled to relief granted.

There may be grounds to object as to a discharge as to all debts or just to certain debts. Refer to 11 U.S.C. 523 for full details.

The categories of debts from which there can be *no* discharge are:

1. Taxes;

2. Debts incurred by fraud;

3. Unscheduled debts;

4. Embezzlement, larceny, and fiduciary's fraud;

5. Alimony, maintenance, and support;

6. Willful and malicious injury;

7. Fines and penalties;

8. Student loans; and

9. Multiple bankruptcies, such as debts from a previous bankruptcy in which discharge was denied.

A. Step-by-Step Procedure for Objecting to a Discharge in Bankruptcy

1. The person wishing to object to the discharge must commence an adversary proceeding by filing a complaint before the deadline set by the court.

2. Thereafter, a summons is issued by the clerk of the bankruptcy court, together with a notice of trial or pretrial conference.

3. The complaint should state a ground for objection.

4. At his option the debtor may contest the complaint by filing an answer. If he does, a trial will be held.

5. The debtor can make motions to dismiss or request a bill of particulars or more definite statements of the objections.

6. The parties may engage in discovery, in accordance with federal court rules in conjunction with the bankruptcy rules governing adversary proceedings.

The following is a list of grounds for denial of discharge:

1. The discharge is for individuals only.

2. Fraudulent transfers or concealment of property.

3. Failure on the part of the bankrupt to keep books and records.

4. Commission of a bankruptcy crime on the part of the bankrupt, such as:

   a. Knowingly and fraudulently making a false oath or account;

   b. Knowingly and fraudulently presenting or using a false claim;

   c. Knowingly or fraudulently getting or receiving a bribe; or

   d. Knowingly and fraudulently withholding records.

5. Failure to explain loss of assets.

6. Refusal to obey a bankruptcy court order or to answer questions (which may be in the form of a subpoena).

7. Commission of prohibited acts in connection with an insider's bankruptcy.

8. Prior discharge within six years.

9. Prior Chapter 13 discharge.

10. Waiver.

B. Revoking a Discharge

There are three reasons for revoking a discharge:

1. Fraud on the part of the debtor.

2. Concealing the acquisition of the property of the estate on the part of the debtor, before the case is closed, or one year after the case is closed.

3. Refusal to obey orders to answer questions. It should be noted that those persons attempting to revoke a discharge may make their request within one year after the granting of a discharge if it is based on fraud or concealment. Other than for fraud or concealment the request must be made before the bankruptcy case is closed.

C. How to Reaffirm a Debt

A bankruptcy debtor may choose to reaffirm an otherwise dischargeable debt under certain circumstances without violating the Federal Bankruptcy Law. Under the law, the attorney must certify in writing that he advised the debtor of the legal ramifications of this action. This certification must also state that the debtor made the reaffirmation voluntarily and was, at the time, advised that this was not required under the discharge.

Restrictions and limitations on reaffirmations are:

1. The reaffirmed debt may be enforced only to the extent that it is enforceable under applicable non-bankruptcy law.

2. To be enforceable, the reaffirmation agreement must have been made before the granting of a discharge.

3. The debtor has the right to rescind the reaffirmation agreement within thirty days after it becomes enforceable.

4. Whenever the case involves an individual and a discharge is either granted or denied, the court is required to hold a hearing at which the debtor either must be informed that the discharge has been granted or given the reason why a discharge has not been granted. If the debtor wishes to reaffirm a discharged debt, the judge is obliged under the code to inform the debtor at a hearing that (1) such reaffirmation is not required under any law or agreement, and (2) there is a legal effect of such reaffirmation and consequences of default.

5. In the case of reaffirming an individual consumer debt, except for obligations secured by a real estate mortgage, the reaffirmation agreement is not enforceable unless the court determines that it does not impose undue hardship on the debtor or his dependents and that it is in the best interest of the debtor to reaffirm.

There is a detailed list of the required language for reaffirmations under 11 U.S.C. 524(k).

EXAMPLES

Reaffirming a debt is a serious financial decision. The law requires you to take certain steps to make sure the decision is in your best interest. If these steps are not completed, the reaffirmation agreement is not effective, even though you have signed it.

. . . .

If you were not represented by an attorney during the negotiation of your reaffirmation agreement, it will not be effective unless the court approves it. The court will notify you of the hearing on your reaffirmation agreement. You must attend this hearing in bankruptcy court where the judge will review your reaffirmation agreement. The bankruptcy court must approve your reaffirmation agreement as consistent with your best interests, except that no court approval is required if your reaffirmation agreement is for a consumer debt secured by a mortgage, deed of trust, security deed, or other lien on your real property, like your home.

What are your obligations if you reaffirm the debt? A reaffirmed debt remains your personal legal obligation. It is not discharged in your bankruptcy case. That means that if you default on your reaffirmed debt after your bankruptcy case is over, your creditor may be able to take your property or your wages. Otherwise, your obligations will be determined by the reaffirmation agreement which may have changed the terms of the original agreement. For example, if you are reaffirming an open end credit agreement, the creditor may be permitted by that agreement or applicable law to change the terms of that agreement in the future under certain conditions.

Are you required to enter into a reaffirmation agreement by any law? No, you are not required to reaffirm a debt by any law. Only agree to reaffirm a debt if it is in your best interest. Be sure you can afford the payments you agree to make.

What if your creditor has a security interest or lien? Your bankruptcy discharge does not eliminate any lien on your property. A "lien" is often referred to as a security interest, deed of trust, mortgage or security deed. Even if you do not reaffirm and your personal liability on the debt is discharged, because of the lien your creditor may still have the right to take the security property if you do not pay the debt or default on it. If the lien is on an item of personal property that is exempt under your State's law or that the trustee has abandoned, you may be able to redeem the item rather than reaffirm the debt. To redeem, you make a single payment to the creditor equal to the current value of the security property, as agreed by the parties or determined by the court.

Chapter 13: Wage-Earner Petition

The wage-earner petition gives the debtor the opportunity to arrange installment payments with his creditors rather than liquidate his assets. But more important, it is aimed to aid the debtor to avoid the stigma of being adjudged a bankrupt. The repayment should take between three and five years, but in no case will it be permitted to exceed five years. The automatic stay provisions are in effect, with some limitations, thereby protecting the debtor from an involuntary petition. The most important provision in this chapter is the ability to save the debtor's home from foreclosure.

A. Who May File Under Chapter 13

Under the Federal Bankruptcy Code, any individual who can establish the stability and regularity of income to ensure that payments can be made to creditors under Chapter 13 may file a Chapter 13 petition. This relief is not available to corporations or partnerships, who must file under Chapter 11, but it is available to those who are self-employed or are operating an unincorporated business. Interesting to note that stock or commodities brokers are not able to file under this chapter, and individuals living on pensions or receiving Social Security benefits and the like are eligible.

There is a kind of inverse "means test" for this relief. Instead of gauging how much a person makes, this test has put a ceiling on the amount owed. The individual may file as long as the total of the unsecured debts is less than $250,000 and the secured debt is less than $750,000. These figures are adjusted to reflect the increases in the consumer price index—they go up as does the cost of living. See section 109(e) of the Bankruptcy Code.

A Chapter 13 proceeding can be commenced only by the filing of a voluntary petition by the individual debtor or, if it is a joint case, by the husband and wife. The procedure for filing a Chapter 13 petition is the same as that used when filing a Chapter 7 petition; that is, the rules governing venue, jurisdiction, transfer, and so forth apply to the wage-earner petition under Chapter 13. As with Chapter 7 petitions, the Chapter 13 petitioner must list all creditors and submit schedules and the statement of affairs.

B. The Plan

Between twenty and fifty days after the filing of the petition, the meeting of creditors will be held. Similar to Chapter 7 proceedings, the debtor is placed under oath to answer questions regarding the terms of the repayment plan and financial affairs. If it is a joint petition, both the husband and wife must appear.

Within fifteen days of the plan meeting, the debtor must file the repayment plan with the court. This plan must provide for certain amounts to be paid and on what schedule. The plan must pay secured creditors in full, as they have priority over unsecured claims.

Within thirty days of the filing (even if the plan has not been approved by the court), the petitioner must start making payments to the trustee in compliance with the proposed plan.

Within forty-five days after the meeting with the creditors, the court will make a decision on the feasibility of the plan. The court must receive twenty-five days' notice prior to this hearing so that they may object to the terms of the repayment if necessary.

It is important to note that the debtor cannot incur any new debt during these three to five years of repayment. Simply stated, it would compromise the ability of the debtor to repay on the past credit. The debtor has found himself in this position because he could not manage his financial affairs; it is not permissible to engage in the conduct that created the problem in the first place. If the debtor does need to incur more debt, he must receive permission from the trustee before doing so.

C. Discharge

There are two modes of relief under Chapter 13, (1) discharge and (2) hardship discharge. A debtor is absolved of all other obligations to the creditors once he has completed the payments under the court-approved plan. Under 11 U.S.C. 1328, at this time he must certify (1) that he is not behind in any domestic support payments, (2) that he has not received a discharge within two years prior to this filing, and (3) that he has completed an approved course of financial management. See Figure 13.8 for the Order of Discharge.

Hardship discharges are available only when circumstances arise that the debtor could not control and that impact his ability to make payments under the court-approved plan. In this case, the court may permit the debtor to be discharged of his obligation early, almost as if he had filed under Chapter 7.

Chapter 11: Business Reorganization of Debts and Assets

A. Who May File for Reorganization Under Chapter 11

Whereas Chapters 7 and 13 give the individual person a fresh start, Chapter 11 gives the business debtor relief from financial distress.

As with other reorganization petitions, Chapter 11 petitions can be instituted by way of either a voluntary petition by the debtor or by way of an involuntary petition filed by the creditors of the debtor.

The Federal Bankruptcy Code states that any business entity that can file a voluntary petition for liquidation is eligible to file a petition for reorganization. The difference in Chapter 11 is that the petitioner is now referred to as the "debtor in possession" as it is able to keep control over its assets during the reorganization without the appointment of a trustee. Essentially, the business functions as its own trustee and has a fiduciary responsibility to take care of those assets that are to be used to repay the business debts. The debtor in possession, however, does not go unchecked. It is responsible for filing reports so that the U.S. trustee can monitor the situation.

B. The Plan

Within 120 days from the filing of the petition, the debtor in possession must file a plan for the repayment and reorganization of the business. While this is similar to the Chapter 13 filing, the creditors' rights regarding this plan are different.

The largest unsecured creditors make up the "creditor committee," and they consult with the debtor in possession with regard to the creation and administration of the plan for reorganization. See Figure 13.9 for the Notice of the Meeting of Creditors under Chapter 11 and Figure 13.10 for the order approving the disclosure statement. If there aren't that many creditors (as in a small business), the trustee performs this oversight function. A small business case is one in which the debtor has less than $2 million total in both secured and unsecured claims.

Because the debtor in possession is continuing to run the business, there may be actions of which the creditor committee does not approve. In that case, they may file motions with the court seeking the appropriate relief.

C. Conversion and Dismissal

Should your attorney decide that it would be in the best interests of the business debtor to convert a Chapter 11 to a Chapter 7, the following should be checked by you to determine eligibility:

1. If the client/debtor, at the time of the application for petition to reorganize, is a *debtor in possession*;

2. If it is an involuntary petition that was originated under this chapter; or

3. If it was petitioned to be converted under Chapter 11 at the request of another, that is, creditor, equity holder, and so forth.

> NOTE: This is a onetime absolute right on the part of the debtor in possession to convert the matter—there is no absolute right to have the case dismissed. The court makes this decision on conversion after a hearing to determine whether that is in the best interests of the estate and its creditors.

In order for the business debtor to qualify for a conversion or dismissal, you must be sure that the following elements exist:

1. That the business debtor has suffered a continuing loss of property and that there is an apparent absence of likelihood for rehabilitation;

2. That the business debtor is unable to effectuate a plan;

3. That there has been an unreasonable delay on the part of the business debtor that is prejudicial to his creditors;

4. That the business debtor has been unable to produce a plan within the time set by the court;

5. That there has been a denial of confirmation of a proposed plan, a denial of a petition for additional time to file another plan, or modification of any previous plan;

6. That there has been a revocation by the court of an order of confirmation of the plan and/or a denial of confirmation of another plan or modification thereof;

7. That there has been, on the part of a business debtor, demonstrated inability to effectuate consummation of a confirmed plan;

8. That there has been on the part of the business debtor a material default with respect to any confirmed plan; and

9. That there has been a termination, by the court, of a confirmed plan, resulting from an occurrence of nonoccurrence of a condition specified in the plan.

Chapter Appendix of Bankruptcy Forms

The following sample forms for use in federal bankruptcy courts illustrate the use of the required debtor and creditor information that has been discussed in this chapter.

In addition to court forms, two specimen bankruptcy problems are included, together with an office form for obtaining necessary information from the client. (See Figures 13.1 through 13.12.)

Figure 13.1

Bankruptcy Information Form

B 22A (Official Form 22A) (Chapter 7) (01/08)

| In re _____
 Debtor(s)

 Case Number: _____
 (If known) | According to the calculations required by this statement:

 ☐ **The presumption arises.**
 ☐ **The presumption does not arise.**

 (Check the box as directed in Parts I, III, and VI of this statement) |

CHAPTER 7 STATEMENT OF CURRENT MONTHLY INCOME
AND MEANS-TEST CALCULATION

In addition to Schedules I and J, this statement must be completed by every individual chapter 7 debtor, whether or not filing jointly. Joint debtors may complete one statement only.

	Part I. EXCLUSION FOR DISABLED VETERANS AND NON-CONSUMER DEBTORS		
1A	If you are a disabled veteran described in the Veteran's Declaration in this Part I, (1) check the box at the beginning of the Veteran's Declaration, (2) check the box for "The presumption does not arise" at the top of this statement, and (3) complete the verification in Part VIII. Do not complete any of the remaining parts of this statement. ☐ **Veteran's Declaration.** By checking this box, I declare under penalty of perjury that I am a disabled veteran (as defined in 38 U.S.C. § 3741(1)) whose indebtedness occurred primarily during a period in which I was on active duty (as defined in 10 U.S.C. § 101(d)(1)) or while I was performing a homeland defense activity (as defined in 32 U.S.C. §901(1)).		
1B	If your debts are not primarily consumer debts, check the box below and complete the verification in Part VIII. Do not complete any of the remaining parts of this statement. ☐ **Declaration of non-consumer debts.** By checking this box, I declare that my debts are not primarily consumer debts.		
	Part II. CALCULATION OF MONTHLY INCOME FOR § 707(b)(7) EXCLUSION		
2	**Marital/filing status.** Check the box that applies and complete the balance of this part of this statement as directed. a. ☐ Unmarried. **Complete only Column A ("Debtor's Income") for Lines 3-11.** b. ☐ Married, not filing jointly, with declaration of separate households. By checking this box, debtor declares under penalty of perjury: "My spouse and I are legally separated under applicable non-bankruptcy law or my spouse and I are living apart other than for the purpose of evading the requirements of § 707(b)(2)(A) of the Bankruptcy Code." **Complete only Column A ("Debtor's Income") for Lines 3-11.** c. ☐ Married, not filing jointly, without the declaration of separate households set out in Line 2.b above. **Complete both Column A ("Debtor's Income") and Column B ("Spouse's Income") for Lines 3-11.** d. ☐ Married, filing jointly. **Complete both Column A ("Debtor's Income") and Column B ("Spouse's Income") for Lines 3-11.**		
	All figures must reflect average monthly income received from all sources, derived during the six calendar months prior to filing the bankruptcy case, ending on the last day of the month before the filing. If the amount of monthly income varied during the six months, you must divide the six-month total by six, and enter the result on the appropriate line.	**Column A** Debtor's Income	**Column B** Spouse's Income
3	**Gross wages, salary, tips, bonuses, overtime, commissions.**	$	$

Figure 13.1 (*continued*)

4	**Income from the operation of a business, profession or farm.** Subtract Line b from Line a and enter the difference in the appropriate column(s) of Line 4. If you operate more than one business, profession or farm, enter aggregate numbers and provide details on an attachment. Do not enter a number less than zero. **Do not include any part of the business expenses entered on Line b as a deduction in Part V.**			
		a.	Gross receipts	$		
		b.	Ordinary and necessary business expenses	$		
		c.	Business income	Subtract Line b from Line a	$	$
5	**Rent and other real property income.** Subtract Line b from Line a and enter the difference in the appropriate column(s) of Line 5. Do not enter a number less than zero. **Do not include any part of the operating expenses entered on Line b as a deduction in Part V.**			
		a.	Gross receipts	$		
		b.	Ordinary and necessary operating expenses	$		
		c.	Rent and other real property income	Subtract Line b from Line a	$	$
6	**Interest, dividends and royalties.**		$	$
7	**Pension and retirement income.**		$	$
8	**Any amounts paid by another person or entity, on a regular basis, for the household expenses of the debtor or the debtor's dependents, including child support paid for that purpose.** Do not include alimony or separate maintenance payments or amounts paid by your spouse if Column B is completed.		$	$
9	**Unemployment compensation.** Enter the amount in the appropriate column(s) of Line 9. However, if you contend that unemployment compensation received by you or your spouse was a benefit under the Social Security Act, do not list the amount of such compensation in Column A or B, but instead state the amount in the space below: Unemployment compensation claimed to be a benefit under the Social Security Act Debtor $ _____ Spouse $ _____		$	$
10	**Income from all other sources.** Specify source and amount. If necessary, list additional sources on a separate page. **Do not include alimony or separate maintenance payments paid by your spouse if Column B is completed, but include all other payments of alimony or separate maintenance.** Do not include any benefits received under the Social Security Act or payments received as a victim of a war crime, crime against humanity, or as a victim of international or domestic terrorism.			
		a.		$		
		b.		$		
		Total and enter on Line 10		$	$
11	**Subtotal of Current Monthly Income for § 707(b)(7).** Add Lines 3 thru 10 in Column A, and, if Column B is completed, add Lines 3 through 10 in Column B. Enter the total(s).		$	$
12	**Total Current Monthly Income for § 707(b)(7).** If Column B has been completed, add Line 11, Column A to Line 11, Column B, and enter the total. If Column B has not been completed, enter the amount from Line 11, Column A.		$	
	Part III. APPLICATION OF § 707(b)(7) EXCLUSION			
13	**Annualized Current Monthly Income for § 707(b)(7).** Multiply the amount from Line 12 by the number 12 and enter the result.			$

Figure 13.1 *(continued)*

B 22A (Official Form 22A) (Chapter 7) (01/08)

14	**Applicable median family income.** Enter the median family income for the applicable state and household size. (This information is available by family size at www.usdoj.gov/ust/ or from the clerk of the bankruptcy court.) a. Enter debtor's state of residence: _____ b. Enter debtor's household size: _____	$
15	**Application of Section 707(b)(7).** Check the applicable box and proceed as directed. ☐ **The amount on Line 13 is less than or equal to the amount on Line 14.** Check the box for "The presumption does not arise" at the top of page 1 of this statement, and complete Part VIII; do not complete Parts IV, V, VI or VII. ☐ **The amount on Line 13 is more than the amount on Line 14.** Complete the remaining parts of this statement.	

Complete Parts IV, V, VI, and VII of this statement only if required. (See Line 15.)

	Part IV. CALCULATION OF CURRENT MONTHLY INCOME FOR § 707(b)(2)	
16	**Enter the amount from Line 12.**	$
17	**Marital adjustment.** If you checked the box at Line 2.c, enter on Line 17 the total of any income listed in Line 11, Column B that was NOT paid on a regular basis for the household expenses of the debtor or the debtor's dependents. Specify in the lines below the basis for excluding the Column B income (such as payment of the spouse's tax liability or the spouse's support of persons other than the debtor or the debtor's dependents) and the amount of income devoted to each purpose. If necessary, list additional adjustments on a separate page. If you did not check box at Line 2.c, enter zero. a. _____ $ _____ b. _____ $ _____ c. _____ $ _____ Total and enter on Line 17.	$
18	**Current monthly income for § 707(b)(2).** Subtract Line 17 from Line 16 and enter the result.	$
	Part V. CALCULATION OF DEDUCTIONS FROM INCOME	
	Subpart A: Deductions under Standards of the Internal Revenue Service (IRS)	
19A	**National Standards: food, clothing and other items.** Enter in Line 19A the "Total" amount from IRS National Standards for Food, Clothing and Other Items for the applicable household size. (This information is available at www.usdoj.gov/ust/ or from the clerk of the bankruptcy court.)	$
19B	**National Standards: health care.** Enter in Line a1 below the amount from IRS National Standards for Out-of-Pocket Health Care for persons under 65 years of age, and in Line a2 the IRS National Standards for Out-of-Pocket Health Care for persons 65 years of age or older. (This information is available at www.usdoj.gov/ust/ or from the clerk of the bankruptcy court.) Enter in Line b1 the number of members of your household who are under 65 years of age, and enter in Line b2 the number of members of your household who are 65 years of age or older. (The total number of household members must be the same as the number stated in Line 14b.) Multiply Line a1 by Line b1 to obtain a total amount for household members under 65, and enter the result in Line c1. Multiply Line a2 by Line b2 to obtain a total amount for household members 65 and older, and enter the result in Line c2. Add Lines c1 and c2 to obtain a total health care amount, and enter the result in Line 19B. 	**Household members under 65 years of age**		**Household members 65 years of age or older**	
---	---	---	---
a1.	Allowance per member	a2.	Allowance per member	
b1.	Number of members	b2.	Number of members	
c1.	Subtotal	c2.	Subtotal			$

Figure 13.1 (*continued*)

20A	**Local Standards: housing and utilities; non-mortgage expenses.** Enter the amount of the IRS Housing and Utilities Standards; non-mortgage expenses for the applicable county and household size. (This information is available at www.usdoj.gov/ust/ or from the clerk of the bankruptcy court).		$
20B	**Local Standards: housing and utilities; mortgage/rent expense.** Enter, in Line a below, the amount of the IRS Housing and Utilities Standards; mortgage/rent expense for your county and household size (this information is available at www.usdoj/ust/ or from the clerk of the bankruptcy court); enter on Line b the total of the Average Monthly Payments for any debts secured by your home, as stated in Line 42; subtract Line b from Line a and enter the result in Line 20B. **Do not enter an amount less than zero.**		
	a.	IRS Housing and Utilities Standards; mortgage/rental expense	$
	b.	Average Monthly Payment for any debts secured by your home, if any, as stated in Line 42	$
	c.	Net mortgage/rental expense	Subtract Line b from Line a.	$
21	**Local Standards: housing and utilities; adjustment.** If you contend that the process set out in Lines 20A and 20B does not accurately compute the allowance to which you are entitled under the IRS Housing and Utilities Standards, enter any additional amount to which you contend you are entitled, and state the basis for your contention in the space below: _____ _____ _____		$
22A	**Local Standards: transportation; vehicle operation/public transportation expense.** You are entitled to an expense allowance in this category regardless of whether you pay the expenses of operating a vehicle and regardless of whether you use public transportation. Check the number of vehicles for which you pay the operating expenses or for which the operating expenses are included as a contribution to your household expenses in Line 8. ☐ 0 ☐ 1 ☐ 2 or more. If you checked 0, enter on Line 22A the "Public Transportation" amount from IRS Local Standards: Transportation. If you checked 1 or 2 or more, enter on Line 22A the "Operating Costs" amount from IRS Local Standards: Transportation for the applicable number of vehicles in the applicable Metropolitan Statistical Area or Census Region. (These amounts are available at www.usdoj.gov/ust/ or from the clerk of the bankruptcy court.)		$
22B	**Local Standards: transportation; additional public transportation expense.** If you pay the operating expenses for a vehicle and also use public transportation, and you contend that you are entitled to an additional deduction for your public transportation expenses, enter on Line 22B the "Public Transportation" amount from IRS Local Standards: Transportation. (This amount is available at www.usdoj.gov/ust/ or from the clerk of the bankruptcy court.)		$
23	**Local Standards: transportation ownership/lease expense; Vehicle 1.** Check the number of vehicles for which you claim an ownership/lease expense. (You may not claim an ownership/lease expense for more than two vehicles.) ☐ 1 ☐ 2 or more. Enter, in Line a below, the "Ownership Costs" for "One Car" from the IRS Local Standards: Transportation (available at www.usdoj.gov/ust/ or from the clerk of the bankruptcy court); enter in Line b the total of the Average Monthly Payments for any debts secured by Vehicle 1, as stated in Line 42; subtract Line b from Line a and enter the result in Line 23. **Do not enter an amount less than zero.**		
	a.	IRS Transportation Standards, Ownership Costs	$
	b.	Average Monthly Payment for any debts secured by Vehicle 1, as stated in Line 42	$
	c.	Net ownership/lease expense for Vehicle 1	Subtract Line b from Line a.	$

Figure 13.1 *(continued)*

B 22A (Official Form 22A) (Chapter 7) (01/08)

24	**Local Standards: transportation ownership/lease expense; Vehicle 2.** Complete this Line only if you checked the "2 or more" Box in Line 23. Enter, in Line a below, the "Ownership Costs" for "One Car" from the IRS Local Standards: Transportation (available at www.usdoj.gov/ust/ or from the clerk of the bankruptcy court); enter in Line b the total of the Average Monthly Payments for any debts secured by Vehicle 2, as stated in Line 42; subtract Line b from Line a and enter the result in Line 24. **Do not enter an amount less than zero.**

a.	IRS Transportation Standards, Ownership Costs	$	
b.	Average Monthly Payment for any debts secured by Vehicle 2, as stated in Line 42	$	
c.	Net ownership/lease expense for Vehicle 2	Subtract Line b from Line a.	$

25	**Other Necessary Expenses: taxes.** Enter the total average monthly expense that you actually incur for all federal, state and local taxes, other than real estate and sales taxes, such as income taxes, self-employment taxes, social-security taxes, and Medicare taxes. **Do not include real estate or sales taxes.**	$
26	**Other Necessary Expenses: involuntary deductions for employment.** Enter the total average monthly payroll deductions that are required for your employment, such as retirement contributions, union dues, and uniform costs. **Do not include discretionary amounts, such as voluntary 401(k) contributions.**	$
27	**Other Necessary Expenses: life insurance.** Enter total average monthly premiums that you actually pay for term life insurance for yourself. **Do not include premiums for insurance on your dependents, for whole life or for any other form of insurance.**	$
28	**Other Necessary Expenses: court-ordered payments.** Enter the total monthly amount that you are required to pay pursuant to the order of a court or administrative agency, such as spousal or child support payments. **Do not include payments on past due obligations included in Line 44.**	$
29	**Other Necessary Expenses: education for employment or for a physically or mentally challenged child.** Enter the total average monthly amount that you actually expend for education that is a condition of employment and for education that is required for a physically or mentally challenged dependent child for whom no public education providing similar services is available.	$
30	**Other Necessary Expenses: childcare.** Enter the total average monthly amount that you actually expend on childcare—such as baby-sitting, day care, nursery and preschool. **Do not include other educational payments.**	$
31	**Other Necessary Expenses: health care.** Enter the total average monthly amount that you actually expend on health care that is required for the health and welfare of yourself or your dependents, that is not reimbursed by insurance or paid by a health savings account, and that is in excess of the amount entered in Line 19B. **Do not include payments for health insurance or health savings accounts listed in Line 34.**	$
32	**Other Necessary Expenses: telecommunication services.** Enter the total average monthly amount that you actually pay for telecommunication services other than your basic home telephone and cell phone service—such as pagers, call waiting, caller id, special long distance, or internet service—to the extent necessary for your health and welfare or that of your dependents. **Do not include any amount previously deducted.**	$
33	**Total Expenses Allowed under IRS Standards.** Enter the total of Lines 19 through 32.	$

Subpart B: Additional Living Expense Deductions **Note: Do not include any expenses that you have listed in Lines 19-32**

Figure 13.1 (*continued*)

34	**Health Insurance, Disability Insurance, and Health Savings Account Expenses.** List the monthly expenses in the categories set out in lines a-c below that are reasonably necessary for yourself, your spouse, or your dependents.	
	a. Health Insurance — $ b. Disability Insurance — $ c. Health Savings Account — $ Total and enter on Line 34 **If you do not actually expend this total amount,** state your actual total average monthly expenditures in the space below: $ _____	$
35	**Continued contributions to the care of household or family members.** Enter the total average actual monthly expenses that you will continue to pay for the reasonable and necessary care and support of an elderly, chronically ill, or disabled member of your household or member of your immediate family who is unable to pay for such expenses.	$
36	**Protection against family violence.** Enter the total average reasonably necessary monthly expenses that you actually incurred to maintain the safety of your family under the Family Violence Prevention and Services Act or other applicable federal law. The nature of these expenses is required to be kept confidential by the court.	$
37	**Home energy costs.** Enter the total average monthly amount, in excess of the allowance specified by IRS Local Standards for Housing and Utilities, that you actually expend for home energy costs. **You must provide your case trustee with documentation of your actual expenses, and you must demonstrate that the additional amount claimed is reasonable and necessary.**	$
38	**Education expenses for dependent children less than 18.** Enter the total average monthly expenses that you actually incur, not to exceed $137.50 per child, for attendance at a private or public elementary or secondary school by your dependent children less than 18 years of age. **You must provide your case trustee with documentation of your actual expenses, and you must explain why the amount claimed is reasonable and necessary and not already accounted for in the IRS Standards.**	$
39	**Additional food and clothing expense.** Enter the total average monthly amount by which your food and clothing expenses exceed the combined allowances for food and clothing (apparel and services) in the IRS National Standards, not to exceed 5% of those combined allowances. (This information is available at www.usdoj.gov/ust/ or from the clerk of the bankruptcy court.) **You must demonstrate that the additional amount claimed is reasonable and necessary.**	$
40	**Continued charitable contributions.** Enter the amount that you will continue to contribute in the form of cash or financial instruments to a charitable organization as defined in 26 U.S.C. § 170(c)(1)-(2).	$
41	**Total Additional Expense Deductions under § 707(b).** Enter the total of Lines 34 through 40	$
	Subpart C: Deductions for Debt Payment	

Figure 13.1 *(continued)*

42	**Future payments on secured claims.** For each of your debts that is secured by an interest in property that you own, list the name of the creditor, identify the property securing the debt, state the Average Monthly Payment, and check whether the payment includes taxes or insurance. The Average Monthly Payment is the total of all amounts scheduled as contractually due to each Secured Creditor in the 60 months following the filing of the bankruptcy case, divided by 60. If necessary, list additional entries on a separate page. Enter the total of the Average Monthly Payments on Line 42.				
		Name of Creditor	Property Securing the Debt	Average Monthly Payment	Does payment include taxes or insurance?	
	a.			$	☐ yes ☐ no	
	b.			$	☐ yes ☐ no	
	c.			$	☐ yes ☐ no	
				Total: Add Lines a, b and c.		$

43	**Other payments on secured claims.** If any of debts listed in Line 42 are secured by your primary residence, a motor vehicle, or other property necessary for your support or the support of your dependents, you may include in your deduction 1/60th of any amount (the "cure amount") that you must pay the creditor in addition to the payments listed in Line 42, in order to maintain possession of the property. The cure amount would include any sums in default that must be paid in order to avoid repossession or foreclosure. List and total any such amounts in the following chart. If necessary, list additional entries on a separate page.				
		Name of Creditor	Property Securing the Debt	1/60th of the Cure Amount	
	a.			$	
	b.			$	
	c.			$	
				Total: Add Lines a, b and c	$

44	**Payments on prepetition priority claims.** Enter the total amount, divided by 60, of all priority claims, such as priority tax, child support and alimony claims, for which you were liable at the time of your bankruptcy filing. **Do not include current obligations, such as those set out in Line 28.**	$

45	**Chapter 13 administrative expenses.** If you are eligible to file a case under chapter 13, complete the following chart, multiply the amount in line a by the amount in line b, and enter the resulting administrative expense.		
	a.	Projected average monthly chapter 13 plan payment.	$
	b.	Current multiplier for your district as determined under schedules issued by the Executive Office for United States Trustees. (This information is available at www.usdoj.gov/ust/ or from the clerk of the bankruptcy court.)	x
	c.	Average monthly administrative expense of chapter 13 case	Total: Multiply Lines a and b	$

46	**Total Deductions for Debt Payment.** Enter the total of Lines 42 through 45.	$

Subpart D: Total Deductions from Income

47	**Total of all deductions allowed under § 707(b)(2).** Enter the total of Lines 33, 41, and 46.	$

Figure 13.1 (*continued*)

	Part VI. DETERMINATION OF § 707(b)(2) PRESUMPTION	
48	**Enter the amount from Line 18 (Current monthly income for § 707(b)(2))**	$
49	**Enter the amount from Line 47 (Total of all deductions allowed under § 707(b)(2))**	$
50	**Monthly disposable income under § 707(b)(2).** Subtract Line 49 from Line 48 and enter the result	$
51	**60-month disposable income under § 707(b)(2).** Multiply the amount in Line 50 by the number 60 and enter the result.	$
52	**Initial presumption determination.** Check the applicable box and proceed as directed. ☐ **The amount on Line 51 is less than $6,575** Check the box for "The presumption does not arise" at the top of page 1 of this statement, and complete the verification in Part VIII. Do not complete the remainder of Part VI. ☐ **The amount set forth on Line 51 is more than $10,950.** Check the box for "The presumption arises" at the top of page 1 of this statement, and complete the verification in Part VIII. You may also complete Part VII. Do not complete the remainder of Part VI. ☐ **The amount on Line 51 is at least $6,575, but not more than $10,950.** Complete the remainder of Part VI (Lines 53 through 55).	
53	**Enter the amount of your total non-priority unsecured debt**	$
54	**Threshold debt payment amount.** Multiply the amount in Line 53 by the number 0.25 and enter the result.	$
55	**Secondary presumption determination.** Check the applicable box and proceed as directed. ☐ **The amount on Line 51 is less than the amount on Line 54.** Check the box for "The presumption does not arise" at the top of page 1 of this statement, and complete the verification in Part VIII. ☐ **The amount on Line 51 is equal to or greater than the amount on Line 54.** Check the box for "The presumption arises" at the top of page 1 of this statement, and complete the verification in Part VIII. You may also complete Part VII.	

	Part VII: ADDITIONAL EXPENSE CLAIMS	
56	**Other Expenses.** List and describe any monthly expenses, not otherwise stated in this form, that are required for the health and welfare of you and your family and that you contend should be an additional deduction from your current monthly income under § 707(b)(2)(A)(ii)(I). If necessary, list additional sources on a separate page. All figures should reflect your average monthly expense for each item. Total the expenses.	

	Expense Description	Monthly Amount
a.		$
b.		$
c.		$
	Total: Add Lines a, b and c	$

	Part VIII: VERIFICATION
57	I declare under penalty of perjury that the information provided in this statement is true and correct. (*If this is a joint case, both debtors must sign.*) Date: _____ Signature: _____ (Debtor) Date: _____ Signature: _____ (Joint Debtor, if any)

Figure 13.2
Petition for Bankruptcy

B 1 (Official Form 1) (1/08)

United States Bankruptcy Court	Voluntary Petition

Name of Debtor (if individual, enter Last, First, Middle):	Name of Joint Debtor (Spouse) (Last, First, Middle):
All Other Names used by the Debtor in the last 8 years (include married, maiden, and trade names):	All Other Names used by the Joint Debtor in the last 8 years (include married, maiden, and trade names):
Last four digits of Soc. Sec. or Indvidual-Taxpayer I.D. (ITIN) No./Complete EIN (if more than one, state all):	Last four digits of Soc. Sec. or Indvidual-Taxpayer I.D. (ITIN) No./Complete EIN (if more than one, state all):
Street Address of Debtor (No. and Street, City, and State): ZIP CODE	Street Address of Joint Debtor (No. and Street, City, and State): ZIP CODE
County of Residence or of the Principal Place of Business:	County of Residence or of the Principal Place of Business:
Mailing Address of Debtor (if different from street address): ZIP CODE	Mailing Address of Joint Debtor (if different from street address): ZIP CODE
Location of Principal Assets of Business Debtor (if different from street address above): ZIP CODE	

Type of Debtor (Form of Organization) (Check **one** box.)	Nature of Business (Check **one** box.)	Chapter of Bankruptcy Code Under Which the Petition is Filed (Check **one** box.)
☐ Individual (includes Joint Debtors) *See Exhibit D on page 2 of this form.* ☐ Corporation (includes LLC and LLP) ☐ Partnership ☐ Other (If debtor is not one of the above entities, check this box and state type of entity below.) _____	☐ Health Care Business ☐ Single Asset Real Estate as defined in 11 U.S.C. § 101(51B) ☐ Railroad ☐ Stockbroker ☐ Commodity Broker ☐ Clearing Bank ☐ Other **Tax-Exempt Entity** (Check box, if applicable.) ☐ Debtor is a tax-exempt organization under Title 26 of the United States Code (the Internal Revenue Code).	☐ Chapter 7 ☐ Chapter 15 Petition for ☐ Chapter 9 Recognition of a Foreign ☐ Chapter 11 Main Proceeding ☐ Chapter 12 ☐ Chapter 15 Petition for ☐ Chapter 13 Recognition of a Foreign Nonmain Proceeding **Nature of Debts** (Check one box.) ☐ Debts are primarily consumer ☐ Debts are primarily debts, defined in 11 U.S.C. business debts. § 101(8) as "incurred by an individual primarily for a personal, family, or house- hold purpose."

Filing Fee (Check one box.)	Chapter 11 Debtors
☐ Full Filing Fee attached. ☐ Filing Fee to be paid in installments (applicable to individuals only). Must attach signed application for the court's consideration certifying that the debtor is unable to pay fee except in installments. Rule 1006(b). See Official Form 3A. ☐ Filing Fee waiver requested (applicable to chapter 7 individuals only). Must attach signed application for the court's consideration. See Official Form 3B.	**Check one box:** ☐ Debtor is a small business debtor as defined in 11 U.S.C. § 101(51D). ☐ Debtor is not a small business debtor as defined in 11 U.S.C. § 101(51D). **Check if:** ☐ Debtor's aggregate noncontingent liquidated debts (excluding debts owed to insiders or affiliates) are less than $2,190,000. - **Check all applicable boxes:** ☐ A plan is being filed with this petition. ☐ Acceptances of the plan were solicited prepetition from one or more classes of creditors, in accordance with 11 U.S.C. § 1126(b).

Statistical/Administrative Information										THIS SPACE IS FOR COURT USE ONLY
☐ Debtor estimates that funds will be available for distribution to unsecured creditors. ☐ Debtor estimates that, after any exempt property is excluded and administrative expenses paid, there will be no funds available for distribution to unsecured creditors.										

Estimated Number of Creditors									
☐ 1-49	☐ 50-99	☐ 100-199	☐ 200-999	☐ 1,000-5,000	☐ 5,001-10,000	☐ 10,001-25,000	☐ 25,001-50,000	☐ 50,001-100,000	☐ Over 100,000

Estimated Assets									
☐ $0 to $50,000	☐ $50,001 to $100,000	☐ $100,001 to $500,000	☐ $500,001 to $1 million	☐ $1,000,001 to $10 million	☐ $10,000,001 to $50 million	☐ $50,000,001 to $100 million	☐ $100,000,001 to $500 million	☐ $500,000,001 to $1 billion	☐ More than $1 billion

Estimated Liabilities									
☐ $0 to $50,000	☐ $50,001 to $100,000	☐ $100,001 to $500,000	☐ $500,001 to $1 million	☐ $1,000,001 to $10 million	☐ $10,000,001 to $50 million	☐ $50,000,001 to $100 million	☐ $100,000,001 to $500 million	☐ $500,000,001 to $1 billion	☐ More than $1 billion

Figure 13.2 (*continued*)

B 1 (Official Form 1) (1/08)

Voluntary Petition *(This page must be completed and filed in every case.)*	Name of Debtor(s):	
All Prior Bankruptcy Cases Filed Within Last 8 Years (If more than two, attach additional sheet.)		
Location Where Filed:	Case Number:	Date Filed:
Location Where Filed:	Case Number:	Date Filed:
Pending Bankruptcy Case Filed by any Spouse, Partner, or Affiliate of this Debtor (If more than one, attach additional sheet.)		
Name of Debtor:	Case Number:	Date Filed:
District:	Relationship:	Judge:

Exhibit A	**Exhibit B**
(To be completed if debtor is required to file periodic reports (e.g., forms 10K and 10Q) with the Securities and Exchange Commission pursuant to Section 13 or 15(d) of the Securities Exchange Act of 1934 and is requesting relief under chapter 11.)	(To be completed if debtor is an individual whose debts are primarily consumer debts.) I, the attorney for the petitioner named in the foregoing petition, declare that I have informed the petitioner that [he or she] may proceed under chapter 7, 11, 12, or 13 of title 11, United States Code, and have explained the relief available under each such chapter. I further certify that I have delivered to the debtor the notice required by 11 U.S.C. § 342(b).
☐ Exhibit A is attached and made a part of this petition.	X _____ Signature of Attorney for Debtor(s) (Date)

Exhibit C

Does the debtor own or have possession of any property that poses or is alleged to pose a threat of imminent and identifiable harm to public health or safety?

☐   Yes, and Exhibit C is attached and made a part of this petition.

☐   No.

Exhibit D

(To be completed by every individual debtor. If a joint petition is filed, each spouse must complete and attach a separate Exhibit D.)

☐   Exhibit D completed and signed by the debtor is attached and made a part of this petition.

If this is a joint petition:

☐   Exhibit D also completed and signed by the joint debtor is attached and made a part of this petition.

Information Regarding the Debtor - Venue
(Check any applicable box.)

☐   Debtor has been domiciled or has had a residence, principal place of business, or principal assets in this District for 180 days immediately preceding the date of this petition or for a longer part of such 180 days than in any other District.

☐   There is a bankruptcy case concerning debtor's affiliate, general partner, or partnership pending in this District.

☐   Debtor is a debtor in a foreign proceeding and has its principal place of business or principal assets in the United States in this District, or has no principal place of business or assets in the United States but is a defendant in an action or proceeding [in a federal or state court] in this District, or the interests of the parties will be served in regard to the relief sought in this District.

Certification by a Debtor Who Resides as a Tenant of Residential Property
(Check all applicable boxes.)

☐   Landlord has a judgment against the debtor for possession of debtor's residence. (If box checked, complete the following.)

_____
(Name of landlord that obtained judgment)

_____
(Address of landlord)

☐   Debtor claims that under applicable nonbankruptcy law, there are circumstances under which the debtor would be permitted to cure the entire monetary default that gave rise to the judgment for possession, after the judgment for possession was entered, and

☐   Debtor has included with this petition the deposit with the court of any rent that would become due during the 30-day period after the filing of the petition.

☐   Debtor certifies that he/she has served the Landlord with this certification. (11 U.S.C. § 362(l)).

Figure 13.2 *(continued)*

B 1 (Official Form) 1 (1/08)	
Voluntary Petition *(This page must be completed and filed in every case.)*	Name of Debtor(s):

Signatures	

Signature(s) of Debtor(s) (Individual/Joint)	**Signature of a Foreign Representative**

Signature(s) of Debtor(s) (Individual/Joint)

I declare under penalty of perjury that the information provided in this petition is true and correct.

[If petitioner is an individual whose debts are primarily consumer debts and has chosen to file under chapter 7] I am aware that I may proceed under chapter 7, 11, 12 or 13 of title 11, United States Code, understand the relief available under each such chapter, and choose to proceed under chapter 7.

[If no attorney represents me and no bankruptcy petition preparer signs the petition] I have obtained and read the notice required by 11 U.S.C. § 342(b).

I request relief in accordance with the chapter of title 11, United States Code, specified in this petition.

X _____
    Signature of Debtor

X _____
    Signature of Joint Debtor

    Telephone Number (if not represented by attorney)

    Date

Signature of a Foreign Representative

I declare under penalty of perjury that the information provided in this petition is true and correct, that I am the foreign representative of a debtor in a foreign proceeding, and that I am authorized to file this petition.

(Check only **one** box.)

☐ I request relief in accordance with chapter 15 of title 11, United States Code. Certified copies of the documents required by 11 U.S.C. § 1515 are attached.

☐ Pursuant to 11 U.S.C. § 1511, I request relief in accordance with the chapter of title 11 specified in this petition. A certified copy of the order granting recognition of the foreign main proceeding is attached.

X _____
    (Signature of Foreign Representative)

    (Printed Name of Foreign Representative)

    Date

Signature of Attorney*

X _____
    Signature of Attorney for Debtor(s)

    Printed Name of Attorney for Debtor(s)

    Firm Name

    Address

    Telephone Number

    Date

*In a case in which § 707(b)(4)(D) applies, this signature also constitutes a certification that the attorney has no knowledge after an inquiry that the information in the schedules is incorrect.

Signature of Non-Attorney Bankruptcy Petition Preparer

I declare under penalty of perjury that: (1) I am a bankruptcy petition preparer as defined in 11 U.S.C. § 110; (2) I prepared this document for compensation and have provided the debtor with a copy of this document and the notices and information required under 11 U.S.C. §§ 110(b), 110(h), and 342(b); and, (3) if rules or guidelines have been promulgated pursuant to 11 U.S.C. § 110(h) setting a maximum fee for services chargeable by bankruptcy petition preparers, I have given the debtor notice of the maximum amount before preparing any document for filing for a debtor or accepting any fee from the debtor, as required in that section. Official Form 19 is attached.

    Printed Name and title, if any, of Bankruptcy Petition Preparer

    Social-Security number (If the bankruptcy petition preparer is not an individual, state the Social-Security number of the officer, principal, responsible person or partner of the bankruptcy petition preparer.) (Required by 11 U.S.C. § 110.)

    Address

X _____

    Date

Signature of Debtor (Corporation/Partnership)

I declare under penalty of perjury that the information provided in this petition is true and correct, and that I have been authorized to file this petition on behalf of the debtor.

The debtor requests the relief in accordance with the chapter of title 11, United States Code, specified in this petition.

X _____
    Signature of Authorized Individual

    Printed Name of Authorized Individual

    Title of Authorized Individual

    Date

Signature of bankruptcy petition preparer or officer, principal, responsible person, or partner whose Social-Security number is provided above.

Names and Social-Security numbers of all other individuals who prepared or assisted in preparing this document unless the bankruptcy petition preparer is not an individual.

If more than one person prepared this document, attach additional sheets conforming to the appropriate official form for each person.

A bankruptcy petition preparer's failure to comply with the provisions of title 11 and the Federal Rules of Bankruptcy Procedure may result in fines or imprisonment or both. 11 U.S.C. § 110; 18 U.S.C. § 156.

Figure 13.3
Bankruptcy Intake Questionnaire

Although we are asking questions about all of your property, it does not mean that you will lose it by filing for bankruptcy.

Complete all questions fully and completely based on all information available to you. If you do not have the information available, make your best effort to obtain the information from all sources.

1. NAME AND RESIDENCE INFORMATION:

    A. Full name: _____

    B. Marital status (if married and separated from your spouse, please state "Separated" or if divorced state "Divorced"):

    _____

    Your spouse's name: _____

    C. Social Security number: _____

    Your spouse's Social Security number: _____

    D. List any other names used by you or your spouse (including maiden name) in the last six years: _____

    _____

    _____

    E. Current address: _____

                     Street   City   County   ZIP

    F. Telephone number: _____

                      Home   Work

    (1) List spouse's current address and telephone number, if different than above:

    _____

    _____

    G. List all addresses you have had in the last six years. If husband and wife are both filing bankruptcy, list addresses for each for the last six years: (Include street, town, and ZIP code)

    _____

    _____

    _____

    _____

    _____

2. OCCUPATION AND INCOME:

    A. Usual type of work you do: _____

    B. Name and address of current employer: _____

    _____

    C. Spouse's usual type of work: _____

    _____

Figure 13.3 (*continued*)

D. Name and address of spouse's current employer: _____

_____

E. How long were each of you at your current job: _____

_____

If not employed by present employer for at least one year, state the names of the prior employers of either of you and nature of your job.

_____

_____

F. When do you receive payment of your salary (weekly, twice monthly, monthly, etc.)?

_____

G. Have you or your spouse been in business by yourself or with others during the last six years? Yes _____ No _____ If yes, give the name of the business, its address, and the names of others in business with you or your spouse.

_____

_____

_____

H. Amount of wages that you and your spouse received for last year:
Your wages: _____
Your spouse's wages: _____
Amount of wages that you and your spouse received for the year before last:
Your wages: _____
Your spouse's wages: _____
Amount and type of payroll deductions:

_____

_____

Amount of any other income received by you and your spouse last year (specify source such as welfare, child support, unemployment compensation, etc.):

_____

Amount of any other income received by you and your spouse for the year before last (specify source): _____

_____

Amount of income which you and your spouse believe you will receive during the next twelve months:

_____

_____

Is your employment or your spouse's employment subject to seasonal change or variation?

_____

_____

Figure 13.3 (*continued*)

3. TAX RETURNS AND REFUNDS: (Bring a copy of your income tax returns with you to our office.)

    A. Did you file a federal income tax return during the last three years? Which year or years? _____

    Did you file a state income tax return during the last three years?

    _____

    Which year or years? _____

    B. Where did you send tax returns for the last two years? Give city and state to which each form was mailed.

    State: _____

    Federal: _____

    State: _____

    Federal: _____

    C. Have you received any income tax refunds this year? Yes ____ No ____

    Amount: State $ _____ Federal $ _____

    D. What income tax refunds do you expect to receive this year? _____

    Amount: State $ _____ Federal $ _____

4. BANK ACCOUNTS AND SAFE DEPOSIT BOXES:

    A. Name and address of each bank in which you have had any account (checking, savings, etc.) during the past two years. Include every name on the account and the name of *every* person authorized to make withdrawals.

    _____

    _____

    B. Name and address of each bank you had any safe deposit box in during the past two years. Include name and address of all persons with a right to open the box, describe the contents of the box, and if given up, when:

    _____

    _____

    C. Are you a member of a credit union? Yes ____ No ____ If yes, give its name and address and how much you have saved there:

    _____

    Name   Address   Amount

5. BOOKS AND RECORDS

    A. Have you kept books of accounts or records of any nature or type whether formal or informal which relate to your finances during the last 2 years? Yes ____ No ____ If yes, where are these books or records now (Give names and addresses and include information about checkbooks, bank statements, invoices, statements of accounts, etc.)?

    _____

    _____

Figure 13.3 *(continued)*

    B. If any of the records of your financial affairs have been lost or destroyed during the past two years, tell when and how:

_____

_____

_____

6. PROPERTY HELD FOR ANOTHER PERSON: Do you have in your possession any property, furniture, etc. that belongs to another person? Yes ___ No ___ If yes, what is the property, who owns it, and what is it worth? Include name and address of the owners:

Type of Property	Value	Owned by	Address	Relative Yes or No

7. PRIOR BANKRUPTCY: Were you ever involved in any prior bankruptcy action? Yes ____ No ____ If yes, bring *all* papers relating to the action to our office.

8. RECEIVERS AND ASSIGNEES:

    A. Is a receiver or trustee holding any of your property? (Generally, a receiver is a person appointed by a court to receive and preserve the property or funds involved in a legal proceeding. A trustee is generally a person appointed by the court who is required by law to care for property and administer its disposition.) Yes ____ No ____ If yes, bring in all papers relating to the property and the person's appointment.

_____

Trustee's Name	Address

    B. Did you give, transfer, deliver, pledge, or assign for any reason whatsoever any of the property (including wages) to a creditor within the past year? Yes ____ No ____ If yes, describe the property, its worth, and give the name and address of the person you gave it to:

Type of Property	Value	Name and Address of Person Who Has It

9. PROPERTY HELD BY ANOTHER PERSON: Does anyone have anything of value that belongs to you? For example, have you loaned any of your property to another person or does a person other than a creditor hold any of your property for any reason?

Figure 13.3 (*continued*)

Yes____ No ____ If yes, who has the article, what is that person's address, and what is the article worth:

Article	Who Has the Article/Address	Value

10. LAWSUITS AND ATTACHMENTS:

    A. Have you been a party to a lawsuit of any kind during the past 12 months? Yes ____ No ____ If yes, bring in all papers pertaining to any lawsuits in which you have ever been involved.

    B. Are you suing anyone, or do you have any possible reason for suing someone, for injuries to yourself or other members of your family? Yes ____ No ____ If yes, who are you suing, for how much are you asking, and why are you suing?

    C. To your knowledge, does anyone have any reason for suing you (e.g., car accident)?

    D. Have you had any property sold in a sheriff's sale or seized by a creditor or creditor's representative during the last 4 months? Yes ____ No ____ If yes, bring any papers concerning those actions. Below, give a description of the property and the names and addresses of any creditors involved, as well as the dates involved.

    E. Has your bank account or paycheck been garnished in the last 4 months? Yes ____ No ____ If yes, give the following:

Who Received the Money	Amount Taken	Dates:	From	To

11. LOANS REPAID:

    A. If you have made any payments within the last 12 months to creditors from whom you have a loan of any type whether secured or unsecured (not medical bills, charge accounts, or other open accounts), give the name of the creditor, the dates of the payments, and the amount of the payments:

Creditor	Payment Dates	Amount of Payment

Figure 13.3 (*continued*)

B. Have you paid off any loans in full in the last 12 months? Yes _____ No _____
If yes, give the following:

Creditor   Address   Date Paid   Amount Paid   Relative   Yes or No

_____

_____

_____

_____

12. PROPERTY TRANSFERS:

A. Describe any gifts other than ordinary and usual presents to family members and charities during the past one year. Include the date of transfer and name and address of who received the gift:

_____

_____

B. Describe any sales or other transfers of any of your property during the past one year. Include the date of the transfer and the names and addresses of the people who received the property:

Property   Amount Received for It   Date   Person It Was Sold To/Address

_____

_____

_____

_____

C. State the amount of money you actually received for the sale or transfer of any of the property you listed in A and B above:

_____

_____

_____

13. REPOSSESSIONS AND RETURNS: If any property was repossessed (taken by a creditor) or returned during the past one year, give the following:

Description of   Date of Return   Creditor   Address   Value
Property   or Repossession

_____

_____

_____

_____

14. LOSSES:

A. If any property was lost in the past one year due to fire, theft, or gambling, describe the property and its value, give the date of the loss, and identify all persons involved.

_____

_____

Figure 13.3 *(continued)*

    B. Did insurance pay for any part of the loss? Yes ____ No ____ If yes, give date of payment _____ and amount paid _____

15. PAYMENTS OR TRANSFERS TO ATTORNEYS:

    A. Give the date, name, and address of any attorney you consulted during the past one year:

    _____

    _____

    B. Give the reason for which you consulted an attorney during the past year:

    _____

    _____

    C. Give the date and amount you have paid an attorney or any property you have transferred to any attorney:

    _____

    _____

    D. If you have promised to pay an attorney within the past year, give the amount and terms of the agreement:

    _____

    _____

16. BUSINESS: If you are in business, list the names of all the partners in your business, or if your business is a corporation, the names of all of the officers, directors, and stockholders of the corporation:

    _____

    _____

    _____

    _____

17. DEPENDENTS:

Does either spouse pay or receive alimony, maintenance, or child support?

Husband: _____ How much? _____

Wife: _____ How much? _____

If support received, for whose benefit is it received? _____

    List all dependents other than present spouse for whose support either spouse is responsible. Also state their relation to you. _____

    _____

    _____

18. BUDGET:

    A. Please estimate what you believe will be you and your spouse's average future monthly income for the next 12 months:

    Others (describe) _____ Amount _____

    _____ Amount _____

Figure 13.3 (*continued*)

B. If there is a cosigner or guarantor for any of your debts, give cosigner's or guarantor's name and which debt he or she cosigned for or guaranteed:

_____

_____

_____

_____

C. Have you ever been a cosigner or guarantor for someone else's debts? Yes ____ No ____ If yes, give the following:

Creditor	Address	Amount Owed	Date You Cosigned	Person You Cosigned For

ASSET LIVING

1. REAL PROPERTY:

Do you own real estate? Yes ____ No ____ Describe and give the location of all real property (lot, house, burial plot, etc.) in which you hold an interest: (If you have the deed or mortgage bring them with you to our offices.)

_____

_____

_____

Outstanding mortgage balance: _____

Name of mortgage company: _____

Purchase price: _____ Year purchased:_____

Address: _____

Present value of your house: _____

Is there a second mortgage? Yes ____ No ____ If yes, give the name and address of the company: _____

2. PERSONAL PROPERTY:

A. Cash on hand: _____

B. Do you have any deposits of money in banks, savings and loan associations, credit unions, utility companies, or with landlords or others? If yes, list the name and address of the company and the amount of deposit:

_____

_____

_____

Husband: _____ (take-home pay)

Wife: _____ (take-home pay)

Figure 13.3 (*continued*)

C. Please set out the estimated average amount of the following monthly expenses you believe will be incurred over the next 12 months

    (1) Rent or mortgage: _____

    (2) Utilities: _____

    _____

    _____

    _____

    _____

    _____

    (3) Food: _____

    (4) Clothing: _____

    (5) Laundry and cleaning: _____

    (6) Newspapers, periodicals, etc. _____

    (7) Medical and drug expenses: _____

    (8) Insurance (not deducted from wages): _____

    (9) Transportation: car loans: _____

                other: _____

    (10) Entertainment and recreation: _____

    (11) Dues (if not deducted from wages): _____

    (12) Taxes not deducted from wages and not included in

    mortgage payment: _____

    (13) Alimony, maintenance, or support: _____

    (14) Other support of dependents not at home: _____

    (15) Other (specify): _____

    _____

    _____

    _____

    _____

CREDITORS

1. SPECIAL CREDITORS:

    A. Do you owe wages to anybody? Yes ____ No ____

       To whom? _____

       Address: _____

       How much: _____

    B. Do you owe taxes to anybody? Yes ____ No ____ If so, to whom and how much:

       U.S.A. _____ Amount _____ State _____ Amount _____

       County _____ Amount _____

    C. List your major personal property items such as furniture, tools, appliances, stove, refrigerator, TV, sewing machine, etc., giving approximate age and value

Figure 13.3 (*continued*)

(what you think you could get for it if you sold it). Itemize as completely as possible:

Item   Approximate Age   Value (what you could get for it if you sold it)

_____

_____

_____

_____

_____

_____

_____

_____

_____

_____

If any of the above items are being financed through a company, list the item and the name and address of the company below and bring the financing papers to our offices:

_____

_____

_____

_____

Give an estimate of the value (what you could get for it if you sold it) of the following:

All your furniture: _____ All your clothing: _____

All minor appliances: _____ All your jewelry: _____

All your other household goods (such as dishes, utensils, food, etc.):

_____

D. CARS, MOBILE HOMES, TRAILERS, AND BOATS:

1. Do you have any cars? Yes _____ No _____ If so, give the year, make, model, value, and who is financing it: (Also give the amount owed and to what company or bank it is owed.)

_____

_____

_____

2. Do you have any mobile homes, trailers, and/or boats? Yes _____ No _____ If so, give brand, year, value, and who is financing it: (Also give amount owed.)

_____

_____

_____

Figure 13.3 (*continued*)

E. ACCESSORIES:

1. Do you own any life insurance policies? Yes _____ No _____
   Company/Address:_____
   How long have you had the policy? _____
   Cash surrender value: _____
2. Do you own any stocks? Yes _____ No _____ Value of stocks: _____
3. Do you own any bonds? Yes _____ No _____ Value of bonds: _____
4. Do you have any interest in or own any machinery, tools, or fixtures used in your business or work? Yes _____ No _____ If yes, describe and state what you could sell it for:

   _____
   _____
   _____
   _____

5. Do you have any books, prints, or pictures of substantial value? Yes _____ No _____ If so, estimate the value of them:

   _____
   _____
   _____
   _____
   _____

6. Do you have any stocks, bonds, certificates of deposit, or the like? Yes _____ No _____ If so, estimate the value of them:

   _____

7. Do you own or claim any other property not mentioned above? (Include livestock or animals other than family pets.) Yes _____ No _____ If so, what: _____
   Value: _____
   Have you had any previous marriages? Yes _____ No _____
   If so, what is the name of your former spouse? _____
8. Does anybody owe you any money, alimony, or child support? Yes _____ No _____ Who: _____
   How much:_____
9. Do you owe any alimony or child support? Yes _____ No _____ If so, how much and to whom: _____
10. Have you been involved in any automobile accidents in the past two years? Yes _____ No _____
11. Do you expect to inherit any money within the next six months? Yes _____ No _____
12. Do you expect to receive any settlements from any insurance companies? Yes _____ No _____ Amount: _____

Figure 13.3 (*continued*)

F. BUSINESS:

    1. If you own or operate a business, does the business have any equipment or furniture of any type used in the business? Yes _____ No _____ If so, list all items and their estimated value:

    _____

    _____

    2. Does the business have any outstanding and unpaid accounts receivable? Yes _____ No _____ If so, list the name and address of each person owing money to the company and the amount owed:

    _____

    _____

    3. Does the company have any inventory of finished or unfinished goods or merchandise for sale? Yes _____ No _____ If so, list and give your best estimate of value:

    _____

    _____

    4. Do you or does your business own or have an interest in any type of property about which we have not asked? Yes _____ No _____
    Please describe the property and the value you would give it:

    _____

    _____

    _____

I certify that the information contained in this application is true and correct to the best of my knowledge.

Dated:_____   _____

                                          _____

                                              Applicant(s)

Figure 13.4
Creditor's Proof of Claim

www.uscourts.gov/rules/bk_forms_1207/B_010_1207f.pdf

UNITED STATES BANKRUPTCY COURT _____ DISTRICT OF _____	**PROOF OF CLAIM**

Name of Debtor:	Case Number:

NOTE: *This form should not be used to make a claim for an administrative expense arising after the commencement of the case. A request for payment of an administrative expense may be filed pursuant to 11 U.S.C. § 503.*

Name of Creditor (the person or other entity to whom the debtor owes money or property):	Check this box to indicate that this claim amends a previously filed claim.
Name and address where notices should be sent:	**Court Claim Number:_____** (*If known*)
Telephone number:	Filed on:_____
Name and address where payment should be sent (if different from above):	Check this box if you are aware that anyone else has filed a proof of claim relating to your claim. Attach copy of statement giving particulars.
Telephone number:	Check this box if you are the debtor or trustee in this case.

1. Amount of Claim as of Date Case Filed: $_____ If all or part of your claim is secured, complete item 4 below; however, if all of your claim is unsecured, do not complete item 4. If all or part of your claim is entitled to priority, complete item 5. Check this box if claim includes interest or other charges in addition to the principal amount of claim. Attach itemized statement of interest or charges.	**5. Amount of Claim Entitled to Priority under 11 U.S.C. §507(a).** If any portion of your claim falls in one of the following categories, check the box and state the amount. Specify the priority of the claim. Domestic support obligations under 11 U.S.C. §507(a)(1)(A) or (a)(1)(B).
2. Basis for Claim: _____ (See instruction #2 on reverse side.)	Wages, salaries, or commissions (up to $10,950*) earned within 180 days before filing of the bankruptcy petition or cessation of the debtor's business, whichever is earlier – 11 U.S.C. §507 (a)(4).

3. Last four digits of any number by which creditor identifies debtor: _____
 	
   3a. Debtor may have scheduled account as: _____
   (See instruction #3a on reverse side.)	

4. Secured Claim (See instruction #4 on reverse side.) Check the appropriate box if your claim is secured by a lien on property or a right of setoff and provide the requested information. **Nature of property or right of setoff:** Real Estate Motor Vehicle Other **Describe:** **Value of Property:**$_____ **Annual Interest Rate___%** **Amount of arrearage and other charges as of time case filed included in secured claim,** **if any: $_____ Basis for perfection:** _____ **Amount of Secured Claim: $_____ Amount Unsecured: $_____**	Contributions to an employee benefit plan – 11 U.S.C. §507 (a)(5). Up to $2,425* of deposits toward purchase, lease, or rental of property or services for personal, family, or household use – 11 U.S.C. §507 (a)(7). Taxes or penalties owed to governmental units – 11 U.S.C. §507 (a)(8).
6. Credits: The amount of all payments on this claim has been credited for the purpose of making this proof of claim. **7. Documents:** Attach redacted copies of any documents that support the claim, such as promissory notes, purchase orders, invoices, itemized statements of running accounts, contracts, judgments, mortgages, and security agreements. You may also attach a summary. Attach redacted copies of documents providing evidence of perfection of a security interest. You may also attach a summary. (*See definition of "redacted" on reverse side.*) DO NOT SEND ORIGINAL DOCUMENTS. ATTACHED DOCUMENTS MAY BE DESTROYED AFTER SCANNING. If the documents are not available, please explain:	Other – Specify applicable paragraph of 11 U.S.C. §507 (a)(__). **Amount entitled to priority:** $_____ *Amounts are subject to adjustment on 4/1/10 and every 3 years thereafter with respect to cases commenced on or after the date of adjustment.*
Date: **Signature:** The person filing this claim must sign it. Sign and print name and title, if any, of the creditor or other person authorized to file this claim and state address and telephone number if different from the notice address above. Attach copy of power of attorney, if any.	**FOR COURT USE ONLY**

Penalty for presenting fraudulent claim: Fine of up to $500,000 or imprisonment for up to 5 years, or both. 18 U.S.C. §§ 152 and 3571.

Figure 13.4 *(continued)*

INSTRUCTIONS FOR PROOF OF CLAIM FORM

The instructions and definitions below are general explanations of the law. In certain circumstances, such as bankruptcy cases not filed voluntarily by the debtor, there may be exceptions to these general rules.

Items to be completed in Proof of Claim form

Court, Name of Debtor, and Case Number:
Fill in the federal judicial district where the bankruptcy case was filed (for example, Central District of California), the bankruptcy debtor's name, and the bankruptcy case number. If the creditor received a notice of the case from the bankruptcy court, all of this information is located at the top of the notice.

Creditor's Name and Address:
Fill in the name of the person or entity asserting a claim and the name and address of the person who should receive notices issued during the bankruptcy case. A separate space is provided for the payment address if it differs from the notice address. The creditor has a continuing obligation to keep the court informed of its current address. See Federal Rule of Bankruptcy Procedure (FRBP) 2002(g).

1. Amount of Claim as of Date Case Filed:
State the total amount owed to the creditor on the date of the Bankruptcy filing. Follow the instructions concerning whether to complete items 4 and 5. Check the box if interest or other charges are included in the claim.

2. Basis for Claim:
State the type of debt or how it was incurred. Examples include goods sold, money loaned, services performed, personal injury/wrongful death, car loan, mortgage note, and credit card.

3. Last Four Digits of Any Number by Which Creditor Identifies Debtor:
State only the last four digits of the debtor's account or other number used by the creditor to identify the debtor.

3a. Debtor May Have Scheduled Account As:
Use this space to report a change in the creditor's name, a transferred claim, or any other information that clarifies a difference between this proof of claim and the claim as scheduled by the debtor.

4. Secured Claim:
Check the appropriate box and provide the requested information if the claim is fully or partially secured. Skip this section if the claim is entirely unsecured. (See DEFINITIONS, below.) State the type and the value of property that secures the claim, attach copies of lien documentation, and state annual interest rate and the amount past due on the claim as of the date of the bankruptcy filing.

5. Amount of Claim Entitled to Priority Under 11 U.S.C. §507(a).
If any portion of your claim falls in one or more of the listed categories, check the appropriate box(es) and state the amount entitled to priority. (See DEFINITIONS, below.) A claim may be partly priority and partly non-priority. For example, in some of the categories, the law limits the amount entitled to priority.

6. Credits:
An authorized signature on this proof of claim serves as an acknowledgment that when calculating the amount of the claim, the creditor gave the debtor credit for any payments received toward the debt.

7. Documents:
Attach to this proof of claim form redacted copies documenting the existence of the debt and of any lien securing the debt. You may also attach a summary. You must also attach copies of documents that evidence perfection of any security interest. You may also attach a summary. FRBP 3001(c) and (d). Do not send original documents, as attachments may be destroyed after scanning.

Date and Signature:
The person filing this proof of claim must sign and date it. FRBP 9011. If the claim is filed electronically, FRBP 5005(a)(2), authorizes courts to establish local rules specifying what constitutes a signature. Print the name and title, if any, of the creditor or other person authorized to file this claim. State the filer's address and telephone number if it differs from the address given on the top of the form for purposes of receiving notices. Attach a complete copy of any power of attorney. Criminal penalties apply for making a false statement on a proof of claim.

_____DEFINITIONS_____

Debtor
A debtor is the person, corporation, or other entity that has filed a bankruptcy case.

Creditor
A creditor is the person, corporation, or other entity owed a debt by the debtor on the date of the bankruptcy filing.

Claim
A claim is the creditor's right to receive payment on a debt that was owed by the debtor on the date of the bankruptcy filing. See 11 U.S.C. §101 (5). A claim may be secured or unsecured.

Proof of Claim
A proof of claim is a form used by the creditor to indicate the amount of the debt owed by the debtor on the date of the bankruptcy filing. The creditor must file the form with the clerk of the same bankruptcy court in which the bankruptcy case was filed.

Secured Claim Under 11 U.S.C. §506(a)
A secured claim is one backed by a lien on property of the debtor. The claim is secured so long as the creditor has the right to be paid from the property prior to other creditors. The amount of the secured claim cannot exceed the value of the property. Any amount owed to the creditor in excess of the value of the property is an unsecured claim. Examples of liens on property include a mortgage on real estate or a security interest in a car.

A lien may be voluntarily granted by a debtor or may be obtained through a court proceeding. In some states, a court judgment is a lien. A claim also may be secured if the creditor owes the debtor money (has a right to setoff).

Unsecured Claim
An unsecured claim is one that does not meet the requirements of a secured claim. A claim may be partly unsecured if the amount of the claim exceeds the value of the property on which the creditor has a lien.

Claim Entitled to Priority Under 11 U.S.C. §507(a)
Priority claims are certain categories of unsecured claims that are paid from the available money or property in a bankruptcy case before other unsecured claims.

Redacted
A document has been redacted when the person filing it has masked, edited out, or otherwise deleted, certain information. A creditor should redact and use only the last four digits of any social-security, individual's tax-identification, or financial-account number, all but the initials of a minor's name and only the year of any person's date of birth.

Evidence of Perfection
Evidence of perfection may include a mortgage, lien, certificate of title, financing statement, or other document showing that the lien has been filed or recorded.

_____INFORMATION_____

Acknowledgment of Filing of Claim
To receive acknowledgment of your filing, you may either enclose a stamped self-addressed envelope and a copy of this proof of claim or you may access the court's PACER system (www.pacer.psc.uscourts.gov) for a small fee to view your filed proof of claim.

Offers to Purchase a Claim
Certain entities are in the business of purchasing claims for an amount less than the face value of the claims. One or more of these entities may contact the creditor and offer to purchase the claim. Some of the written communications from these entities may easily be confused with official court documentation or communications from the debtor. These entities do not represent the bankruptcy court or the debtor. The creditor has no obligation to sell its claim. However, if the creditor decides to sell its claim, any transfer of such claim is subject to FRBP 3001(e), any applicable provisions of the Bankruptcy Code (11 U.S.C. § 101 *et seq.*), and any applicable orders of the bankruptcy court.

Figure 13.5
Power of Attorney for Bankruptcy
www.uscourts.gov/bkforms/official/b11a.pdf

United States Bankruptcy Court

_____ District Of_____

In re _____,
        Debtor

Case No. _____

Chapter _____

GENERAL POWER OF ATTORNEY

To _____ of * _____, and
_____ of * _____.

The undersigned claimant hereby authorizes you, or any one of you, as attorney in fact for the undersigned and with full power of substitution, to vote on any question that may be lawfully submitted to creditors of the debtor in the abo ve-entitled case; [*if appropriate*] to vote for a trustee of the estate of the debtor and for a committee of creditors; to receive dividends; and in general to perform any act not constituting the practice of law for the undersigned in all matters arising in this case.

Dated: _____

Signed: _____

By _____

as _____

Address: _____

_____

[*If executed by an individual*] Acknowledged before me on _____.

[*If executed on behalf of a partnership*] Acknowledged before me on _____,
by _____, who says that he [*or* she] is a member of the partnership named above and is authorized to execute this power of attorney in its behalf.

[*If executed on behalf of a corporation*] Acknowledged before me on _____,
by _____, who says that he [*or* she] is _____ of the corporation named above and is authorized to execute this power of attorney in its behalf.

_____

_____

[*Official character.*]

* State mailing address.

Figure 13.6
Petition for Involuntary Liquidation

www.uscourts.gov/rules/bk_forms_1207/b_005_1207f.pdf

<table>
<tr>
<td colspan="2">UNITED STATES BANKRUPTCY COURT
_____ District of _____</td>
<td>INVOLUNTARY
PETITION</td>
</tr>
<tr>
<td colspan="2">IN RE (Name of Debtor – If Individual: Last, First, Middle)</td>
<td>ALL OTHER NAMES used by debtor in the last 8 years
(Include married, maiden, and trade names.)</td>
</tr>
<tr>
<td colspan="2">Last four digits of Social-Security or other Individual's Tax-I.D. No./Complete EIN
(If more than one, state all.):</td>
<td></td>
</tr>
<tr>
<td colspan="2">STREET ADDRESS OF DEBTOR (No. and street, city, state, and ZIP code)</td>
<td>MAILING ADDRESS OF DEBTOR (If different from street address)</td>
</tr>
<tr>
<td colspan="2">COUNTY OF RESIDENCE OR PRINCIPAL PLACE OF BUSINESS

ZIP CODE</td>
<td>ZIP CODE</td>
</tr>
<tr>
<td colspan="3">LOCATION OF PRINCIPAL ASSETS OF BUSINESS DEBTOR (If different from previously listed addresses)</td>
</tr>
<tr>
<td colspan="3">CHAPTER OF BANKRUPTCY CODE UNDER WHICH PETITION IS FILED

Chapter 7   Chapter 11</td>
</tr>
<tr>
<td colspan="3" align="center">INFORMATION REGARDING DEBTOR (Check applicable boxes)</td>
</tr>
<tr>
<td>Nature of Debts
(Check one box.)

Petitioners believe:

Debts are primarily consumer debts
Debts are primarily business debts</td>
<td>Type of Debtor
(Form of Organization)
Individual (Includes Joint Debtor)
Corporation (Includes LLC and LLP)
Partnership
Other (If debtor is not one of the above entities,
check this box and state type of entity below.)
_____</td>
<td>Nature of Business
(Check one box.)
Health Care Business
Single Asset Real Estate as defined in
11 U.S.C. § 101(51)(B)
Railroad
Stockbroker
Commodity Broker
Clearing Bank
Other</td>
</tr>
<tr>
<td>VENUE

Debtor has been domiciled or has had a residence, principal place of business, or principal assets in the District for 180 days immediately preceding the date of this petition or for a longer part of such 180 days than in any other District.

A bankruptcy case concerning debtor's affiliate, general partner or partnership is pending in this District.</td>
<td colspan="2">FILING FEE (Check one box)

Full Filing Fee attached

Petitioner is a child support creditor or its representative, and the form specified in § 304(g) of the Bankruptcy Reform Act of 1994 is attached.
[If a child support creditor or its representative is a petitioner, and if the petitioner files the form specified in § 304(g) of the Bankruptcy Reform Act of 1994, no fee is required.]</td>
</tr>
<tr>
<td colspan="3" align="center">PENDING BANKRUPTCY CASE FILED BY OR AGAINST ANY PARTNER
OR AFFILIATE OF THIS DEBTOR (Report information for any additional cases on attached sheets.)</td>
</tr>
<tr>
<td>Name of Debtor</td>
<td>Case Number</td>
<td>Date</td>
</tr>
<tr>
<td>Relationship</td>
<td>District</td>
<td>Judge</td>
</tr>
<tr>
<td colspan="2" align="center">ALLEGATIONS
(Check applicable boxes)</td>
<td align="center">COURT USE ONLY</td>
</tr>
</table>

1. Petitioner (s) are eligible to file this petition pursuant to 11 U.S.C. § 303 (b).
2. The debtor is a person against whom an order for relief may be entered under title 11 of the United States Code.
3.a. The debtor is generally not paying such debtor's debts as they become due, unless such debts are the subject of a bona fide dispute as to liability or amount;

     or
  b. Within 120 days preceding the filing of this petition, a custodian, other than a trustee receiver, or agent appointed or authorized to take charge of less than substantially all of the property of the debtor for the purpose of enforcing a lien against such property, was appointed or took possession.

Figure 13.6. (*continued*)

Name of Debtor_____

Case No._____

TRANSFER OF CLAIM
Check this box if there has been a transfer of any claim against the debtor by or to any petitioner. Attach all documents that evidence the transfer and any statements that are required under Bankruptcy Rule 1003(a).

REQUEST FOR RELIEF

Petitioner(s) request that an order for relief be entered against the debtor under the chapter of title 11, United States Code, specified in this petition. If any petitioner is a foreign representative appointed in a foreign proceeding, a certified copy of the order of the court granting recognition is attached.

Petitioner(s) declare under penalty of perjury that the foregoing is true and correct according to the best of their knowledge, information, and belief.

x_____
Signature of Petitioner or Representative (State title)

Name of Petitioner   Date Signed

Name & Mailing
Address of Individual   _____
Signing in Representative
Capacity   _____

x_____
Signature of Attorney   Date

Name of Attorney Firm (If any)

Address

Telephone No.

---

x_____
Signature of Petitioner or Representative (State title)

Name of Petitioner   Date Signed

Name & Mailing
Address of Individual   _____
Signing in Representative
Capacity   _____

x_____
Signature of Attorney   Date

Name of Attorney Firm (If any)

Address

Telephone No.

---

x_____
Signature of Petitioner or Representative (State title)

Name of Petitioner   Date Signed

Name & Mailing
Address of Individual   _____
Signing in Representative
Capacity   _____

x_____
Signature of Attorney   Date

Name of Attorney Firm (If any)

Address

Telephone No.

PETITIONING CREDITORS

Name and Address of Petitioner	Nature of Claim	Amount of Claim
Name and Address of Petitioner	Nature of Claim	Amount of Claim
Name and Address of Petitioner	Nature of Claim	Amount of Claim

Note:	If there are more than three petitioners, attach additional sheets with the statement under penalty of perjury, each petitioner's signature under the statement and the name of attorney and petitioning creditor information in the format above.	Total Amount of Petitioners' Claims

_____continuation sheets attached

Figure 13.7
Summons to Debtor in an Involuntary Petition
www.uscourts.gov/bkforms/official/b250e.pdf

United States Bankruptcy Court

_____ District of _____

In re _____
          Debtor

Case No. _____

Chapter _____

SUMMONS TO DEBTOR IN INVOLUNTARY CASE

To the above named debtor:

A petition under title 11, United States Code was filed against you on _____
                                                                                                  (date)
in this bankruptcy court, requesting an order for relief under chapter _____ of the Bankruptcy Code

(title 11 of the United States Code).

YOU ARE SUMMONED and required to file with the clerk of the bankruptcy court a motion or answer to the petition within 20 days after the service of this summons. A copy of the petition is attached.

Address of Clerk

At the same time, you must also serve a copy of your motion or answer on petitioner's attorney.

Name and Address of Petitioner's Attorney

If you make a motion, your time to serve an answer is governed by Federal Rule of Bankruptcy Procedure 1011(c).

If you fail to respond to this summons, the order for relief will be entered.

_____
Clerk of the Bankruptcy Court

_____   By:_____
      Date   Deputy Clerk

_____
*Set forth all names, including trade names, used by the debtor within the last 6 years. (Fed. R .Bankr. P. 1005).

Figure 13.7 *(continued)*

Case No._____

CERTIFICATE OF SERVICE

I
of**
certify:

     That I am, and at all times hereinafter mentioned was more than 18 years of age;
     That on the   day of   ,19
I served a copy of the within summons, together with the petition filed in this case, on

the debtor in this case, by *[describe here the mode of service]*

the said debtor at

I certify under penalty of perjury that the foregoing is true and correct.

Executed on _____   _____
                 [Date]   *[Signature]*

_____

**State mailing address.

United States Bankruptcy Court

_____ District Of _____

In re _____   Case No. _____

Debtor*

Address: _____   Chapter 13

_____

Last four digits of Social-Security or Individual Taxpayer-
Identification (ITIN) No(s).,(if any): _____
Employer Tax-Identification (EIN) No(s).(if any): ____

_____

DISCHARGE OF DEBTOR AFTER COMPLETION
OF CHAPTER 13 PLAN

It appearing that the debtor is entitled to a discharge,

IT IS ORDERED:

The debtor is granted a discharge under section 1328(a) of title 11, United States Code, (the Bankruptcy Code).

BY THE COURT

Dated: _____   _____

United States Bankruptcy Judge

SEE THE BACK OF THIS ORDER FOR IMPORTANT INFORMATION.

_____

* *Set forth all names, including trade names, used by the debtor(s) within the last 8 years. For joint debtors, set forth the last four digits of both social-security numbers or individual taxpayer-identification numbers.*

Figure 13.8 (*continued*)

EXPLANATION OF BANKRUPTCY DISCHARGE IN A CHAPTER 13 CASE

This court order grants a discharge to the person named as the debtor after the debtor has completed all payments under the chapter 13 plan. It is not a dismissal of the case.

Collection of Discharged Debts Prohibited
The discharge prohibits any attempt to collect from the debtor a debt that has been discharged. For example, a creditor is not permitted to contact a debtor by mail, phone, or otherwise, to file or continue a lawsuit, to attach wages or other property, or to take any other action to collect a discharged debt from the debtor. *[In a case involving community property:* There are also special rules that protect certain community property owned by the debtor's spouse, even if that spouse did not file a bankruptcy case.] A creditor who violates this order can be required to pay damages and attorney's fees to the debtor.

However, a creditor may have the right to enforce a valid lien, such as a mortgage or security interest, against the debtor's property after the bankruptcy, if that lien was not avoided or eliminated in the bankruptcy case. Also, a debtor may voluntarily pay any debt that has been discharged.

Debts That Are Discharged
The chapter 13 discharge order eliminates a debtor's legal obligation to pay a debt that is discharged. Most, but not all, types of debts are discharged if the debt is provided for by the chapter 13 plan or is disallowed by the court pursuant to section 502 of the Bankruptcy Code.

Debts That Are Not Discharged
Some of the common types of debts which are <u>not</u> discharged in a chapter 13 bankruptcy case are:

a. Domestic support obligations;

b. Debts for most student loans;

c. Debts for most fines, penalties, forfeitures, or criminal restitution obligations;

d. Debts for personal injuries or death caused by the debtor's operation of a motor vehicle, vessel, or aircraft while intoxicated;

e. Debts for restitution, or damages, awarded in a civil action against the debtor as a result of malicious or willful injury by the debtor that caused personal injury to an individual or the death of an individual (in a case filed on or after October 17, 2005);

f. Debts provided for under section 1322(b)(5) of the Bankruptcy Code and on which the last payment is due after the date on which the final payment under the plan was due;

g. Debts for certain consumer purchases made after the bankruptcy case was filed if prior approval by the trustee of the debtor's incurring the debt was practicable but was not obtained;

h. Debts for certain taxes to the extent not paid in full under the plan (in a case filed on or after October 17, 2005); and

i. Some debts which were not properly listed by the debtor (in a case filed on or after October 17, 2005).

This information is only a general summary of the bankruptcy discharge. There are exceptions to these general rules. Because the law is complicated, you may want to consult an attorney to determine the exact effect of the discharge in this case.

Figure 13.9

Notice of Meeting of Creditors under Chapter 11

www.uscourts.gov/rules/bk_forms_1207/form_9e_1207.pdf

B9E (Official Form 9E) (Chapter 11 Individual or Joint Debtor Case) (12/07)

UNITED STATES BANKRUPTCY COURT_____District of_____

Notice of
Chapter 11 Bankruptcy Case, Meeting of Creditors, & Deadlines

[A chapter 11 bankruptcy case concerning the debtor(s) listed below was filed on _____ (date).]
or [A bankruptcy case concerning the debtor(s) listed below was originally filed under chapter_____on
_____ (date) and was converted to a case under chapter 11 on_____(date).]

You may be a creditor of the debtor. **This notice lists important deadlines.** You may want to consult an attorney to protect your rights. All documents filed in the case may be inspected at the bankruptcy clerk's office at the address listed below. NOTE: The staff of the bankruptcy clerk's office cannot give legal advice.

See Reverse Side for Important Explanations

Debtor(s) (name(s) and address):	Case Number:
	Last four digits of Social-Security or Individual Taxpayer-ID (ITIN) No(s)./Complete EIN:
All other names used by the Debtor(s) in the last 8 years (include married, maiden, and trade names):	Attorney for Debtor(s) (name and address): Telephone number:

Meeting of Creditors

Date: / /   Time: (   ) A. M.   Location:
                              (   ) P. M.

Deadlines:
Papers must be *received* by the bankruptcy clerk's office by the following deadlines:

Deadline to File a Proof of Claim:
Notice of deadline will be sent at a later time.

Creditor with a Foreign Address:
A creditor to whom this notice is sent at a foreign address should read the information under "Claims" on the reverse side.

Deadline to File a Complaint to Determine Dischargeability of Certain Debts:

Deadline to File a Complaint Objecting to Discharge of the Debtor:

First date set for hearing on confirmation of plan
Notice of that date will be sent at a later time.

Deadline to Object to Exemptions:

Thirty (30) days after the *conclusion* of the meeting of creditors.

Creditors May Not Take Certain Actions:
In most instances, the filing of the bankruptcy case automatically stays certain collection and other actions against the debtor and the debtor's property. Under certain circumstances, the stay may be limited to 30 days or not exist at all, although the debtor can request the court to extend or impose a stay. If you attempt to collect a debt or take other action in violation of the Bankruptcy Code, you may be penalized. Consult a lawyer to determine your rights in this case.

Address of the Bankruptcy Clerk's Office: **Telephone number:**	**For the Court:** Clerk of the Bankruptcy Court:
Hours Open:	Date:

Figure 13.9 (*continued*)

Filing of Chapter 11 Bankruptcy Case	A bankruptcy case under Chapter 11 of the Bankruptcy Code (title 11, United States Code) has been filed in this court by or against the debtor(s) listed on the front side, and an order for relief has been entered. Chapter 11 allows a debtor to reorganize or liquidate pursuant to a plan. A plan is not effective unless confirmed by the court. You may be sent a copy of the plan and a disclosure statement telling you about the plan, and you might have the opportunity to vote on the plan. You will be sent notice of the date of the confirmation hearing, and you may object to confirmation of the plan and attend the confirmation hearing. Unless a trustee is serving, the debtor will remain in possession of the debtor's property and may continue to operate any business.
Legal Advice	The staff of the bankruptcy clerk's office cannot give legal advice. Consult a lawyer to determine your rights in this case.
Creditors Generally May Not Take Certain Actions	Prohibited collection actions are listed in Bankruptcy Code § 362. Common examples of prohibited actions include contacting the debtor by telephone, mail, or otherwise to demand repayment; taking actions to collect money or obtain property from the debtor; repossessing the debtor's property; starting or continuing lawsuits or foreclosures; and garnishing or deducting from the debtor's wages. Under certain circumstances, the stay may be limited to 30 days or not exist at all, although the debtor can request the court to extend or impose a stay.
Meeting of Creditors	A meeting of creditors is scheduled for the date, time, and location listed on the front side. *The debtor (both spouses in a joint case) must be present at the meeting to be questioned under oath by the trustee and by creditors.* Creditors are welcome to attend, but are not required to do so. The meeting may be continued and concluded at a later date without further notice. The court, after notice and a hearing, may order that the United States trustee not convene the meeting if the debtor has filed a plan for which the debtor solicited acceptances before filing the case.
Claims	A Proof of Claim is a signed statement describing a creditor's claim. If a Proof of Claim form is not included with this notice, you can obtain one at any bankruptcy clerk's office. You may look at the schedules that have been or will be filed at the bankruptcy clerk's office. If your claim is scheduled and is *not* listed as disputed, contingent, or unliquidated, it will be allowed in the amount scheduled unless you filed a Proof of Claim or you are sent further notice about the claim. Whether or not your claim is scheduled, you are permitted to file a Proof of Claim. If your claim is not listed at all *or* if your claim is listed as disputed, contingent, or unliquidated, then you must file a Proof of Claim or you might not be paid any money on your claim and may be unable to vote on a plan. The court has not yet set a deadline to file a Proof of Claim. If a deadline is set, you will be sent another notice. A secured creditor retains its rights in its collateral regardless of whether that creditor files a Proof of Claim. Filing a Proof of Claim submits the creditor to the jurisdiction of the bankruptcy court, with consequences a lawyer can explain. For example, a secured creditor who files a Proof of Claim may surrender important nonmonetary rights, including the right to a jury trial. **Filing Deadline for a Creditor with a Foreign Address:** The deadline for filing claims will be set in a later court order and will apply to all creditors unless the order provides otherwise. If notice of the order setting the deadline is sent to a creditor at a foreign address, the creditor may file a motion requesting the court to extend the deadline.
Discharge of Debts	Confirmation of a chapter 11 plan may result in a discharge of debts, which may include all or part of your debt. *See* Bankruptcy Code § 1141 (d). Unless the court orders otherwise, however, the discharge will not be effective until completion of all payments under the plan. A discharge means that you may never try to collect the debt from the debtor except as provided in the plan. If you believe that a debt owed to you is not dischargeable under Bankruptcy Code § 523 (a) (2), (4), or (6), you must start a lawsuit by filing a complaint in the bankruptcy clerk's office by the "Deadline to File a Complaint to Determine Dischargeability of Certain Debts" listed on the front side. The bankruptcy clerk's office must receive the complaint and any required filing fee by that Deadline. If you believe that the debtor is not entitled to receive a discharge under Bankruptcy Code § 1141 (d) (3), you must file a complaint with the required filing fee in the bankruptcy clerk's office not later than the first date set for the hearing on confirmation of the plan. You will be sent another notice informing you of that date.
Exempt Property	The debtor is permitted by law to keep certain property as exempt. Exempt property will not be sold and distributed to creditors, even if the debtor's case is converted to chapter 7. The debtor must file a list of property claimed as exempt. You may inspect that list at the bankruptcy clerk's office. If you believe that an exemption claimed by the debtor is not authorized by law, you may file an objection to that exemption. The bankruptcy clerk's office must receive the objection by the "Deadline to Object to Exemptions" listed on the front side.
Bankruptcy Clerk's Office	Any paper that you file in this bankruptcy case should be filed at the bankruptcy clerk's office at the address listed on the front side. You may inspect all papers filed, including the list of the debtor's property and debts and the list of the property claimed as exempt, at the bankruptcy clerk's office.
Creditor with a Foreign Address	Consult a lawyer familiar with United States bankruptcy law if you have any questions regarding your rights in this case.

Refer to Other Side for Important Deadlines and Notices

Figure 13.10

www.uscourts.gov/bkforms/official/b13.pdf

Official Form 13
(12/03)

Form 13. ORDER APPROVING DISCLOSURE STATEMENT AND FIXING TIME FOR FILING ACCEPTANCES OR REJECTIONS OF PLAN, COMBINED WITH NOTICE THEREOF

[Caption as in Form 16A]

ORDER APPROVING DISCLOSURE STATEMENT AND FIXING TIME FOR FILING ACCEPTANCES OR REJECTIONS OF PLAN, COMBINED WITH NOTICE THEREOF

A disclosure statement under chapter 11 of the Bankruptcy Code having been filed by _____, on _____ [*if appropriate*, and by _____, on _____], referring to a plan under chapter 11 of the Code filed by _____, on _____ [*if appropriate*, and by _____, on _____ respectively] [*if appropriate*, as modified by a modification filed on _____]; and

It having been determined after hearing on notice that the disclosure statement [*or* statements] contain[s] adequate information:

IT IS ORDERED, and notice is hereby given, that:

A. The disclosure statement filed by _____ dated _____ [*if appropriate*, and by _____, dated _____ is [are] approved.

B. _____ is fixed as the last day for filing written acceptances or rejections of the plan [*or* plans] referred to above.

C. Within _____ days after the entry of this order, the plan [*or* plans] *or* a summary *or* summaries thereof approved by the court, [and [*if appropriate*] a summary approved by the court of its opinion, if any, dated _____, approving the disclosure statement [*or* statements]], the disclosure statement [*or* statements], and a ballot conforming to Official Form 14 shall be mailed to creditors, equity security holders, and other parties in interest, and shall be transmitted to the United States trustee, as provided in Fed. R. Bankr. P. 3017(d).

D. If acceptances are filed for more than one plan, preferences among the plans so accepted may be indicated.

E. *[If appropriate]* _____ is fixed for the hearing on confirmation of the plan [*or* plans].

F. *[If appropriate]* _____ is fixed as the last day for filing and serving pursuant to Fed. R. Bankr. P. 3020(b)(1) written objections to confirmation of the plan.

Dated: _____

BY THE COURT

_____

United States Bankruptcy Judge

[If the court directs that a copy of the opinion should be transmitted in lieu of or in addition to the summary thereof, the appropriate change should be made in paragraph C of this order.]

Figure 13.11
Specimen Problem 1

Using a Chapter 13 (wage-earner petition) to restrain your creditors:

Harold M. has been sued by a finance company. They are demanding that he pay them $800. Harold had borrowed from them and gave them a "chattel mortgage" on his furniture. Harold could not pay the $800, so he went instead to downtown Los Angeles and filed a Chapter 13. Here is what Chapter 13 is doing for Harold.

It took about two hours for Harold to file his Chapter 13. As soon as he did so, the lawsuit brought against him by the finance company was "frozen." The finance company could not go ahead with the lawsuit.

Harold did not have to give up his furniture. He kept it. Through the Chapter 13, the chattel mortgage on the furniture was "avoided" or done away with. The finance company cannot ever get it.

The Chapter 13 operates as a restraining order on *all* creditors. The finance company had to stop telephoning him and demanding payment. The collection agencies had to stop harassing him—no more telephone calls to his employer, or to his home. Chapter 13 stops all such.

Harold had an old judgment outstanding against him, and that creditor sent the marshal to Harold's place of work to run an "attachment" against his earnings. Harold and his boss told the marshal that a Chapter 13 had been filed and gave him the number. The marshal then left, as he had been restrained from running the attachment.

Harold added up his debts, and they came to a total of $4,200. He added up his living expenses—rent, food, gasoline, and so forth—and figured out that the most he could pay his old creditors was $50 a month. He then arranged through the Chapter 13 plan that he would pay $50 a month for a period of thirty-six months, and that is what the creditors got. The creditors, including the finance company that had sued him, received less than half of what they wanted, but under the Chapter 13, they were entitled only to what Harold could afford. Harold did not have to pay the balance of the money he owed.

As shown by the foregoing, the new Chapter 13 plan was designed with the purpose of permitting a debtor to get full relief from his debts by paying what he can afford, and not the whole amount. This way he is able to avoid bankruptcy, and he does not have to borrow money.

Figure 13.12
Specimen Problem 2: The New Consolidation Plan

If you use the new Consolidation Plan, you do not have to borrow money, and you do not have to file bankruptcy. It is a new way to handle your creditors.

As soon as you must file your application for a Consolidation Plan, the creditors *must* leave you alone. They cannot sue you, cannot telephone you any more, cannot telephone your employer to put pressure on you, cannot tie up your paychecks, cannot pick up your automobile, and cannot even write a letter to you.

How would you like to pay your creditors only what you can afford (not what they want), and as long as you are doing this, the creditors *must* leave you strictly alone? This can be done through the new Consolidation Plan. Here is how it works:

First, you write down on a sheet of paper how much money you bring home each month. Next, add up your ordinary monthly living expenses—rent, food, medical, utilities, transportation, and so forth. Subtract the monthly living expenses from the amount you bring home. What is left is what you can afford to pay on the old bills. That is all you have to pay. This is divided up among the creditors.

What you do is to pay into the Consolidation Plan once a month the amount that you can afford to pay. You make these payments for a limited period, usually twenty-four months. By then, the creditors may have been paid very little, but that is all they get, and they cannot come at you to make you pay the rest of it.

If you are buying things on time, like a car, a TV, stereo, or the like, you can either tell them to come and get it or work out a deal to pay the reasonable value of the property in reduced monthly payments.

Foreclosure on your home: The new Consolidation Plan stops the foreclosure immediately, and you have a period of time within which to get on your feet, so you will not lose your equity in the real property.

CHAPTER FOURTEEN

Setting Up a Business Entity

This chapter deals primarily with, and gives an overview discussion of, the pitfalls, questions which may arise, and steps to be considered when setting up any type of business venture. It will therefore outline certain step-by-step procedures regarding the accumulation of the proper documents, such as articles of incorporation, which can now be found online in a myriad of places. We state this simply because it will be your duty as the attorney's paralegal to gather these documents and do the legal research pertinent thereto.

There are four general categories of business organizations:

1. The corporation,

2. The limited liability company,

3. The partnership, and

4. The sole proprietorship.

There are important differences between these entities, including structure, liability and tax consequences, and, of course, method of creation, for which you as the paralegal may be responsible. In every state, the secretary of state has the responsibility for maintaining records of all these business organizations. The secretary of state also serves as a resource for business information. Links to each of these offices can be found at State and Local Government on Net (www.statelocalgov.net/50states-secretary-state.cfm).

Corporations

First and foremost, what is a corporation? Legal theory tells us that a corporation is considered to be an entity, a legal "person" separate and apart from persons interested in controlling it.

There are several classes of corporations which we will discuss. Please note in your research that these different classes of corporations are organized under different statutes and may not be the same in your state.

1. The *public corporation*, which includes such entities as the cities, towns, tax districts, irrigation districts, departments of water and power, etc., and may also include the Federal Deposit Insurance Corporation and the Federal Savings and Loan Insurance Company.

2. The *corporations not for profit*, which are organized for purposes other than monetary gain. These types of corporations are normally for religious, social, educational, or charitable purposes. And the designation as a nonprofit corporation bestows a preferred tax exempt status under the Internal Revenue Code.

3. The *corporations for profit*, which are organizations that issue stock and sell the same for profit. These corporations can be classified as publicly owned corporations, closed corporations, or professional corporations.

   The closely held corporation, often called an "S" corporation, normally concerns itself with a small group of stockholders (usually seventy-five or fewer), and oftentimes they are all members of the same family. You will need to research this in your state to see if special corporate laws are applicable.

   Another decision that needs to be made is whether the corporation will be publicly or privately held. See Figure 14.1 for a comparison between the advantages and disadvantages of public versus private corporations.

4. The *professional corporation*, commonly known as the "professional association," which we see all the time with lawyers and doctors, etc. These corporations often have the designation "P.C." after their names.

In addition to the above classifications of corporations, you also have what is called the "de jure corporation" and the "de facto corporation."

The de jure corporation is one which has been formed in compliance with all of the applicable state laws and may have the right to sue and be sued.

Figure 14.1

Comparison Between Public and Private Corporations

PUBLICLY HELD CORPORATIONS

Advantages	Disadvantages
1. Easier to raise capital.	1. Difficulty in borrowing money since no one in the corporation will be personally responsible; and the corporation does not have adequate assets.
2. Keeps the officers more honest because of the requirement to file report with the SEC and annual report to the stockholders.	2. Profit must be distributed upon demand even if the officers wanted to retain it in the business.
3. Easier to purchase or merge with other businesses or corporations.	3. Extensive paperwork, bookkeeping, financial reports, etc.
4. Easier to expand business: i. sale of stock ii. issuance of debt securities, bonds, etc. iii. issuance of additional class of stocks.	4. Decisions of directors subject to attack by stockholders.

PRIVATELY HELD CORPORATIONS

Advantages	Disadvantages
1. Higher profit for individual owner.	1. Higher risk for individual owner—bankruptcy.
2. Decisions can be made quickly and without too much resistance.	2. Easier to dissolve the corporation.
3. If necessary, profit can be retained in the business for reinvestment and expansion.	3. Since there will be more difficulty in raising money, it will be harder to expand the business.
4. Easier to borrow money, if the officers are willing to cosign a note.	4. Much harder to sell stock to private investors for expansion of the business.

Opposed to the de jure corporation is the de facto corporation, which merely exercises corporate powers and franchises under the color of law, absent compliance to applicable state laws. Here again, you are cautioned to research your state corporate laws to see if there are any peculiar laws pertinent to these two corporations in your state.

After you have decided which type of corporation you will recommend to your employer for his client, then you have to determine under which tax laws it should be governed.

The newly formed corporation can be treated either as a "C" corporation or as a subchapter "S" corporation for purposes of federal income tax. A "C" corporation is automatically taxed unless its shareholders elect to be treated as an "S" corporation.

The "C" corporation is considered separate and apart from its shareholders, as opposed to the "S" corporation, which treats its shareholders as similar to partners. Generally, an "S" corporation's income, gains, and losses are passed on to the shareholders, rather than remaining with the corporation. Each state, however, can treat its "S" corporations differently; some may allow a corporate tax, but at a different rate. In this connection, you should review and research both the Internal Revenue Code, election by a small business corporation, and your applicable state code.

Key Factors to Be Researched

1. *Determine how much capital or credit* will be required and if the client will be supplying all of it.

2. *What will be the liability?* Unlimited personal liability is a characteristic of a sole proprietorship and a general partner. You do not have this disadvantage under a corporate structure.

3. *Transferability of interest.* The corporation offers easy transferability of ownership interest, which makes it easy for one to liquidate his investment.

4. *Legal status.* It is important to know whether or not the proposed corporation (a) holds property, (b) can transfer ownership, and (c) can sue or be sued. All of these rights are available to a corporation.

5. *Longevity.* A partnership or sole proprietorship has a severe disadvantage in this area: *Reason:* death or withdrawal by a partner. A corporation goes on forever.

6. *The abilities and background of the promoters.* If a promoter can provide capital but does not have experience or management abilities, consider carefully the risks and liabilities associated with them.

7. *Tax ramifications.* For corporations, you are talking about the issuance of stock, if at all. In considering other forms, you will need to consider the protections

against personal liability for taxes and the rate at which the entity (or partners) will be taxed.

The Model Business Corporation Act (MBCA) is a definitive guide to corporate law published by the ABA as adopted by the Committee on Corporate Laws of the Section of Business Law. It can be accessed online at www.abanet.org/buslaw/library/onlinepublications/mbca2002.pdf.

Corporate Stock Issuance

The result of the issuance of several classes of stock, who owns them, and how much will affect the control of the operation. The two principal classes of stock issued by a corporation under the laws of its state and the provisions of its articles of incorporation are (1) common stock and (2) preferred stock.

Common stock is the most common type of stock issued by a corporation. It is the responsibility of the common stockholder to elect the board of directors, which has the responsibility of hiring persons to manage and operate the corporation. A common stockholder has no voice in the running of the corporation beyond the annual vote for the board of directors. And further, common stockholders are only entitled to share the assets of a corporation upon its dissolution.

Preferred stock is a type in which investors have certain privileges over common stockholders. Preferred stock is issued with any (or all) of the following rights: (1) priority to assets upon liquidation, (2) special voting rights, including certain veto powers, (3) priority in the distribution of dividends, (4) conversion and redemption rights for the preferred stock, and (5) protection against dilution of the stocks' value due to splits or other manipulation of the outstanding stock.

Value of the Stock

Stock can either be par-value stock or no-par-value stock. Stock, which has on its face the value thereof, is considered to be par-value stock. Stock upon which there is no value assigned is considered to be no-par-value stock. Preferred stock, as a general rule, has a par value, while common stock, on the other hand, can either be par-value or no-par-value. The trend is to eliminate the par-value stock, as it has very little meaning anyway regarding the actual value of the stock.

Other types of stock can be "treasury stock," which is stock previously sold by the corporation and later reacquired by the corporation. Then there is "watered stock," which is stock when issued as fully paid up, but the purchase price therefor was paid with property of inflated value.

In discussing this with your attorney, either in a memorandum or a face-to-face conversation, be sure to bring up the Securities Act of 1933, which regulates the sale of securities in interstate commerce, as well as the Securities Exchange Act of 1934, which regulates initial offerings and the over-the-counter markets. This latter act requires the registration of stock exchanges traded in interstate commerce and SEC-regulated, publicly held corporations.

To underscore what I have said, let us now deal with a hypothetical case scenario to bring the point home.

Your office has been consulted by A, B, and C to give an analysis with regard to the operation of Special Metals Inc. They have need for capitalization. They seek advice as to the methods for distributing the stock to the public to raise capital.

The background of the company is as follows:

A. The Company

Special Metals Inc. was incorporated under the laws of the State of Ames, which follows the Uniform Securities Act and the Model Business Act in regulating corporations. Its principal asset consists of a "new process" for handling special metals. It has its executive offices and plant in the city of Langdell. Special Metals Inc. has been organized to serve as a supplier of special metals and plastics, primarily for the electronics industry, and to act as a specialist consultant in the use and handling of special metals for electrical components.

The company will be working in research and development of new processes in the handling of special metals geared to the special needs of consumer problems.

The company is a new business, has no history of earnings or operations, and has no established competitive position. Investors, therefore, will have to assume the usual risks associated with any new business venture. Although the company has conducted various market surveys which indicate a broad potential market for its special process, no assurance can be given that Special Metals Inc. will be successful in selling its product or realize any profits.

B. Incorporators

A, B, and C, individually, have very little money or equity in personal or real property to sustain a corporation. Together they can raise $60,000, which is inadequate to establish a space-age type of corporation, let alone buy the necessary equipment, plant site, raw materials, etc., needed to get a corporation of this nature off the ground.

A, B, and C, for the majority of their adult lives, have been employees, never employers, with the accompanying knowledge of business management and operation.

A, B, and C's prime assets lie in the area of their expertise in scientific procedures and metal processing, as well as creation of ideas; the know-how in experimentation; and their complete dedication to and conviction about their process. The creation of ideas was their job while in the employ of "X" Corporation.

It would appear, therefore, that the role to be played by A, B, and C in Special Metals Inc. would be in the nature of control and decision-making in the area of research and development; training of personnel; and survey of markets for the sale and use of the process.

For this reason, it is conceivable that A, B, and C would be of great help in selling not only the product of the company to the public, but the stock of the corporation as well.

C. Stock

The price of the stock to be sold hereunder has been based upon the funds estimated by the company to be reasonably required to begin operations and not on book value, earnings, asset value, or any other recognized criteria.

The threefold purpose of going public with stock is to raise money, determine interest in the company for the sale of the product of the company, and for profit.

One of the problems of Special Metals Inc. is that the cash reserve is quite thin, i.e., $60,000, reduced to $59,700 since $300 was used as a deposit on a ninety-day option to buy or lease a plant in Langdell. Furthermore, the only real asset of the company is the "new process" for handling special metals. Additionally, the lack of a business track record of A, B, and C will cloud the matter and make it difficult to get financing. With this in mind, let us proceed to analyze the offers of financing proposed to date, in light of the federal and state restrictions in the sale and purchase of securities.

D. Available Sources

1. L and P, a young lawyer and accountant, friends of A, B, and C, offered their services in exchange for stock in the company. This would net them between $2,000 and $5,000 and might place some restrictions on the stock as to any tax exemptions.

   The law is gray as to whether you can exchange stock for services, but it is clear that L and P can buy stock in the company for cash. As to the accountant: The Tax Commission looks down on the transfer of stock in exchange for services. *Reason:* The Registration Statement required to be filed with the Securities Exchange Commission must be certified by an "independent public accountant" before it is filed as a step in going public with its stock, or to distribute its stock under the Securities Act of 1933. This act prohibits issuance of stock to an accountant for his services in connection with the organization of a company, "if these services include preparation of the Registration Statement."

   This provision is intended to protect the public investor and secure for the benefit of the public "detached objectivity" as to the financial status of the company. It is felt that an accountant with a financial interest in the company might lose his objectivity in preparing the Registration Statement.

   As to the lawyer, the law is quite clear, and leaves the decision pretty much up to the business ethics of the lawyer as to whether or not he will accept stock in the company in exchange for his services. It is the position of the commission that "though he owes a responsibility to the public, his first duty is to his client; and the protection of the interest and rights of said client." Therefore, it might not be a good idea for the lawyer to accept stock in Special Metals Inc. because of the friendly relationship and the potential legal malpractice liability. On the other hand, should he choose to do so, he should fully disclose the nature and extent of his interest in Special Metals Inc.

Perhaps L and his clients would be willing to furnish money and/or property needed, in exchange for securities of the corporation, which could be one or more types of stock and/or bonds.

2. L then put A, B, and C in touch with a small investment firm, which offered a "best effort underwriting," assuming all risks and guaranteeing approximately $400,000, but it wanted a 15 to 20 percent commission. A, B, and C should reject this offer, as the commissions alone would leave approximately $200,000 for the new company, and their projection figure is $500,000 minimum. They must still allow for costs of legal fees, accountant charges, printing, sales promotion, etc.

3. A, B, and C then contacted a large public underwriting company, who offered a $500,000 guaranteed capitalization, which would have included the cost of equipment, but who wanted a controlling interest in the company in exchange. This procedure should be rejected, as it would wipe out any tax exemption available under the Securities Act. This act provides for continued control of the company to qualify it for said exemption, i.e., 80 percent of the shares of stock immediately upon the transfer of outstanding stock in the company. Under the terms of the foregoing proposition, this would not be the case.

4. Sometimes a potentially large supplier or bank may provide money on notes of the company to be cosigned by the promoters. Such was the case when A, B, and C visited an industrial commission and a small business investment company. The problem here was the feasibility of securing a bank loan, which would insist on some type of security for the loan. Furthermore it would have required A, B, and C to cosign a loan, making them personally liable, instead of the corporation. This procedure too should be rejected, inasmuch as the company is too new and the market too speculative at this point. Plus, it would entail a great deal of time and expense to work out the financing arrangements. A loan from a finance company would not be in the best interest of Special Metals Inc. at this time.

5. D, a stockbroker friend of A, B, and C, suggested that they return to their original idea of private solicitation as a means of financing their company and its operations. There are a few wealthy individuals willing to pay five times more for the stock than the asking price. This measure would have the effect of set-

ting up a small-knit corporation. This might be the way to go, provided, however, that Special Metals Inc. could qualify as a small business corporation.

E. Litigation

None pending, but possible.

Reason: As indicated earlier, A, B, and C were employees of "X" Corporation. While so employed, A, B, and C developed a "new process" for handling special metals used in the component parts of "X" Corporation. This process is the prime and principal asset of Special Metals Inc. All of the experimentation was done on company time, in the company plant, using company materials. A, B, and C received salaries all during these procedures.

Admittedly, A, B, and C advised the officers of "X" Corporation of the results of said experimentation, but they did not disclose the precise nature of the production processes that they had developed. While "X" Corporation was not interested in utilizing the new process in connection with its component parts (though aware of the "bright prospects" and future of the process), it is conceivable that it may change its mind when Special Metals Inc. displays the success of the new process.

The question therefore arises as to whether or not A, B, and C had a right to use the new process developed at the expense of "X" Corporation for their own use and benefit, and to the possible detriment of "X" Corporation.

The scope of unfair competition is not limited to any particular type of deception. The legal concept of unfair competition has evolved as a broad and flexible doctrine with the capacity for further growth to meet changing conditions. There is no complete list of activities that constitute unfair competition. In this example, A, B, and C developed a process at the request of their employer for its business activity. It was to be used by said employer. The slightest use, therefore, or invasion of information subsequently developed, would be advantageous to any competitor to the detriment, however remote, of "X" Corporation. A, B, and C's misappropriation and/or conversion thereof could be considered an act of unfair competition in setting up Special Metals Inc. using this new process.

F. Summary of Analysis

Special Metals Inc. is a small business. It has no business track record and its incorporators have always been employees. They have no business track record or business management experience.

It will be difficult to raise money for this type of small business, and the investors will have to assume all the normal risks (and perhaps more) associated with any new business venture.

The capital investment of Special Metals Inc. is very thin.

The authorized shares of stock to be issued are only 122,000, the sale of which would net approximately $500,000, with no other shares of stock outstanding or in issue. This status of affairs would result in the necessity of issuing either additional shares of stock or securing debt bonds to raise more money, if and when needed. The stock structure should be revamped to allow for this contingency.

A possible lawsuit to enjoin the use of the "process" should be given careful consideration as a future substantial problem which could affect the sale of stock and the success in growth of the business.

Incorporation

Step-by-Step Procedures

(Be sure to check your local state statutes and corporations code before implementing these procedures.) In bringing a corporation into existence, there are certain steps which are necessary and prerequisite to be followed by your attorney; the role that you play is as follows:

1. Determine from the client the name of the corporation. (In our hypothetical case, the name was "Special Metals.") If not already accomplished, this name should be reserved with your local state department applicable. In California, it is the Secretary of State Division of Corporations.

   In most states, there is a "reservation" fee. This can be accomplished by calling the branch of the Corporation Division of the Secretary of State, if applicable in your state.

2. Then you prepare the necessary incorporating papers, such as the Articles of Incorporation. (See Figure 14.2 for a general form. Figure 14.3 is an example of the online form available from the secretary of State of North Carolina.)

3. It is also at this juncture that you prepare a Certification of Authority to issue stock. This is secured from the State Securities Department. Simultaneously, you should prepare the corporation's bylaws. There, again, are a number of resources available online from the sites mentioned or from Westlaw and Lexis form databases.

4. The next step is to have these documents, above described, executed by the pertinent partners and/or directors.

5. Thereafter, documents should be filed with the appropriate state department of your state. Here again, you should check your local state statutes regarding this procedure.

6. Prepare the notice and/or letter advising the incorporators of their first meeting. The date and time of this meeting should have been discussed with the incorporators.

7. Then prepare the necessary letter or notice regarding the first meeting of the directors. This would have been done at the meeting of the incorporators (who may also be the original stockholders), when normally the board of directors would have been elected.

8. Then the stock certificates for the outstanding issue of stock should be prepared. The delivery of the stock certificates would have been determined at the board of directors meeting.

Figure 14.2
Articles of Incorporation

I

The name of this corporation is:_____.

II

The purpose of this corporation is to engage in any lawful act or activity for which a corporation may be organized under the general corporation law of the State of _____, other than the banking business, the trust company business or the practice of a profession permitted to be incorporated by the _____ Corporation Code.

III

The name and address in the State of _____ of this corporation's initial agent for service of process is _____.

IV

This corporation is authorized to issue only one class of stock; and the total number of shares which this corporation is authorized to issue is _____.
DATED: _____, 20___

_____

I hereby declare that I am the person who executed the foregoing Articles of Incorporation, which execution is my act and deed.

_____

The above is an example of an alternative set of articles of incorporation. Of course, there are others which can be created which are in more detail and which may include the name and address of the incorporators as well as the names and addresses of the initial directors, and the duration of the corporation. A sample of a set of articles of incorporation for a nonprofit organization is also attached.

Figure 14.3
State of North Carolina

Department of the Secretary of State

ARTICLES OF INCORPORATION

Pursuant to §55-2-02 of the General Statutes of North Carolina, the undersigned does hereby submit these Articles of Incorporation for the purpose of forming a business corporation.

1. The name of the corporation is:_____

2. The number of shares the corporation is authorized to issue is:_____

3. These shares shall be: *(check either a or b)*

☐   all of one class, designated as common stock; or

☐   divided into classes or series within a class as provided in the attached schedule, with the information required by N.C.G.S. Section 55-6-01.

4. The street address and county of the initial registered office of the corporation is:
Number and Street_____
City_____State_____ZIP Code_____County

5. The mailing address, *if different from the street address*, of the initial registered office is:
Number and Street_____
City_____State_____ZIP Code_____County

6. The name of the initial registered agent is:_____

7. Principal office information: *(must select either a or b)*
☐   The corporation has a principal office.
The street address and county of the principal office of the corporation is:
Number and Street_____
City_____State_____ZIP Code_____County
The mailing address, *if different from the street address*, of the principal office of the corporation is:
Number and Street_____
City_____State_____ZIP Code_____County
☐   The corporation does not have a principal office

8. Any other provisions, which the corporation elects to include, are attached.

9. The name and address of each incorporator is as follows:
_____
_____
_____

Figure 14.3 (*continued*)

10. These articles will be effective upon filing, unless a date and/or time is specified:

_____
_____
_____
_____

This the_____day of_____ 20_____

_____

Signature

_____

Type or Print Name and Title

Partnerships

Where two or more people are interested in doing business together as co-owners, they are able to form a partnership. A general partnership encompasses all sorts of activities that would generate a profit for the partners. Whereas a joint-venture partnership is an arrangement entered into for a specific purpose and for a limited time.

There are very few formalities required in a partnership. No papers, other than a "trade name certificate" need to be filed in order for the partnership to exist. A sample from New Jersey is included in Figure 14.4. It is for this reason that the agreement between the partners is well written. The flexibility and lack of regulations can make this a situation susceptible to problems.

The biggest disadvantage counterbalancing this flexibility in management and profit-sharing is the personal liability of the partners for the debts of the company.

Professionals, like accountants, attorneys, doctors, and architects, can form LLPs—limited liability partnerships, which essentially operate like LLCs. The main benefit of LLPs is to maintain the flexibility of a general partnership but also to insulate partners from each other's professional malpractice claims.

Figure 14.4
Certificate of Trade Name (New Jersey)

This is to certify that:
The following statement is made by the undersigned pursuant to the provisions of N.J.R.S. 56:1-1 et seq. ("Business and Partnership Names").
1. The name under which the business is now or about to be conducted is

_____

Figure 14.4 *(continued)*

2. The nature of the business is _____
_____

3. The address where said business is now or is about to be conducted is
_____

4. The full name and residence or post-office address of each person connected with the said business as a member of the firm, partner or owner conducting or about to conduct the said business is

_____
_____
_____

Business Telephone No. ( ) _____

The person or partners or members of the firm or partnership conducting or transacting the said business, who are not resident in this State, do hereby constitute the Clerk of the County wherein nonresident person or persons, partner or partners upon whom all original process may be served (a) in an action or legal proceeding against said firm or partnership of (b) in an action against said person or persons for any debt, damages, or liability contracted or incurred by them in or growing out of the conduct or transaction of said business. It is agreed that such original process which may be served upon the County Clerk shall be of the same force and validity as if served upon said nonresident person or persons, partners, or members of the firm or partnership. The authority hereof shall as to such nonresidents, continue in force so long as they shall do, conduct, or transact the said business in this State under such name.

Witnessed by:

_____
_____
_____

Dated: _____
_____

State of New Jersey,
County of
_____, who I am satisfied is/are the person(s) named in the foregoing certificate, has/have personally appeared before me and, after being duly sworn, has/have certified that the statements contained therein are true.

Sworn to and Subscribed before me this
_____ day of _____
_____

Limited Liability Companies

A limited liability company (LLC) is a relatively recent creation in business organizations. It is a legal entity that has characteristics of both a corporation and a partnership. It permits companies to maintain the flexibility of management of a partnership with the protection of individual members from the liabilities of the company. It will be necessary to check the laws in your state to determine the tax status of the LLC. The Uniform Limited Liability Company Act of 2006 can be accessed directly at www.law.upenn.edu/bll/archives/ulc/fnact99/1990s/ullca96 .htm.

Forming an LLC requires the filing of a Certificate of Formation with your secretary of state. It has much of the same information as the articles of incorporation for a corporate entity. The certificate includes the name of the LLC, its address, the registered agent for service of process, its organizers, the duration of its existence and purpose. See www.secstate.wa.gov/_assets/corps/llc.pdf for a sample form from the State of Washington.

The members (as opposed to shareholders) enter into an operating agreement which states how the business is going to be run, who may make decisions, who has authority to enter into agreements and incur liabilities, disposition of assets, dissolution, and other provisions. It is the duty of the paralegal to assemble all the necessary information regarding the following:

1. The availability of the name for the LLC.

   NOTE: The company must include "LLC" in its name.

2. The names of all the managers and organizers of the LLC along with their addresses.

3. The name and address of the person who will act as the registered agent.

   NOTE: This cannot be a PO box.

4. The purpose of the LLC, if it is not general, and its duration, if not in perpetuity.

Sole Proprietorships

This is the simplest form of a business. One owner controls all aspects of its operation and takes on all profits and losses. This also means that all liability rests upon that sole owner and the taxes are passed through to the individual.

Any business can operate as a sole proprietorship. The owner can either run the business under his own name or under a fictitious name or a d/b/a ("doing business as") name. The Small Business website mentioned earlier in the chapter has a page with a direct link to the fictitious name forms for all fifty states. It can be accessed at www.business.gov/guides/business-law/business-name/dba.html.

The benefit to running a sole proprietorship, aside from having the complete control over the business decisions, is that no operating expenses need to be raised through others willing to invest in your dream. Often, a sole proprietor is able to raise money on his own credit. This, of course, leads straight to the downside of operating a sole proprietorship—the credit of the owner is at risk. All financial matters are directly reflected in the personal finances of the owner.

CHAPTER FIFTEEN

How to Assist in a Criminal Law Practice

A paralegal should be familiar not only with the classification and types of crimes, but also with all aspects of criminal procedure, including pretrial and post-trial motions. The paralegal should be able to conduct initial interviews with the client, when appropriate, and know what information is necessary to determine what court documents are needed in preparation for the defense of the case. More important, the paralegal should be fully aware of the fiduciary relationship between the client and the attorney.

Additionally, the paralegal must have a working knowledge of specialized areas of criminal law and procedures that arise most often in criminal cases, such as: legality of arrests; searches and seizures (both with and without warrants); the admissibility of confessions or other statements of the defendant; the hearsay rule and its exceptions; the names of the various crimes as stated in the applicable criminal statutes. The paralegal should also know the elements of the crime, that is, that combination of intent and act that makes up the crime and that must specifically be proved in order to secure a conviction.

The following discussion is based upon the Federal Rules of Criminal Procedure, Evidence, and Appellate Practice. Some state-specific material will be included by way of example only. Be sure to check your jurisdiction's criminal code for both substantive law and procedure rules.

General Discussion

Criminal law deals with what is and what is not a crime. A crime is that which is considered an offense against the State. It is prosecuted and punishable by the State.

The burden is on the state to prove "beyond a reasonable doubt." All the defendant has to do is appear; no affirmative defense is necessary. If he determines or feels from the State's witnesses that the State has not proven its case, he does not need to offer proof or testimony in his defense.

This zealous prosecution of offenses must be tempered with the concerns of Constitutional Due Process, which guarantees certain rights to the criminal defendant. Bear the concepts of the Fourth, Fifth, Sixth, and Eighth Amendments in mind when reviewing the process by which the prosecution arrested, gathered evidence, and prosecutes the case.

Elements

For every crime, the state sets forth elements that need to be satisfied in order to find a violation of that statute. Each and every element of the crime must be found in the matter, otherwise the defendant cannot be found guilty of its commission.

EXAMPLE

Burglary: Traditionally, the definition called for "breaking and entering into the dwelling place of another—in the nighttime—with *an intent* to commit a felony or serious crime therein." Many states have eliminated the strict requirements that the entry be into a dwelling place and that it take place at night. Compare: North Carolina still retains the dwelling requirement while Minnesota considers entry into a dwelling as first degree burglary and other kinds of buildings as burglary in the third degree. This exemplifies why it is so critical to find the relevant statute in your jurisdiction!

Using the traditional definition, a person would have to commit each element of the definition of "burglary" to be found guilty of its commission:

1. First element: *breaking and entering*—this could be opening a window or screen door, or just walking through an open door. What the offender is doing is breaking past the barriers of privacy expectations.

2. Second element: into the *dwelling place* of another (could be a driveway or backyard, etc., any place where the occupant had an expectation of privacy and security).

3. Third element: it has to have been *in the nighttime*.

4. Fourth element: with the *intent* to commit a serious crime therein. This intent is the "*mens rea*," the "mental state" of the offender. This is *vitally* important: *the intent to do the act.*

If a person were pushed by another through the front door of a dwelling place at nighttime, he would not be found guilty, because he did not have the required mental state to commit the crime of burglary. He did not intend to enter into the house, he was pushed involuntarily through it.

Actus Reus

The *actus reus* is the "guilty act." It assumes both the requisite mental state and the action in furtherance of the criminal purpose. A criminal intent unaccompanied by a criminal act is not punishable in law.

There *must be* some affirmative action. Just thinking about performing an act is not a crime. (Planning an act *may* be a crime where it involves other persons—this can be considered "conspiracy.")

Issues in determining whether the *actus reus* exists are as follows:

1. A person is *responsible* not only for actions directly taken by him, but also those that he:

   a. Originates,

   b. Sets in motion,

   c. Solicits,

   d. Supports, or

   e. Incites.

2. A person may play any number of *roles* in committing the *actus reus*. A person can be:

   a. A principal,

   b. An accessory,

   c. An aider,

   d. An abettor, or

   e. An agent.

3. Does this conduct or act really *cause* the injury or harm? The State must prove that a *causal relationship* exists:

a. Between the act done and

b. The harm resulting therefrom.

In other words:

a. That the defendant acted and

b. That the defendant's action was the proximate cause of the harm suffered.

The problem arises in making the determination of "proximate cause." The defendant's actions must have been close enough to the result to be related to those actions. It is helpful to think in terms of dominoes. Once one falls, all the others that are close enough to it as an immediately preceding link fall as well. If however, something comes between the dominoes, the initial act no longer causes the final result of having them all fall. Something else may then set them in motion again; however, the subsequent tumbling is no longer tied to the initial tip-over.

Potential defenses include:

- Defendant not responsible because of an "intervening cause,"

- Defendant not responsible because of "concurrent causes,"

- Defendant not responsible because of an "independent intervening cause," and

- Defendant not responsible because of a "superseding cause."

EXAMPLE
"A" beats up "B" and throws "B" into the street. "B" is subsequently run over by a car and dies.

Question: Is A liable for murder?

- Was there a break in the chain of responsibility?

- Is B's death caused totally by independent causes?

- When do third parties become partially responsible?

A did not run over B, which was the actual cause of death. However, A should have known that B *could* get run over if A threw him in the street. B was only in the street because of A's actions. The last question goes to the avoidability of the accident on the part of the driver. Generally speaking, causation is *not* broken where the initial actor can foresee the problems or risks that his actions will cause to occur or arise. There might be a different result if B was struck by lightning as he lay in the street. The act of nature would be random and not related to A's actions.

1. Attempt:

   a. Finding the accused guilty *does not* require successful completion of a crime.

   b. An "attempt" is an unfinished crime.

2. Is it impossible to commit the actus reus?

   a. *Physically impossible:*

      i. Pickpocket who attempts to steal from a person who has no wallet or

      ii. Drug buyer wanting to purchase drugs from a dealer, who has none.

         NOTE: The actor can still be guilty of the "attempted" crime.

   b. *Factually impossible:*

      i. Assault on a store "mannequin" or

      ii. Shooting a pillow thought to be a human body.

   c. *Legally impossible:*

      i. Perjury committed outside a legal proceeding;

      ii. Juvenile committing an "adult" crime (if the court finds that the person acted as a juvenile that means that he could not form the requisite intent to commit the "adult crime"; a minor can be tried as an adult only if the court finds that he could form the adult intent); or

      iii. Rape where the party clearly consented at the time of the act.

Conclusion: If the *act* is impossible to *commit*, the *actus reus* may not be properly proven for the purposes of establishing criminal liability. *It must be accompanied by a mental state—mens rea—an intent to commit.*

Classification of Crimes

1. *Felony:* very serious and punishable by imprisonment in state penitentiary.

2. *Misdemeanor:* less serious and generally punishable by a fine or commitment to a county jail.

Pleas

1. *Guilty:* This can be either to the offense charged or to a less serious offense pursuant to an agreement with the prosecuting attorney.

2. *Nolo contendere,* "no contest." The party accepts responsibility for the punishment

without having to admit or deny that the crime was committed. This is available in some jurisdictions and has the same effect as a plea of guilty, except that it cannot be used against the defendant in civil actions arising out of the same incident that gave rise to the criminal charges.

3. *Not guilty:* Self-explanatory.

4. *Not guilty by reason of insanity:* This is sometimes pled in conjunction with the not guilty plea. The party is claiming to have such a mental impediment that he could not have formed the requisite intent to commit the crime.

5. *Double jeopardy:* A party may only be tried once for the same crime in the same tribunal. *Key:* "in the same tribunal." O. J. Simpson was tried for murder once in the criminal courts and once in the civil courts. There was no double jeopardy. Double jeopardy also does not apply where the defendant successfully secures a new trial after an appeal, or after a motion for new trial is granted by the trial court.

Rather than entering one of the above pleas, a defendant, in some jurisdictions, can enter a demurrer, which in effect states that the complaint or information does not state a cause of action against him. After a hearing on the demurrer, the court can either "sustain" the demurrer (and thus either dismiss the complaint or allow the prosecution to amend it) or can "overrule" the demurrer, at which point the defendant must enter a plea.

Crimes fall into three basic categories:

1. Crimes against the person,

2. Crimes against property, and

3. Crimes against the habitation.

The most common types of crimes are the following:

1. First- or second-degree murder,

2. Voluntary or involuntary manslaughter,

3. Grand or petty burglary, robbery, or theft,

4. Arson,

5. Sexual offenses, and

6. Kidnapping.

Crimes Against the Person

A. Homicide

1. *Murder:* Purposely or knowingly done, or is committed recklessly, manifesting extreme indifference to human life.

2. *Manslaughter:* An act of passion. An act of extreme mental or emotional disturbance that has a reasonable explanation.

3. *Felony Murder Rule:* Addresses itself to any and all members of a "conspiracy to commit a major criminal felony . . . where murder is a foreseeable result."

B. Assault

Assault is an intentional, unlawful offer of corporal injury to another by force to create well-founded fear of imminent peril, with apparent present ability to execute, if not prevented.

1. *Simple assault:* One committed with no intention to do any other injury, falls short of actual battery

2. *Aggravated assault:* One committed with the intention of committing some additional crime; or one attended with circumstances of peculiar outrage or *atrocity*

3. *Reckless endangerment:* Reckless taking of *chance* without intent that accident or injury would occur

C. Kidnapping

Kidnapping is the forcible removal of any person from his own country and/or home and/or confinement, and may include "for the purposes of":

1. Ransom, reward, shield, or hostage;

2. Facilitating commission of a felony;

3. Inflicting bodily injury or terrorizing victim; and/or

4. Interfering in the performance of any governmental function.

D. Sexual Offenses

1. Rape/aggravated sexual assault elements:

    a. Sexual intercourse (penetration),

    b. Lack of consent (implying force or threat of harm), and

c. Both males and females may assert the claim as rape has become gender "neutral."

2. *Sexual conduct:* Lewd and lascivious behavior and public exposure of "naked body."

> **NOTE:** As it is apparent that crime throughout the country is ever increasing, some of the formerly indispensable elements that make up violent crimes against persons may not be needed for the courts to interpret that there has been a violent crime committed.

For example, you might want to check your local state codes to determine the applicability of the need for penetration in rape. It may be that now, in some states, molestation may have superseded the actual act. This means that any improper touching of a person such as a child under age or a woman who did not agree to the act of sex, even with her husband or a date, could be considered molestation or rape.

Then there are the federal laws regarding what constitutes sexual harassment. These are brought to your attention since they were deliberately not discussed in the employment law section. In other words, check your local state codes with reference to what elements are necessary and/or mandatory to a felony conviction as to violent crimes against persons.

Crimes Against Property

A. Larceny/Theft
The taking away of property to which the person has no lawful right of possession.

Elements of larceny/theft:

* Taking of property of value;

* No lawful right to possession; and

* Movement, transfer, or "asportation" of the property.

B. Theft by Deception and Fraud
Must relate to material issues of fact. Scams; cancer cures; door-to-door rip-offs; consumer protection: purposely creating an impression in the mind of the owner to induce consent when the impression is false.

C. Theft of Services/Public Utilities

1. Restaurant: check or tab not paid and the restaurant is left with no means of collection

2. Nonpayment of utility bills, etc.

D. Theft of Lost or Abandoned Property

Anyone who comes into control of property, knowing it to be mislaid, lost or delivered by mistake, commits a theft, if he or she does not take reasonable measures to return the property to the person.

EXAMPLE

Say you found a brown bag in an alley containing $50,000 in unmarked bills and no identifying markings. You turn the bag and its contents over to the police to process. They have to hold it for six months (this time may vary in your state) while they check for the owner. Thereafter you have to wait an additional thirty days before you can legally claim the money as yours.

E. Theft by Extortion

Found under larceny/theft statutes, often used by organized crime—when a person obtains by a threat, to:

1. Inflict bodily injury or other offense,

2. Falsely accuse anyone of an offense,

3. Expose secrets,

4. Take or withhold official action,

5. Cause a strike or boycott,

6. Withhold legal testimony, or

7. Threaten any harm.

F. Receiving Stolen Property

One who pays a bargain price for goods, knowing that it was a "low" price for the value, can be viewed as knowing the goods were stolen. Example: $35 for an iPod. Actual knowledge can be inferred from the facts.

G. Robbery

Primary difference between "robbery" and "larceny" is the amount of force exerted. Robbery inflicts serious bodily injury, or threatens another with, or purposely puts him in fear of immediate, serious bodily injury.

Robbery, therefore, is an offense of the person as well as property.

Crimes Against the Habitation

A. Burglary

1. Entry,

2. Without a license or privilege, and

3. With the intent to commit a crime therein.
   (Again, note that most states have done away with the nighttime and dwelling-place requirements.)

B. Arson

Does *not* require a successful destruction—mere charring is sufficient—but does require intent to burn, destroy, and set fire to property, and done with knowledge that this conduct involves substantial risks.

Crimes Classified as "Inchoate"

An inchoate crime is one in which no harm has actually occurred; however, public policy requires that the crime be punished as a disincentive to criminal behavior.

A. Conspiracy
Two or more people:

1. Have conspired to engage in conduct constituting a crime,

2. Have agreed to aid in the planning or commission of the crime, and

3. Have committed an overt act in furtherance thereof.

B. Solicitation
Hiring a hit man. Individuals who: promote, facilitate, command, incite, or encourage others to commit criminal offenses. Both are equally liable.
Defenses:

* Notified the person solicited that you renounced the crime, and

* Gave timely warning to appropriate law enforcement, or

* Tried to stop the criminal behavior.

In all cases where you will need to establish the criminal elements of the crime, it will be necessary to do the legal research in your jurisdiction. Of course, the statutory elements will need to be researched, but even more important, how your courts have interpreted those elements. Statutory law is very broad. The language is susceptible to ambiguities. Case law will help you better understand the intent and application of the statute in a variety of situations.

Justifiable Defenses

An act may be justified (excused) where there exists a legitimate reason for taking that action. The person committing the act does not have criminal intent in connection with the action. Rather, the intent to commit the act has a different result.

A. Public Authority
The State has authority through its agents to commit an act that would be a criminal act if it were committed by an ordinary individual. Police officers have public authority to use force, even deadly force, where necessary.

B. Domestic Authority
Parents and schoolteachers inflicting non-deadly force upon children where it is necessary to maintain control of their safety.

C. Self-Defense
Permits an individual to use force, including deadly force, that is reasonably necessary to terminate a physical attack on the person. The key is that the person must meet the force with equal force, not excessive force. Only when you are faced with deadly force can you use deadly force in response.

D. Defense of Others
In most jurisdictions, the general law is that you may only defend others if you stand in some kind of *public* or *family* or *personal relationship* with them.

E. Defense of Property
You do not have the right to "shoot" aggressors simply because they are on your property. Again, the equal force requirement pertains here.

F. Crime Prevention
Force may be used as reasonably necessary to protect against a "breach of peace." This breach must be a felony.

G. Excuses and Mitigating Factors
Where justification for the act is imperfect, the court may still consider the following factors in making the determination as to the true intent rather than criminal

intent. The act may then be excused without criminal penalty or the crime charged may be lessened to reflect these extenuating circumstances:

1. *Infancy:* The court presumes that there is no capacity to form the *mens rea* of the crime.

   a. Below age seven it is absolute;

   b. Seven to fourteen, it is rebuttable.

2. *Insanity* (not rising to the level of an absolute defense)

3. *Involuntary intoxication*

4. *Mistake of fact*

5. *Mistake of law:* Ignorance of law is no excuse as a matter of practicality.

6. *Duress* (coercion): When you can show you have acted under the threat of another, in fear of your life or serious bodily harm.

7. *Necessity:* For example, if the party is caught out in a storm, needing someplace to stay, and he breaks into a vacant house. The party had no alternative *but to open and use the house.*

8. *Coverture:* "My husband made me do it." Committing a crime at the direction of another.

9. *Conduct of the victim:*

   a. *Consent:* "Affective" consent will be a defense to the commission of the crime.

   b. *Ineffective consent:* Fraud, misrepresentation.

   c. *The guilt of the victim:* An individual who deals with a "fence," or someone who left himself wide open to a criminal act.

10. *Victim condoning an act after it has been committed:* It is totally irrelevant. It is a crime against our society, not just the individual victim.

11. *Entrapment:* When law enforcement participates in the setting up of a crime, which would not have happened without the intervention of the agency.

The Client Interview

More than in any other phase of law practice, your attitude toward and treatment of a client in criminal law should be professional. There will be times when you are appalled at the alleged crime, or not in sympathy with the alleged act of violence, or shocked by the indulgence in a sex act or by participation in the use of narcotics or other drugs, but you are not there to sit in judgment—you are there to help the client.

The initial interview of a client charged with a criminal offense is one of the most crucial steps in a criminal proceeding, since you are dealing with a person's life and freedom of movement as opposed to loss of, or damage to, property.

Time is of the essence, since the period between arrest and trial is very short as compared to a civil action, which may not come to trial within eighteen months or two years from the date of filing the complaint. For this reason, the time in which discovery can be initiated and conducted is compressed. In this connection you should be doubly careful: First, obtain from the client the minute details of the arrest to determine if his rights were violated in any way and if there were any illegal acts committed by the arresting officers. Second, if the client is a member of any minority, by race, creed, color, or sex, or is poor and indigent, you may be faced with the additional problem of communication. Hence, you should be well versed and knowledgeable about the concerns and customs of various cultures and ethnic groups with whom you may have to deal. The following are some of the factors you should bear in mind when interviewing a client in a criminal matter.

The Cultural Gap

1. Client's interests

2. Client's capabilities

3. Client's motivation

4. Behavioral patterns: those normally accepted in his world are controlling to him

5. Language barrier: This could be just the slang he uses or a foreign language necessitating his translating English (in his head) to his own language. Often the words do not mean the same in his language, or the word might have two meanings in our language.

Family Structure

1. Who is the head of the household, if any?

2. What is the client's responsibility in the home?

3. What is the earning power of the husband? The wife?

4. Who and how many people are depending on him?

These facts help shape the client's attitude about himself and will aid you in preparing the client for both trial and the rehabilitation process. It will give you insight into his behavior and what, if anything, your attorney can do to help. Also, depending where he is in the family structure, you might get an insight as to why he really committed the crime, if he did. Sometimes too much pressure or responsibility or an unfaithful spouse is the real culprit. Your attorney, in any event, should be aware of these and any other possible motivating factors that may become apparent during the interview.

Attitude Toward the Establishment

If you are interviewing a member of a minority, how he feels about crime and punishment is vitally important. His cooperation in implementing the trial strategy to be planned by your attorney is a must. You should be aware that punishment by the establishment may not be as important to him as is the punishment of his peers. Committing a crime could be a way of obtaining "approval" or to "be a man" in the eyes of someone close, or would not be considered a crime by your client, period. Hence, going to jail could be a reward or a means of making his point.

Finally, be aware of your client's shrewdness and possibly comprehensive knowledge of the law and the sentences accompanying his particular crime. If he is not a first offender, he is probably much more educated than you are in this area. Even first offenders seem to know the "ropes." On the other side of the coin, the client may be too willing to talk or cooperate. There is the other feeling of being prepared or willing to say whatever is expected, rather than what he really wants to say.

This short course in practical psychology will aid in determining what the truth really is, as told by the client, or will perhaps help you draw the truth from him and win his confidence. This will make your attorney's job much easier.

Your Attitude

The information that you are able to obtain from the client may depend on your attitude during the interview. It is important to be cognizant of the following:

1. Let the client explain his side of the story in full detail. This gives him some control of this potentially intimidating situation. Do not interrupt or make any judgments. It is in this way that you will be able to find out what his intentions may have been before things went wrong.

2. Treat him with respect. Ask questions about the client, including: personal history, marital status, finances, education, work experience, occupation, hobbies. You, after all, work for him in the representation.

3. Explore the details of the story. Be sure to ask if he has any prior record of violence, any prior felony convictions.

4. Explain the procedures that your office will follow. Your client will feel more at ease if he knows what to expect from *you*, not just the justice system.

Pretrial Procedure

In many jurisdictions, when the client is charged with having committed a misdemeanor, a complaint is filed against him. The defendant appears in court for the "arraignment" (usually within a specific statutory period after the filing of the complaint), to enter the "plea." He may plead guilty and have the matter set for sentencing, or he may plead not guilty and have the matter set for trial. (Of course, the other alternatives set forth earlier are also available.) Depending on the verdict reached after the trial, either the case will be dismissed or the defendant will be ordered to return for sentencing.

When a felony is charged against the client, the subsequent procedure may become somewhat more complicated, since the offense charged is more serious.

For instance: After the arrest, the defendant must be arraigned within a specific time period, and assuming a guilty plea is not entered, the court may set the matter for preliminary hearing (again within a set time period). If, after the preliminary hearing, the court decides that sufficient cause exists to hold the defendant for trial, the client may then be re-arraigned in another court, and the matter may be set for trial.

Time limitations are almost always set by law, and if the prosecution deviates from them without the defendant's consent, you can proceed to prepare a motion to dismiss.

Pretrial Motions

1. *Motion to reduce bail:* If an excessive bail has been set, the following is a sample motion to reduce the bail:

(Name)
(Address)
(Telephone No.)
Attorney for Defendant, John Doe
SUPERIOR COURT OF THE STATE OF CALIFORNIA
FOR THE COUNTY OF _____

PEOPLE OF THE STATE	)	No._____
OF _____	)	MOTION TO REDUCE
	)	EXCESSIVE BAIL
Plaintiff,	)	
v.	)	
	)	
JOHN DOE,	)	
	)	
Defendant	)	
_____	)	

Defendant John Doe, through his counsel (name of counsel), hereby moves the Court for an Order reducing defendant's bail from the previously set sum of $500,000, which is unconstitutionally excessive, to the sum of $100,000, an amount that should guarantee defendant's appearance at all stages of the proceedings.

This motion is based upon the transcript of the preliminary examination, which the Court has read and considered, the declaration of John Doe, attached hereto as Exhibit A.

Exhibit A : [The accompanying affidavit:]

John Doe, being first duly sworn, deposes and says:

1. I am the defendant, John Doe, named in this proceeding.

2. I am currently in the custody of the sheriff of the County of [county], State of [state], pursuant to an order of arrest issued by the court on the ground that [specify ground for arrest].

3. On [date], the court fixed the bail in the sum of 500,000.

4. This sum is excessive for the following reasons: [set forth reasons].

Therefore, defendant requests that the court reduce the amount of bail to $100,000.

This sample motion illustrates a format for all pretrial motions in criminal case.

2. *Motion to quash or set aside complaint or indictment:* If there was no "probable cause" to arrest the defendant or, in matters heard by a grand jury, if the evidence was not properly presented to the grand jury, a motion to quash may be used in some jurisdictions. See also Motion to Dismiss following.

3. *Motion to dismiss:* This may be made based on formal defects in the information or indictment. The attorney must decide whether it is wise to make such a motion, as it may educate the prosecutor unnecessarily—ref. F.R.C.P. 6(b)(2) and 12(b).

The following is a sample motion to dismiss stating several possible grounds (use only the grounds applicable to your particular case):

In the United States District Court for the
_____ District of _____
_____ Division

UNITED STATES OF AMERICA

v.   No. . . . .

John Doe

MOTION TO DISMISS INDICTMENT

The defendant moves that the indictment be dismissed on the following grounds:

1. The court is without jurisdiction because the offense, if any, is cognizable only in the _____ Division of the _____ District of _____.
2. The indictment does not state facts sufficient to constitute an offense against the United States.
3. The defendant has been acquitted (convicted, in jeopardy of conviction) of the offense charged therein in the case United States v. _____ in the District Court for the _____ District of _____, Case No. _____ terminated on _____.
4. The offense charged is the same offense for which the defendant was pardoned by the President of the United States on _____ day of _____, 20_____.
5. The indictment was not found within three years next after the alleged offense was committed.

Signed:_____

_____
Address

Dated: _____, 20_____

4. *Motion for change of venue:* This order can be done on the court's own motion, but you can file the same if your attorney feels her client will not get a "fair and impartial trial" within the county where the alleged crime was committed.

5. *Motion for discovery under court rules of criminal procedure:* Your attorney has the right to be aware and informed of the district attorney's case and possible witnesses. That was not so in the "good ole days."

6. *Motion to suppress evidence:* You would use this motion where evidence has been obtained through illegal search and seizure. It applies to physical evidence, statements made by the defendant when not advised by counsel or through wiretapping, prior convictions, and so forth. Dee F.R.C.P. 12(b)(3) and Federal Evidence Code.

This motion is normally presented days prior to the date of trial or at the preliminary hearing, but most criminal court rules allow it to be filed at any time before trial.

A sample of a motion to suppress evidence and for the return of the seized property follows:

In the United States District Court for the
_____ District of _____,
_____ Division

United States of America
                    Plaintiff,

v.   No._____

John Doe
                    Defendant.

_____

MOTION TO SUPPRESS

John Doe hereby moves this Court to direct that certain property of which he is the owner, a schedule of which is annexed hereto, and which on the night of _____, 20_____ , at the premises known as _____ Street, in the city of the District of _____, was unlawfully seized and taken from him by two deputies of the United States Marshal for this District, whose true names are unknown to the petitioner, be returned to him and that it be suppressed as evidence against him in any criminal proceeding.

The petitioner further states that the property was seized against his will and without a search warrant.

The Certification of defense counsel for John Doe, Petitioner, is attached hereto as Exhibit A in support of this Motion to Suppress Evidence.

_____

Attorney for Petitioner

Address

Dated: _____, 20_____

Exhibit A. Certification of Defense Counsel in Support of the Motion to Suppress Evidence.

© 11 Am. Jur. Pl. & Pr. Forms Federal Criminal Procedure §163

I, *[attorney for the defendant]*, being first duly sworn, state:

1. I am the attorney for defendant *[name of defendant]* and am fully familiar with all the facts and proceedings previously had in the above-captioned case.

2. On *[date of search and seizure]*, at premises belonging to and occupied by defendant and known as *[location of search and seizure]*, *[agents/ [other title of law enforcement officers]]* of *[the Federal Bureau of Investigation/[other name of federal law enforcement entity]]* searched for and seized certain papers and property belonging to defendant. An inventory of such papers and property, which was prepared by the *[agents/[other title of law enforcement officers]]* is attached to this affidavit, marked Exhibit *[exhibit designation]*, and incorporated by reference.

3. The search and seizure was conducted under the authority of a search warrant dated *[date of search warrant]*, and issued by *[a United States Magistrate Judge for the [name of district] of [name of state]/[other title of official issuing search warrant]]*.

4. The affidavit of *[name of affiant]* in support of the issuance of the search warrant was insufficient in the following respects:
   a. The affidavit contained no allegation of probable cause to believe that the property seized was being concealed on the premises searched.
   b. The affidavit contained no allegation or proof of probable cause for believing that defendant possessed the property seized with intent to use it as the means of committing a criminal offense.

7. *Motion to sever:* This motion is used when there are two defendants charged with the same crime or who acted jointly in the commission of a crime and either attorney feels it would be in his client's best interest it they had separate trials. In federal cases and in some states the prosecutor can also request relief from prejudicial joinder on motion and order of court. See F.R.C.P. 14 and 12(b)(5).

8. *Motion for appointment of an expert:* This motion is used if the attorney feels that an expert witness, that is, psychiatrist, pathologist, and so forth, will be necessary for the defense and if the client does not have sufficient funds to hire an expert. You are referred to your local court rules to determine how an expert can be appointed at court expense for an indigent defendant. Psychiatric examination on motion of the federal prosecuting attorney is governed by F.R.C.P. 12.2(c). It is imperative to give adequate and timely notice to the prosecution of the defendant's intent to rely upon the insanity defense. If the defendant fails to give adequate notice or fails to submit to the examination, the defendant will be barred from asserting that defense at trial.

A state court sample order for an examination at the request of the defendant follows:

(Name)
(Address)
(Telephone No.)
Attorney for Defendant.

SUPERIOR COURT OF THE STATE OF _____

FOR THE COUNTY OF _____

PEOPLE OF THE STATE OF CALIFORNIA,	))	CASE NO._____
Plaintiff,	))	MOTION FOR ORDER
v.	))	APPOINTING PSYCHIATRIST (_____ Evid. Code,
JOHN DOE,	))	Sections _____, _____, _____)
Defendant.	))	
_____	)	

(Name), counsel for defendant herein, moves the court for an order appointing _____ M.D. as psychiatrist for defendant herein, to examine said defendant and to report her findings to defendant's counsel only.

A confidential psychiatric examination is necessary and material, and is authorized by Sections 370, 952, and 1017 of the Evidence Code, so that counsel can be fully advised and can advise defendant whether to present a defense based on insanity or on defendant's mental or emotional condition.

Dated: _____, 20_____

_____
Attorney for Defendant

Order for Pretrial Examination (from the State of Arizona, by way of example)

STATE OF ARIZONA Plaintiff

-v-

Defendant (FIRST, MI, LAST **)**

NOTICE OF
APPOINTMENT OF
MENTAL HEALTH
EXPERT
(COMPETENCY)

The Court, having granted the motion for competency examination pursuant to Rule 11.2, Rules of Criminal Procedure, and the defendant having been charged with:

_____

IT IS HEREBY ORDERED appointing

_____

And _____

as mental health experts, to prepare and send to the Court a written report of the experts' opinions and findings as to the defendant's competency to stand trial (i.e., the defendant's ability to understand the nature of the proceedings and to assist counsel in the preparation of the defense). If a mental health expert finds the Defendant is incompetent to stand trial at this time, an opinion shall also be rendered as to:

(A) The mental disease, defect, or disability which is the cause of the Defendant's incompetency;

(B) Whether there is a substantial probability the Defendant will become competent within a reasonable period of time;

(C) The most appropriate form and place of treatment in this state, based on the defendant's therapeutic needs and potential threat to public safety;

(D) The defendant's prognosis; and

(E) Whether the defendant is incompetent to refuse treatment and should be subject to involuntary treatment.

IT IS FURTHER ORDERED that the report name each mental health expert who examines the defendant; that it describe the nature, content, extent, and results of the examination and any test conducted; and that it include the facts on which the findings are based.

IT IS FURTHER ORDERED that if the defendant is not in custody, defense counsel is to contact the experts at [names and phone numbers]_____ within two (2) working days of this order to schedule a time for the defendant's examination and use due diligence to secure the defendant's attendance at the examination.

IT IS FURTHER ORDERED that the prosecutor and defense counsel provide to the experts at [addresses] _____ the motion to have defendant's mental condition examined, copies of police reports, previous mental health reports, and any other appropriate material for the examination.

IT IS FURTHER ORDERED that payment of the cost of the examination of the defendant is the responsibility of the _____ pursuant to ARS § 13-4505.

IT IS FURTHER ORDERED that a competency hearing will be held in _____court on the _____day of _____, 20 at_____ a.m./p.m.

IT IS FURTHER ORDERED that the experts will submit the written reports at least 10 days prior to the competency hearing date to which will seal the originals and provide copies to defense counsel. Defense counsel shall provide redacted copies of the reports to the court and the prosecutor's office within 24 hours of receipt.

_____

Signature of Judicial Officer

Date

Pretrial Discovery in a Criminal Case

In a criminal case, pretrial discovery may be made by deposition. Some criminal court rules and Federal Rules of Criminal Procedure 15 require a court order to take a necessary deposition. Some state courts have more liberal pretrial deposition rules. Check your criminal court rules.

Even though deposition may be taken only on order of court and even though interrogatories, as such, are not available under criminal court rules of procedure, pretrial discovery is possible under other rules that require disclosure of evidence and other information by the prosecutor to the defense lawyer. Some of these rules are mandatory and some are permissive.

Federal Rules of Criminal Procedure 16 provides for reciprocal disclosure by the prosecutor and the defendant. The reciprocal rules require disclosure of names and addresses of witnesses and statements (written or recorded), as well as documents and tangible objects that are in the custody and control of the government and that are either material to the preparation of the defense or intended for use as evidence.

Certain information is not subject to disclosure.

Some state criminal procedure rules have a "notice of alibi" rule similar to that of Federal Rules of Criminal Procedure 12.1. The prosecutor must make the first move (a written demand) to invoke this rule under the federal and many state rules.

Your attorney may not want to take advantage of the reciprocal rules of disclosure, and the prosecutor may not want to take advantage of the notice of alibi rule, for practical strategic reasons, but the paralegal should be aware of these rules in case either one does want to use them.

EXAMPLES

1. Motion for deposition alleging reasons, see F.R.C.P. 15.

2. Notice of defense based on mental condition, see F.R.C.P. 12.2.

3. Written demand by prosecutor stating time, date, and place at which the alleged offense was committed. It is in response to that written demand that a notice of alibi, listing names and addresses of alibi witnesses, must be served on the prosecution by the defense attorney (usually ten days), see F.R.C.P. 12.1.

4. Request by defendant for disclosure, see F.R.C.P. 16(a) and (b).

Check your local criminal court rules or rules of criminal procedure for other strategies available by pretrial written motion or written request.

Jury Selection

Unless the attorney wishes to challenge the entire grand or petit jury panel (for example, on the grounds of racial or sexual discrimination, which may, of course, give rise to overall investigatory problems), the paralegal's main concern as the trial approaches is in assisting in the preparation of the voir dire examination by the attorney on the day of trial.

This may involve the preparation of specific questions to be directed to the various members of the jury by your attorney, questions that are designed to elicit information showing pretrial bias on the part of any and all members of the panel.

Very often, however, your attorney will prepare his own voir dire questions just prior to the court's calling the jury, since questioning may vary with the nature of the offense charged and the special peculiarities inherent in certain classes of offenses, or the attorney may have a standard list of voir dire questions upon which he may elaborate prior to each trial.

Useful data on potential jurors may be compiled as follows by:

1. Obtaining the areas of their residence from the local Department of Voter Registration, tax assessor's office, and so forth;

2. Checking their political affiliations;

3. Checking what petitions they may have signed;

4. A basic Google search of their names; and

5. Determining if they have any children, animals, and the like—anything you feel might give the attorney insight as to their personality.

Trial Preparation Procedure

Preparing the case for trial involves:

1. Coordinating the activities pertinent to the trial;

2. Interviewing witnesses;

3. Setting up depositions of witnesses;

4. Preparing witnesses for examination and cross-examination;

5. Preparing exhibits;

6. Preparing list of names and addresses of witnesses to be subpoenaed, if any; and

7. Preparing the trial book (similar to the exhibit book in a civil action), which contains:

   a. A police report,

   b. Profile of the witnesses and their testimony,

   c. Investigation file, and

   d. Research memoranda.

If there are physical items of evidence to be offered by the defense, such as photographs and the like, be sure the attorney has them in his possession on the day the trial begins. In this connection, it has been our experience that a brief memo explaining the various items of evidence and when they are to be first identified and marked during the trial is quite helpful to your attorney.

At the trial itself, you should be familiar with the standard of "proof beyond a reasonable doubt" applicable in a criminal proceeding, as opposed to "proof by a mere preponderance of the evidence" or the "clear and convincing proof" standards applicable to a civil matter.

An initial thoroughgoing effort at discovery before the trial, as described earlier in this chapter, will enable your attorney to evaluate the nature and strength of the evidence to be presented by the prosecution, so that he may plan how best to present the defense.

At times the prosecution's case will be so weak as to be unable to withstand a defense motion to dismiss at the close of the prosecution's case. But do not expect this blessing too often, if at all, since many weak cases are weeded out either before they are formally filed or at the preliminary examination.

All defense witnesses should be thoroughly interviewed by you and your attorney, since, unlike in civil proceedings, depositions in criminal proceedings are somewhat rare. Make notes of statements made by witnesses as you interview them or, if the interviewed witness agrees, record the questions and answers.

Witnesses

Witnesses can be of several types: (1) direct witnesses, (2) alibi witnesses, (3) character witnesses, (4) expert witnesses, and so forth. If any of your witnesses testified under oath previously concerning the offense charged, it is important that you secure a transcript of that testimony to ensure that there is no variance in later testimony.

If there is a variance due to a memory lapse, then the witness will want to refresh his recollection before testifying, and this is done by review of the transcript. Here you can be of great assistance to your attorney, for if you suspect that the witness's variance is attributable to intentional misrepresentation, or perjury, you can advise your attorney so that he may avoid the pitfalls that will result from calling that particular witness to the stand.

The foregoing procedure, that is, reviewing the transcript with a potential witness, aids your attorney in achieving the best results and cuts down the possibility of embarrassment or of being caught by surprise in the middle of a trial.

1. *Direct witness:* a person who saw the actions of the accused at the scene of the crime or saw actions of others that are relevant to the case.

2. *Alibi witness:* a witness who can testify to facts that place the defendant somewhere other than at the scene of the crime. (See Notice of Alibi criminal court rule and annotations of cases interpreting that rule.)

3. *Character witness:* a witness who may know nothing about the facts of the alleged crime but who knows the reputation in the community of the defendant, for the character quality involved in the offense such as:

   a. Larceny—honesty

   b. Assault—peace-loving

   c. Sex crime—morality and chastity

4. *Expert witness:* a person qualified in a scientific or other relevant field, to answer a hypothetical question by stating an opinion or by giving demonstrative or opinion evidence.

Prior to subpoenaing character witnesses, it is important to find out, through pretrial evidence disclosure as discussed earlier, whether or not the defendant has a prior criminal record. If so, get the details of the charge and the disposition of the prior case.

If the defendant has a criminal record, it may not be wise to raise the issue of his reputation by calling character witnesses.

NOTE: In some states, the issues of credibility of the defendant as a witness may be raised as soon as he takes the witness stand in his own behalf, and the prior criminal record can be introduced, whether or not character witnesses are called.

Know, by studying the appropriate provisions of your evidence statutes (and by consulting with the attorney on case law), how much of the "rap sheet" the prosecution will be able to get before the jury, if you put on character witnesses or he calls the defendant to testify.

Preparing Jury Instructions

Proper preparation of jury instructions is critical. Many jurisdictions have standard jury instructions which can be accessed through the various legal databases. Certainly, the easiest place to find them is through the criminal court website in your jurisdiction.

Each aspect of the case (elements of the crime, defenses, etc.) has a separate jury instruction associated with it. A sample of Florida's Standard Jury Charge for the defense of insanity follows:

Insanity

An issue in this case is whether (defendant) was insane when the crime allegedly was committed.

A person is considered to be insane when:

1. [He] [She] had a mental infirmity, disease, or defect.

2. Because of this condition
   a. [he] [she] did not know what [he] [she] was doing or its consequences or
   b. although [he] [she] knew what [he] [she] was doing and its consequences, [he] [she] did not know it was wrong.

Give if applicable.

A defendant who believed that what [he] [she] was doing was morally right is not insane if the defendant knew that what [he] [she] was doing violated societal standards or was against the law.

All persons are presumed to be sane. The defendant has the burden of proving the defense of insanity by clear and convincing evidence. Clear and convincing evidence is evidence that is precise, explicit, lacking in confusion, and of such weight that it produces a firm belief, without hesitation, about the matter in issue.

In determining the issue of insanity, you may consider the testimony of expert and nonexpert witnesses. The question you must answer is not whether the defendant is insane today, or has ever been insane, but whether instead the defendant was insane at the time the crime allegedly was committed.

Give if applicable.

Unrestrained passion or ungovernable temper is not insanity, even though the normal judgment of the person is overcome by passion or temper.

Give if applicable.

If the evidence establishes that the defendant had been adjudged insane by a court, and has not been judicially restored to legal sanity, then you should assume the defendant was insane at the time of commission of the alleged crime, unless the evidence convinces you otherwise.

If you find that (*defendant*) committed the crime but you find by clear and convincing evidence that the defendant was insane, then you should find [him] [her] not guilty by reason of insanity.

> If your verdict is that the defendant is not guilty by reason of insanity, that does not necessarily mean [he] [she] will be released from custody. I must conduct further proceedings to determine if the defendant should be committed to a mental hospital, or given other outpatient treatment or released.

There are, however, instances in which your attorney will want special jury instructions typed "to order." You should know when these jury instructions must be presented to the court. In California, jury instructions ordinarily must be handed in to the judge prior to commencement of the argument of counsel.

Documenting Opening and Final Arguments

Your attorney may want you to assist in preparation of his opening and final arguments. As a guide, you should briefly outline the facts of both the prosecution and defense case, and note the items of evidence that are to be or have been introduced and which of these, if any, would be most helpful to your attorney's argument. Your attorney will advise you what other items or arguments he may wish to include. Then develop a legal memorandum accordingly.

After the verdict has been rendered, if it is adverse to the client, your attorney may want you to interview, or assist him in interviewing, the jury, to determine what led them to the verdict and if there were any irregularities during the deliberations that might give rise to a motion for new trial. This is not allowed in some states or may be counterproductive.

Post-Trial Procedure in a Criminal Case

If the jury returns a not guilty verdict, the proceedings are usually at an end then and there, unless the client is held to answer on other charges.

If a guilty verdict is returned, various post-trial motions may be in order. Very often, a motion for new trial may be made. In addition, the defendant may apply to the court for probation. If the client has the funds, the attorney may, if an appeal is to be filed, move that the court admit the defendant to bail pending appeal.

Practical Step-by-Step Post-Trial Procedure After Verdict

1. After the verdict has been rendered, file a motion for new trial (if applicable) or a motion for release from custody on bail pending sentence.

2. Interview the jurors after the trial to determine how they reached the verdict.

3. Assuming that your motion for a new trial is denied and the client is sent to jail or released on bail pending sentencing, he can be given:

   a. Time in jail or prison;

b. Straight probation; or

   c. Probation conditioned upon certain community service, medical treatment, or other condition.

After conviction, a great deal can be done by the paralegal in preparing the defendant for the inquisition of the probation department. The report of the assigned probation officer is analogous to a civil service personnel file in that it follows the defendant not only to the jail, but becomes a matter of public record and can affect the defendant's status in the community for the rest of his life.

The paralegal, therefore, not only interviews the defendant after conviction as to prior offenses, employment history, and so forth, but delves into areas which could mitigate the punishment and/or reduce the sentence, such as a feeling of remorse and penitence or a desire for possible psychiatric examination or treatment and, of course, job rehabilitation.

If an application for probation is submitted, every effort should be made to present the probation officer with the strongest justification for admitting the defendant to probation. Very often, letters of recommendation can be presented to the probation officer from friends, family, employers, clergymen, and so forth, and these letters can be reviewed by the court at the time of sentencing without running afoul of the hearsay rule.

If delegated the responsibility, you should instruct the client to be perfectly candid and remorseful (that is, if the client is in fact guilty) when talking with the probation officer. As a practical matter, the attorney often deals directly with the probation officer, not only to secure the best possible recommendation for sentencing, but also to determine if the probation officer arrived at the recommendation fairly and properly.

If the client's criminal record is extensive, the probation officer will often recommend that the client spend a period of time in the county jail or state prison. (Mandatory death penalty statutes involve special problems of "finality" and of constitutionality which will not be discussed here.) And for this reason, sometimes the client will be psychologically prepared to "do time." In this connection, sometimes your attorney, or you (if delegated this task), must assume the duties of a parent-confessor-psychologist in preparing the client for incarceration.

In any event, the preparation for the sentencing hearing by your attorney, or you, can often be more important than the trial itself. This can especially be seen in cases where the client pleads guilty and waives the constitutional rights attached to a trial by jury. To this end, you should review all the various classes of post-trial motions authorized by statute in your jurisdiction, so that you may be best prepared to utilize many or all of them for your attorney and his client.

Appeal in a Criminal Case

If a motion for new trial is denied, the defendant may want to appeal. Although procedures on appeal may vary from jurisdiction to jurisdiction, you will very often find that a prepared "notice of appeal" must be filed within a specified time period after judgment is rendered.

Your duties, once the notice of appeal is filed, may include a formal request for the preparation, by the clerk of the Record on Appeal, which consists of, for example, the Clerk's Transcript (Record during Trial), the Reporter's Transcript, copies of all motions filed, jury instructions, and so forth. In short, the appellate court must have before it a complete picture of these proceedings.

You must be aware of the strict time limits within which requests must be made, briefs filed, and motions made to the appellate court. See the Appellate Rules of Procedure for the appellate court to which the appeal is being taken.

Oral arguments made by the attorneys are often as important as the written brief, and you may be called upon to assist in the research needed to prepare the written brief and in the preparation of oral arguments, or both.

Even after an appellate decision is rendered, various jurisdictions permit the defendant to file a "petition for rehearing" (if the decision is adverse), and you may be called upon to draft the petition for rehearing. Appellate court rules usually require that the reasons for need of rehearing be set forth in the petition.

If that petition for rehearing is denied, file a petition for hearing in, or review by, the state's highest court (*certiorari*). Or, if a constitutional question has been raised in the state courts, there may be grounds for an eventual appeal to the Supreme Court of the United States. See 1980 Revised Rules of the U.S. Supreme Court or the rules volumes of the U.S. Code Annotated.

Summary: General Procedure of the Criminal Process

A. Arraignment

This is when the accusatory instrument has been filed—*information* or *indictment*—and the defendant is informed of the charge against him and informed of his rights, especially the assistance of an attorney. An attorney is needed at this critical stage.

1. *Custodial interrogation:* "Custody" is a much broader term than "arrest." A person is in custody when the circumstances would lead a reasonable person to believe he is not free to go.

2. *Interrogation:* Statements made in the presence of the suspect, although not specifically directed to him, that invite an incriminating response have been held to be "interrogation."

B. Bail or ROR (Release on Own Recognizance)

Factors considered in these are:

1. Nature of offense,

2. Penalty that may be imposed,

3. Probability of voluntary appearance of the defendant or flight to avoid punishment,

4. The pecuniary and social status of the defendant,

5. The general reputation and character of the defendant, and

6. The nature and strength of the proof as bearing on the probability of his/her conviction.

C. Disposition Without Plea of Guilty

Upon or after arraignment in a local criminal court on an information or misdemeanor complaint and before (a) entry of a guilty plea or (b) the commencement of trial, the court may, on its own motion or that of the prosecutor or defendant, and with the *consent* of *both parties*, order that the action be "adjourned in contemplation of dismissal." Reasons: no witnesses; state's case is so trivial that it will not endanger the community.

D. Specialized Hearings or Dispositions

To adjudicate:

- First-time/or small-time drug offenders,

- Youthful offenders and violent juveniles,

- First-time offenders, or

- Candidates whose crimes are so small that their disposition should be accelerated.

E. Preliminary Hearings

Arraignment of a felony complaint, which is indictable by a grand jury and which cannot be disposed of in the local criminal court. The purpose is:

- To determine whether there is sufficient evidence to bring the matter before the grand jury;

- To test the sufficiency of the evidence and whether or not it establishes "prima facie evidence." If not, then the case can be dismissed. Sufficient evidence will cause the defendant to be held over for grand jury action.

F. Grand Jury

Ten to twenty-three citizens hear testimony presented by the prosecution. Does *not* determine *guilt* or *innocence*, just sufficiency of evidence to prosecute. There is *no* judge. Returns an "indictment for felonies" *and* indictable misdemeanors, recommends to prosecutor to file an "information" in the criminal court *or* dismisses the charge by returning a "no true bill."

G. Plea Bargaining

1. Can dispose of heavy *criminal* loads;

2. Is used when witnesses are not available or reluctant to testify;

3. Is used when prosecutor's evidence is lacking or questionable;

4. Enables prosecution to dispose of an indictment on a reasonable basis, and in the interest of the public;

5. Eliminates a long trial or conviction of a higher degree of crime for the defendant.

H. Omnibus Motions Filable

1. Motion for severance

2. Motion for suppression of evidence

3. Motion for psychiatric examination

4. Motion to quash the indictment or information

5. Motion for change of venue

6. Motion to excuse the trial judge

7. Motion to dismiss—speedy trial, sufficiency of evidence

8. Motion to continue

9. Motion to suppress identification testimony

I. Trial Process

1. *Jury selection*—voir dire

2. *Opening statements:* Recitation of strategy and tactics, interpretation of law as applied to the facts

3. *Direct examination*—witnesses

4. *Cross-examination*—witnesses

5. *Redirect or rebuttal*

6. *Summation or closing:* Counsel summarize their positions

7. *Jury instructions:* Judge instructs jury in the law as it relates to the facts

8. *Verdict:* Jury deliberates, returns verdict

J. Post-Verdict Motions

1. *Petition for Writ of Habeas Corpus:* filed within ten days after finding of guilt

2. *N.O.V.:* Discharge on the basis of insufficient evidence

3. *Motion for New Trial* and *In Arrest of Judgment:*

   a. Verdict contrary to law and evidence

   b. Verdict against weight of evidence

   c. Court erred in not suppressing testimony

   d. Court erred in not admitting confession

   e. Court erred in its instructions to jury

4. *Application for Modification of Sentence*

Hypothetical Case

Johnny, a twenty-two-year-old male, who is mentally the age of seven, is walking down the street at dusk one warm summer eve.

Mary, a twenty-five-year-old woman, is preparing for bed. She has, in error, left up the window shade on her ground floor bedroom window, and the window is open.

Johnny sees Mary. After Mary gets into bed and turns out the lights, Johnny walks over to the window. He places his hands on the windowsill. Mary, thinking it is her lover, calls out, "Is that you, darling? Come in."

Johnny climbs through the window and into Mary's bed. Mary realizes her mistake and screams. Johnny is frightened and leaps from the bed. Mary turns on the light, screams a second time, and reaches for a gun she keeps in the side table by the bed.

Johnny picks up a bookend and throws it at Mary, knocking her unconscious.

Johnny heads toward the front door. Halfway there, he sees an expensive camera. Picking it up, he calls out, "Can I have this?" Getting no response, he takes it and leaves.

Define the crimes and defenses of Johnny and Mary.

Your attorney has given you the above facts and has asked you to do a preliminary analysis of said facts and come up with a recommendation as to what crime or crimes have been committed, if any, and what defenses to said crimes are available to the client. Consider the following: The defendant, Johnny, is mentally retarded and has the thinking capacity of a seven-year-old. Would he therefore be capable of attempted rape? Would he be guilty of trespass? And what about breaking and entering? And lastly, would he be guilty of assault and battery? Or guilty of a house robbery?

If any of the above are true, would his defense be that he was mentally retarded and did not know what he was doing, or was not capable of understanding what he was doing? This being true, all things being equal, is he guilty of any crime at all?

As to Mary, what was her culpability in this scenario? Is she guilty of contributory negligence or negligence in preparing for bed leaving the shade to her window up and the window open? Was this an open invitation to anyone walking by her window, seeing her prepare for bed? Was she negligent in assuming that it was her lover and inviting in the person without a confirmation?

This hypothetical case sets forth some of the questions that you would have to determine and for which you would have to do some legal research.

CHAPTER SIXTEEN

How to Handle a Contract Action

Since the basic substantive law of contracts is an extremely broad and vast field of law, no attempt to delve into every aspect of it is intended here. Contracts are involved in just about every relationship, from buying your morning coffee to multimillion-dollar acquisitions. This chapter contains a brief overview of the basic elements you should understand to draft a contract.

What Is a Contract?

A "contract" is a legally enforceable agreement between two or more parties. It may be oral or written, and for the most part, both are equally enforceable, although the terms of the oral contract may be harder to prove. Both parties must mutually agree to act upon some promise(s) made by one or both of them. The law recognizes a duty to perform these promises and allows the recovery of damages for the lack or failure of performance of said agreements or promises.

Unilateral vs. Bilateral Contracts

Unilateral contract: In this type of contract, one party (the offeror) promises to do something if and when the other (the offeree) performs a requested act. It is the exchange of a promise for an act. The contract does not become binding on the offeror until the offeree substantially completes the act requested. This means that the offeror can rescind the contract up until that time.

EXAMPLE

A promises B that he will pay B $100 if B enrolls in and completes a stop smoking program. B enrolls in the program and completes the course. A owes B $100 upon completion of the program.

Bilateral contract: In this contract both parties make promises. The contract becomes binding upon the offeror at the time the offeree makes his return promise to do something. This is the kind of contract that we are most used to seeing and that the courts prefer because it sets a definite moment of formation of the contract and the time of breach can be readily determined.

EXAMPLE

A promises B that A will sell B a certain farm in return for B's promise to A that B will pay A a certain amount of money and execute a note and mortgage for the balance of the purchase price on the closing date specified in the deed.

Elements Necessary to Create a Contract

Following is a list of elements necessary to create a contract:

1. Offer (oral or written, if not required by law to be written),
2. Acceptance (oral or written, if not required by law to be written),
3. Consideration (money or promise),
4. Capacity of the parties to contract (not a minor or incompetent or drunk or drugged),
5. Intent of the parties to contract (objective meeting of the minds), and
6. Object of the contract (it must be lawful *and* not be against public policy).

Offer

An offer is a definite expression or overt action which signals that the offeror is willing to enter into a contract. It cannot be ambiguous. It must be spelled out in terms that are specific and certain; the offeree must be able to identify the nature of the object (quality and quantity) which is being offered and under what conditions and/or terms (such as time for performance) it is offered. If the offer is accepted by the offeree, the offer can be enforced as a contract.

The offeror is generally able to rescind the offer at any time prior to its acceptance by the offeree, either by making a reciprocal promise or by performance. The formal exception to this rule is made by forming an "option contract." This is an agreement that the offeror will keep the offer open for a certain period of time. This gives the offeree time to think about the offer or obtain some sort of necessary financing or fulfill some other condition precedent without the fear of losing the opportunity to accept. Option contracts must be supported by separate consideration.

Negotiations: Negotiations of a contract between prospective parties to a contract are not offers in the true sense of the word. The individuals involved are merely discussing the possibility of offering something.

Advertisements: These generally do not contain a specific promise to sell. They are usually statements that certain items are available for an offer to purchase at the advertised price by the unknown members of the public who may read the ad.

NOTE: There are many consumer protection laws that prohibit deceptive advertising.

Rewards. A reward offer is a unilateral contract. If the act to be rewarded is performed with the intent of accepting the offer, the unilateral contract may be enforced by the person who performed as long as he had knowledge of the offer.

Commercial sales offers: An offer between merchants as defined in your state commercial code must be communicated. It should be noted, however, that under the Uniform Commercial Code, which has been adopted by all states, an offer of a contract of sale does not fail for lack of an in-depth statement of terms, even though one or more terms are left open, if the parties have intended to make a contract and there is a reasonably certain basis for giving an appropriate remedy. The Uniform Commercial Code can be accessed through the Cornell website directly at www.law .cornell.edu/ucc/ucc.table.html.

Acceptance

As a general proposition of law, the acceptance of the offer creates the contract; the parties are bound to perform the obligations undertaken by them under the terms of the offer. This acceptance, as a general rule, cannot be withdrawn; nor can it vary the terms of the offer, or alter it, or modify it. To do so makes the acceptance a counteroffer. Though this proposition may vary from state to state, the general rule is that there are no conditional acceptances by law. In fact, by making a conditional acceptance, the offeree is rejecting the offer and replacing it with another. The original offeror now becomes the offeree and has the power to accept or reject this counteroffer.

Here again, the Uniform Commercial Code, as it has been adopted in your state, governs acceptance by a merchant (including manufacturer sellers of commercial goods to wholesale buyers of commercial goods) of an offer made by a merchant. The rules differ somewhat between a merchant and a consumer and between non-merchants.

Consideration

Consideration for a contract may be money or may be another right, interest, or benefit, or it may be a detriment, loss, or responsibility given up to another. Consideration is a necessary element of a contract. Each party must give something of value to the other. The essence of consideration is the "bargained-for exchange" of obligations.

> **CAUTION:** The consideration must be expressly agreed upon by both parties to the contract or be implied in fact by the express terms of the contract. A possible or accidental benefit or detriment alone is not a valid consideration. The consideration must be explicit and sufficient to support the promise to do or not to do, whichever is applicable. However, it need not be of any particular monetary value.

It should be noted that mutual promises are adequate and valid consideration as to each party, as long as they are binding. This general rule goes to conditional promises as well.

To take it a step further, the general rule is that a promise to perform an act which you are already legally bound to do is not a sufficient consideration for a contract. The application of this general rule may differ from jurisdiction to jurisdiction, as the courts tend to sustain agreements involving liquidated or undisputed debts where there has been a partial payment of a preexisting obligation.

Furthermore, it has been held that an express promise to pay or perform made to the party entitled to such performance under a contract will be enforced. It is suggested, because of these variances in holdings, that you consult case law in your case for ordinary contracts and your state commercial code for sales of goods between merchants.

Variations of Contract

Void contract: This is an agreement that was unenforceable from its inception. There was no contract. Examples of such a contract would be illegal contracts (such as gambling or price fixing in violation of federal law). A contract can be void as a matter of public policy. It is possible for it to meet every other requirement of a valid contract, such as an offer, acceptance, consideration, and so forth, but as a matter of public policy, or because it is illegal, be void.

Voidable contract: Such a contract may bind only one of the parties to the contract and give an option to the other party to withdraw if he so chooses. This type of contract normally arises when there is some sort of defect in the formation of the contract. For example, when one of the parties has been induced by fraudulent misrepresentation to make his promise, and he later discovers the misrepresentation, he can either hold the other party to the performance of his duties under the contract and perform his part or he may rescind the contract and not perform his part. This also occurs in contracts with minors. Note that only the party suffering from the defect (the defrauded party or the minor) can avoid the contract. The other party cannot claim this as a defense to performance.

Quasi-contract: This contract is implied by law even though it could not be implied in fact, and even though the parties did not enter into an expressed agreement. A contract is implied in law where one person actually performed with the knowledge and consent of the other, and the person thereby accepted the benefit of the performance and would be unjustly enriched if the law would not imply a contract. This is an equitable remedy, not a contractual one.

Capacity of the Parties

It is a general presumption of law that people have a capacity to enter into a contract. A person who is trying to avoid a contract would have to plead his lack of capacity to contract against the party who is trying to enforce the contract; that is, he was a minor, an incompetent, otherwise impaired (drunk or drugged), or so forth.

When filing a suit to enforce a contractual promise, you allege an offer, acceptance, and consideration, as well as a failure to perform, with resulting damages. You do not plead lack of capacity unless you are trying to avoid the contract.

The capacity to enter into the contract must go to the heart of the matter. It must be shown that the person was incapable of understanding the fact that he was entering into a contract. Eccentricity or lack of judgment do not rise to the level of avoidance of a contract.

Minors can disaffirm a contract at any time before they reach their age of majority, and within a reasonable time after they become of age. In the case of a minor, this incapacity is presumed unless the object of the contract was to obtain necessities or certain other matters of public policy. For example, here a minor, seventeen years of age, enters into a contract to buy school clothes on the installment plan, and upon reaching the age of majority he still owes on the debt, he can be forced to pay the balance due. Further, school loans and military enlistments, child support agreements and the like can be enforced as against a minor on public policy grounds.

Intent of the Parties

It is a basic prerequisite to the formation of any contract (oral or written) that there must be a mutual assent or a "meeting of the minds" of the parties on all essential elements and terms of the proposed contract. There can be no contract unless all the parties involved intended to enter into one. This intent is determined by the outward words or actions of the parties, not their secret intentions. That is why mere negotiations to arrive at a mutual assent to a contract are not considered offer and acceptance, even though the parties agree on some of the terms being negotiated. That is also why fraud or certain mistakes may make a contract voidable.

EXAMPLES

1. A mistake resulting from the ambiguity of the language contained in the contract where the meaning placed thereon by each party could reasonably vary, though it is an honest interpretation. Under these circumstances, the court will generally determine that there is no mutual agreement—hence no contract. This is the defense of "mutual mistake."

2. A mistake as to a material fact is, as a general rule, a mistake of the mind, where one party reasonably thought something was present or expected, when in fact it was not. There can be no meeting of the minds in this instance because the parties hold different underlying beliefs as to the object of the contract. Courts will grant relief in this instance, if there is not resulting injury to innocent third parties.

3. A unilateral mistake will not necessarily void a contract unless there are other elements present, such as misrepresentation or ambiguous language, or the other party to the contract had knowledge of the mistake and took advantage of it.

4. A mistake in the drafting or typing of the contract may be remedied through reformation, if the parties really did agree and intend to contract. In this instance, your attorney would have to prove it was clearly a typographical error made in the typing of the instrument or that the words were transposed, rearranged, and the like, by mistake, as opposed to a lack of understanding by the parties of the language used. This is important to you, since as the paralegal you will be drafting the contract. The basic action or pleading for reformation would be one in equity.

Object of the Contract

Contracts can be entered into to accomplish just about any goal. Contracts proliferate in every aspect of our lives; it hardly seems possible to go through one day without encountering at least a dozen!

There are restrictions on the consideration permissible. A contract is not enforceable if its object is illegal or against public policy.

In many jurisdictions contracts predicated upon horse races, dog races, lotteries, and other forms of gambling are illegal contracts. Yet in some states these types of contracts are valid. Of course, contracts that have as their object an illegal goal are per se invalid. These are, in actuality, criminal conspiracies. For example, murder, insurance fraud, drug smuggling, etc.

Federal and some state laws make contracts in restraint of trade, in price-fixing, and in monopolies illegal. Therefore, a contract that violates those statutes would be illegal and unenforceable.

In some states an overly broad noncompetitive clause in an employment contract is against the public policy of free enterprise or against a statute making unlimited noncompetitive contracts illegal. For that reason, such clauses should be carefully drafted and used only where necessary to protect trade secrets. Most states require that such a clause be limited in both time and geographical area. Thorough research in your jurisdiction as to the clauses' enforceability is encouraged.

If the legality of part of a contract may be in doubt, the contract should contain a severance clause.

EXAMPLE

Should any portion of this agreement be judicially determined to be illegal, the remainder of the agreement shall not be affected by such determination and shall remain in full force and effect.

Any contract governed by the Uniform Commercial Code (U.C.C.) as adopted in your state is subject to the unconscionable provision of U.C.C. §2-302.

In pleading to avoid a commercial contract, facts should be alleged which would show that the contract or a provision thereof is unconscionable.

Statute of Frauds
Purpose and Effect

The Stature of Frauds requires certain contracts to be in writing in order to avoid problems of proof in certain circumstances that lend themselves to fraudulent misconduct. Each state has its own version of this statute, but the general tenets of the law hold true throughout the country.

NOTE: Just because the contract is not in writing does not render it void. The parties are free to perform on the contract. This issue is in the enforcement of the contract should one (or more) party decide not to fulfill his obligation under the unwritten agreement.

Areas of Application of This Doctrine

Contracts for the following need to be in writing in order to be enforceable in court:

1. *The sale/transfer of real property interests:* This includes mortgages, leases for a term of greater than one year, transfers of shares in real estate cooperatives, easements, and liens on property. Further, most of these transactions must be recorded in a clerk's office so that the interests in the real estate are of public record. Requiring a writing under the Statute of Frauds protects that governmental interest and assures certainty and security in real estate dealings.

2. *Contracts that are not performable within one year:* Due to the fuzzy nature of memory, the courts will not enforce a contract where the terms were purportedly written so far back in time. Only if it is not possible to perform the contract within one year is the statute's writing requirement triggered. For example, an eighteen-month employment contract is not performable within one year and therefore must be in writing. However, a contract to build a house, even where the contractor usually takes eighteen months to finish, is not under the statute because the builder could finish in less than one year. The contract does not specify that it must take longer than one year.

3. *Contracts in consideration of marriage (not the marriage contract itself):* This is most often a prenuptial agreement that deals with distribution of assets should the marriage terminate, or other conditions that are related to the marriage.

4. *Sureties and guarantees (answering the debt of another):* Anyone who voluntarily takes on paying for someone else's debt must put that promise in writing.

5. *Uniform Commercial Code provisions regarding the sale of goods priced at over $500.00.*

Nature of Writing

It can be a mere scrap of paper, an email, a formal contract, or a written agreement. The agreement can be contained in several documents as long as they all can be related to one another. The key is whether the writing contains sufficient information for the court to reconstruct the intent of the parties. Additionally, the writing must be "signed by the party to be charged." This means that the writing(s) must be signed or otherwise authenticated by the person against whom enforcement is sought. Recall, the purpose for the Statute of Frauds is to avoid fraudulent conduct or "overreaching" by one party to the disadvantage of another.

Conditions to Contract
Conditions Precedent, Subsequent, and Concurrent

Condition precedent: This is where one party must do something *before* performance by the other party is required.

For example, a buyer's ability to get a certain amount or proportion of financing may be a condition precedent for a contract to sell land, or in an insurance contract, if there is a condition that a claim must be made within a certain period after an accident, that is a condition precedent to the insurance company's obligation to pay the claim.

Conditions subsequent: This is where a valid contract is terminated or a required performance is changed if a specified thing happens after performance of the contract has begun.

EXAMPLE

The payment of the required premium is a condition subsequent to an insurance contract. If the premium is not paid on time or within any prescribed grace period, the condition subsequent is broken. Any condition requiring for future performance under a contract is a condition subsequent. Breach of that condition is a breach of contract unless the breach is waived or consented to by the other party.

Conditions concurrent: If there is something to be done on both sides and no time for performance is set, these conditions are concurrent.

EXAMPLE

"I will give you my car for $100."

The performance is assumed to be meant to happen at the same time. Performance on each side is dependent on performance of the other side at the same time.

Third-Party Beneficiary Contracts

A contract made between two or more people may be made for the benefit of a person who is not a party to the contract. That type of contract is called a "third-party beneficiary contract."

The general rule in most states relating to third-party beneficiaries is that these persons have the right, in their own name, to enforce contracts made for their benefit, despite the fact that they are not a party to the contract. That right usually arises once the party learns of the contract. Prior to that, the parties may be free to terminate or change the benefit to be received by the third party.

Under present law the courts, in enforcing the rights of third-party beneficiaries under this circumstance, look to the intent of the contracting parties, to determine if they, in fact, intended that the third party benefit from the contract.

You should be aware at this juncture, however, that although this third-party doctrine is applicable to various types of contracts, for it to be applied there must be more than an incidental, indirect, or consequential benefit inuring to the benefit of the third-party beneficiary by reason of the contract.

EXAMPLE

Creditor beneficiary: A owes B money. A makes a contract with C, who promises to pay A's debt to B. A and C are the initial contractual parties, but the nature of the contract is purely for the benefit of B, who is in fact the creditor of A. As a creditor beneficiary under the contract between A and C, B can exercise some rights.

Furthermore, under present law, a third-party-donee beneficiary also has the right to enforce a contract made for his benefit, since most courts no longer require privity of obligation between the donee-beneficiary and the promisee.

Finally, you should know that the third-party beneficiary rights, as set forth there, vest immediately upon the making of the contract between the promisor and the promisee, even if the actual benefits will not take place until a later date.

EXAMPLE

Donee beneficiary: Father has a son he wishes to be well cared for. Father contracts with the bank to draw a trust on behalf of his son. Then later, the father says that the bank is not doing a satisfactory job for the benefit of the needs of his son.

The son is a donee beneficiary of the contract between the father and the bank, and as a result can enforce his rights under that contract.

Assignment and Delegation of Contract

In most states, the rights under a contract are assignable, unless the contract provides otherwise. Duties to perform may be delegable unless the contract requires the performance of some unique service (as a particular actor or opera singer or a particular handcraftsman).

A right to assign or delegate may be conditioned on some other action or event, or the right to assign or delegate may be denied.

EXAMPLE

This contract [or mortgage] is not assignable by the buyer [or mortgagor or other appropriate party].

Assignment can also occur where one person to a contract conveys his "beneficial rights" to another person. *Note that only "the right" is assignable. It does not extinguish the duty.* Though the rights are assignable, the duty to perform can *only* be *delegated*, but the person to whom the right is assigned must accept the duty to perform. Further, if a duty to perform is delegated to another person, the original party remains liable for the performance should the delegate fail to perform.

EXAMPLE

Landlord rents an apartment to Tenant. Landlord can assign his right to collect the rent to another person generally without Tenant's permission. Landlord is no longer responsible to Tenant for collecting the rent. It really doesn't matter whom the Tenant pays. However, Tenant usually cannot delegate to another his duty to pay rent without the consent of Landlord. If Landlord does grant permission for Tenant to delegate his duty (by a sublease to Subtenant), the original Tenant remains liable for the rent should Subtenant fail to perform the delegated duty to pay. It does not matter who is in the position of payor.

Note further that you *cannot* assign claims for wages, workers' compensation, personal services, insurance, credit, future rights, or any assignment or delegation that may be in violation of public policy.

Types of Assignments

1. Gratuitous or outright as a gift (*These are revocable.*)

2. Assignments for value, as in a contract between assignor and assignee (collection agencies) (*These are irrevocable.*)

Breach of Contract
Definitions of a Breach

What is a breach of contract? When one of the parties fails and refuses to perform under the terms of the contract without a valid or legal reason or excuse.

Should this occur, the *injured party* to the contract can opt for any of the following:

1. Rescind the contract, *period*;

2. Sue to recover any monies expended;

3. Sue for the value of services rendered to date; or

4. Maintain the contract and sue for damages because of the breach.

The non-breaching party must mitigate the damages associated with the breach. Therefore, which option he should choose is also based on which would do the least damage to his position. The non-breaching party must also establish that the breach was material. A breach is material if it affects the underlying reason for entering into the contract in the first place. Minor deviations in form of performance are tolerable. A breach seriously impacts the anticipated benefit that the non-breaching party was to receive under the contract and there is no means for remedying the situation.

Defenses

Where there are legal reasons for one's failure to perform the terms of a contract, the court permits the following as defenses:

1. *Prevention:* Exists when one party acts in a manner as to prevent the other party from carrying out its contractual obligation.

   EXAMPLE

   I contract with you to clean my house. You arrive and find that the house is surrounded by a ten-foot wall with guard dogs. Clearly, you would not attempt to scale that wall and come in to my house for fear of the dogs attacking you.

   NOTE: The fact that you may lose money on the contract is not a defense of prevention. You cannot be forced to carry out a nonprofitable contract that may send you into bankruptcy. This is not prevention, just bad faith and/or bad business.

2. *Anticipatory breach:* This occurs when a party to the contract acts or says things in a manner that indicates that he will not perform the contractual obligations.

   EXAMPLE

   Say you claim a delivery of widgets and that I am going to pay you after the first delivery of said widgets. After the first order is made, I tell you I will not pay for them or that I will not pay for any more. Here, the words convince you that the other party is not going to pay you. Therefore, validity is excused from the contract. In other words, the contract speaks.

3. *Prospective inability to perform:* Exists when the actions or circumstances surrounding the contract indicate that the party will not perform according to his words.

EXAMPLE

"Going Out of Business Sale" posted on the door.

EXCEPTION: Having title in an escrow. Here, we find that you did not own the property in question. But title to the property may be there when escrow closes. The key is whether or not you have title at the time of the closing of the escrow.

You are forgiven for performing, if the other party fails to perform, when one side breaches a contract, or does not perform their part of the contract. This constitutes a breach, but the breach has to be a "material" breach.

EXAMPLE

The tenant and the landlord each has, among other things, an obligation to deliver three gallons of bottled water every three weeks. No water is delivered for five weeks. This failure is not a "material breach." On the other hand, if you are a chemist and you use water for your experiments, the water becomes a material breach, since water is used in the main line of your work.

4. *Waiver of duty to perform:* Running with the example of the bottled water, let us assume that you did not need as many bottles of water, or that you do not need any more water, period. This is a waiver of a duty to perform by the landlord to you.

Here, for your own protection and that of your employer, you should get any and all modifications in writing, additionally, the description of a job. This, because the job may be one which is impossible to perform.

EXAMPLE

The car you are going to paint has been destroyed. Hence, you cannot paint the car.

5. *Personal service contracts:* These types of services are special and unique and therefore cannot be transferred to another. A defense to these types of contracts is death or illness of the person for whom you are to perform the service.

EXAMPLE

Asking Van Gogh to paint your portrait.

6. *Frustration of property:* This exists when performance is possible, but the value of the service no longer exists. To explain: renting a room or buying a house near the ocean, when a highway, or even a toxic dump, is placed near the room/house or the ocean.

7. *Mutual discharge and cancellation:* This occurs when both parties agree that the terms have been carried out, or want to withdraw from the contract.

Note that in most states, the superficial procedure distinctions between law and equity have been abolished, but the complaint to be filed must contain statements of fact which will state a proper cause of action in either law or equity. Alternative counts may be pleaded in most states.

8. *Other defenses:* Some affirmative defenses (legal excuses) that can be raised in a law action for damages for breach of a contract are:

   a. Disclaimer written or agreed to in the contract

   b. Unconscionability (sale of goods, contract security agreement, or other contract subject to the U.C.C.)

   c. Waiver

   d. Accord and satisfaction

   e. Payment or completed performance

   f. Excuse for nonperformance

   g. Novation

   h. Estoppel

   i. Failure of consideration on the part of the plaintiff

   j. Statute of Frauds

   k. Statute of Limitations

   l. Illegality

   m. Others

   Some affirmative defenses that can be raised in an action for specific performance of a contract are:

   a. Subject matter of the contract is not unique, so damages would suffice to make plaintiff whole

   b. Estoppel

   c. Laches

   d. Fraud

   e. Duress

   f. Mistake

   g. Illegality

   h. Others

Facts to state a cause of action for rescission would include facts to show:

a. Breach

b. Anticipatory breach

c. Damages

d. Fraud

e. Duress

f. Mistake

Drafting the Pleadings

A breach of contract was defined in the foregoing section. Excuses for nonperformance were also discussed in that section. A cause of action is based upon that failure to perform. The cause of action is stated in the complaint. The excuses for nonperformance are stated as affirmative defenses in the answer.

Complaint

In preparing a complaint for a breach of contract, be direct and to the point, and use as many theories as you can. *Reason:* If you fail in one, your attorney may be able to win in another. This procedure is used to ensure that the client will come out whole, or as if the contract had in fact been performed, the latter being the overall purpose of a breach of contract action. Use separate counts for each alleged course of action.

EXAMPLE

In an action for specific performance, which can force a seller to sell to a buyer, when the seller, for whatever reason, decides that he does not want to sell, you should draft your complaint to include facts and prayer not only for specific performance of the contract, but also for the return of the deposit and damages for the breach as it relates to, for example, the buyer, who had to put his furniture in storage until the house was out of escrow, and so forth. If the house was being built to specifications, then any monies expended in this effort, that is, purchase of special rugs, linoleum, fixtures, and so forth, and any other allegations that would support money damages would be recoverable.

The following counts are for law actions involving contracts:

1. *Indebitatus assumpsit:* A promise to pay upon a debt

2. *Quantum meruit:* Work and labor (reasonable value for services)

3. *Quantum valebant:* Goods, sold and delivered (implied contract)

4. Open book account (account stated)

5. Action for the contract price paid and consequential damages

In your complaint, there must be allegations of fact to show (1) the existence of the contract, (2) the violation of the contract rights of the plaintiff by the defendant, (3) a statement to the effect that demand for performance, payment, and so forth, was made, and (4) that the defendant "failed and refused" and "continues to fail and refuse" to perform in accordance with the contract or to pay for performance rendered by the plaintiff.

In these counts you must allege an express promise to pay an amount agreed upon between the parties, together with the reasonable amount of the services and damages sustained as a result of the breach. Further, the actions taken in mitigation (or reasons why not) must be stated as well.

A defense, most commonly used to a common count, is that of pleading a "set off" such as a counterclaim or cross-complaint, which is filed concurrently with the answer to the complaint, or by way of affirmative defenses included in the answer to the complaint.

The following are some examples of notice of pleading of some of the more usual contract counts:

GOODS SOLD AND DELIVERED

1. Within two years last past, and on or about _____, 20__, at (CITY), (STATE), plaintiff sold and delivered to defendant goods, wares, and merchandise of the reasonable value of $_____, for which said defendant agreed to pay plaintiff. (A copy of the agreement is attached hereto as Exhibit A.)

2. No part of said sum has been paid (except the sum of $_____), and there is now due, owing, and unpaid the sum of $_____.

3. On or about _____, 20__, plaintiff demanded said amount from the defendant.

4. Defendant has failed and refused to pay said amount.

ACCOUNT STATED

1. Within four years last past, and on or about _____, 20__, at (CITY), (STATE), plaintiff was furnished to defendant at his special instance and request, upon an open book account, goods, wares, and merchandise of the aggregate-agreed (reasonable) value of $_____.

2. No part of said sum has been paid (except for the sum of $_____), and

there is now due, owing and unpaid from defendant to plaintiff, the sum of $_____.

3. On or about _____, 20__, plaintiff demanded said amount from the defendant.

4. Defendant has failed and refused to pay said amount.

WORK AND LABOR

1. Between _____, 20___, and _____, 20___ at (CITY, (STATE), plaintiff rendered services to defendant as a _____. Such services were rendered and performed at the special instance and request of defendant, and defendant then and there promised to pay plaintiff the reasonable (or agreed amount) value thereof.

2. The reasonable value (or agreed amount) of such services at the time they were rendered and at the time defendant promised to pay, was the sum of $_____.

3. No part of said sum has been paid (except for $_____).

4. On or about _____, 20___, plaintiff demanded said amount from the defendant.

5. Defendant has failed and refused to pay said amount.

MONEY HAD AND RECEIVED

1. On _____, 20___ at (CITY), (STATE), defendants became indebted to plaintiff in the sum of $_____ for money lent by plaintiff to defendants, and each of them, at their instance and request.

2. On or about _____, 20___, and before the commencement of this action, plaintiff demanded payment from the defendants.

3. No part of the sum loaned has been repaid, although payment has been demanded, leaving the balance due, owing, and unpaid to plaintiffs in the amount of $_____ plus interest at the legal rate from and after _____, 20___,

NOTE: Where an action is based on a written contract, whether the action is in law or equity, most court rules of civil procedure require that a copy of the executed contract be attached to the complaint or counterclaim alleging it.

The first step a paralegal should take before preparing a breach of contract complaint is to read the contract carefully.

A practical hint is to make a photocopy of the contract so that you can "mark it up" as you read it, when you locate provisions relevant to the client's problem.

Answer

The answer may just consist of a general denial. Or it may contain affirmative defenses and possibly a counterclaim.

The various affirmative defenses available in both a law action and an equitable action for breach of contract have been listed earlier in this chapter.

If a contract involves the sale of goods between merchants, see the implied warranty sections in your state's version of the Uniform Commercial Code 2-312 (title and against infringement); 2-313 (express warranty of description); 2-314 (implied warranty based on dealing or usage of trade); 2-315 (goods fit for particular use); 2-316 (goods are merchantable for ordinary use); 2-317 (goods will conform to sample); 2-318 (to third parties as to consumer goods). Also see exclusion and modification of warranties and sections in your commercial code for performance by seller and performance by buyer.

Research into your jurisdiction's interpretations of the provisions of the Uniform Commercial Code is vital in situations involving merchants. There are many "gap-filling" provisions that must be understood before you can either draft an effective pleading or assert a valid defense.

If either the cause of action or affirmative defense to a contract action is fraud, the facts constituting the alleged fraud must be spelled out with particularity.

EXAMPLE

Do not allege "The contract was procured by fraud of the seller" and then stop. Do allege:

1. The contract was procured by fraud of the seller against the buyer as follows:

    a. The seller-distributor did not have a full output contract with the manufacturer, as he specifically stated to the buyer that he had to induce the buyer to place his Christmas order with him and pay $5,000 in advance to the seller.

    b. The seller knew or should have known that he could not deliver to buyer in time for the Christmas season because of his lack of the above contract with the manufacturer.

    c. The seller intended to use the advance payment demanded of the buyer for . . .

    d. The seller agreed with X Company, a direct competitor of buyer, that he would do these alleged actions for the purpose of harming buyer's Christmas business.

2. And further allege that the buyer had a right to rely on the seller's statement and did rely on it.

    a. The buyer had a right to rely and did rely on the representation of the seller when he placed the order that seller did have a full output contract with the manufacturer.

    b. And so forth.

Damages

Damages is the sum of money that the fact-finder (the judge in a nonjury case or the jury) by its verdict awards the contract claimant as compensation, recompense, or satisfaction for the wrong sustained by reason of the breach of contract.

There must be not only a breach of the contract (a wrong or injury done), but also damages resulting from the wrong. Only nominal damages (in equity) can be awarded if no evidence of damage is given by the person who alleges breach of contract.

The damages ordinarily recovered in an action for breach of contract are compensatory and/or consequential and/or incidental damages.

1. *Compensatory damages* are those that are the natural or necessary result of the breach, such as the difference between the value of the actual performance and the contract price. You can sue to be compensated for any actual dollar injury that is clearly identified in the contract.

> **EXAMPLE**
>
> You can sue for the cost differential to mitigate your damages. That is, get another person to finish a job someone else started. In this instance, you can sue for the difference between the amount you paid the first person and what it actually cost you.

    Compensatory damages may also take the form of the equitable remedy of "Rescission/Restitution." In this instance, you are asking the court to cancel the contract and give you back whatever you put in it. You are saying, "I do not want damages, I just want my money back."

2. *Consequential damages* are special damages that are a direct, foreseeable, and calculable result of the nonperformance by the other party.

3. *Incidental damages* are a special form of consequential damage. They are not necessarily foreseeable as a natural consequence of the breach, but their potential was brought to the attention of the parties to the contract at the time of its making.

EXAMPLE

You have contracted with the Airport Car Company to take you to the airport for your flight to Dallas. As a result of their failure to pick you up, you have missed your flight. Consequential damages might be the cost to reissue a ticket for you. If you had made a point that you must get to the airport to meet an important client on that flight, the loss of profits from that meeting might be incidental damages.

4. *Equitable remedies* may be appropriate where money will not make the plaintiff whole. This may include specific performance, injunctions, or declaratory judgment.

EXAMPLE

In real estate, every piece of land/house is considered to be unique. If Seller refuses to sell the property to Buyer, then Buyer may be able to force the sale because money is not what Buyer wants back; he wants that particular piece of property.

If none of these damages is appropriate or calculable, the damages may be controlled by the contract itself as either:

- *Liquidated damages:* A contract may provide that in the event of a breach, in order to avoid complicated calculations of damages, the breaching party will be required to pay a certain amount in liquidated damages. The amount must be reasonable in light of the contract. This is something that each court decides on a case-by-case basis, and as long as damages are not punitive in nature, they will be upheld.

- A *Limitation of Damages clause* sets a maximum amount that can be awarded in a claim for damages.

The two kinds of damages that are never awarded in contract damages are those that are:

1. *Speculative:* If the amount of harm cannot be reasonably determined by objective means then damages cannot be recovered. It is not permissible to merely guess at the amount.

2. *Punitive:* These are equity damages that are normally awarded only in circumstances where the behavior of a party is offensive, so offensive that the court wants to discourage any repetition. In other words, to punish the defendant. These types

of awards are normally given in medical malpractice cases, and cases involving insurance companies or automobile companies.

It is vital to bear all these potential damages in mind while initially drafting a contract. The goal of the paralegal should be to protect and insulate the client from as much damage should there be a breach of contract.

Glossary

Ambiguous: Having two or more meanings. Not clear; vague.

Assignment: A transfer of a contractual right.

Bilateral Contract: Where it is contemplated by the offeror that the offeree shall make a return *promise* to give certain performance.

Condition Concurrent: A type of condition precedent that exists when the parties to a contract are bound to render performance at the same time.

Condition Precedent: A condition that delays the establishment of a right until a specified event has happened.

Condition Subsequent: A condition that has the effect of terminating liability for a breach that has already occurred.

Consideration: That which is bargained for and given in exchange for a promise.

Constructive Condition: A condition which does not arise out of the agreement of the parties but is imposed by the courts as a matter of fairness and justice.

Counteroffer: A manifestation by the offeree of a present willingness to deal on different terms.

Credit Beneficiary: A third party qualifies as a creditor beneficiary where no purpose to make a gift appears and performance by the promisor will satisfy an obligation owing by the promisee to the beneficiary.

Disputed Claim: An unsettled assertion of a right.

Divisible Contract: A contract wherein the performance of the parties is divided into two or more separate units, and performance of each part by one party is the agreed exchange for a corresponding performance by the other party.

Donee Beneficiary: A third party qualifies as a donee beneficiary where it appears that the intent of the promisee in obtaining the promisor's promise of performance is to make a gift to the beneficiary.

Equivocal: Having two or more meanings; purposely ambiguous.

Estoppel: An admission or declaration by which a person is prevented from bringing evidence to controvert it, or prove the contrary.

Gratuitous Assignment: An assignment for which no consideration is given.

Gratuitous Promise: A promise for which the promisor does not bargain for anything in exchange for his promise.

Illusory Promise: One which by its terms imposes no obligation upon the person making it.

Incidental Beneficiary: A third person who will benefit from performance of a contract, but who does not qualify as a donee or creditor beneficiary.

Insolvency: The state of one who has no property sufficient for the full payment of his debts, or who is unable to pay his debits as they fall due in the usual course of business.

Irrevocable: Incapable of being revoked.

Legal Detriment: Unilateral contracts: Promisee is doing something that he was not previously obligated to do, or is giving up a legal right.

Liquidated Debt: Fixed; ascertained. The exact amount that must be paid.

Meeting of the Minds: A requirement that all the parties to the contract agree to, understand, and interpret the terms in the same way.

Mortgage: A conveyance of property, real or personal, to a person called the mortgagee, to secure the performance of some act, such as the payment of money, by the mortgagor.

Novation: A new contract which works on immediate discharge of a preexisting contractual duty and creates a new duty in its stead.

Option Contract: An agreement to keep the offer open for acceptance for a certain period of time.

Prenuptial: A contract entered into before marriage to determine control over disposition of the individual assets of each party.

Quasi Contract: Recovery based upon the theory that the defendant has been unjustly enriched at the plaintiff's expense and that, as a matter of fairness, the defendant should reimburse the plaintiff for the benefit conferred.

Reformation: The correction of an instrument so as to make it express the true intentions of the parties.

Rejection: A manifestation by the offeree that he does not intend to accept the offer or to give it further consideration.

Repudiation: An apparent inability to perform.

Rescission: Rescinding or putting an end to a contract by the parties, or one of them.

Restitution: A restoring of whatever benefits have been conferred under a contract.

Revocation: A manifestation by the offeror that he no longer intends to enter into the proposed contract.

Unilateral Contract: Where it is contemplated by the offeror that he shall not be bound by his offer until he has received *performance* by the offeree.

Usury: Originally, interest charged for the use of money. Now illegal interest only.

Vendee: One to whom something is sold.

Vendor: One who sells something.

Voidable Promise: Of imperfect obligation, so that it may be legally annulled or, on the other hand, cured or confirmed at the option of one of the parties.

Waiver: A surrendering of a right to decline to take advantage of.

CHAPTER SEVENTEEN

How to Assist in Estate Planning and Administration

General Duties

The general duties of a paralegal in estate planning and administration involve the gathering and recording of financial information for use by the attorney in his advisory function in estate planning and his guidance in the administration of a decedent's estate.

1. *Planning:* interviewing the client for information after the client's initial interview with the attorney; gathering facts; and assembling assets in preparation for drafting a will

   Administration: similar duties in preparation for the probate of a will or intestate (without a will) administration of a deceased client's estate

2. *Planning:* drafting the initial inventory of assets and appraisal documents

   Administration: gathering assets and preparing court inventory

3. Researching the federal tax laws and their ramifications for possible application in the estate-planning process or their application to the estate of a deceased client

4. *Administration:* developing financial data required for the completion of the appropriate state and federal tax forms

5. *Planning:* preparing for the attorney memoranda regarding the estate planning

6. *Planning:* drafting of initial trust agreements

7. *Administration:* initiating administration of an estate; preparing court documents; and preparing filing and notice procedures necessary for obtaining an appointment to administer a decedent's estate

8. *Administration:* accumulating, marketing, acquiring, listing, and inventorying the assets of the estate

9. *Administration:* preparing interim and final accounting documents; preparing petitions for sale or distribution; preparing court petitions; and following discharge of executor or administrator, or trustee in case of a trust.

10. *Planning:* reviewing and updating wills to keep abreast of the changes in the law and of the status of the client.

This chapter will deal with the theory and concept of preparing wills and trusts, as opposed to the completion of routine estate administration forms.

As a paralegal you will be primarily responsible for the drafting portion of your attorney's estate practice on behalf of his client. It is important for you to understand the meaning of the clauses in order to make your drafting more efficient and more interesting. Further, you will need to be able to sift through the plethora of choices of clauses available through electronic research.

Types of Wills

There are three basic types of testamentary wills: (1) formal, statutory wills, (2) holographic wills, and (3) nuncupative wills.

You have probably heard of another kind of will—the living will, also known as a health care proxy. This kind of will does not dispose of property after death, but rather provides directives for health care issues when the person is not able to make those decisions. It is extremely important to check the laws in your jurisdiction regarding the making and using of the living will before attempting to draft one.

This chapter will focus on the three kinds of testamentary wills:

1. The "formal, witnessed will," which category includes the self-proved will provided for in Section 2-504 of the Uniform Probate Code, which has been adopted in some states. (At the time of this writing, eighteen states have adopted most of the provisions of the Uniform Probate Code; others have adopted parts of it, some with significant modifications.)

2. The "holographic will," which must be totally in the handwriting of the tester to be valid, including the signature and date signed. Note that this form of will is only valid as to personal property, and in half the jurisdictions it is not recog-

nized at all. You should consult your local statutes for this procedure. For example, in Alabama the holographic will is not recognized because of the strict requirements for two witnesses; but next door in Tennessee, the holographic will is recognized as long as two witnesses can verify the testator's handwriting.

3. The "nuncupative will," which is an oral statement subsequently reduced to writing (within a statutory time limit) by the person who heard the testator make the statement. This latter type of will could be a deathbed statement of intent or a "battlefield expression," and the like, and is only applicable to personal property. Here again you should consult your state statutes, since the treatment of nuncupative wills varies and is only permissible in a minority of states.

The foregoing wills can be further broken down into mutual and joint wills, though the latter is not very often used, and is discussed only for your information and comparison. The propriety of their use would, of course, be in accordance with state statutes.

The joint will is one document containing the desire and intent of two testators as to the disposition of their property. It is a testamentary gift document signed by two or more testators. It is administrable on the death of one of the testators. If the will is revoked as to one, it is still in force as to the non-revoking testator.

Mutual wills are considered to be wills with contracts incorporated within the document wherein each testator agrees not to revoke the terms thereof. In some states, there are accepted rules under the law of contracts where a party may contractually agree to do or not to do something in his will, in consideration of another's promise or other consideration. Because of this variance in recognition and procedure, you should check your local statutes relating to mutual wills and their contents, and independent contracts to make a will.

Elements of a Will

As a general rule, the basic elements required to be present for a valid will to exist, with caution taken, however, to incorporate them in accordance with local state laws, are as follows:

1. It must have been executed with testamentary intent.

2. Testator must have had testamentary capacity. That is, he must have had the ability, at the time the will was drawn and executed, to do that which he intended.

3. The execution, assuming capacity, must be done of testator's own free will, that is, without undue influence, duress, or the like.

4. It must have been duly executed and be in compliance with statutory requirements.

A will cannot be accepted for probate if it is not "duly executed."

A will, even though accepted for probate, may be canceled or set aside by a "will contest" if it was executed as a result of fraud, undue influence, or duress, or if the testator lacked testamentary intent or capacity. This is not easy to prove and can only be asserted by a person with "standing." A person has standing if (1) they are named in the will or (2) they would normally take under the will or intestacy if the will were found invalid.

Your local probate court rules will contain the procedure to raise the question (as by contest or petition to set aside the will). Carefully research your jurisdiction's opinions on will contests and the standards which apply.

The Codicil

A codicil is a subsequently drawn document, which can be a part of the original will or a separate document in place of the original will and may revoke a portion of or amend a previously drawn will, or it may just name an executor. In any and all such events, a codicil must have all the testamentary elements of a will, unless otherwise provided by law.

Other aspects of a codicil are that it can republish a will, it can and may invalidate a prior will, or it may make valid that which had become a revoked prior will.

This being true, a will speaks of the date of the latest codicil to that will. The date of the codicil becomes the date of the entire will and for all purposes of intent, you would use the date of the codicil for interpretation of the will.

Watch out for ambiguities in your codicils. A patent ambiguity appears obvious on the face of the document. A latent ambiguity does not. To avoid latent ambiguity, be specific in describing property to be bequeathed or devised.

EXAMPLE

A testator may have several homes, or may have since sold the home mentioned in the original will and purchased another. The best practice is to describe the house to be devised with specificity, giving the legal description and the common street address.

Revoking a Will or Codicil

There are primarily four ways in which a will or codicil can be revoked:

- By the execution (dating and signing) of a new formal will;

- By drawing a codicil that is inconsistent with the original will;

- By destroying the will or codicil; and

- By a change in the circumstances of the testator, that is, marriage, divorce, death of a beneficiary, and so forth.

Any revocation must be done by a person who has the testamentary intent to revoke and the testamentary capacity to revoke. There must be an overt, undeniable expression to revoke. You should check your probate codes to determine the overt acts that can be done to destroy a will, for only those physical acts set forth in the applicable code or statute will be effective as to the destruction of a will. If there is no such statute authorizing this type of revocation, the testator cannot destroy or effectively revoke his will in this manner. Almost all states have this type of statute.

Some of the overt, physical acts to destroy and thereby revoke a will are as follows:

- The testator can burn the entire will,

- The testator can just severely burn or scorch an existing will or codicil, or

- The testator can tear up the will or codicil or just tear it enough to show the intent to revoke.

Implied Revocation

Implied revocation may arise by word or deed of the testator.

Generally, an implied revocation can exist if there are inconsistencies in the will or codicils to that will. Partial inconsistencies in a will can be integrated by reasonable interpretation and made into a valid will, but total inconsistencies render both the will and the codicil to that will invalid and of no force and effect.

An example of an implied revocation by an act of the testator rather than by an ambiguity in the will itself could be the following:

EXAMPLE

Testator executed will 1, then later on executed will 2, which expressly or impliedly revoked will 1; later on, Testator (though not creating another will) performed some physical act (such as tearing or burning it), which in effect revoked will 2.

In the last example, the key factor in determining which will was in force and effect is the intent of the testator—what was really meant by the physical act performed by the testator.

Independent Relative Revocation

This doctrine merely means that the alleged revocation was dependent on, and relative to, certain facts being mistaken by the testator. That is, if the testator knew the truth (true facts) or was mistaken about the truth (or true facts), he would not have done what he did in his will. This would render any revocation ineffective. It is a presumption in the law, and the language of the will supports this presumption unless it is express revocation.

To invoke this theory of Independent Relative Revocation there must be a revocation to begin with; the intent to revoke must have been predicated upon a mistake of fact or law; and the truth must not be within the knowledge of the testator making the revocation. Had the truth been known by the testator, the revocation would not have taken place, and the revocation would not have been consistent with the intent of the testator.

By way of example, let us say that through trickery or some other devious device, you prevent your boyfriend from changing his will after he left everything to you; then he dies. If the legal heirs can show that the testator would have revoked his will except for your trickery or deceit, the will will be totally ineffective. As a matter of course, the law will not allow a person to profit by his unlawful act. He would merely be the trustee in a constructive trust for the benefit of the true heirs.

The doctrine here described is comparable to the fraud doctrine available to set aside a will that was duly executed.

The Legal Checkup

Alice and Boyd marry and make wills, leaving property to each other. At the time of the dissolution of the marriage, generally speaking, if the dissolution is the result of a legal proceeding, gifts from one spouse to another as contained in a will will be invalidated unless there is some language in the will making it clear that the testator intends to give the gift regardless of whether he is divorced. However, in some states the entire will is revoked by a divorce.

The attorney should be aware of the client's change of status or circumstances and should explain to the client who is in a divorce proceeding as plaintiff or respondent what effect divorce may have on the client's present will. The client may want to rewrite his or her will, or at least add a codicil to the will, changing the beneficiary and/or leaving only the spousal rights required under the laws of Intestate Succession and such other rights as provided by law. It saves a lot of headaches later on.

However, this change or possibility is sometimes covered in a property settlement agreement, wherein it is stated that each spouse, among other things, shall have no interest in the other's estate, or take any inheritance. It repudiates and/or surrenders any right to a gift in the testator's will. It is not, however, applicable to the children of the parties, unless the testator specifically writes them out of his will.

Updating Wills and Trust Agreements

Giving a client's will or estate-planning documents a legal checkup in today's modern law office can be accomplished with relative ease and your clients should be encouraged to do so.

> **EXAMPLE**
>
> When reviewing and/or auditing your probate files, if you determine that some of the clients have been divorced, or a spouse or child has died, or a child has reached the age of majority, or a child has been adopted, or some other pertinent condition or clause in the will or trust agreement has been invalidated for whatever reason, you should contact the client for his "checkup."

It is a good idea to develop an "electronic library" of pertinent business, probate, estate planning, and probate tax liability forms and the like which have been written and developed in your office. This makes it much simpler to retrieve the appropriate clauses that both you and your attorney are comfortable using. You can also annotate these clauses so that you can recall the circumstances in which they are most useful. Further, you can attach citations to recent cases and developments in your state to keep the information up-to-date. It is effective use of your time to check your legal newspaper weekly for these developments and append them to the appropriate files.

Thereafter, you can review the client's will together with the will on the screen and, merely by switching paragraphs around or making word changes, print out the addition or clause or phrase that your client wants. This can be done in a matter of twenty to thirty minutes.

Drafting a Will

We will include here a checklist for drafting a will, a sample of a basic simple will, and practical hints for using electronic word and data processing in preparing a will or drafting a codicil.

Checklist for Drafting a Will

1. *Introductory clause* introduces the testator and gives instructions for payments of last debts.

2. *Declaratory clauses* spell out the desires of the testator for disposition of his personal and real property, that is, "bequests" of personal property and "devises" of real property. Such bequests or devises may be specific or general.

EXAMPLES

For a specific bequest, specifically identify the object being given. You should describe the property. "I give A my ten (10) shares of General Motors stock." Not "I give my stock to A." Anything that tends to identify the nature or specificity of a gift is a specific gift. A gift of personal property is usually called a bequest. A gift of real property is usually called a devise.

In some states, the person who drafts the will must be very precise in using the appropriate gift transfer word.

3. *Appointment clause* sets forth the name of the executor (and trustee, if applicable) and the powers of said individuals.

4. *Residuary clause* disposes of any and all property not otherwise disposed of in the will.

5. *Signature clause*, which is self-explanatory.

> **NOTE:** When drafting a will, you are cautioned to *always* (and I cannot emphasize this too greatly) keep the line for the testator's signature on the same page with at least two lines of the attestation clause at the bottom. This is vitally important. If the attestation clause with the signatures becomes detached and lost, the will will be considered invalid.

6. *Attestation clause* is also self-explanatory. Note, however, that in some states only two witnesses are required, and in some states it may be three. You are cautioned to check with your local probate code for the required number.

In states where the self-proving will is allowed as provided in the Uniform Probate Code, the specific statutory language must be used. Two witnesses are required plus a notary public. See Figure 17.1 for a sample form of a self-proving attestation clause.

Even though a will was not self-proved at the time of its execution, Uniform Probate Code 2-504(b) (and the states that have adopted it) allows an attested formal will to be made self-proving at a later date by the same witnesses and the testator executing the appropriate form and attaching it to the original attested will. See Figure 17.2.

Figure 17.1
Self-Proving Attestation Clause

I, _____, the testator, sign my name to this instrument this _____ day of _____, 20 _____, and being first duly sworn, do hereby declare to the undersigned authority that I sign and execute this

Figure 17.1 (*continued*)

instrument as my last will and that I sign it willingly (or willingly direct another to sign for me), that I execute it as my free and voluntary act for the purpose therein expressed, and that I am eighteen years of age or older, of sound mind, and under no constraint or undue influence.

_____
(Testator)

We, _____ and _____, the witnesses, sign our names to this instrument, being first duly sworn, and do hereby declare to the under-signed authority that the testator signs and executes this instrument as his last will and that he signs it willingly (or willingly directs another to sign for him), and that each of us in the presence and hearing of the testator, hereby signs this will as witness to the testator's signing, and that to the best of our knowledge the testator is eighteen years of age or older, of sound mind, and under no constraint or undue influence.

_____ _____
(Witness)   (residence of witness)

_____ _____
(Witness)   (residence of witness)

State of _____

County of _____

Subscribed, sworn to and acknowledged before me by _____, the testator and subscribed and sworn to before me by _____ and _____ witnesses, this _____ day of _____, 20 _____.

_____
(Notary Public)
My commission expires:

Figure 17.2
Self-Proving Attachment to Attested Will

State of _____

County of _____

We, _____, _____, and _____, the testator and witnesses respectively, whose names are signed to the attached or fore-going instrument, being first duly sworn, do hereby declare to the undersigned authority that the testator signed and executed the instrument as his last will and that he had signed willingly (or willingly directed another to sign for him), and that he executed it as his free and voluntary act for the purposes therein expressed, and that each of the wit-nesses, in the presence and hearing of the testator, signed the will as witness and that to

Figure 17.2 *(continued)*

the best of his knowledge the testator was at that time eighteen years of age or older, of sound mind, and under no constraint or undue influence.

_____
(Testator)

_____ of _____
(Witness)   (residence of witness)

_____ of _____
(Witness)   (residence of witness)

Subscribed, sworn to and acknowledged before me by _____, the testator, and subscribed and sworn to before me by _____ _____, and _____, witnesses, this _____ day of _____, 20 _____.

_____
(Notary Public)

My commission expires:

Sample Form of Simple Will

LAST WILL AND TESTAMENT OF MARY ANN JONES

1. Opening paragraph: [not numbered]

I, MARY JONES, of 123 Magnolia Boulevard, Los Angeles, California, being of sound mind and disposing mind and memory, do hereby make, publish, and declare this instrument to be my Last Will and Testament, hereby revoking any and all previous wills or codicils that may have been executed by me.

[It may be wise to note here some other personal identifying information, such as name of husband and children, if any. If the testator is divorced, indicate the name of the former spouse and date of dissolution of the marriage.]

2. [*The body of the will:* The paragraphs in this section usually bear numbers and these numbers are normally spelled out in capital letters, such as <u>FIRST</u> and <u>SECOND</u> and underlined.]

<u>FIRST</u>: I direct that my executor, hereinafter named, pay all my legal obligations and just debts as soon after my demise as may be possible.

<u>SECOND</u>: [set forth specific bequests] I give, devise, and bequeath unto my brother, John Doe, etc. my car, a Pontiac Grand Prix 2008, my home audio equipment, etc. [be as specific as possible to avoid confusion].

[Use separate, numbered paragraph for each specific bequest if there is more than one.]

<u>THIRD</u>: I give, devise, and bequeath all the rest, residue, and remainder of my real, personal, or mixed property wherever situate to my husband, John Jones, his heirs and assigns forever.

[It is important to have a "residuary clause" in any will. If there is no residuary clause,

Figure 17.2 *(continued)*

most states treat the residuary estate as intestate and it would be distributed as provided in the state intestate succession laws, not to the other person or persons named as specific beneficiary in the will.]

FOURTH: [optional, but practical] If any beneficiary under this Will does not survive me by 30 days, then I shall be deemed to have survived such person.

FIFTH: I hereby make, constitute, and appoint my husband, John Jones, as Executor [or personal representative in some states] of this my Last Will and Testament. If he is unable or unwilling to serve, then I name _____ as alternate Executor. My Executor and alternate shall have all powers granted by applicable laws of my state to carry out all provisions of this Will, may use provisions and procedures for the simplified handling of estates, may hold in trust the share of any minor beneficiary until s/he reaches age 18, and shall not be required to post a bond.

[The last paragraph before the signature is not numbered. It is called the witness clause.]

IN WITNESS WHEREFORE, I, MARY ANN JONES, have hereunto set my hand and seal this _____ day of _____, 20_____.

_____

MARY ANN JONES,
Testatrix

WITNESSETH:

The foregoing instrument, consisting of four (4) pages, including this page was at the date hereof, by MARY ANN JONES, signed as and declared to be her will, in the presence of us, who at her request and in her presence, and in the presence of each other, have subscribed our names as witnesses thereto. Each of us observed the signing of the will by MARY ANN JONES and by each other subscribing witness and knows that each signature is the true signature of the person whose name is signed.

Each of us is now more than twenty-one (21) years of age, and a competent witness and resides at the address set forth after his name.

We are acquainted with MARY ANN JONES, and aver that she has the legal capacity to make this will, is of the age of majority (or in accordance with local statute), and to the best of our knowledge is of sound mind and is not acting under duress, menace, fraud, misrepresentation, or undue influence.

We declare, under penalty of perjury (or such other provision as required by local statute), that the foregoing is true and correct.

Executed on this _____ day of _____, 20 ____, at _____,
(COUNTY)   (STATE)   (CITY)

_____, _____
_____ residing at _____
                                                          _____
_____ residing at _____
                                                          _____

Instead of the above "attestation clause," you may use the one that complies with your particular state statute.

Be sure that the testatrix initials each and every page of the will and thereafter give her a copy and put the original in the attorney's safe deposit box at the bank or wherever he keeps original wills. It often happens that the client will want to keep the original. In either such event, govern yourself according to the policy of your employer, the wishes of the client, and the state in which you work.

Information Checklist for Estate Planning

This may be prepared by the paralegal and submitted to the attorney for planning.

Family and Personal Information

Name and address of client: _____

Occupation of client: _____

Name and address of employer: _____

Client's date of birth; place of birth: _____

Wife (or husband's) name; date of birth; place of birth: _____

Children's names and dates of birth: _____

_____

Other relatives to be mentioned in will: name, addresses, and relationships:

Persons who would take if there is no will (state's intestate succession law):

Previous marriages (names and dates):

Other pertinent facts about family relationships: names of grandchildren; personal resources of beneficiaries (e.g., earnings in profession or occupation, legal and equitable interests, powers of appointment); disability of beneficiaries.

General Outline of Estate Plan

PRIMARY BENEFICIARIES:

Name   Relationship   Property or shares of estate—how given (outright or otherwise)

OTHER BENEFICIARIES:

Name   Relationship   Property or share of estate—how given (outright or otherwise)

Inventory of Assets

BUSINESS INTERESTS

Is business conducted as a sole proprietorship, partnership, or close corporation?

_____

Name and address of the business: _____

_____

Names of the client's business associates. How many shares of stock (or what percentages of the business) are owned by each associate and by client?

What office is held by each associate and by client?

Who are the directors, if a corporation?

What functions in the business are carried on by the client and by each associate?

Are there any key employees? What are their names, addresses, and titles?

Where are the corporation's legal and bookkeeping records kept? Name of accountant?

Have the stockholders or partners entered into a business continuation agreement with the client? Is there a partnership agreement in writing? A stockholder's agreement? A buy and sell agreement? Stock redemption agreement with corporation?

What is the estimated value of the client's interest in the business?

BANK ACCOUNTS

Names and addresses of all banks in which accounts are held; _number of each account;_ names on each account (i.e., joint, tentative trust, etc.); nature of account (i.e., checking, savings and loan, building and loan, etc.); amounts at present in each account.

Where are bank books, checkbooks, and bank statements kept?

SAFE DEPOSIT BOXES

Name of safe deposit company, address, box number, names and addresses of other persons having access. Who has keys? Where are the keys kept?

FINANCIAL INVESTMENTS, STOCKS, AND BONDS

Names of brokerage houses where accounts are maintained; addresses; names of persons who handle client's accounts.

Where are statements and other records kept?

Are stocks owned individually in client's names, or jointly with others? Does he own any stock as custodian for a minor?

Where are the stock certificates kept?

What is estimated value of stock owned?

What is estimated value of bonds owned?

What other property interests does client have in this area, such as stock options, etc.? What is estimated value of such interests?

Does client own any U.S. savings bonds? Are they in individual, co-owner, or beneficiary form? What are names of co-owners and beneficiaries? What is the face amount of bonds owned? What is their present value?

REAL ESTATE, HOMES

Does client own home, condominium, or cooperative apartment? Is it owned in his individual name, as joint tenant with right of survivorship, as tenant in common, as tenant by the entirety, etc.? What is name of other owner and relationship to client? Where is the property located?

What is approximate description of property? What is value of property? What is the amount of the mortgage, or mortgages, and other liens of the property? What is value of client's equity interest? What is total equity in property?

What other property does client own for his own use, i.e., summer homes, winter homes, or hunting lodges, etc.?

Fire, title, and other insurance on above property; name and address of insurance company, kind of insurance and coverage; policy number; amount; expiration dates; name and address of broker familiar with client's property and liability insurance?

REAL ESTATE, INVESTMENTS

Location, description, ownership, valuation, and equity in real property owned as an investment. Names and addresses of associates, amounts of mortgages and other liens on property, and by whom held. Addresses of mortgagees and lienors. Fire, title, and other insurance on above property. All pertinent information with regard to this realty.

MORTGAGES OWNED

Amount and nature of each mortgage owned; property on which mortgage owned-location, description, ownership, valuation; other liens on said property;

names and addresses of associates in ownership of mortgage. Value of client's interest in mortgage.

PENSION, PROFIT-SHARING, OR STOCK BONUS PLAN; KEOGH PLANS AND IRA ACCOUNTS

Name of plan; name and address of plan trustee; name of insurance company if group annuity or other insured retirement plan; number of group annuity certificate; is plan contributory or noncontributory; how much has client contributed; option already elected; options still available; amount of annuity or other distribution on retirement; amount of death benefit?

Where are copies of plans, certificates of participation, and client's account books kept?

BENEFIT PLANS OF CLIENT'S EMPLOYER

Group life insurance plan; split dollar life insurance; other death benefit plan; stock option plan; disability income, accident, sickness, medical, or hospitalization plan; name of insurance company or service organization; number of policy or certificate of participation; amount; names, addresses, and relationships of beneficiaries; options still available under policy; option already elected?

Where are copies of plans, policies, and certificates of participation kept?

DEFERRED COMPENSATION AGREEMENT WITH EMPLOYER

Date of execution; provisions for retirement and death benefits; funded by insurance policy purchased by employer; name of insurance company issuing policy; number of policy; amount; options still available; option already elected; other funding arrangement?

Where is agreement kept?

LIFE INSURANCE AND ANNUITY POLICIES

Name of insurance company issuing each policy; number of policy; amount; names, addresses, and relationships of beneficiaries; any loans under policy; any assignment; options still available under policy; option already elected; settlement agreement; any dividends at interest or applied to purchase of additional insurance; life insurance trust; participation in life insurance (group or individual) program of employer; National Service Life Insurance?

Other types of personal insurance policies owned by client (disability income, accident, sickness, hospitalization, etc.); name of insurance company; number of policy; participation in program of employer?

Policies owned by client on lives of others; name of insurance company; number of policy; amount; names, addresses, and relationships of beneficiaries; cash values; who pays premiums?

Where are policies and certificates of participation in employer's insurance plans kept?

Family or other noncommercial annuities?

SOCIAL SECURITY AND VETERANS ADMINISTRATION BENEFITS

Social Security account number; veteran or not; serial number, branch of service, dates of service?

OTHER PROPERTY

Money owed client personally as distinct from business credits; all facts in connection with said credits.

Rights of client under living trusts set up by himself or others; all facts in connection therewith.

Rights of client under testamentary trusts; all facts, etc.

Interest of client in unadministered estates of relatives or others; client's expected inheritance from parents or others; all facts, etc.

General or special powers of appointment held by client; all facts, etc.

All facts in connection with jewelry, furs, silverware, art works, books, stamp collections, coin collections, and similar property owned by client.

Value of household furniture owned by client.

Automobiles; boats.

All other property or interests in property not covered previously.

All facts relating to insurance on any of above property.

Cemetery plot; location, custody of deed, owned in what names; perpetual care or not?

Documents Requested of Client

Previous will or wills

Spouse's will

Prenuptial or other property agreement with spouse

Other instruments as indicated by answers to questions on foregoing pages

Examples: Partnership or stockholders' agreement; life insurance and annuity policies; pension, profit-sharing, and other benefit plans; deferred compensation agreement; deeds of house and business property; leases; tax receipts; maps; surveys; fire and other insurance policies; mortgages and notes owned; copies of trust agreements and wills under which client has power of appointment or other rights; copies of income and gift tax returns; bills of sale and other evidences of ownership.

Tax Outline

PROPERTY UNDER WILL

Real estate valued at	$ _____	
Securities valued at	$ _____	
Business interests valued at	$ _____	
Other property valued at	$ _____	
		A. $ _____

Life insurance
includible in gross estate

B. $ _____

PROPERTY OWNED WITH OTHERS (at value includible in gross estate)

Joint bank accounts	$ _____
Jointly owned real estate	$ _____
Jointly owned securities	$ _____
Jointly owned other property	$ _____
Property owned by the entireties	$ _____
Community property	$ _____

(Note: Exclude property listed above under "Property under Will")

C. $ _____

OTHER PROPERTY NOT UNDER WILL (to extend includible in gross estate)

Living trusts	$ _____
Powers of appointment	$ _____
Gift taxes paid on taxable gifts within 3 years of death	$ _____
Other	$ _____

D. $ _____

COMPUTATION OF TAX

(1) Gross estate [Total of A, B, C, & D] $ _____

(2) Estimated administration and funeral expenses,
    and debts of decedent $ _____

(3) Marital deduction $ _____

(4) Other deductions (e.g., charitable transfers) $ _____

(5) Taxable estate [(1) − [(2) + (3) + (4)] $ _____

(6) Taxable gifts made after 1976 $ _____

(7) Tentative tax base [(5) + (6)] $ _____

(8) Tentative tax [from table] $ _____

(9) Gift taxes paid on gifts made after 1976 $ _____

(10) Tax before unified credit [(8) − (9)] $ _____

(11) Allowable unified credit [from table] $ _____

(12) Approximate federal estate tax payable [(10) − (11)] $ _____

UNIFIED ESTATE AND GIFT TAX RATES

Amount Subject to Tax ($)	Amount of tax ($)	% Rate on Excess
less	18% of amount transferred	—
10,000	1,800	20
20,000	3,800	22
40,000	8,200	24
60,000	13,000	26
80,000	18,200	28
100,000	23,800	30
150,000	38,800	32
250,000	70,800	34
500,000	155,800	37
750,000	248,300	39
1,000,000	345,800	41
1,250,000	448,300	43
1,500,000	555,800	45
2,000,000	780,800	49
2,500,000	1,025,800	53
3,000,000	1,290,800	(*) 55

Subject to unified tax credit of $192,000 to U.S. citizens and residents.

(*) There's an additional 5% tax on so much of the taxable amount that's over $10,000,000 but not more than $21,040,000.

The tax computed by use of the foregoing table is without allowance for any credit for state or foreign death taxes paid or credit for tax on prior transfers.

MAXIMUM UNIFIED CREDIT AGAINST ESTATE TAX

LIFETIME EXEMPTIONS UNDER 2001 TAX CUT LAW

	Estate Tax Lifetime Exemption	Gift Tax Lifetime Exemption
2001	$675,000	$675,000
2002	$1,000,000	$1,000,000
2003	$1,000,000	$1,000,000
2004	$1,500,000	$1,000,000
2005	$1,500,000	$1,000,000
2006	$2,000,000	$1,000,000
2007	$2,000,000	$1,000,000
2008	$2,000,000	$1,000,000
2009	$3,500,000	$1,000,000
2010	(estate tax repealed)	$1,000,000
2011†	$1,000,000	$1,000,000

Drafting a Trust Agreement

A. Definition and Nature of a Trust

A trust is a legal entity designed to ensure that the testator's last wishes are carried out. A trust agreement creates a fiduciary relationship between two or more persons wherein one is entrusted with the property, real or personal, of another and holds legal title thereto, for the use and benefit of the other(s). The "beneficiaries" have an "equitable title" or interest in the property so held in trust. The trustee has the legal title.

The trustee has complete control of the trust property subject to the terms of the trust agreement and state law regulating trusts. The consequences of this power of the trustee are far-reaching. For this reason, but not necessarily limited thereto, a will containing trust agreements should be meticulously and carefully drawn and reviewed by your attorney. It can be one of the most important documents you will ever draft in a probate matter because of the long-range effect on the property of the testator and the heir-recipients thereof.

Hence, it is vitally important that during the initial interview with the client, he states with specificity his intent as to the trust agreement and the powers of the trustee and reviews the tax ramifications applicable to the gifts therein set out.

Trusts are normally established to ensure the future support of the surviving spouse, the future support and education of the children of the testator, and to preserve the capital or body of the estate. The trust agreement usually provides for particular payment income to specified beneficiaries. Accumulating income from the trust property is limited by tax law.

Trust agreements may be "testamentary" or *inter vivos*.

B. Parties to a Trust

1. The "trustor," or "settlor," who is the party who creates the trust.

2. The "trustee," who is the party of the second part with fiduciary responsibility as to the property being entrusted to him. He holds the legal title to the property so entrusted. This can be an individual or an institution like a bank.

3. The "beneficiary," who is the party for whom the property is being held by the trustee.

    In an *inter vivos* trust, the trustor or settlor may also be a beneficiary during his lifetime.

C. Elements of a Trust

1. *Intent:* There must be an intent to create a trust. You do not have to use the word "trust," just prove that there was an intent to create a fiduciary relationship and a fiduciary duty. You may use words which express hope or desire without their being a demand or command. But be sure to make it effective immediately.

2. *Property or trust res:* The property must be identifiable. You must describe the trust *res* with great particularity. (Note that a debt owed by the trustor is not a specific property; it is merely a general obligation of the estate.)

3. *Parties:* The parties to the trust (who may be a class of persons) must be designated. Any incompleteness as to the designation of a trustee or beneficiary would make the trust ineffective. There must be an appointment and designation of people *now.* The parties must have the capacity of a settlor or trustor as with any other document, that is, capacity, and so forth. The actual name of the trustee is not too important or necessary, but the provision for a trustee should be spelled out in the document. The court can always name a trustee, but it cannot name the other parties.

4. *It must be for a legal purpose:* That is, it must be a trust that is not against public policy.

D. Types of Trusts

All trusts, regardless of what they are called, fall into two basic categories, active or passive, depending on the duties of the trustee: In an active trust the trustee has to do a lot; in a passive trust the trustee has little to do in managing the trust. The various types of trusts are as follows:

1. A "private trust" is an express trust for a particular individual or named individuals or designated class of individuals.

2. A "charitable trust" is an express trust for undesignated persons of a definite class for a charitable purpose.

3. An "express trust" is one which is expressly and definitely created by the trustor (settlor) by his conduct, words, writing, or all together. There is specific intent on the part of the trustor to create the trust.

4. A "resulting trust" is one inferred by operation of law. This is declared when a court finds that a person *intended* a trust but did not effectively create a trust by a written or oral statement.

5. A "constructive trust" is one resulting by operation of law. It is normally used to prevent fraud or unjust enrichment. It is a sort of remedial device and is a trust merely because the law says so. Such a trust could be one decreed by a court to avoid fraud against creditors or to avoid fraud against heirs of a decedent's estate where the testator had made an absolute deed to a person before his death but intended that person to hold the property in trust for the heirs of others. This type of trust could be declared by the court on petition of the creditors or heirs. The trustee under this circumstance would be the record title owner holding the property for the benefit of the creditors.

6. The "spendthrift clause" protects the beneficiary against his own folly. If a spendthrift clause or clauses is included in a trust agreement, the beneficiary's creditors cannot attach the property; and the beneficiary cannot encumber the same.

7. An "*inter vivos* trust" is a trust created by the settlor (trustor) while he is living. The settlor may also be the beneficiary during his lifetime of an *inter vivos* trust created by him. The *inter vivos* trust may be "revocable" or "irrevocable."

   If it is revocable, it is one in which the trustor has power comparable to total ownership. This is a totally flexible instrument. In California, if the trust does not say anything about it, it is presumed to be a revocable trust. Therefore, if you want to make it an irrevocable trust, you must spell it out in detail; otherwise, the court will presume that the trust is revocable.

   This revocable trust can be set up during life and can be funded or unfunded. The funded *inter vivos* trust is payable immediately upon death, without benefit of probate, directly to the beneficiaries named in the trust. The unfunded *inter vivos* trust is payable upon death to the trustee rather than to the members of the family directly. This vehicle is sometimes called the "pour-over trust," and its advantage is that the assets of the estate cannot be attacked by creditors; it also has certain tax advantages.

   A pour-over trust is an existing trust recognized under the terms and provisions of a will. The trustee performs the provisions of the trust, or the will. The will in this instance merely provides funds for the trust.

8. A "totten trust" is created by the deposit of one person of his own money in a bank in his own name, as a trustee for another. It is a tentative trust, revocable at will until the depositor dies or completes the gift in his lifetime. It becomes an absolute trust at his death, if it was not disposed of entirely during the life of the trustor.

EXAMPLE

B. Jones goes to the bank and opens a bank account in the name of "B. Jones, in trust for my wife C. Jones."

This type of trust does not go through probate.

Checklist of Clauses That Can Be Included in Testamentary Trust Agreements

It is in this area of your duties that the word processing system can be most helpful and time-saving, as generally most trust agreements are long and complicated, with many paragraphs and subparagraphs. Furthermore, most of these paragraphs and subparagraphs are boilerplate and repetitive, as they are used in most types of trust agreement. In this connection, therefore, consider the following clauses, among others, that can be described as boilerplate clauses:

1. Trust for spouse and family not qualifying for the marital deduction-beneficial interest.

2. Trust for spouse to qualify under the Economic Recovery Tax Act of 1981 (ERTA). Note suggestion to put specific reference to the act in the clause concerning unlimited marital exemption, see Section 403 of ERTA.

3. Trust for several individuals

4. Trust for one individual

5. Trust for a class of persons

6. Spendthrift trust clauses

7. Annuity trust clauses

8. Income accumulation trust clauses

9. Cemetery trust clause

10. Exculpatory clauses

11. Power to terminate trust clauses

12. Invasion of principal clauses

State Laws Affecting Estate Planning

Some state common laws or statutes that may affect estate planning and the drafting of a will are as follows:

1. *Integration rule:* This is the rule in some states that requires every page of a will to be present and connected at the time of the signing of the will by the testator. This is the basis for requiring each and every page of a will to be initialed by the testator and for the inclusion in the attesting paragraph of the will the number of pages of the will.

2. *Law of the situs:* The courts will look to the laws of the state in which the will was drawn when probating an estate to determine if it is a valid will, even if it is being probated in a different state.

   NOTE: A will is offered for probate in the state where the deceased resided at the time of his death.

   EXAMPLE

   The testator lives in California and owns property in Missouri. His personal property will be disposed of according to the laws of California, but the real property will be disposed of according to the laws of Missouri. An ancillary administration may have to be instituted in Missouri.

   It should be noted that most states try to uphold the provisions of a will made in another state if possible and will change the practical effect of provisions therein contained only if they conflict to a great extent with the laws of their state.

3. *The cy-pres doctrine:* The rule of "cy-pres" is a common-law rule for the construction of instruments in equity by which the intention of the party is carried out as near as can be, when it would be impossible or illegal to give it literal effect. Thus, where a testator attempts to create a gift to a charity that is no longer in existence, the court may endeavor, instead of making the devise entirely void, to explain the will in such a way as to carry out the testator's general intentions and allow the gift to a similar charity. Some states do not apply the cy-pres doctrine or apply it only in very limited situations.

4. *The rule against perpetuities:* This rule was originally an English common-law rule. Some states have adopted statutes to get a similar result.
   In California, the Rule Against Perpetuities applies to trusts that are geared to the accumulation of money over a period of fifty years or more. The common

rule stated that property of any type must vest, if at all, not later than twenty-one years, plus a life (or lives) in being, but a charitable beneficiary with a "now" vesting interest may accumulate property.

> NOTE: A baby within the womb has been considered to be a life in being within the definition and terms of the Rule Against Perpetuities.
>
> In some courts, where an interest violates the Rule Against Perpetuities, only that interest is void; the balance of the interest is not affected. This is because the courts will do anything within their power to avoid forfeitures and losses. This is a good point to remember when preparing and working with trusts or wills and the interests conveyed to others therein.

5. *Intestate succession:* While these rules do not affect properly drafted and executed wills, it is important to understand them, as they may apply in a situation where a will is only partially satisfactory or has been challenged. Every state has different rules on the disposition of estates in the absence of a will. It behooves the paralegal to be able to explain these rules to a client who has yet to draft a will. Some clients may be very uncomfortable at the thought of disposition of property under these rules and should therefore be counseled regarding them. This may just be the impetus the client needs to get his will drafted!

Under the Uniform Probate Code, the surviving spouse receives either the entire estate if there are no descendants or all the descendants are also descendants of the surviving spouse. If the parent(s) of the decedent is (are) alive, the spouse receives the first $200,000, plus three fourths of any balance of the intestate estate. If there are descendants that are qualified to take, the cash amount is either the first $150,000 or $100,000 plus one half of any balance of the intestate estate. If the decedent leaves no spouse, then there is a series of rules for distribution to parents, grandparents, and siblings, and their descendants.

Federal Tax Law Affecting Estate Planning

As you know, the federal estate tax, as provided for in the Internal Revenue Code, is a tax imposed on all of the property owned by the decedent jointly or severally at the time of the death, be it real or personal, tangible or intangible, and wherever located. It includes not only the value of property owned outright, but also the value of any interest he may have had in the property as of the time of his death (jointly owned).

The value of the taxable estate is determined by deducting from the value of the gross estate (as described here) the exemptions, credits, and deductions allowed in the estate-tax section of the Internal Revenue Code.

The Economic Recovery Tax Act of 1981 (ERTA) made major and revolutionary changes in the exemptions, credits, and other tax benefits allowable in estate planning. It should be made clear, however, that the basic statute, the Internal Revenue Code of

1954, remains in effect. The Economic Recovery Tax Act of 1981 (hereinafter referred to as ERTA) made changes by amendment to the Internal Revenue Code of 1954.

These new provisions are of such a highly sophisticated and complicated nature that any attempt here to set forth a fully detailed discussion would be an exercise in futility. Furthermore, because of the major surgery performed by the amendments made to the Internal Revenue Code of 1954, resulting from the enactment of ERTA, you, the paralegal, should immediately check the estate-planning files, wills, and trust documents of your attorney's clients so that he can determine the need for changes or additions to these documents by reason of ERTA.

The Administration of and Probating of Estates

The following step-by-step procedures are geared to California practice and set forth by way of example what you should look for and be guided by. It is suggested that you look to your local court rules and statutes for the procedures used in your jurisdiction.

Initial Steps (Generally)

Generally, as to both intestate and testate probate proceedings, you should:

1. Search for burial instructions and/or will to dispose of the body;

2. If applicable, open safe deposit box for burial instructions, and/or will;

3. Determine if a special administrator is needed;

4. Have copies made of will for later use in administration procedures;

5. Locate witnesses to prove the will; or if it is a holographic will, someone who can prove the handwriting of the decedent;

6. Prepare petition for issuance of letters testamentary, letters of administration with the will annexed, or letter of administration, whichever is applicable;

7. Determine who is to be the petitioner; and

8. Ascertain names, addresses, ages of heirs at law, and/or named beneficiaries.

Probating the Estate

A. Intestate
Step-by-step procedure:

1. File petition for Letters of Administration.

2. Notice of hearing. (Be sure any and all heirs or suspected heirs are notified of

the hearing date via registered mail at least ten days prior to the date of said hearing; or whatever time limit is the policy of your state.)

3. File any contest to petitioner, petitioning for Letters of Administration.

4. Preparation for hearing:

   a. Testimony establishing death,

   b. Residency requirements, and

   c. Known heirs and unknown heirs, etc.

5. *Order appointing administrator:* This should be prepared in original and three copies and placed in your attorney's file so that he may have same at the hearing.

6. *Letters of Administration:* These should be prepared before the hearing and placed in the attorney's file so that he may have them on the date of the hearing. Make an original and three copies; others may be secured when and as needed.

7. Administration of the estate:

   a. Publication of Notice to Creditors. All claims should be filed within four months from the date of publication.

   b. Request appointment of an appraiser. In some states this is now automatically done by the court.

   c. Prepare an original and three copies of the Inventory and Appraisement. An original and one for the court, one for the appraiser, and one copy for your file.

      NOTE: In each of the above documents, be sure that the petitioner has signed in all spaces provided for the signature.

   d. Powers and duties of administrator:

      i. Liquidate assets,

      ii. Raise funds by selling property and/or collecting outstanding debts due the estate,

      iii. Pay all outstanding debts as soon as possible, including state and federal taxes due and inheritance taxes, if any, and

      iv. Pay expenses of administration and attorney's fees, if any.

8. Distribution and Settlement of Estate:

   a. Preliminary distribution (if warranted)

   b. Final distribution:

    i. A period of six months from date of first publication of Notice to Creditors must have lapsed before there can be a distribution (time element may be peculiar to your state).

    ii. Current and final accounting should be prepared before there can be a final distribution to heirs, etc.

    iii. If first and final accounting is approved by the court, then the attorney can distribute the funds in the estate.

    iv. File application to the court for final discharge.

    v. File application for termination of proceedings when the estate is exhausted.

B. Testate

1. File petition to probate will and for Letters Testamentary (or for Letters of Administration with Will Annexed if appropriate).

2. Send out notice of hearing to all named heirs, beneficiaries, etc., and unknown.

3. Prepare the necessary documents for issuance of your Letters before the hearing date so that the attorney may have them in the file.

    a. Order for Letters Testamentary

    b. Letters Testamentary

    c. Subscribing witness affidavit and proof of will (in some states this procedure has been changed and a printed document is now used, and in some states a certified copy of the original will must be submitted to the witness for verification as to signature)

    d. Prepare the order admitting will to probate

    e. Secure bond, if required

4. *Administration of estate:* Use the same procedure as set forth under the General Outline for probating an estate wherein there was no will, and the paragraphs a through d of subparagraph 7 and 8 regarding distribution and settlement of the estate.

C. Estates Involving Minors and Guardians
The provision for the appointment of guardians on behalf of minors or incompetents is in many state statutes, or is governed by committees for the insane, with the appointments being made by the court.

The duties and trust of the guardian are administered under the control of the court, and the power to remove a guardian for cause is generally vested in the court making or approving the appointment.

These guardianships can be generally classified as follows:

1. A constructive guardianship,

2. A natural guardianship,

3. A testamentary guardianship,

4. A general guardianship, or

5. A guardian *ad litem*.

Since the basis for their determination may vary from state to state, it is conceivable that the procedure for their administration and control will also vary from jurisdiction to jurisdiction. Hence, you are referred to your local probate rules for the controlling procedures. The following procedures are set forth as examples only, and emphasize the duties that can be performed by paralegals in this area of an attorney's practice, and are guided by California practice and policy.

The powers and duties of a guardian are basically the same as those for any "estate" except that you must be sure to keep accurate and complete records of any and all expenditures for the support and care of the minor and/or incompetent; you also must make semiannual or annual accountings to the court (whichever time limit has been established by the court); and any and all expenditures, regardless of how small, must be approved by the court *before* they are expended.

Although all sales or transfer of any asset in any "estate" must receive the approval of the court, it is most important in that of a minor and/or incompetent, in order that the minor may have an income or money when he has attained the age of majority; and/or for the incompetent's protection.

Termination of these types of guardianships occurs when:

1. The minor has reached the age of majority and you make a full and complete accounting to him and the court; and

2. When the incompetent has been restored to capacity in the eyes of the court or has died. Then his estate becomes a true "estate" matter and should be handled accordingly.

You should also secure final discharge papers and termination of proceedings documents when the duty of the guardians has been discharged completely and to the satisfaction of the court.

The following is a step-by-step procedure for dealing with estates involving minors and incompetents:

MINORS

1. File petition for Letters of Guardianship.

2. Send out notice of hearing to interested parties.

3. Prepare the following for hearing:

   a. Order appointing guardian;

   b. Letters of Guardianship; and

   c. Secure bond, if required.

INCOMPETENTS

1. File petition for Letters of Guardianship.

2. Send out notice of hearing to all interested parties, including relatives, creditors, etc.

3. Prepare the following for hearing:

   a. Order appointing guardian;

   b. Letters of Guardianship; and

   c. Bond, if required.

Chronological Step-by-Step Procedure in Handling an Estate Matter

Source: Oregon Department of Education, Curriculum Development Unit, Vocational and Career Education

1. Collect and compile personal data needed to handle estate.

2. Evaluate data needed to write legal and correct will(s).

3. Write will(s).

4. Collect and compile information for trust agreement.

5. Write legal and correct trust agreement.

6. Transfer assets to a Trust.

7. Write specific Power of Attorney Document.

PROBATING DECEDENT'S ESTATE

1. Compile personal data of decedent.

2. Determine whether probate is necessary from personal data.

3. Evaluate data to develop a petition for probate.

4. Document legal petition for probate.

5. Write affidavit of minutes to the will.

6. Document bond for estate executor.

7. Write text of court order to admit will to probate.

8. Compile information for heirs.

9. Write a Note to Interested Persons.

10. Arrange required publishing of death notice with newspaper.

11. Locate and inform heirs of the death and arrange required actions.

12. Locate and establish control of estate assets.

13. Appraise value of estate assets.

14. Document assets and their value.

15. Pay off liens and/or court judgments against the estate.

16. Determine necessity of ancillary probate.

17. Write documents required for ancillary probate.

18. Pay or reject claims against the estate.

19. Compile needed data and write out income tax return.

20. Write out fiduciary tax returns.

21. Prepare Federal estate tax return.

22. Request final audit in writing.

23. Apply for release of assets.

24. Administer checking account.

25. Estimate total cash needed to close the estate.

26. Advise heirs and devisees of the status of the estate.

27. Accomplish a final accounting for the estate.

28. Write a Notice of Final Accounting.

29. Write court order approving the Final Accounting.

30. Arrange transfer of assets to heirs.

31. Prepare receipts.

32. Assemble information for Supplementary Final Accounting.

33. Prepare Supplementary Final Accounting.

34. Compile and write court order to close estate.

35. File Claim against estate.

36. File objection to final accounting.

Chronological Step-by-Step Procedure in Handling a Conservatorship

1. Collect and organize data needed to set up conservatorship.

2. Compile petition for appointment of conservator.

3. Prepare Order for citation.

4. Prepare citation.

5. Prepare Acceptance of Service of Citation and Waiver.

6. Write document needed to place Conservator under.

7. Write court order appointing Conservator.

8. Document Inventory of assets under Conservatorship.

9. Administer conservator checking account.

10. Provide annual accounting for conservatorship.

11. Compile tax returns affected by conservatorship.

12. Write court order approving annual accounting.

13. Compile conservatorship final accounting.

14. Write court order approving conservatorship final accounting and direct distribution.

15. Fill out conservatorship direct distribution receipt.

16. Write court order closing conservatorship.

17. Prepare conservator's petition for sale of real property.

18. Prepare and serve citation for Sale.

19. Write court order to sell real property under conservatorship.

20. Write conservator's petition for sale of personal property.

21. Write court order to sell personal property under conservatorship.

Glossary

Administrator: An individual appointed by the court to manage the estate of a decedent who has died without leaving a will (feminine is an administratrix, although the masculine is generally universally used).

Administrator with Will Annexed: An individual appointed by the court when a decedent has left a will in which there has been no executor or executrix appointed or the named executor fails to act.

Codicil: An addition to or change in a will that has already been executed by the testator or testatrix.

Devise: A gift of real property under a will.

Devisee: An individual to whom real property is given under a will.

Executor (Executrix): An individual (or entity such as a bank) appointed by a decedent in his will to carry out the terms and provisions of his will.

Holographic Will: A will entirely written by hand, dated and signed by the testatrix and/or testator.

Intestate: The state of an individual not having prepared and left a valid will for probate.

Legatee: An individual to whom personal property is bequeathed under the terms of a will.

Letters of Administration: The formal instruction of authority and appointment given to an administrator by the proper court, empowering him to enter upon the discharge of his office as administrator.

Letters Testamentary: The formal instruction of authority and appointment given to an executor by the proper court, empowering him to enter upon the discharge of his office as executor (executrix).

Living Will: Also known as a Health Care Proxy. It is a written directive that specifies who should make health decisions and how they should be made in the instance where the writer is no longer able to make those decisions for himself.

Nuncupative Will: An oral will declared, or dictated, by a testator, *before witnesses,* and *afterward* reduced to writing.

Public Administrator: A public official who has prior right to administer an estate, when no other qualified person seeks appointment as administrator.

Residuary Legatee: One who receives the residue of an estate after payment of the testator's (testatrix's) debts, devises, and legacies.

Special Administrator: An individual who is appointed, by the court, under certain conditions when the circumstances of the estate require an immediate appointment of a personal representative.

Testate: The state of having died leaving a valid will for probate.

Will: An instrument in which a qualified person legally and intentionally directs the disposition of his or her property to become effective after his or her death.

CHAPTER EIGHTEEN

How to Handle a Family Law File

One of the prime functions of a paralegal in a law office with a family law practice is that of interviewing the client and obtaining the necessary facts relating to the marriage, the children, if any, and the property of the parties. Thereafter, he will be able to analyze and determine what marital state was created, whether there is a child custody problem, and what is the separate, personal property of the parties as opposed to the community property or joint property (depending on the state where the parties reside).

The most common mistake made is that of assuming all property automatically upon marriage becomes community or jointly owned (depending on the state where the parties reside) property. It is for this reason that a paralegal should know the difference between the two and how they interact and can change their character.

One of the causes of emotional distress and bitterness at the time of the dissolution of a marriage is the improper division of the property of the parties.

Inasmuch as the format and procedures used in pursuing a family law matter vary from state to state, an in-depth, step-by-step procedure would be impractical.

Hence, this section on family law will be an overview discussion of the theory and concept of the marital state and a capsule breakdown of property before, during, and after a marriage.

What Is the State Called Marriage?

Marriage is a civil contract, the parties to which are (1) a man, (2) a woman, and (3) the state. It is not a commercial contract in that it cannot be contracted away. It can be dissolved only by the state law, in conformity with "public policy."

Throughout all discussions with clients regarding a marital problem, bear in mind these two words—"public policy"—since they are the underlying determining factor of all laws relating to marriage and the dissolutions of marital bliss.

Elements of Statutory Marriage

A so-called legal marriage is a marriage authorized by state statute. The statute usually requires a license to marry plus a marriage ceremony by a person authorized to perform marriage, such as a minister, priest, notary public, captain of a ship, judge, and the like.

Absent a license to marry issued by the state, it is a void marriage in spite of a marriage ceremony, regardless of its formality, except in a state that recognizes common law marriage.

Furthermore, "mandatory statutes," directed to the parties, state that the parties shall not be validly married if there is a preexisting marriage not dissolved by law.

And "directory statutes" advise county clerks that they shall not issue a marriage license unless there is evidence that a blood test has been taken. But it is a valid marriage even though the clerk may not have had the blood certificate physically present at the time of issuing the certificate.

The general rule as to statutory marriage or another state's recognition of a common law marriage is that a marriage valid where celebrated is valid everywhere except where it is against public policy.

Elements of Common Law Marriage

Most states do not recognize common law marriages. The minority of states that do are:

Alabama	Iowa	Oklahoma
Colorado	Kansas	Pennsylvania (if created before 1/1/05)
District of Columbia	Montana	Rhode Island
Georgia (if created before 1/1/97)	New Hampshire (for inheritance purposes only)	South Carolina
Idaho (if created before 1/1/96)	Ohio (if created before 10/10/91)	Texas
		Utah

There is a sharp disagreement and conflict as to the validity of such a marriage, but in a state or court jurisdiction where it is accepted this type of marital arrangement carries with it all rights of inheritance, descent, and distribution, as well as other property rights. Hence, the prerequisites should be clear-cut and defined as follows:

1. There must be a mutual consent and agreement between the parties;

2. There must be cohabitation between the parties; and

3. There must be full and complete representation and a holding out to the community at large that the parties are living as husband and wife for a specified (statutory provision) period of time. If there is no statutory provision, it is deemed to be a "common law" marriage as each of the above elements are present.

According to the full faith and credit clause, states that do not recognize a common law marriage created there must recognize a common law marriage created in a state that does.

Another method sometimes used to establish a marriage is the proxy marriage. Where recognized, it is considered a valid marriage. It is allowable without cohabitation if an authorized representative of each party is present at the proxy ceremony. Absent such statutory regulation, such a marriage is void and of no force and effect. Though this doctrine of the proxy marriage is not recognized in every state, most states have such a statute on the books.

Other Relationships Distinguished

1. *Putative relationship:* A "putative relationship" exists when one or both of the parties enter into an invalid marriage but do so in good faith, believing that neither one has any impediment affecting the validity of the marriage. In jurisdictions where this type of relationship is recognized, as in New York and Texas, a mistake of fact or law may be present and still not negate the lawfulness of a putative relationship, or, in this instance, only the innocent spouse of the putative spouse. The one who knows that the marriage is invalid is the "meretricious spouse."

2. *Meretricious relationship:* A meretricious relationship exists where both parties have knowledge of the invalidity of the marriage performed or where they are just living together. It is not a sufficient community and does not constitute any legally recognized relationship.

3. *Rights of the parties in meretricious and putative relationships:* One of the major problems arising in these types of relationships is the status of any property accumulated and the disposition thereof when the relationship is terminated. The laws relating to the disposition of property vary in the states recognizing these relationships, but most tend to favor the putative spouse.

EXAMPLE

In the case of the wife as the putative spouse, should she find that her husband has a living wife somewhere and thereafter obtain an annulment of the marriage, her rights as the innocent spouse in the putative relationship are fully protected, and she is entitled to the same share that she would have been entitled to had it been a valid marriage.

In the case of a "legal wife" who survives a meretricious husband, cases treat the husband as having had two surviving spouses. As a result of this treatment, one half of the property of the husband goes to the putative wife and one half goes to the legally recognized community, or the legal wife. The reasoning is that since the putative innocent spouse contributed to the putative community, she is entitled to what she contributed; and of course, the legal wife is entitled to one half of the legal community.

The recent trend to couples living together without benefit of matrimony or statutory or common law has changed some of the former legal rules about the rights of parties to a meretricious relationship.

The Common Law Methodology of marriage appears to have taken on a new legal status, and the state of flux in the law relating to alimony, maintenance, and support appears to have stabilized as the result of the recent judicial decision in the California case of *Marvin v. Marvin*, 18 Cal 3rd 660, (1976); 122 Cal App 3rd 871 (8-11-1981). Since the Marvin case, some other jurisdictions have recognized and applied some of its principles where there was no marriage intended.

As you will recall, in that case the parties were living together without the benefit of a traditional marriage ceremony or other *prima facie* evidence of a legal marriage or intent to marry, and the court made its decision based on the relationship as between the parties over the many years of their living together as "husband and wife."

The effect of the decision in the *Marvin v. Marvin* case on family law practice and the legal precedents set established the following:

1. An unmarried person can recover from a person with whom he or she had lived, in accordance with an agreement; or if

2. By way of the conduct between the parties it could be *implied* that there was a contract; or

3. The court can consider equitable remedies based upon the value of the relationship or on the basis of a "constructive trust"—*quantum meruit.*

In dealing with a large divorce case, such as the Marvin case, perhaps you should consider "bifurcating" the property settlement agreement and/or division of property from the actual divorce proceeding because of the possible tax ramifications. It is suggested that you check with your attorney about this.

Same-Sex Marriage

The debate concerning same-sex marriages or civil unions continues to play out in the individual states. Each jurisdiction can decide how to construct and/or limit the legal relationship between same-sex couples. A handful of Northeastern states permit civil unions and give traditional spousal rights to those partners. California and Massachusetts are the only states (so far) that issue marriage licenses to these partners. (This can change depending on ballot initiatives.) New York, while it does not permit civil unions within its state, recognizes civil unions from other states that permit them.

In those states without regulations touching on same-sex rights, courts can decide to permit the principles underlying putative spouses to be used in probate and other contractual relationships. This is a developing area of the law. If your office handles family law, you should stay apace with the decisions in your jurisdiction.

Some states have also adopted the Defense of Marriage Act of 1996, which "ensures that whatever definition of 'spouse' may be used in Federal law, the word refers only to a person of the opposite sex." However, it reserves to the states their individual power to decide for themselves whether they wants to grant legal status to same-sex "marriage."

Marital Agreements

A "prenuptial agreement" between a husband and a wife before marriage, but in contemplation of marriage, regarding separate personal property must contain a complete disclosure of all separate property of the parties, and, as well, a representation of each party by an attorney of his or her own choosing. A sample Financial Disclosure Statement is provided in Figure 18.1 and a sample Prenuptial Agreement is included as Figure 18.2.

If the wife is not represented by counsel, the agreement may be invalidated by the court. Therefore, in drafting your agreement, be sure to include a statement to the effect that there was a full disclosure of all separate property of the parties, and that each party was represented by counsel.

Since there is a duty, established by law, that a husband should support his wife, he cannot contract away that duty. He can sometimes contract away "spousal support," but in your agreement you must show that the wife has fair and reasonable means to support herself.

A "post-marital agreement" may be made by the parties and enforced by the court where divorce is contemplated or where the parties intend to continue the marriage relationship if there is full disclosure and separate representation by attorneys.

Since the Marvin case, some homosexuals living together have called upon attorneys to draft a "non-marital agreement" for them.

The section of family law of the American Bar Association has published an excellent and informative paperback book with sample forms for all the above contracts. Its title is *Pre-Marital and Marital Contracts* by Lewis Becker and Edward L. Winer, and it's available at the ABA store online (www.abanet.org/abastore).

Figure 18.1
Sample Financial Disclosure Statement from FindLaw.com

Before entering into a prenuptial or premarital agreement, each prospective spouse must make a complete and honest financial disclosure to the other. The following form, used in conjunction with the advice and counsel of your family law attorney, can be useful in putting together your own financial statement and verifying that the information you receive from your spouse is complete.

A. Gross Monthly Income

Source/Amount _____ /$ _____

Source/Amount _____ /$ _____

Source/Amount _____ /$ _____

TOTAL: $ _____

B. Deductions from Gross Income

State Income Tax $ _____

Federal Income Tax $ _____

Social Security $ _____

Self-Employment Tax $ _____

Health Insurance $ _____

Union Dues $ _____

Pension/Retirement $ _____

Support Orders $ _____

Other $ _____

TOTAL: $ _____

C. NET MONTHLY INCOME (gross income minus total deductions):

$ _____

Figure 18.1 (*continued*)

D. Assets & Liabilities

	Value	Owe
Primary Home	$ _____	$ _____
Vacation Home	$ _____	$ _____
Other Home/Property	$ _____	$ _____
Vehicle(s)	$ _____	$ _____
Recreational Vehicle	$ _____	$ _____
Boat(s)	$ _____	$ _____
Furniture	$ _____	$ _____
Home Furnishings	$ _____	$ _____
Appliances	$ _____	$ _____
Artwork	$ _____	$ _____
Jewelry	$ _____	$ _____
Computer(s)	$ _____	$ _____
Personal Property	$ _____	$ _____
Cash	$ _____	$ _____
Stocks/Bonds/Funds	$ _____	$ _____
Stock Options	$ _____	$ _____
Checking Account(s)	$ _____	$ _____
Savings Account(s)	$ _____	$ _____
Retirement/Pensions	$ _____	$ _____
Profit Sharing	$ _____	$ _____
IRA(s)	$ _____	$ _____
Business(es)	$ _____	$ _____
Professional Practice	$ _____	$ _____
Life Insurance	$ _____	$ _____

Figure 18.1 (*continued*)

Other Assets

Description   Value

_____
_____
_____
_____
_____
_____

TOTAL ASSETS: $ _____   TOTAL LIABILITIES: $ _____

E. NET WORTH (assets minus liabilities): $ _____

F. Educational Degrees

_____
_____
_____

Figure 18.2
Sample Prenuptial Agreement from FindLaw.com

_____, hereinafter referred to as Pro-
spective Husband, and _____, hereinaf-
ter referred to as Prospective Wife, hereby agree on this _____ day of _____,
in the year _____, as follows:

1. Prospective Husband and Prospective Wife contemplate marriage in the near future
   and wish to establish their respective rights and responsibilities regarding each other's income and property and the income and property that may be acquired, either
   separately or together, during the marriage.
2. Prospective Husband and Prospective Wife have made a full and complete disclosure
   to each other of all of their financial assets and liabilities, as more fully set forth in the
   accompanying Financial Statements, attached hereto as Exhibits A and B.
3. Except as otherwise provided below, Prospective Husband and Prospective Wife
   waive the following rights:
   1. To share in each other's estates upon their death.
   2. To spousal maintenance, both temporary and permanent.

Figure 18.2 *(continued)*

3. To share in the increase in value during the marriage of the separate property of the parties.

4. To share in the pension, profit sharing, or other retirement accounts of the other.

5. To the division of the separate property of the parties, whether currently held or hereafter acquired.

6. To any claims based on the period of cohabitation of the parties.

4. [SET FORTH RELEVANT EXCEPTIONS HERE.]

5. [ADDITIONAL PROVISIONS HERE. These can range from prescribing that the children will be raised in a particular religion to allocating household chores between the parties.]

6. Both Prospective Husband and Prospective Wife are represented by separate and independent legal counsel of their own choosing.

7. Both Prospective Husband and Prospective Wife have separate income and assets to independently provide for their own respective financial needs.

8. This agreement constitutes the entire agreement of the parties and may be modified only in a writing executed by both Prospective Husband and Prospective Wife.

9. In the event it is determined that a provision of this agreement is invalid because it is contrary to applicable law, that provision is deemed separable from the rest of the agreement, such that the remainder of the agreement remains valid and enforceable.

10. This agreement is made in accordance with the laws of the state of _____, and any dispute regarding its enforcement will be resolved by reference to the laws of that state.

11. This agreement will take effect immediately upon the solemnization of the parties' marriage.

I HAVE READ THE ABOVE AGREEMENT, I HAVE TAKEN TIME TO CONSIDER ITS IMPLICATIONS, I FULLY UNDERSTAND ITS CONTENTS, I AGREE TO ITS TERMS, AND I VOLUNTARILY SUBMIT TO ITS EXECUTION.

_____   _____
Prospective Husband   Prospective Wife

Divorce (Dissolution of Marriage)

In all states a statutory marriage must be dissolved by order of court. In states where a common law marriage is recognized, divorce or dissolution of marriage proceedings would be the only definitive way to end such a marriage (children, property rights, and so forth).

Many states still require specific grounds for divorce to be stated in the petition or complaint. Others have adopted the "no-fault divorce" concept. In the latter, it is sufficient to allege that the marriage is irretrievably broken without stating the specific reasons for the breakup. Check your state divorce code or statutes for the grounds you must allege. State case law interprets those statutes.

State court rules of civil procedure and local court rules govern what court documents must be filed and the times for filing.

Dissolution of Marriage (No-Fault Divorce)

About fifteen of the fifty states still require a complaint in divorce to state grounds for divorce other than the mere ultimate fact that the marriage is "irretrievably broken." The grounds to be stated may not be the real reasons the plaintiff (petitioner) wants a divorce, but at least one of the grounds must be alleged in the complaint (petition) to state a cause of action in divorce.

State statutes provide the basis for getting a divorce. They state the grounds: irretrievable breakdown of the marriage (no-fault), adultery, desertion, mental or extreme cruelty, physical cruelty, impotence (not infertility), nonsupport or willful neglect, insanity, alcoholism, drug addiction, and conviction of a felony, among others.

In all states, the "substantive grounds" for divorce must be stated in the complaint to state the cause of action. In no-fault divorce states, it is sufficient to state that the marriage is irretrievably broken, without stating grounds or facts showing why. In other states, the particular ground for obtaining the divorce must be stated in the complaint, and the defendant may demand a bill of particulars or motion for more definite statement to get the facts if the divorce is being contested.

In all states the "jurisdictional grounds" for divorce must also be stated in the complaint (petition). Jurisdiction is based on the place and length of residence of the parties. Residence requirements (immediately preceding the filing of the action) vary from none in Alaska and six weeks in Idaho and Nevada to one year in Iowa, Rhode Island, South Carolina, and West Virginia. Some of the states with longer residence requirements have exceptions where the plaintiff was married in the state, if the cause of action for divorce arose in the state, or if both parties reside in the state.

Important: Check your state court rules for divorce procedure. Check your state statute(s) for the grounds for divorce in your state.

In most no-fault divorce states, the plaintiff (petitioner) must include allegations in the complaint (petition) that will entitle him or her to other relief if he or she wants it: division of property, custody of children, attorney's fees, partition of jointly held property, and so on.

The court will apply equitable principles of law in deciding those questions.

NOTE: If grounds or jurisdictional facts are not stated in the complaint for divorce, it is subject to a motion for dismissal (demurrer). If facts that show the petitioner is entitled to any or all of the other relief mentioned here are not stated in the complaint and prayer, the court may not even consider those questions.

A. Jurisdiction

Jurisdiction is the authority and capacity of the court and its judicial officers to take cognizance of and decide the case before it. It must have jurisdiction over both the subject matter and the parties. The question of "domicile" goes to the subject matter in a divorce case.

Jurisdiction over the parties is obtained by "service of process." See Chapter 4 on court systems and procedures.

Service: Service in a divorce court (with certain limitations) can be:

1. Personal service, which is the physical service of process on the person of the defendant. This must be accomplished to have *in personam* in jurisdiction.

2. Constructive service, where the individual has been served by publication, which is merely a notice of pending in *rem* proceeding.

3. Marital status is considered a thing (*rem*), so constructive service may be made in a divorce or dissolution case to determine the right to divorce or dissolution (of the marital status), but other matters cannot be disposed of unless there is personal service.

Domicile: Domicile can be of the following types:

1. Marital domicile, which is the place where the husband and wife established a home in which they live as husband and wife and where the marriage contract is being performed. Since in some states this element of domiciliary may be relevant as it relates to the question of jurisdiction at the time of a separation between the parties, you should consult your state statutes for resolution.

2. Domicile of origin is where the person was born or lived with his parents, and

3. It can be where the person chose to live.

Domicile itself has two necessary elements: (1) To establish domicile of the plaintiff sufficient to give a court jurisdiction of a divorce where the defendant resides in another state, the plaintiff must be physically present in the state and must (2) have the subjective intent to remain in said state for an indefinite period of time.

Additionally, all states have a further domiciliary requirement for the plaintiff, that is three months, six months, six weeks, one year, and so forth, immediately prior to the filing of the complaint or petition.

Where a husband and wife are domiciled in one state and the respondent is personally served, a divorce granted by that state is given full force and effect everywhere.

Divisible divorce: The doctrine of divisible divorce allows a valid *ex parte* divorce to be granted in one state and property rights to be settled by a court in another state.

EXAMPLE

A wife secured a divorce in Nevada and remains there. There is no property owned jointly by the parties in Nevada. The husband lives in Arizona, where there is property. Wife cannot sue for support and alimony or for the division of the property in Arizona. Nevada can grant the divorce, but the State of Arizona would have to order support and alimony payments and divide the property, since these require *in personam* jurisdiction. This is called a divisible divorce.

B. Procedure

Documents to be filed in an uncontested divorce: In most states a divorce proceeding is started by a petition for dissolution of marriage or complaint in divorce. If a response document is not filed by the respondent within the statutory period, for example, thirty days in California, the divorce decree is automatic, after the filing of the Interlocutory Decree and normal confidential and financial declaration papers. (Of course, these procedures vary from state to state.)

In California, for example, there is now the summary judgment type of proceeding, which requires the following qualifications, but serves as an uncontested divorce proceeding. See Figure 18.3 for this petition as adapted from the form available at www.courtinfo.ca.gov/forms/fillable/fl800.pdf.

Figure 18.3
Petition for Divorce or Legal Separation

Attorney or Party without Attorney (Name, State Bar number, and address):

_____

_____

SUPERIOR COURT OF CALIFORNIA, COUNTY OF _____
MARRIAGE OF
      Husband: _____
      Wife: _____
JOINT PETITION FOR SUMMARY DISSOLUTION OF MARRIAGE
We petition for a summary dissolution of marriage and declare that all the following conditions exist on the date this petition is filed with the court:
1. We have read and understand the *Summary Dissolution Information* booklet.
2. We were married on: (date). **(A summary dissolution of your marriage will not be granted if you file this petition more than five years after the date of your marriage.)**

Figure 18.3 *(continued)*

3. One of us has lived in California for at least six months and in the county of filing for at least the three months preceding the date of filing.

4. There are no minor children who were born of our relationship before or during our marriage or adopted by us during our marriage. The wife, to her knowledge, is not pregnant.

5. Neither of us has an interest in any real property anywhere. **(You may have a lease for a residence in which one of you lives. It must terminate within a year from the date of filing this petition. The lease must not include an option to purchase.)**

6. Except for obligations with respect to automobiles, on obligations incurred by either or both of us during our marriage, we owe no more than $6,000.

7. The total fair market value of community property assets, not including what we owe on those assets and not including automobiles, is less than $36,000.

8. Neither of us has separate property assets, not including what we owe on those assets and not including automobiles, in excess of $36,000.

9. We each have filled out and given the other an *Income and Expense Declaration*

10. We each have filled out and given the other copies of the worksheets on pages 8, 10, and 12 of the *Summary Dissolution Information* booklet (form FL-810) used in determining the value and division of our property. We have told each other in writing about any investment, business, or other income-producing opportunities that came up after we were separated based on investments made or work done during the marriage and before our separation. This meets the requirements of preliminary declaration of disclosure.

11. (Check whichever statement is true)
    a. We have no community assets or liabilities
    b. We signed an agreement listing and dividing all our community assets and liabilities and have signed all the papers necessary to carry out our agreement. A copy of our agreement is attached to this petition.

12. Irreconcilable differences have caused the irremediable breakdown of our marriage, and each of us wishes to have the court dissolve our marriage without our appearing before a judge.

13. The wife desires to have her former name restored. Her former name is: _____. The husband desires to have his former name restored. His former name is: _____.

14. Upon entry of judgment of summary dissolution of marriage, we each give up our rights to appeal and to move for a new trial.

15. **Each of us forever gives up any right to spousal support from the other.**

16. We agree that this matter may be determined by a commission sitting as a temporary judge.

17. Mailing address of husband:

Figure 18.3 *(continued)*

18. Mailing address of wife:
19. Number of pages attached:

I declare under penalty of perjury under the laws of the State of California that the foregoing and all attached documents are true and correct.

Date:
Signature of Husband:

_____

    Date:
    Signature of Wife:

_____

NOTICES:
Your divorce will not be final until husband or wife files a *Request for Judgment, Judgment of Dissolution of Marriage, and Notice of Entry of Judgment* **(form FL-820) and receives a stamped copy back from the court. Either husband or wife can file form FL-820 with the court six months after you file this petition. Until husband or wife files form FL-820, either one of you can stop the divorce by filing a** *Notice of Revocation of Petition for Summary Dissolution* **(form FL-830)**

Dissolution may automatically cancel the rights of a spouse under the other spouse's will, trust, retirement plan, power of attorney, pay-on-death bank account, transfer-on-death vehicle registration, survivorship rights to any property owned in joint tenancy, and any other similar thing. It does not automatically cancel the rights of a spouse as beneficiary of the other spouse's life insurance policy. You should review these matters, as well as any credit card accounts, other credit accounts, insurance policies, and credit reports to determine whether they should be changed or whether you should take any other actions. However, some changes may require the agreement of your spouse or a court order.

In other jurisdictions, the case can be set for hearing immediately after the time for filing an answer has passed.

Documents to be filed in a contested divorce: The following preparation must be made when filing for a contested divorce:

1. Prepare summons (marriage), the reverse side of which (in some states) tells you what other documents should be prepared to accompany it for filing with the court. These additional documents may vary from state to state, so check your state divorce statute or code. Often a Case Information Statement specific to the divorce proceeding must be filed. See Figure 18.4 for a CIS from New Jersey.

Figure 18.4

Case Information Statement for Divorce Proceedings

[Appendix V]

FAMILY PART CASE INFORMATION STATEMENT

Attorney(s):
Office Address
Tel. No./Fax No.
Attorney(s) for:

v.	Plaintiff, Defendant.

SUPERIOR COURT OF NEW JERSEY
CHANCERY DIVISION, FAMILY PART
COUNTY

DOCKET NO.
CASE INFORMATION STATEMENT
OF _____

NOTICE: This statement must be fully completed, filed and served, with all required attachments, in accordance with Court Rule 5:5-2 based upon the information available. In those cases where the Case Information Statement is required, it shall be filed within 20 days after the filing of the Answer or Appearance. Failure to file a Case Information Statement may result in the dismissal of a party's pleadings.

PART A - CASE INFORMATION:

Date of Statement_____
Date of Divorce (post-Judgment matters)_____
Date(s) of Prior Statement(s)_____
_____
Your Birthdate_____
Birthdate of Other Party_____
Date of Marriage_____
Date of Separation_____
Date of Complaint_____

ISSUES IN DISPUTE:

Cause of Action_____
Custody_____
Parenting Time_____
Alimony_____
Child Support_____
Equitable Distribution_____
Counsel Fees_____
Other issues [be specific]_____
_____

Does an agreement exist between parties relative to any issue?   [ ] Yes   [ ] No.   If Yes, ATTACH a copy (if written) or a summary (if oral).

1. Name and Addresses of Parties:

Your Name _____
Street Address _____ City_____ State/ZIP_____
Other Party's Name _____
Street Address _____ City_____ State/ZIP_____

2. Name, Address, Birthdate and Person with whom children reside:

a. Child(ren) from This Relationship

Child's Full Name	Address	Birthdate	Person's Name
_____	_____	_____	_____
_____	_____	_____	_____
_____	_____	_____	_____

b. Child(ren) from Other Relationships

Child's Full Name	Address	Birthdate	Person's Name
_____	_____	_____	_____
_____	_____	_____	_____
_____	_____	_____	_____

Figure 18.4 (*continued*)

PART B - MISCELLANEOUS INFORMATION:
1. Information about Employment (Provide Name & Address of Business, if Self-employed)
Name of Employer/Business _____ Address _____

_____

Name of Employer/Business _____ Address _____

_____

2. Do you have Insurance obtained through Employment/Business? [ ] Yes [ ] No. Type of Insurance:
Medical [ ]Yes [ ]No; Dental [ ]Yes [ ]No; Prescription Drug [ ]Yes [ ]No; Life [ ]Yes [ ]No; Disability [ ]Yes [ ]No
Other (explain) _____
Is Insurance available through Employment/Business? [ ] Yes [ ] No Explain:_____

_____

3. ATTACH Affidavit of Insurance Coverage as required by Court Rule *5:4-2* (f) (See Part G)

4. Additional Identification:
Confidential Litigant Information Sheet: Filed [ ]Yes [ ] No

5. ATTACH a list of all prior/pending family actions involving support, custody or Domestic Violence, with the Docket
Number, County, State and the disposition reached. Attach copies of all existing Orders in effect.

PART C. - INCOME INFORMATION: Complete this section for self and (if known) for spouse.
1. LAST YEAR'S INCOME

	Yours	Joint	Spouse or Former Spouse
1. Gross earned income last calendar (year)	$_____	$_____	$_____
2. Unearned income (same year)	$_____	$_____	$_____
3. Total Income Taxes paid on income (Fed., State, F.I.C.A., and S.U.I.). If Joint Return, use middle column.	$_____	$_____	$_____
4. Net income (1 + 2-3)	$_____	$_____	$_____

ATTACH to this form a corporate benefits statement as well as a statement of all fringe benefits of employment. (See Part G)

ATTACH a full and complete copy of last year's Federal and State Income Tax Returns. ATTACH W-2 statements, 1099's,
Schedule C's, etc., to show total income plus a copy of the most recently filed Tax Returns. (See Part G)
Check if attached: Federal Tax Return [ ]   State Tax Return [ ]   W-2 [ ] Other [ ]

2. PRESENT EARNED INCOME AND EXPENSES

	Yours	Other Party (if known)
1. Average gross weekly income (based on last 3 pay periods – ATTACH pay stubs) Commissions and bonuses, etc., are: [ ] included [ ] not included* [ ] not paid to you.	$_____	$_____

*ATTACH details of basis thereof, including, but not limited to, percentage overrides, timing of payments, etc.
  ATTACH copies of last three statements of such bonuses, commissions, etc.

	Yours	Other Party
2. Deductions per week (check all types of withholdings): [ ] Federal [ ] State [ ] F.I.C.A. [ ] S.U.I. [ ] Other	$_____	$_____
3. Net average weekly income (1 - 2)	$_____	$_____

3. YOUR CURRENT YEAR-TO-DATE EARNED INCOME
Provide Dates: From _____ To _____
                                        Number of Weeks_____
1. GROSS EARNED INCOME: $
2. TAX DEDUCTIONS: (Number of Dependents:)

Figure 18.4 (*continued*)

a. Federal Income Taxes   a. $_____
b. N.J. Income Taxes   b. $_____
c. Other State Income Taxes   c. $_____
d. FICA   d. $_____
e. Medicare   e. $_____
f. S.U.I. / S.D.I.   f. $_____
g. Estimated tax payments in excess of withholding   g. $_____
h.   h. $_____
i.   i. $_____
           TOTAL $_____

3. GROSS INCOME NET OF TAXES $ $_____

4. OTHER DEDUCTIONS   If mandatory, check box
   a. Hospitalization/Medical Insurance   a. $_____ [ ]
   b. Life Insurance   b. $_____ [ ]
   c. Union Dues   c. $_____ [ ]
   d. 401(k) Plans   d. $_____ [ ]
   e. Pension/Retirement Plans   e. $_____ [ ]
   f. Other Plans—specify   f. $_____ [ ]
   g. Charity   g. $_____ [ ]
   h. Wage Execution   h. $_____ [ ]
   i. Medical Reimbursement (flex fund)   i. $_____ [ ]
   j. Other: j. $_____ [ ]
           TOTAL $_____

5. NET YEAR-TO-DATE EARNED INCOME: $_____

NET AVERAGE EARNED INCOME PER MONTH: $_____

NET AVERAGE EARNED INCOME PER WEEK $_____

4. <u>YOUR YEAR-TO-DATE GROSS UNEARNED INCOME FROM ALL SOURCES</u>
(including, but not limited to, income from unemployment, disability and/or social
security payments, interest, dividends, rental income and any other miscellaneous
unearned income)

Source	How often paid	Year to date amount
_____	_____	$_____
_____	_____	$_____
_____	_____	$_____
_____	_____	$_____
_____	_____	$_____
_____	_____	$_____
_____	_____	$_____
_____	_____	$_____
_____	_____	$_____

TOTAL GROSS UNEARNED INCOME YEAR TO DATE $_____

Figure 18.4 (*continued*)

5. <u>ADDITIONAL INFORMATION</u>:

1.   How often are you paid? _____

2.   What is your annual salary? $ _____

3.   Have you received any raises in the current year? [ ]Yes [ ]No. If yes, provide the date and the gross/net amount.
_____

4.   Do you receive bonuses, commissions, or other compensation, including distributions, taxable or non-taxable, in addition to your regular salary? [ ]Yes [ ]No. If yes, explain:_____
_____

5.   Did you receive a bonuses, commissions, or other compensation, including distributions, taxable or non-taxable, in addition to your regular salary during the current or immediate past calendar year? [ ] Yes [ ] No If yes, explain and state the date(s) of receipt and set forth the gross and net amounts received: _____
_____

6.   Do you receive cash or distributions not otherwise listed? [ ] Yes [ ] No If yes, explain. _____
_____

7.   Have you received income from overtime work during either the current or immediate past calendar year? [ ]Yes [ ]No If yes, explain. _____

8.   Have you been awarded or granted stock options, restricted stock or any other non-cash compensation or entitlement during the current or immediate past calendar year? [ ]Yes [ ]No If yes, explain. _____
_____

9.   Have you received any other supplemental compensation during either the current or immediate past calendar year? [ ]Yes [ ]No. If yes, state the date(s) of receipt and set forth the gross and net amounts received. Also describe the nature of any supplemental compensation received._____
_____

10. Have you received income from unemployment, disability and/or social security during either the current or immediate past calendar year? [ ]Yes [ ]No. If yes, state the date(s) of receipt and set forth the gross and net amounts received._____

11.   List the names of the dependents you claim:_____

12. Are you paying or receiving any alimony? [ ]Yes [ ]No. If yes, how much and to whom paid or from whom received?   _____

13. Are you paying or receiving any child support? [ ]Yes [ ]No. If yes, list names of the children, the amount paid or received for each child and to whom paid or from whom received. _____
_____

14. Is there a wage execution in connection with support? [ ]Yes [ ]No If yes explain._____
_____

15. Has a dependent child of yours received income from social security, SSI or other government program during either the current or immediate past calendar year? [ ]Yes [ ]No. If yes, explain the basis and state the date(s) of receipt and set forth the gross and net amounts received _____
_____

16. Explanation of Income or Other Information:
_____
_____
_____
_____
_____
_____
_____
_____

Figure 18.4 (*continued*)

PART D - MONTHLY EXPENSES (computed at 4.3 wks/mo.)
Joint Marital Life Style should reflect standard of living established during marriage. Current expenses should reflect the current life style. Do not repeat those income deductions listed in Part C – 3.

	Joint Marital Life Style Family, including _____ children	Current Life Style Yours and _____ children

SCHEDULE A: SHELTER

If Tenant:

	Joint Marital Life Style	Current Life Style
Rent	$_____	$_____
Heat (if not furnished)	$_____	$_____
Electric & Gas (if not furnished)	$_____	$_____
Renter's Insurance	$_____	$_____
Parking (at Apartment)	$_____	$_____
Other charges (Itemize)	$_____	$_____

If Homeowner:

	Joint Marital Life Style	Current Life Style
Mortgage	$_____	$_____
Real Estate Taxes (if not included w/mortgage payment)	$_____	$_____
Homeowners Ins (if not included w/mortgage payment)	$_____	$_____
Other Mortgages or Home Equity Loans	$_____	$_____
Heat (unless Electric or Gas)	$_____	$_____
Electric & Gas	$_____	$_____
Water & Sewer	$_____	$_____
Garbage Removal	$_____	$_____
Snow Removal	$_____	$_____
Lawn Care	$_____	$_____
Maintenance	$_____	$_____
Repairs	$_____	$_____
Other Charges (Itemize)	$_____	$_____

Tenant or Homeowner:

	Joint Marital Life Style	Current Life Style
Telephone	$_____	$_____
Mobile/Cellular Telephone	$_____	$_____
Service Contracts on Equipment	$_____	$_____
Cable TV	$_____	$_____
Plumber/Electrician	$_____	$_____
Equipment & Furnishings	$_____	$_____
Internet Charges	$_____	$_____
Other (itemize)	$_____	$_____
TOTAL	$_____	$_____

SCHEDULE B: TRANSPORTATION

	Joint Marital Life Style	Current Life Style
Auto Payment	$_____	$_____
Auto Insurance (number of vehicles:)	$_____	$_____
Registration, License	$_____	$_____
Maintenance	$_____	$_____
Fuel and Oil	$_____	$_____
Commuting Expenses	$_____	$_____
Other Charges (Itemize)	$_____	$_____
TOTAL	$_____	$_____

Figure 18.4 (*continued*)

SCHEDULE C: PERSONAL..	Joint Marital Life Style Family, including _____children	Current Life Style Yours and _____ children
Food at Home & household supplies............................	$_____	$_____
Prescription Drugs..	$_____	$_____
Non-prescription drugs, cosmetics, toiletries & sundries......	$_____	$_____
School Lunch...	$_____	$_____
Restaurants...	$_____	$_____
Clothing..	$_____	$_____
Dry Cleaning, Commercial Laundry............................	$_____	$_____
Hair Care...	$_____	$_____
Domestic Help...	$_____	$_____
Medical (exclusive of psychiatric)*...........................	$_____	$_____
Eye Care*..	$_____	$_____
Psychiatric/psychological/counseling*.........................	$_____	$_____
Dental (exclusive of Orthodontic)*............................	$_____	$_____
Orthodontic*...	$_____	$_____
Medical Insurance (hospital, etc.)*............................	$_____	$_____
Club Dues and Memberships.....................................	$_____	$_____
Sports and Hobbies...	$_____	$_____
Camps...	$_____	$_____
Vacations...	$_____	$_____
Children's Private School Costs................................	$_____	$_____
Parent's Educational Costs......................................	$_____	$_____
Children's Lessons (dancing, music, sports, etc.)..............	$_____	$_____
Baby-sitting..	$_____	$_____
Day-Care Expenses...	$_____	$_____
Entertainment..	$_____	$_____
Alcohol and Tobacco...	$_____	$_____
Newspapers and Periodicals.....................................	$_____	$_____
Gifts...	$_____	$_____
Contributions..	$_____	$_____
Payments to Non-Child Dependents............................	$_____	$_____
Prior Existing Support Obligations this family/other families (specify)...	$_____	$_____
Tax Reserve (not listed elsewhere).............................	$_____	$_____
Life Insurance...	$_____	$_____
Savings/Investment...	$_____	$_____
Debt Service (from page 7) (not listed elsewhere).............	$_____	$_____
Parenting Time Expenses..	$_____	$_____
Professional Expenses (other than this proceeding)...........	$_____	$_____
Other (specify)..	$_____	$_____

*unreimbursed only..

TOTAL $_____ $_____

Please Note: If you are paying expenses for a spouse and/or children not reflected in this budget, attach a schedule of such payments.

Schedule A: Shelter...	$_____	$_____
Schedule B: Transportation......................................	$_____	$_____
Schedule C: Personal...	$_____	$_____
Grand Totals...	$_____	$_____

Figure 18.4 (*continued*)

PART E - BALANCE SHEET OF ALL FAMILY ASSETS AND LIABILITIES
STATEMENT OF ASSETS

Description	Title to Property (H, W, J)	Date of purchase/acquisition. If claim that asset is exempt, state reason and value of what is claimed to be exempt	Value $ Put * after exempt	Date of Evaluation Mo./Day/ Yr.
1. Real Property				
2. Bank Accounts, CD's				
3. Vehicles				
4. Tangible Personal Property				
5. Stocks and Bonds				
6. Pension, Profit Sharing, Retirement Plan(s) 40l(k)s, etc. [list each employer]				
7. IRAs				
8. Businesses, Partnerships, Professional Practices				
9. Life Insurance (cash surrender value)				
10. Loans Receivable				
11. Other (specify)				

TOTAL GROSS ASSETS: $_____

TOTAL SUBJECT TO EQUITABLE DISTRIBUTION: $_____

TOTAL NOT SUBJECT TO EQUITABLE DISTRIBUTION: $_____

Figure 18.4 (*continued*)

STATEMENT OF LIABILITIES

Description	Name of Responsible Party (H, W, J)	If you contend liability should not be considered in equitable distribution, state reason	Monthly Payment	Total Owed	Date
1. Real Estate Mortgages					
_____	___	_____	___	___	___
_____	___	_____	___	___	___
_____	___	_____	___	___	___
2. Other Long Term Debts					
_____	___	_____	___	___	___
_____	___	_____	___	___	___
_____	___	_____	___	___	___
3. Revolving Charges					
_____	___	_____	___	___	___
_____	___	_____	___	___	___
_____	___	_____	___	___	___
_____	___	_____	___	___	___
_____	___	_____	___	___	___
_____	___	_____	___	___	___
_____	___	_____	___	___	___
_____	___	_____	___	___	___
_____	___	_____	___	___	___
4. Other Short Term Debts					
_____	___	_____	___	___	___
_____	___	_____	___	___	___
_____	___	_____	___	___	___
5. Contingent Liabilities					
_____	___	_____	___	___	___
_____	___	_____	___	___	___

TOTAL GROSS LIABILITIES: $_____
(excluding contingent liabilities)

NET WORTH: $_____
(subject to equitable distribution)

Figure 18.4 (*continued*)

PART F - STATEMENT OF SPECIAL PROBLEMS

Provide a Brief Narrative Statement of Any Special Problems Involving This Case: As example, state if the matter involves complex valuation problems (such as for a closely held business) or special medical problems of any family member etc.

I certify that the foregoing information contained herein is true. I am aware that if any of the foregoing information contained

therein is willfully false, I am subject to punishment.

DATED: _____   SIGNED: _____

PART G - REQUIRED ATTACHMENTS

CHECK IF YOU HAVE ATTACHED THE FOLLOWING REQUIRED DOCUMENTS

1. A full and complete copy of your last federal and state income tax returns
   with all schedules and attachments. (Part C-1)   _____

2. Your last calendar year's W-2 statements, 1099's, K-1 statements.   _____

3. Your three most recent pay stubs.   _____

4. Bonus information including, but not limited to, percentage overrides, timing of payments, etc.;
   the last three statements of such bonuses, commissions, etc. (Part C)   _____

5. Your most recent corporate benefit statement or a summary thereof showing the nature, amount
   and status of retirement plans, savings plans, income deferral plans, insurance benefits, etc. (Part C)   _____

6. Affidavit of Insurance Coverage as required by Court Rule 5:4-2(f) (Part B-3)   _____

7. List of all prior/pending family actions involving support, custody or Domestic Violence, with the
   Docket Number, County, State and the disposition reached. Attach copies of all existing Orders in
   effect. (Part B-5)   _____

8. Attach details of each wage execution (Part C-5)

9. Schedule of payments made for a spouse and/or children not reflected in Part D.   _____

10. Any agreements between the parties.   _____

11. An Appendix IX Child Support Guideline Worksheet, as applicable, based upon available information.   _____

The summons must be personally served on the defendant if the defendant can be located. The plaintiff must have resided in the state where the divorce is filed for the length of time prescribed by state statutes.

2. Then prepare the petition for divorce or complaint in divorce. If you use a printed form, be sure you choose the appropriate one.

3. Look to the state statutes and local court rules to determine the grounds for divorce and if you need to attach to the petition for divorce any exhibits, such as a property settlement agreement, inventory of household goods and furnishings, financial statements, and so forth.

4. If there is a danger of physical harm to your client by the spouse, the attorney may want you to prepare a temporary restraining order to be signed by the court.

5. A confidential conciliation statement may not be applicable in your state. The same caution should be used in completing this document as is outlined in number 3 above.

6. The financial declaration is called the financial statement in some states. It is also a vital document, as it advises the court of the financial condition of both parties, thereby aiding the court in making a ruling as to who pays what, and when. Be sure it is as complete and correct and as current as possible.

   NOTE: Your attorney and the client must sign this document. In some states the financial statement must be made under oath but need not be signed by the attorney.

7. In preparing notices and orders to show cause and other various notices— motions and orders to show cause regarding contempt, modification, joinder of parties, and so forth—you should work closely with your attorney and check your local rules applicable regarding service, and so on.

These documents should be meticulously and carefully prepared, since they deal with the needs of the petitioner relating to child support, alimony, and the ability of the respondent to pay same, as well as the disposition or hypothecating of real and personal property of the community property in California and other community-property states.

1. To prepare the request or declaration regarding default (marriage), do the following:

   a. Check to determine if a current financial declaration is of record; if not, attach a carbon copy to your request for default.

   b. A copy of this request for declaration must be mailed to the last known address of the respondent. You *cannot show* "unknown" as it relates to the address of the respondent.

    c. In some states you cannot get a default judgment for the petitioner, but the case can be set for trial and tried *ex parte.*

2. Your checklist preparing your attorney for trial ends in preparing your attorney for the hearing (or trial) in a dissolution proceeding; therefore, be sure to include the following:

    a. The required number of copies of the interlocutory judgment of dissolution (regarding marriage), which you had prepared beforehand;

    b. Copies of any property settlement agreement, as well as the original for filing with the court, if necessary; and

    c. Notice of entry of judgment regarding marriage.

> NOTE: Naturally, if it is a full-blown trial, then all documents normally prepared and included for a trial would be applicable here.

Alimony and Child Support

Alimony and child support are usually decided in a divorce (dissolution of marriage) case.

The following are basic issues in a divorce case:

1. Jurisdiction of court (based on the residence of plaintiff)

2. Required grounds for divorce

3. Custody of minor children, if any

4. Division of property by agreement of the parties or by order of court

> NOTE: In dealing with a large divorce settlement, perhaps you might want to consider "bifurcating" the property settlement and/or division of property from the actual divorce proceeding because of the possible tax ramifications. It is suggested that you discuss this possibility with your attorney-employer.

5. Child support if there are minor or disabled children

6. Spousal support (If this is determined to be income to the wife and therefore taxable to the wife, husband can deduct this spousal support. Check the Internal Revenue Code and the Code of the Federal Regulations on the subject.)

    Further note: In some states, a trial court has in its jurisdiction whether to terminate jurisdiction over spousal support, unless the record clearly shows that the wife cannot take care of herself once the spousal support is terminated.

To determine whether or not the wife can take care of herself and appraise the assets of the husband, if he is the respondent, the paralegal should gather the kind of evidence to be submitted to the court that would indicate that the wife can or cannot take care of herself at the time of the termination of the spousal support.

This should include a financial declaration as to both parties, supporting schedules, earning capacity of each party, separate property of each party, historical background as to education and work experience of the wife, and so forth.

In connection with this, your attorney may consider discovery at this point, such as depositions, interrogatories, and so forth, to determine the separate assets and earning capacity of each party. This is to support the plaintiff's ability to obtain employment, once the divorce is final.

7. Attorneys' fees and costs

8. In some states, jointly owned property that is held as "tenants by the entireties" by husband and wife during the marriage remains jointly owned, but the divorced partners are tenants in common instead of tenants by the entireties from the moment the divorce or dissolution decree is entered.

> NOTE: In some of those states, a spouse may prove a "special equity" in the jointly owned property by proving that he or she paid for the property from funds unconnected with the marriage (as by inheritance or part of a former divorce settlement). That spouse must also prove that no gift to the other spouse was intended when the property was put in both names.

9. In some states the jointly owned property may be ordered partitioned by the court if grounds for partition were alleged in the petition or complaint for divorce and that relief was asked for in the prayer contained in the petition or complaint.

The general rule in most states is that a husband is liable for the support of the wife. This duty is based upon and is an integral part of the marriage contract.

The husband's liability as to support is based upon the wife being his agent with express or implied authority to pay, as a matter of law, for the necessities of life, that is, food, clothing, education, support and maintenance for the children of the parties, medical expenses, and the like. To this end, the wife has the power to pledge the husband's credit to produce these necessities—as long as they are still married, whether physically together or not.

Once a divorce or separate maintenance decree is made by a court, obtaining money ordered by the court for the support and maintenance of the children and for alimony is another matter. There is a definite procedure for exercising these rights and fulfilling the decree of the court; these step-by-step procedures can be found under the domestic relations or family law section of your state civil code or code of procedure.

For example, in California once there has been a hearing on a petition for dissolution of a marriage, the court issues its orders to the respondent (if by default, he does not have to be present; but the petitioner is required to forward him a copy of all pleadings and minute orders of the court), requiring him to do or not to do certain things, including but not limited to (1) paying a specified sum of money to the petitioner for the support and maintenance of the children of the parties, if any; (2) paying alimony (if not waived); (3) paying attorney's fees; (4) making provision for visitation rights; (5) making provision for the disposition of any property: and (6) abiding by any restraining order pertinent thereto.

Hence, you have the following orders that may be issued by the court:

1. Order for support and maintenance,

2. Order for child custody,

3. Order regarding visitation rights of the parties,

4. Order for attorney's fees and costs, and

5. Injunctive or restraining orders.

Enforcing Support Orders

California procedure is set forth here by way of example only.

There are basically two methods that may be used to proceed to enforce these orders of the court: (1) civil and (2) criminal. A step-by-step procedure follows.

A. Civil Method

1. This could be a contempt order or modification order in which a declaration is made as to the amount of the arrearage, the amount ordered to be paid and when, and the balance due. If it is a modification, then a statement should be included setting forth a change in circumstances, requiring a reduction in payments.

2. This document is filed with the court and a failure of compliance on the part of the respondent (or defendant) results in a money judgment being entered upon which is obtained a writ of execution.

3. This writ is delivered to the marshal to levy on the property of the respondent (or defendant), that is, bank account, automobile, salary, and the like.

4. The proceeds are physically taken from the bank, or the marshal will take the car, and so forth, in satisfaction of the money judgment for back support payments.

This method may be followed for attorney's fees, alimony payments, and child support.

B. Criminal Method

This procedure is used when the party is in contempt of a court order for which he can be imprisoned. But there must be a hearing to determine his violation and disobedience of a lawful court order. Since it is a quasi-criminal proceeding, he has to be personally served and physically present at the hearing, though he need not take the stand to testify. He can remain silent, but the initiating party must prove beyond a reasonable doubt that:

1. He had knowledge of the order, either by being in court on the day it was decreed, or had been personally served with a true copy thereof;

2. He has the ability to comply with the order; and

3. He willfully disobeyed the court's order at the time he had the ability to pay.

Custody

Custody is a problematic area in family law practice. It is ongoing and changeable. You will need to keep up with your client's (and your client's dependant children's) changing needs in order to best serve them. The court retains jurisdiction over the children until they reach the age of majority. Either parent can file a complaint for modification if necessary. Again, FindLaw.com provides links to all the state forms relating to child custody at http://family.findlaw.com/child-custody/custody-forms/state-child-custody-forms.html. See Figure 18.5 for an example of Complaint for Child Custody/Visitation and Support from North Carolina.

Types of Custody

1. *Joint custody:* Both parents share in making the decisions concerning the child(ren). This is the most common form of custody, as the courts tend to believe in parental involvement from both the mother and father.

   a. As a practical consequence of the divorce, the child will have to maintain a primary residence with only one parent. That parent has "residential custody." The other parent has visitation rights. The child(ren) will spend a certain amount of time (generally some weekends and vacation time) with the nonresidential parent. In some circumstances the parents can share residential custody (if they live very close to each other and they are cooperative).

Figure 18.5
Complaint for Child Custody/Visitation and Support (NC)

STATE OF NORTH CAROLINA

COUNTY OF MECKLENBURG

IN THE GENERAL COURT OF JUSTICE
DISTRICT COURT DIVISION
_____-CVD-_____ (   )

_____,)
)
               Plaintiff,   )
)
               v.   )
)
_____,)
)
               Defendant.   )

COMPLAINT FOR CHILD CUSTODY
OR VISITATION AND/OR
CHILD SUPPORT

Plaintiff, complaining of defendant, alleges and says:

PARTIES, JURISDICTION AND VENUE

1.   Plaintiff is a citizen and resident of _____.
                                                    (County and State)

2.   Plaintiff's address is_____.

3.   Plaintiff's Social Security Number is_____.

4.   Defendant is a citizen and resident of _____.
                                                    (County and State)

5.   Defendant's address is_____.

6.   Defendant's Social Security Number is_____.

7.   Defendant's relationship to child:_____.
                                              (Mother, Father, etc.)

8.   The name(s), age(s) and birth date(s) of the child or children at issue in this case is/are as follows:

_____
_____
_____

9.   Explain your standing to bring this civil action (e.g., I am the mother/father/other relative of the child/children):

_____
_____
_____

Figure 18.5 (*continued*)

10.   That during the past five years (or since birth if the child is less than five years old), the (child) (children) have lived with:

Name of child _____, birthdate _____, birthplace _____.

PERIOD	**ADDRESS**	**PERSON LIVED WITH**	**PRESENT ADDRESS**
____ to present	_____	_____	_____
____ to _____	_____	_____	_____
____ to _____	_____	_____	_____

Name of child_____, birthdate_____, birthplace_____.

PERIOD	**ADDRESS**	**PERSON LIVED WITH**	**PRESENT ADDRESS**
____ to _____	_____	_____	_____
____ to _____	_____	_____	_____
____ to _____	_____	_____	_____

(If there are more than two children, insert additional sheets.)

11.   That I (have) (have not) participated as a (party) (witness) (other capacity) in litigation concerning the custody of the minor child in (this) (another) State, viz.
_____ on _____, ___.
(if answer is affirmative, give details, stating capacity, name and address of court.)
_____
_____
_____
_____

12.   That I (have) (do not have) information of any custody proceeding concerning a child mentioned above pending in a Court of this or any other State.
(If answer is affirmative, give details) _____
_____
_____

13.   That I (know) (do not know) of a person who has physical custody of the child viz.
_____, or

(Name)	(Address)

Figure 18.5 (*continued*)

claims to have custody or visitation rights with respect to the child, viz.:

_____

(Name)   (Address)

14.   The District Court of Mecklenburg County has personal jurisdiction over the parties and subject matter jurisdiction (including jurisdiction under the Uniform Child Custody Jurisdiction Act) to decide the claim(s) and render a custody determination in this action.

15.   Venue of this action is pro in Mecklenburg County, North Carolina.

CUSTODY OR VISITATION CLAIM

16.   Plaintiff is a fit and proper person to have primary custody/visitation of the aforesaid minor child/children and an award of custody/visitation to her/him would best promote the interests and welfare of the aforesaid minor child/children.

CHILD SUPPORT CLAIMS

17.   The aforesaid minor child/children is/are in need of support and maintenance for his/her/their health, education and welfare.

18.   Defendant is an able-bodied man/woman regularly and gainfully employed, or capable of gainful employment, and is capable of providing support for the aforesaid minor child/children.

19.   Plaintiff is entitled to have and recover child support from and of the defendant.

20.   Attached hereto as Exhibit B, and incorporated by reference as if fully set forth herein, is Plaintiff's Affidavit of Financial Standing setting forth his/her needs and the needs of the child/children as required by the Local Rules of Court.

PRAYER FOR RELIEF

WHEREFORE, plaintiff prays the Court for relief as follows:

1.   _____ That custody/visitation of the minor child/children be awarded to plaintiff.

2.   _____ That defendant be ordered to pay reasonable child support.

3.   _____ That defendant be taxed with the costs of this action.

4.   _____ That plaintiff have and recover such other and further relief as the court may deem just and proper.

Figure 18.5 (*continued*)

This _____ day of _____, _____.

_____
(Signature of Plaintiff)

ADDRESS AND TELEPHONE NUMBER OF PLAINTIFF:

_____
_____
_____

Figure 18.5 (*continued*)

STATE OF NORTH CAROLINA)

)   <u>VERIFICATION</u>

COUNTY OF MECKLENBURG)

_____, being first duly sworn, deposes and says that he/she is the plaintiff in the foregoing action, that he/she has read the foregoing COMPLAINT and knows the contents thereof to be true of his/her own personal knowledge except for those matters and things alleged therein upon information and belief, and as to those matters and things, he/she believes same to be true.

_____

Sworn to and subscribed before me
this ____ day of _____, _____.

_____
      Notary Public

My Commission expires _____

b. *Legal custody* is the shared right to make the parental choices affecting the child(ren). This is an equal right.

2. *Sole custody:* All the decisions are made by one parent, who also has sole physical custody of the child(ren). The visitation rights of the other parent may be severely limited. This happens in situations where the other parent is unavailable or found unfit.

3. *Divided custody:* This is rare. The children of the marriage are split between the two parents. One child lives with one parent and another child with the other. There are provisions for reciprocal visitation rights.

4. *Non-parental custody:* If the court finds both parents unfit to care for the child(ren), it can grant custody to another family member or other appropriate person or agency.

Uniform Child Custody and Jurisdiction Act

The Uniform Child Custody and Jurisdiction Act was revised in order to provide a method of dealing with interstate visitation and custody cases. The act recognizes that: "As with child support, state borders have become one of the biggest obstacles to enforcement of custody and visitation orders. If either parent leaves the State where the custody determination was made, the other parent faces considerable difficulty in enforcing the visitation and custody provisions of the decree. Locating the child, making service of process, and preventing adverse modification in a new forum all present problems." The act states that its purposes are to:

> (1) Avoid jurisdictional competition and conflict with courts of other States in matters of child custody which have in the past resulted in the shifting of children from State to State with harmful effects on their well-being; (2) Promote cooperation with the courts of other States to the end that a custody decree is rendered in that State which can best decide the case in the interest of the child; (3) Discourage the use of the interstate system for continuing controversies over child custody; (4) Deter abductions of children; (5) Avoid re-litigation of custody decisions of other States in this State; and (6) Facilitate the enforcement of custody decrees of other States.

This act is not automatically reciprocal. Each state needs to incorporate the act's provisions into its statutes. Check your jurisdiction's family laws to determine whether the act has been enacted. If it has, it will be necessary to follow it and plead the necessary allegations in all child custody cases and in divorce proceedings that pray for determination of child custody. The full text of the act can be found at www.familylaw.org/uccja.htm. And links to each state's family law codes can be found at www.familylaw.org/familylawcode.htm.

Division of Marital Property
In Community-Property States

As indicated earlier, one of the greatest problems to be resolved in a family law matter is the division of the property accumulated during the marriage of the parties. The courts and legislators had the presence of mind to develop a means by which this could be accomplished on a more equitable basis with the least amount of trauma; hence the classification of property into personal and community in community-property states.

1. *Personal property:* This kind of property is normally that which consists of things temporary and movable, such as animals, furniture, jewelry, books, and cars; or stocks, bonds, patents, and copyrights. It can include cash on hand and separate checking and savings accounts, all of which were acquired, in this instance, prior to a marriage between the parties.

2. *Community property:* Under this classification, husband and wife form a kind of partnership and the property acquired by either during the marriage belongs to both. It is therefore necessary, when dealing with dissolution where there is community property, to consider the date of the acquisition of the property in order to fully determine the rights of the parties therein.

This community-property plan regulates property rights as between a husband and a wife in the United States and is based upon express legislation, and it is controlling in the following states: Arizona, California, Idaho, Louisiana, Nevada, New Mexico, Texas, and Washington. Oklahoma has an optional community-property plan.

In California, all property that is owned by married persons can be one of only three things:

1. Husband's separate property,

2. Wife's separate property, or

3. Community property.

Under this plan, the property acquired during the marriage as the result of the efforts of both husband and wife belongs to the community. This type of property may include any and all property, other than gifts, devises, or inheritance.

One of the problems in dividing the property in a dissolution of marriage proceeding is to be able to place the property into the proper category. This is done by tracing the source of the property.

For your state's marital property laws, FindLaw.com provides a list of links. See http://law.findlaw.com/state-laws/marital-property.

A. Sources of Community Property

What does community property include? Earnings and real property acquired during the marriage are the community property of both, while gifts received from third parties are the personal property of either the husband or wife.

Earnings include whatever benefits are appended to employment such as pensions, profit sharing plans, bonuses, stock options, and the like. If these other sources flow from the employment, they are community property.

1. *Pension plans:* Whatever the plan stipulates as to the rights of the husband thereunder is applicable to the interest of the wife in said plan.

   EXAMPLES

   Husband was to be in the plan for fifteen years to be eligible. The lump sum is $10,000 at maturity, or $200.00 per month. Wife's interest in the plan, as determined at the date of divorce, would be one half of $10,000 or one half of $200. If one spouse had a completely perfected right prior to marriage, then that property would be separate property of that spouse.

   Husband buys an automobile prior to marriage. He makes the down payment out of his separate property. He then gets married and thereafter makes the monthly payments out of his earnings. These payments would be community property. He would then own one half of the automobile and the wife would own one half. The amount of the down payment, being separate property, would be apportioned at the time of the divorce between the parties.

   An author is writing a book and it takes him six months to do so. He gets married upon completion of the manuscript. Thereafter, the book is published and he receives $10,000. His right to this money was a perfected right since no income was involved. This money would not be apportioned at a divorce hearing.

   By way of explanation, simply put: A perfected right says, "I do not have to do anything else to get the money. It is due me." The non-perfected right says, "I have to do something before I get the money." This right would be subjected to apportionment out of community property.

2. *Apportionment of insurance proceeds:* You have to prove the source of the money used to purchase the insurance policy. If paid by community funds, the proceeds from the policy will be in the same ratio as the proceeds used from community funds. So it would be apportioned.

   EXAMPLE

   Husband buys a $10,000 policy (before marriage) and (after marriage) pays $500 in premiums before he dies. This would be apportioned as to the amount of premiums paid. Look to the ratio of the premiums to determine the community interest.

If the husband uses separate property in community property to purchase this life insurance and names the wife as the beneficiary, then this is a gift to the wife and she is entitled to the whole thing. The children would not have an interest in the policy and would not be successful in attacking the policy.

If the marriage is terminated by divorce, a problem arises as to the insurance policy, which has a value only at the time of death. A mathematical formula as to the cash value is the determining factor, and it is then apportioned as to what is separate and what amount is community property.

3. *Gifts, bequests, devises, and inheritances:* All are separate property of the recipient, unless there is some agreement to the contrary between the parties. To prove a gift, there must be a showing of actual or constructive delivery of the gift of property.

"Constructive delivery" means the gift was never actually placed in the hands of the person, but rather was placed in a bank, or in trust in the donee's name (compare and distinguish a totten trust). This shows the intent to make a gift. It can be inferred.

"Actual delivery" is where the gift is physically handed to the person. The intent at the time of the delivery of the gift is determinative of whether or not it was a gift of separate property, either to the wife or husband. If it is not community property, it is the separate property of each. If no intent was shown as to distribution when given, they each have a one-half individual interest in the gift.

4. *Damages (money) from personal injury:* The general rule is that the cause of action is community property, but the funds received therefrom would be separate property. The present state of the law in California has lumped them together, so that the entire personal injury recovery is community property. It is suggested, therefore, that you check your local statutes in this regard.

Exceptions to the foregoing are that any personal injury recovery will be separate property in the following ways:

a. If at the time of the receipt of the money there is a final judgment of dissolution, or

b. If the parties are living separate and apart pursuant to a decree of legal separation or interlocutory judgment of dissolution.

If either of the foregoing exists, the proceeds are then the separate property of the recipient except that if the wife is the injured spouse, then you need only physical separation for her funds to be separate property. The community is entitled to reimbursement for any money paid out for expenses arising out of this accident. Even if the personal injury funds are community property, the wife would have management and control over her own personal injury property.

Formerly, the cause of action was common property, and since the husband had management and control of the community property, he could select the attorney and authorize the settlement. The wife could have management and control only after receipt of the funds.

That used to be the case. Today, the wife has management and control from the time of the accident.

5. *Credit acquisitions:* The general rule is that credit is property. The status of property acquired on credit is determined by the status of the credit involved. If the property is acquired on the basis of either spouse's separate credit, then that property is separate property.

If community funds were used to make the payments, even though the intent of the creditor was to look to the separate property of the husband, there is a "presumption in the law" that it is a community asset, though it may be considered a separate liability of the husband because of his management and control. If it is a worthwhile asset, the law will divide it between the parties; but if it is worthless or nil in value, the husband may have to pay.

6. *Rents, issues, and profits:* Coming from common property, these remain common property; and the rents, issues, and profits from separate property remain separate property, unless during the marriage there has been some service rendered by the spouse on a particular piece of separate property that may increase its value.

EXAMPLE

Husband owns a house before marriage. From the income he pays taxes and so forth. He takes over the management of the house (say, an apartment house), wherein he renders maintenance and painting services, and the like, thereby increasing the value of the separate property. If this occurs, you may have a community interest.

B. Change of Character Property

The character change of property is governed by the transmutation doctrine, which defines transmutation as any act taken by the parties that changes the character of property. This character change is not to be confused with change in form. (Check your local code to determine the applicability of this doctrine in your state.)

EXAMPLE

Say you have $100,000 in the bank. You take it out of the bank and buy an apartment building. This is merely an exchange of cash for real property. It is still considered separate property. In other words, money change in form does not change the character of the property. Examples of changes in character of property would be: (1) conversion of community property to separate property; and (2) separate property to community property by agreement.

These can be accomplished by way of an oral agreement. (Joint-tenancy property may be transferred only by means of a written agreement.) The oral agreement, however, will operate only as a change of status of property, not as a conveyance of the property. To create a joint tenancy, it *must be* in writing to fulfill the requirements of the four unities of (1) interest, (2) time, (3) title, and (4) possession.

Neither spouse can make a gift of community property to him or herself in an attempt to change the character of the community property to personal property.

C. How Do You Change the Character of Property?

Transmutation can be accomplished in three ways: (1) ratification, (2) waiver, and (3) estoppel.

EXAMPLES

Husband attempts to change the character of the property by making a third party the beneficiary of an insurance policy, using community property to pay the premiums. This is invalid, but the wife can ratify the act and make it legal by doing some overt, affirmative act or by orally agreeing to it.

The waiver approach is merely negative-type conduct or is passive ratification. Using the foregoing insurance policy situation, the wife does nothing about it. She neither agrees to the payment of the premiums nor does anything overt or affirmative to approve it. In other words, she has knowledge of what the husband did but does nothing, thereby waiving her right to object to the change in character of the community property

Estoppel is the detrimental reliance of one party on the acts of the spouse. Husband says to the wife, "I am thinking of purchasing a life insurance policy and naming a third person as the beneficiary." Wife says it is a good idea. Husband, then relying upon her agreement, buys the policy naming his mother as the beneficiary. The wife is estopped from taking any adverse action, since the husband based his action on her accord.

In Other States—Equitable Distribution

The division of marital property in states which do not have community-property laws usually allows one of the divorced parties to keep the property according to its record title unless the other party proves some special equity in the jointly owned property.

The division of the property will be determined under "equitable distribution" principles which attempt to make the allocation of assets *fair* rather than a simple

50/50 split. The court tries to determine what the actual financial situation of the parties will be after the divorce and then shifts assets to compensate each party in a way that is most appropriate. This is a very subjective determination and therefore, if this is the situation in your jurisdiction, it will be hard to advise your client with any sort of probability of outcome. The court considers the following in making equitable distribution:

1. The relative and potential earning power of the spouses

2. The value of the separate property of the spouses

3. By whose work/earnings was the property acquired?

4. The worth of the "homemaker"

5. Spending habits of the spouses (Did one waste or dissipate the assets in common?)

6. Duration of the marriage and the standard of living

7. Age and health of the spouses

8. Who will be responsible for providing for the housing, feeding, clothing, and educating of the children?

9. Fault of a spouse (Was there abuse or marital infidelity? The court has the power to "penalize" the offending spouse.)

Since a *tenancy by the entireties* in a special common law tenancy applies only to husband and wife, most state statutes provide that these tenants by the entireties become *tenants-in-common* of the jointly owned property after the decree in divorce or no-fault dissolution of marriage. There are presumptions of gift to a spouse to be reckoned with. There are special contributions of funds unconnected with the marriage to be considered.

The paralegal must be familiar with the case law in the state which has interpreted the no-fault dissolution of the marriage statute or the divorce code to determine what information should be obtained from the client before preparing a petition for dissolution or divorce.

> **NOTE:** Don't take the client's word for anything. Have the client bring in car titles, deeds, mortgages, stock certificates, or get these items by request for documents under the discovery rules of most states.

Common Sense Advice

The following is a list of some common sense advice that is worth passing along to your client during your interview, or in a form letter if a divorce or dissolution action is being contested:

1. Take a vacation from each other to let irrational anger cool off before negotiations begin.

2. Understand the benefits of a careful balance between alimony, child support, and unallocated maintenance payments, and satisfy yourself that your lawyer has calculated them to the optimum advantage of both parties.

3. Consider whether there are good reasons to reverse the usual practice of automatically granting custody of the children to the mother. Agree on a visitation schedule and stick to it.

4. Make a list of joint assets built up since the marriage. Be realistic, especially concerning the wife's intangible contribution. Remember that the house, the furniture, and the car traditionally go to the spouse who will be maintaining a home for the children.

5. Discuss assets each partner owned before the marriage, and leave them out of the settlement.

6. Investigate the tax ramifications of who gets the house. If you have joint ownership and the wife gets the house, the husband will in effect be selling his half and may have to pay a capital gains tax on half of the difference between the acquisition price and the current market value.

7. Remember a divorced wife has no rights to her ex-husband's estate. A life insurance policy is often used to provide her with financial security in the event of his death. Determine whether it is more advantageous, from a tax standpoint, to make her the owner of the policy—in which case the premiums, in the form of alimony, would be deductible. If the wife remains the beneficiary, she will have to check to see that payments are kept up and that the policy is not canceled.

8. Take into account the fact that the husband usually pays the fees of both lawyers, although it may be possible to pay the wife's fees in the form of deductible alimony. Remember that the husband normally provides health insurance coverage for the wife. The children are usually covered by his business health plan; check to see if the company plan provides a rider for the ex-spouse.

9. A divorced spouse can obtain benefits under a former husband's Social Security record if the marriage lasted at least ten years and the divorced spouse is sixty-

two years of age or older and unmarried. Prerequisite: The husband must be sixty-two years of age. The parties may have been divorced for two years and get those benefits even if the worker is not retired.

10. Try to get divorced in your own state. Quickie divorces are still available in Haiti and the Dominican Republic, but they might be declared invalid if contested. A trip to a divorce-mill state or territory like Idaho, Nevada, or the Virgin Islands creates extra costs—transportation, hotel bills, and duplicate legal fees—all of which further deplete the post-divorce assets available to either partner.

CHAPTER NINETEEN

How to Assist in a Real Estate Practice

As a paralegal working in a law office with a heavy real estate practice, your duties may vary, from accumulating data and information needed to complete the various instruments of conveyance, such as deeds or mortgages, to monitoring mortgage foreclosures and real estate closings, examining title reports, and in some law offices, preparing and plotting legal descriptions of land.

In some jurisdictions, you will also be preparing all types of leases, land sale contracts, and secured transactions agreements, as well as drafting complaints, answers, and other documentation dealing with unlawful detainer proceedings such as attachments and undertakings, quiet title, and partition actions.

Because of this continuing contact with the operation and effect of the laws relating to the changes in the character, purchase and sale, and transfer of real property from one person to another, you should know the rules affecting ownership and transferability of real estate.

Examining the Nature of Real Property Law

Real estate almost always deals with a portion(s) of the original land and objects which are permanently affixed to it. In actuality, it is the study of the rights to the use of a portion of the earth. For example, a building can be bulldozed, yet it is considered to be real property because of the difficulty in removing it from the earth upon which it was built. It was intended to remain there indefinitely. Lighting fixtures are in the same category. Crops of wheat and the like can be covered by real estate law if they are considered to be permanent fixtures on the land. Until they are physically removed, then, they are considered a part of personal property.

What are some of the rights that run with the ownership of property? Most of us look at buying property like buying a television set. When you buy the television, what you acquire is absolute and free title and total unencumbrance. There is no body of law that can restrict your use of your television. But buying a piece of real property is different.

The bundle of rights that run with the ownership of property has relationship with other people who own property and hence limits and restricts your use of your property. It will never be free and clear of this series of encumbrances.

What Is Real Property?

Real property is land and personal property that is affixed in a permanent way to it as part of the land. Trade fixtures and equipment may or may not be so attached to the land as to become real property. A mobile home may become so affixed to the land as to become real property. Whether personal property has become part of the land is a question of fact in most cases. A contract may specify whether personal property that is attached to the land becomes real property. This could create a question of both law and fact if a dispute arises.

> **NOTE:** A "mortgagee" of land would be particularly interested in knowing what is included as part of the mortgaged land. If there is any doubt, the mortgagee should be given a "security interest" in the personal property in plain language in the mortgage or in a separate security agreement. A "financing statement" should then be filed to perfect the security interest under the applicable state commercial code.

Interests in Real Property

Some interests a person may have in real property are:

Fee simple: An estate in fee simple is an absolute interest in land.

Life estate: A life estate is an estate in land for the length of one's life or the life of another. The life tenant has the right to possession during his life or the life of that other person named in the deed.

Reversionary interest: A reversionary estate is a non-possessory interest in land, the residue of an estate remaining in the grantor after he has conveyed away some lesser estate. It will be possessory only on the termination of the lesser state transferred.

EXAMPLE

A to B for life with the reversion to A on B's death.

Remainder interest: A remainder estate is also a non-possessory interest in land, which vests after a precedent estate ends. It is created by an act of the grantor in favor of some person other than the grantor. It remains out of possession of the grantor forever, rather than reverting back to the grantor.

EXAMPLE

A gives to B for life, and at B's death, to B's son.

This is a typical remainder interest. The property remains out of the possession of the grantor and is non-possessory until it vests in the heirs of B.

Periodic estate (leasehold interest): This is a tenancy for a designated period of time. An example of this type of estate is month-to-month tenancy.

Tenancy at will: This is a tenancy created for an uncertain term by agreement between the landlord and tenant. Either party may terminate by giving notice at any time. It may be oral or in writing. A tenancy at will cannot be assigned.

Easement: Another possible interest or right in the use of land is the easement. Though the theory of, and laws relating to, easements may vary from state to state, as a general proposition, an easement is a right of interest in the land of another, existing apart from the ownership of land. It can be a positive or negative right and/or interest in land. It may be created by a conveyance giving limited or unlimited use or enjoyment to someone other than the owner. This type of interest in land is attached to the land and will continue even if the original owner conveys his ownership interest.

An easement is to be distinguished from a mere "license" to use land for a specific purpose. A license is a personal, revocable, and unassignable privilege to do certain acts on land (such as place a billboard in a field). A license may be created orally, but it is wiser to have it in writing. A license does not attach to the land like an easement. It does not flow through a conveyance like an easement.

An easement may be an affirmative easement where the owner of the easement has the right to enter upon another's land, or it may be a negative easement under which the owner of the land cannot use a specified part of his own land.

An easement can be "appurtenant" or "in gross":

1. An easement appurtenant is established where there are at least two tracts of land and the owner's use and enjoyment of one tract is benefited by the easement. The easement is appurtenant to the other tract of land. The land benefited is called the "dominant estate" and the tract burdened by the benefit is called the "servient estate." Example is the right to ingress and egress over another's land.

2. An easement in gross, on the other hand, is generally a personal right benefiting the owner personally, *not* any land he owns. These rights are generally granted to install and maintain electric power or sewers.

An "easement by prescription" is obtained by adverse use for a continuous period prescribed by the statutes or common law of the state in which the land being used is located.

Simply put, it is virtually the same as gaining land by adverse possession. The elements required to establish an easement by prescription are as follows:

1. Hostile intent and possession,

2. Open and notorious use, and

3. Continuous and uninterrupted use.

This use applies, generally, only to an easement, as opposed to getting the land by adverse possession, together with title to the land. See Figures 19.1 and 19.2 for sample forms of easement.

Condominium ownership: This is a type of ownership of real estate wherein the owner doesn't actually own the land upon which his dwelling rests. The condominium purchaser gets a recordable deed to a unit or apartment in a condominium complex. It is subject to the terms of the Condominium Declaration which has been filed by the developer. The owner is required to pay the taxes and insurance for his unit or apartment. He may sell, lease, mortgage, or even include his condominium premises in his will. See Figure 19.5 for a basic form of condominium *lease*. Additionally, he shares with other unit owners certain rights to use common areas and facilities such as halls, basements, lobby, elevators, and storage space located on the land upon which the condominium apartments are built. A condominium association is usually formed by the unit owners. The association then deals with the developer on behalf of the owners.

The condominium concept of real estate ownership is created and held together by the Master Deed (Condominium Declaration), which spells out and affirms separate ownership of the individual units and the sharing of the obligation for commonly used areas.

To ensure the aforementioned separateness of ownership and joint sharing of obligations, the residents may elect a Board of Managers to supervise all activities and enforce the rules and regulations of the Master Deed or Condominium Declaration.

Cooperative ownership: The cooperative form of ownership, on the other hand, though similar in some ways to the condominium ownership, provides individual buyers a stockholder position in the cooperative corporation that actually owns the multiple unit property. The cooperative corporation stockholders receive a *proprietary lease* from the corporation instead of a deed to their respective units.

And, unlike condominium owners, renters of a cooperative own only a percentage of the corporation and are assessed sums of money periodically (monthly, quarterly, and so forth) to cover the payment of taxes, mortgages, repairs, and the like. A cooperative owner cannot sell or otherwise dispose of his co-op, as he does not "own" his own apartment. The sale of his stock in the cooperative corporation is governed by the terms and conditions of the articles and bylaws of the cooperative corporation.

The obligations and rights of the tenant-stockholder will be spelled out in his proprietary lease from the corporation, which usually incorporates the bylaws of the corporation by reference.

House rules and bylaws that govern the activities of the tenant-owner will be incorporated in the proprietary lease by reference or be spelled out in the lease.

The board of directors of the corporation manage the cooperative complex, pay taxes, make repairs, enforce rules, and so on.

Ownership in Real Property

Sole and Individual Ownership
The grantee's title to property will be sole and individual if his name only appears on the deed (in some states a spouse has an inchoate dower interest).

Joint Ownership with Another
If there is more than one grantee named in a deed, or joint ownership of the real estate is created, a remainder interest or reversionary interest may result, depending on the language of the deed.

Joint tenancy: If the deed names two or more grantees and includes the words "with right of survivorship," a joint tenancy is created in the whole of the land, which cannot be disposed of without the consent of all until the last survivor is the sole owner.

When a joint tenancy exists between two or more people, each is theoretically considered to own the entire property until the death of the other joint tenant(s). In effect, then, a joint tenancy merely creates an estate that vests in the last surviving joint tenant. Only the last surviving tenant can dispose of the property by will.

A joint tenancy between spouses is called a "tenancy by the entirety." See below.

Tenancy-in-common: If the deed names two grantees without words of survivorship (see exception in case of husband and wife in comment following), a tenancy-in-common is created in most states.

This type of tenancy exists between two or more persons who each own an individual interest in the property, but each can, during his or her lifetime, dispose of that undivided interest by deed and can, of course, bequeath it by will. A tenancy in common may be specifically created by such words as: "I, AB, do hereby grant to JS and LY, as tenants in common, each as to an undivided one half interest in the following described real property: (here you should insert the legal description)."

In most states, the undivided interest owned by a tenant-in-common may be the subject of a partition action, whereas a joint tenancy or tenancy by the entireties may not be partitioned.

Tenancy by the entireties (between spouses): The deed language required to create this particular type of tenancy varies widely from state to state and can depend on whether the state in question is a community-property state or not.

Some states that are not community-property states require that a deed to husband and wife use the words "with right of survivorship" to create the joint tenancy, which is then called a "tenancy by the entireties." Some states hold that any deed naming both husband and wife as grantees and including the description "his wife" or "her husband," automatically creates a tenancy by the entireties even though there are no specific words of survivorship. Some states will allow a court to declare that a tenancy by the entireties was created if the two grantees are in fact husband and wife, even though the relationship was not spelled out in the deed.

Obviously, the surest way to create a tenancy by the entireties (other than calling it by that name outright) would be to give the two names plus the relationship, plus the words "with right of survivorship."

EXAMPLE

John Doe and Mary Doe, his wife, with right of survivorship.

General Duties of the Paralegal

Now that we know the categories of real property, what can the paralegal do in this practice? The answer is almost everything! This is one of those areas of practice in which the paralegal is most valuable. The general duties of the paralegal in a real estate practice are as follows:

- Accumulating data and information needed to complete various instruments of conveyance
- Preparing contracts for purchase and sale of land

- Preparing and plotting legal descriptions of land

- Preparing deeds, mortgages, leases

- Examining title reports, abstracts, or preliminary title insurance binders

- Preparing statements for real estate closing (Use your office closing statement form as a checklist for information and documents you will need at the closing.)

- Drafting complaints, answers, and other legal pleadings (breach of contract to purchase or sell land, action for specific performance of contract to sell land, landlord-tenant actions, and the like)

- Monitoring mortgage foreclosures

- Preparing secured transaction agreements where personal property is being sold with real property, as in the sale of a business or the selling of a residence with a mobile home or selling a business real property with movable equipment

The following is a sample list of what a paralegal might do in a case where two people want to form a partnership or execute a joint venture agreement to purchase a certain piece of real estate:

1. After your attorney has held the initial meeting with the client, use your form checklist of questions and basic information to review and complete any unanswered questions. If you do not have such a checklist, develop one from the attorney notes in the file.

2. Do your research relating to the tax ramifications of the real estate transactions, as well as any other legal aspects.

3. Develop and then prepare a Time and Responsibility Schedule to aid you and your attorney to keep on top of certain things to be done, that is, documents placed in escrow, money due from lender, title search begun or received from title company, and the like.

4. Prepare the partnership agreement or joint venture agreement as directed by your attorney.

5. Prepare or review the real estate purchase and sale agreement.

6. Gather your exhibits to be attached to the purchase and sale agreement, that is, plot plans, schedules, assignments of leases, subleases, notes, deed of trust, and the like. Make sure all the exhibits have been dated and properly and completely executed.

7. After approval, have the agreements typed and have them mailed out for signatures with exhibits attached.

8. Prepare your escrow instructions.

9. After the foregoing has been accomplished, draft your consent to assignments and subleases and prepare estoppel certificates.

10. Send out a request for a preliminary title report from the title company.

11. Once the entire package has been executed by all parties, including the sales agreement and partnership agreement and initialing the exhibits, have the certificate of partnership recorded in the county where the property is located. If a limited partnership is involved, check the state limited partnership statute.

   NOTE: As with all voluminous documents, check and recheck to see that every page requiring a signature has been signed and that every page requiring notarization has been so notarized.

12. Then draft any and all remaining documents needed to be deposited into escrow.

13. Check all closing documents and prepare the closing statement, showing amounts to be paid by the respective parties at closing.

14. Deliver all closing documents and the closing statement to your attorney for his use at the closing.

Instruments of Transfer of Interests in Real Property

As the title, effect, and description of instruments of transfer may vary from state to state, the following are submitted as guidelines so that you will at least know what to look for when gathering information and completing these documents.

Deeds

A deed to real property is the legal instrument by which the grantor transfers title to his interest to the grantee.

A deed should contain the following:

1. Name of the grantor;

2. Words of conveyance, that is, I give, I hereby grant, sell, or transfer;

3. Name of the grantee;

4. Legal description (not just the address) of the property being conveyed;

5. Signature of the grantor;

6. Witnesses to the grantor's signature, if required by state law where the property is located;

7. Date on which the signature was affixed; and

8. A notary acknowledgment of said signature.

> **PRACTICAL HINTS:** When conveying property, the grantor must use the same name as when he received the property, that is, "D. Bard Smith to Mary Smythe" and then "Mary Smythe to Jane Oslow," not "Mary Smith to Jane Oslow."

A deed must be acknowledged to be recorded; however, it is valid as between the grantee and grantor without acknowledgment.

There are various types of deeds:

1. *Grant deed (special warranty deed)* applies provided

    a. That the grantor has not previously conveyed the property to another, and

    b. That the grantor has not made any liens or other encumbrances in or on the property.

2. *General warranty deed* is one that contains a covenant of warranty of title and an obligation to defend that title for the grantee against anyone. See Figure 19.1 for a general form of a warranty deed from Oklahoma.

3. *Quitclaim deed* is a deed of conveyance the purpose of which is to convey all the interest of the grantor, whatever it is. He does not warrant anything. Its use is intended to pass any title, interest, or claim that the grantor may have in the property.

    It can be used in an easement situation or if there is a break in the chain of title. In giving a quitclaim deed, the grantor is not giving any implied warranty to the grantee as to title in the property. The grantor is merely giving whatever interest, if any, he possesses, in the property. It could be nothing, but he or the grantee thinks he may have an interest, and the quitclaim deed will clear the title of any claim the quitclaim grantor may have.

    Simply put, a quitclaim deed is generally used where a person has an interest that cannot be defined, has no monetary value, or where the grantor wants to pass his title but is not willing to make any warranties. The Illinois statutes provide that the following language is enough to convey a quitclaim deed:

    > The grantor [here insert grantor's name or names and place of residence], for the consideration of [here insert consideration], convey and quit claim to [here insert grantee's name or names] all interest in the following described real estate [here insert description], situated in the County of . . . , in the State of Illinois.

4. *Void deed* is a deed that is void from inception and cannot be cured.

5. *Voidable deed* is one given to a minor who cannot acquire title, or because there are statutes to the granting of title. This can be by virtue of fraud, mistake, or receipt from someone mentally or legally incapable of transferring property.

Figure 19.1
General Warranty Deed (Oklahoma sample)

WARRANTY DEED

KNOW ALL PERSONS BY THESE PRESENTS:

That _____ *("Grantor")*, in consideration of the sum of _____ Dollars and other valuable consideration, in hand paid, the receipt of which is hereby acknowledged, does hereby grant, bargain, sell and convey unto _____, husband and wife (collectively "Grantees"), as joint tenants and not as tenants in common with full rights of survivorship, the whole estate to vest in the survivor in the event of the death of either, the following described real property and premises, situate in _____ County, State of Oklahoma, to wit:

[Insert description of real property]

together with all the improvements thereon and the appurtenances thereunto belonging (the "Property"), LESS AND EXCEPT any interest in and to oil, gas, coal, metallic ores and other minerals therein and thereunder previously reserved or conveyed of record and all rights, interest and estates of whatsoever nature incident thereto or arising thereunder; and warrant the title to the same, subject to the permitted exceptions attached hereto as Exhibit "A" (the "Permitted Exceptions").

TO HAVE AND TO HOLD the Property unto Grantees as joint tenants with full right of survivorship and not as tenants in common, and to the heirs and assigns of the survivor, forever, free, clear and discharged of and from all former grants, charges, taxes, judgments, mortgages and other liens and encumbrances of whatsoever nature, subject to the Permitted Exceptions.

Signed and delivered this _____ day of _____ 20 _____.

_____

Name: _____

Recording Non-Court Documents: The Deed, Only Evidence of Title

In the majority of states, the deed must be recorded in the County or City Registrar's Office. The recordation does not affect the validity of the conveyance itself. The conveyance is valid if it is unrecorded; however, all other rights rely upon the recordation of the transfer.

If a deed were not recorded, a Complaint to Quiet Title would be in order.

RECORDABLE INSTRUMENTS

1. Any writing, signed and delivered from one person to another giving an interest, right, or duty; and in payment of a debt.

2. Those specifically provided for by statute. Statutes affecting the recordation of conveyance:

a. *Notice Recording Statute:* e.g., A to B, then A to C, thereafter B records and C records later.

> NOTE: In a *Notice Recording Statute* state, in the above example, B is under a duty to give *notice of conveyance* to C. Failure to give such notice could cause him to lose against C in a quiet title action.

b. *Race Statute:* e.g., A to B; then A sells the same property to C.

i. C immediately records, and thereafter B records.

ii. C would win the lawsuit under the theory of this statute, obtaining clear title to the property.

iii. B would have recourse against A for damages.

iv. It would not matter whether C knew about B or not. Under the Race Statute, it is *first in time, first in right.*

c. *Race Notice Statute:* This is peculiar to the State of California, and applies to people who have no notice of a recorded document regarding property purchased, or to be purchased. As a result, "a buyer without notice is unprotected as against an unrecorded transfer."

WHAT CONSTITUTES NOTICE—TWO TYPES

1. *Constructive notice:* which is actual recordation of the instrument of conveyance—notice to the world.

2. *Actual notice:* This is being aware of negotiations or agreements for purchase and sale of property between others: e.g., A actually knew about a transfer to B, because someone told him about it.

Easements

Figure 19.2
Right of Way for Ingress and Egress for Limited Time, Allowing Joint Use

1. This agreement made in the City and County of _____ on this _____ day of _____, 20____, by JOHN DOE who lives at _____, hereinafter called the party of the first part and JOHN SMITH, residing at _____, in the City, County, and State of _____, hereinafter called the party of the second part.

WITNESSES AS FOLLOWS:

2. That the party of the first part, his heirs and assigns, grants and conveys unto the party of the second part to his heirs and assigns an easement in, to, upon, and over all that paved portion of a certain roadway situated at:

Figure 19.2 (*continued*)

NOTE: Once again, give a full detailed legal description of the property to be conveyed.

3. It is understood that said easement is for the sole purpose of ingress and egress, and it is agreed and understood that it is not to be construed as an easement given to the exclusion of the party of the first part or his heirs and assigns, or to others later granted a similar right.
4. That the party of the second part, and his heirs and assigns, covenants with the party of the first part, and to his heirs and assigns, to at all times maintain and repair, at his or their expense, said easement for its proper upkeep and maintenance.
5. That the party of the second part is to hold the said right-of-way easement for a period of _____ years. (Here put a time limitation, such as five years, twelve years, and so forth.)
6. IN WITNESS WHEREOF, the parties hereto have executed this agreement on the date above first written.

_____

(Owner of servient land)

NOTE: Be sure to add an acknowledgment for recording the easement in the county where the servient land is located.

Figure 19.3
Easement, Basic Form

LIMITED USE EASEMENT FOR UNLIMITED TIME

This agreement made in the City and County of _____ on this _____ day of _____, by JANE DOE, who lives at _____, in the City of _____, hereinafter called the party of the first part, and MARY SMITH, residing at _____, in the City, County, and State of _____, hereinafter called the party of the second part;

WITNESSES AS FOLLOWS:

That the party of the first part represents and warrants that she owns and has fee simple title to that parcel of real property located in the City of _____, County of _____, and State of _____, bounded and described as follows:

NOTE: Here you should set out the complete legal description of said property including the tract, block, and boundary lines.

That the party of the second part desires to use said property for:

NOTE: Here you should describe completely and with clarity the exact nature and type of easement desired, that is, walkway, to build a fence, and so forth.

Figure 19.3 (*continued*)

It is mutually agreed as between the parties under the following conditions as follows:

The party of the first part does hereby grant, assign and set over to the party of the second part:

NOTE: Describe the nature and type of easement granted, with any and all *restrictions* that your client may deem necessary. Also include servient owner's right to share use, if that is desired.

Except as herein granted, the party of the first part shall continue to have the full use and enjoyment of the property.

The party of the second part shall bear full responsibility for the use and enjoyment of the property and shall hold the party of the first part harmless from any claim of damages to person or premises resulting from the use, occupancy, and possession of said property by the party of the second part.

Furthermore, to have and to hold said easement unto the party of the second part and to her successors and assigns forever.

IN WITNESS WHEREOF, the parties hereto have executed this agreement on the date above first written.

_____
(Owner of servient land)

Mortgages

Depending on the state, a mortgage is treated as creating a lien or title. Most states apply the "lien theory."

A mortgage may be created by an instrument called a mortgage (which may secure a note or a bond), a mortgage deed, a trust deed, or an agreement for deed.

1. "Trust deed" gives the trustee legal title to the real property until the debt is paid. The elements of a trust deed are:

   a. The trustor or debtor,

   b. The trustee who holds the legal title for security of the debt,

   c. The beneficiary or lender, and

   d. An obligation.

   You should also include in the trust deed words of conveyance and a description of the property as heretofore mentioned.

EXAMPLE

A to B for $20,000. B pays $5,000 down, then borrows $15,000 from C, a banking institution, or other, and obtains promissory note for $15,000. B is the maker of the promissory note, and the bank is the holder of the note. The note is for $15,000 plus interest. The bank is also the lender beneficiary and obtains security for the note that is the trust deed; or it could obtain a lien on stock commensurate to the $15,000 borrowed by the trustor. This promissory note must contain the following:

a. The name of the borrower-lender, and a description of the trust deed (or other collateral) with specificity;

b. The signature of the borrower, dated and acknowledged by a notary public; and

c. A complete description of the property herein.

When the note is paid in full, a reconveyance is signed and recorded in favor of the borrower.

2. Mortgage

a. Mortgagor who is the debtor retains title.

b. Mortgagee who is the lender acquires a lien on the property.

This document should contain the operative words of the mortgage, a description of the property, and of course, incorporation reference or attachment of the note or bond that is being secured by the mortgage.

3. Mortgage deed

a. Mortgagor who is the debtor gives conditional title to the mortgagee.

b. Mortgagee acquires title to the land only if the mortgagor fails to pay the note or bond that is being secured by the mortgage deed.

4. Land sale contract (agreement for deed). This is another means of creating what amounts to a mortgage on real property and is done without giving title to the property. It is a written agreement for the purchase and sale of real property between a vendor and a vendee.

The vendee gets an equitable title to the property and possession thereof so long as he complies with the terms of the contract or agreement for deed.

The vendor has the legal title and no possession, as opposed to a grantor and a grantee relationship, where the grantor gives away all of his right, title, and interest in and to the real property.

Some of the restrictions or limitations to the vendor-vendee relationship are:

a. The contract or agreement can be rescinded or foreclosed (depending on the jurisdiction where the property is located) if the purchaser doesn't pay or comply with other terms of the contract of agreement.

b. The purchaser or vendee cannot change the property without the consent of the vendor.

Leases

In some states a leasehold interest in real property is considered personal property. A lease is at least a possessory interest in real property, even if it is not considered an estate in real property.

Drafting Guide for Leases

A lease must describe the demised premises with sufficient certainty to avoid ambiguity. Language similar to that required in the drafting of a deed may be used in describing leased premises but is not required in most cases.

The same general rules that apply to reservations and exceptions in deeds apply equally to reservations and exceptions in leases. If a reservation or exception set forth in a lease is repugnant to any estate previously granted, the lease is inferior to that prior interest in the land. See Figure 19.4 for a general and basic form of Residential Lease.

Checklist

Consider the following checklist of those elements to be considered when drafting a lease of residential property.

1. Date

2. Names and status of the prties, and their interests in the property

3. Demise or conveyance clause

4. Description of, and reservations or exceptions affecting, the property leased, including any garages or parking spaces or other common facilities (such as pool or tennis courts) that may be pertinent

5. Duration of and limitation of terms of occupancy and date on which the occupancy commences

6. Any restrictions relative to use of the demised premises

7. Limitation on number of occupants, if applicable

8. Amount of and mode, place, and time for payment of rent

Be aware of state statutes creating special landlord and tenant laws and court rules for summary procedure in landlord and tenant cases.

NOTE: Most states require a lease for a year or more to be written. If that is required, an oral lease for such a period is unenforceable. Check your state statute on fraud.

Figure 19.4
Basic Residential Lease

A. (DATE)
This lease agreement, entered into on this _____ day of _____, 20___.

B. (PARTIES)
By and between _____, hereinafter referred to as the lessor, and _____, hereinafter referred to as the lessee.

C. (PREMISES)
In consideration of the rental below-described and of the covenants stipulated herein, the lessor agrees to lease the following-described premises located at _____ Avenue, _____ City, _____ County, State of _____, and legally described as follows:

NOTE: Here should be set forth the full legal description of the commonly described rental unit; for example, Lot 1, Block 2, in Tract 40, City and County of Los Angeles, State of California, as per map recorded in the office of the County Recorder, in Book 100, at page 67.

D. (TERM)
To have and to hold the premises unto the lessee, its successors and assigns, for the term of _____ (years or months) commencing on the _____ day of _____, 20 _____, and ending on the _____ day of _____, 20___.

E. (RENT)
That the rent for the term of this lease is _____ Dollars ($_____), payable without demand or notice in monthly installments of _____, on the _____ day of each and every month of the term beginning on the _____ day of _____, 20___.

NOTE: Here again, you can incorporate at this juncture the acknowledgment of the first and last month's rent in advance, as well as a security deposit. In some instances, this is optional and/or negotiable, as between the parties.

F. (USE)
The use of the premises shall be for _____, and for no other purpose except with the written consent of lessor.

G. (ASSIGNMENT)
The lessee may not assign this lease or sublease any part of said premises without the written consent of the lessor.

Figure 19.4 (*continued*)

H. (LESSOR'S MAINTENANCE RESPONSIBILITIES)

The lessor hereby agrees to keep the entire exterior portion of the premises in good repair and maintenance.

NOTE: Here is an opportunity for you to insert any other responsibilities of the lessor that your client may wish to have spelled out for clarity to avoid confusion in the future.

I. (LESSEE'S MAINTENANCE RESPONSIBILITIES)

The lessee hereby agrees to maintain the interior portion of the premises in good repair at all times.

NOTE: Here is an opportunity for you to insert any other responsibilities of the lessee which your client may wish to have spelled out for clarity to avoid confusion in the future.

J. (DEFAULT REMEDIES)

Said lessee hereby covenants and agrees that if a default shall be made in the payment of rent or if the lessee shall violate any of the covenants of this lease, then the lessee shall become a tenant at sufferance, waiving all right of notice, and the lessor shall be entitled to re-enter and take possession of the demised premises.

NOTE: This is tantamount to your three-day or thirty-day notice that leads to an unlawful detainer action.

K. (TERMINATION)

The lessee agrees to quit and deliver up said premises at the end of the term of this lease in good condition, ordinary wear and tear accepted.

L. (OPTION)

The lessee has the option to renew the lease for a further term of _____ (years), beginning with the _____ day of _____, and ending with the _____ day of _____, for a total rent of _____, payable _____ Dollars ($) per month. All other terms and conditions of the lease agreement shall remain in full force and effect.

IN WITNESS WHEREOF, . . .

M. (SIGNATURES AND WITNESSES)

NOTE: Residential leases are not usually recorded, so an acknowledgment is not necessary. If, for any reason, the lease is to be recorded, an acknowledgment should be added and executed.

Figure 19.5
Proprietary Lease (Cooperative Apartment)

This Proprietary Lease, dated the _____ day of _____, 20 ___ by and between _____ a (State of Incorporation of the cooperative corporation) having an office at _____ hereafter "Lessor"; and _____ hereinafter called "Lessee."

WHEREAS, the Lessor is the owner of the property and building in the City and County of _____, commonly known as _____ *(number of street)* _____, hereafter called the "Building"; and

WHEREAS, the Lessee is the owner of _____ shares of the Lessor, to which this lease is appurtenant and which had been allocated to Unit Number _____ in the Building;

TERM

NOW, THEREFORE, in connection of the premises, the Lessor hereby leases to the Lessee, and the Lessee hires from the Lessor, subject to the terms and conditions hereof, Unit Number _____ in the Building (hereinafter referred to as the Apartment). (It is here that any other terms and conditions can be placed that bear on the lease to the apartment.)

1. Rent (basis upon which it is set)
2. Lessor's repairs
3. Services by Lessor
4. Damage to Apartment or Building
5. Inspection of books of account/annual report
6. Changes in terms and conditions of Proprietary Lease
7. Penthouses, terraces, and balconies
8. Assignment of Lessor's rights against occupant
9. Cancellation of prior agreements
10. Quiet enjoyment of premises
11. Indemnity/hold harmless
12. Payment of rent
13. House rules
14. Use of premises
15. Subletting
16. Assignment of lease or transfer of shares
    a. Consent: of debt of Lessee
    b. Consents generally as it relates to stockholders' and directors' obligations to consent
    c. Release of Lessee upon assignment of subletting, resale
17. Pledge of shares and proprietary lease
18. Repairs by Lessee
19. Lessor's right to remedy Lessee's default
20. Increases in rate of fire insurance
21. Alterations
22. Proprietary lease subordination to mortgage and ground lease

Figure 19.5 *(continued)*

23. Mechanic's lien
24. Right of entry (the right of the Lessor to have a key to each unit apartment).
25. Waivers
26. Notices
27. Reimbursement of Lessor's expenses
28. Lessor's immunities
29. Termination of lease by Lessor
30. Lessor's right after Lessee's default
31. Waiver of right redemption
32. Surrender of possession
33. Lessee's option to cancel
34. Extension of option to cancel
35. Continuance of a cooperative management after all leases have been terminated
36. Unsold shares
37. Foreclosure procedures
38. Covenants
39. Waiver of trial by jury
40. Lessor's Additional Remedies (Lessee can be more than one person)
41. Effect of partial invalidity
42. Notice to Lessor of default
43. Unity of shares and lease
44. Charges of utilities
45. No discrimination as to race, creed, or religion, etc.
46. All changes to be in writing

NOTE: This form and checklist is just a skeleton, giving basic subjects that should be covered in a proprietary lease.

Be further guided by your state's general real estate and contract laws and any specific statute pertaining to cooperative apartments.

The Total Real Estate Paralegal*
Acquisition Responsibilities

Purchase Agreement

- Prepare initial draft of purchase agreement from attorney notes or interview.

---

* Courtesy of NFPA.

- Coordinate with other parties (buyer, seller, title company, opposing counsel, lender).

- Take comments about purchase agreement and revise as necessary.

- Arrange for execution of purchase agreement.

- Review purchase agreement for critical dates and contingencies and calendar same.

- Prepare closing checklist.

- Draft deed.

Due Diligence Responsibilities

Matters of Title

- Conduct or arrange for title search and request abstract of title. Order title commitment and/or preliminary title report.

- Negotiate title insurance coverage.

- Review legal description of the property and track against map, if available.

- Review exceptions (standard exceptions regarding survey, taxes and assessments, etc.) and cumbrances of record.

- Arrange for discharge/satisfaction of deed trust/mortgage (existing mortgages of record on the property) and obtain payoff figures.

- Draft and review any permits and easements. If necessary, plot against legal description.

- Review and determine validity of mineral claims through search of Bureau of Land Management records.

- Draft escrow instructions.

- Arrange for issuance of title policy.

Existent Contracts/Lease Declarations

- Review contracts and leases for assignment, due on sale and due on encumbrance provisions; prepare abstracts regarding same.

- Draft requisite assignment, amendment, or extension documentation.

- Review condominium declaration/resale certificate for due on sale provisions/rights of first refusal.

Purchaser/Seller Representations

- If necessary, obtain corporate organizational documents, including authorization of the applicable parties to purchase and/or sell, for all parties.

- Review corporate documents for prohibitions against borrowings, power of decision-making bodies, and so forth.

- If necessary, obtain certificates of good standing/certificates of existence.

- Conduct public records search of the parties, including judgments, tax liens, and U.C.C. filings.

Environmental

- If necessary, order environmental assessment.

- Review environmental assessment and prepare releases.

Insurance

- If residential, provide purchasers with information about homeowner's insurance.

- Coordinate with lender and purchaser to ascertain lender insurance requirements.

- Obtain and review required evidence of insurance from purchaser or insurance agent.

Closing Matters

Prorations

- Prorate real and personal property taxes and utilities, and adjust for closing figures.

- Obtain closing figures from bank and prorate all closing costs.

- Exchange all figures with other parties.

- Review figures with client.

Purchase Money Loan

Loan Documentation

- Perform financial calculations (amortization, net present value, discounting, annual percentage rate).

- Draft loan agreement, promissory note, deed of trust/mortgage, security agreement, assignment of leases and rents, guaranties, and Truth-in-Lending disclosure statements.

- Obtain and/or draft necessary corporate, partnership, or limited liability company documentation and resolutions in connection with loan transaction. (See Business/Corporate Section, *supra*, for more detailed information.)

- As necessary, draft any leases and/or assignments, extensions, or modifications to lease.

- If necessary, draft U.C.C. financing statements, amendments, extensions, and/or terminations.

Closing

- Finalize closing checklist.

- Organize closing folders.

- Attend closing and assist attorney in activities regarding execution of closing documents.

- Educate signatories with respect to the documents being executed.

- If appropriate, notarize documents upon execution.

- Coordinate recording of real estate documents and filing of U.C.C. financing statements.

Post-Closing

- Obtain documents to be executed post-closing.

- Coordinate with all parties concerning post-closing questions and, if necessary, provide documents.

- Follow-up on recorded/filed documents.

- Prepare closing binders.

Tax-Related Matters

- Obtain solicitation form from seller, if applicable, and prepare and file Form 1099.

- Record capital gains/loss on client's income tax return.

- Draft appropriate capital gains tax affidavit.

- Assemble tax bills and payments.

- Obtain and analyze property information and current valuation.

- Draft complaint on real property assessment.

- Draft discovery requests and responses to discovery requests in conjunction with real property assessment.

- Coordinate formal property appraisal and report.

- If appropriate, prepare notice of appeal on valuation of property.

Leases

- Obtain terms of lease from attorney notes or interview.

- Prepare initial draft of lease.

- If necessary, negotiate and revise lease.

- Conduct due diligence to the extent necessary.

- Arrange for any existent contract modifications.

- If necessary, draft subleases.

- If necessary, prepare memorandum of lease.

- Facilitate execution of lease and memorandum of lease.

- If necessary, record memorandum of lease.

- Review or draft estoppel certificates and/or subordinates, non-disturbance and attachment agreements.

Foreclosure

- Prepare notice of intent to accelerate.

- If necessary, appoint substitute trustee.

- Draft foreclosure notice.

- Facilitate posting of foreclosure notice.

- Attend foreclosure sale.

- Prepare judicial foreclosure documentation.

- As necessary and appropriate, negotiate with owner/lender.

- See Foreclosure Section, *supra*, for more detailed information.

Miscellaneous

- Prepare subdivision, condominium, and timeshare registrations for in-state and out-of-state registrations.

- Prepare registrations of recreational subdivisions for federal registrations.

- Assist with probate and trust transfers and property investigations.

- Draft notice of mechanic's lien; determine validity of existing mechanic's liens; prepare releases or waivers of rights and assist with foreclosing mechanic's liens. (See Construction Section, *supra*, for more detailed information.)

CHAPTER TWENTY

How to Handle a Tort Action

Section 1: Theory

As a working paralegal, you will not be required to have complete comprehension of the substantive law of torts, but you will need a working knowledge of the concept and theory of the laws affecting tort actions or casualty claims. For in-depth explanations of any area of tort law, almost every judge and practitioner turns to the Restatement of Torts (2d). As you may recall, these treatises are published by the American Law Institute (www.ali.org) and are considered definitive guides on the various area of law.

This chapter will give you much of the basic knowledge you will need to properly prepare a complaint in a personal injury, property damage, products, or strict liability lawsuit or a medical malpractice claim. To this end, emphasis is placed on the basic elements of tort law relating to negligence, duty owed, liabilities of the parties, and some of the defenses used in defending a claim based on negligence.

Theory and Concept of Negligence

As a general proposition a tort is any wrongful act or omission against another. There must be the existence of a legal right held by one person and a violation of this right by another who is under a legal duty to the first that would give rise to a cause of action in tort. Specifically, a tort has been defined as a private wrong or injury to person or property or other violation of a right not dependent upon contract. The wronged person can pursue remedies under civil law.

A crime can also be a tort, if the crime committed injures the person, property, or rights of another. The injured person may file a civil action against the "criminal" to recover the damages suffered. The crime itself is a public wrong, but the damage to the victim is a private wrong. Again, easy reference can be made to the O. J. Simpson case. His purported actions were prosecuted as a crime by the State and as a civil damages suit.

A crime must be proved beyond a reasonable doubt. A tort must be proved by the preponderance of the evidence. This means that the fact-finder must only believe that it is more likely than not to have occurred.

Most crimes require intent. A tort may be the result of carelessness (negligence), regardless of the intent.

Generally, to establish a valid cause of action based on negligence, the following elements must be present:

1. A duty owed to the plaintiff by the defendant,

2. A breach of that duty by the defendant,

3. Breach of the duty being the actual or proximate cause of the injury to the plaintiff, and

4. Damages resulting from the breach of the duty.

The Duty of Care

Every negligence action is based on the "duty of care," which the defendant owes to the plaintiff. That duty may be a statutory duty or just a duty to exercise the reasonable care under the circumstances that would be expected of a reasonable, prudent person. It should be noted that the duty of care may vary depending on the factual situation and may or may not be governed by statutes.

These variances in types of duty owed between the parties may be based on the status, capacity, and age of the persons involved.

These variances may also be due to the special relationships between the parties, that is, employer-employee relationships, parent-child relationships, landlord-tenant relationships, master-servant relationships, expert-client relationships, and the like.

Where no statute has been violated by the defendant, case law is the precedent for determining whether his actions constitute breach of his duty of care to the plaintiff.

General Legal Doctrines Affecting Liability

In every tort action, liability of the defendant must be established before the plaintiff can recover damages for his injury. A plaintiff cannot recover damages just because there was an "accident."

The plaintiff must prove liability (breach of the duty of care, and the breach was the cause of the injury complained of).

In determining whether you can prove liability, you should look to the following doctrines most often and generally applied in most states:

A. The Prudent/Reasonable Person Test

This is applied in common law cases and may be used where no statutory duty is involved. The test is what a reasonably prudent person would do under the circumstances. In making this determination, the fact-finder must take individual characteristics and the particular circumstances surrounding the event into consideration. For example, a person with superior experience or knowledge in a given situation can be held to a higher standard (e.g., an off-duty policeman can be held to a higher standard of care in a dangerous situation).

B. Doctrine of *Res Ipsa Loquitur*

This is the "but for" test and states in essence that "but for the negligent act of defendant, the accident would not have occurred." Translated from the Latin, it means "the thing speaks for itself"; there is no explanation by expert testimony necessary, negligence is inferred through ordinary knowedge. To apply this doctrine, the following elements must be proved:

1. That the accident could not have occurred unless the defendant was negligent. Even though the plaintiff cannot prove the precise act of negligence, the happening of that particular type of accident is circumstantial evidence that the defendant was negligent.

2. That the defendant has exclusive control over the thing or condition that caused the injury.

3. That the plaintiff did absolutely nothing to contribute to the accident.

The *Exxon Valdese* oil spill is an example of a case in which the doctrine of *res ipsa loquitur* can be applied. Ordinarily, oil spills do not and cannot occur without some sort of mishandling on the part of the defendant. Exxon had a duty to secure the oil cargo; it must have done something wrong for the spill to occur. Further, Exxon had exclusive control over the transport of the oil, so anything that went wrong was the responsibility of Exxon. There was no one else to blame. Therefore, any plaintiffs injured by the oil spill were injured due to the breach of the duty of care by Exxon— *res ipsa loquitur*. (In certain circumstances involving dangerous activities, the doctrine of strict liability would apply instead. This higher standard is discussed later in this chapter.)

C. Doctrine of "Last Clear Chance"

This doctrine stands for the proposition that the contributory negligence of the plaintiff will not prevent his recovery, if it appears that the defendant, by the exercise of reasonable care and prudence, had the last clear chance to avoid the accident.

Some states now apply the "comparative negligence" rule in tort actions instead of the strict "contributory negligence" rule. Contributory negligence bars the recovery of the plaintiff because he is found to be, at least in part, responsible for his own injury. Comparative negligence softens this all-or-nothing stance by permitting some recovery. (A detailed discussion of these theories follows below.) Whether there was a last clear chance to avoid injury would be relevant to determining the comparative negligence of the parties in those states. It would allocate a greater percentage of fault to the defendant who failed to avoid further injury to the plaintiff.

D. Doctrine of Negligence Per Se

Violation of a statute by the defendant may create "negligence per se" (by itself).

For this doctrine to operate, the statute that was violated must have been designed to prevent the type of injury the plaintiff suffered. In some jurisdictions proof of violation of the statute is treated as proof of negligence. In other states, proof of the violation of the statute is only some evidence of negligence.

Check your state case law to determine which rule your courts apply.

EXAMPLE

Mary, driving in excess of the legal speed limit, runs a red light and in so doing hits a pedestrian in the crosswalk who was crossing the street with the green light.

In this instance, Mary has violated the following statutes designed to protect this class of persons, that is, the pedestrian:

1. Driving in excess of the speed limit set by law,

2. Running through a red light in violation of the law, and

3. Hitting an innocent bystander, a pedestrian.

This is a typical negligence per se factual situation. The act was in violation of a state statute. The statute sets forth the standard of care owed. You would look to the legislative intent to determine if the plaintiff was a member of the class of persons intended to be protected under the statute violated as described by courts in your state.

E. Cause

Liability for negligence must be based upon a causal connection between the defendant's act and the plaintiff's injury.

The cause of the injury may be primary, intervening, or concurrent. The defendant's liability depends on whether his acts were the proximate cause of the plaintiff's injury, regardless of other cause.

1. *Primary cause* is the actual action that directly inflicted injury upon the plaintiff. A punch to the plainitff's face is the direct cause of his broken jaw.

2. *Proximate cause* is the cause of an injury or damage which is established by showing that the plaintiff's injury was not only the natural, but also the probable consequence of the primary negligent act of the defendant. A punch to the plaintiff's face caused him to reel backward into the wall, hitting his head and causing a concussion. The punch was the proximate cause of the concussion.

3. *Intervening cause* may or may not be the proximate cause of the injury to the plaintiff. If it supersedes the prior wrongful act or is an unforeseeable, independent act that destroys the causal connection between the negligent act of the defendant and the wrongful injury, the intervening cause becomes the proximate cause of the injury. Under this circumstance, damages would not be recoverable from the original wrongdoer, as his act would not have been the proximate cause of the injury.

   A third person shoots the plaintiff after the first defendant punches him. This criminal act of a third party is not related, or intended or foreseeable, by the original defendant who caused only a broken jaw and/or a concussion.

4. *Concurrent cause* is the negligent act of two persons occurring at the same time and where the accident would not have happened absent the negligence of both parties. In this instance, both parties are liable, and the acts of both are deemed to be the proximate cause of the accident. For example, suppose a plaintiff is shot while he and his two friends are out hunting. Both friends negligently shot toward the plaintiff; only one hit the plaintiff, but it cannot be determined whose bullet caused the injury. Both defendant-friends would be the concurrent cause of the injury.

F. Doctrine of Contributory Negligence

This is a "defense" to a tort action based upon the negligence of the plaintiff. It is a common law doctrine. Negligence in this instance means that the plaintiff has failed to exercise that standard of care that a person of ordinary prudence would exercise for his own safety. This is the reasonable and prudent person test applied to the conduct of the plaintiff.

It has been our experience, and you will find, that a client will not always understand that simply because he was rear-ended while driving along the highway does not mean that the defendant is liable to him for his damages. It may have happened that in the defendant's rush to get to work, he changed lanes without looking through his rearview mirror and did not see the car behind him changing lanes; or he may have suddenly decided to get off the freeway onto an off-ramp he almost missed, causing the vehicle behind him to swerve and hit him.

The defendant did have a duty to the plaintiff to have his car under control, but the plaintiff's own inattention and carelessness contributed to the cause of his damage. In a state which applied the doctrine of contributory negligence, the plaintiff could not recover. The result may be different in a state which applies the doctrine of comparative negligence.

G. Doctrine of Comparative Negligence

This doctrine determines the degree of liability of the plaintiff and how much he may recover based upon his contribution to the accident or injury. It is based on the doctrine of contributory negligence, wherein the defendant may raise the plaintiff's contributory negligence as an affirmative.

EXAMPLE

In the automobile accident case described under contributory negligence, the jury may find (in a comparative negligence state) that the plaintiff was 50 percent wrong (or other percentage). In such case the plaintiff could recover only 50 percent of his damages. Check your state comparative negligence statute as to percentage limits of recovery.

H. Doctrine of *Respondeat Superior* (Imputed Negligence)

When two persons have some legal relationship to each other, one may have the duty to require the other to use care in regard to a third party. Examples are principal–agent, employer–employee, family car owner–family driver.

Even though the principal employer or owner was not present, he may be held liable for the negligent acts of the agent, employee, or family driver under some circumstances where the doctrine of *respondeat superior* is applied. The negligence of the one is imputed to the other where the negligence was done within the scope of the agency, employment, or purpose.

EXAMPLE

Store owner is responsible for injury to a customer as a result of employee's failure to clean up a greasy substance on the floor where the employee knew or should have known that the substance was there where customers walked.

I. Doctrine of Assumption of Risk

If a plaintiff assumes the risk of injury by the defendant by the plaintiff's own actions and the plaintiff is injured, the defendant may invoke the doctrine of assumption of risk as a defense in states that apply the contributory negligence doctrine. In comparative negligence states, the assumption of risk may go only to the amount of recovery.

Under this doctrine, the plaintiff must have known and understood the danger and assumed the risk of said danger voluntarily. Very often, people are required to sign a waiver before a party in control of a potentially dangerous situation will permit them to participate. This is true for sports teams, recreational facilities, exercise classes, etc.

EXAMPLE

Waiver of Liability

I/we hereby release and forever discharge the City of _____, its elected and appointed officials, directors, officers, boards, commissions, agents, representatives, servants, and employees from any and all claims of any kind or character which I/we have or may have against them due to my participation in a City Recreation Program. This waiver includes all damages, losses, costs, expenses, and injuries that allegedly occur during the course of this recreation program. In that regard, I/we covenant to indemnify, defend, and hold harmless to the fullest extent permitted by law the foregoing persons and entities from any loss or damages, including reasonable attorneys' fees and litigation expenses, which may be incurred by them in the event any such claims are asserted against them or any of them. I/we understand that medical claims are my/our responsibility. This waiver does not extend to any such claim or liability that is caused by the sole and exclusive intentional acts or gross negligence of the City or its officers, employees, or agents.

The two significant limitations upon this defense of assumption of risk is that the plaintiff is not barred from recovery (1) where the participation in the activity was not a free and voluntary choice and/or (2) where the defendant acted intentionally or with gross negligence toward the plaintiff.

J. Doctrine of Strict Liability

In certain cases, legal liability for harm may be imposed even where there is no proof of carelessness or fault (negligence) on the part of the person or company that caused the injury. Because the party has chosen to engage in an inherently dangerous activiy, he wil be responsible for all outcomes stemming from that activity. Examples are product liability cases, dangerous instrumentality cases (such as use of dynamite), or animal cases.

The theory is based on public policy and is prescribed by statute or ordinance in some instances.

For example, under the general common law rule the liability of a dog owner whose dog injures a person depends upon knowledge or notice of this dangerous tendency. In some jurisdictions, the law has been broadened by statute or ordinances to hold the owner of any animal (wild or domesticated) liable for the damages suffered by any person harmed by that animal while in a public place or lawfully in a private place, which includes the property or home of the owner. Such statutes or ordinances create "strict liability." Where strict liability is not imposed by statute or ordinance, the injured person may recover from a pet owner only if the owner had actual or constructive knowledge of the animal's tendencies for causing injury and had failed to warn the injured person.

Strict liability is based upon presumed knowledge of the tendencies of an animal to do harm. Liability of an owner may be established on the negligence theory if there is no statute or ordinance.

EXAMPLE

Say you own a German shepherd, who is a guard dog, and you keep him locked up most of the time, but he gets out of the house while you are away because you left the door ajar when you took off in a hurry. As a result, he injures your next-door neighbor. Your neighbor may recover on the theory of negligence if he can prove your lack of care.

Another area where the doctrine of strict liability is used is that of the ultrahazardous activity. Under this doctrine, liability is established for extrahazardous activities that may involve the escape of dangerous substances brought onto the land, a dangerous use of land or water, or the use of inherently dangerous instruments anywhere.

To determine the applicability of this doctrine is a question of law. The court determines whether the activity is ultrahazardous or whether an inherently dangerous instrument is being used.

In some states there are statutes defining such activities or instruments.

K. Automobile Guest Statutes

The occupant or guest statutes and the liability of the driver in these instances vary from state to state and are generally dependent upon whether or not the person was an invited guest, an occupant by sufferance, a trespasser, or a passenger for hire.

The law in most states, however, follows the general rule that the duty owed to such a guest is that of ordinary or reasonable care in the operation of the vehicle. However, in some states automobile guest statutes require that gross negligence on the part of the driver must be present to establish liability on the part of the driver.

Product Liability

In spite of increased government regulation of manufactured products and their labeling, injuries do result from the use of such products. A useful site for offices involved in product liability cases is the U.S. Consumer Product Safety Commission at www.cpsc.gov.

Whether or not an injured person can recover damages for his injuries depends on the facts in the case.

The basis of the lawsuit may be negligence, breach of warranty, or strict liability. The law on this subject is in a state of flux.

In any case, the following facts must be proved to establish product liability:

1. The defendant manufactured or sold the product.

2. The product is defective or dangerous.

3. The defect was a hidden defect or the product was dangerous and had no warning labels. (Instructions may not constitute a warning.)

4. The product, because of the defect, caused injury or damage to plaintiff.

5. The plaintiff used the product in the way and in the manner for which it was intended or in a reasonably foreseeable manner. (Allegations or proof of this need to be made only if the manufacturer or seller claims, as an affirmative defense, that the product was not properly used.)

The defense of the manufacturer or seller may be:

1. Assumption of risk,

2. Unreasonable or unforeseeable use of the product, or

3. Limited warranty (if the action is based on breach of warranty).

The Restatement of Torts 2d sets forth the following elements of a strict liability claim (§402A. Special Liability of Seller of Product for Physical Harm to User or Consumer):

1. One who sells any product in a defective condition unreasonably dangerous to the user or consumer or to his property is subject to liability for physical harm thereby caused to the ultimate user or consumer, or to his property, if

   a. The seller is engaged in the business of selling such a product, and

   b. It is expected to and does reach the user or consumer without substantial change in the condition in which it is sold.

2. The rule stated in Subsection (1) applies although:

a. The seller has exercised all possible care in the preparation and sale of his product, and

b. The user or consumer has not bought the product from or entered into any contractual relation with the seller.

The Restatement of Torts 2d gives the following example of a manufacturer's liability for a defective product:

> A manufactures and packs a can of beans, which he sells to B, a wholesaler. B sells the beans to C, a jobber, who resells it to D, a retail grocer. E buys the can of beans from D, and gives it to F. F serves the beans at lunch to G, his guest. While eating the beans, G breaks a tooth, on a pebble of the size, shape, and color of a bean, which no reasonable inspection could possibly have discovered. There is satisfactory evidence that the pebble was in the can of beans when it was opened. Although there is no negligence on the part of A, B, C, or D, each of them is subject to liability to G. On the other hand E and F, who have not sold the beans, are not liable to G in the absence of some negligence on their part.

Certain materials or working situations may also prove to be inherently dangerous and defective, and without a warning to the employees, the manufacturer and/or employer may be held strictly liable for the ensuing medical problems. This is true for the massive ongoing asbestos litigation matters. The plaintiff in such matters must show not only that there was no warning of the dangerous nature of the work, but also that the plaintiff would have heeded that warning by acting to minimize risk of injury if there was a reasonable ability to so avoid it.

Professional Malpractice

To constitute professional malpractice, the conduct of the accused professional must be below the standard established by law for the protection of his patients or clients.

An unreasonable lack of skill in performing his professional duties or the display of illegal or immoral conduct which caused the injury or damage to the patient or client may be the basis of a cause of action for malpractice. In the case of attorneys and paralegals, a breach of the relevant ethical code is also considered professional malpractice. This is why it is critical for you to understand the ethical codes that bind you and your supervising attorney.

The standard of performance required in most states is the exercise of the degree of skill and learning ordinarily possessed and used by other members of the profession. This standard is proven by expert testimony at the hearing or trial.

A specialist is held to a higher standard of care than a general practitioner.

Malpractice cases against physicians have proliferated in the past. Malpractice suits against lawyers are becoming more common.

In medical malpractice suits, some states apply the "respectable minority rule" (choice of several recognized courses of treatment for the patient) or the "error in judgment rule" (made a wrong decision but otherwise followed professional standards).

The statute of limitations for bringing the action usually starts when the injury is reasonably discovered rather than at the time of the misconduct.

EXAMPLE

A sponge or surgical instrument was left in the patient's abdominal cavity during surgery. He suffered stomach pains after the surgery, but thought it was normal, until an X-ray was taken six months later, by another doctor, which revealed the foreign object. The action against the surgeon must be brought within the statutory limitation time from the date the new X-ray was interpreted by the new doctor.

An attorney may be liable to a client for malpractice even after he no longer represents the client (as where he damages a client by breach of his duty of confidentiality after he has completed his representation).

The attorney must perform for his client in accordance with the professional skills of the profession. He must also obey the ethical rules of the profession and the fiduciary duty he owes to a client. To be the basis of a malpractice suit, his failure in any of these areas must cause damages to the client. Otherwise, the remedy may be a complaint to the appropriate bar association for disciplinary action.

Section 2: Practice
Initial Steps

Before drafting a complaint or an answer in a tort case, the paralegal must understand the basic tort law applicable to the facts in the particular case. Getting all the facts and applying the theory of the case can be accomplished initially by using the following checklist. (Also read Chapters 6 and 7.)

I have found the following reminders to be most helpful in drafting a complaint or in preparing an answer to a complaint for personal injury and/or property damage claims:

1. Was there a duty of care owed to the plaintiff by the defendant, which was violated?

2. Was the duty breached by the defendant the result of his failure to act (or not act) as a reasonable, prudent person?

3. Did the defendant violate a statute at the time he breached this duty of care?

4. Did plaintiff, in fact, sustain damages or injury as a result of the breach of duty?

5. Was the defendant's breach of duty the actual and proximate cause of the plaintiff's injury or damage?

6. Was the plaintiff in any way negligent, thereby contributing to the breach?

7. Are there any affirmative defenses to defendant's breach of duty, if owed?

Drafting a Complaint in a Tort Action

Let us now turn to specifics with a simple personal injury case and property damage claim to put it all together. (See Chapter 6.)

It is well established that where there is concurrent injury to two separate properties, that is, personal injury and property damage, you can bring two separate causes of action for damage: complaint for personal injury or complaint for property damage.

In the alternative, the property damage claim can be an additional count within the complaint for personal injury.

In utilizing either approach, you should be aware of the statute of limitations governing the filing of these claims so as not to blow the statute as to either. In most jurisdictions, the time for filing a claim for personal injury is shorter than the time for filing a claim for property damage. If the injured person died, most states have wrongful death statutes of limitations, which are even shorter than those for personal injury where death does not result.

Use the facts obtained in the answer to the questions in the preceding seven-point checklist. State those facts in separate paragraphs in the complaint. (See Chapter 6.) You should consult state statutes for the time restrictions in your state if the action is to be brought there.

Claims Against Governmental Entities

If the client's claim involves the federal government, read the special federal courts section in Chapter 5.

Although the Federal Tort Claims Act allows many federal claims to be filed directly in special courts, some federal claims require preliminary agency hearings. In any event, before you can file a lawsuit naming the federal government as a defendant, a formal petition or claim for damages must be presented within the prescribed time period to the appropriate federal agency for an administrative determination.

These petitions or claim forms can be obtained from the agency itself, and the filing procedures can be found in the U.S. Code creating the special court or the Administrative Act that created the agency involved.

State statutes usually regulate the procedures for making claims against the state, and waive sovereign immunity (recovery is usually limited in amount by those statutes).

If a claim is against a municipality or county or other local government entity, read any pertinent state statute and also the municipal or public authority charter and/or ordinances.

CLAIM AGAINST A MUNICIPALITY (LOS ANGELES, CALIFORNIA)

1. You have one hundred days in which to file a claim after the date of the accident or incident.

2. Thereafter, you have forty-five days' waiting period in which the claim is deemed rejected if you do not get a response.

3. You then have a six-month period in which you must file a lawsuit or be forever barred from bringing an action to prosecute the claim.

   NOTE: All the above statutory limitations should be checked with your local state statutes so as to not blow a statute.

Specific Step-by-Step Procedure

The first step is to file the claim, which is usually a printed form that can be secured from the particular municipality. (See Figure 20.1.)

Figure 20.1
Claim Against Public Entity

In the matter of the claim of_____, claimant, v. CITY OF _____; COUNTY OF _____; DEPARTMENT OF HIGHWAYS; DEPARTMENT OF STREET MAINTENANCE AND REPAIR:

_____hereby presents this claim to the City of _____; County of _____; Department of Highways; Department of Street Maintenance and Repair, pursuant to Section of the _____ Government Code.

1. The name and post office address of the claimant's attorney is: _____, Attorney at Law, _____, _____, _____.
2. All notices, letters, and documents regarding this claim are requested by claimant, _____, to be mailed to her attorney at the address set forth here.
3. On October 11, 20____, at or near the _____ block of Wilshire Boulevard, County of _____, State of _____, claimant received personal injuries under the following circumstances: On October 11, 20____, at approximately 8:15 p.m., claimant was

Figure 20.1 (*continued*)

exiting the premises of the _____ Restaurant, located in the City and County of _____, _____. Claimant descended some steps outside said _____ building and was heading in a direction toward the sidewalk located at or near the _____ block of Wilshire Boulevard in the City of _____, County of _____, State of _____. When claimant reached the end of the premises of the restaurant building and reached the sidewalk, claimant slipped and fell by virtue of a negligent and adjoining restaurant-building property. Claimant is informed and believes and upon such information and belief alleges that the City of _____, County of _____, Department of Highways and Streets and Department of Street Maintenance and Repair are responsible in some manner for the defective condition set forth above.

4. That as a proximate result of the negligence of the public entities here described, claimant slipped and fell, injuring her right hand and breaking a finger, and further, sustained cuts and bruises on her head and jaw. Claimant further sustained injuries to her shoulder, all of which have caused her great mental and physical injury and damage, and claimant is informed that said injuries will continue for a period of time presently unknown to claimant herein. As a further and proximate cause of the negligence of the above public entities here described, claimant suffered loss of earnings in an amount presently unknown to claimant.

5. So far as is known to claimant, _____, at the date of the filing of this claim, _____ has incurred damages as follows:
   a. General damages
   b. Special damages
   c. Loss of earnings

6. At the time of the presentation of this claim, _____ claims damages in the amount of $25,000, together with her medical damages and loss of earnings according to proof.

DATED: _____

_____
CLAIMANT

_____
Attorney for _____

Check applicable state code sections for appropriate procedures and law.

If the client is late in obtaining the services of your attorney, then obtain an application for leave to present a late claim form, as shown in Figure 20.2, which follows this discussion. This latter document should be accompanied by a notice of petition for relief from governmental restrictions and order that suit may be filed. A declaration in support thereof and a copy of the proposed claim should accompany the notice.

Your office will receive notification of the hearing on this request. If the petition is approved, prepare the order, file the original and copy with the court clerk, and serve a copy on the board of directors. If the board does not object, the judge will sign the original order and return a conformed copy within a two-week period. You thereafter have forty-five days in which to file your complaint.

Figure 20.2
Application for Leave to Present Late Claim

Claimant

_____

                                                Claimant,

                                                                APPLICATION FOR LEAVE TO
v.   PRESENT LATE CLAIM ON
                                                                BEHALF OF CLAIMANT

STATE OF _____, STATE
BOARD OF CONTROL,

                        Defendants.

_____

TO THE STATE BOARD OF CONTROL:

1. Application is hereby made for leave to present a late claim founded on a cause of action for personal injuries which accrued on July 16, 20___, and for which a claim was not presented within the 100-day period provided by Section 911.2 of the Government Code. For additional circumstances relating to the cause of action, reference is made to the proposed claim attached to this application.

2. The failure to present this claim within the 100-day period specified by Section _____ of the Government Code was through mistake, inadvertence, surprise, and excusable neglect, and the State of _____ was not prejudiced by this failure, all as more particularly shown by the attached declaration of _____.

3. This application is being presented within a reasonable time after the accrual of this cause of action, as more particularly shown by the attached declaration of _____.

WHEREFORE, it is respectfully requested that this application be granted and that the attached proposed claim be received and acted on in accordance with Sections _____ of the government code.

DATED: _____

_____
Signature of Claimant
By _____
Attorneys for Claimant

> **PRACTICAL SUGGESTION:** All the above documentation should be sent by certified or registered mail, return receipt requested.

Medical Malpractice Claim

The complaint in an action for medical malpractice must state facts that, if proved, would show both a breach of due care by the doctor and damage to the patient as the proximate result thereof. Medical malpractice is a tort.

Care should be taken when filing a complaint for professional malpractice. There may be a procedural requirement to also file an "Affidavit of Merit" in conjunction with the Complaint (eleven states have this requirement). This is a sworn statement from a professional in the same field as the defendant. The New Jersey statute reads as follows:

2A:53A-27. AFFIDAVIT REQUIRED IN CERTAIN ACTIONS AGAINST LICENSED PERSONS

In any action for damages for personal injuries, wrongful death or property damage resulting from an alleged act of malpractice or negligence by a licensed person in his profession or occupation, the plaintiff shall, within 60 days following the date of filing of the answer to the complaint by the defendant, provide each defendant with an affidavit of an appropriate licensed person that there exists a reasonable probability that the care, skill or knowledge exercised or exhibited in the treatment, practice or work that is the subject of the complaint, fell outside acceptable professional or occupational standards or treatment practices. The court may grant no more than one additional period, not to exceed 60 days, to file the affidavit pursuant to this section, upon a finding of good cause.

In the case of an action for medical malpractice, the person executing the affidavit shall meet the requirements of a person who provides expert testimony or executes an affidavit as set forth in section 7 of P.L.2004, c. 17 (C.2A:53A-41). In all other cases, the person executing the affidavit shall be licensed in this or any other state; have particular expertise in the general area or specialty involved in the action, as evidenced by board certification or by devotion of the person's practice substantially to the general area or specialty involved in the action for a period of at least five years. The person shall have no financial interest in the outcome of the case under review, but this prohibition shall not exclude the person from being an expert witness in the case.

The standard of care required of a physician is based upon the degree of learning and skills ordinarily possessed by other members of the profession in his field, as well as the use of ordinary care and diligence in applying and learning the skills.

Since the level of learning and degree of skills are different for a general practitioner than they are for a specialist, the standard of care, therefore, for a medical specialist is higher. Should a general practitioner, for whatever reason, fail to consult with a specialist or refer the patient to a specialist upon determining that this is what the patient needs, this failure may constitute malpractice, if the general practitioner should have recognized the need for consultation with a specialist.

There are some other facts that may constitute a breach of the doctor's duty to a patient:

1. A physician may be considered negligent if he fails to hospitalize a patient where the standard of care indicates this to be necessary.

2. A physician may be considered to be in violation of his duty of care by his lack of diligence in attending his patient.

3. A physician may be considered in violation of his duty of care if he unjustifiably abandons or neglects his patient absent sufficient notice, excuse, or mutual agreement.

4. A physician may be considered to be in violation of his duty of care if he promises results that are not reasonably forthcoming as the result of the treatment prescribed or surgery performed.

5. A physician may be considered to be in violation of his duty of care if he fails to explain to and inform a patient as to the nature of proposed surgery and if he fails to obtain an informed, intelligent consent to said surgery. The exception to this rule, in some jurisdictions, is emergency surgery.

A plaintiff has no medical malpractice case unless he can establish that the doctor breached his duty of care and that the same was the proximate cause of the injury or death of the patient.

NOTE: In some states there is statutory provision for a preliminary hearing before the complaint can be filed in court. Check your state malpractice statute before proceeding with any malpractice claim. Also read the state case law involving similar cases. See Chapter 8, "Legal Research Tools."

Answering a Complaint in a Tort Action

When a complaint filed against your client comes into the office, you should immediately do the following:

1. Set up a file and index card, and if applicable obtain an extension of time in which to answer. Enter the same on your follow-up calendar. Place in the appropriate docket book.

2. Examine the complaint to determine if a routine answer, general denial, or affirmative defense is needed (see Section I of this chapter for some possible affirmative defenses).

3. Examine the proof of service to determine if proper service was made, and if not, whether you can file a motion to strike or a special demurrer or other similar type document.

4. If you find that you can file a simple answer, then draft such a document and attach it to the file and give it to your attorney.

5. If the complaint has more than one count, it is always best to determine the theory under which each count is being alleged, that is, common count, alterego, breach of contract, and so forth. This will aid you in stating your affirmative defenses. They may differ for each count. For example, the plaintiff's first cause of action is based on an alleged breach of warranty, the second is based on alleged negligence, and the third on alleged acts creating strict liability.

A useful, personal practice is to put notations of proposed answers in the margin of the complaint-pleading, next to each paragraph, as follows:

Margin	
(deny)	Paragraph V
(admit)	Paragraph VI

This type of notation makes it easier for your employer to review your work and make any additions, embellishments, or suggestions for your final draft of the answer.

Medical Malpractice Defense

Both the attorney and the paralegal may have to use a little psychology when working with the physician.

Generally speaking, as with the average layman, most doctors know very little about the law, the legal process, and/or the daily routine involved in court procedures. What they are fully aware of, however, is the time, and the fact that everything done in the legal process takes up too much of their time—time which they feel belongs to their patients.

Add to this fact that someone has filed a lawsuit against them, alleging misconduct or incompetence in their performance as doctors, and you have problems. Doctors, generally, do not understand how someone they have treated, perhaps for years and sometimes since childhood, could possibly sue them for anything. It is more of a personal affront than, say, with an ordinary personal injury action where an individual has been allegedly injured by a stranger.

For these reasons alone, defending a physician in a medical malpractice suit is one of the more difficult tasks of your attorney; hence, you as his paralegal should be aware of these emotional and psychological obstacles in order to aid your attorney in his dealings with a physician client.

Therefore, consider the following practical hints:

1. *Immediately* upon service of process upon the doctor, he needs sympathy and an interpretation and explanation of the charge made in the legal language of the complaint.

2. Your attorney will explain to the doctor the nature of the doctor's responsibility and liability, if any.

3. You must explain the time restrictions, that is, twenty or thirty days in which to answer, as the case may be.

4. Explain why you need the doctor's help—hence some of his time—to get the facts from his point of view in order to answer the complaint and set forth affirmative defenses, if applicable.

5. Although your attorney will have discussed it with him, reiterate the role being played by your attorney and the doctor's insurance company (malpractice insurance carrier) to defend him against the action.

6. You do the above by explaining to the doctor that your attorney's expertise is medical malpractice (as is the insurance carrier's) and they are there to help him in every way they can.

7. Explain each step involved in defending the lawsuit, that is, the discovery process—what it is and what is involved, such as interrogatories; depositions, including his own; the possibility of his records being subpoenaed for copying and inspection; and so forth.

If you do all the above at the beginning of the defense of the lawsuit, it has been our experience that the doctor will be much more cooperative when he is needed in each step of the discovery process and trial, should it come to that.

Although the plaintiff is the aggressive party, in most cases, the defendant in a medical malpractice suit may become the moving party and as such may immediately initiate the discovery process by sending out interrogatories and/or request for admission, or both concurrently. Bearing this in mind, consider the following tried and proven procedures:

1. When a complaint is received in your office, your attorney will tell you how he thinks it should be answered. He will often want you to review the complaint yourself to determine if he has overlooked anything.

   EXAMPLE

   A possible demurrer to a request for punitive damages. Should you discover this, advise your attorney and obtain permission to file a special demurrer to this allegation.

2. Or the attorney may have noted on the complaint to go forward and file an answer alleging affirmative defenses.

   EXAMPLE

   A "good Samaritan" defense or "contributory negligence."

   If, in fact, plaintiff sustained any injury and damage of any nature whatsoever by reason of anything done or omitted to be done by the defendant, which fact is not admitted, but is merely stated for the purpose of this defense, said injury and damage, if any, was approximately caused by the negligence of the plaintiff in failing to take proper and reasonable measure for his own well being before and after the surgery as instructed to do by the defendant.

   NOTE: It is vitally important in this type of lawsuit to include affirmative defenses. Hence, if your attorney, for whatever reason, overlooked to instruct you to allege affirmative defenses, bring this oversight to his attention if you have found any facts to support it.

3. Thereafter, or concurrently therewith, prepare and cause to be filed a set of interrogatories and requests for admission directed to the plaintiff. It is suggested that you mark these documents First Set of _____, since it has been our experience in this type of lawsuit that more than one set of interrogatories and requests for admissions are required to obtain the information needed and wanted by your attorney.

4. Oftentimes, you will find that you have to compel answers to the interrogatories or requests for admissions, and since you are defending the action, upon the expiration of the statutory time within which plaintiff has to file said answers (twenty to thirty days), you should immediately prepare your motion to compel answers or compelling further answers (see Chapter 9).

5. In the preceding connection, your duty in relation to answering the interrogatories served on the doctor is one of meticulous scrutiny, review, editing, and in some instances, rewriting. One major factor you should look for is the name or names of other doctors who may have worked with the patient, or may perhaps have been involved in the surgical procedure (or whatever the complaint is) to determine if there is a possible conflict of interest, that is, your office representing him as general counsel or otherwise.

6. Furthermore, check to see if in the interrogatories there was a request for information as to the finances of the doctor. If so, check the complaint to see if there was an allegation for punitive damages. If punitive damages were not pleaded, or pleaded incorrectly, then the doctor does not have to answer to the interrogatory as to his finances, since the request for punitive damages will not stand. If, initially, you had filed a demurrer to the allegation regarding punitive damages

and said demurrer was overruled, this would allow the allegation on punitive damages to stand, having the effect of allowing the plaintiff to inquire into the financial stature of the doctor. The doctor would then have to answer the interrogatory.

7. Obtain copies of any and all medical reports by other doctors retained by the plaintiff in the possession or under the control of the plaintiff for your attorney and the insurance company (get copies from your doctor also for comparison).

8. Schedule (on notice) the taking of the deposition of the plaintiff.

9. Upon receipt of the notice of the Trial Setting Conference (TSC) and Mandatory Settlement Conference (MSC) or your state court's equivalent, notify the insurance company and the doctor. Especially notify the doctor, since unless he has signed a Consent to Settlement of the lawsuit, he does have to appear. You should consult with your attorney, however, to determine if he wants the doctor present at the Mandatory Settlement Conference. Then too, the doctor may want to be present just to be on top of what is going on in the case. You will find that if attorneys' schedules permit, they like to be present.

10. Should the case go to trial, the step-by-step procedure is the same as with any other litigated matter.

Other Torts

Along with an action based on negligence, there are four other basic tort actions that were not previously discussed. We generally answered the question, "What is a tort?" Now let us discuss the "intentional tort," which is one that causes a personal harm. It is a nonconsensual relationship in which society does not have a stake. It is a relationship between individuals.

The intentional torts are those where the person being sued has done something that has caused harm to another person. For example:

Battery: When the defendant intentionally inflicts a harmful or offensive touching on someone. The key here is that it must be a voluntary action on the part of the defendant and it must have caused a harmful or offensive touching.

Another example: someone kissing you in public, or the boss patting his secretary on the behind. In other words, any touching that is embarrassing can be offensive and will give rise to a tort dollar damage recovery. Some of these actions are also included in a sexual harassment complaint.

Assault: Assault is not and does not include physical contact. It is the creation of apprehension of harmful or intentional touching, merely frightening or creating fear. This is assaulting the plaintiff. Words alone do not create "fear." But, if you are blind, then the hearing of words may create "fear" and apprehension.

More important, the defendant must have the clear and apparent ability to carry out and commit the act and create the emotional fear. In other words, it must be immediate. The defendant cannot say, "I'm going to beat you up if you do that again." The defendant must say, "I am going to beat you up now, this minute, this second." *It must be immediate.*

Another type of intentional tort is called "false imprisonment." In this area of tort law, the plaintiff has to know that he or she has been imprisoned and is being restrained intentionally by the defendant in a restricted area.

EXAMPLES

(a) The defendant has placed the plaintiff in a room with locked doors and no means of exit; (b) Locked doors with a window open gives the plaintiff a reasonable means of exiting the premises unless the defendant has threatened to harm a member of the family if the plaintiff leaves by that open window. Both of these would constitute false imprisonment.

The Private Nuisance

Trespass and *non-trespass:* These are unreasonable interferences and/or invasions of your property, those things that interfere with the peace and tranquility of the enjoyment of your property.

A trespassory tort indicates that a person who was not invited or permitted by license or other arrangement has entered upon your land. A non-trespassory tort includes excessive noise, pollution, or other invasion by a thing, rather than the person, that interferes with your enjoyment or use of your property.

The defense to these property torts is the reason of necessity. If a person finds themselves in danger and the only way to avoid it is to trespass on your land, he will be excused for this invasion.

Torts Relating to Real and Personal Property

Conversion: The taking of a piece of property belonging to another. If taken permanently, one can sue for the full dollar value.

Now compare this to "trespass," an example of which is joyriding. When you invade, but do not permanently deprive someone of, personal property, this is a trespass. The loss, in this case, would be for damages to the property when the defendant was using the property. But if the defendant takes the car and drives it across the state line or to a location where it is inconvenient or unreasonable, or you are unable to find it, then this is "conversion."

Again, the defense of necessity or emergency exists here. If you needed to use the car to escape imminent danger, you could be excused of the commission of the tort.

For both trespass and conversion, the police have the right to exercise their authority in a situation where they are protecting the public. In either circumstance, the damage to the property will be reimbursed.

Harm to Nonphysical Property

This type of tort relates to one's reputation, emotional distress, embarrassment, etc.

A. Defamation of Character

This occurs when someone communicates something defaming or embarrassing in the community, and it is heard by someone else and understood that way. These remarks do not have to be true or be read in the newspaper or heard on television. Defamation can take place in a classroom, a living room, a cafeteria, or by making a statement in front of others. It occurs in the setting up of a telephone call and asking for a reference as to your actions on a job.

We all, in our lifetime, have had to get a reference from an employer. We all know that a potential new employer will call the ex-employer and ask what kind of employee we were. The remarks that follow could be defamation. For example, your ex-employer could say that you are lazy; that you stole from the office; that you embezzled the petty cash. These are accusations that could conceivably cost you your new job; hence, they are defaming.

Another example of this would be if, while in the office, your boss walks up to you in the presence of other employees and says, "You are fired because you are incompetent and you are lazy and I have caught you in too many mathematical mistakes in your bookkeeping." This too is defamation of character.

In discussing defamation of character, be advised that it comes in two forms: (1) libel, which is in writing, or (2) slander, which is oral. The defense to defamation of character is the defense of truthfulness of the statements made.

B. Wrongful Invasion of Privacy

You are entitled to certain private thoughts and papers and facts. Violation of these rights is the basis for a good cause of action from which you may recover.

C. Right to Privacy

Misappropriation of likeness: The unauthorized use of a person's picture and likeness is an invasion of the right to privacy.

You cannot present the plaintiff in a false light and hold that person up to public embarrassment.

Additionally, you cannot invade another person's physical solitude, or private conversations by bugging a personal telephone with electronic devices without permission. The violation of the statutes in this connection and the individual's right to privacy is the subject of a lawsuit from which the plaintiff could recover.

D. Intentional Infliction of Emotional Distress

This is best explained by way of example: seeing your child or parent or spouse killed in front of you by a car or other deadly weapon; being told that, because you are black, or Chinese, or a Jew, short or fat, you cannot enter this restaurant or join a health center, etc.—anything that causes you embarrassment or humiliation in public, causing you wrongful emotional distress, can be the basis of a lawsuit from which a plaintiff could recover. The caveat is that the offender must be aware of this sensitivity. Inadvertent tactlessness or callousness does not rise to the level of this tort.

E. The Right to Rely on Things Said

You have the right to rely on things said to you and not be unjustly harmed through misrepresentation. This occurs when someone provides you with a false, but material, misrepresentation of facts, which is known to be false but done with the intent to cause you to rely on it; you then rely on it to your injury.

Say you are going to buy my car and I tell you that the car has only 3,000 miles on it, when in fact I had eliminated three zeros. This is a material fact that is also false. The test, then, is: Would you have bought the car if you had known that it had 300,000 miles on it instead of 3,000?

F. Disparagement

Disparagement is a little like defamation: false statements made to others about the plaintiff that cause injury to the plaintiff's business. An example of this is a disgruntled customer standing out in front of a market, telling people not to go in because the food is bad; it is poisonous; they cheat you; the cashiers cheat you on your change; they have rats in the building; etc. This is disparagement upon which a plaintiff could file a lawsuit and recover.

G. Interference with Contracts

You have an existing contract and the defendant undertakes a course of action to cause injury to that contractual relationship. For example, the defendant goes to the other party, the contractor, and says negative things about you, such as that you will not pay the bill, that you are hard to get along with, and such other remarks. And as a result, the defendant contractor withdraws from the contract. Under these conditions, a lawsuit can be filed to recover money damages.

H. Interference with Prospective Economic Advantage

Where someone wrongfully interferes with future business contracts or business. For example, someone says, "This guy is a bum. Do not go into business with him." As a result of this, a potential investor changes his mind and does not go into business with the plaintiff.

I. Malicious Prosecution or Abuse of Process

Wrongfully filing a lawsuit against someone for which there is no justification in law or in fact. This is a growth area in the law, and the trend is now to punish persons who frivolously use the court system and bog it down. A good example of this concerns inmates who are always filing frivolous lawsuits to get their sentences reduced or to complain about the food or to complain about the conditions in the prisons. Since they are allowed to file lawsuits without a filing fee, they have, in fact, bogged down the court system so that those in the civilian world are unable to get their lawsuits heard in a timely manner.

Further, attorneys are susceptible to sanctions under Rule 11 of the Federal Rules of Civil Procedure for filing a pleading or other court submission without reasonably believing the contents, or using it for an improper purpose such as harassment, delay, or embarrassment of the opposing party. Check your local rules of procedure for this equivalent. This is also an ethical obligation on the part of attorneys. See the ABA Model Rule 3.1 and its equivalent in your jurisdiction.

Some Defenses

A. Consent

Where the plaintiff gives permission to the defendant to touch her, she cannot then sue for battery unless the defendant exceeds the permission given.

1. Actual or expressed consent;

2. Expressed or implied consent (when a reasonable person would assume that defendant had permission to touch her);

3. Consent implied by law (to save life or property).

All of the above are valid defenses—as it relates to a female plaintiff, up to the part where she says no. Then anything thereafter would be battery.

B. Self-Defense

As a general rule, a plaintiff is privileged to use force to defend himself. But you cannot rise to deadly force unless you can reasonably conclude that it is necessary. For example, in California, the law was recently changed so that if you walked into your home and discovered a burglar, you could use deadly force to defend yourself provided that the defendant had in his hands a deadly weapon, or if the defendant was the size of, say, the Incredible Hulk, and you are five foot even, weighing a hundred pounds.

Consider another example: a twelve-year-old weakling coming through your window at night, and you alone in bed. The only condition under which you could use deadly force is if you could prove to the court and sway the jury that you were in fear of your life. Then the question would be, how could a twelve-year-old hurt you, unless of course you saw what appeared to be a deadly weapon.

Another self-defense that would stand up in court would be the defense of third persons. A person may be legally entitled to defend someone else against attack under certain circumstances. This is usually applied to persons with whom the defender has a relationship or when circumstances warranted the intervention. And here again, it would be a reasonable defense under the circumstances.

C. Defense of Land

You may not use deadly force to protect land or personal property. But you can use non-deadly force. (Please check your local criminal code to verify this law.)

D. The Shopkeeper Rule

This rule should speak for itself. For example, a person walking through a department store lifts a piece of jewelry and upon exiting the store is approached by the store detective inquiring about the jewelry, which (it is apparent) has not been paid for. The defendant thereafter is locked in a room while the detective goes for authorities. This could be construed as false imprisonment.

As long as the "imprisonment" in the room is done in a reasonable manner, within a reasonable time, there is no defense against it. If, on the other hand, the detective leaves the suspect in the room for the rest of the day with no contact from anybody, then there is a possible lawsuit for false imprisonment. Once again, whether or not this defense can be used depends on the facts and circumstances.

Preparation for Trial

After establishing the claim and/or defenses, it will be necessary to discuss with the lawyer the follow-up steps such as the schedule for sending out interrogatories, setting up depositions, developing requests for admissions, and the need or desire for a jury trial if the latter was not requested in the complaint.

1. Should you receive answers to a set of interrogatories propounded by you, review them by comparing the answers and studying the evasions and incomplete responses. Flag them for your attorney and discuss them, together with the possible need for a motion to produce or to compel further answers.

2. If you receive a set of interrogatories to be answered by your client, your attorney may want to object to some of the interrogatories propounded. Remember the time restriction for this type of action (Motion for Protective Order).

3. After or instead of the foregoing, consider requests for admissions. These requests for admissions may be based upon plaintiff's answers to your interrogatories, statements of witnesses or their testimony at a deposition, or information obtained as the result of a motion to produce documents or as a result of private investigation.

4. Should number 3 be implemented, the next step would be to move for an order that certain facts be admitted if that is the procedure in your court. Under some court rules, facts contained in a request for admissions are automatically admitted if they are not denied or objected to within a specified number of days (usually thirty).

5. If the plaintiff files a response to a request for admissions, review the responses of plaintiff, determine the need to request more admissions, and report your findings to your attorney. Here it may be possible to file a motion for summary judgment. If not, you are probably ready to have the case set for trial, if the plaintiff has not set it for trial.

6. If not already prepared and filed by the plaintiff, prepare and file an at-issue memorandum (or its equivalent in your court) with the court. In some states, this is a printed form and does not have to be signed by opposing counsel. Merely mail a copy to him.

7. In some states, after three or four weeks, the court will send out a document entitled Certificate of Eligibility to File Certificate of Readiness. This is a printed document wherein the court is advising all parties that the case is now on the civil active list and that the parties may now obtain a trial date. In other states an order setting trial date and a date for a pretrial date and a date for a pretrial conference will be sent to you by the court.

8. In some states, you can now prepare for filing with the court your Certificate of Readiness, which is a printed form. In other states, you prepare your pretrial conference memorandum as required by the court and have your client available for settlement decision during the pretrial conference.

9. Notify the client of the trial date and settlement conference date by letter. This will prevent misunderstanding.

10. Notify all potential witnesses of the trial date.
    Suggestion: Send out a copy of the letter to be returned to you, confirming the witnesses' appearance at the trial and setting a possible office conference prior to the date of the trial to review the facts of the case.
    Complete your in-office trial preparation (refer back to Chapter 3).

    a. Review the file and determine what witnesses are to be subpoenaed;

    b. Prepare the subpoenas and hold them in the file until needed;

c. Marshal all trial documents, photos, exhibits, and the like;

d. Start your trial brief (or briefs);

e. Draft your proposed jury instructions;

f. Draft appropriate motions, including notice of appeal, just in case; and

g. Draft closing documents, arguments, and so forth.

For help in making the final trial preparation, three checklists follow. They are master trial checklists for office calendar, trial book outline, and instructions for preparing the trial book.

Master Trial Checklist for Office Calendar

Date	Event
Six weeks before trial	**1.** Confirm availability of witnesses for trial.
	2. Determine and acquire all necessary evidence and documents.
	3. Complete the taking of all oral depositions.
One month before trial	**1.** Review pleadings for any possible amendments (due to new facts found during discovery).
	2. Make decision in regard to additional pretrial discovery.
	3. Review any depositions.
Three weeks before trial	**1.** Complete all depositions analyses.
	2. Arrange for the appearance of witnesses, including making any hotel reservations needed.
Two weeks before trial	**1.** Complete the research of any legal questions (read carefully all pleadings to determine the legal questions involved in the lawsuit).
	2. Set the pretrial client conference for your attorney or complete the arrangements for pretrial client conferences.
One week before trial	**1.** Have the attorney complete preparation for direct and cross-examination of witnesses, including expert witnesses, if any.
	2. Docket call (if required by court rules).
	3. Organize trial exhibits (prepare the trial book, if necessary).
	4. Organize evidence in regard to attorney's fees, if applicable.

Date	Event
	5. For jury trial:
	a. Prepare motion in limine.
	b. Complete voir dire outline.
	c. Complete preparation of special issues.
	d. Prepare written stipulations.
	e. Draft your instructions to be requested.
One day before trial	**1.** Have your attorney meet with the client in preparation for testimony at the trial, unless it is routine and he instructs you to handle it.

Trial Book Outline

1. Jury

    a. Voir dire examination

    b. Argument

    c. Opening argument

    d. Closing argument

2. Testimony

    a. Witness list

    b. Client's statement

    c. Witnesses' statements

3. Evidence

    a. Defendant's deposition

    b. Plaintiff's deposition

    c. Exhibit list

    d. Instructions

    e. Legal authorities and case decisions

4. Pleadings

    a. Plaintiff's original petition or complaint

    b. Defendant's answer

    c. Last-minute pleadings (*motion in limine*)

Preparing the Trial Book

Interrogatories: Print each question on a blank sheet followed by the answer (if necessary for clarity). Otherwise arrange, as filed, in logical order.

Depositions: Prepare a deposition analysis or summary and put it into the book under Testimony.

Witness list: Set up the columns as follows: Name, Address and Telephone Number, Topic, and Time/Date for Testimony.

Prepare the witness list before the pretrial conference. Give one copy of the witness list to your attorney to take to the trial; keep one copy at the office for you or the secretary. Locate and schedule all witnesses (get assistance, if necessary). Fill in the list as each witness is scheduled.

Expert witness conference: Have the attorney organize the experts' testimony so that they buttress one another, cover gaps, and eliminate inconsistencies. Set and attend the expert witness conference with the attorney. Take notes at the conference to prepare a memo of the conference. The position of each expert should be summarized by you for the attorney. Background data on each expert must be itemized by you for the attorney. A memo of the expert witness conference should be circulated among all the experts. Place the conference memo in the testimony section of the trial book.

Preparing and serving subpoenas: Prepare subpoenas or have them prepared. Use a standard form. Send to the process server or sheriff.

Exhibits list: Set up the columns as follows: Exhibit Number, Description, In/Out. The name of the case and your office file number (if any) should appear at the top. Prepare before the pretrial conference. Use In/Out for admission (in) or rejection (out). Use the same exhibit numbers throughout the pretrial and court hearings for easy cross-referencing.

Color coding (if used by your office): *Red:* the client's testimony outline, deposition analysis, and interrogatories. *Yellow:* the adverse party's deposition analysis, statement, and interrogatories. *Green:* general trial matters such as outline of the case and voir dire opening argument. *Blue:* legal authorities relevant on evidentiary and substantial law points. *Purple:* procedural portions.

CHAPTER TWENTY-ONE

How to Assist in
Collecting a Judgment

After you have concluded a successful lawsuit on behalf of your client, it will be necessary to turn that judgment into real money. The laws governing the enforcement of money judgments are controlled by state statutes in the state where the money or property of the judgment debtor is located. This chapter addresses itself primarily to the procedures involved in the enforcement and collection of debts that have been reduced to judgment in the same state where the judgment debtor's property is located. The practice and procedure for the collection of judgments under "sister state" reciprocal judgment statutes is also discussed.

The advanced information available through legal research sites and other electronic support systems in this area of the law is essential to this type of practice. Familiarizing yourself with those asset search engines will be of enormous help.

This type of law practice seeks to collect numerous money judgments in volume on behalf of the client (such as a large department store or medical association or other organization). Because it is a volume practice, the paralegal will also be handling a substantial load of work in preparing complaints for money owed, open book accounts, and so forth.

Most Common Procedures Used to Enforce Money Judgments

In securing satisfaction of a money judgment, the most commonly used vehicles to reach the property of the judgment debtor are:

1. Prejudgment attachment, which is attachment of the alleged debtor's property before the trial where the debtor is expected to secrete or move his assets before the judgment can be obtained. There are very strict rules for obtaining this relief and you will need to check your local rules for the prerequisites and procedures.

2. Garnishment

3. Writ of execution (possession)

4. Such other remedies as may be provided in your state statutes and court rules

Step-by-Step Procedure for Prejudgment Attachments
Prejudgment Attachment: Plaintiff Step-by-Step Procedure

This is the process of securing possession of property in controversy or of creating a security for the debt in controversy before the final judgment of the court on the merits of the case.

1. At the time of filing the complaint, or any time thereafter, the plaintiff may apply for an order and Writ of Attachment by filing an application for the Order and Writ.

2. This application, executed under oath, should include the following:

    a. A statement setting forth facts which indicate the validity of the claim and that the debtor is likely to secrete or remove his property from the jurisdiction (check your state statute for necessary allegations);

    b. A statement of the full amount owed or special payment;

    c. A statement that the Writ of Attachment is not sought for any other property than that upon which the attachment is based;

    d. A statement to the effect that the applicant has no knowledge, information, or belief that the claim is dischargeable in bankruptcy or that it has been discharged in bankruptcy; and

    e. A full and clear description of the property to be attached, and that to the best of his knowledge the property is subject to attachment, that is, not homesteaded, and so forth.

NOTE: The defendant must be served with the following documents prior to the date of a hearing on the request for issuance of an order and writ of attachment:

1. A copy of the summons and complaint;

2. A notice of application and hearing; and

3. A copy of the application and any affidavits in support of the application. The plaintiff must show that the plaintiff has satisfied the statutory requirements with regard to the right to attach that particular kind of property and that the plaintiff will probably prevail in the action entitling him to access the property and that the property is not exempt from such attachment.

Thereafter the court must first make a determination at the time of the hearing on the request for issuance of a writ of attachment that the defendant's assets exceed the amount necessary to satisfy the money judgment or secured by the attachment. When this has been accomplished, the court will order a levy on the appropriate assets.

This package should be served on the defendant not less than five days before the date of the hearing (or other appropriate time restriction) on the Application, Request for Order, and Writ of Attachment.

It should be noted, if applicable in your state, that you can obtain an *exparte* hearing for issuance of a Writ of Attachment, provided you can show that it would cause great and irreparable harm to the plaintiff if the issuance was delayed until the matter could be heard on notice. Reasons for your fear must be stated in the petition for prejudgment Writ of Attachment.

Furthermore, do not forget that the plaintiff must file an undertaking bond to pay for any money damages the defendant may recover for wrongful attachment by the plaintiff in the action. The amount of this undertaking depends on the value of the property to be attached, which must not exceed the monetary jurisdiction of the court in which the action was filed. (You should check your local state statute and court rules for this procedure.)

Step-by-Step Procedure for Collecting a Judgment Debt

First note that you will need to know what kind of assets the judgment-debtor possesses and where they are. Assume that the judgment-debtor will not voluntarily give up this information. Many states provide that the prevailing party can serve an information subpoena upon those parties that have had an order of judgment rendered against them. You will need to check your local rules for the exact content and service requirements for the information subpoena. Figure 21.1 contains the New Jersey Information Subpoena form found in its court rules.

Figure 21.1
Information Subpoena (NJ)

APPENDIX XI-L.
INFORMATION SUBPOENA AND WRITTEN QUESTIONS

IMPORTANT NOTICE--PLEASE READ CAREFULLY

FAILURE TO COMPLY WITH THIS INFORMATION SUBPOENA MAY
RESULT IN YOUR ARREST AND INCARCERATION

NAME: SUPERIOR COURT OF NEW JERSEY
ADDRESS: LAW DIVISION: SPECIAL CIVIL PART
                                          _____ COUNTY
TELEPHONE NO.:   DOCKET NO.
Attorneys for:

            Plaintiff   CIVIL ACTION
                                          INFORMATION SUBPOENA

   -v-

            Defendant

THE STATE OF NEW JERSEY, to: _____

Judgment has been entered against you in the Superior Court of New Jersey, Law Division, Special Civil Part, _____ County, on _____, 20__, in the amount of $_____ plus costs, of which $_____ together with interest from _____, 20__, remains due and unpaid.

Attached to this Information Subpoena is a list of questions that court rules require you to answer within 14 days from the date you receive this subpoena. If you do not answer the attached questions within the time required, the opposing party may ask the court to conduct a hearing in order to determine if you should be held in contempt. You will be compelled to appear at the hearing and explain your reasons for your failure to answer.

If this judgment has resulted from a default, you may have the right to have this default judgment vacated by making an appropriate motion to the court. Contact an attorney or the clerk of the court for information on making such a motion. Even if you dispute the judgment you must answer all of the attached questions.

You must answer each question giving complete answers, attaching additional pages if necessary. False or misleading answers may subject you to punishment by the court. However, you need not provide information concerning the income and assets of others living in your household unless you have a financial interest in the assets or income. Be sure to sign and date your answers and return them to the address in the upper left hand corner within 14 days.

Dated: _____, 20__

_____   _____
Attorney for   Clerk

Figure 21.1 (*continued*)

QUESTIONS FOR INDIVIDUALS

1. Full name _____

2. Address _____

3. Birthdate _____

4. Social Security # _____

5. Driver's license # and expiration date _____
   _____

6. Telephone # _____

7. Full name and address of your employer _____
   _____
   (a) Your weekly salary: Gross _____ Net _____
   (b) If not presently employed, name and address of last employer. _____
   _____

8. Is there currently a wage execution on your salary?
   Yes ____ No ____

9. List the names, addresses and account numbers of all bank accounts on which your name appears.

10. If you receive money from any of the following sources, list the amount, how often, and the name and address of the source:

Type	Amount & Frequency	Name & Address of Sources
Alimony		
Loan Payments		
Rental Income		
Pensions		
Bank Interest		
Stock Dividends		
Other		

Figure 21.1 (*continued*)

11. Do you receive any of the following, which are exempt from levy? Any levy on disclosed exempt funds may result in monetary penalties including reimbursement of the debtor's out-of-pocket expenses.

Social Security benefits　　　　Yes ___ Amount per month　　No __

S.S.I. benefits　　　　　　　　Yes ___ Amount per month　　No __

Welfare benefits　　　　　　　Yes ___ Amount per month　　No __

V.A. benefits　　　　　　　　　Yes ___ Amount per month　　No __

Unemployment benefits　　　　Yes ___ Amount per month　　No __

Workers' compensation benefits Yes ___ Amount per month　　No __

Child support payments　　　　Yes ___ Amount per month　　No __

Attach copies of the three most recent bank statements for each account listed in Question 9 that contains funds from these sources.

12. Do you own the property where you reside?
Yes ___ No ___ If yes, state the following:
(a) Name of the owner or owners _____
(b) Date property was purchased _____
(c) Purchase price _____
(d) Name and address of mortgage holder _____
_____
(e) Balance due on mortgage _____

13. Do you own any other real estate?
Yes ___ No ___ If yes, state the following for each property:
(a) Address of property _____
(b) Date property was purchased _____
(c) Purchase price _____
(d) Name and address of all owners _____
_____
(e) Name and address of mortgage holder _____
_____
(f) Balance due on mortgage _____
_____
(g) Names and address of all tenants and monthly rental paid by each tenant _____
_____

Figure 21.1 (*continued*)

14. Does the present value of your personal property, which includes automobiles, furniture, appliances, stocks, bonds, and cash on hand, exceed $1,000?

    Yes ___ No ___   If the answer is "yes," you must itemize all
                       personal property owned by you.

    Cash on hand: $_____

    Other personal property: (Set forth make, model and serial number. If financed, give name and address of party to whom payments are made).

Item	Date Purchased	Purchase Price	If Financed Balance Still Due	Present Value

15. Do you own a motor vehicle?

    Yes ___ No ___ If yes, state the following for each vehicle owned:
    (a) Make, model and year of motor vehicle _____

    (b) If there is a lien on the vehicle, state the name and address of
        the lienholder and the amount due to the lienholder _____

    (c) License plate # _____

    (d) Vehicle identification # _____

16. Do you own a business?

    Yes ___ No ___ If yes, state the following:
    (a) Name and address of the business _____

    (b) Is the business a Corporation _____, sole proprietorship _____
        or partnership _____?
    (c) The name and address of all stockholders, officers and/or partners

    (d) The amount of income received by you from the business during the
        last twelve months _____

17. Set forth all other judgments that you are aware of that have been entered against you and include:

Creditor's Name	Creditor's Attorney	Amount Due	Name of Court	Docket #

Figure 21.1 (*continued*)

I hereby certify that the foregoing statements made by me are true. I am aware that if any of the foregoing statements made by me are willfully false, I am subject to punishment.

Date: _____   _____

QUESTIONS FOR BUSINESS ENTITY

1. Name of business including all trade names. _____
   _____

2. Addresses of all business locations. _____
   _____

3. If the judgment-debtor is a corporation, the names and addresses of all
   stockholders, officers and directors.
   _____
   _____
   _____

4. If a partnership, list the names and addresses of all partners.
   _____
   _____
   _____

5. If a limited partnership, list the names and addresses of all general
   partners.
   _____
   _____
   _____

6. Set forth in detail the name, address and telephone number of all
   businesses in which the principals of the judgment-debtor now have an
   interest and set forth the nature of the interest.
   _____

7. For all bank accounts of the judgment-debtor business entity, list the
   name of the bank, the bank's address, the account number and the name in
   which the account is held.
   _____
   _____

8. Specifically state the present location of all books and records of the
   business, including checkbooks. _____
   _____

9. State the name and address of the person, persons, or entities who

Figure 21.1 (*continued*)

prepare, maintain and/or control the business records and checkbooks.

_____
_____

10. List all physical assets of the business and their location. If any asset
    is subject to a lien, state the name and address of the lienholder and
    the amount due on the lien.

    _____
    _____
    _____

11. Does the business own any real estate? Yes ____ No ____
    If yes, state the following for each property:
    (a) Name(s) in which property is owned _____
    (b) Address of property _____
    (c) Date property was purchased _____
    (d) Purchase price _____
    (e) Name and address of mortgage holder _____
        _____
    (f) Balance due on mortgage _____
    (g) The names and addresses of all tenants and monthly rentals paid by
        each tenant.

    NAME AND ADDRESS OF TENANT   MONTHLY RENTAL

12. List all motor vehicles owned by the business, stating the following for
    each vehicle:
    (a) Make, model and year _____
        _____
    (b) License plate number _____
    (c) Vehicle identification number _____
    (d) If there is a lien on the vehicle, the name and address of the
        lienholder and the amount due on the lien

        _____
        _____

13. List all accounts receivable due to the business, stating the name,
    address and amount due on each receivable.
    NAME AND ADDRESS   AMOUNT DUE

14. For any transfer of business assets that has occurred within six months
    from the date of this subpoena, specifically identify:
    (a) The nature of the asset _____
        _____
    (b) The date of transfer _____
    (c) Name and address of the person to whom the asset was transferred ____
        _____
    (d) The consideration paid for the asset and the form in which it was
        paid (check, cash, etc.) _____

Figure 21.1 (*continued*)

(e) Explain in detail what happened to the consideration paid for the asset _____

15. If the business is alleged to be no longer active, set forth:
    (a) The date of cessation _____
    (b) All assets as of the date of cessation _____
    _____

    (c) The present location of those assets _____
    _____

    (d) If the assets were sold or transferred, set forth:

        (1) The nature of the assets _____
        _____

        (2) Date of transfer _____
        (3) Name and address of the person to whom the assets were
            transferred _____
            _____

        (4) The consideration paid for the assets and the form in which it
            was paid _____
            _____

        (5) Explain in detail what happened to the consideration paid for
            the assets _____
            _____

16. Set forth all other judgments that you are aware of that have been entered
    against the business and include the following:

Creditor's Name	Creditor's Attorney	Amount Due	Name of Court	Docket Number

17. For all litigation in which the business is presently involved, state:
    (a) Date litigation commenced _____
    (b) Name of party who started the litigation _____
    _____

    (c) Nature of the action _____
    _____

    (d) Names of all parties and the names, addresses and telephone numbers
        of their attorneys _____
        _____
        _____

    (e) Trial date _____
    (f) Status of case _____
    (g) Name of the court and docket number _____
    _____

18. State the name, address and position of the person answering these
    questions. _____
    _____

Figure 21.1 (*continued*)

I hereby certify that the foregoing statements made by me are true. I am aware that if any of the foregoing statements made by me are willfully false, I am subject to punishment.

Date: _____   _____

[Note: Former Appendix XI-K adopted June 29, 1990, effective September 4, 1990; amended July 14, 1992, effective September 1, 1992; redesignated as Appendix XI-L and amended July 13, 1994, effective September 1, 1994; amended July 28, 2004 to be effective September 1, 2004.]

Garnishment

"Garnishment" is a form of attachment that utilizes the appropriation of an individual's wages or credits held by third persons such as a bank or employer (under circumstances allowed by law). You may be able to secure up to 25 percent of the wages earned from the judgment-debtor. Title III of the Consumer Credit Protection Act sets the limits and also protects against a discharge by the employer should the defendant-employee be subject to wage garnishment.

The garnishment proceeding requires applying for a Writ of Garnishment from the court, or its equivalent in your state. Please visit www.fair-debt-collection.com/state-garnishment-laws.html for a list of links that will take you to each state's garnishment laws. You will serve the necessary papers on the judgment debtor's bank or employer as a warning or notice not to pay out monies or deliver property to the defendant which may be in their possession until further order of court.

In California, the Memorandum of Garnishee (or Garnishment), as it is called, served upon the third party (garnishee) is a document which is to be completed and returned to the court within a ten-day period and allows the garnishee to explain why he cannot comply, if that is the case. Absent that, the garnishee must list the property and/or monies due and owing to the judgment debtor. The judgment creditor (the plaintiff who won the money judgment) is the garnishor. See Figure 21.2 for an example from Arizona.

On the reverse side of this memorandum the garnishee will find, for his or its convenience, a list of the various exempt properties, if applicable.

Once again, remember that this document, and any accompanying document simultaneously served on the third party, must be completed and returned according to the statutory time period in your state. Therefore, look to your applicable

Figure 21.2
Application for Writ of Garnishment

(1) Person Filing:_____

Mailing Address:_____

City, State, ZIP Code:_____

Daytime Phone:_____ Alternate Phone:_____

Representing: [ ] Self   [ ] Attorney   [ ] Other

State Bar No. (if applicable):_____

(2) [ ] JUSTICE COURT _____, **COUNTY OF** _____

(3) [ ] MUNICIPAL COURT_____, **COUNTY OF** _____

(4) [ ] ARIZONA SUPERIOR COURT, COUNTY OF _____

(5) Petitioner/Plaintiff [ ] Judgment Creditor [ ] Judgment Debtor
Name:_____

Address:_____

City, State, ZIP Code:_____   **(8)** Case No.:_____

Phone(s):_____

(6) Respondent/Defendant [ ] Judgment Debtor [ ] Judgment Creditor
Name: _____

Address:_____   **APPLICATION FOR WRIT OF**

City, State, ZIP Code:_____   **GARNISHMENT (EARNINGS)**

Phone(s): _____   **(A.R.S. §§ 12-1598 through -1598.17)**

(7) Garnishee:
Name:_____

Address:_____

City, State, ZIP Code:_____

Phone(s):_____

Attorney:_____

1. I am the judgment creditor. I was awarded a money judgment or order against the judgment debtor.

2. I have asked the judgment debtor to pay, and the judgment debtor has not paid.

Figure 21.2 (*continued*)

Case No. **(8)** _____

3. The amount of the outstanding balance on the judgment or order, including accrued interest and allowable costs, is **(9)** $_____. Interest accrues at the rate of **(10)** _____% per **(11)** _____. The cost of serving the Writ of Garnishment will be shown on the Affidavit of Service and may be added to the Judgment along with allowable costs.

4. I believe garnishee employs judgment debtor or owes or will owe judgment debtor disposable earnings within 60 days.

5. I have provided garnishee name and address in **(7)**.

6. The statement checked below is true:
(12) (check one)

    [ ] I have not been notified that judgment debtor intends to sign an agreement for debt scheduling.

    [ ] I was notified that judgment debtor intends to sign an agreement for debt scheduling, but I objected timely in writing, therefore I am not subject to the debt scheduling.

    [ ] Judgment debtor signed an agreement for debt scheduling, but I was notified that the agreement is not good anymore.

7. I have attached a completed Writ of Garnishment and Summons form and ask that the Writ be issued.

(13) _____   _____
     Date   Signature of Judgment Creditor or Authorized Agent

Civil Code section and be guided thereby, whether you represent a garnishee who was served or the judgment creditor.

In some states it is considered in violation of the law and in contempt of court for failure to comply with a garnishment proceeding. You should check your state statute and court rules for the applicability of this penalty or others.

Writ of Execution

The Writ itself is normally prepared by the clerk of the court where the judgment was entered, upon receipt of an Application for Writ of Execution prepared by you. This application is delivered to the court with a nominal fee. The fee may vary from state to state, so check your rules of court.

It has always been our practice to prepare the original application and two copies. The original is for the court (sheriff). It is his authority to levy on the real or personal property wherever situated in his jurisdiction or a particular property, depending on state law. The second copy is for the attorney's file, and, as a courtesy, one is for the client. An example from California's Superior Court for a Writ of Execution can be found at www.courtinfo.ca.gov/forms/fillable/ej130.pdf.

> **NOTE:** In some states one writ of execution is sufficient for all future levying. Other state court rules may require that a new application for a writ be prepared each time you require a new writ to be issued. Check your court rules for this procedure.

A copy of the Writ of Execution and levying instructions describing the property of the judgment debtor that is to be levied on and its location is delivered to the sheriff (or other levying officer).

Additionally, I have found it a good idea to call ahead to the levying officer's offices to get a ballpark figure as to the costs involved in levying on the property of the judgment-debtor, wherever situated.

> **NOTE:** *Not more than one Writ per county can be issued by the court clerk at one time.* I always liked to have them ready so that when the 180 days expires (time restriction in California), the next one is ready to be delivered to and issued by the court clerk and shot off to the next county without delay. (Check your state code and court rules for this procedure.)

Remember that the sale thereafter of the land (or other property) also has a statutory time limitation. You should check your state statute and court rules for this time restriction and procedures.

The Writ of Execution directs the sheriff to levy. The levy is the act of the sheriff in taking the judgment-debtor's property into the custody of the sheriff pursuant to the Writ of Execution.

To levy on the property of the judgment-debtor:

1. Take actual physical possession of the property (such as a car or other moveable personal property); or

2. Serve a copy of the Writ on the judgment debtor-owner and post the property with a notice of levy, which usually contains a notice of the date of the sheriff's sale of the property.

Enforcement of Out-of-State Judgments

The Uniform Enforcement of Foreign Judgments Act provides a method to enforce judgments that have been entered in one state to be collected in another. Its essence lies in the "Full Faith and Credit" article of the U.S. Constitution. The full text can be found at www.law.upenn.edu/bll/archives/ulc/fnact99/1920_69/ruefja64.pdf.

Be sure to check your own state statutes governing judgments and execution to find out if your state has adopted this Uniform Act and what the procedures are for enforcing that judgment. The Uniform Act makes the right of the judgment-creditor to bring an action in the sister state to enforce his judgment optional. He may proceed with the filing or registration of his judgment under the Uniform Act or proceed under other court procedure.

As in any proceeding, the key is jurisdiction. In order for a sister state to acknowledge or have the power to hear and determine the matter or honor your state's judgment, it must have the jurisdiction of the person or the action and in some instances the property.

EXAMPLE

The judgment-debtor moved to New York to avoid the collection of the judgment. You can bring an action on the judgment obtained against him in California, by filing a lawsuit in the State of New York, which gives the New York court jurisdiction of a judgment-debtor and the case before the California Bar. The State of New York must give "full faith and credit" to the judgment obtained in California. Thereafter, you can obtain a Writ of Execution issued in New York and have it levied on any property, real or personal, belonging to the judgment-debtor, in his possession, or under his control to satisfy the judgment.

Under the Uniform Act here described, if it had been adopted in New York, the lawsuit would be unnecessary. In that instance, the out-of-state judgment would need to be filed in the appropriate clerk's office and then would be effective as if it were issued from that office.

Procedure for Collection of Sister-State Judgments in California

The foregoing being true, consider the following California procedure as an example of what you may have to do in complying with your local state statute relating to collecting sister-state money judgments. The following procedure allows a judgment-creditor to apply for the entry of a judgment based upon a sister-state judgment by filing an application with the superior court (or other appropriate court in your state) for the county in which any judgment-debtor resides; or if no judgment-debtor is a resident, then any county in the state.

The application which must be executed under oath must include the following:

1. A statement that an action in this state on a sister-state judgment is not barred by the applicable statute of limitations;

2. A statement based on the applicant's information and belief that no stay of enforcement of the sister-state judgment is currently in effect in the sister state;

3. A statement that the amount remains unpaid under the sister-state judgment;

4. A statement that no action based on the sister-state judgment is currently pending in any court in this state and that no judgment based on the sister-state judgment has previously been entered in any proceeding in this state;

5. Where the judgment debtor is an individual, a statement setting forth the name and last known residence address of the judgment-debtor (except for facts which are matters of public record in this state, the statements required by this paragraph may be made on the basis of the judgment-creditor's information and belief); and

6. A statement setting forth the name and address of the judgment-creditor.

A properly authenticated copy of the sister-state judgment must be attached to the application. See www.courtinfo.ca.gov/forms/fillable/ej105.pdf for the official form for making this application.

> **NOTE:** The normal closing paragraph follows, as in any application, and we suggest that it be under penalty of perjury, or if applicable in your state, have it notarized.

Another uniform act would aid in the collection in our state courts of judgments obtained by a foreign country. It is called the Uniform Foreign Money-Judgments Recognition Act.

"The Act states rules which have long been applied by the majority of courts in this country," according to the National Conference of Commissioners on Uniform

State Laws. The act does not prescribe a uniform judgment enforcement procedure. It allows each state to use its own procedures or the procedures of the Uniform Enforcement of Foreign Judgments Act (sister states) if it has been adopted or the state wants to use it for judgments rendered in foreign countries as well as sister states in the United States.

The preceding discussion should give you some hope for collecting out-of-state or even out-of-country judgments where a country has a reciprocal provision, by treaty or otherwise.

CHAPTER TWENTY-TWO

What You Should Know About Trademarks— Protectable Business Marks

Trademarks (and other such marks) are a protectable business commodity because they serve to identify the quality and goodwill of a particular company. Customer loyalty to a brand, known through its mark, is extremely valuable in commerce.

Though there is both federal and state protection available to individuals relative to protecting their trademarks, most consideration is in and under the protection of federal law. Federal protection arises from the Trademark Act of 1946, as set forth in the U.S. Code, and commonly referred to as "the Lanham Act." (15 U.S.C.A. §1051 et seq., accessible through Cornell Law at www.law.cornell.edu/uscode/html/uscode15/usc_sup_01_15_10_22.html.)

This act recognizes four protectable marks:

1. Trademark,

2. Service mark,

3. Certification mark, and

4. Collective mark.

It has been our experience that the ones most commonly used (and abused) are the service and trademarks.

Definitions and Explanations
Trademark

A "trademark" is any mark, letter, or word (and the like) used to identify and distinguish goods of a particular person. The primary intent of a trademark is to protect—to prevent the confusion of the consuming public. *It must be affixed to the goods in a commercial sense.*

A further purpose of a trademark is to identify and distinguish the goods of one from those of another.

It should be noted that a trademark may not be a word or phrase that is:

- Generic or common to the goods in question—for example, peas, carrots, etc.;

- Descriptive of the goods or contents (malted milk);

- Geographically denoting place of origin;

- A personal name of person or manufacturer; or

- Scandalous or indecent or otherwise violative of public policy.

Further, generally, the color or shape of the container is not trademark-able. However, there have been exceptions to this rule. One of the most famous "color" trademarks is the pink Owens' Corning insulation. The court found that because the pink was so unnecessary to the functioning of the product, its only purpose was to distinguish it from the competition, and the company had spent a considerable amount of time and money in developing the pink's significance as a secondary meaning in the market. *In re Owens-Corning Fiberglas Corp.* 774 F.2d 1116 (C.A. Fed. 1985). However, color was found not to be trademark-able in the *NutraSweet* case. *NutraSweet Co. v. Stadt Corp.*, 917 F.2d 1024 (Ill. 1990). The court found that the exclusion of color designations for the different tabletop sweeteners would actually present a bar to competition. All "pink packets" of artificial sweeteners like Sweet 'N Low were permitted to use the pink designation and all NutraSweet-like products could use Equal's blue packaging. This is a terrific example of the care and attention to detail needed in trademark practice.

Protectable Trademarks
There are basically two protectable trademarks, and they are as follows:

1. One which has become distinctive of applicant's goods; and

2. One which has attained a secondary meaning. This secondary meaning is a protection to personal names and geographical designations that were not initially

protectable under the act, but, because of extensive use on the common market, became distinctive of the product.

As a general rule, the more arbitrary or fanciful a name is, the more trademark-able it is. For example, Starbucks coffee. Neither the word "star" nor "bucks" does anything to suggest coffee products, whereas Band-Aid does suggest first aid. The closer the name is to its actual function, the more difficult the argument for protection. Indeed, Band-Aid is almost the generic term for an adhesive bandage and appears even in slang terms—a Band-Aid solution.

Technical Trademarks
This is applicable where the surname is not primary, but merely a surname. The test here is whether a term would be immediately recognized as a surname without any other possible connotation.

The composition of a trademark may consist of the following:

1. A letter, several letters, numbers, words, combinations of words, or even entire sentences;

2. A picture or symbol or emblem (commonly called a "logo"); or

3. Any combination of permissible devices.

Service Mark

Recall that a "trademark" is any word, name, symbol, or device or any combination thereof adopted and used by a manufacturer or merchant to identify his goods and distinguish them from those manufactured or sold by others. This is distinguishable from service marks. The "service mark" identifies and distinguishes a service performed.

This mark (service) is used in the sale or advertisement of services, the purpose of which is to identify the services of one person and, in so doing, distinguish these services from those of another. This may include, but not necessarily be limited to, marks, names, symbols, titles, resignations, slogans, character names, and any distinctive and unique features of radio or other advertising used in commerce.

Certification Mark

The "certification mark" is related to the service mark. These include such marks as the Good Housekeeping Seal of Approval, which are used by persons other than the owner of a trademark or service mark, to certify that the goods or services meet certain standards or have a certain regional origin. The person using a service mark or certification mark must exercise control over the use of this mark so that the certified standards may be met at all times. (This is protected under the Federal Protection Act of 1946, commonly called the Lanham Act.)

Collective Mark

Then we have the "collective mark," which is a trademark or service mark used by the members of a cooperative, an association, or other collective group or organization; it includes marks to indicate membership in a union, association, or other organization. (This type of trademark or service mark is also protected under the Federal Act, commonly called the Lanham Act.)

It should be noted that this "collective mark" is used primarily to indicate membership in an organization such as the ABA , AAfPE, NALA, and NFPA. But it may be used to identify the goods of individual members of the group, for example, "R.P." (NFPA controls the use of this designation.) In this instance, the organization owns the collective mark and exercises control of its use by the members.

Trade Secret

A "trade secret," as defined by *Black's Law Dictionary* (8th edition 2004), is:

> A formula, process, device, or other business information that is kept confidential to maintain an advantage over competitors; information—including a formula, pattern, compilation, program, device, method, technique, or process—that (1) derives independent economic value, actual or potential, from not being generally known or readily ascertainable by others who can obtain economic value from its disclosure or use, and (2) is the subject of reasonable efforts, under the circumstances, to maintain its secrecy.

Factors considered by the court in determining protective or trade secrets may be the following:

1. Expenditure of money, time, and labor in developing the trade secret;

2. The novelty of the secret;

3. Whether or not it is—in fact—a secret;

4. The conscious and continuing effort on the part of the owner to keep and/or maintain this secrecy of the product;

5. The value of the secret to the business entity;

6. The extent to which it may be isolated; and

7. The relationship between the parties having knowledge of the secret, e.g., employee and employer.

It should be noted that, though the law of trade secrets falls within the law of unfair competition, it gives much significance to the concept of fairness. Therefore, the relationship between the parties is carefully examined by the court before any equitable remedy is made available.

An employer may protect his trade secret in one of two ways:

1. A written agreement between himself and his employee. See Figure 22.1 for a typical clause as printed in American Jurisprudence Legal Forms 2d. There is an entire body of law regarding the enforceability of these employment restraint clauses. You would do well to research them carefully in your jurisdiction with regard to the limitations on enforcement.

2. By way of an oral agreement ("gentleman's pact") or an implied promise on the part of the employee to the employer that he or she would not divulge the secret of his operation.

Figure 22.1

§147:5.1. Contractual Provision—Right to injunction to restrain unauthorized use or disclosure of confidential information—Employment agreement

Employee agrees not to use or disclose or make available to anyone for use outside Employer, either during the term of this Agreement or for one year subsequent to the expiration of this Agreement, for any reason, any **trade secret** or proprietary information, including but not limited to training procedures, employee procedures, product processes, ingredients and formulation, business strategies, overall *[type of business]* operations and any related data and information (collectively called "Confidential Information"). Employee further agrees that upon expiration of this Agreement that Employee shall promptly deliver to Employer all *[description of types of property]*, documents, data or material belonging to or concerning Employer or relating to Employer's affairs and, without limiting the foregoing, will promptly deliver all documents and materials (including *[description of types of property]* provided by Employer) containing or constituting Confidential Information. It is mutually understood and agreed that Employer has no adequate remedy at law for Employee's unauthorized use or disclosure of Confidential Information and that Employer shall be entitled to equitable **relief** by way of **injunction** or otherwise without further proof of irreparable harm for any actual or threatened violation of this paragraph by Employee.

Trade Secrets and Federal Preemption

Since the law controlling and governing trade secrets is so fact-sensitive and somewhat inconsistent across jurisdictions, it is suggested that you read or reread some of the landmark cases involving patent law, license estoppels, and the interpretations of the court as to what other product may be considered a trade secret. For example, some of these cases have held that an invention, design, process, or even an idea may be a trade secret, and that these types of products may receive a license, which license may or may not be patentable; or that the object so licensed may not be patentable. See, for example, *Lear Inc. v. Adkins*, 395 U.S. 653, 895, Sup. Ct. 1902, 23 L.Ed.2d 610 (1969).

The decisions reached in these cases have caused attorneys to be cautious in advising the client in the area of trade secrets. The following case excerpt demonstrates just how tricky these determinations can be.

United States District Court, N.D. Illinois, Eastern Division.
FAST FOOD GOURMET INC., Plaintiff,

v.

LITTLE LADY FOODS INC., and Kraft Foods Global Inc., Defendants.
No. 05 C 6022.

April 3, 2008.

. . . . .

A. Counts I and II

In Count I of FFGI's second amended complaint, FFGI alleges that LLFI violated the Illinois Trade Secrets Act (the "ITSA"), 765 ILL. COMP. STAT. 1065/1, *et seq.*, by "misappropriat[ing] FFGI's trade secrets for its own benefit and for the benefit of Kraft." Specifically, FFGI alleges that LLFI "made pizzas or pizza crusts for its own benefit and for the benefit of Kraft using FFGI's equipment line and other trade secrets." In Count II, FFGI alleges that "Kraft knew or had reason to know that [LLFI] acquired FFGI's trade secrets by improper means, or knew or had reason to know that [LLFI's] knowledge, use and disclosure of FFGI's trade secrets was improper. . . ."

Defendants move for summary judgment on the trade secret misappropriation counts, arguing that FFGI's alleged trade secrets are not secret, and that FFGI cannot demonstrate misappropriation by LLFI or Kraft. Specifically, defendants argue that FFGI's alleged trade secrets are not secret because: (1) Rheon stress-free sheeting is widely used; (2) using brick ovens to bake pizza is not unique; (3) the combination of stress-free sheeting and conveyorized oven is not unique; (4) FFGI's president admits LLFI can use a brick or stone oven, Rheon stress-free sheeting, and a combination of the two; (5) FFGI previously disclosed its alleged trade secrets; and (6) FFGI failed to designate its equipment as confidential, as required by the Agreement. (LLFI Mem. in Supp. of Mot. for Summ. J. at 8-17; Kraft Mem. in Supp. of Mot. for Summ. J. at 8-16.) LLFI argues FFGI cannot demonstrate misappropriation because the Agreement allowed LLFI to use FFGI's equipment. (LLFI Mem. in Supp. of Mot. for Summ. J. at 17-19.) And Kraft argues FFGI cannot demonstrate misappropriation because the Agreement allowed LLFI to use FFGI's equipment, Kraft did not know or have reason to know of LLFI's alleged misappropriation, and Kraft independently developed its pizza. (Kraft Mem. in Supp. of Mot. for Summ. J. at 16-20.)

To succeed on a claim for misappropriation of trade secrets under the ITSA, a plaintiff must demonstrate that the information was: (1) a trade secret; (2) misappropriated; and (3) used in the defendant's business. *Learning Curve Toys Inc. v. Play-Wood Toys Inc.*, 342 F.3d 714, 721 (7th Cir.2003). The ITSA defines a "trade secret" as information that "(1) is sufficiently secret to derive economic value, actual or potential, from not being generally known to other persons who can obtain economic value from its disclosure or use; and (2) is the subject of efforts that are reasonable under the circumstances to maintain its secrecy or confidentiality." 765 ILL. COMP. STAT.. 1065/2(d).

The first requirement-that the information be sufficiently secret-"precludes trade secret protection for information generally known or understood within an industry even if not to the public at large." *Learning Curve*, 342 F.3d at 722 (internal quotation omitted). The second requirement-that the information be subject to reasonable efforts to keep it secret-"prevents a plaintiff who takes no affirmative measures to prevent others from using its proprietary information from obtaining trade secret protection." *Id.* (citation omitted). In addition, Illinois courts refer to six Restatement factors as "instructive guidelines for ascertaining whether a trade secret exists under the Act," but not as "a list of requisite elements." *Id.* These factors include:

(1) the extent to which the information is known outside of the plaintiff's business; (2) the extent to which the information is known by employees and others involved in the plaintiff's business; (3) the extent of measures taken by the plaintiff to guard the secrecy of the information; (4) the value of the information to the plaintiff's business and to its competitors; (5) the amount of time, effort, and money expended by the plaintiff in developing the information; and (6) the ease or difficulty with which the information could be properly acquired or duplicated by others.

Id. (citations omitted). "The existence of a trade secret ordinarily is a question of fact." *Id.* at 723.

"A trade secret can exist in a combination of characteristics and components, each of which, by itself, is in the public domain, but the unified process, design and operation of which, in unique combination, affords a competitive advantage and is a protectable secret." *3M v. Pribyl*, 259 F.3d 587, 595 (7th Cir.2001) (addressing claim for misappropriation of trade secrets under Wisconsin Uniform Trade Secrets Act, and citing *Syntex Ophthalmics Inc. v. Tsuetaki*, 701 F.2d 677, 684 (7th Cir.1983) (applying Illinois trade secret law)); *RRK Holding Co. v. Sears, Roebuck & Co.*, No. 04 C 3944, 2007 WL 495254, at *3 (N.D.Ill. Feb. 14, 2007) (Coar, J.) (citing *3M*, 259 F.3d at 595, and denying defendant's motion for summary judgment on ITSA trade secret misappropriation count). A combination does not constitute a trade secret unless it transforms the individual features into something that is itself secret, i.e., not generally known or easily duplicated by the industry. *See Computer Care v. Serv. Sys. Enters. Inc.*, 982 F.2d 1063, 1074-75 (7th Cir.1992).

According to defendants' expert, Faubion, high oven temperature "in excess of 700 degrees", stone hearth oven, stress-free sheeting, and thin sheeting as well as dough temperature out of the mixer of "68-72°F" (for which using "ice in a dough formulation is simply one means to achieve the target temperature goals"), floor time of 90-120 minutes, and eliminating artificial dough conditioners are generally known in the pizza industry. [FN omitted] Specifically, Faubion's report states "all items identified in the Plaintiff's Identification of Trade Secrets are generally known in the commercial pizza industry, either individually and/or in combination[.]" In addition, Faubion's report indicates that "the items identified as [FFGI's] crust making methodology are generally known in the commercial industry, individually and/or in combination[.]" FFGI responds by arguing that Faubion's report fails to "suggest that anybody else in the industry is utilizing the combination of techniques identified by FFGI in conjunction with a stone-hearth oven of any kind, much less a conveyorized impingement stone-hearth oven." Moreover, FFGI has presented evidence that: the Gouet conveyorized impingement stone-hearth oven is uncommon for the commercial manufacture of frozen pizza, Hoseney never heard of anyone using a stone impingement oven to manufacture frozen pizzas, the only such oven sold in the United States was the one purchased by FFGI, and FFGI is the only company Parr is aware of using a combination of stress-free sheeting and extremely high baking temperature in a thinly sheeted pizza crust. [FN omitted]

" 'Simply being the first or only one to use certain information does not in and of itself transform otherwise general knowledge into a trade secret.' " *Computer Care*, 982 F.2d at 1073 (quoting *Service Ctrs. of Chicago Inc. v. Minogue*, 180 Ill.App.3d 447, 455, 129 Ill.Dec. 367, 535 N.E.2d 1132, 1137 (Ill.App.Ct.1989)); *see Learning Curve*, 342 F.3d at 723. But, here, there is additional evidence that FFGI's process is not generally known in the industry. First, Hoseney testified that he "would argue that the whole process is unique." Also, Kraft changed the process and formula developed in its pilot plant once it began making pizza at LLFI on FFGI's equipment line. Prior to entering into a co-manufacturing relationship with LLFI, Kraft developed a pizza crust over a period of approximately four months, which was not prepared using a stone hearth oven, extremely high baking temperatures, or sheeting equipment. After commencing its relationship with LLFI, over the course of several months, Kraft altered its dough formula and process by using ice to achieve cool dough temperature, providing for lengthy floor time before sheeting and baking, and removing SALP, baking soda, and Fermaid P.

Moreover, the extent of LLFI's involvement in Kraft's development process is disputed. There is also evidence that Kraft chose to use LLFI as co-manufacturer because of its crust.

Further, there is evidence that FFGI's pizza production technique may satisfy several of the Restatement factors as well. For example, FFGI has presented evidence that it expended a great deal of time and money to develop its pizza production technique; [FN omitted] that it took some measures to guard the secrecy of its process; [FN omitted] and that this information was valuable to its business [FN omitted] and to its competitors [FN omitted] Overall, I cannot conclude on these motions that FFGI's pizza production process does not constitute a trade secret.

FFGI must not only establish that its process qualifies as a trade secret, but FFGI must also demonstrate that defendants misappropriated its trade secret. The ITSA defines "misappropriation" as:

(1) acquisition of a trade secret of a person by another person who knows or has reason to know that the trade secret was acquired by improper means; or (2) disclosure or use of a trade secret of a person without express or implied consent by another person who: (A) used improper means to acquire knowledge of the trade secret; or (B) at the time of disclosure or use, knew or had reason to know that knowledge of the trade secret was: (I) derived from or through a person who utilized improper means to acquire it; (II) acquired under circumstances giving rise to a duty to maintain its secrecy or limit its use; or (III) derived from or through a person who owed a duty to the person seeking relief to maintain its secrecy or limit its use.

765 ILL. COMP. STAT. 1065/2(b). Thus, LLFI would be liable for trade secret misappropriation under section 1065/2(b)(2)(B)(II) if it improperly disclosed a trade secret in violation of a duty to maintain secrecy or limit use; and, if LLFI improperly disclosed FFGI's trade secret, then Kraft would be liable for misappropriation under section 1065/2(b)(1) if it "knew or had reason to know that the trade secret was acquired by improper means."

Domain Names

The newest issues in trademark protection stem from the ubiquitous use and innumerable presences on the Internet. "Domain names" are the electronic equivalent of trademarks in cyberspace. The interesting phenomenon of "cybersquatting" has arisen in an attempt to profit from this characteristic of the Internet. A "cybersquatter" is a person who attempts to register a name that he believes a trademark owner would desire, in order to sell it back to the mark's owner. Under the traditional Lanham Act, it would not have been infringement if the cybersquatter did not intend to use the domain name commercially. The code has been updated to reflect this new development.

§1125. FALSE DESIGNATIONS OF ORIGIN, FALSE DESCRIPTIONS, AND DILUTION FORBIDDEN

(d) Cyberpiracy prevention

(1)

(A) A person shall be liable in a civil action by the owner of a mark, including a personal name which is protected as a mark under this section, if, without regard to the goods or services of the parties, that person—

(i) has a bad faith intent to profit from that mark, including a personal name which is protected as a mark under this section; and

(ii) registers, traffics in, or uses a domain name that—

(I) in the case of a mark that is distinctive at the time of registration of the domain name, is identical or confusingly similar to that mark;

(II) in the case of a famous mark that is famous at the time of registration of the domain name, is identical or confusingly similar to or dilutive of that mark; or

(III) is a trademark, word, or name protected by reason of section 706 of title 18 or section 220506 of title 36.

Duties of a Trademark Paralegal

The first order of business should be to familiarize yourself with the United Sates Patent and Trademarks Office's website. This extremely helpful website can be accessed at www.uspto.gov/main/trademarks.htm. All the forms can be found in the TEAS (Trademark Electronic Application System) at www.uspto.gov/teas/index .html.

As a paralegal working in an office whose specialty is copyright/patent law, your duties, generally, would be as follows:

1. To determine, through research, what name, symbol, or trademark the client can place on its product. This job is made easier through the Trademark Electronic Search System (TESS), available at http://tess2.uspto.gov/bin/gate.exe?f= tess&state=6cns.1.1. This procedure is similar to the one used in setting up a corporation and selecting a name for the corporation. In this instance, you must also submit several ideas for names, or trademarks, or symbols to your attorney after investigation as to their current use in the marketplace.

2. Once a name has been chosen, your job really becomes hectic as you must do further meticulous research as to a possible conflict or superior right in the use of the name so chosen, not only in this country, but on a worldwide basis if the client has an international company. In this connection, you do research as to not only the use of the name, but also possible conflicts in trademark law in the various countries where the client's product is to be used. This is made easier by checking the status of the potentially conflicting mark in the

Trademark Applications and Registrations Retrieval system (TARR), at http://tarr.uspto.gov.

3. The matter may necessitate conferences, negotiations, and resulting agreements with third parties currently using the name or symbol, or one very similar to it (which would cause a conflict in the eyes of the public), to allow your attorney's client to use the name (or continue to use the name).

4. Once this has been accomplished, it is incumbent upon you to see that either of the marks is registered immediately. This is essential because registration under the Lanham Act is prima facie evidence of exclusive right to the use of the mark, and a strong presumption in favor of the validity is the fact that registration exists.

5. Finally, be prepared to file a lawsuit to protect the name, enjoining others from using a similar or identical name or symbol. An extensive sample from American Jurisprudence Pleading and Practice Forms is included as Figure 22.2.

6. One other element that is a prerequisite to validity and ownership of the service or trademark is continued use in commerce for a period of five years after its registration. This makes the right to use a mark incontestable and the registration thereof conclusive rather than presumptive.

Figure 22.2

§101. Complaint in Federal District Court—Under Anticybersquatting Consumer Protection Act and Lanham Act—Domain name cybersquatting—False designation or representation—Misappropriation of right of publicity

COMPLAINT

Plaintiff _____ *[name]*, professionally known as _____ *[name]*, alleges as follows:

JURISDICTION AND VENUE

1. This action arises under the trademark laws of the United States and under the common-law right of publicity laws of the State of _____. This court has federal question jurisdiction over this matter pursuant to 15 U.S.C.A. § 1125(a), (d), and 28 U.S.C.A. § 1331, and 1338(d), and supplemental jurisdiction over plaintiff's claims arising under _____ *[state]* law pursuant to 28 U.S.C.A. § 1367, because they flow from a common nucleus of operative facts.

2. Venue is proper in this district pursuant to 28 U.S.C.A. § 1391(b), (c). Defendants, and each of them, are subject to personal jurisdiction in this district. A substantial part of the events or omissions giving rise to the claims here occurred in this district.

Figure 22.2 *(continued)*

THE PARTIES

3. Plaintiff _____ *[name]*, professionally known as _____ *[name]*, is a resident of the City of _____, _____ County, _____ *[state]*.

4. Plaintiff is informed and believes, and on the basis of such information and belief alleges, that defendant _____ *[A.B.]* is an individual residing in the City of _____, _____ County, _____ *[state]*.

5. Plaintiff is informed and believes, and on the basis of such information and belief alleges, that defendant _____ *[C.D.]* is an individual residing in _____ *[city, state]*.

6. Plaintiff is informed and believes, and on the basis of such information and belief alleges, that defendant _____ *[E.F.]* is an entity of unknown form with its principal place of business in _____ *[foreign country]*.

7. Plaintiff is informed and believes, and on the basis of such information and belief alleges, that the fictitiously named defendants sued here as Does 1 through 10, inclusive, and each of them, were in some manner responsible or legally liable for the events, actions, transactions, and circumstances alleged here. The true names and capacities of these fictitiously named defendants, whether individual, corporate, associate, or otherwise, are at present unknown to plaintiff, who will seek leave of this court to amend this complaint to assert the true names and capacities of these fictitiously named defendants when their names and capacities have become known to plaintiff.

8. Plaintiff is informed and believes, and on the basis of such information and belief alleges, that defendants, and each of them, were the agents, employees, partners, joint-venturers, coconspirators, owners, principals, and employers of the remaining defendants, and each of them, and are, and at all times here mentioned were, acting within the course and scope of agency, partnership, employment, conspiracy, ownership, or joint venture. Plaintiff is informed and believes, and on the basis of such information and belief alleges, that the acts and conduct here alleged of each such defendant were known to, authorized by, and/or ratified by the other defendants, and each of them.

FACTS COMMON TO ALL CAUSES OF ACTION

9. _____ *[Describe plaintiff's facts, such as accomplishments, talent, popularity, hard work, and any artistic and commercial successes, indicating the value of the plaintiff's name, both commercially and with the public.]* Based on _____ *[his or her]* talent, popularity, and hard work, and the artistic and commercial success of many of _____ *[his or her]* films, plaintiff has, for a number of years, been highly sought after as a motion picture actor, all of which has given _____ *[his or her]* name tremendous value in the entertainment industry, and great commercial value with the public. Accordingly, plaintiff has a substantial investment in the drawing power and commercial value of _____ *[his or her]* name.

Figure 22.2 *(continued)*

10. Plaintiff has enjoyed an exceedingly valuable reputation and good will among the consuming public as a result of _____ *[his or her]* many motion pictures, public persona, and widespread recognition through unsolicited media attention. Plaintiff's reputation and good will are associated with, and designated and represented by, _____ *[his or her]* professional name, _____, which is widely recognized throughout the United States and the rest of the world by millions of fans and the general public.

11. Plaintiff has been using _____ *[his or her]* professional name to identify _____ *[himself or herself]*, _____ *[his or her]* image, and _____ *[his or her]* performances since the beginning of _____ *[his or her]* acting career in the late _____ *[range of years]*. Plaintiff's professional name, throughout this time, has undoubtedly acquired a "secondary meaning" worthy of protection under the United States Trademark Act.

A. THE "_____ *[Summary name for defendants 1, 2, and DOES 1-20]*"

12. Plaintiff is informed and believes, and on the basis of such information and belief alleges, that defendant _____ *[name of defendant web owner]* is the owner of the commercial internet domain name "_____.com" and that this defendant registered this domain name with _____ *[domain registration company]* without the prior knowledge, permission, or consent of plaintiff. Defendant _____ *[name of defendant web owner]* has undertaken, and is continuing to undertake, efforts to sell the domain name "_____.com" for thousands of dollars, including offering to sell the domain name to plaintiff for the sum of $ _____. On information and belief, defendant _____ *[name of defendant web owner]* posted on a website the domain name "_____.com" during _____ *[date or year]* which stated, in its entirety: "This domain name is for sale. Contact _____ *[email address]* and state your offer!"

13. Plaintiff is informed and believes, and on the basis of such information and belief alleges, that defendant _____ *[name of administrative contact defendant]* is the administrative contact, technical contact, and billing contact for the domain name "_____.com", has acted and is continuing to act as an agent for defendant _____ *[name of defendant web owner]*, is a participant and joint tortfeasor in the scheme to sell the domain name "_____.com" for a substantial profit, and has admitted that _____ *[he or she]* stands to benefit financially from _____ *[his or her]* role in the scheme to sell the domain name "_____.com" for a profit.

14. Plaintiff is informed and believes, and on the basis of such information and belief alleges, that defendants _____ *[Defendants web owner and administrative technical contact]* and DOES 1 through 20, inclusive (here referred to collectively as the "_____ *[summary name for defendants 1, 2, and DOES 1-20]*"), and

Figure 22.2 (*continued*)

each of them, were the agents, employees, partners, joint-venturers, coconspirators, owners, principals, and employers of one another and are, and at all times here mentioned were, acting within the course and scope of that agency, partnership, employment, conspiracy, ownership, or joint venture. Plaintiff is further informed and believes and, based on such information and belief, alleges that the acts and conduct here alleged of each of the _____ *[summary name for defendants 1, 2, and DOES]* were known to, authorized by, and/or ratified by the other _____ *[summary name for Defendants 1, 2, and DOES]*, and each of them.

B. THE "_____ *[summary name for defendant net domain*
name owner and DOES 21-50]"

15. Defendant _____ *[domain name owner]* is the owner of the domain name "_____.net" and registered the domain name without the prior knowledge, permission, or consent of plaintiff. Defendant _____ *[net domain name owner]* currently operates a website at the domain name "_____.net" that contains numerous photographs of plaintiff, sells merchandise including books and movies pertaining to plaintiff, posts advertisements, and operates a fan club called the "_____ Club," which issues a membership card featuring the name and photograph of plaintiff. All of the above activities are being done without plaintiff's consent, and in contravention of plaintiff's affirmative demands that defendant _____ *[net domain name owner]* cease and desist from such practices that infringe on plaintiff's rights.

16. Plaintiff is informed and believes and, based on such information and belief alleges, that defendants _____ *[net domain name owner]* and DOES 21 through 50, inclusive, (here referred to collectively as the "_____ *[summary name for defendant net domain name owner and DOES 21-50]*"), and each of them, were the agents, employees, partners, joint-venturers, coconspirators, owners, principals, and employers of one another, and are, and at all times here mentioned were, acting within the course and scope of that agency, partnership, employment, conspiracy, ownership, or joint venture. Plaintiff is further informed and believes and, based on such information and belief, alleges that the acts and conduct here alleged of each of the _____ *[summary name for defendant net domain name owner and DOES 21-50]* were known to, authorized by, and/or ratified by the other _____ *[summary name for defendant net domain name owner and DOES 21-50]*, and each of them.

C. THE DOMAIN NAMES

17. The domain names "_____.com" and "_____.net" are sometimes below collectively referred to as the "Domain Names."

Figure 22.2 (*continued*)

18. Each of the defendants' registration and use of the Domain Names is likely to cause confusion among the consuming public, who will be led to believe that plaintiff is affiliated with defendants, and each of them, and/or has approved of defendants' use and registration of the Domain Names and the contents contained on the websites at those Domain Names, including the promotion and sale of merchandise on those websites.

19. Each of the defendants' registration and use of the Domain Names also dilutes the distinctiveness of the name and distinctive mark, _____ *[name actor goes by]*, and reduces the ability of the name and mark, _____ *[name actor goes by]*, to distinguish any goods and services offered by plaintiff from the goods and services offered by others, including defendants.

20. Plaintiff has no ability to control the quality of the goods and services offered and sold by defendants, nor to control the information contained on any of the websites located at the Domain Names, including information pertaining to plaintiff, nor to control defendants' use of the Domain Names, or the websites located at such Domain Names.

FIRST CAUSE OF ACTION

(Cybersquatting Pursuant to 15 U.S.C.A. § 1125(d))

(Against the _____ *[summary name for defendants 1, 2, and DOES 1-20]*)

21. Plaintiff repeats, realleges, adopts, and incorporates each and every allegation contained in Paragraphs 1 through 20, inclusive, as though fully set forth here.

22. Plaintiff's name is a distinctive and famous mark, and was a distinctive and famous mark at the time the domain name "_____.com" was registered with _____ *[domain registration company]*, and at all other times relevant here, pursuant to the Anticybersquatting Consumer Protection Act of 1999, 15 U.S.C.A. § 1125(d) (referred to below as the "Anticybersquatting Act"), and specifically Section 3002(a) of the Act, 15 U.S.C.A. § 1125(d)(1).

23. Plaintiff is informed and believes, and on the basis of such information and belief alleges, that the _____ *[summary name for defendants 1, 2, and DOES 1-20]*, and each of them, have had, and continue to have, a bad faith intent to profit from the name _____ *[plaintiff actor's name]*, which is protected as a distinctive mark and personal name under Section 3002(a) of the Anticybersquatting Act, 15 U.S.C.A. § 1125(d)(1). Specifically, the _____ *[summary name for defendants 1, 2, and DOES 1-20]* registered the domain name "_____.com" without the prior knowledge, permission, or consent of plaintiff, have undertaken efforts to sell the domain name for a substantial profit and have demanded, and continue to demand, payment in the amount of $_____ for ownership

Figure 22.2 *(continued)*

of such domain name. Such actions are a violation of Section 3002(a) of the Anticybersquatting Act, 15 U.S.C.A. §§ 1125(d)(1)(A)(ii)(I), (II); (d)(1)(B)(i)(II), (VI); and (d)(1)(E).

24. Plaintiff is therefore entitled to a judgment from this court compelling the _____*[summary name for defendants 1, 2, and DOES 1-20]*, and each of them, to transfer all ownership in the domain "_____.com" to plaintiff, or in the alternative for cancellation of the domain name, pursuant to Section 3002(a) of the Anticybersquatting Act, 15 U.S.C.A. § 1125(d)(1)(C).

25. Plaintiff is further entitled to a preliminary and permanent injunction enjoining the _____ *[summary name for defendants 1, 2, and DOES 1-20]* from any use of the domain name "_____.com" pursuant to Section 3003 of the Anticybersquatting Act, 15 U.S.C.A. § 1116(a).

26. Plaintiff is further entitled to a judgment from this court awarding plaintiff all actual damages proximately caused by the _____ *[summary name for defendants 1, 2, and DOES 1-20]* or, in the alternative, statutory damages of not less than $1,000 and not more than $100,000, as the court considers just, pursuant to Section 3003(b) of the Anticybersquatting Act, 15 U.S.C.A. § 1117(a), (d).

SECOND CAUSE OF ACTION

**(False Designation or Representation Pursuant to the Lanham Act,
15 U.S.C.A. § 1125(a))**

(Against the _____ *[summary name for defendants 1, 2, and DOES 1-20]*)

27. Plaintiff repeats, realleges, adopts, and incorporates each and every allegation contained in Paragraphs 1 through 20, inclusive, as though fully set forth here.

28. Plaintiff is informed and believes, and on the basis of such information and belief alleges, that the _____ *[summary name for defendants 1, 2, and DOES 1-20]*, and each of them, have violated Section 43(a) of the Lanham Act, 15 U.S.C.A. § 1125(a), by expressly and impliedly making false designations or in registering the domain name "_____.com", and by using the domain name for a commercial purpose, namely, attempting to sell the domain name for a profit. These false designations or representations include, without limitation, the implied representation that plaintiff endorses, sponsors, operates, and/or is affiliated with the domain name "_____.com" and/or any and all information, products, and services offered on any website located at this domain name.

29. Plaintiff is informed and believes, and on the basis of such information and belief alleges, that the conduct of the _____ *[summary name for defendants 1, 2, and DOES 1-20]*, and each of them, has caused, and is continuing to cause, confusion

Figure 22.2 (*continued*)

among Internet users in that persons accessing the domain name "_____. com" are led to believe that such domain name, and any website accessed by using that domain name, owned, operated, sponsored, endorsed by, and/or affiliated with plaintiff, which they are not. Moreover, Internet users are further led to believe that, if plaintiff does not operate a website on the domain name "_____.com", or one of the other Domain Names (which use plaintiff's name as the Internet domain name), plaintiff must not have a domain name or website of _____ *[his or her]* own.

30. Plaintiff is informed and believes, and on the basis of such information and belief alleges, that unless enjoined and restrained by order of this court, the continuing acts of the _____ *[summary name for defendants 1, 2, and DOES 1-20]* will cause plaintiff irreparable injury, which cannot adequately be compensated by money damages. By reason of the above, plaintiff is entitled to temporary, preliminary, and permanent injunctive relief, enjoining the _____ *[summary name for defendants 1, 2, and DOES 1-20]* from any use of the domain name "_____.com" and further compelling defendants to transfer ownership in the domain name to plaintiff, or in the alternative for cancellation of the domain name.

31. Plaintiff is informed and believes, and on the basis of such information and belief alleges, that, as a direct and proximate result of the wrongful conduct by the _____ *[summary name for defendants 1, 2, and DOES 1-20]*, and each of them, plaintiff has suffered and will continue to suffer general and special damages including, but not limited to, damage to _____ *[his or her]* business, profession, reputation, character, and property, which will result in loss of earnings and profits in an amount that has yet to be ascertained. When plaintiff ascertains the exact amount of these damages, _____ *[he or she]* will seek leave of court to amend this complaint to set forth the amount.

THIRD CAUSE OF ACTION

(Common-Law Misappropriation of Right of Publicity)

(Against the _____ *[summary name for defendants 1, 2, and DOES 1-20]*)

32. Plaintiff repeats, realleges, adopts, and incorporates each and every allegation contained in Paragraphs 1 through 20, inclusive, as though fully set forth here.

33. The _____ *[summary name for defendants 1, 2, and DOES 1-20]* registration and commercial use of domain name "_____.com" constitutes a violation and misappropriation of plaintiff's common-law right of publicity in that the _____ *[summary name for defendants 1, 2, and DOES 1-20]* misappropriated plaintiff's name and used it for the purpose of receiving financial gain.

34. The _____ *[summary name for defendants 1, 2, and DOES 1-20]* have

Figure 22.2 *(continued)*

continued to own and use the name "_____.com" despite demands by plaintiff to cease such use and to transfer all ownership in the domain name to plaintiff.

35. Plaintiff is informed and believes, and on the basis of such information and belief alleges, that the _____ *[summary name for defendants 1, 2, and DOES 1-20]* appropriated plaintiff's name for the purpose of creating and enhancing defendants' pecuniary gain and profit through the registration and eventual sale of the domain name "_____.com."

36. Plaintiff is informed and believes, and on the basis of such information and belief alleges, that unless enjoined and restrained by order of this court, the _____ *[summary name for defendants 1, 2, and DOES 1-20]* continuing acts will cause plaintiff irreparable injury, which cannot adequately be compensated by money damages. By reason of the above, plaintiff is entitled to temporary, preliminary, and permanent injunctive relief enjoining the _____ *[summary name for defendants 1, 2, and DOES 1-20]* from use of the domain name "_____.com" and further compelling the _____ *[summary name for defendants 1, 2, and DOES 1-20]* to transfer all ownership in the domain name to plaintiff, or in the alternative for cancellation of the domain name.

37. Plaintiff is informed and believes, and on the basis of such information and belief alleges, that, as a direct proximate result of the wrongful conduct by the _____ *[summary name for defendants 1, 2, and DOES 1-20]*, and each of them, plaintiff has suffered and will continue to suffer general and special damages including, but not limited to, damage to _____ *[his or her]* business, profession, reputation, character, and property, which will result in loss of earnings and profits in an amount that has yet to be ascertained. When plaintiff ascertains the exact amount of the damages, plaintiff will seek leave of court to amend this complaint to set forth the amount.

FOURTH CAUSE OF ACTION

(Cybersquatting Pursuant to 15 U.S.C.A. § 1125(d))

(Against the _____ *[summary name for defendant net domain name owner and DOES 21-50]*)

38. Plaintiff repeats, realleges, adopts, and incorporates each and every allegation contained in Paragraphs 1 through 20, inclusive, as though fully set forth here.

39. Plaintiff's name is a distinctive and famous mark, and was a distinctive and famous mark at the time the domain name "_____.net" was registered with _____ *[domain name registration company]*, and at all other times relevant to this action, pursuant to Section 3002(a) of the Anticybersquatting Act, 15 U.S.C.A. § 1125(d)(1).

Figure 22.2 (*continued*)

40. Plaintiff is informed and believes, and on the basis of such information and belief alleges, that the _____ *[summary name for defendant net domain name owner and DOES 21-50]*, and each of them, have had, and continue to have, a bad faith intent to profit from the name _____ *[actor's name and mark]*, which is protected as a distinctive mark and personal name under Section 3002(a) of the Anticybersquatting Act, 15 U.S.C.A. § 1125(d)(1). Specifically, the _____ *[summary name for defendant net domain name owner and DOES 21-50]* registered the domain name "_____.net" without the prior knowledge, permission, or consent of plaintiff, and have operated and are continuing to operate a website that contains numerous photographs of plaintiff, sells merchandise, including books and movies pertaining to plaintiff, posts advertisements, and operates a fan club called the "_____ Club" (an abbreviation for _____.net, which issues a membership card featuring the name and photograph of plaintiff). All of the above activities are being done without plaintiff's consent, and in contravention of plaintiff's affirmative demands that _____ *[name of defendant net domain name owner]* cease and desist from such practices, which infringe on plaintiff's rights. Accordingly, the actions of the _____ *[summary name for defendant net domain name owner and DOES 21-50]*, and each of them, as alleged here constitute a violation of Section 3002(a) of the Anticybersquatting Act, 15 U.S.C.A. §§ 1125(d)(1)(A)(ii)(I), (II); (d)(1)(B)(i)(II), (V) and (d)(1)(E).

41. Plaintiff is therefore entitled to a judgment from this court compelling the _____ *[summary name for defendant net domain name owner and DOES 21-50]*, and each of them, to transfer all ownership in the domain name "_____.net" to plaintiff, or in the alternative for cancellation of the domain name, pursuant to Section 3002(a) of the Anticybersquatting Act, 15 U.S.C.A. § 1125(d)(1)(C).

42. Plaintiff is further entitled to a preliminary and permanent injunction enjoining the _____ *[summary name for defendant net domain name owner and DOES 21-50]* from any use of the domain name "_____.net" pursuant to Section 3003 of the Anticybersquatting Act, 15 U.S.C.A. § 1116(a).

43. Plaintiff is further entitled to a judgment from this court awarding plaintiff actual damages proximately caused by the _____ *[summary name for defendant net domain name owner and DOES 21-50]* or, in the alternative, statutory damages of not less than $1,000 and not more than $100,000, as the court considers just, pursuant to Section 3003 of the Anticybersquatting Act, 15 U.S.C.A. § 1117(d).

FIFTH CAUSE OF ACTION

(False Designation or Representation Pursuant to The Lanham Act,
15 U.S.C.A. § 1125(a))

Figure 22.2 (*continued*)

44. Plaintiff repeats, realleges, adopts, and incorporates each and every action contained in Paragraphs 1 through 20, inclusive, as though fully set forth here.

45. Plaintiff is informed and believes, and on the basis of such information and belief alleges, that the _____ *[summary name for defendant net domain name owner and DOES 21-50]*, and each of them, have violated Section 43(a) of the Lanham Act, 15 U.S.C.A. § 1125(a), by expressly and impliedly making false designations or representations when registering the domain name "_____.net" and by operating a website that contains numerous photographs of plaintiff, sells merchandise concerning plaintiff, posts advertisements (including announcements regarding plaintiff's latest motion pictures) and otherwise appears to be an official website for plaintiff. These false designations or representations include, without limitation, the implied representation that plaintiff endorses, sponsors, operates, and/or is affiliated with the domain name "_____.net" and/or any and all information, products, and services offered on the website located at the domain name "_____.net."

46. Plaintiff is informed and believes, and on the basis of such information and belief alleges, that the conduct of the _____ *[summary name for defendant net domain name owner and DOES 21-50]*, and each of them, has caused, and is continuing to cause, confusion among Internet users in that persons accessing the domain name "_____.net" are led to believe that such domain name, and the website located at that domain name, are owned, operated, sponsored, endorsed by, and/or affiliated with plaintiff, which they are not. Moreover, Internet users are further led to believe that, if plaintiff does not operate a website at the domain name "_____.net" or one of the other Domain Names (which use plaintiff's name as the domain name), plaintiff must not have a domain name or website of _____ *[his or her]* own.

47. Plaintiff is informed and believes, and on the basis of such information and belief alleges, that unless and until enjoined and restrained by order of this court, the continued acts of the _____ *[summary name for defendant net domain name owner and DOES 21-50]* will cause plaintiff irreparable injury, which cannot adequately be compensated by money damages. By reason of the above, plaintiff is entitled to temporary, preliminary, and permanent injunctive relief enjoining the _____ *[summary name for defendant net domain name owner and DOES 21-50]* from any use of the domain name "_____.net" and compelling them to transfer ownership of the domain name to plaintiff, or in the alternative for cancellation of the domain name.

48. Plaintiff is informed and believes, and on the basis of such information and belief

Figure 22.2 (*continued*)

alleges, that, as a direct and proximate result of the wrongful conduct by the _____ *[summary name for defendant net domain name owner and DOES 21-50]*, and each of them, plaintiff has suffered and will suffer general and special damages including, but not limited to, damage to _____ *[his or her]* business, profession, reputation, character, and property, which will result in loss of earnings and profits, in an amount that has yet to be ascertained. When plaintiff ascertains the exact amount of the damages, _____ *[he or she]* will seek leave of the court to amend this complaint to set forth the amount.

49. Plaintiff is informed and believes, and on the basis of such information and belief alleges, that, as a direct and proximate result of the above-mentioned acts by the _____ *[summary name for defendant net domain name owner and DOES 21-50]*, and each of them, the _____ *[summary name for defendant net domain name owner and DOES 21-50]* have earned profits from the commercial use of plaintiff's name and the domain name "_____.net" in an amount that has yet to be ascertained. Plaintiff is entitled to an accounting, setting forth all revenues and profits received by the _____ *[summary name for defendant net domain name owner and DOES 21-50]* as a result of their unauthorized use of plaintiff's name for commercial purposes, and for disgorgement of all such profits.

50. Plaintiff is informed and believes, and on the basis of such information and belief alleges, that the officers, directors, and/or managing agents of the _____ *[summary name for defendant net domain name owner and DOES 21-50]* authorized, directed, and/or ratified the wrongful acts of the _____ *[summary name for defendant net domain name owner and DOES 21-50]* and are consequently liable to plaintiff.

SIXTH CAUSE OF ACTION

(Common-Law Misappropriation of Right of Publicity)

(Against the _____ *[summary name for defendant net domain name owner and DOES 21-50]*)

51. Plaintiff repeats, realleges, adopts, and incorporates each and every allegation contained in Paragraphs 1 through 20, inclusive, as though fully set forth here.

52. The registration and commercial use of the domain name "_____.net" by the _____ *[summary name for defendant net domain name owner and DOES 21-50]* constitutes a violation and misappropriation of plaintiff's right of publicity in that the _____ *[summary name for defendant net domain name owner and DOES 21-50]* misappropriated plaintiff's name and used it for the purpose of receiving financial gain.

53. The _____ *[summary name for defendant net domain name owner and DOES 21-50]* have continued to own and use the domain name "_____

Figure 22.2 (*continued*)

.net" despite demands by plaintiff to cease such use and to transfer all ownership in the domain name to plaintiff.

54. Plaintiff is informed and believes, and on the basis of such information and belief alleges, that the _____ *[summary name for defendant net domain name owner and DOES 21-50]* appropriated plaintiff's name for the purpose of receiving financial gain and profits by registering the domain name "_____.net" and operating a website that sells merchandise concerning plaintiff, posts commercial advertisements, and operates a fan club called the "_____ Club," among other commercial activities.

55. Plaintiff is informed and believes, and on the basis of such information and belief alleges, that unless and until enjoined and restrained by order of this court, the _____ *[summary name for defendant net domain name owner and DOES 21-50]* will continue their actions, as alleged here, and will cause plaintiff irreparable injury, which cannot adequately be compensated by money damages. By reason of the above, plaintiff is entitled to temporary, preliminary, and permanent injunctive relief enjoining the _____ *[summary name for defendant net domain name owner and DOES 21-50]* from any use of the domain name "_____.net" and compelling them to transfer ownership of the domain name to plaintiff, or in the alternative for cancellation of the domain name.

56. Plaintiff is informed and believes, and on the basis of such information and belief alleges, that, as a direct proximate result of the wrongful conduct by the _____ *[summary name for defendant net domain name owner and DOES 21-50]*, and each of them, plaintiff has suffered and will continue to suffer general and special damages including, but not limited to, damage to _____ *[his or her]* business, profession, reputation, character, and property, which will result in loss of earnings and profits in an amount that has yet to be ascertained. When plaintiff ascertains the exact amount of the damages, plaintiff will seek leave of the court to amend this complaint to set forth the amount.

57. Plaintiff is informed and believes, and on the basis of such information and belief alleges, that, as a direct and proximate result of the above-mentioned acts by the _____ *[summary name for defendant net domain name owner and DOES 21-50]*, and each of them, the _____ *[summary name for defendant net domain name owner and DOES 21-50]* have earned profits from the commercial use of plaintiff's name and the domain name "_____.net" in an amount that has yet to be ascertained. Plaintiff is entitled to an accounting, setting forth all revenues and profits received by the _____ *[summary name for defendant net domain name owner and DOES 21-50]* as a result of their unauthorized use of plaintiff's name for commercial purposes, and for disgorgement of all such profits.

58. Plaintiff is informed and believes, and on the basis of such information and belief alleges, that the officers, directors, and/or managing agents of the _____ *[summary*

Figure 22.2 (*continued*)

name for defendant net domain name owner and DOES 21-50] authorized, directed, and/or ratified the wrongful acts of the _____ *[summary name for defendant net domain name owner and DOES 21-50]* and are consequently liable to plaintiff.

WHEREFORE, plaintiff requests judgment against defendants, and each of them, as follows:

AS TO THE FIRST CAUSE OF ACTION:

1. For an order of this court compelling the _____ *[summary name for defendants 1, 2, and DOES 1-20]*, and each of them, to transfer all ownership in the domain name "_____.com" to plaintiff, or in the alternative for cancellation of the domain name;

2. For a preliminary and permanent injunction enjoining the _____ *[summary name for defendants 1, 2, and DOES 1-20]* from further use of the domain name "_____.com";

3. For general and special damages against the _____ *[summary name for defendants 1, 2, and DOES 1-20]*, and each of them, jointly and severally, according to proof at the time of trial or, in the alternative, for statutory damages in an amount not less than $1,000, nor in excess of $100,000;

AS TO THE SECOND CAUSE OF ACTION:

4. For an order of this court compelling the _____ *[summary name for defendants 1, 2, and DOES 1-20]*, and each of them, to transfer all ownership in the domain name "_____.com" to plaintiff, or in the alternative for cancellation of the domain name;

5. For a preliminary and permanent injunction enjoining the _____ *[summary name for defendants 1, 2, and DOES 1-20]* from further use of the domain name "_____.com";

6. For general and special damages against the _____ *[summary name for defendants 1, 2, and DOES 1-20]*, and each of them, jointly and severally, according to proof at the time of trial;

AS TO THE THIRD CAUSE OF ACTION:

7. For an order of this court compelling the _____ *[summary name for defendants 1, 2, and DOES 1-20]*, and each of them, to transfer all ownership in the domain name "_____.com" to plaintiff, or in the alternative for cancellation of the domain name;

8. For a preliminary and permanent injunction enjoining the _____ *[summary name for defendants 1, 2, and DOES 1-20]* from further use of the domain name "_____.com";

Figure 22.2 *(continued)*

9. For general and special damages against the _____ *[summary name for defendants 1, 2, and DOES 1-20]*, and each of them, jointly and severally, according to proof at the time of trial;

AS TO THE FOURTH CAUSE OF ACTION:

10. For an order of this court compelling the _____ *[summary name for defendant net domain name owner and DOES 21-50]*, and each of them, to transfer all ownership in the domain name "_____.net" to plaintiff, or in the alternative for cancellation of the domain name;

11. For a preliminary and permanent injunction enjoining the _____ *[summary name for defendant net domain name owner and DOES 21-50]* from further use of the domain name "_____.net";

12. For an accounting setting forth all revenues and profits received by the _____ *[summary name for defendant net domain name owner and DOES 21-50]*, and each of them, in connection with the use of plaintiff's name, including, without limitation, all sales and advertising revenues and profits received by such defendants from the website located at "_____.net";

13. For general and special damages against the _____ *[summary name for defendant net domain name owner and DOES 21-50]* and each of them, jointly and severally, according to proof at the time of trial or, in the alternative, for statutory damages in an amount not less than $1,000, nor in excess of $100,000;

AS TO THE FIFTH CAUSE OF ACTION:

14. For an order of this court compelling the _____ *[summary name for defendant net domain name owner and DOES 21-50]*, and each of them, to transfer all ownership in the domain name "_____.net" to plaintiff, or in the alternative for cancellation of the domain name;

15. For a preliminary and permanent injunction enjoining the _____ *[summary name for defendant net domain name owner and DOES 21-50]* from further use of the domain name "_____.net;"

16. For general and special damages against the _____ *[summary name for defendant net domain name owner and DOES 21-50]*, and each of them, jointly and severally, according to proof at the time of trial;

17. For an accounting setting forth all revenues and profits received by the _____ *[summary name for defendant net domain name owner and DOES 21-50]*, and each of them, in connection with the use of plaintiff's name, without limitation all sales and advertising revenues and profits received by such defendants from the website located at "_____.net;"

Figure 22.2 (*continued*)

18. For an award of the _____ *[summary name for defendant net domain name owner and DOES 21-50]* profits attributable to the commercial use of plaintiff's name;
19. For an order declaring that the _____ *[summary name for defendant net domain name owner and DOES 21-50]* hold such profits trust for plaintiff.

AS TO THE SIXTH CAUSE OF ACTION:

20. For an order of this court compelling the _____ *[summary name for defendant net domain name owner and DOES 21-50]*, and each of them, to transfer all ownership in the domain name "_____.net" to plaintiff, or in the alternative for cancellation of the domain name;
21. For a preliminary and permanent injunction enjoining the _____ *[summary name for defendant net domain name owner and DOES 21-50]* from further use of the domain name "_____.net";
22. For general and special damages against the _____ *[summary name for defendant net domain name owner and DOES 21-50]*, and each of them, jointly and severally, according to proof at the time of trial;
23. For an accounting setting forth all revenues and profits received by the _____ *[summary name for defendant net domain name owner and DOES 21-50]*, and each of them, in connection with the use of plaintiff's name, including, without limitation, all sales and advertising revenues and profits received by such defendants from the website located at "_____.net";
24. For an award of the _____ *[summary name for defendant net domain name owner and DOES 21-50]* profits attributable to the commercial use of plaintiff's name;
25. For an order declaring that the _____ *[summary name for defendant net domain name owner and DOES 21-50]* hold such profits in trust for plaintiff.

AS TO ALL CAUSES OF ACTION:

26. For costs of suit incurred in this action;
27. For interest on the above-requested damages at the maximum legal rate as provided by law; and
28. For such other and further relief as the court deems just and proper.

REQUEST FOR JURY TRIAL

Plaintiff demands a jury trial pursuant to Rule 38 of the Federal Rules of Civil Procedure (F.R.C.P. 38).

Dated: _____.

Unfair Competition
Definition

What is competition? The right of the individual to engage in private enterprise—and the collateral right of freewheeling competition between individuals.

Unfair competition *need not* actually involve competition between the parties, and the parties *need not* be intentionally unfair. While there is such a thing as a "tortious unfair competition," this type of unfair competition may be the result of an innocent competitive act.

The remedy for unfair competition is an equitable one in the nature of injunctive relief and, in addition, money damages whenever incurred.

Legal Remedy Pitfalls

Legal remedies in an action for unfair competition are inadequate for the following reasons:

1. Money damages arising from a business setting generally involve the loss of anticipated profits evolving from a speculative and unascertainable commodity; and

2. The conduct of the moving party, if continued, would create multiple lawsuits for which money damages would hardly provide adequate compensation.

NOTE: You, as a paralegal, should look to your applicable state civil code sections to determine if these grounds are prevailing in your state.

In order to protect the trade secrets of your client, it may be necessary to file a lawsuit to enjoin a former employee in order to prevent substantial harm from their disclosure. A sample from American Jurisprudence Pleading and Practice forms is included in Figure 22.3.

Developing a Complaint in an Unfair Competition Lawsuit (Injunctive Relief) Based on a "Trade Secret"

PRACTICAL HINTS

1. Remember to show that the plaintiff was harmed.

2. Remember to set forth that the plaintiff used every acceptable and reasonable means to protect his "trade secret."

3. Remember to spell out that the defendant had fiduciary knowledge of the "trade secret" and access thereto.

Figure 22.3

§100. Complaint in Federal Court—Disclosure of tradesecrets by former employee and use by present employer—For damages, injunctive relief, and accounting

COUNT ONE.

1. Plaintiff is a corporation incorporated under the laws of *[name of state A]*, and has its principal place of business in *[name of city]*, *[name of county]* County, *[name of state A]*.
2. Defendant *[name of defendant]* is a corporation incorporated under the laws of *[name of state]*, and has its principal place of business in *[name of city]*, *[name of state B]*.
3. Defendant *[name of individual defendant]* is a citizen of *[name of state B]*, and is a resident of *[name of city]*, *[name of state B]*.
4. The matter in controversy, exclusive of interest and costs, exceeds $*[dollar amount of monetary jurisdiction]*. The court has jurisdiction under the provisions of 28 U.S.C.A. § 1332.
5. Plaintiff designs and manufactures *[specification of product]* and other *[specification of type of devices]* devices, which operations require the extensive use by plaintiff of its secret and confidential information and processes.
6. Defendant *[name of individual defendant]* was employed by plaintiff as its *[job title of individual defendant]* from *[begin date of employment]*, until *[his/her]* discharge by plaintiff on *[date of discharge]*.
7. Prior to being employed by plaintiff, defendant *[name of individual defendant]* had no knowledge of plaintiff's **secret** or confidential information, plaintiff's processes, or the production methods utilized by plaintiff in the production of *[specification of product]*, among other things.
8. While employed by plaintiff, defendant *[name of individual defendant]* acquired knowledge of numerous **tradesecrets** and **secret** and confidential information of plaintiff, utilized, among other things, in the manufacture of *[specification of product]*, and relating to plaintiff's customer lists and other confidential customer information.
9. Subsequent to being discharged by plaintiff, defendant *[name of individual defendant]* knowingly and willfully disclosed such **tradesecrets** and confidential information belonging to plaintiff to defendant *[name of corporate defendant]*.
10. Such **tradesecrets** and confidential information are a primary asset of plaintiff, and plaintiff has carefully guarded these **tradesecrets** and confidential information, and there has been no public disclosure of these **tradesecrets** by plaintiff.
11. Defendant *[name of individual defendant]* knew and now knows that plaintiff regarded such proprietary matter as **tradesecrets** and confidential information.
12. By reason of the willful and knowing disclosure by defendant *[name of individual defendant]* of plaintiff's **tradesecrets** and confidential information, plaintiff has

Figure 22.3 *(continued)*

been and, unless defendant *[name of individual defendant]* is enjoined from further making such disclosures, will continue to be greatly and irreparably harmed and injured, and will suffer the threat of loss of competitive advantage, income, profits, and customers, without having an adequate remedy at law.

COUNT TWO.

13. Plaintiff realleges Paragraphs 1 through 5 of Count One of this complaint and makes them a part of this Count Two as if fully set forth.

14. Defendant *[name of corporate defendant]* is a competitor of plaintiff, engaged in the design and production of *[specification of products]* for industrial and military applications.

15. Plaintiff realleges Paragraphs 6 through 8 of Count One of this complaint and makes them a part of this Count Two as if fully set forth.

16. In *[name of month]*, of *[identification of year]*, defendant *[name of individual defendant]* was employed by defendant *[name of corporate defendant]* as *[job title of individual defendant]*. Shortly afterwards, defendant *[name of corporate defendant]* began actively to solicit orders for *[specification of product]* from some of plaintiff's customers. *[List of names of known customers solicited, and specification of reason showing why names of others cannot be specified at present.]*

17. Plaintiff's *[specification of products]* are produced by the use of secret information, processes, and production methods, and defendant *[name of individual defendant]* was responsible for supervising such items, among others, while *[he/she]* was in the employ of plaintiff.

18. Plaintiff realleges Paragraphs 9 through 11 of Count One of this complaint and makes them a part of this Count Two as if fully set forth.

19. Defendant *[name of corporate defendant]* has appropriated and used, for its benefit, the confidential information and secrets of plaintiff, including those relating to its production of *[specification of product]* without plaintiff's consent, and in violation of plaintiff's rights. Such appropriation and use by defendant *[name of corporate defendant]* has been, and will be, of great value to defendant *[name of corporate defendant]*, and has resulted, and will result, in its unjust enrichment.

20. Plaintiff's competitive advantage in the development, manufacture, and marketing of its products, including *[specification of product]*, will be seriously impaired, if not completely destroyed, and plaintiff will therefore suffer great and irreparable injury without having an adequate remedy at law, unless the unlawful invasion by defendant *[name of corporate defendant]* of plaintiff's rights in the above-described confidential information and secrets is enjoined.

Figure 22.3 *(continued)*

WHEREFORE, plaintiff requests:

1. A preliminary and permanent injunction:
    (a) preventing defendant *[name of individual defendant]* from using, divulging, and communicating to others any of plaintiff's trade secrets and confidential information, the knowledge of which *[he/she]* acquired by reason of or during *[his/her]* employment by plaintiff;
    (b) ordering defendant *[name of individual defendant]* to return to plaintiff all drawings, documents, and other tangible materials of plaintiff in the possession of *[name of individual defendant]* obtained from plaintiff, or from others, and any and all copies; and
    (c) ordering defendant *[name of individual defendant]* to deliver to plaintiff all drawings, documents, or other materials based on or utilizing any aspects of the **tradesecrets** and confidential information of plaintiff;
2. A preliminary and permanent injunction:
    (a) preventing defendant *[name of corporate defendant]* from eliciting or acquiring from defendant *[name of individual defendant]* any of plaintiff's **tradesecrets** and confidential information, knowledge of which defendant *[name of individual defendant]* acquired by reason of or during *[his/her]* employment by plaintiff, and from using any such **tradesecrets** and confidential information;
    (b) ordering defendant *[name of corporate defendant]* to return to plaintiff all drawings, documents, and other materials of plaintiff in the possession of *[name of corporate defendant]* obtained or received by *[name of corporate defendant]* from *[name of individual defendant]*, or others, and any and all copies; and
    (c) ordering defendant *[name of corporate defendant]* to deliver to plaintiff all drawings, documents, and other materials in the possession of *[name of corporate defendant]* based on or utilizing any aspects of the trade secrets and confidential information of plaintiff;
3. An accounting by defendant *[name of corporate defendant]*, and a judgment for the amount found to be due on such accounting in favor of plaintiff, for all profits realized by that defendant, and for all damages and loss of profits ascertained to have been sustained by plaintiff by reason of the unlawful conduct of defendants;
4. Damages against defendants in the sum of $*[dollar amount of damages]*;
5. Exemplary damages against defendants in the sum of $*[dollar amount of exemplary damages]* by reason of the willful and deliberate nature of defendants' actions, involving malicious injury or a reckless indifference to the interests of plaintiff;
6. Plaintiff's reasonable costs and expenses, including attorney's fees, incurred in connection with the prosecution of this action; and
7. Such other and further relief as the court may deem just and equitable.

4. Remember to spell out that the defendant converted the same for his own use and benefit.

5. Remember to explicitly set forth that the defendant, in using and converting plaintiff's trade secret, *intended* to mislead and defraud the public.

6. Remember to allege that the defendant, in doing the acts above referenced, violated the fiduciary relationship as between employee and employer.

7. Remember to allege the "secret" converted by defendant was not of a nature or type that could be legitimately retained in the mind of a defendant, and therefore could not be legally used by defendant for his own use and benefit.

Documents Required to Accompany an Unfair Competition Complaint

1. Notice of Motion for Preliminary Injunction;

2. Memorandum of Points and Authorities in support of said Motion; and

3. Declaration of your attorney, and, if applicable, Declaration of Affidavit by the client.

CHAPTER TWENTY-THREE

Workers' Compensation

"Workers' compensation" is an insurance plan that all employers must participate in to provide insurance coverage for medical care and other recompense for employees who are hurt during the course of employment. This can either be at the place of employment or while performing some off-site task at the direction of the employer. One of the provisions of this coverage means that the employee no longer has a right to sue the employer for negligence in connection with the injury.

General information and links to your state's program can be accessed through the U.S. Department of Labor, Employment Standards Administration, Office of Worker's Compensation Programs (www.dol.gov/esa/owcp_org.htm) and the National Workers' Compensation Service Center, a private affiliation (www.workerscompen sation.com).

Here is a common misunderstanding: Whenever an employee is injured on the job, whether or not he is at fault, filing a claim against said "employer" is actually *not* against the employer. Rather, it is against the workers' compensation insurance carrier. All employers by law have to carry insurance to protect the employee against mishaps.

Additionally, in workers' compensation claims, it is unimportant whether or not the employee was at fault. The law is clear in this regard. What may differ is the procedure for filing said claim against the insurance carrier of the employer.

A Legal Conflict

Another common misunderstanding: *You can receive state disability and workers' compensation payments simultaneously.* The procedure is that, upon injury, the employee, after the doctor has certified that the injury is work-related, should immediately apply for state disability to receive such sums that are due and owed as a result of employment. The application form for this state disability includes a question relative to whether or not the employee has received workers' compensation benefits.

At the time that the employee receives the first temporary disability check from the workers' compensation insurance carrier of the employer, then he must, under the law, advise the state disability office of such receipt. To do otherwise is fraud and can result in either a penalty or imprisonment.

Please be sure to check your local statutes to see whether or not this process is applicable.

In order to properly interview a client and complete the applicable claim form, then to follow the industrial claim to a successful conclusion, a paralegal must know and have a full understanding of the workers' compensation laws in his particular state and how they operate. For example, states such as Louisiana, Alabama, New Mexico, Tennessee, and Wyoming have what is called "court-administered systems" in workers' compensation procedures. What this means is that all of the workers' compensation procedures are processed through the "court" systems.

In the State of Wyoming, for example, the industrial accident procedure is encased in an "industrial accident fund," and the employer must be in good standing in order to qualify for joining "the fund."

After the paralegal has prepared the original application, a filing fee must be paid to the district court where the application is ultimately filed. In this instance, the employee is represented by a court-appointed attorney or prosecuting attorney, if the injured employee lacks other representation. Your attorney should be aware that in the State of Wyoming, there are limitations as it relates to fees awarded to the attorney.

In the initial application, you as a paralegal must be sure to include the following: (1) the need for applying for an award, and (2) you should stress the need for temporary and/or permanent disability. Because temporary and permanent disability claims are not automatic, they must be filed and requested by the employee (or the representative of the injured person).

Additionally, any and all claims, either by employee or employer, are made to the district court in the county in which the injury occurred. If disputed, they are handled as regular civil matters with appeal privileges to the supreme court of the state.

Though, like California, there is a Subsequent Injuries Fund procedure, there is no serious and willful application under the laws of Wyoming's Compensation Act.

Note that the employee cannot sue his employer; and if the employee fails to file for disability, he has to pay for all hospitalization, doctors, and other medical bills himself.

For our purposes, however, this chapter will be discussing the procedures of the workers' compensation practice in the State of California.

General Principles of Workers' Compensation (Under the Federal Employment Compensation Act)

The laws in workers' compensation can change frequently. It is crucial that you as the paralegal in a workers' compensation office be aware of these changes. Continuing legal education opportunities, weekly review of the relevant legal newspapers, journals, or bulletins, and online alerts should be part of your repertoire. Be sure to check the relevant website(s) in your jurisdiction for updates.

Further, it will be necessary to have contacts with the local workers' compensation carriers. Workers' compensation does not start in the courts, rather it starts with the insurance carrier and notice to the employer. §8119 of the Federal Employment Compensation Act (hereinafter referred to as "Act") provides that notice of injury or death shall:

1. Be given within thirty days after the injury or death;

2. Be given to the immediate superior of the employee by personal delivery or by depositing it in the mail properly stamped and addressed;

3. Be in writing;

4. State the name and address of the employee;

5. State the year, month, day, and hour when and the particular locality where the injury or death occurred;

6. State the cause and nature of the injury, or, in the case of death, the employment factors believed to be the cause; and

7. Be signed by and contain the address of the individual giving the notice.

In any state, the employer must receive written proof that the employee has been injured. This can normally be accomplished by the claimant (employee) securing a physician's report and submitting it to his immediate supervisor. (See §8123 of the act.) Figure 23.1 contains a sample of the format for this kind of report from American Jurisprudence Legal Forms 2d for Workers' Compensation. The next step is on the part of the employer who must file with the insurance carrier. (See Figure 23.2.)

Figure 23.1

§267:35. Report—Physician to Workers' Compensation Commission—First Diagnosis and Treatment of Injury or Disease

PHYSICIAN'S FIRST REPORT OF OCCUPATIONAL INJURY OR ILLNESS

A. Insurer
    1. Name: *[name of insurer]*
    2. Address: *[address of insurer]*
B. Employer
    3. Name: *[name of employer]*
    4. Address: *[address of employer]*
    5. Nature of business: *[nature of business]*
C. Employee
    6. Name: *[name of employee]*
    7. Address: *[address of employee]*
    8. Telephone: *[telephone number of employee]*
    9. Social Security Number: *[Social Security number of employee]*
    10. Sex: *[male/female]*
    11. Date of birth: *[date of birth of employee]*
    12. Occupation: *[occupation of employee]*
    13. Date last worked: *[date last worked]*
    14. Has worker been previously treated by you or your office? *[yes/no]*
D. Injury or illness
    15. Date and hour of injury or onset of illness: *[date and hour of injury]*
    16. Date and hour of first examination or treatment: *[date and hour of first examination or treatment]*
    17. Employee's description of how the accident or exposure happened: *[employee's description of accident]*
E. Diagnosis
    18. Subjective **complaints** of employee: *[subjective complaints of employee]*
    19. Physical examination findings: *[description of physical examination findings]*
    20. X-ray and laboratory results: *[description of X-ray and laboratory results]*
    21. Diagnosis: *[description of diagnosis]*
    22. Other current condition that will impede or delay employee's recovery: *[description of other conditions]*
    23. In your opinion, was injury or disability the result of accident or exposure described above? *[yes/no]*
F. Treatment
    24. Date of first treatment: *[date of first treatment]*
    25. Date of most recent treatment: *[date of most recent treatment]*

Figure 23.1 *(continued)*

26. Treatment employed on initial visit: *[description of treatment employed on initial visit]*
27. Treatment employed on subsequent visits: *[description of treatment employed on subsequent visits]*
28. Name(s) and address(es) of other physician(s) employee was referred to: *[list of names and addresses of other physicians]*
29. Name and location of hospital, if hospitalized: *[name of hospital]*, *[address of hospital]*
30. Further treatment required: *[description of further treatment required]*

G. Work status
31. Expected duration of disability: *[expected duration of disability]*
32. Estimated time off from work—regular work: *[estimated time off from regular work]*
33. Estimated time off from work—modified work: *[estimated time off from modified work]*
34. Restrictions: *[description of restrictions]*

H. Rehabilitation
35. Is rehabilitation treatment recommended? *[yes/no]*
36. If so, has referral been made? *[yes/no]*

Figure 23.2
§267:36. Employer's Report of Industrial Injury—To Compensation Commission and Insurance Carrier

EMPLOYER'S REPORT OF OCCUPATIONAL INJURY OR ILLNESS

A. Employee
1. Name: *[name of employee]*
2. Home address: *[address of employee]*
3. Telephone: *[telephone number of employee]*
4. Birth date: *[date of birth of employee]*
5. Social Security No. *[Social Security number of employee]*
6. Sex: *[male/female]*
7. Marital status: *[marital status]*
8. Occupation and job title at time of injury or onset of illness: *[occupation and job title of employee]*

B. Employee's wage data
9. Length of employment to date of injury: *[length of employment]*
10. Employment temporary or permanent? *[temporary/permanent]*

Figure 23.2 *(continued)*

If temporary, for: *[period of temporary employment]*

    11. Wage rate of employee: $*[dollar amount of hourly wage rate]* per hour

    12. Number of hours per week employee usually worked: *[number of hours per week]*

    13. Number of hours per day employee usually worked: *[number of hours per day]*

    14. Was employee on overtime at time of accident? *[yes/no]*

    15. Was employee paid for day of injury? *[yes/no]*

    16. Actual gross earnings of employee for *[number of days]* days preceding injury: $ *[dollar amount of gross earnings of employee for period of days preceding injury]*; for *[number of months]* months preceding injury: $*[dollar amount of gross earnings of employee for period of months preceding injury]*

    17. Overtime rate of pay, if any: $*[dollar amount of overtime hourly pay]* per hour

    18. Number and relationship of dependents claimed by employee: *[number and relationship of dependents]*

C. Employer

    19. Name: *[name of employer]*

    20. Nature of business: *[nature of business]*

    21. Compensation policy no.: *[policy number]*

    22. Office mail address: *[office mailing address of employer]*

    23. Telephone: *[telephone number of employer]*

D. Injury or illness

    24. Date of injury or onset of illness: *[date of injury]*

    25. Time injury or illness occurred: *[time of injury]*

    26. Date employer notified: *[date employer notified]*

    27. Date last worked: *[date last worked]*

    28. Date returned to work: *[date returned to work]*

    29. Number of workdays lost (actual or estimated—state which): *[number of workdays lost]*, *[actual/estimated]*

    30. Location where event or exposure occurred: *[location where event occurred]*

    31. Department where event or exposure occurred: *[department where event occurred]*

    32. On employer's premises? *[yes/no]*

    33. How did injury/illness occur? *[description of how injury occurred]*

    34. Equipment, materials, chemicals, machines, tools, or objects employee was using when event or exposure occurred: *[description of equipment, materials, chemicals, machines, tools, or objects employee was using]*

    35. State activity the employee was performing when event or exposure occurred: *[description of activity employee was performing when event occurred]*

    36. Did event or exposure occur during employee's regular duty hours? *[yes/no]*

Figure 23.2 *(continued)*

37. Was accident directly related to the duties to which employee was assigned? *[yes/no]*
38. Were mechanical safeguards, respiratory masks, or similar apparatuses provided for task in which employee was engaged? *[yes/no]*

    Specify: *[description of mechanical safeguards, respiratory masks, or similar apparatuses]*

    Was employee using apparatus at time of injury? *[yes/no]*
39. General nature of injury: *[description of nature of injury]*
40. Was accident fatal? *[yes/no]*
41. Part of body affected: *[part of body affected]*
42. Attending physician:

    Name: *[name of physician]*

    Office address: *[office address of physician]*
43. Name of hospital, if employee hospitalized: *[name of hospital]*

    Address of hospital: *[address of hospital]*

E. Claim for compensation:

44. Is claim filed or to be filed by employee? *[filed/to be filed]*
45. Will employee resist claim, in whole or in part? *[yes/no]*
46. Does employer believe claim is not compensable, in whole or in part? *[yes/no]*

    If not compensable, state grounds: *[grounds for claim not being compensable]*
47. Was accident the result, in whole or in part, of employee's own misconduct? *[yes/no]*

    If so, specify: *[description of employee's misconduct]*
48. Names and addresses of witnesses to accident: *[list of names and addresses of witnesses]*
49. Name and title of person preparing this report, if different from person signing: *[name of person preparing report]*, *[title of person preparing report]*

The employee is entitled to compensation for medical care/treatment and out-of-work benefits that may include lost wages and an award to compensate for the injury. All plans have a schedule of injury compensation. It is interesting (in kind of a morbid way) to see the valuation apportioned to different injuries. See Figure 23.4 for some of the injury valuations from the Federal Compensation Schedule §8107. The primary treating physician (PTP) is authorized to take those steps in medical care that would "cure, give relief, reduce the degree or the period of disability, or aid in lessening the amount of the monthly compensation" of the injured employee. (See §8103.)

Figure 23.4
Federal Compensation Schedule under §8107

. . .

(c) The compensation schedule is as follows:

(1) Arm lost, 312 weeks' compensation.

(2) Leg lost, 288 weeks' compensation.

(3) Hand lost, 244 weeks' compensation.

(4) Foot lost, 205 weeks' compensation.

(5) Eye lost, 160 weeks' compensation.

(6) Thumb lost, 75 weeks' compensation.

(7) First finger lost, 46 weeks' compensation.

(8) Great toe lost, 38 weeks' compensation.

(9) Second finger lost, 30 weeks' compensation.

(10) Third finger lost, 25 weeks' compensation.

(11) Toe other than great toe lost, 16 weeks' compensation.

(12) Fourth finger lost, 15 weeks' compensation.

(13) Loss of hearing—

(A) complete loss of hearing of one ear, 52 weeks' compensation; or

(B) complete loss of hearing of both ears, 200 weeks' compensation.

Award of benefit is based on either the termination of temporary disability and/ or when it has been adjudged by a physician that the employee's condition has become permanent and stationary (which means that further treatment will neither improve the condition nor make it worse).

Once this fact has been determined, it is appropriate to start the inquiry and process for vocational rehabilitation. This type of rehabilitation is entered into between the employer and the employer's workers' compensation insurance carrier. This process or procedure will be discussed in detail later on in the chapter.

Covered Parties

There are two general categories of workers, one of whom is covered and one who is not: true employees and independent contractors, respectively. There are many instances where the line is a fine one between these two classifications, and it matters a great deal once a compensable event has occurred.

At its most basic, "an independent contractor is a person 'who, in carrying on an independent business, contracts to do a piece of work according to his own methods without being subject to the control of the employer as to the means by which the result is to be accomplished, but only as to the result of the work.'"* Evidence of the

---

Bahrle et al. v. Exxon Corporation et al., 145 NJ 144, 158 (1996), citing *Wilson v. Kelleher Motor Freight Lines Inc.*, 12 NJ 261, 264 (1953).

"right to control" is expressed in terms of the employer's right to direct not only what should be done, but also how it should be done. Employees are under more control than independent contractors. Other factors in determining whether a worker is an employee or not are (1) provision of the equipment used to perform the work and (2) how that worker is compensated. It is more likely that a worker is an employee if the employer provides all the supplies, machinery, and space to perform the work. Being on the company's regular payroll is also an indicator of employee status.

Factors to consider under the Restatement of Agency §220:

1. The extent of control which, by the agreement, the master may exercise over the details of the work;

2. Whether or not the one employed is engaged in a distinct occupation or business;

3. The kind of occupation with reference to whether, in the locality, the work is usually done under the direction of the employer or by a specialist without supervision;

4. The skill required in the particular occupation;

5. Whether the employer or the workman supplies the instrumentalities, tools, and the place of work for the person doing the work;

6. The length of time for which the person is employed;

7. The method of payment, whether by time or by the job;

8. Whether or not the work is a part of the regular business of the employer; and

9. Whether or not the parties believe they are creating the relationship of master and servant.

Covered Events

There are generally two types of events that can be covered under workers' compensation. The first is a single traumatic accident and the other is a continual exposure to certain materials or conditions that lead to the development of a health condition. Either type of injury must be shown:

1. To have "arisen out of" the employment,

2. To have occurred "during the course of" employment,

3. To have occurred on the premises of the employer, or

4. If it did not occur on the premises, to have been covered under the "going and coming rule" (if the employer directed the employee to be off-site and the injury occurred during the travel to or from that location; it does not cover travel to and from work),

5. To have been an "accident" covered by workers' compensation (it cannot be the result of intentional wrongdoing), and

6. To be traceable in time to an occurrence or exposure at work.

EXAMPLE

If you are employed in a grocery store and it is your job to put away heavy bags of potatoes or lift heavy slabs of meat or boxes of canned goods from one place to another within the store, and in doing any of the above, you injure your back or sustain a severe strain or sprain of a muscle, necessitating medical treatment or hospitalization, this is an "on-the-job" injury entitling you to file an industrial accident claim, or workers' compensation claim.

An industrial illness, on the other hand, is any injury or disease that is caused or aggravated by a person's work or working conditions; and may include damage to artificial limbs, dentures, hearing aids, eyeglasses, etc., if incidental to the injury. Examples include chemical poisoning; stress or strain, which may aggravate arthritis; latent diabetes; and psychological problems. These injuries are described as follows:

- *Specific:* occurring as the result of one incident or exposure;

- *Cumulative*: occurring repeatedly over an extensive period of traumatic activities, which combination causes a disability; and

- *Occupational disease:* one in which the cumulative effect of continuous exposure to the harmful elements of one's employment results in the disability, as in the stress and strain of your back and the chemical poisoning mentioned above.

Venue

1. Application filed in the county where the employee or dependent resides on the date of filing; or

2. Cumulative trauma/disease claims where the last alleged injurious exposure occurred.

Composition of the Appeals Board (California, by Way of Example)

1. It is a seven-member board:

   a. Five attorneys appointed by the governor to serve four-year staggered terms;

   b. Two laymen.

   Judicial powers are vested and provided for in the California Labor Code.

2. *The Benefit Unit:* Monitors and insures that the employer gives prompt payment of disability benefits, and/or *prompt* notice of nonpayment on a claim to the employee.

3. *The Medical Bureau:*

    a. This division examines injured employees at the request of the Referee to determine the nature and extent of the industrial accident.

    b. It also evaluates the disability if requested.

    c. There are seven physicians with offices in Sacramento, Oakland, Los Angeles, and Long Beach.

    d. It maintains a panel of independent medical examiners (IMEs) who are appointed upon recommendations of the Medical Advisory Committee.

4. *The Medical Advisory Committee:*

    a. This is a seven-member committee of physicians in specialized areas of medicine and disease.

    b. It is their responsibility to review and approve panels of doctors when and if the injured employee, via attorney, requests a change of treating physician.

    c. These are appointed by the administrative director of the Division of Industrial Accidents.

5. *The Legal Staff:*

    a. The Workers' Compensation Appeals Board (WCAB) maintains a staff of attorneys whose responsibilities include:

        i. Processing cases pending on reconsideration,

        ii. Legal and factual research, and

        iii. Preparation of legal memoranda for the board.

6. *The Rating Bureau:* Not to be confused with the Medical Bureau—totally different function. These are twenty-one specialists, with the following responsibilities:

    a. Issuance of informal ratings in uncontested cases,

    b. Preparation of recommended ratings in contested cases,

    c. Preparation of pretrial estimates prior to pretrial hearings,

    d. Receiving Compromise and Release forms to determine their adequacy, and

    e. Consultation services.

7. *Purpose of the Board:*

   a. Guarantee support for employee and family while employee is unable to work;

   b. Provide medical support and treatment free of charge;

   c. Furnish money award for any permanent disability, or life pension if necessary; and

   d. In case of death of injured employee, provide adequate compensation to family.

8. *The Hearing:*

   a. It is an "administrative-type" proceeding *controlled by* and under the *supervision* of the WCAB; and

   b. The procedures are governed by the rules and regulations of the Government and Labor Code of the State.

Key: Unlike in personal injury cases, the employee can be *grossly* negligent and still recover for injuries sustained.

However, he cannot recover the pain and suffering as in a personal injury case.

In industrial accident cases, *it is unimportant* who is at fault. *It is only important* that the injury occurred "during the course and scope of employment."

Practice and Procedure Before the Workers' Compensation Appeals Board (California Procedure)

The Industrial claim has three dimensions: the informal procedures; the formal procedures; and the appeal.

Informal Procedures (Consent of Both Parties)

Voluntary provision of benefits. The parties are also permitted to settle or release claims without involvement from the WCAB.

Formal Procedures

A. Filing the Workers' Compensation Claim (Adjudication of Industrial Claim)

Who may file a claim? Answer: Anyone privy to the circumstances surrounding the injury, e.g., employer on behalf of the employee; employee on behalf of himself; medical provider (lien claimant); and the legal representative of said employer. (If you as the paralegal are preparing the claim on behalf of the employee, though you are allowed by law to do so, you should notify the Workers' Compensation Appeals

Board *prior* to filing the formal application.)

What is included on the claim form? Answer: a short statement of the facts concerning how the injury occurred and on what date it occurred; a request for normal compensation benefits (temporary disability, permanent disability, medical and legal costs, etc.); and a request for death benefits, if the employee died as a result of the injury.

Under the new rules, you may also include on this initial form a claim for serious and willful misconduct; and you may also include a request for vocational rehabilitation if you discern that the injury suffered by the employee will require it.

B. Death Benefits

The deadline for filing death benefits is one year after the date of death of the employee (or one year from the date of the accident); you should check the local state statute as to this ruling.

Children or spouses living within the home at the time of the incident are covered as it relates to the receipt of said death benefits.

> **NOTE:** It is the responsibility of the spouse to inform you or your attorney that the injury suffered by the employee was the result of a work-related injury and, therefore, death benefits are applicable. However, there are some exceptions, and as the paralegal, it would be your responsibility to check the local labor code and/or the statutes as set forth in your local workers' compensation volumes.

Both of these formal documents (original application and death benefit application) have to be personally served on the employer and/or his insurance company, whichever is applicable in your state.

These should be served immediately upon your receipt, from the applicable Workers' Compensation Appeals Board, of the conformed copy. By conformed copy we mean a copy which includes the board's number.

Thereafter you have fifteen days, under the new rules, within which to contact the opposing parties in an attempt to resolve the matter.

During the interim period, however, you should have been receiving medical reports from the pertinent doctors—both your doctor and the insurance company doctors for comparison and resolution. Once you have received these medical reports and you have attempted to resolve the matter outside of litigation, you are now prepared to file a Declaration of Readiness to Proceed. This is a form which can be obtained from the Workers' Compensation Appeals Board when you are ready to present the claim to them for a hearing on the issues. If you have not already done so, you should procure and file with the Declaration all copies of the doctors' reports heretofore received by your offices so that the WCAB will have something with which to work and make a decision.

C. Filing the Answer to the Application

If you are on the receiving end of an Adjudication Claim, you have ten days after you are served with the Declaration of Readiness to file an answer.

In your answer, you should deny the allegations in the Application and at the same time file any and all reports you have from doctors. (For those of you who are unfamiliar with this procedure, be advised that you can obtain a form copy of an answer from the WCAB.)

Other Formal Procedures

1. *The Subsequent Injuries Fund Benefit application:*

   a. You can file a Subsequent Injuries Fund Petition when the employee has had a partial disability from any cause at the time he was injured on the job and

   b. When the degree of disability caused by a combination of previous disability and subsequent injury is greater than would have resulted from the subsequent injury alone. (See your labor code for this definition and explanation.)

   c. The application must show all the facts concerning the previous disability and

   d. When the employee is entitled to benefits for a previous disability.

   NOTE: The deadline for filing this Petition is the same as when filing the original application for normal benefits.

2. *Petition for New and Further Disability Benefits:* This petition can be filed when the injury has caused a "new and further" disability. This occurs when the employee was able to return to work but is again temporarily or permanently disabled; or when the employee needs further medical treatment.

   The deadline for filing a Petition for New and Further Disability occurs five years after date of injury where the benefits were already provided; or at the time the original application was filed on time; when the case was previously adjudicated; or one year after the last provision of benefits, even though five years from the date of injury; or if the employee did *not* file for benefits before.

   The petition should contain facts that show a new or further disability and/or if an original application had not been filed.

3. *Petition for Serious and Willful Misconduct:* The grounds for filing a Petition for Serious and Willful Misconduct arise when an employer or employee has caused an employee's injury by serious and willful misconduct. That is to say, there has been an intentional or reckless violation of a safety order or an intentional act with knowledge that serious injury is a probable result of such an act.

The petition should include the basis of the claim, e.g., violation of an established safety order, and facts supporting the claim. An example of this would be a correct citation of the subject safety order; the specific manner in which the employer violated the safety order; facts that the employer knew about the violation or the violation was obvious, and that the condition created a probability of serious injury.

It is vitally important that each theory relied on state the facts and allegations separately for each alleged theory of misconduct. Further, the employer's misconduct allegation must be filed within twelve months after injury. As previously noted, this application may be included in the original claim for adjudication.

Appeal Procedures

1. *Petition for Reconsideration:* To file a Petition for Reconsideration, the Workers' Compensation Appeals Board must have made an award, or a decision against the client. The decision must have exceeded the board's or workers' compensation judge's power; or the decision was procured by fraud; or the evidence did not justify the findings of fact; or the findings of fact did not support the decision; and there has been newly discovered evidence. As it relates to all of the above, please be sure to check your Workers' Compensation Appeals Board statutes, as well as the Labor Code.

    If you, as the paralegal, have been instructed to serve this document, note that you have twenty days within which to serve this petition after the order, decision, or award if you want to challenge it. If you determine that this is applicable, you have twenty-five days to mail the petition if it occurs within the State of California. If you live outside the State of California, you have thirty days within which to mail it; and if the recipient lives out of the country, then you have forty days. Note again that you should check your local Workers' Compensation Appeals Board and the Labor Code applicable in your state for this procedure.

    The deadline for filing an answer to this petition, if personally served, is ten days after receipt. If served by mail within California you have fifteen days; or twenty days if mailed outside of California; and/or thirty days if mailed outside of the United States.

2. *The Petition for Writ of Review:* This petition can be filed after you have petitioned for reconsideration in order to seek and obtain a review in the appellate court, based on the following facts:

    a. The Workers' Compensation Appeals Board acted without or in excess of its power;

    b. The order, decision, or award was procured by fraud;

    c. The order, decision, or award was unreasonable;

d. The order, decision, or award was not supported by substantial evidence; or

e. The findings of fact were made and the findings do not support the order, decision, or award under review.

As to the deadline for filing this petition, you have only forty-five days after the board files either an order denying reconsideration or an order following the Petition for Reconsideration. You might want to check your Code of Civil Procedure regarding the deadline within which to file the Petition for Writ of Review. In any and all events, note that you have only twenty days after the petition is served within which to file an answer; and ten days after answer has been served.

3. *Petition to Reopen for Good Cause:* This ability arises when you can show good cause to reopen the proceedings in order to rescind, alter, or amend a previous order, decision, or award. In this connection, "good cause" means you have new evidence that was not previously available or reasonably obtainable; and the same was not presented to the board; or that the law has been changed to support your position that could result in a change in the order, decision, or award.

Please note that you cannot file a petition based on good cause to reopen to have issues of employment reconsidered once the Workers' Compensation Appeals Board has made its decision.

The deadline for filing a Petition to Reopen for Good Cause is five years from the date of the injury.

4. *Miscellaneous claims:* Another claim that can be filed in today's society is a claim for stress. The prerequisite for filing such a claim by an employee is that he must have been employed by the employer for six months or more; or the injury must have been caused by sudden and extraordinary employment conditions, such as long hours or overwork or the conditions under which the employee worked. In addition, the stress claim must be related to a physical injury. For example, an employee who had been previously physically injured on the job came back to work before he was well enough to perform the duties required, and as a consequence, it became stressful for the employee to work in pain and/or discomfort. As the paralegal, you should check your local labor codes to determine when this claim can be filed and if the injury sustained is applicable.

Another miscellaneous claim that can be filed is one on behalf of minors and incompetents. In this instance, time does not run against a minor or incompetent until a guardian *ad litem* or trustee has been appointed by the Workers' Compensation Appeals Board. This relates to any individual under the age of majority and/or any individual under the age of majority who is deemed to be incompetent by the court for any physical or mental reasons. Here again, you should check with your local labor code and statutes to determine when such a claim is viable before the Court.

Vocational Rehabilitation

Nowhere in the area of law is there a more personalized suffering sustained by an entire family as is an industrial accident. The misery and pain inflicted upon the family of the injured employee when he becomes unemployable because of such an incident cannot be measured in damages for "pain and suffering" as in the accepted personal injury case. In many cases, as a result of an industrial incident, these persons are maimed for life; or at the very least, unable to secure gainful employment in the same or similar job activity. In most cases, the adverse residual effects of an industrial incident will remain throughout a lifetime. That is why vocational rehabilitation is so very important.

In most states, this is considered a mandatory program which is entered into between the employee and employer, together with the workers' compensation insurance carrier and the state department of rehabilitation. Some attorneys, as a practical matter, will look to the WCAB to assist in setting up this rehabilitation or retraining program. See Figure 23.5 for a sample from the American Jurisprudence Legal Forms 2d for Workers' Compensation.

Figure 23.5
§267:58. Vocational Rehabilitation Agreement

VOCATIONAL REHABILITATION AGREEMENT

Date *[date of agreement]*

Employee

Name *[name of employee]*

Address *[address of employee]*

Telephone *[telephone number of employee]*

Social Security No. *[Social Security number of employee]*

Birthdate *[date of birth of employee]*

Injury Rehabilitation representative

Name *[name of rehabilitation representative]*

Address *[address of rehabilitation representative]*

Telephone *[telephone number of rehabilitation representative]*

Date of injury *[date of injury]*

Type of injury *[type of injury]*

Earnings at injury *[earnings at injury]*

Claim No. *[number of claim]*

Employer

Name *[name of employer]*

Address *[address of employer]*

Insurance Carrier

Name *[name of insurance carrier]*

Address *[address of insurance carrier]*

DESCRIPTION OF PLAN

Description of the type of injury and medical limitations of employee: *[description of type of injury]*.

Figure 23.5 (*continued*)

Employee's educational and vocational background: *[description of employee's educational background]*.

Vocational objective: *[description of vocational objective]*.

Type of plan: *[type of plan]*.

Description of rehabilitation program: *[description of rehabilitation program, including actual time, place and cost of program]*.

Plan commencement date: *[date of plan commencement]*.

Description of fiscal provisions of rehabilitation program: *[description of fiscal provisions of rehabilitation program]*.

RESPONSIBILITIES

Responsibilities of employer. Employer/insurer shall timely provide all vocational rehabilitation services and benefits necessitated by the approved vocational rehabilitation plan and as required by *[citation of statute]*.

Responsibilities of employee. Employee shall be available, participate in all scheduled activities, follow the requirements of all facilities and persons providing vocational rehabilitation services, and shall cooperate in the provision of vocational rehabilitation services.

PLAN AGREEMENT

Subject to the approval of the *[name of governing board]*, employer and employee agree to comply with the terms and provisions of the above-described vocational rehabilitation plan. Failure of the employee to comply with the provisions of this plan may result in termination of the employer's liability for rehabilitation services.

Under this program, the employee is entitled to receive temporary disability payments and advances against any permanent disability to which he/she may be entitled until the rehabilitation or job training program is completed. It is suggested that you look to your labor code for the exact procedure in applying for these benefits. In California, for example, the following procedure is in place:

1. Public agencies, the insurance carrier, and the state Department of Rehabilitation are charged with the responsibility of formulating selected procedures and referral of individuals who may benefit by rehabilitation services or retraining programs.

2. The employer of said injured applicant and/or the insurance carrier for the employer is charged with the duty of notifying the employee of the availability of

such rehabilitation or retraining program. Note that a rehabilitation plan and/or request for approval of said plan has a deadline which you as the paralegal should calendar so that it will not be defeated because you let the statute go by. Under the new rules, the deadline to submit the plan after the employee and employer have agreed is fifteen days.

3. The employee who is seeking rehabilitation is entitled to a "subsistence allowance" in an amount to sustain the employee, but not as a replacement of lost earnings.

4. Finally, of great importance to the success of the plan is the cooperation of the employee. A failure or refusal to cooperate or comply with the plan or program may cause his rights to a subsistence allowance to be terminated or suspended.

   You should be aware that, although the benefits are not automatic, the injured employee, once advised by his doctor that his injury will incapacitate him for at least a year, can file a claim for Social Security disability benefits. Note, however, that these benefits, once applied for, do not commence until six months after the disability begins. It is therefore extremely important, once you find out that the disability will last beyond a year, that you file for the Social Security benefits.

The Compromise and Release

One vehicle used to dispose of a workers' compensation claim is by way of a settlement without a formal hearing. It is the Compromise and Release agreement which must be approved by the Workers' Compensation Appeals Board. This procedure is used to protect the applicant as to the amount of the settlement and attorney's fees requested.

> **NOTE:** This procedure may not be valid in your jurisdiction. Please consult your local rules. See Figure 23.6 for a sample from the American Jurisprudence Legal Forms 2d for Workers' Compensation.

Procedure: This document is usually prepared by the workers' compensation insurance company with a copy to the appeals board. All medical lien forms or reasonable medical expenses, or reasonable value of living expenses for the applicant's family, are attached to the copy of the Compromise and Release form mailed to the appeals board.

This form of settlement is a final disposition that forever closes the case. The applicant can never reopen a claim against the insurance carrier for this particular injury once the Compromise and Release has been approved by the appeals board.

This document is normally a form which can be obtained from the Workers' Compensation Appeals Board. To complete it, you do the following:

Figure 23.6
Settlement and Release

This agreement is made *[date of agreement]*, between *[name of employee]*, of *[address of employee]* ("employee"), *[name of employer]*, of *[address of employer]* ("employer"), and *[name of insurer]*, the insurer of employer, a corporation organized and existing under the laws of *[name of state]*, with its principal office located at *[address of insurer]* ("insurer"). Insurer is authorized to transact business and is transacting business as an insurer within this state under the *[title of workers' compensation statute]* of *[name of state]*, and has been approved as insurance carrier by the *[title of director of compensation]*.

RECITALS

A. Employee has been employed by employer as a *[job title or description]* since *[date of start of employment]*, and at the time of injury earned weekly wages of $*[dollar amount of weekly wages]*, with average weekly earnings of $*[dollar amount of average weekly earnings]*.

B. On *[date of injury]*, while employed at *[location of injury]* by employer, employee sustained the following injuries arising out of and in the course of employment: *[description of injury, stating portion or portions of body injured]*.

C. Prior to the date of this agreement, employer or insurance carrier made the following *[temporary/permanent]* disability payments to employee: *[description of disability payments, with weekly rate and periods covered for temporary disability payments]*, and paid medical and hospital bills on behalf of employee totaling $*[dollar amount of medical and hospital bills]*.

D. Employee claims the following benefits to be due and owing from employer or insurance carrier: *[description of benefits claimed by employee to be due from employer or insurance carrier, including medical and hospital bills paid by employee, unpaid medical and hospital expense, estimated future medical expense, and amount of disability indemnity due and unpaid]*.

E. Employer and insurer deny *[description of allegation of employee denied by employer and insurer]*, so that there now exists a dispute between claimant on the one hand, and employer and insurer on the other, as to whether *[description of dispute]*.

F. The parties desire to compromise and settle the dispute between them. This agreement is made for the purpose of settling between the parties the claims and differences arising from the injury described above.

In consideration of the matters described above, and of the mutual benefits and obligations set forth in this agreement, the parties agree as follows:

1. The parties agree to settle any and all claims on account of the above-described injury by the payment of $*[dollar amount of settlement payment]* in addition to any sums pre-

Figure 23.6 (*continued*)

viously paid by employer or insurer to employee, to be payable as follows: *[description of time and manner of settlement payment].*

2. On approval of this agreement by *[the Workers' Compensation Appeals Board/a referee]*, employee releases and forever discharges employer and insurance carrier from all claims and causes of action, whether now known or ascertained, or which may subsequently arise or develop as a result of the above-described injury, including any and all liability of employer and insurance carrier and each of them to the dependents, heirs, executors, representatives, administrators or assigns of employee.

3. *[OPTIONAL: Approval of this agreement releases any and all claims of employee's dependents to death benefits relating to the injury covered by this agreement. The parties have considered the release of these benefits in arriving at the sum stated above.]*

4. *[OPTIONAL: Approval of this agreement does not release any claim applicant may now or subsequently have for rehabilitation or benefits in connection with rehabilitation.]*

5. The parties agree that this agreement will not be effective unless and until it has been approved by *[the Workers' Compensation Appeals Board/a referee].*

The parties execute this agreement at *[place of execution]* on *[date of execution].*

The Board thereafter will approve the Compromise and Release. However, if the judge, in his discretion, feels that the proposed settlement amount is not adequate, he can disapprove the same and/or amend it in any manner he sees fit, such as requiring that the applicant get more medical treatment, or determining that the settlement amount is excessive.

In any case, be sure to calendar the date you receive the order approving the Compromise and Release, so that you can advise your attorney as to whether or not the monies settled upon have been received or not received, so that he may take the proper action.

This is opposed to the Findings and Award, which is the decision, opinion, and award of the judge who heard the matter before the Workers' Compensation Appeals Board. This disposition of the claim is far better for the applicant inasmuch as the Workers' Compensation Appeals Board retains jurisdiction of the case.

The judge, at his discretion, has decided upon a monetary award based on the evidence, which is testimony from witnesses, experts, and medical reports of doctors. The judge can also order that the applicant receive future medical treatment and/or lifetime medical treatment, and such other benefits as he deems necessary and appropriate.

1. Insert the attorney's fees;

2. State the reason and purpose for the Compromise and Release;

3. Obtain a waiver from the Department of Unemployment as to its lien, if applicable;

4. Check all liens against the gross settlement figure to make sure they are accurate; and

5. Ensure that the applicant has signed and approved the Compromise and Release.

Thereafter, secure all signatures of the appropriate legal representatives for both parties; then submit the original document to the WCAB with copies to the proper legal representatives.

A Hypothetical Case for You to Review Your Skills

Those of you who specialize in workers' compensation matters and/or are students of the workers' compensation field are aware that the two main mandates for circumstances of injury are those "arising out of employment" and those "in the course and scope of employment." In this connection, workers' compensation would be *the remedy* for an employee claiming intentional or negligent infliction of emotional distress. This is well documented in the case of *Livitsanous v. Superior Court* (1992) 1 C.4th 744,7 C.R.2d 808. However, since certain employees are not covered specifically by workers' compensation for the above, it is imperative that you check with your local labor codes to determine the validity of the coverage.

All of this has been said to introduce you to the case that follows, which concerns itself with the course and scope of employment and whether or not the employee therein was covered by insurance at the time of his alleged injury. It would behoove you to check this case out to determine (1) your ability to recognize what is the underlying rule therein and (2) your ability to do the legal research required. Good luck.

Legal Research Problem—A Real Case; Find It

Your client, Sam Jones, was employed by the Pill Drug Company as a salesman. His duties required him to call on doctors and hospitals to sell them supplies. He lived in Utopia, and his territory was the southeastern portion of the State of Bliss.

His employer's headquarters were in Big Town. On occasions he was required to go to the headquarters store of the company. He was to be in the headquarters store in Big Town on the first and fifteenth of each month, and at other times when in the area.

On Thursday, December 17, he left Utopia and worked accounts in various towns in his territory, then went to Little Town, where he spent the night with his mother. On Friday morning, December 18, he called on accounts in various towns and then drove to the store in Big Town. He arrived at the store at about 2:00 or 2:30 p.m. He had some orders from doctors which he wrote up and left at the store. He obtained a purchase order from the store, and went to a gift store to pick up a gift, which was his personal business. He then drove back to Little Town and stayed overnight at his mother's home.

On Saturday, December 19, he left Little Town, drove to the store in Big Town, checked his mail file, waited on customers, talked with the president of the company about his car allowance, and made up an expense voucher for the week. He also picked up some items to deliver to customers, to save the customers freight bills.

On Saturday afternoon he returned to Little Town to get his personal things, which were at his mother's home. He remembered he did not have a spare tire. He was unable to get the tire mounted at that time, and went back and visited with his mother for a while. At about 6:00 or 6:30 p.m., he returned to the service station to pick up his used tire. He then started west on U.S. Highway A. He stopped at Dogtown for coffee, and then went on to Ghost Town. When he arrived at Ghost Town, he was tired, so he stopped for another cup of coffee. He left Ghost Town; about three miles east of Utopia, his home, an accident occurred between his car and a semi-truck. The accident happened at about 10:30 p.m. on a Saturday night.

After leaving Big Town at about 1:00 p.m. that day, Sam Jones *had nothing further to do for his employer*, and had only to return to his home in Utopia. *He did not intend to perform any duties* in Little Town, did not make any solicitations or calls on customers, and *his usual hours of service* were Monday through Friday.

A claim for workers' compensation was filed for the injuries Sam sustained in the accident. The Workers' Compensation Court dismissed the claim. An appeal was taken to the district court, and compensation was allowed. The employer has now appealed to the Supreme Court of the State of Bliss, asking that the claim be dismissed.

ENDNOTES

1. *A Guide to Medical Records* by Arleen Kaizer, Esq., pages 57 and 63–66. Published by OMA Enterprises Inc., Las Vegas, NV. Used with permission.
2. *Johnson v. Sears Roebuck*, 355 F. Supp 1065 (1973); *Berg v. U.S.*, 806 F. 2nd 978 (1986) (hospital negligent in maintaining equipment and training staff); *Rose v. Hakim*, 506 F. 2nd 806, 335 F. Supp 1221, (1971) (strict liability applied to hospital for use of defective machinery).
3. *Gaines v. Comanche County Medical Hosp.*, 143 P.3d 203 (Okla. 2006) (JCAHO standards admissible as evidence of proof of the standard of care), but see *Lykins v. Miami Valley Hosp.*, 157 Ohio App.3d 291, 811 N.E.2d 124 (Ohio App. 2 Dist. 2004). (Guidelines of the Joint Commission for Accreditation of Healthcare Organizations along with the hospital's own policies and procedures were irrelevant and inadmissible to prove the standard of care to be applied in the matter. These contrasting holdings illustrate the importance of doing your research in your jurisdiction!)
4. Id. At 681–682, citing *State v. Tollardo*, 134 N.M. 430, 77 P.3d 1023, 1029 (Ct. App. 2003).

PERMISSIONS

Page 148 (Figure 8.1): "The Restricted Shepard's Summary for the Miranda Decision" has been reproduced by permission of LexisNexis. Further reproduction of any kind is strictly prohibited.

Pages 149–51 (Figure 8.2): "KeyCite Result List for the Miranda Deicion" copyright © 2009 by FindLaw, a Thomas Reuters business. Reprinted with permission.

Pages 425–27 (Figure 18.1): "Sample Financial Disclosure Statement" copyright © 2009 by FindLaw, a Thomas Reuters business. Reprinted with permission.

Pages 427–28 (Figure 18.2): "Sample Prenuptial Agreement" copyright © 2009 by Find-Law, a Thomas Reuters business. Reprinted with permission.

Pages 543–57 (Figure 22.2): "§101. Complaint in Federal District Court—Under Anti-cybersquatting Consumer Protection Act and Lanham Act" copyright © 2009 by Find-Law, a Thomas Reuters business. Reprinted with permission.

INDEX

Page numbers in **bold** indicate tables; those in *italic* indicate figures.

American Law Institute, 486

ancillary and pendant jurisdiction, 78

Annotated Law Reports (ALR), 159

annotated statutes, 156

annuity policies, estate planning, 401–2

answer/answering

    breach of contract, 381

    court systems and procedures, 62, 63, 65, 66–67

    federal court practice and procedure, 79

    interrogatories, 176–78

    removal of state court action to federal court system, 82–84

    Request for Admissions, 180–81

    tort action, 502–6

    See also responsive pleadings; writing effectively

anticipatory breach defense, 375

appeals

    civil law, 237, *238*

    criminal law, 357, 359

    electronic trial preparation, 248

    workers' compensation, 577–78

appearance of defendant, service of process (civil), 123–24, 125

appellant, 101

appellate courts, 57–58

appellate jurisdiction, 56, 57, 61, 71, 72

Application for Leave to Present Late Claim, 499–500, *500*

Application for Modification of Sentence, 362

Application for Writ of Garnishment, 526, *527–28*

appointment clause, wills, 394, *397*

arbitration, 80, 229–30, *230–32*, 232–33

Arizona, 6, 33, 73, 74, *350–51*, 454, 526, *527–28*

Arizona, Miranda v., 146, *148*, *149–51*, 152, 160

Arkansas, 6, 73, 74

arraignment, 345, 359

arrests, 331

arson, 336, 340

Article III of the Constitution of the United States, 70, 71

as-needed basis, paralegals, 33

assault, 337, 355, 506–7

asset case, 259

assignment and delegation of contract, 373–74, 384

assists, schedule of, 253, *254*, 255, *286*

associate attorneys and paralegals, 20, 21, 22, 25, 31

associate's degree, 32

Association of Legal Writing Directors (ALWD), 154, 160

Association for Legal Professionals (NALS), 4

associations, service of process, 82

assumption of risk, 492

"at issue," 62, 63, 136, 220, 233

attempt, unfinished crime, 335

attestation clause, wills, 394, *394–95*

attorneys and paralegals, 19, 20–21, 24

authenticated by testimony, 204–5

automatic stay, 268–70

automobile guest statutes, 493

bad faith letters, 28, 29

bail, 357, 360

Band-Aid, 535

bank accounts, estate planning, 399

bank loans, 322

Bankruptcy Abuse Prevention and Consumer Protection Act of 2005 (BACPA), 251, 252

"Bankruptcy Basics" (Administrative Office of the Court), 261

bankruptcy courts, 72, 75

bankruptcy (federal), 34, 251–314

Bankruptcy Information Form, 252, *278–85*

bargained-for exchange of obligations, 367

battery, 506

Becker, Lewis, 425

beneficiaries, 398, 405, 406

benefit plans of employer, estate planning, 401

benefits, changes in, 32–33

Benefit Unit (WCAB), 573

bequests, 393–94, *396*, 456

best evidence rule, 212–13

best offer underwriting, 322

bifurcating property settlement, 423

bilateral vs. unilateral contracts, 364–65, 384, 385

billing systems, 243, 244, 245

Black's Law Dictionary, 159, 210–11, 536

BlueBook, 154, 160

Boolean-type searches, 144, 145

breach of contract, 96, 374–84

breach of duty of care, 487, 488

breach of peace, 341

Bridgeport Music Inc. v. Universal Music Group Inc., 160

Burdine, Texas Dep't of Community Affairs v., 215

burglary, 332–33, 336, 340

burn out, 52

Bush, George W. (President), 251

business entity, setting up, 35–36, 315–30

business marks, protectable, 42, 533–62

business reorganization of debts and assets (Chapter 11), 253, 259, 263–64, 274, 275–77, *310–12*

business summons, 121–22

but for test, 488

calendar, 34, 133, 242, 245, 513–14

California

    business entity, setting up, 324

    cause of action in civil case, 105

prenuptial agreements, 371, 385, 403, 424, *427–28*
"presumption in the law," 457
presumption of law, 210–11
pretrial conference memorandum, 220–21
pretrial discovery, 170–201
    See also admissibility and use of evidence; electronic trial preparation procedures; summaries, preparing
pretrial motions, 65–66, 68, 69
    federal court practice and procedure, 78–79
    removal of state court action to federal court system, 85, 86–87
    responsive pleadings, 133–39
pretrial practice and procedure (civil), 117–39
    See also cause of action in civil case; court systems and procedures; federal court practice and procedure; responsive pleadings (answer and/or counterclaim); service of process, civil; state court practice and procedure
pretrial practice and procedure (criminal), 345–57
    See also criminal law practice
prevention defense, breach of contract, 375
Pribyl, 3M v., 539
price-fixing, 370
prima facie, 215, 360
primary beneficiaries, estate planning, 398
primary cause, 490
primary sources, 155–59, *157*
principle in complaint, 106
printed vs. drafted forms, 27–28
prison inmate "attorney" as paralegals, 32
private family trusts or estates, 263
private law libraries, 155
privately held corporations, 316, *317*
private nuisance, 507
private solicitation of funds, 320–21, 322–23
private trusts, 407
privileged information, 172
privilege rule of testimony, 216, 217–19
probate and estate specialist, 45–46
probate courts, 55, 61
probating the estate, 411–15
probation, 357, 358
procedural facts, 164
production of documents and things, 189–91, *190–91*
product liability, 494–95
products liability cases, 194–95
professional corporations, 316
profits, community property, 457
profit-sharing plans, estate planning, 401
progress of case through trial and appeal, 236–37, *238*

promoters, abilities and background of, 318, 320, 321
"proof beyond a reasonable doubt," 332, 354
Proof of Certificate of Mailing, 111
Proof of Claim, 257–58, 259, *301–2*
Proof of Summons and Complaint, 122–23, *123*
property, crimes against, 336, 338–39
property of trust, 406
propria persona (litigant representing himself), 55, 62, 100
Proprietary Lease (Cooperative Apartment), *479–80*
prorations, real estate, 482
pro se appearance (litigant representing himself), 62
prospective inability to perform defense, breach of contract, 375–76
protectable business marks, 42, 533–62
protective orders, 178–79, *179*
proximate cause, 334, 490
prudent/reasonable person test, 488
public acts or codes, 156
public administrator, 419
public authority, justifiable defense, 341
public benefits specialist, 46–47
public defenders' offices and paralegals, 33
publicly held corporations, 316, *317*
public policy and marriage, 421
Puerto Rico, 73, 74
punitive damages, 383–84, 505–6
purchase agreements, real estate, 480–81
purchase money loan responsibilities, real estate, 483
purchaser representations, real estate, 482
purpose of document, writing effectively, 161
putative relationships, 422–23

qualified general denials, 129–30
qualities to look for in paralegals, 25
quantitative vs. qualitative matches, 146
quantum meruit (constructive trust), 378, 407, 423
quantum valebant, 379
quarter sessions (criminal courts), 61
quasi-contract, 368, 385
questionnaire, bankruptcy, 255, *289–300*
question (quoting) in general correspondence, 162
questions, asking attorney, 165
questions of fact, 63
questions of law, 63
quickie divorces, 461
quitclaim deeds, 470
quotations, writing effectively, 168, 187

Race Notice Statute, 472
rainmaking clients, 20–21